Tarragon / salad, chicken, soup, fish, vinegar, sauces

Thyme / tomatoes, lamb, veal, pork, stock

Fines Herbes / a combination of chopped herbs, usually parsley, basil,
chives and chervil, added to omelets, sauces, cream soups

Bouquet Garni / a combination of herbs tied together in a cheesecloth
bag and put in soups, stews and ragouts.
Typically, 3 sprigs parsley, 2 sprigs thyme,
white part of 1 leek, 1 celery stalk.

SPICES:

Allspice / pickles, relishes, cakes, cookies, pot roast,
stew, meatloaf

Cardamom / marinade, mulled wine, coffee, bread, cake,
swedish meatballs

Cloves / ham, mulled wine, tea, fruit, chutney,
pickles, boiled meats, soup

Curry Powder / curry, eggs, marinade, sauce

Ginger / cookies, cakes, puddings, pot roast, fruit,
sweet potatoes, squash, carrots

Nutmeg / eggnog, spice cake, compote, applesauce,
meatloaf, spinach

Pepper / WHITE with sausages, pale-colored foods and sauces;
BLACK with dark sauces, red meats, salads;
CAYENNE in some sauces, used sparingly.

A TREASURY *of* GREAT RECIPES

To many hands in many lands.

*Our home is the achievement of many hands laboring
with love to make it beautiful. Our luble
reflects the many lands we have traveled in and
the hands that fed us. We thank them all
for enriching our lives in so many ways and hope that
through the pages of this book we may
enrich yours as well.*

INTRODUCTION I

by Cleveland Amory

I FIRST met Mary and Vincent Price many years ago on a trip to the West Coast. "You'll love them," I was told. "They've never 'gone Hollywood.'"

I soon learned that this was indeed true. Although Mary and Vincent are *of* Hollywood, they are far from being *from* Hollywood. But I also learned that Mary and Vincent do not look down on Hollywood. Although this would be easy for them to do — Vincent is, after all, six feet four, and Mary is statuesque — neither of them looks down on anything or anybody. They know that they owe to Hollywood their fame and fortune — Vincent as a brilliant actor and Mary as a brilliant costume designer — and they are grateful to Hollywood, acknowledging at the same time the fact that Hollywood could never be their be-all and end-all. In fact, it was never for them even the beginning-all. Vincent is a St. Louisian — a background which gives him, both geographically and culturally, an almost ideal perspective — part Western, part Southern, and part Eastern. As for Mary, her background is British, which gives her even more objectivity.

But if Mary and Vincent do not look down, neither do they look up. They meet you evenly, without pretense or show, and upon this firm base rests the very special quality — of which my wife will shortly tell you more — of their truly inspirational entertaining. I should like to say a word about another quality of these highly civilized human beings, which to me seems most special of all — their humor. Whatever the situation, the Prices live with humor — at all times and particularly under pressure. Courage has been defined as grace under pressure — and I think that is a fine definition. But the singular Price quality is, I think, humor under pressure.

Let me give you two examples. Once, during the fifties — at a time when the stock market and all the Prices' Hollywood friends seemed to be doing well — one of their well-doing and well-meaning friends took Vincent aside and told him he really shouldn't be buying art, he should be sensible and put his money in stocks and bonds. "Should I?" Vincent smiled. "I've never heard of anybody jumping out a window because a Rembrandt went down."

At another time, on a Hollywood tour of their famous house, a particularly irritating tour lady pointed crossly to one of their pictures. "What on earth," she snapped, "do you call that?" To this Mary and Vincent replied almost in unison. "We call it," they said politely, " 'We Like It.' "

Vincent called his famous book on art, *I Like What I Know* — which is in itself, I think, not only a memorable answer to modern-art criticism but also to why, now, a Price cookbook. The reason is simple. The world knows the Prices for their artistic and designing abilities, but their friends know them as highly skilled amateur chefs and talented connoisseurs of fine cooking — indeed, experts in everything associated with fine food and fine dining.

Here are the dishes, then, collected from all over the world, which the Prices have liked cooking and eating and which they serve to their own special "We Like Them" friends with their own special "We Like It" verve. You can never be sure, at a Price dinner party, what you'll get. You might sit down to anything from *gazpacho* to gumbo. But you can be sure of one thing — you, too, will like it.

INTRODUCTION II

by Martha Hodge Amory

TASTE in everything is, I believe, the touchstone of the individualist, and everything Mary and Vincent do is individualistic, beautiful, amusing and yet simple. When I say "simple" I mean uncluttered, unpretentious and spontaneous. Nothing is done to impress or bowl you over — it is done because it is their way of living. Their home is a continual education, which they generously share with friends and visitors alike, and when you walk into it, the vibrant colors, the works of art, the many "eye surprises," the subtleties are beautifully coordinated, and all have an air of balance and perfection which you realize, of course, didn't just happen. But none of the feeling of the rightness of it all, and the wondrous good taste, diminishes the warmth which makes it homey for their dynamic daughter, Mary Victoria, two "people" poodles named Prudence and Pasqualle, and a plain personality mutt named Joe. All contribute in their characteristic and inimitable way to the general gaiety and vitality of family and home.

An invitation to dine with Mary and Vincent conjures up the feelings of excitement and anticipation of real adventure. Vincent, with his enormous, overflowing charm, greets you at the door, and at his side is Mary, gracious and twinkling but calm and cool, too. No breathless, hectic, excuse-making hostess she. For all is planned and ready, and you feel they are looking forward to the evening as eagerly as you. They are true professionals at everything associated with excellent dining. Mary has even been known to gold-luster a complete set of dinnerware in her own kiln for a particular occasion. I remember after one of their evenings saying, "What a memorable and fabulous occasion! Where *do* you get all your ideas?" Vincent smiled. "From Mary of course," he said. "No," promptly countered Mary, "that's not true. I get as many ideas from Vincent as he gets from me. Let's just say the ideas were there and we didn't want them to get away so we married them."

And here at last are all the "wedded" secrets, collected between hard covers. Like everything else of Mary and Vincent's, they, too, are unique and unpretentious.

Overleaf:
Art and nature combine to make a still life in our
entrance hall that says "Welcome" to our guests.
The painting is late seventeenth-century Neapolitan,
the food an assortment of cheeses from all over the world;
celery in our baby's silver christening cup;
crisp English biscuits; fresh fruit to set off the cheese;
and a full-bodied Chianti to cast a mellow glow
over the evening. Simple foods artfully presented: that is
the keynote of our hospitality—and of this book.

A
TREASURY
OF
GREAT
RECIPES

By

MARY *and* VINCENT PRICE

Famous Specialties of the World's Foremost
Restaurants Adapted for the American Kitchen

PUBLISHED BY
AMPERSAND PRESS, INC.

EDITED BY DARLENE GEIS

ILLUSTRATED BY FRITZ KREDEL

RECIPES TESTED BY ANN SERANNE

DESIGNED BY ARTHUR HAWKINS

 Published by Ampersand Press, Inc.
Manufactured in the United States of America.

Library of Congress Catalog Card Number: 65-10310

FIRST PRINTING

CONTENTS

INTRODUCTION: Cleveland and Martha Amory 6

AN INVITATION AND A PROMISE 21

FRANCE

France 25
Restaurant de la Pyramide, *Vienne* 27
La Réserve, *Beaulieu-sur-Mer* 34
Lasserre, *Paris* 41
La Boule d'Or, *Paris* 45
Hostellerie de la Poste, *Avallon* 51
Tour d'Argent, *Paris* 65
Hôtel de la Poste, *Beaune* 75
Baumanière, *Les Baux* 80

ITALY

Italy 85
Tre Scalini, *Rome* 89
Passetto, *Rome* 94
Casina Valadier, *Rome* 95
The Royal Danieli Roof Terrace, *Venice* 99
Harry's Bar, *Venice* 108

HOLLAND

Holland 113
Amstel Hotel, *Amsterdam* 117
Dikker and Thijs, *Amsterdam* 123
The Bali, *Amsterdam* 125

SCANDI-NAVIA	Scandinavia	131
	Belle Terrasse, *Copenhagen, Denmark*	135
	La Belle Sole, *Oslo, Norway*	139
	Restaurant Blom, *Oslo, Norway*	142
ENGLAND	England	149
	The Ivy, *London*	153
	Boulestin, *London*	161
	Hole in the Wall, *Bath*	167
	Woburn Abbey, *Buckinghamshire*	171
	Levens Hall, *Westmorland*	174
	Harrods, *London*	181
SPAIN	Spain	187
	Sobrino de Botín, *Madrid*	191
	Jockey, *Madrid*	195
	Ritz Hotel, *Madrid*	196
	Palace Hotel, *Madrid*	198
	Restaurante Horcher, *Madrid*	199
	Soley, *Barcelona*	201
MEXICO	Mexico	205
	Rivoli, *Mexico City*	209
	La Mallorquina, *Puerto Rico*	217
	Dorado Beach Hotel, *Puerto Rico*	219
UNITED STATES	United States	223
	Pierre Grill, *New York*	227
	Trader Vic's, *New York*	232
	House of Chan, *New York*	233
	Lüchow's, *New York*	237
	Sardi's, *New York*	251
	The Four Seasons, *New York*	261
	Le Pavillon, *New York*	266
	Gage and Tollner's, *Brooklyn*	271
	Forum of the Twelve Caesars, *New York*	277

14

Wayside Inn, *South Sudbury*		281
Stonehenge, *Ridgefield*		286
Beau Séjour, *Long Island*		287
La Crémaillère, *Banksville*		288
Locke-Ober's, *Boston*		291
Durgin-Park, *Boston*		298
Virginia Museum of Fine Arts, *Richmond*		301
Grisanti's, *Memphis*		307
Old Original Bookbinder's, *Philadelphia*		311
The Warwick, *Philadelphia*		317
Antoine's, *New Orleans*		321
The Royal Orleans, *New Orleans*		327
UNITED STATES	Galatoire's, *New Orleans*	328
	The Sante Fe Super Chief	331
	The Whitehall Club, *Chicago*	341
	The Pump Room, *Chicago*	348
	The Red Carpet, *Chicago*	350
	The Stockyard Inn, *Chicago*	352
	Hotel Hana-Maui, *Hawaii*	355
	The Racquet Club, *Palm Springs*	369
	Scandia, *Los Angeles*	379
	Perino's, *Los Angeles*	385
	The Blue Fox, *San Francisco*	389
	Ernie's, *San Francisco*	395
	Bush Garden, *Portland*	396
	Chavez Ravine, *Los Angeles*	399

Specialties of Our House	405
Blender Magic	423
Frozen Assets	433

INDEX	445
HERBS AND SPICES	FRONT END PAPERS
WEIGHTS AND MEASURES	BACK END PAPERS

ILLUSTRATIONS

Frontispiece—William Claxton   10

The Whitehall Club   19

The Prices in Their Kitchen—William Claxton   20

FRANCE

La Pyramide—Eliot Elisofon - Life Magazine   29

Truite Farci Fernand Point—Tosh Matsumoto   30

Restaurant Lasserre   39

Casserolettes Lasserre—Tosh Matsumoto   40

Hostellerie de la Poste   49

The Prices' Mobile Home—William Claxton   50

Tour d'Argent—Eliot Elisofon - Life Magazine   63

Soufflé au Grand Marnier—Tosh Matsumoto   64

Hôtel de la Poste: Kitchen   73

Steak Chevillot—Tosh Matsumoto   74

ITALY

Tre Scalini: Sidewalk Café and Buffet (2)   87

Spaghetti alla Bolognese—Tosh Matsumoto   88

Royal Danieli—Eliot Elisofon - Life Magazine   97

Osso Bucco—Tosh Matsumoto   98

HOLLAND	Restaurant of the Amstel Hotel	115
	Carré de Veau à la Duxelles—Tosh Matsumoto	116
SCANDI-NAVIA	Belle Terrasse	133
	Wild Duck Flambé—Tosh Matsumoto	134
ENGLAND	The Ivy	151
	Roast Beef—Tosh Matsumoto	152
	Woburn Abbey: High Tea	169
	Tea at the Prices' Pool—William Claxton	170
	The Food Halls at Harrods	179
	Farmers' Market—William Claxton	180
SPAIN	Sobrino de Botín	189
	Mediterranean Fish Soup—William Claxton	190
MEXICO	Rivoli Restaurant	207
	Canapés, Mexican Style—William Claxton	208
UNITED STATES	Pierre Grill	225
	Curry at the Prices'—William Claxton	226
	Christmas at Lüchow's	235
	Flaming German Pancake—Tosh Matsumoto	236
	Sardi's West	249
	Boccone Dolce—Tosh Matsumoto	250
	The Four Seasons	259
	Dinner Party at the Prices'—William Claxton	260
	Gage and Tollner's	269
	Preparing Mixed Grill—William Claxton	270
	Thanksgiving at the Wayside Inn	279
	Thanksgiving at the Prices'—William Claxton	280
	Locke-Ober's	289

17

	New England Boiled Dinner—Tosh Matsumoto	290
	Virginia Museum of Fine Arts	299
	Green Salad—Tosh Matsumoto	300
	Old Original Bookbinder's	309
	Snapper Soup—Tosh Matsumoto	310
	Antoine's Wine Cellar	319
	Café Brûlot at the Prices'—William Claxton	320
	The Santa Fe Super Chief	329
	Library Breakfast—William Claxton	330
	The Whitehall Club: Kitchen	339
UNITED STATES	Chocolate Roll—Tosh Matsumoto	340
	Hotel Hana-Maui	353
	Hawaiian Fish	354
	The Racquet Club	367
	Cracked Crab—William Claxton	368
	Scandia Restaurant	377
	Stuffed Cabbage—Tosh Matsumoto	378
	The Blue Fox	387
	Scampi alla Livornese—Tosh Matsumoto	388
	Chavez Ravine—William Claxton	397
	Ball-Park Hot Dog—Tosh Matsumoto	398

Indoor Barbecue—William Claxton	403
The Prices' Moroccan Room—William Claxton	404
Blender Butter—Tosh Matsumoto	421
Basic Sauces—Tosh Matsumoto	422
Beef Stock—Tosh Matsumoto	431
Molded Ices—Tosh Matsumoto	432

The photographs by Eliot Elisofon © 1958 Time Inc.

After a fine dinner at Chicago's Whitehall Club, the last and best course of all was the one I took with Tony, who taught me the secret of his great crepes suzette.

Back home in our own kitchen Mary and I cook for each other, for our friends, and for the sheer pleasure of creating good and beautiful things to eat.

AN INVITATION
AND A PROMISE

COME into our kitchen" is an invitation we extend to all of you reading this book. It is an invitation which has been extended to us in many languages, in many lands, by some of the world's most famous chefs—and many an obscure one too—in great restaurants and quiet little bistros, in one of England's stately homes and even, in one case, in a museum. Our treasury of great recipes has been lovingly collected from all sorts of places, wherever in the world we have enjoyed good food.

For gourmet cooking is where you find it, and connoisseurs of the culinary art are found wherever there is good eating. It is not only in Europe, it is not always in the grand places, nor is it necessarily exotic or expensive. The finest food, like the best in every art, is simply a matter of excellence of preparation, imagination and performance.

The purpose of this book is to invite you to dine, wine, break bread with us, to partake with us of our favorite dishes gleaned from kitchens all over the world. We have gone straight to the source, to the great chefs and to those dedicated to seeing to it that the world eats well. Mary and I have accepted not only their invitation to eat, but also the challenge of trying to find out what we were eating, why it was so good, and how it got that way. Behind the scenes we've met the alchemists in tall white hats who have initiated us into their mysteries. So far they've all been wonderful to us, and not a skillet has been raised in high dudgeon when we invaded their domain. Somehow it has gotten around that we are collectors of everything, all the arts, folk art, decorative art, fine art and the art of enjoying food—and preparing it.

When we come back home from any trip to anywhere we try to bring something of that place with us, including menus from the restaurants and recipes. Sometimes there has been some aspect of a place that made us feel we could do something more to decorate our house when we returned, to remind us of that place. Or there came a day when we got home and it occurred to us, "How lovely it would be if we could have a meal such as the one we had in that tiny old restaurant in Spain."

Then we would have fun cooking it and telling our guests where we first had it and how ours was different. Maybe we would serve it on dishes brought home from our trip. The whole thing was a wonderful glamorous recreation of the experience. And that is what we really want to try to do for people with this book. So in these pages you will see how we have brought home treats for the eye as well as for the palate.

It is comparatively easy to hang pictures and place objects, but the recipes literally take some doing, and so we did them. Over the years, we did them and did them and did them again ("Mary is a marvelous cook"—Vincent) ("Vincent is a good cook, too"—Mary) until at last the results are as delicious as our memories of the originals.

All those irritating measurements, strange ingredients and complicated procedures are now geared to the American kitchen, to its equipment and to one housewife with only two hands—and a husband who loves to dabble in the kitchen. Together we have tried out on our friends, and on each other, all the good things we've eaten at home and abroad. The famous and the off-beat recipes have been translated—or adapted if you will—for use in the home kitchen. Your kitchen as well as ours, we hope.

Now for that promise, and we intend to keep it. We would like to assure you that the recipes in this treasury are, for the most part, never grand, not too difficult, and well within your ability and budget to achieve. So we hope you will accept our promise that is this book's first premise—that you can be a memorable host or hostess by learning to create extraordinary food and attractive settings for it. The recipes, suggestions and photographs in this book are designed to help you do just that. We promise.

Mary and Vincent Price

A TREASURY *of* GREAT RECIPES

FRANCE

Tourists, like armies, travel on their stomachs, and one reason that France rates so high as a tourist attraction is very probably because she feeds us so well. Obviously, the French love to eat and therefore they have learned to love to cook. It is pretty hard to eat badly anywhere in France—small villages, big cities, provincial towns, famous restaurants or obscure bistros, wherever you go you can always count on good food.

Right after the war Mary and I bought a fifth-hand little car and drove up, down and across France to prove the point—and it's true. Today, with postwar restrictions eased, it's even truer and, sad to say, much more expensive. The little table d'hôte with *vin ordinaire* is a thing of the past. But apparently as long as a Frenchman has any money, he puts it in his stomach, and gladly.

A couple of years ago, after a six months' stay in Rome, we took off a week to eat ourselves out of shape in Paris. Mary was pregnant and found that she yearned only for Chinese food. Darned if Paris didn't come up with a half dozen top Oriental restaurants. Still, to eat Chinese food in that capital of French gastronomy is about on a par with dropping in at the Louvre just to buy postcards. You'll get what you went after all right, but oh, what treasures you will have missed!

In Paris you can eat with elegance and even grandeur, but the really classic French cuisine is simplicity itself. It depends upon the quality of ingredients and painstaking care in their preparation. The result may be a perfect consommé, a superb chicken gently cooked in its own juices, thin pancakes, puffy soufflés, but everything with its own pure flavor and marvelous texture. Even a ham sandwich at a little bistro is perfection—a slab of pink, ham-tasting ham placed between two halves of a small crusty loaf that has been spread with sweet butter.

The point is that whether you dine at one of the fabled restaurants in Paris—and pay a fabulous price for the experience—or at an inexpensive little hole-in-the-wall, you will eat food that has been well prepared. The French are *serious* about their cooking, and that's what makes it such fun to eat there. They are scrupulous in the way they treat the God-given gifts of field, stream, vine and barnyard. Rather than waste a shred of precious food, they put their ingenuity to work and dream up a masterpiece made from bits of this and that.

Everyone has their favorite French dish, but the first thing I look for in a French restaurant is the *pâté maison;* the second is the sauces. Sauces are the secret of French cooking, the *pâté,* the secret of the house. In little country restaurants you can get the most marvelous little turnovers filled with *pâté.* Maybe they tossed together a few anchovy fillets, a bit of leftover ham, some herbs, an egg, some brandy or port, baked the mixture in a little crust, and *voilà,* a memorable morsel.

The country restaurants of France have great charm. But more than that, many of them have great chefs. It is evidently every chef's dream, not to go to heaven but to find a haven in the French countryside where he can quietly exercise his genius. Some of France's most famous chefs are tucked away in little villages and towns, running small country restaurants that are rustic and unpretentious. But their food is legendary, and a steady stream of pilgrims, both from France and abroad, beats a path to their door. You will understand why when you read some of their recipes in this section. Read them and drool!

RESTAURANT
DE LA PYRAMIDE

Just say "Pyramide" to any Frenchman who cares about food, and then sit back and listen. One and all they will tell you that without question it is the greatest restaurant in France, which is perhaps another way of saying the greatest in the world. You don't often find a unanimous opinion among Frenchmen, so that in itself is a clue. Then each person will tell you, as though he were reliving an old love affair, about some remarkable meal, some perfect dish that he once had there. And sooner or later you feel that you have to try it yourself.

Now this temple of gastronomy is located in a rather drab little town called Vienne, halfway between Paris and the Riviera. There is not much reason to go to Vienne or even to stop over—except to enjoy the gastronomic experience of a lifetime. The town has been plodding along since the first century B.C. and was once one of Julius Caesar's Roman colonies. On your way to the restaurant you pass a tall pyramid standing on a base with four arches, right in the middle of the street. It once marked the center of a Roman circus where chariots raced. Today traffic slows here, for much of it is heading for the restaurant nearby, which took its name from this old Roman landmark.

The Pyramide is a small, neat country house set in a quiet garden behind a high wall. A sign on the gate says simply "FERNAND POINT, RESTAURATEUR." But most of the people who pass through that gate are well aware that Fernand Point was the *greatest* restaurateur of this century. His ideas about gastronomy have influenced much of the fine cooking of our day.

27

It was Point, for instance, who first insisted that great food must be pleasing to all the senses—taste, smell, sight and even touch and sound. His china and glassware were chosen to please the eye, but he also paid attention to the clinking sound his plates and goblets made. In some restaurants the crockery clatters. In the Pyramide, so help me, it seems to have a musical tinkle. The table linens are spotless white and their freshly laundered fragrance adds to the pleasure of country dining.

In the spring and summer, tables are set out on the terrace under the trees where you lunch in the cool shade. The setting has been carefully designed to complement the pleasures of dining. The sunny garden beyond is a sweep of neat lawn surrounded by flower beds and gravel walks, all very simple but elegant in its perfection. And that is the secret of the classic *grande cuisine* for which the Pyramide is famed. Their food is not fancied up unnecessarily. The original flavor of each dish is artfully enhanced, and a great deal of thought goes into an attractive presentation, but the food itself is never disguised to look or taste like something else. It too is elegant in its simple perfection.

This kind of cooking can only be done by a master chef, an artist, a Rembrandt among cooks. Madame Point has never allowed her late husband's recipes to be published, but she very generously gave us three of Fernand Point's most famous creations, written out so that we could understand them. Believe me, it was a proud moment for the Prices, and we are delighted to share it with you. When we are in the mood to recreate that heavenly lunch at the Pyramide, we get to work with one of these recipes—to do them all at one sitting would be a bit beyond us. The results are delicious, reminding us all over again of that memorable afternoon at the Pyramide in much the way that a good art reproduction can reawaken your memory of an original Rembrandt.

The bounty of summer and the genius of a master chef result in this treasure-laden table set in the quiet garden of the Pyramide.

Fresh from the brook, these trout are stuffed and sauced according to Fernard Point's great recipe. Beautiful to look at, beautiful to eat.

Restaurant de la Pyramide

FERNAND POINT
VIENNE (ISÈRE)

7 Mars 1964
—

Brioche de Foie gras
Pâté chaud Beurre Blanc
Mousse de Saumon Périgueux
Escargots de Bourgogne

ou
=

Truite farcie braisée au Porto
Quenelle de Brochet Nantua
—

Pintadeau poêlé en Cocotte

ou
=

ou 2 couverts Caneton Nantais grillé Béarnaise
Gratin Dauphinois

Fromages

Choix à la Carte

Caviar Extra
Huîtres pleine mer
Terrine de Foie gras
Terrine de Grives
Jambon et Saucisson
de campagne
Gratin de Queues d'Ecrevisses
saumon frais
Chevreuil — Bécasse
Asperges de Cavaillon

Glace et Sorbet
Gâteaux Succès
Friandises
Corbeilles de Fruits

45 Francs sans vin

TRUITE FARCIE FERNAND POINT (*Stuffed Trout Fernand Point*)

SERVES 2 FOR ENTRÉE; 4 FOR FIRST COURSE

At the Pyramide, the fabulous trout they serve are caught in a nearby brook and kept alive in an outdoor aquarium near the kitchen until the chef is just ready to cook them. Moral: Only the freshest fishes are truly delicious.

carrots
onion
mushrooms
truffle
celery
butter
salt, pepper
flour
eggs
milk
trout
thyme
port
shrimp
cream
lemon
parsley
fish stock (see index)

STUFFING

1 Cut into thin strips: **1 small carrot.** Cover with boiling water and simmer for 10 minutes. Drain and mince.

2 Add to carrot: **2 medium mushrooms, minced, 1 truffle, minced,** and **1 small center stalk of celery, minced.**

3 In saucepan melt: **2 tablespoons butter** and in it cook the vegetable mixture over low heat for 10 minutes, or until vegetables are soft. Sprinkle with **a little salt** and **pepper** and stir in **2 tablespoons flour.**

4 Combine: **2 egg yolks** and **¼ cup milk.** Add to vegetable mixture and cook, stirring rapidly, until mixture becomes thick. Pour into a shallow dish, cool, then chill.

FISH

1 Preheat oven to moderate (350° F.).

2 Stuff: **2 ready-to-cook trout** with the vegetable-egg mixture, and sew fish up with needle and heavy thread.

3 **Butter** a shallow oval casserole and sprinkle bottom with: **½ carrot, chopped, ½ onion, chopped,** and **a pinch of thyme.**

4 Add: **1 cup fish stock** and **¼ cup port.**

5 Place the fish in the casserole, cover with an oval piece of **buttered** brown or parchment paper, and bake in the moderate oven for 30 minutes.

GARNITURE

1 Poach: **6 medium shrimp.** Shell, devein and keep warm.

2 Sauté: **4 small mushroom caps** in **½ tablespoon butter** until lightly brown and keep warm.

3 Transfer fish from baking dish to platter and keep warm.

4 Strain cooking liquid into a saucepan and add: **¼ cup cream.** Correct seasoning with **salt** and **pepper,** and gradually stir in: **2 tablespoons flour** mixed to a smooth paste with **2 tablespoons soft butter** (or use **2 tablespoons** *beurre manié*).

5 Cook, stirring rapidly until sauce is thickened.

6 Add: **1 tablespoon port** and a **squeeze of lemon juice,** and pour the sauce over the fish.

7 Garnish each trout with 3 shrimp and 3 mushrooms. Put a small slice of **truffle** on each mushroom and garnish platter with **parsley** and **wedges of lemon.**

VOLAILLE PYRAMIDE (*Chicken Pyramide*)

SERVES 4

A marvelous trick this, to loosen the skin of poultry and insert seasonings, butter or, in this case, truffles between skin and flesh. Try it with turkey sometime, using little pats of very cold butter, and see how moist and flavorful your bird will be.

CHICKEN

1 Slice thinly: **1 large** and **1 small truffle.**

2 Loosen the skin at neck of **a large roasting chicken** and insert hand all the way down, under the skin, as far as the narrow part of the drumstick, carefully separating the skin from the flesh of the

truffles
chicken
butter
leeks
onion
carrots
white wine
lemon
chicken stock
(see index)
salt
cloves
peppercorns
flour
eggs

chicken. Insert truffle slices, using the small slices for the points of the breasts and narrow parts of legs, and placing the large slices over breast, thigh, and thick part of drumsticks. Secure neck skin beneath wing tips, and truss.

3 In large casserole melt: **2 tablespoons butter.**

4 Add: **the white part of 8 leeks, well washed, and 8 young carrots.** Place the chicken on the vegetables, and cook over moderate heat, turning the chicken until lightly browned on all sides. Finish with chicken lying on one side.

5 Add: **2 cups white wine** and about **6 cups chicken stock,** or enough to half cover the chicken, **½ teaspoon salt,** and **½ teaspoon peppercorns.** Bring liquid to a boil, cover tightly, and braise the chicken for 1½ hours, turning from side to side at 20 minute intervals, and adding more stock if necessary to keep the chicken half covered at all times. When cooked, keep hot in the stock.

SAUCE

1 In saucepan heat: **¼ cup butter.**

2 Stir in: **½ cup flour** and cook, stirring, for a few minutes, without letting the mixture brown.

3 Gradually stir in: **3 cups of the broth from the chicken** and cook, stirring, until sauce is smooth and thickened. Add: **1 small carrot** and **1 small onion, stuck with 3 cloves,** and cook the sauce over low heat for about 1 hour.

4 Remove carrot, onion, and cloves.

5 Stir in bit by bit: **1 tablespoon butter.**

6 Beat: **3 egg yolks** with a little of the hot sauce, add to remaining sauce, and cook, stirring briskly, for about 1 minute. Add: **a squeeze of lemon juice,** or to taste, and correct seasoning.

PRESENTATION

Place the chicken in center of a warm serving platter, and surround with the leeks and carrots. Spoon the sauce over the chicken.

GÂTEAU MARJOLAINE (*Marjolaine Cake*)

SERVES 10

This cake is Fernand Point's masterpiece of pastry. *Marjolaine* means sweet marjoram, though neither flower nor herb have anything to do with it. For decoration the chef stencils the famous pyramid on the sugared top of the cake and they serve it every day at the Pyramide. I, for one, would never tire of it.

MERINGUE-NUT CAKE

blanched almonds
hazelnuts
sugar
eggs
salt
cream of tartar
semisweet
chocolate pieces
sweet butter
vanilla
praline powder
(see index)
confectioners' sugar

1 Preheat oven to very hot (450° F.).

2 In separate pans or pie plates put **1½ cups blanched almonds** and **1 full cup skinned hazelnuts.** Bake in the hot oven for 20 minutes, or until brown, shaking pans occasionally. Remove from oven and cool. Grind 1 cup at a time in an electric blender on high speed for about 5 seconds, and empty into a bowl. Mix ground nuts with **1½ cups sugar.**

3 Reduce oven to very slow (250° F.).

4 Beat until stiff: **8 egg whites** (reserve

yolks for butter cream), **a pinch of salt,** and **¼ teaspoon cream of tartar.**

5 Gradually fold in the sugar-nut mixture.

6 Line baking sheets with waxed paper and **butter** paper lightly. On it mark 4 bands about 12 inches long and 4 wide. Spread these bands thickly with the meringue-nut mixture, and bake in the slow oven for about 30 minutes, or until crusty on top, but still pliable. Invert on waxed paper, and carefully remove waxed paper from bottom of bands. Cool.

CHOCOLATE WAFERS

1 Melt: **6 ounces semisweet chocolate pieces** over hot water. Cut circles 2½ inches in diameter from waxed paper and spread these rounds with a thin coating of the melted chocolate. Place rounds on a cookie sheet and chill in refrigerator.

BUTTER CREAM

1 In saucepan combine: **1 cup sugar, ⅓ cup water,** and **⅛ teaspoon cream of tartar.** Bring to a boil and boil rapidly to 240° F. on a candy thermometer, or until syrup spins a long thread. Gradually beat the hot syrup into **8 egg yolks,** and continue to beat until the mixture is cool and thick.

2 Beat in bit by bit: **1½ cups sweet butter.** This makes 1 quart butter cream.

3 Measure 1 cup of the butter cream and flavor it with **1 teaspoon vanilla.** Meas-

ure a second cup and flavor it with ¼ **cup praline powder.** Melt: **3 ounces semisweet chocolate pieces** with **1 tablespoon water** and stir into remaining butter cream. Chill all cream until firm enough to spread.

PRESENTATION

Place a meringue band on a serving plate and spread with the vanilla cream. Top with second meringue band and spread with half the chocolate cream. Top with the third meringue band and spread with praline cream. Top with fourth meringue band. Frost sides with remaining chocolate cream and sprinkle top heavily with **confectioners' sugar.** Carefully peel waxed paper from bottom of the chocolate wafers and decorate the sides of the cake by overlapping the wafers all the way around.

LOUP RÉSERVE BEAULIEU (*Baked Stuffed Fish with Wine Sauce*)
SERVES 2

The Hotel Réserve in Beaulieu, on the Mediterranean, is one of the most beautiful resorts we know. The hotel is famous for its food as well as its view, and does the dishes of the South of France particularly well. This recipe for *loup,* a fish found only in the Mediterranean, is a favorite of ours. We have to make it with bass or snapper, but whenever we can get back to the Réserve, we enjoy the real thing.

saltwater fish
sweet butter
eggs
bread
milk
chives
salt, white pepper
dry white wine

FISH

1 Wash and scale a very fresh **2-pound saltwater fish** such as a striped bass or red snapper. With a sharp knife make deep slits along both sides of the backbone. Sever bone at neck and tail ends and remove the backbone and entrails. Wash thoroughly, scraping out any clots of blood, and dry on paper towels.

2 Combine: **½ cup soft sweet butter** and **2 egg yolks.**

3 Soak: **3 slices bread, trimmed,** in ¼ **cup milk.** Squeeze dry and mix into the butter-egg yolk mixture.

4 Stir in: **1 tablespoon chopped chives,** ½ **teaspoon salt,** and ¼ **teaspoon white pepper.** Stuff the fish with this mixture and sew up the opening.

5 Preheat oven to moderate (325° F.).

6 Put fish in a **buttered** baking dish. Add: **1 cup dry white wine** and bake in the moderate oven for 30 minutes.

PRESENTATION

Remove fish and place on warm serving platter. Cook liquid remaining in the baking pan over high heat until reduced by half. Strain over the fish and serve.

BROCHETTE DES CORSAIRES (Assorted Seafood on Skewers)

SERVES 4

This dish from Provence is traditionally served with *Riz Pilaf à la Valencienne* (Rice Stewed with Vegetables), and *Sauté de Scupions à la Niçoise* (Squid with Tomato and Anchovies). "Scupions" is a local name for baby squid. The seafood *en brochette* may, however, be served independently of these dishes, and the rice pilaf is so delicious it bears repeating as an accompaniment to many other meat or fish dishes. On its own, the Squid *Niçoise* makes a piquant appetizer served hot or cold. The Hotel Réserve, our favorite Mediterranean resort, gave us this recipe too.

SEAFOOD

whitefish
large shrimp
sea scallops
large mussels
flour
lemon
eggs
salt, pepper
cooking oil
bread crumbs
Dijon mustard
butter

1 Cut: **1 pound whitefish** (whiting, sole, flounder, bass), free of skin and bones, into 8 pieces.

2 Poach: **8 large shrimp** in **salted** water for 5 minutes and drain.

3 Steam: **8 large mussels** in **¼ cup water** until shells open. Remove mussels and discard the shells.

4 Wash and dry: **8 sea scallops.**

5 Arrange the seafood on 4 skewers about 8 inches long, alternating 2 chunks of the whitefish, 2 shrimp, 2 mussels, and 2 scallops on each skewer.

6 Roll the seafood in **flour**. Coat with a mixture of **2 eggs**, beaten with **½ tea**-spoon salt, **¼ teaspoon pepper**, and **1 tablespoon cooking oil**. Then roll in **fine fresh bread crumbs** and dab the seafood on each skewer with a little **Dijon mustard**, using about 1 teaspoon mustard per serving.

7 In large skillet heat: **½ cup butter** and when very hot sauté the seafood on the skewers for about 4 minutes on each side or until golden brown.

PRESENTATION

Serve with **lemon wedges** or the traditional garnishes that follow: **Rice Stewed with Vegetables,** and **Squid with Tomato and Anchovies.**

RIZ PILAF À LA VALENCIENNE (Rice Stewed with Vegetables)

SERVES 4

RICE

butter
eggplant
zucchini or summer squash
large mushrooms
garlic
tomato
pimientos
salt, pepper
rice
canned chicken broth
mussels

1 In saucepan melt: **½ cup butter.**

2 Add: **1 cup diced, peeled eggplant, 1 small zucchini or summer squash, diced, 2 large mushrooms, sliced, 1 clove garlic, minced, 1 ripe tomato, peeled, seeded and chopped, 3 pimientos (a 7-ounce can), minced, 1 teaspoon salt,** and **¼ teaspoon pepper.** Cook over moderate heat for 10 minutes, stirring occasionally.

3 Stir in: **1 cup rice.**

4 Add: **1 can (13¼ ounces) chicken broth** and bring to a boil. Cover tightly and cook over low heat for 30 minutes.

5 While rice is cooking, scrub thoroughly **12 mussels**. Put them into a saucepan with **½ cup water**, cover, and cook over high heat for 5 minutes, or until shells open. Keep warm.

PRESENTATION

Turn the rice onto a warm serving dish and top with the mussels in their shells. When this pilaf is served with the **Brochette des Corsaires,** it is placed in a little mound alongside the brochette, with a mound of *Scupions à la Niçoise* on either side.

35

SAUTÉ DE SCUPIONS À LA NIÇOISE
(Squid with Tomato and Anchovies)
SERVES 2 OR 4

SQUID

tomatoes
tarragon
salt, pepper
white pepper
onion
squid
flour
olive oil
anchovy fillets
bread crumbs
lemon

1 Peel and chop: **2 very ripe tomatoes** (or use **whole canned tomatoes**). Cook over high heat with: **1 tablespoon chopped fresh tarragon** (or **1 teaspoon dried tarragon**), **¼ teaspoon salt**, **⅛ teaspoon pepper**, and **1 small onion, minced**, for 20 minutes, or until very soft. Press through a fine sieve or blend for 20 seconds in an electric blender. Spread the puree in the bottom of a shallow baking dish.

2 Clean: **1 pound squid** (2 medium or 4 small). Pull the head from the body, discard the transparent "spine," and wash out the ink. (This ink, by the way, is the sepia used by artists.) Cut the tentacles from the head, discarding head and attached innards. Cut the bodies in half or quarters, depending on the size.

3 Preheat oven to hot (400° F.).

4 **Flour** the squid lightly, sprinkle with **¼ teaspoon salt** and **⅛ teaspoon white pepper**, and sauté in **6 tablespoons hot olive oil** for about 5 minutes on each side, or until golden brown and cooked.

PRESENTATION

Arrange the squid on the bed of tomato puree. Sprinkle with **2 ounces (1 small can) anchovy fillets, chopped**. Sprinkle with **½ cup fine fresh bread crumbs** and **2 tablespoons olive oil**. Bake in the hot oven for 10 minutes. Garnish with **thin lemon slices.**

LE POUSSIN EN SURPRISE
(Boned Stuffed Rock Cornish Hens with Sauce Diable)
SERVES 2

At the Réserve they serve the local Provençal dishes, but they also go all out for the most elegant classic French cookery. These small chickens or game hens are an interesting combination of the two. The spicy herb-olive oil marinade is very South of France, but the small birds, boned, stuffed and cooked in paper are *haute cuisine*. The result is marvelously good.

GAME HENS

1 Bone: **2 Rock Cornish game hens**. With sharp knife, slit birds down backbone. Carefully cut away flesh on both sides of the ribs exposing wing and leg joints. Cut through joints and remove carcass.

2 Put the boned birds in a glass or earthenware bowl and add: **4 tablespoons olive oil**, **¼ teaspoon each of thyme, marjoram, basil, rosemary**, **1 teaspoon salt**, and **¼ teaspoon pepper**. Let marinate in this savory mixture, turning occasionally to coat all sides with oil.

3 Sauté: **¼ pound chicken livers, chopped**, in **½ cup butter** with **2 shallots, chopped**, **1 small onion, minced**, **¼ teaspoon thyme**, and **½ bay leaf** for 5 minutes. Discard bay leaf and press mixture through a fine sieve or blend for 20 seconds in an electric blender. Stir in: **1 tablespoon cognac**, **¼ teaspoon salt**, **⅛ teaspoon pepper** and chill.

4 Preheat oven to moderate (350° F.).

5 Remove hens from the marinade, reserving the marinade, and place skin side down on work table. Spread with the liver pâté, dividing the pâté between the 2 birds. Close up and sew with kitchen

Rock Cornish
game hens
olive oil
thyme
marjoram
basil
rosemary
salt, pepper
chicken livers
cayenne pepper
butter
shallots
onion
bay leaf
cognac
dry red wine
dry white wine
bacon
brown sauce
(see index)

thread. Truss legs and wings close to body and sauté the hens in **2 tablespoons hot butter** until browned on all sides. Place them in a shallow roasting pan, pour the marinade over, and roast in the moderate oven for 50 minutes, basting several times with the liquid in the pan. Remove hens from oven and increase oven temperature to hot (400° F.).

SAUCE

While the birds are cooking make a sauce *diable*. In saucepan combine: ¼ **cup dry red wine** and ¼ **cup dry white wine**. Add: **1 tablespoon minced shallots** and boil until wine is reduced by one-third. Add: **¾ cup brown sauce** (or **gravy**), **salt to taste**, and from **⅛ to ¼ teaspoon cayenne pepper**, or to taste.

Sauce should be hot. Simmer for 20 minutes, then swirl in **2 tablespoons butter** and keep hot.

PRESENTATION

Cook: **4 slices bacon** until crisp and drain on absorbent paper.
Cut parchment or heavy brown, unglazed paper large enough to enclose each hen. Rub both sides with **soft butter**. Fold paper in center and place a hen on one side on top of 2 slices bacon. Cover with 2 tablespoons of the sauce *diable*. Bring edges of paper together, fold over in a double fold and crimp to seal tightly. Bake in the hot oven for 10 minutes. Serve in the "surprise" packages with the remaining sauce on the side.

LE SOUFFLÉ AUX FRAMBOISES *(Fresh Raspberry Soufflé)*
SERVES 6

There is nothing quite so delicate as a soufflé flavored with fresh fruit. This one, another specialty of the Hotel Réserve, is made with fresh raspberries and tastes as though it were made in heaven. Just one word of warning: it cannot be made with frozen berries—we tried it to our sorrow. But it is great with the fresh raspberries, and consequently it is a lovely way to celebrate the season.

SOUFFLÉ

milk
sugar
framboise
flour
butter
fresh raspberries
salt
eggs

1 In saucepan heat to simmering: **2 cups milk**.
2 In another saucepan combine: **8 egg yolks** and ½ **cup sugar**.
3 Stir in: **4 tablespoons flour**.
4 Add the hot milk and cook, stirring rapidly, for about 3 minutes, or until cream is smooth and thick. Remove from heat and top with **1 tablespoon butter**. Let cool.
5 Stir into the cream: **3 tablespoons framboise**.
6 Preheat oven to hot (400° F.).

7 Beat: **8 egg whites** with **a pinch of salt** until stiff. Fold in **1 cup fresh raspberries**. Add the cream and fold until cream and egg whites are lightly mixed.
8 Turn soufflé mixture into a **buttered** 8-cup soufflé mold and put into the hot oven. Immediately reduce oven temperature to 375°F. and bake for 40 minutes. Serve hot with raspberry sauce.

RASPBERRY SAUCE

Cook: **1½ cups fresh raspberries** with ⅓ **cup sugar** for about 10 minutes. Press through a fine sieve or blend in electric blender and strain. Stir into the raspberry purée **1 tablespoon framboise**.

LE GRAND SUCCÈS RÉSERVE *(Ice Cream Cups)*
SERVES 6

This dessert is a great success no matter where it's served. At the Réserve they top the whole thing off with a fluff of spun sugar, but that is a trick that only a master pastry chef can perform. We spin not, neither do we toil. We simply whip some cream and squeeze it through a pastry tube for an attractive garnish, and the result is still magnificent.

sugar
thin slice *Génoise*
or sponge cake
semisweet chocolate
butter
Grand Marnier
vanilla ice cream
fresh fruit
cream
fresh strawberries

CHOCOLATE CUPS

Heat: **6 squares semisweet chocolate** and **2 tablespoons butter,** stirring until chocolate is melted and mixture is smooth. Using a flexible spatula, swirl mixture around bottom and sides of 6 large paper baking cups, covering the entire inner surface with a thin layer. Place cups in muffin pans and chill. Peel off paper and keep in refrigerator until ready to fill.

FRESH FRUIT

Dice or slice any combination of **fresh fruit to measure 1 cup.** Use berries, pineapple, melon, banana, or orange. Sprinkle fruit with **2 tablespoons sugar** and **2 tablespoons Grand Marnier.**

PRESENTATION

Cut: **a thin slice *Génoise* or sponge cake** into 6 rounds, 2 inches in diameter. Dip each slice into **Grand Marnier** and place one in bottom of each chocolate cup. Put **a large spoonful of vanilla ice cream** on each cake round and cover with a spoonful of the fresh fruit. Garnish with **a dab of whipped cream** and top with **a whole strawberry.**

In this sumptuous dining room at Lasserre some of the finest food in Paris is served. The elegance of the setting dramatizes both the dinner and the diners.

Lasserre's famous *casserolettes* typify the charm and imagination of French cooking at its very best.

LASSERRE RESTAURANT

F. KREDEL

THERE are all kinds of charming and unpretentious little places in Paris where you can get a good meal. Dine under an umbrella at the Place du Tertre, under the trees in the Bois de Boulogne, under an awning at a sidewalk café or in a crowded little bistro where the owner and his wife prepare the food and you rub elbows with the workingmen of Paris. You almost can't go wrong—gastronomically, that is—in this city. But at least once it is fun to eat at one of the handsome and fashionable establishments where the cuisine is superb and the decor rather formal.

Lasserre fills the bill for us. It is everything a chic Parisian restaurant should be. The food is beautiful, the service impeccable, and the best-dressed women in the fashion capital are to be seen there. This could all add up to just another stuffy, high-class restaurant, but René Lasserre's imaginativeness prevents that. For though you dine indoors, under crystal chandeliers and seated on cut-velvet chairs, you can still dine under the Paris sky. The center section of the ceiling slides back, and at night you can look up and see the star-spangled sky, and smell the inimitable Paris air.

The open ceiling is also used on special occasions for a flock of white doves, who flutter down and alight on some of the tables—*after* dinner, naturally. The doves have become a sort of trademark of the restaurant and are even woven into the design of the carpeting. Where for my money they could just as well remain. We do love some of Lasserre's tricks with food, however. Many of their fish and seafood dishes are served in little tart shells made of the flakiest puff pastry. We've learned to make these wonderful *casserolettes*, and so can you. Whatever you serve in them becomes "instant Lasserre," and very stylish indeed.

❦ ENTRÉES ❦

LE PLAT DU JOUR

LE POUSSIN POELÉ PERIGOURDINE 17

LE STEAK DUMAS (AVEC OU SANS MOELLE) 18   GOURMAND DE VEAU « LASSERRE » 18

LE DEMI COQUELET GRAND PALAIS 16,   LA COTE DE VEAU EN PAPILLOTTE 18

CANARD A L'ORANGE ENTIER (POUR 2 3 OU 4 PERS) PAR PERSONNE 18

GRATIN DE RIS DE VEAU LASSERRE 18   ROGNONS DE VEAU FLAMBES LASSERRE 20

QUARTIER D'AGNEAU PERSILLÉ POMMES NOUVELLES 19

PINTADEAU ENTIER ROTI (POUR 2 PERSONNES) 36

DEUX CAILLES EN COCOTTE PAYSANNE 20

LA COTE DE VEAU POELEE AUX ENDIVES MEUNIERE 17

ROGNONS DE VEAU ENTIER DANS SON FOND AU XERES 19

LE DEMI COQUELET AU CURRY 16

L'ESCALOPE DE FOIE GRAS FRAIS AUX POMMES REINETTES (CHAUD) 21

POUSSIN GRILLE MOUTARDE 16

LE TOURNEDOS ROSSINI 26

DEUX CERVELLES D'AGNEAU MEUNIERE 16

★ GRILLADES ★

CHATEAUBRIANT SAUCE BEARNAISE (PAR PERSONNE) 20   STEAK MINUTE POMMES SOUFFLEES 17

MIXED GRILL AMERICAINE 17   FOIE DE VEAU GRILLÉ A L'ESPAGNOLE 17

COTES D'AGNEAU HARICOTS VERTS 19

TRONCON DE SELLE D'AGNEAU GRILLE 19

LE PLATEAU DE FROMAGES 7   LES SALADES DE SAISON 7

DESSERT DU JOUR

TARTE NORMANDE 8

PANNEQUET SOUFFLE FLAMBE LASSERRE 9   PROFITEROLES GLACEES AU CHOCOLAT 9

TIMBALE ELYSEE 9   DEMI ANANAS CLUB DE LA CASSEROLE 8

CYGNE ROYAL 8   PECHE MERINGUEE 9   DESIR DE LA POMPADOUR 8

SORBET AU CITRON 7   GROSSES FRAISES 13

TARTELETTE MAISON 8   FRUITS RAFRAICHIS AU MARASQUIN 8   BABA AU RHUM 7

POIRE BELLE HELENE 8   ORANGES A L'ORIENTALE 7

GLACES TOUS PARFUMS 7   ANANAS FRAIS AU KIRSCH 8   CREPES SUZETTE 10

MERINGUE GLACEE CHANTILLY 7   CORBEILLE DE FRUITS 8   CREME RENVERSEE AU CARAMEL 7

CASSEROLETTES DE FILETS DE SOLE LASSERRE
(Little Pastry Casseroles of Fillet of Sole)

SERVES 4

If you use the frozen puff pastry and roll it out to suit yourself, you too can do all the great dishes that call for this most complicated pastry. Even Lasserre's famous *casserolettes* are possible.

frozen patty shells
flour
butter
mushrooms
asparagus
salt, pepper
fillets of sole
shallots
fish stock (see index)
béchamel sauce
(see index)
egg
truffle (optional)

CASSEROLETTES

1 Defrost overnight in refrigerator **4 unbaked frozen puff patty shells.**

2 Next day, preheat oven to very hot (450° F.).

3 Roll out patty shells very thin, on lightly **floured** pastry board with **floured** rolling pin, and cut into circles 8 inches in diameter. Roll out trimmings and cut 4 strips for "handles." Line 4 tartlet pans, 4½ inches in diameter, with the circles. Press dough firmly against edge of pans and prick with tines of a fork. Line with waxed paper, fill with rice or beans, and bake with the "handles" in the hot oven for 10 minutes. Remove "handles" to cool. Discard rice or beans and paper, and bake casserolettes for 3 minutes longer. Cool.

4 Reduce oven temperature to hot (400° F.).

FILLING

1 In skillet heat: **3 tablespoons butter** and in it stew **6 mushrooms, finely chopped,** for about 5 minutes, or until tender. Set aside.

2 Cook: **16 asparagus tips** in boiling salted water for 6 minutes, or just until tender. Drain and keep warm.

3 In a **buttered** baking dish, poach: **4 small fillets of sole,** each cut into 3 portions, with **2 shallots, chopped, 2 mushrooms, sliced, salt** and **pepper,** and **1 cup fish stock.** Cover with waxed paper and cook in the hot oven for 10 minutes. Set aside.

PRESENTATION

Line each pastry shell with ¼ of the cooked mushrooms. On top, arrange 4 tips of cooked asparagus, and on the asparagus place 3 pieces of fish fillet. Keep warm.

Cook liquid in which fillets were poached over high heat until it is reduced to about ½ cup. Stir in: **½ cup béchamel sauce** and **1 tablespoon butter.** Beat: **1 egg yolk** with a little of the hot sauce and stir into remaining sauce. Pour sauce over the fish in the pastry shells, garnish each with **chopped truffle** (optional) and put a pastry "handle" in each shell so it looks like a small saucepan. Heat in the hot oven for 8 minutes. Serve piping hot.

GOURMANDISE BRILLAT-SAVARIN *(Fillet of Veal with Mushrooms)*

SERVES 1

This unusual dish is a specialty of Lasserre and is a fine example of inventive cookery at its best. Imagine wrapping a fillet of sautéed veal in a thin pancake and then baking it! The result is indeed worthy of Brillat-Savarin who defined gourmandism *(gourmandise)* as combining, "the elegance of Athens, the luxury of Rome and the delicacy of France." Quite a combination, and so is this.

fillet of veal
butter
shallots
mushrooms
sherry
salt, pepper
Parmesan cheese
unsweetened crepe
(see index)

For each serving, make a thin crepe without sugar, from 8 to 9 inches in diameter.
Preheat oven to hot (400° F.).

VEAL

In skillet heat: **1 tablespoon butter** and in it sauté: **1 fillet of veal**, about 1 inch thick and weighing about 6 ounces, for 6 minutes on each side, or until browned and almost cooked. Set aside and keep warm.

FILLING

To skillet add: **1 tablespoon butter** and in it sauté: **½ teaspoon chopped shallots** and **3 mushrooms, sliced**, for about 3 minutes. Add: **¼ cup sherry** and cook, stirring, for 3 minutes longer. Sprinkle with **a little salt** and **pepper**.

PRESENTATION

Spread half the mushroom mixture in the center of the crepe. Place the fillet on top and cover with remaining mushroom mixture. Fold sides of crepe over the filling, completely enclosing it, and place on a **buttered** fireproof dish. Dot with **1 teaspoon butter** and sprinkle with **1 tablespoon freshly grated Parmesan cheese**. Bake in the hot oven for 5 minutes, and serve immediately.

PANNEQUETS SOUFFLÉS FLAMBÉS *(Flaming Soufflé Pancakes)*
SERVES 6

Another favorite of ours at Lasserre is this dessert, a delicate and original variation of that old standby, crepes suzette. There is nothing quite so festive as flaming a dessert at the table, and it brings out the actor in every host.

crepes (see index)
thick pastry cream
(see index)
eggs
liqueur (kirsch, framboise, Grand Marnier, curaçao—
your favorite)
butter
confectioners' sugar

Make 12 6-inch crepes.
Make thick pastry cream.
If pastry cream has been made in advance or has been stored in freezer, heat it over low heat until slightly warm.
Preheat oven to very hot (450° F.).

SOUFFLÉ MIXTURE

1 Beat into pastry cream: **2 egg yolks**, **1 whole egg**, and **4 tablespoons of a favorite liqueur**, using a wooden spoon.

2 Beat until stiff: **6 egg whites** and fold into the egg yolk mixture.

STUFFED CREPES

Spread crepes out on a working surface, and spread each with about ⅓ cup of the soufflé mixture. Lap two sides of each crepe over the filling, allowing some of the filling to come out at each end.

PRESENTATION

Arrange crepes on a large, **buttered** flameproof platter or in 6 individual au gratin dishes that have been **buttered**, and bake in the hot oven for 6 to 8 minutes, or until soufflé is puffed and lightly browned.

Remove from oven, sprinkle heavily with **confectioners' sugar**, and flame with **¼ cup of a favorite liqueur**.

QUICHE LORRAINE *(Cheese and Bacon Tart)*
SERVES 6

Last time we were in Paris we were introduced to a charming little bistro called La Boule d'Or, The Golden Ball, not far from the outdoor markets. The night we were there we had little individual *quiches Lorraines*, puffy and golden brown, and swore they were the best we've ever tasted. The owner gave us this recipe for one large *quiche*—still the best we've ever tasted and the classic way to serve it.

PASTRY

flour
eggs
butter
salt, pepper
bacon
Gruyère cheese
cream
dry mustard

1 Preheat oven to hot (425° F.).

2 Measure onto pastry board **1 cup flour.** Make a well in center and in the well put: **1 egg yolk, ½ cup butter, a pinch of salt,** and **1 tablespoon water.** Mix center ingredients to a smooth paste, then quickly work in flour to make a soft dough. Chill for 30 minutes, then roll out thinly on **floured** board. Line a 9-inch pie plate with the dough, trim edge and crimp. Cover pastry with waxed paper, partially fill with rice or beans, and bake in the hot oven for 8 minutes. Discard rice or beans and paper and bake the pastry for 3 minutes longer.

TART

1 Reduce oven temperature to moderate (350° F.).

2 Cook in skillet: **½ pound bacon** until golden and crisp. Drain on absorbent paper. Crumble and sprinkle into partially baked pastry shell.

3 Add: **½ pound (1¼ cups) diced Gruyère cheese.**

4 Combine: **8 egg yolks, 2 cups cream, ¼ teaspoon salt, ¼ teaspoon dry mustard,** and **⅛ teaspoon freshly ground black pepper.** Pour mixture into pastry shell and bake in the moderate oven for 45 minutes. Serve hot or warm.

SOUPE À L'OIGNON *(Onion Soup)*
SERVES 6

After a late night in Paris we used to like to go to Les Halles, the large outdoor markets, where we could get steaming bowls of savory onion soup to revive us. Late or early, this hearty soup is one of my all-time favorites. If we serve it before a big meal, we use just one piece of bread and no cheese. But if we want to make a meal of the soup, with perhaps just a salad on the side, we use more bread and lots of cheese, run under the broiler to give it a crust. You will find both methods in this recipe.

onions
butter (optional)
bacon drippings
flour
dry white wine
salt, pepper
chicken stock
(see index)
French bread
cognac
Parmesan cheese
(optional)
garlic
parsley
thyme

1 In a deep saucepan heat: **3 tablespoons bacon drippings.**

2 Sauté in the drippings: **4 large onions, chopped fine.** Cook over medium heat until onions are just soft.

3 Add: **2 tablespoons flour, ½ teaspoon salt, ⅛ teaspoon pepper,** and **1 clove garlic, mashed.** Cook until mixture is golden brown but not burned.

4 Add: **a sprig of parsley, a pinch of thyme, 1 quart chicken stock, 1 cup dry white wine,** and simmer for ¾ hour. Add: **1 tablespoon cognac.**

PRESENTATION

Serve in individual ovenproof bowls, with **1 slice of toasted French bread** in each.

If you want to serve onion soup *gratinée*, place in each bowl 3 layers of toasted French bread, each layer sprinkled with grated **Parmesan cheese.** Pour soup into bowls, top with more grated Parmesan cheese and **a little melted butter,** and place under broiler until the cheese melts and forms a brown crust.

TOURNEDOS MASSÉNA (*Beef Fillets with Madeira and Truffle Sauce*)

SERVES 2

Tournedos, or little fillets of beef, are great favorites on nearly every French menu. There are endless variations on the theme of sautéed steaks with a little wine sauce. This one from the Boule d'Or is rich and filling because of the added garnishes and is an excellent recipe for making a little fillet go a long way.

fillets of beef
salt, pepper
artichoke bottoms
beef marrow
bread
butter
Madeira
beef stock
(see index)
truffles

TOURNEDOS

1 Sprinkle: **2 fillets of beef**, each weighing about 6 ounces, with **salt** and **pepper.**

2 Heat: **2 canned artichoke bottoms** in a little of the liquid from the can and keep warm.

3 Poach: **8 slices beef marrow** in simmering **salted** water for 3 minutes. Keep warm.

4 Sauté: **2 3-inch rounds of bread** in **2 tablespoons hot butter** until golden on both sides. Drain on absorbent paper.

5 Heat in skillet: **1 tablespoon butter** and in it cook the fillets over high heat for about 5 minutes on each side until well browned but still rare. Transfer to warm serving dish, placing each fillet on a round of sautéed bread. Pour off excess butter and fat in pan.

SAUCE

Add to pan: **½ cup Madeira** and cook until wine is reduced by half. Add: **½ cup beef stock** and **2 tablespoons finely chopped truffles.** Swirl in **2 tablespoons butter.**

PRESENTATION

Arrange an artichoke bottom on top of each fillet, put 4 slices of the poached marrow in each artichoke "cup," and spoon sauce over all.

QUENELLES AMBASSADE (*Fish Dumplings Embassy*)

SERVES 4

The Boule d'Or makes these luscious, light-as-a-feather *quenelles*, known less elegantly as fish dumplings (ugh!). "What's in a name?" indeed. We like to make a double batch of the *quenelles*, poach them, and freeze them wrapped individually in transparent wrap. They reheat beautifully, and the sauce can be cooked fresh in a matter of half an hour.

SAUCE AMÉRICAINE

1 Sauté: **6 shallots, minced, 1 small onion, minced,** and **2 cloves garlic, minced,** in **3 tablespoons butter** for 5 minutes, without letting the vegetables brown.

2 Add: **¼ cup cognac** and simmer for 5 minutes.

3 Add: **1½ cups white wine** (not too dry), **4 tablespoons tomato puree, 2 tablespoons minced parsley,** and **1 tablespoon minced fresh tarragon** (or 1 teaspoon dry tarragon). Simmer for about 20 minutes, or until sauce is reduced by one-third.

4 Season with: **¼ teaspoon salt,** or to taste, and **⅛ teaspoon cayenne pepper.** Swirl in **2 tablespoons butter.** Set aside.

FISH DUMPLINGS (*Quenelles*)

1 In saucepan bring to a boil: **½ cup milk, ¼ cup butter, ½ teaspoon salt,** and **⅛ teaspoon white pepper.**

2 Add, all at once: **½ cup flour** and cook, stirring rapidly, until mixture

shallots
small onion
garlic
butter
cognac
white wine
tomato puree
parsley
tarragon
salt, white pepper
cayenne pepper
milk
flour
eggs
whiting
sauce hollandaise
(see index)

forms a ball in middle of pan. Empty into mixing bowl or bowl of an electric beater.

3   Beat in: **2 eggs**, one at a time, beating well after each addition until paste is smooth and glossy. Chill. Makes 1 cup or ½ pound panada.

4   Dice: **½ pound very cold raw whiting** to make 1½ cups diced fish. Pound in a mortar to a smooth paste, or blend half at a time in an electric blender. Work the ground fish through a food mill into a mixing bowl or the bowl of an electric beater.

5   Beat in: **the panada, 1 whole egg**, and **2 egg yolks**, beating well after each addition. Gradually beat in: **¾ cup cold butter, ¼ teaspoon salt, ⅛ teaspoon**

white pepper, and **1 tablespoon cream**. Chill for at least 2 hours.

6   Shape the fish forcemeat into small croquettes on a **floured** board, using a good tablespoon of the mixture for each dumpling. Carefully lower the dumplings into a skillet containing 1 inch simmering **salted** water and poach for 10 minutes, without letting the water boil. Remove with slotted spoon onto a towel to drain. Makes 20 *quenelles*.

PRESENTATION

Heat the sauce *Américaine* to simmering. Strain it into **1 cup of sauce hollandaise** and heat, stirring, over simmering water. Arrange the *quenelles* on a warm serving platter and pour the sauce over them.

The enchantment of French country dining is captured in the courtyard of the Hostellerie de la Poste. Napoleon slept here; the Windsors, Eisenhowers, Hemingway and the Kennedys have eaten at this famous old inn, which prides itself on one of the finest kitchens in France.

A picnic dinner in our mobile home is informal but luxurious. No gypsy caravan could ever have been more fun than this, no painted landscape more beautiful than the one framed in the window.

HOSTELLERIE
DE LA POSTE

THE old duchy of Burgundy is the traveler's delight. You pass through it driving south from Paris to the Riviera, and it is one of the most picturesque parts of France. The wines of Burgundy are famed and, since wine and food are inseparable in France, some of the country's greatest cooking is naturally to be found in its greatest wine-growing section.

Burgundy is dotted with charming inns where, over the centuries, travelers have stopped on their way to Paris. One of the best is the Hostellerie de la Poste in Avallon. The coaching inn is built around a quiet cobblestone courtyard where the horse-drawn carriages of another era used to pull up after a day of bumpy travel. Now this little yard is set with tables where you can enjoy some of the most illustrious food in France. The proprietor of the inn, René Hure, knows a thing or two about fine food and wine. His cellar is a treasure-trove of more than four hundred different wines, and as for the food! Who can choose among the treasures of the menu either? Mary and I usually put ourselves in the hands of the proprietor at a time like this and let him choose for us.

In California we enjoy quite a different kind of country dining. Then, our coaching is done in a brand new Clark Cortez mobile home. We drive out into the country or to the seashore, park where we please and picnic in style on a meal prepared in the galley. A bottle of good California wine sets off our repast to perfection. We can spend the night, too, because the Cortez sleeps four—though I'd hate to put it to the test after a big meal! As we've said before, gourmet food is where you find it, and under the proper circumstances a cold chicken wing at the beach can taste almost as wonderful as any of M. Hure's heavenly dishes that follow.

Gostellerie de la Poste
AVALLON
(YONNE)

LE PATE DE BROCHET
avec la Salade de Fontaine
La Mousseline de Cresson
et la Sauce Corail

CHABLIS BEUGNON 1961

-:-:-:-:-:-:-:-:-:-:-:-

LE JAMBON BRAISE A LA CHABLISIENNE "PAPA BERGERAND"
avec les quatre purées à la crème

-:-:-:-:-:-:-:-:-:-:-:-

LE POULET EN CIVET AU VIEUX BOURGOGNE
avec les Pommes Nouvelles sautées au beurre

CORTON POUGETS 1953

-:-:-:-:-:-:-:-:-:-:-:-

LES FROMAGES ASSORTIS

-:-:-:-:-:-:-:-:-:-:-:-

LA TARTE AUX POMMES DES DEMOISELLES TATIN

-:-:-:-:-:-:-:-:-:-:-:-

LES FRUITS

GUIRLANDE DE SUPRÊMES EN GELÉE
(Garland of Chicken Breasts in Aspic)
SERVES 6

At the Hostellerie de la Poste, this cold buffet dish is made with quail, which have been boned and stuffed with a rich chicken forcemeat. The dish is garnished before service with the heads of the quail. We would sooner have ours without the heads, and have made this delicious facsimile of their recipe, using breasts of chicken in place of the quail.

chicken breasts
cognac
Madeira
foie gras (liver pâté, canned)
truffles
eggs
salt, white pepper
nutmeg
chicken stock (see index)
cream
plain gelatin
sliced boiled ham
watercress
apple
romaine lettuce
lemon
sour cream

CHICKEN BREASTS

Bone and skin **3 whole chicken breasts**, and cut in half lengthwise. Remove the small muscle on the underside of each and set aside. Place each half breast between pieces of waxed paper and pound as thin as possible with a heavy cleaver or side of a large knife. Trim each into a neat triangle, reserving the trimmings. Put the breasts into a china dish with **6 tablespoons cognac** and **6 tablespoons Madeira** and let marinate for 3 hours. Cut trimmings and small muscles into small pieces and measure 1 cup to make the forcemeat.

CHICKEN FORCEMEAT

1 Into container of an electric blender put: **1 cup raw chicken meat, 2 tablespoons foie gras, 1 small truffle, diced, 1 egg white, ½ teaspoon salt, dash white pepper,** and **⅛ teaspoon nutmeg.** Cover and blend on high speed until mixture is smooth, stopping to stir down if necessary.

2 Add: **1 cup cold heavy cream** and blend on high speed for about 20 seconds, or until cream is blended into the chicken meat.

Drain chicken breasts, reserving the marinade. Spread each breast with a layer of this forcemeat, roll up like tiny jelly rolls, and tie each in a piece of cheesecloth. Arrange in a skillet, add the marinade and **enough chicken stock** to cover the breasts. Bring to a boil, cover, and cook over low heat for 20 minutes. Strain cooking liquid into saucepan and add enough **chicken stock to measure 1 quart.** Cool. Cover chicken breasts with waxed paper and chill.

ASPIC

1 In saucepan beat: **2 egg whites, 2 envelopes plain gelatin,** and **½ cup cracked ice** until egg whites are frothy. Gradually beat in the cool chicken stock. Bring to a boil, stirring constantly. Correct flavor with **salt, pepper,** and a **dash of Madeira** and strain through a sieve lined with several thicknesses of moist cheesecloth. Cool to room temperature. This makes 1 quart of aspic.

2 Pour a ¼-inch layer of the cool, but still liquid, aspic into a 6-cup ring mold, and chill until aspic is set. Arrange **6 slices of foie gras with truffle in center** around the mold and cover with a thin layer of the aspic. Chill again. Place a cooked chicken breast, unwrapped from cheesecloth, on each slice of foie gras. Add liquid aspic to half the height of the chicken breasts and chill. Add liquid aspic to just cover the breasts.

3 Cut: **6 thin slices of ham** into 2-inch rounds. Dip the rounds in liquid aspic, and overlap them all around the mold. Add more aspic to fill the mold, and chill.

PRESENTATION

When ready to serve, unmold on a cold serving plate. Garnish with **watercress,** and fill the center with apple and truffle salad.

APPLE AND TRUFFLE SALAD

1 Combine: **1 apple, peeled and diced, 1 large truffle, thinly sliced, 1 heart romaine lettuce, shredded, salt, pepper,** and the **juice of ½ lemon.**

2 Mix: **½ cup sour cream** and **¼ cup cream.** Pour over the salad and toss lightly.

LE POULET EN CIVET AU VIEUX BOURGOGNE
(Ragout of Chicken with Onions, Bacon and Mushrooms)
SERVES 4

The classic French cuisine is probably the greatest in the world, but their hearty peasant food is wonderful, too, in its own way, and we are particularly fond of some of the country dishes we've had in France. At the Hostellerie de la Poste they do both superbly, and we think this Burgundy-style chicken can hold its own with their grander dishes.

bacon
onion
carrot
chicken
marc de Bourgogne
or cognac
flour
red Burgundy
chicken stock
(see index)
salt
peppercorns
garlic
parsley
thyme
bay leaf
butter
small onions
large mushrooms
bread
garlic butter
(see index)

CHICKEN

1 In braising kettle put: **3 strips bacon, diced, 1 medium onion, chopped,** and **1 carrot, chopped.** Cook over moderate heat until bacon is crisp and vegetables are lightly browned.

2 Add: **a 3-pound chicken, quartered,** and cook until chicken is lightly browned on both sides.

3 Add: **¼ cup *marc de Bourgogne* or cognac,** and ignite. When the flame burns out, sprinkle with **4 tablespoons flour** and stir until flour is well mixed with bacon drippings in pan.

4 Add: **2 cups good red Burgundy, 1 cup chicken stock, 1 teaspoon salt, 2 cloves garlic, minced, 6 sprigs parsley, ¼ teaspoon thyme, ¼ teaspoon peppercorns,** and **1 small bay leaf.**

5 Bring liquid to a boil, cover, and simmer over low heat for 45 minutes.

GARNITURE

1 While the chicken is cooking, sauté:

4 strips bacon until crisp.

2 Boil: **8 small onions, peeled,** until tender.

3 Sauté: **4 large mushrooms in 1 tablespoon butter** until lightly browned.

4 Set aside and keep warm.

5 Toast: **4 slices bread.** Trim, spread with **garlic butter,** and cut into triangles to make garlic croutons.

PRESENTATION

When ready to serve, correct seasoning of the sauce with **salt** and **pepper.** Arrange chicken pieces on a warm serving platter and strain the sauce over them. Garnish the platter with the onions, bacon, mushrooms, and garlic croutons.

At this famous restaurant in Avallon, the sauce of this chicken dish is thickened at the last moment with the blood of the chicken. (*Civet* is a ragout in which the blood of the animal is added to the sauce.) In addition to the garniture suggested above, they add cooked kidneys and cocks' combs.

LA FONDUE DE POULET PAPA BERGERAND
(Chicken with Curry Sauce)
SERVES 4

René Hure has dedicated this dish to the master chef, Papa Bergerand—many of his recipes are named for special friends. "Papa" evidently liked his chicken poached in the French style and then finished off with a creamy curry sauce, delicate and flavorful. We do too.

CHICKEN

1 Into large kettle put **a 3½-pound tender chicken,** ready to cook and trussed, breast side down.

2 Add: **2 small or 1 large carrot, chopped, 1 medium onion, chopped, 1 clove garlic or 4 shallots, chopped, 6 sprigs parsley, 1 stalk celery with leaves,**

chicken
carrots
onions
garlic or shallots
parsley
celery
bay leaf
thyme
peppercorns
salt
Chablis
butter
apple
curry powder
flour
cream
lemon
rice

chopped, **1 bay leaf, ¼ teaspoon thyme, ¼ teaspoon peppercorns, 1½ teaspoons salt, 6 cups water,** and **2 cups Chablis.**

3 Bring liquid to a boil, cover and poach the chicken for 55 minutes. Keep hot in the chicken broth.

SAUCE

1 In skillet heat: **3 tablespoons butter,** and in it sauté **½ large apple, peeled and minced,** and **2 small onions, minced (⅓ cup),** and cook over moderate heat for 3 minutes, stirring occasionally.

2 Stir in: **1 tablespoon good curry powder** and cook, stirring, for 2 minutes.

3 Stir in: **3 tablespoons flour.**

4 Gradually stir in: **2 cups of the hot chicken stock** and cook over low heat for 25 minutes, stirring occasionally.

5 Strain sauce through a fine sieve, and return to the heat.

6 Stir in: **½ cup cream, ¼ teaspoon salt,** or to taste, and **1 teaspoon lemon juice.**

PRESENTATION

Remove chicken from stock and cut into quarters. Arrange the parts on a warm serving platter, and pour the sauce over. Serve with **plain steamed rice.**
Strain and refrigerate or freeze remaining stock for future use. It's much too good to waste.

LE COQUELET À LA MOUTARDE (*Roast Game Hens with Mustard*)
SERVES 2 OR 4

butter
Dijon mustard
salt, pepper
Rock Cornish
game hens
béchamel sauce
(see index)
lemon
bread
cream

GAME HENS

1 Preheat oven to hot (400° F.).

2 Combine to a smooth paste: **2 tablespoons butter, 1 tablespoon Dijon mustard, ½ teaspoon salt,** and **¼ teaspoon pepper.**

3 Spread this paste over breast, legs, and wings of **2 ready-to-cook Rock Cornish game hens,** about 1¼ to 1½ pounds each.

4 Put the birds in a **buttered** roasting pan and roast in the hot oven for 60 minutes, basting occasionally with juices in pan.

5 When the birds are cooked, remove from oven, and cut each in half or quarters with poultry shears. Arrange pieces in a shallow pan and keep hot.

SAUCE

1 Make **½ cup béchamel sauce.**

2 Mince: **the yellow rind of ½ lemon.** Cover with water, bring to a boil and simmer for 10 minutes. Drain and reserve the rind.

3 To liquid in roasting pan add: **1 tablespoon Dijon mustard** and cook, stirring in all the juices in the pan.

4 Add: **½ cup béchamel sauce** and **¼ teaspoon salt.**

5 Stir in: **1 cup cream** and bring sauce to a boil. Correct seasonings with **salt,** if necessary. Add: **the blanched lemon peel, a little freshly ground pepper,** and **1 teaspoon butter.**

PRESENTATION

Sauté: **2 or 4 round cut-outs of bread,** depending on whether you are serving 2 or 4 persons, in **a little hot butter** until golden on both sides. Drain on absorbent paper, and arrange these croutons on serving platter.

Place the Rock Cornish hens in the sauce, turn to coat and heat them, then transfer to the croutons on the serving platter. Strain the sauce over all.

LA SOLE FOURRÉE AU FUMET DE MEURSAULT
(Stuffed Sole Poached in Meursault)
SERVES 2

Every so often it's fun to go overboard with a dish that is rich and elegant and out of the ordinary. This one takes a bit of fussing, but it is worth it just to watch the expressions of delight and disbelief when your guests first taste it and realize you did it yourself. Another of the Hostellerie's gems.

sole
eggs
cream
salt, white pepper
nutmeg
butter
mushrooms
truffles
shallots
fish stock (see index)
lemon
fish *velouté*
(see index)
dry white wine
(preferably
Meursault)

FISH
For each two people to be served, buy **a small sole**, weighing about 12 ounces. With kitchen scissors cut off fins. Lay the sole on a cutting board, white skin side up. With a very sharp knife, slit the skin from head to tail down center bone of fish. Using the knife, carefully strip away the flesh from either side, exposing the bone. Cut through center bone at head and tail end and, with kitchen scissors, cut through the fine rib bones on both sides, about 1 inch from edge of fish. Lift up one end of center bone and, again using the knife, strip flesh away from underside of bone, being careful not to cut the skin. Discard the viscera from the pouch below the mouth of the fish, and wash inside and out. This makes a large pocket in the fish, free of bones, which is going to be stuffed.

Preheat oven to moderate (350° F.).

STUFFING
1 In skillet heat: **2 tablespoons butter.**

2 Add: **2 mushrooms, minced, and 1 truffle, minced,** and cook over low heat for 5 minutes, or until mushrooms are tender, stirring occasionally.

3 Make fish forcemeat (for blender method, see index): Dice: ¼ **pound raw sole,** free of skin and bones, and

pound in a mortar with a pestle until it is reduced to a paste. Work the paste through a food mill. Set bowl containing the fish puree in a pan of ice and slowly work in the **white of 1 small egg.** Add gradually, stirring constantly, about ½ **cup cream** to make a creamy mixture that will hold its shape when a half teaspoon is dropped into hot, but not boiling water. Test, then season lightly with **salt, white pepper,** and **nutmeg.** Stir in the mushroom-truffle mixture.

4 Stuff the pocket in the fish with the fish forcemeat. Place fish in a **buttered** baking dish, sprinkle with a little **salt** and **pepper,** and **2 shallots, chopped.** Add: **1 cup fish stock** and ½ **cup dry white wine (preferably Meursault).** Cover with **buttered** paper and bake in the moderate oven for 30 minutes. Transfer fish to a serving dish and keep warm.

SAUCE
Reduce liquid the fish was cooked in by half. Stir in ½ **cup fish *velouté*.** Combine: **2 egg yolks** and ¼ **cup cream** with a little of the hot sauce. Stir into remaining sauce and cook, stirring rapidly, for 2 minutes. Add: **a squeeze of lemon juice** and swirl in **1 tablespoon butter.** Pour sauce over fish and garnish with **thin slices of truffles.**

GRATIN DE QUEUES D'ÉCREVISSES
(Crayfish Tails with Sauce Nantua)
SERVES 4

This is one of the great dishes of French cookery with a sauce that you could swoon over. Lots of good butter, fresh eggs and cream and subtle seasonings, plus infinite care and patience go into the making of this kind of culinary masterpiece. M. Hure gave us the recipe, and it really works. So do we when we make it—but it is worth every minute.

FISH STOCK

ish bones and heads
onions
carrots
garlic
celery
salt, peppercorns
parsley
bay leaf
shallots
dry white wine
white tarragon
vinegar
frozen Danish
crayfish tails
butter
flour
white pepper
milk
cream
eggs
lemon
cayenne pepper
cognac

Into a saucepan put: **2 pounds fish bones and heads, 1 large onion, chopped, 2 small carrots, chopped, 1 clove garlic, 1 stalk celery, chopped, 2 teaspoons salt, ¼ teaspoon peppercorns, a few stalks parsley,** and **a bay leaf.** Add: **2 quarts water, 1½ cups dry white wine,** and **4 tablespoons white tarragon vinegar.** Bring to a boil and simmer for 15 minutes.

CRAYFISH TAILS (Écrevisses)

Add to the fish stock **2 pounds (about 36) defrosted Danish crayfish tails** and simmer for 5 minutes. Remove the crayfish, let cool a little, then slit shells on under part of tail with scissors and remove the meat. Set aside. (Strain the delicious fish stock remaining and freeze for future use.)

CRAYFISH BUTTER

Crush the **shells of the crayfish** in a mortar with **½ cup butter** and put through a food mill to remove pieces of shell.

SAUCE NANTUA

1 In saucepan melt: **4 tablespoons butter.** Stir in: **6 tablespoons flour, 1 teaspoon salt,** and **¼ teaspoon white pepper.** Add, off the heat: **2 cups hot milk.** Stir rapidly, return to heat, and cook for about 2 minutes, stirring, until sauce is smooth and thickened.

2 Stir in: **½ cup cream.** Add: **1 small onion, chopped,** and cook over low heat for 1 hour, or until sauce is reduced by one-third, stirring occasionally. Stir in the **crayfish butter** and set aside.

SAUCE HOLLANDAISE

1 Into a small bowl put: **4 egg yolks, 2 tablespoons cream, 1 tablespoon lemon juice, ⅛ teaspoon salt,** and **a pinch of cayenne pepper.**

2 Put the bowl in a skillet of hot water and beat well over low heat until sauce begins to thicken.

3 Beat in, bit by bit, **½ pound butter.** Set aside.

PRESENTATION

1 In skillet heat: **2 tablespoons butter.** Add the crayfish tails, **1 tablespoon finely chopped shallots, ¼ teaspoon salt,** and **a pinch of cayenne pepper.** Stir until shallots are cooked and the crayfish are heated through. Add: **3 tablespoons cognac,** ignite, and stir until flame dies.

2 Strain the sauce *Nantua* over the fish and cook, stirring, until sauce is hot and bubbling. Remove from heat and gradually stir in the hollandaise sauce.

3 Divide the mixture into 4 au gratin dishes and brown for about 2 minutes under hot broiler.

PÂTÉ DE BROCHET (Cold Pike Pâté)
SERVES 8

I've had any number of meat and liver pâtés, but this fish pâté from the Hostellerie de la Poste is one of the greatest and most unusual. Served cold and in thin slices, it is a beautiful hors d'oeuvre or summer lunch dish. We bake it in an attractive terrine and it looks very festive when it is brought to the table.

PIKE

Cut: **1 pound pike fillets** into strips about 4 inches long. Put them in a glass or earthenware bowl and add: **2 tablespoons cognac, 2 tablespoons olive oil, ½ teaspoon salt, ⅛ teaspoon white pepper, ½ tablespoon chopped chives, 1 tablespoon minced parsley, 1 teaspoon fresh tarragon** (or **½ teaspoon dried tarragon**), and **1 teaspoon chopped shallots.** Pour over **½ cup dry white wine** and marinate in refrigerator for several hours.

FISH FORCEMEAT

pike fillets
cognac
olive oil
salt, white pepper
chives
parsley
tarragon
shallots
dry white wine
panada (see index)
eggs
butter
anchovy fillets
plain gelatin
lemon
fish stock (see index)

1 Make: **1 cup or ½ pound panada.**

2 Dice: **1 pound cold raw pike fillets,** free of bones and skin. Pound in a mortar or blend 1 cup at a time in an electric blender. Work the ground fish through a food mill into a mixing bowl, or the bowl of an electric beater, if possible. Put the panada through the food mill and beat into the fish puree.

3 Beat in one at a time: **4 egg whites** and **3 whole eggs.** If working by hand, set the bowl over a pan of cracked ice. If using an electric beater, all ingredients should be very cold.

4 Beat in bit by bit: **½ pound cold butter** and beat vigorously until the forcemeat is very smooth and thick. Chill.

PÂTÉ

1 Dry fish fillets on absorbent paper (reserve the marinade) and sauté in **2 tablespoons hot butter** for about 3 minutes, or until just cooked. Set aside.

2 Preheat oven to hot (425° F.).

3 Put alternate layers of the forcemeat and the fish fillets in an 8-cup loaf pan, using half the forcemeat and half the fillets to half fill the pan. Over the last layer arrange the drained fillets from a **2-ounce can of anchovies.** Add the marinade and the butter remaining in the pan in which the fillets were sautéed. Continue to fill the pan with alternate layers of forcemeat and fillets, ending with forcemeat.

4 Bake in the hot oven for 10 minutes, reduce oven temperature to 325° F. and continue to bake for 40 minutes longer.

5 Chill and, when cold, cover with a layer of fish aspic.

FISH ASPIC

1 In saucepan combine: **2 cups fish stock, 1 envelope plain gelatin, ½ cup dry white wine, ¼ teaspoon salt,** or to taste, **2 egg whites, beaten,** and **a sprig of fresh tarragon** (or **¼ teaspoon dried tarragon**). Bring to a boil, stirring constantly. Set off the heat for 5 minutes, then strain through a sieve lined with moist flannel.

2 Stir in: **1 tablespoon cognac** and **1 teaspoon lemon juice.**

COEUR À LA CRÈME (*Cream Cheese Hearts*)
SERVES 12

This is a favorite dessert of ours in France where it is made with one of their fabulous fresh cheeses and served with little wild berries. We have arrived at this very acceptable substitute for the French cheese through trial and error, and find this a beautiful dessert to serve when California berries are at their lushest, ripest best. You do have to have the little heart-shaped baskets in order to make these properly, but they are generally available in stores that carry gourmet housewares.

cottage cheese
cream
confectioners' sugar
eggs
vanilla extract
fresh berries

1 Strain: **1 pound cottage cheese** through a sieve. Add: **3 tablespoons confectioners' sugar** and **½ teaspoon vanilla extract.**

2 Whip: **1 cup cream** and mix with the cheese until smooth and well blended.

3 Add: **the stiffly beaten whites of 3 eggs** and fold into mixture. Blend well.

4 Line 12 heart-shaped wicker baskets with squares of cheesecloth rung out in cold water. Spoon the cheese mixture into the baskets, mounding it up a little. Fold cheesecloth over the cheese and place baskets on a tray in refrigerator to drain overnight.

PRESENTATION

You can unmold the hearts on dessert plates, or serve the *coeur à la crème* in the baskets and let your guests unmold their own. Serve with a bowl of **fresh raspberries** or **sliced fresh strawberries** on the side.

LA TERRINE DE RIS DE VEAU *(Terrine of Sweetbreads)*
SERVES AT LEAST 16 FOR APPETIZER

This is a beautiful dish to take along on a picnic. It is cooked in its own attractive earthenware casserole, or terrine, a day or two ahead of time and then chilled in the refrigerator. We serve it sliced right out of the terrine, with a loaf of crusty bread and a crisp salad. It is also a sensational appetizer accompanied by a very cold, very dry white wine.

SWEETBREADS

sweetbreads
truffles
butter
onion
carrot
shallots
garlic
bay leaf
thyme
salt, pepper
dry white wine
Madeira
cognac
ground lean pork
ground fresh fat pork
ground lean ham
eggs
brandy

1 Soak: **3 pairs of sweetbreads** in ice water for 45 minutes. Drain, cover with cold water, bring to a boil and simmer for 3 minutes. Drain and chill in ice water. Remove covering tissue and connecting cords. Make small slits in the sweetbreads and insert small strips of truffles, using about **3 large or 4 small truffles** in all. Weigh down with a dinner plate for 15 minutes.

2 In skillet heat: **3 tablespoons butter.**

3 Add: **1 small onion, minced, 1 small carrot, finely chopped, 2 shallots, minced, ½ clove garlic, minced, ½ bay leaf,** and **a pinch of thyme.** Cook for 5 minutes, stirring occasionally. Arrange the sweetbreads on the bed of vegetables, sprinkle with **¼ teaspoon salt** and **a little freshly ground pepper.**

4 Add: **1 cup dry white wine, 2 tablespoons Madeira,** and **2 tablespoons cognac.** Cover and cook over low heat for 20 minutes. Remove sweetbreads and cook liquid in pan over high heat until reduced to half the quantity. Strain.

5 Preheat oven to moderate (350° F.).

PORK FORCEMEAT

Combine: **1 pound ground lean pork, 2 pounds ground fresh fat pork,** and **1 pound ground lean ham.** Add: **2 teaspoons salt, 1 teaspoon pepper, 2 eggs,** and **2 tablespoons brandy** and mix well with hands into a smooth paste.

TERRINE

Line bottom and sides of a 10-cup terrine or loaf-shaped casserole with a ¼-inch layer of the forcemeat. Sprinkle with some of the reduced cooking liquid. Arrange the truffled sweetbreads in two layers in the terrine, covering each layer with forcemeat and sprinkling the forcemeat with more of the cooking liquid. Cover terrine tightly and bake in the moderate oven for 1½ hours. Cool with a weight resting on the contents, then chill overnight before cutting and serving.

DODINE DE CANARD *(Boned Stuffed Duck)*
SERVES 6

This is a remarkable preparation, and another of the specialties of the Hostellerie de la Poste in Avallon. It is so rich that it is best served in very small slices as a hot appetizer. But it is so fantastically good that you will almost wish you could eat more. As it was explained to us, a *dodine* differs from a *ballottine* of duck by being a roasted, boned and stuffed bird rather than a poached one. It is an ancient preparation, seldom made now. One of the recent times on record was when Escoffier cooked a *dodine de canard* for Sarah Bernhardt. I hope, for the sake of the lady's figure, she was only expected to nibble at it.

DUCK

duck
salt, pepper
allspice
Armagnac
ground pork
ground veal
chicken livers
Chablis
eggs
truffles
Madeira or truffle juice
cooking oil
watercress

1 Cut: wing tips and first wing joint from a ready-to-cook duck. Bone duck completely, except for the small leg bone. (To bone a fowl: see index.) Remove as much of the solid fat as possible and put duck into a shallow dish.

2 Sprinkle with: 1 teaspoon salt, ¼ teaspoon pepper, ⅛ teaspoon allspice, and 3 ounces Armagnac. Put in refrigerator to marinate for several hours or overnight.

STUFFING

1 Make a pork-veal forcemeat. Combine: 1 pound twice-ground lean pork and 1 pound twice-ground veal. Clean: 6 chicken livers, remove connecting tissue and chop finely. Add to meat. Mash duck liver, remove sinews and beat in:

⅓ cup Chablis, 2 eggs, 1 teaspoon salt, and 8 tablespoons Madeira or truffle juice. Beat thoroughly and stir in: 3 large truffles, diced.

2 Preheat oven to moderate (350° F.).

3 Spread duck out on table, skin side down, and spread entire surface with the stuffing. Fold neck skin over filling, bring up sides of duck, reforming it neatly, and sew up skin. Put duck into an oiled baking pan and bake in moderate oven for 2 hours.

PRESENTATION

Remove duck to hot serving platter. Pour off all fat in pan. Add: ¼ cup Armagnac or Madeira and cook over direct heat, stirring constantly, for 3 minutes. Strain juice over the duck. Serve with a garnish of watercress.

LE JAMBON CHAUD À LA CHABLISIENNE
(Braised Ham with Chablis)
SERVES 12

Everything tastes excitingly different at the Hostellerie de la Poste. Even ham, which can be quite ordinary, becomes interesting when it is cooked this way and served with this unusual sauce.

a ready-to-eat ham
Chablis
shallots
tarragon
salt, pepper
brown stock
(see index)
tomato puree
flour
butter
cream

1 Preheat oven to moderate (350° F.).

2 Put a 12- to 14-pound ready-to-eat ham in a heavy casserole with tight-fitting lid. Or place on a baking sheet over two long strips of heavy-duty aluminum foil placed at right angles, and cup the foil up around the ham. Add to pan or foil 1½ cups Chablis (½ bottle). Cover tightly or seal in the foil and bake in the moderate oven for 1 hour.

While the ham is braising prepare the sauce:

SAUCE

1 In saucepan put: 1½ cups Chablis (½ bottle), 2 shallots, chopped, 1 tablespoon minced fresh tarragon (or 1 teaspoon dry tarragon), ½ teaspoon salt,

and ¼ teaspoon black pepper. Bring to a boil and boil rapidly for 10 to 15 minutes, or until wine is reduced by half.

2 Add: 1 quart brown stock and ¼ cup tomato puree and bring to a boil. Stir in: 4 tablespoons flour mixed to a paste with 4 tablespoons butter and cook over low heat for 45 minutes, stirring occasionally. Strain through a sieve into a clean saucepan. Stir in: 1 cup cream and 1 teaspoon chopped fresh tarragon and correct seasoning with salt and pepper to taste.

PRESENTATION

Slice the ham and serve hot with the sauce served separately.

LE GRATIN SAVOYARD *(Potatoes in Cream au Gratin)*
SERVES 4

One summer we were traveling through the mountains of Savoy, near the Italian and Swiss borders, and lunched at a little inn in Mégève. The dairy products and cheeses are typically Alpine in that part of France — in other words, extraordinarily good. We were particularly taken with the potatoes cooked in cream with Gruyère cheese, and then given a marvelous crust under the broiler. If you like garlic, you can rub the baking dish with a clove of it before putting in the potatoes, but then be sure it won't overpower the rest of your meal.

potatoes
light cream
butter
salt, pepper
Gruyère cheese

1 Slice: **8 medium potatoes** very thinly. Put into a saucepan with **salted** water to cover, bring to a boil and boil for 3 minutes. Drain.

2 In **buttered** oval baking dish, about 12 inches long, put a layer of half the potatoes. Sprinkle with: **½ teaspoon salt** and **freshly ground pepper.** Sprinkle

with: **1 cup shredded Gruyère cheese,** and cover with remaining potatoes.

3 Add: **2 cups light cream** and sprinkle with: **1 cup shredded Gruyère.** Bring to a boil over direct heat and simmer for 15 minutes. Run under broiler heat for 2 to 3 minutes, or until browned.

GÂTEAU GRAND MARNIER *(Orange Liqueur Cake)*
SERVES 10

What we think of as French pastry in this country is just a small part of the enormous cake repertoire of France. Although there are only eight basic pastry doughs used there, with all the variations added by generations of ingenious chefs, the number of different cakes made from them now is staggering. We have eaten rich cakes and poor ones, fancy cakes and plain ones, and have liked nearly all of them. Mary is the cake baker in our family ("If you can lay brick you can frost a cake," she explains simply.) and hers are always triumphs. This unfrosted cake, saturated with orange juice and orange liqueur, is a special favorite, marvelous with tea or coffee. Mary was given the recipe at a little inn in Lorraine, a province of France noted for its fruits and liqueurs, and where the rum-saturated cakes known as *babas* were invented.

butter
sugar
eggs
Grand Marnier
flour
baking powder
baking soda
sour cream
oranges
walnuts
slivered almonds

CAKE

1 Preheat oven to moderate (350° F.).

2 Cream: **1 cup butter** with **1 cup sugar** until pale and fluffy.

3 Beat in: **3 egg yolks,** one at a time.

4 Add: **1 teaspoon Grand Marnier.**

5 Sift together: **2 cups all-purpose flour, 1 teaspoon baking powder,** and **1 teaspoon baking soda.**

6 Add dry ingredients to batter, alternating with **1¼ cups sour cream,** beginning and ending with dry ingredients and mixing until smooth.

7 Stir in: **grated rind of 1 orange** and **1 cup chopped walnuts.**

8 Beat until stiff: **3 egg whites** and fold into batter. Pour batter into a **greased** 9-inch tube pan.

9 Bake in the moderate oven for 50 to 55 minutes, or until cake tests done.

TOPPING

Combine: **½ cup sugar, 1 cup orange juice,** and **⅓ cup Grand Marnier.** Pour over hot cake while it is in pan. Sprinkle with **blanched slivered almonds** and let cake cool before removing from pan.

Imagine yourself sitting at this table,
enjoying a glorious meal, impeccably served,
with all Paris spread out beyond the window!
That is dining at the Tour d'Argent,
one of the gastronomic thrills of a lifetime.

Soufflé au Grand Marnier, aristocrat of desserts,
springs from humble beginnings. Eggs, butter,
flour, milk, sugar, and flavoring — what could be
more commonplace? But see how these simple
ingredients are transformed by the magic
formula of a kitchen wizard.

TOUR D'ARGENT

ONE of the oldest and most famous restaurants in Paris is the Tour d'Argent—the Silver Tower. On the Left Bank of the Seine, in the heart of Old Paris, the Tower was built in 1582—just about the time that forks replaced fingers at the tables of the high-born and wealthy, and mere eating became dining.

The Tour d'Argent has been renowned for its magnificent cuisine for nearly 400 years, and it is one of our favorite places in Paris. The view through its large windows, over the Seine to the Gothic towers and flying buttresses of Notre Dame, is inspiring enough, heaven knows. But all this and a superlative lunch or dinner too! It is almost too much. (As we have sometimes felt when our tab was presented: about $12.00 for lunch, $20.00 for dinner, per person!)

Although pressed duck is the great specialty here, we have only ordered it once, out of curiosity. Maybe we're wrong—over a quarter million ducks have been served here in this fashion in the past seventy years. They number each one, so their count is really accurate.

We are going to give you *our* favorite recipes from the Tour d'Argent, ones which we found we could duplicate quite successfully at home. From soup to soufflé each has some special touch that sets it apart, the secrets imparted to us by Pierre Descreux, the Tour d'Argent's Chef de Cuisine. All of this has been done, we hasten to add, with the blessings of the restaurant's dynamic owner, Monsieur Claude Terrail.

LA TOUR

Couvert

Caviar ✳ Blinis
Saumon fumé
Grape-Fruit-Cocktail
Fines de Belon

POTAGES

Potage "Tour d'Argent"
Potage Claudius Burdel
Consommé Fabiola
Consommé
Julienne

ŒUFS

Œufs Bénédictine
Œufs cocotte à la crèm...
Œufs brouillés aux tru...
Œufs brouillés *garniture au ...*
Omelette *garniture au cho...*
Œufs frits tomate
Œufs Mornay

POISSONS

Filets de Sole Sully   Filets de Sole Cardinal
Filets de Sole Caravelle *sur Commande*
Filets de Sole Mornay   Sole frite du Maire
Filets de Sole grillés Frédéric
Barbue Dugléré *sur Commande*   Sole Meunière
Croustade de Barbue Lagrené
Langouste Winterthur   Truite en Chemise
Goujonnettes de Mostelle Tartare
Langouste Mayonnaise   Quenelles de Brochet

Petits Pois
Haricots verts
Champignons
à la Bordelaise

Endives Meunière
Epinards à la crème
Fonds d'Artichauts
soufflés

ENTRÉES

Côtes d'Agneau   Côte de Veau Charlemagne
Carré d'Agneau rôti   Côte de Veau casserole
Médaillon de Ris de Veau braisé
Escalope de Veau Viennoise   Tournedos Yella
Filet Tour d'Argent   Noisettes des Tournelles
Châteaubriand sauce Béarnaise
Filet sauté de Lauzières   Cervelle au beurre noir
Le Filet Charolais aux quatre poivres
Rognons grillés Béarnaise   Rognons Saint-Louis
Terrine de Foie gras à la Gelée de Porto

LÉGUMES

Pommes sautées
Pommes soufflées
Pommes allumettes

LÉGUMES

Salade Roger

Salades de saison

ROTS

Caneton Tour d'Argent

Caneton Raphaël Weill
Caneton à l'Orange
Aiguillettes de Caneton
à la Gelée de Porto
Caneton Marco Polo
Caneton aux Ananas
Caneton aux Olives
Caneton grillé aux Pommes
de Reinette

Poularde à la Broche   Poularde grillée Henry III
Poularde Tour d'Argent   Poularde sautée canaille
sur Commande (vingt-quatre heures)   *pour deux personnes*
Poularde Suédoise   Poulet Sigaud
sur Commande   *sur Commande*
Poularde en Papillote

TEMPS ET SAISONS

Coquilles St-Jacques Duchesse de Gesvres
Selle d'Agneau rôtie Duchesse de Berry
Le Pintadeau Truffé Madame de Parabère
Sorbet oui et non de la belle Aïssé

Faites nous la faveur a'ordonner par avance

Glaces
Sorbets
Crêpes Suzette
Crêpes Flamandes
Crème Américaine
Soufflé Kocisky
Soufflé Valtesse
Soufflé Sainte-Geneviève
Petits Fours *(la pièce)*
Profiterolles au Chocolat

ENTREMETS

Pêches flambées
Ananas au Kirsch
Compotes
Fruits de Saison
Poires Bourdaloue
Poires Wanamaker
Pannequets des Tournell
Beignets Vert Bocage

ENTREMETS

CAFÉ

POTAGE TOUR D'ARGENT *(Bean Soup)*
SERVES 8

This is a good, hearty soup, easy to make and one of the treasures you are apt to discover when you beg a recipe from a great chef. There is something special, something different, about this bean soup, and the surprise ingredient that gives it a lift is the last-minute addition of the sorrel. We could never have guessed it.

kidney beans
lentils
celery
carrot
onions
parsley
garlic
bay leaf
salt, pepper
butter
sorrel or sour grass
parsley or chervil
chicken stock
(see index)

1 Soak: **1 pound kidney beans** and **½ pound lentils** overnight in water to cover. Drain and put into a large soup kettle.

2 Add: **1 stalk celery, chopped, 1 carrot, chopped, 2 onions, chopped, 4 sprigs parsley, 2 cloves garlic, chopped, 1 bay leaf, 1 teaspoon salt, ¼ teaspoon butter, and 8 cups good chicken stock.** Bring to a boil, cover, and cook over low heat for 1½ hours, or until beans are very tender. Blend, 2 cups at a time, in an electric blender on high speed for 20 seconds, and strain into a clean saucepan. Reheat, and correct seasoning with **salt** and **pepper.** Makes 9 cups puree.

3 Heat: **3 tablespoons butter.**

4 Add: **4 cups finely shredded sorrel** or **sour grass,** and **½ cup minced parsley** or **chervil.** Cook, stirring, until the sorrel is wilted and loses color.

Add sorrel mixture to the hot bean puree. Stir in **2 tablespoons butter,** and serve very hot with a sprinkling of **freshly ground pepper.**

CROUSTADE DE BARBUE LAGRENE *(Fish with Soufflé Sauce)*
SERVES 2

Eating at a great restaurant like Tour d'Argent is an adventure because their chefs cook with imagination as well as skill. Here they have made something magnificent out of mere potatoes, fish fillets and the ingredients for a cheese soufflé. At Tour d'Argent the fish used is brill, a European flat fish similar to our sole, flounder or the dabs found on the West Coast. We use whatever is available, and it is unfailingly delicious.

potatoes
cream
salt, white pepper
fillets of flounder,
sole or dabs
fish stock (see index)
white Bordeaux
lemons
Parmesan cheese
fine bread crumbs
(see index)
béchamel sauce
(see index)
eggs
butter
watercress
cayenne pepper

CROUSTADE

Boil until tender: **2 large potatoes, peeled and quartered.** Drain, mash, and beat in: **¼ cup cream, ¼ teaspoon white pepper,** and **½ teaspoon salt.** Set aside.

FISH

Poach: **2 large fillets of flounder, sole, or dabs** in **¾ cup fish stock** with **¼ cup white Bordeaux** for 10 minutes. Keep warm in the liquid.
Preheat oven to hot (400° F.).

SOUFFLÉ SAUCE

1 In saucepan heat: **4 tablespoons** grated Parmesan cheese and **½ cup béchamel sauce** and cook, stirring, until sauce is smooth. Stir in: **1 egg yolk** and season with **cayenne pepper.**
2 Beat until stiff: **3 egg whites** and fold into the egg yolk mixture.
3 Combine: **2 tablespoons grated Parmesan cheese** and **2 tablespoons fine bread crumbs.** Set aside.

PRESENTATION

On a heatproof au gratin dish or oval stainless steel platter, 12 inches long, spread a bed of mashed potatoes. (This is the *croustade,* a foundation of bread or other starch in which a preparation is baked.) Arrange the poached fillets on this bed and cover with the soufflé mixture. Sprinkle with bread crumb-cheese mixture and dot with small pieces of **butter, about 1 tablespoon** in all. Bake in the hot oven for 15 minutes.

While dish is cooking, cook liquid in which the fillets were poached over high heat until reduced to half the quantity. Swirl in **2 tablespoons butter.** Beat: **1 egg yolk** with a little of the hot sauce, stir into remaining sauce and cook, stirring, for about 1 minute. Strain into serving dish and serve on the side. Garnish platter with **watercress** and **lemon wedges.**

NOISETTES DES TOURNELLES *(Fillets of Lamb with Onion Sauce)*
SERVES 4

Almost any kind of meat tastes marvelous with this classic onion sauce, called soubise, but it is especially delicious with the boned lamb chops and artichoke bottoms as served at the Tour d'Argent—*and* at the Prices', and now at your house, too, we hope.

onions
butter
béchamel sauce
(see index)
salt, white pepper
flour
eggs
artichoke bottoms
rib lamb chops
Madeira
chicken stock
(see index)

ONION SAUCE *(Soubise)*

1 Mince: **4 large onions,** or enough to measure 2 cups. Cover with water, bring to a boil, and simmer for 3 minutes. Drain.

2 In saucepan melt: **4 tablespoons butter.** Add onions, and cook slowly for 10 minutes, without letting them brown.

3 Stir in: **¾ cup béchamel sauce, ¼ teaspoon salt,** and **¼ teaspoon white pepper.** Cover and cook over low heat for 20 minutes. Blend in an electric blender on high speed for 15 seconds and strain through a fine sieve, or puree in a food mill.

4 Combine to a paste: **2 tablespoons flour, 2 tablespoons soft butter,** and **2 egg yolks.** Beat a little of the hot sauce into this mixture, then add mixture to sauce and cook, stirring rapidly, until thick and almost boiling.

5 Set aside.

Heat in simmering water: **8 cooked artichoke bottoms, fresh or canned**

NOISETTES

1 Preheat broiler.

2 Remove bone and fat from **8 small rib lamb chops.**

3 In skillet heat: **1 tablespoon butter** and in it sauté the chops over high heat for 3 to 4 minutes on each side, or until brown. Remove from skillet and keep hot.

MADEIRA SAUCE

Pour off fat remaining in skillet and add: **½ cup Madeira** and **¼ cup chicken stock.** Cook over high heat for 4 minutes, or until liquid is reduced by half. Swirl in **2 tablespoons butter** and season with **a little salt** and **pepper.**

PRESENTATION

Arrange the artichoke bottoms on a heatproof platter and fill with onion sauce, reserving about ½ cup. Place a lamb *noisette* on top of each artichoke bottom, and top with 1 tablespoon of the onion sauce.

Put the dish under the broiler for a few minutes, or until sauce is hot and tinged with brown. Serve the Madeira sauce on the side.

FILETS DE SOLE CARDINAL *(Fillets of Sole with Crayfish)*

SERVES 2

In the classic French cuisine there are probably several hundred ways to serve fillets of sole. The Tour d'Argent's recipe for *Filets de Sole Cardinal* is one of the great dishes, combining sole and crayfish in a delectable sauce. Now that the frozen Danish crayfish tails are available in this country there is nothing to prevent us from duplicating this famous recipe at home.

whiting
egg
cream
frozen Danish
crayfish tails
fillets of sole
cognac
Madeira
fish stock (see index)
shallot
parsley
salt, white pepper
nutmeg
tomato sauce
(see index)
butter
flour

FISH FORCEMEAT

(For blender method, see index.)

Dice: ¼ **pound raw whiting**, free of skin and bones, and pound in a mortar with a pestle until it is reduced to a paste. Work the paste through a food mill. Set bowl containing the fish puree in a pan of ice, and slowly work in the **white of 1 small egg**. Add gradually about ½ **cup cream** to make a creamy mixture that will hold its shape when a half teaspoon is dropped into hot, but not boiling water. Test, then season lightly with **salt, white pepper**, and **nutmeg**.

FISH

1 Cut lengthwise: **2 fillets of sole** and spread the four pieces with the fish forcemeat. Roll up the fillets like small jelly rolls.

2 Defrost **4 Danish crayfish tails** and slit the membrane on the under part of the shell with scissors.

3 Put fillets and crayfish tails in a **buttered** skillet. Add: **2 tablespoons cognac**, **6 tablespoons Madeira**, and **1 cup fish stock**. Sprinkle with **1 shallot, chopped**, **1 tablespoon minced parsley**, and a little **salt** and **pepper**. Bring liquid to a boil, cover, reduce heat and poach for 10 minutes. Remove fillets and crayfish and keep warm.

SAUCE

Add to fish liquid: ½ **cup basic tomato sauce**. Bring to a boil and cook until sauce is reduced by half. Stir in **1 tablespoon cognac**. Stir in **1 tablespoon butter** mixed to a paste with **1 teaspoon flour** and cook, stirring, until sauce is slightly thickened. Correct seasoning with **salt** and **pepper**.

PRESENTATION

Arrange stuffed fillets down center of a hot serving platter. Top each with a crayfish tail. Strain sauce over all and sprinkle with a little **finely chopped parsley**.

POULARDE EN PAPILLOTE
(Chicken with White Wine Sauce in Paper)

SERVES 4

At the Tour d'Argent the chicken in paper is brought to the table in its spectacular wrapping which has puffed up like a balloon. Deftly the waiter cuts it open, releasing a steamy cloud of fragrance. The advantage of cooking in paper is that the moisture of the food is retained in spite of the oven's heat. Actually, you can get the same result in a tightly covered baking dish, but it does not make nearly as good a show and besides, *"en papillote"* sounds so much fancier.

CHICKEN

chicken
salt, pepper
butter
shallots
mushrooms
dry white wine
dry vermouth
brown stock
(see index)
cooked ham
fresh tarragon
flour

1 Cut: **a 3-pound frying chicken** into quarters. Wipe parts with a damp cloth, sprinkle with **1 teaspoon salt** and **¼ teaspoon pepper**, and sauté in **½ cup butter** over low heat until lightly browned on both sides. Remove chicken parts and keep warm.

2 Add to pan: **1 tablespoon chopped shallots** and cook for 1 minute longer. Add: **4 tablespoons chopped mushrooms** and cook for 5 minutes. Add: **½ cup dry white wine** and **¼ cup dry vermouth** and cook until wine is reduced by half. Add: **½ cup brown stock** and replace chicken parts. Cover and cook for 20 minutes.

3 Remove chicken and keep warm.

SAUCE

Add to pan: **2 tablespoons finely sliced cooked ham** and **1 tablespoon chopped fresh tarragon.** Stir in, bit by bit, **1 tablespoon flour** mixed to a smooth paste with **1 tablespoon soft butter.** Cook, stirring, until sauce is smooth and has thickened.

Preheat oven to hot (400° F.).

PRESENTATION

Cut parchment or heavy brown, unglazed paper large enough to envelop a piece of chicken. Rub on both sides with **soft butter.** Fold paper in the center and place a piece of chicken on one side. Cover with 3 or 4 tablespoons of the sauce. Bring edges of paper together, fold over in a double fold and crimp to seal tightly. Bake in the hot oven for 10 minutes. Serve the chicken in its paper wrapping, and let each guest unwrap his own portion at the table.

CANETON TOUR D'ARGENT (Frederic's Pressed Duck)
SERVES 2

The Tour d'Argent's chef gave us this recipe for their most famous dish, but we have never tried it. We possess neither a duck press nor a taste for pressed duck, but for those hardy souls who do—here's the unadapted recipe in the chef's own words as he gave it to us.

duck
port
Madeira
lemon
salt, pepper
cognac

The duck used for this recipe must be very young (8 weeks), fattened the last 15 days. They kill this bird by suffocation (strangling) in order to keep all its blood. (*Author's note:* This begins to sound as though the Tour d'Argent chef writes my movie scripts!)

Make about **½ cup of consommé of a duck.**

The **liver of the duck** has been taken away and crushed.

Roast **the duck** about 15 minutes, no more. Then it may be very rare.

Put the crushed liver in a dish with **1 wineglass of port, ⅔ glass Madeira, ⅓ glass good cognac (brandy).**

Slice the duck in small pieces. Send the legs to the kitchen to be broiled.

Crush the bones in the special machine called "Press Duck" in order to extract all the blood, and pour in about **½ cup consommé of a duck.** This juice coming from the press will be poured over the pieces, the crushed liver, the mixture of port, Madeira and cognac, and the **juice of 1 lemon.**

Then this preparation is cooked on an alcohol lamp (chafing dish) until the sauce becomes thick and similar to the color of melted chocolate. **Salt** and **pepper** according to the taste.

The sauce must be beaten without interruption for 20-25 minutes. (*Author's note:* Not possible in my house.)

Serve very hot.

The broiled legs are served separately as a second course.

SOUFFLÉ AU GRAND MARNIER *(Grand Marnier Soufflé)*

SERVES 4

confectioners' sugar
eggs
flour
butter
milk
Grand Marnier
ladyfingers
salt
granulated sugar

One of the best dessert soufflés I know is this one made with Grand Marnier. The Tour d'Argent adds the nice little surprise of ladyfingers soaked in the liqueur and hidden in the middle of the soufflé. You pay a lot extra for that touch at the restaurant, but not at home.

1　In saucepan beat: **¼ cup confectioners' sugar** and **5 egg yolks.**

2　Stir in: **3½ tablespoons flour.**

3　Add: **1¾ cups hot milk** and cook, stirring rapidly, until mixture is smooth and thickened. Do not let it boil. Remove from heat. Add: **1 tablespoon butter,** and cool. Stir in: **3 tablespoons Grand Marnier.**

4　Soak: **2 ladyfingers, halved,** in **3 tablespoons Grand Marnier.**

5　Preheat oven to hot (400° F.).

6　Beat: **6 egg whites** with **a pinch of** **salt** until stiff and fold into the egg yolk mixture.

7　**Butter** a 6-cup soufflé dish and sprinkle with **a little granulated sugar.** Put in half the soufflé mixture. Place the ladyfingers on top and cover with remaining soufflé mixture.

8　Put soufflé into the hot oven. Immediately reduce oven temperature to 375° F. and bake for 30 minutes. Sprinkle top with **1 tablespoon granulated sugar** and continue to bake for 10 minutes longer. Serve immediately.

In the kitchen of the Hôtel de la Poste, we see the makings of a noble meal. Burgundian snails, a rack of lamb, fish from a local stream, vegetables fresh from the garden, and a battery of fine copper pots. The boy apprentice will learn, as we did, from the master chef.

The rich red wine of Burgundy complements the rare red beef. Cook them both together and you have Steak Chevillot, a happy blending of flesh and spirits that will nourish and sustain your own.

HÔTEL DE LA POSTE

A T THE heart of one of the richest wine-growing regions of Burgundy is the medieval city of Beaune. Here, every autumn after the grape harvest, a famous wine auction is held in the courtyard of the ancient hospital for the poor. The Hospices de Beaune has been housing the poor for more than 500 years on the proceeds of the great vineyards which it owns. It also owns a fine painting by Roger van der Weyden, among other treasures, and this handsome Gothic building remains one of the unforgetable pleasures of our visit to Beaune.

The other is the Hôtel de la Poste. I would trade you every chromium-plated motel in the United States for one such French inn. This one stands on the Street of the Cask-Makers — after all, wine is Beaune's chief industry. Its present owner and chef, Marc Chevillot, is the grandson of the founder of the hotel. Like his grandfather and his father before him, young M. Chevillot is a wine dealer as well as a gifted chef. He started as a kitchen apprentice in his father's kitchen, and later was employed by the incomparable Fernand Point at La Pyramide.

When you sit down to a meal at the Hôtel de la Poste, what you get is a distillation of a long tradition of fine wines and food, and the realization that great cooking doesn't just come about overnight. Out of respect for our amateur standing, however, M. Chevillot gave us some recipes which are excellent without being at all difficult to follow, as you will see.

 HEVILLOT A BEAUNE

L E   M E N U

Terrine de Faisan
à la Gelée au Porto

Truite au bleu
Sauce Hollandaise

Civet de Lièvre
au Corton

Volaille de Bresse Rôtie

Pommes Chips

Plateau de Fromages

Corbeille de Fruits

35 Francs, service compris

LES VINS

Pouilly-Fuissé 1961	11	
Saint-Romain 1961	11	
Beaune - Clos des Mouches 1961	18	
Beaune du Château	15	*Bourgognes Blancs*
Puligny-Montrachet 1961	17	
Meursault 1960	17	
Corton-Charlemagne 1961	35	
Savigny-les-Beaune 1961	12	
Aloxe-Corton 1959	14	
Volnay - Clos des Chênes 1959	20	
Pommard - Clos de la Commaraine 1959	20	
Beaune-Toussaints 1957	14	
Beaune du Château	14	
Beaune-Teurons 1959	15	
Beaune - Clos de la Féguine 1953	18	
Corton-Bressandes 1955	25	
Corton-Grancey 1959	25	*Bourgognes Rouges*
Clos de Vougeot, Château de la Tour 1957	35	
Nuits-Saint-Georges - Les Cailles 1957	28	
Chambolle-Musigny 1959	19	
Charmes-Chambertin 1955	33	
Chambolle-Musigny - Les Amoureuses 1959	28	
Gevrey-Chambertin 1959	20	
La Tâche 1953	55	
Grands-Echezeaux 1955	50	
Echezeaux 1937	55	
Meursault 1958, Cuvée Jehan Humblot	20	
Beaune 1957, Cuvée Nicolas Rolin	45	*Hospices de Beaune*
Beaune 1959, Cuvée Estienne	45	
Volnay-Santenots 1952	35	

BROCHET AU VOLNAY (*Pike in Red Wine*)

SERVES 2

Naturally, any wine used in Burgundy is bound to be one of the great local vintages. The Volnay, in which this pike was prepared at the Hôtel de la Poste, is an excellent red Burgundy. At home in California we like to use our local wines, and a good Pinot Noir, we find, can hold its own with any good red wine of Burgundy.

pike
onion
carrot
garlic
shallots
salt, pepper
peppercorns
Volnay (or a domestic red Burgundy)
red wine vinegar
sweet butter
watercress

FISH

1 In long fish kettle put: **½ onion, chopped, ½ carrot, chopped, 1 clove garlic, chopped, 4 shallots, chopped, ½ teaspoon salt,** and **¼ teaspoon peppercorns.**

2 Add: **1 bottle Volnay (or a domestic red Burgundy)** and **1 quart water.** Bring to a boil, and simmer for 12 minutes.

3 In the liquid place **a 2-pound pike,** ready to cook, with head and tail intact. Reduce heat, cover kettle, and poach the fish for 15 minutes.

BUTTER SAUCE

Into small saucepan put: **1 tablespoon minced shallots, 1 tablespoon red wine vinegar,** and **¾ cup sweet butter.** Season with **¼ teaspoon salt** and **⅛ teaspoon pepper.**

PRESENTATION

Just before the pike is ready to be served, stir the butter mixture over the high heat with a wooden spoon until butter is melted and sauce is boiling. Transfer pike to a warm serving dish. Garnish with **watercress** and serve the hot butter sauce on the side.

JAMBON PERSILLÉ À LA BOURGUIGNONNE
(*Jellied Ham with Parsley*)

SERVES 8

At the Hôtel de la Poste in Beaune they serve this traditional Burgundian Easter dish. We were delighted to get M. Chevillot's recipe as it is a beautiful and original solution to the problem of leftover ham.

shinbones with some meat
calf's feet
ham bone
parsley
fresh tarragon
bay leaves
thyme
salt, peppercorns
shallots
dry white wine
eggs
cooked ham
tarragon vinegar

STOCK

1 Into large kettle put: **2 shinbones with some meat, 2 calf's feet, 1 ham bone, ¼ bunch parsley, 1 large sprig tarragon, 2 bay leaves, 1 teaspoon thyme, 1 teaspoon salt, ½ teaspoon peppercorns, 3 shallots,** and **1 bottle dry white wine.**

2 Add: **2 quarts water** to barely cover the bones and meat with liquid. Bring to a boil and simmer for 3 hours. Strain the stock into a saucepan. Cool and remove fat from surface.

3 Add: **2 egg whites, beaten,** bring to a boil, stirring, and let stand for 5 minutes over low heat. Strain through a sieve lined with moist flannel. Makes 1 quart clarified stock for aspic.

JELLIED HAM

1 Take: **6 cups diced cooked ham (2½ pounds).** Mix with 2 cups of the hot clarified stock and press the mixture into an 8-cup serving bowl. Chill.

2 To remaining stock add: **1 tablespoon tarragon vinegar, ¼ cup dry white wine,** and **1 cup minced parsley.** Chill, but just before it sets, stir and pour over surface of ham. Chill until set.

PRESENTATION

Bring serving bowl to table, and slice portions out of it. There will be a layer of pink jellied ham topped with a layer of green parsleyed aspic in each slice.

STEAK CHEVILLOT

SERVES 4

The French prefer their steaks small and sautéed in a pan rather than large and broiled as we usually prepare them here. For four people or fewer this steak, as Chef Chevillot prepares it, is ideal and we find it a perfect chafing dish recipe.

STEAK

butter
fillets of beef
shallots
red Burgundy
flour
marrow bones
(optional)

In skillet heat: **1 tablespoon butter** and in it cook over high heat **4 fillets of beef,** each 1½ inches thick, for about 4 minutes on each side, or until browned and done to taste. Remove fillets to warm serving platter and keep warm. Drain fat from skillet and return skillet to moderate heat.

SAUCE

1 Add: **½ tablespoon butter** and **1 tablespoon minced shallots** and cook for 30 seconds.

2 Add: **½ cup red Burgundy** and cook until wine is reduced to about half its quantity.

3 Stir in: **1 teaspoon flour** mixed to a smooth paste with **1 teaspoon butter** and cook, stirring, for 30 seconds.

4 Swirl in: **1 tablespoon butter** and when butter is melted, add: **2 tablespoons red Burgundy.**

PRESENTATION

Spoon 2 tablespoons of the sauce over each fillet, and serve immediately. If desired, top each fillet with **a slice of poached beef marrow.**

FILETS DE SOLE AU VERMOUTH
(Fillets of Sole with Vermouth Sauce)

SERVES 4

Bistro cooking can be delicious, and is usually a lot simpler than restaurant preparations. This is a very good recipe for sole from the Boule d'Or, excellent and easy to do.

SOLE

sole
fish stock (see index)
butter
dry vermouth
eggs
cream
salt, cayenne pepper
fried bread

1 Remove the fillets from **3 sole,** each weighing about 1½ pounds.

2 Skin and cut each fillet in half lengthwise. Roll like little fat jelly rolls, and fasten each with a wooden pick.

3 With the head and bones of the fish make a small quantity of fish stock.

4 Arrange the fillets in a **buttered** 9-inch skillet and moisten with **1 cup dry vermouth** and ⅓ **cup fish stock.** Sprinkle with **½ teaspoon salt.** Bring liquid to a boil, cover skillet, and poach the fillets for 12 minutes. Remove fillets to a small heatproof platter, discard the picks, and keep warm.

SAUCE

1 Boil the liquid in which the fish were poached over high heat until it is reduced to ¼ cup.

2 In a small bowl beat: **2 egg yolks** and **1 tablespoon cream.** Place bowl in a pan containing 1 inch simmering water. Use a wire whisk and whisk in the reduced fish stock and a **pinch of cayenne pepper.** Continue to whisk until the sauce begins to thicken. Then whisk in, bit by bit, ¾ **cup butter** until the sauce is the consistency of thin hollandaise.

PRESENTATION

Pour the sauce over the rolled fish fillets, decorate the platter with **triangles of fried bread,** and broil for 2 to 3 minutes, or until sauce is lightly browned.

COQUILLES ST. JACQUES BAUMANIÈRE *(Scallops in Cream Sauce)*

SERVES 4

Of all the many recipes for seafood served in scallop shells, this is one of the most delicious—and simple and quick to make into the bargain. We like the fact that the *coquilles* can be prepared in advance and need only be heated in the oven at the last minute.

SCALLOPS

scallops
shallots
salt, white pepper
dry vermouth
cream
flour
butter
parsley

Wash **1½ pounds scallops**. If these are large sea scallops, cut them into quarters. Put in saucepan with: **1 tablespoon chopped shallots, ¼ teaspoon salt, dash white pepper**, and **½ cup dry vermouth**. Bring liquid to a boil, cover saucepan, and simmer over low heat for 2 minutes only. Remove scallops with slotted spoon, and divide into 4 scallop shells. Cook liquid remaining in saucepan over high heat until reduced to half.

SAUCE

1 Add to reduced liquid: **1 cup cream**. Boil rapidly until cream is reduced and sauce is the consistency of syrup.

2 Combine: **1 tablespoon flour** and **4 tablespoons soft butter**. Reduce heat and gradually stir in butter bit by bit.

PRESENTATION

Pour the sauce over the scallops, sprinkle with **minced parsley**, and heat in the very hot oven for 5 minutes.

ROGNONS DE VEAU *(Veal Kidneys)*

SERVES 1

Veal kidneys have a delicate flavor and do not need long cooking. Beef kidneys are tougher and I would not recommend using them for this recipe which makes a delightful little entrée or luncheon dish. It is another excellent specialty from the Baumanière, not difficult to prepare and marvelous to taste.

KIDNEYS

kidney
butter
Armagnac
dry white wine
Dijon mustard
port
salt, pepper
cream
flour
parsley
shallot

1 For each serving, cut out the fat from **1 veal kidney**.

2 In skillet heat: **1 tablespoon butter**. In it sauté the kidney over high heat until browned on all sides.

3 Add: **2 tablespoons Armagnac**, ignite, and let the flame die out.

4 Add: **¼ cup dry white wine**, cover, and cook over low heat for 3 minutes. Do not overcook, or kidney will be tough. Transfer kidney to a small casserole, and keep warm.

SAUCE

1 Cook liquid in skillet until reduced to almost nothing.

2 Stir in: **½ teaspoon Dijon mustard** and **¼ cup port**. Sprinkle with **a little salt** and **freshly ground pepper** and cook until port is slightly reduced.

3 Stir in: **3 tablespoons cream** mixed with **½ tablespoon flour** and cook, stirring, until sauce is slightly thickened. Cook over low heat for 5 minutes.

4 Stir in: **1 tablespoon butter**.

PRESENTATION

As soon as butter is melted, strain the sauce over the kidney. Sprinkle with **a little chopped parsley** and **1 shallot, minced**.

COUPE GLACÉE BAUMANIÈRE
(Ice Cream with Chestnuts and Chocolate Sauce)
SERVES 6

If you keep a can of sweetened chestnut puree and a jar of glacéed chestnuts on your party shelf, you too can toss together this most gala dessert at the drop of an invitation. So easy to do, so delicious to taste, the effectiveness of this *coupe glacée* depends to a large extent upon the kind of oversized glass in which it is served.

semisweet chocolate
cream
chestnut puree with
sugar
vanilla ice cream
glacéed chestnuts

1 Put into small saucepan: **4 ounces semisweet chocolate** and **½ cup cream.** Cook over low heat, stirring constantly, until chocolate is melted and sauce is smooth. Keep warm.

2 Into bottom of each *coupe* glass or brandy snifter put: **1 good tablespoon chestnut puree with sugar.** Cover the puree with **a scoop of vanilla ice cream.** Spoon 2 tablespoons chocolate sauce over the ice cream in each glass and garnish with a **glacéed chestnut.**

TARTE AUX FRAMBOISES *(Raspberry Tart)*
SERVES 6

all-purpose flour
butter
sugar
eggs
milk
cornstarch
framboise
raspberries (or
strawberries)
confectioners' sugar

PASTRY SHELL

1 Measure into a small bowl **1 cup all-purpose flour.** Make a well in center.

2 Into well put: **½ cup soft butter, 1 tablespoon sugar, 1 egg yolk,** and **1 tablespoon cold water.**

3 Mix center ingredients with your hand to a smooth paste, then gradually work in the flour. Gather dough into a ball, flatten out into a small circle on waxed paper and chill for 1 hour.

4 Preheat oven to hot (425° F.).

5 Roll out pastry on a **floured** pastry cloth with a covered rolling pin into a circle 9 inches in diameter. Transfer dough gently to an 8-inch flan ring placed on a baking sheet, or to an 8-inch pie plate. Fit the dough lightly into the pan without stretching. Trim away excess dough, leaving about ⅜ inch of dough above rim of ring or plate. Turn edge of dough back and flute in tiny standing fluted edge.

6 Cover dough with waxed paper, fitting paper down into shell, and covering it with beans or rice. Bake in hot oven for 15 minutes. Remove beans or rice and paper and cool.

7 Reduce oven to moderate (350° F.).

THICK PASTRY CREAM

1 Scald: **2 cups milk.**

2 In saucepan combine: **4 egg yolks, 6 tablespoons sugar, 6 tablespoons flour,** and **1 teaspoon cornstarch.**

3 Gradually add the hot milk and cook, stirring rapidly, for about 3 minutes or until cream is smooth and thick.

4 Dot with **1 teaspoon butter** and cool, stirring occasionally.

5 Stir in: **1 tablespoon framboise.**

TART

1 Pour or strain the cooled pastry cream into the baked pie shell and bake in the moderate oven for 20 minutes.

2 Remove from oven and immediately cover the hot cream with **2 cups raspberries** and sprinkle with **1 tablespoon confectioners' sugar.** Serve at room temperature.

Halved **strawberries** may be used in place of the raspberries.

MOULES À LA NORMANDE (*Mussels in Cream*)

SERVES 4

One of the things we admire about French cooking is the fact that inexpensive foods are given the same loving treatment as the luxury items, and frequently turn out to taste even better. Take mussels. Yours for the picking at any ocean beach, yours for pennies a pound at fish markets where every other finny or shelled creature now fetches a king's ransom. Still, mussels are not used much in this country. We had them once in a little coastal town near Le Havre, prepared in the Normandy manner, and if they were the rarest, scarcest treasure they could not have made a more delectable dish. See for yourself when you try this recipe.

mussels
shallots
parsley
celery (optional)
cream
butter
dry white wine
French bread

Allow about 60 mussels for 4 persons. That would be about 4 pounds, depending upon size. Scrub well with a stiff brush and scrape off any seaweed or beard or barnacles sticking to shells. Discard any mussels that are broken or open, and put others in bowl of cold water in refrigerator until you are ready to use them. You can clean them the day before, if you wish.

1 In a large heavy pot put: **1 cup dry white wine, 2 tablespoons minced shallots, 1 tablespoon minced parsley, 1 tablespoon minced celery leaves** (optional), and **2 tablespoons butter.** Place **cleaned mussels** in pot, cover, and turn heat on high. When liquid boils, remove cover, and as soon as mussels open remove them with slotted spoon.

2 Remove empty top shells from mussels and discard. Keep cooked mussels warm.

3 Let mussel stock boil until it is reduced by half.

4 In a small pan put: **⅓ pint cream.** Let it boil and thicken until it is syrupy.

5 Add the thickened cream to the mussel stock. Stir, and swirl in: **1 tablespoon butter.** Turn off heat and put mussels into sauce. Sprinkle with: **1 tablespoon chopped parsley** and serve at once.

PRESENTATION

Serve right from the large pot, or divide into large shallow soup bowls. Have one empty bowl for shells, a soup spoon and a cocktail fork for each person. Serve **a loaf of warm French bread** cut in thick slices for mopping up the sauce.

PETITS POIS À LA FRANÇAISE (*Little Peas with Lettuce*)

SERVES 6

These tiny fresh green peas are my favorite vegetable in all the world. In France they serve a dish of these young peas as a separate course, they are that wonderful, but we prefer to serve them right with our meal. Even the frozen ones are good prepared this way, but the garden-fresh kind are, of course, much, much better.

butter
peas
small onions
lettuce
thyme
parsley
sugar
salt, pepper

1 In a saucepan melt: **2 tablespoons butter.**

2 Add: **2 pounds young green peas, shelled, 1 head lettuce, shredded, 10 small white onions, 2 sprigs fresh thyme, 4 sprigs parsley, 1 teaspoon sugar, ½ teaspoon salt,** and **⅛ teaspoon pepper.** Stir to mix well.

3 Cover pan tightly and allow to simmer on low heat. Moisture from the lettuce should be sufficient, but you must stir occasionally, and can add a spoonful of water if necessary.

4 Cook for about 45 minutes or until peas are tender. Add: **1½ tablespoons butter,** mix well, and serve.

ESCARGOTS BOURGUIGNONNE *(Burgundian Snails)*
SERVES 8

The plump snails from Burgundy are considered one of the great French delicacies. You either love them or hate them — there is no middle ground where snails are concerned. If you are a snail-lover, you will be happy to know that the recipe for them is simple, but to serve them properly you should have the metal snail dishes with little depressions for each shell, and a slim, two-pronged snail fork for digging the snail out of its shell. If you are a snail-hater, you might like the green butter mixture in which they are cooked, and never mind the gastropod itself. Just make the butter and use it in baked potatoes, on broiled meat or fish, or as a stuffing for broiled mushroom caps. This is the recipe we were given in Burgundy and which we use with the canned snails available here. Good — and garlicky.

snails and shells
sweet butter
shallots
garlic
parsley
salt, pepper
nutmeg
d crumbs (optional)
dry white wine
French bread

SNAIL BUTTER

1   In a mixing bowl cream: **¾ pound sweet butter.**

2   Add: **2 tablespoons finely chopped shallots, 1 clove garlic, mashed, 2 tablespoons finely chopped parsley, ¼ teaspoon salt, a dash of pepper,** and **a pinch of nutmeg.** Mix thoroughly until you have a smooth green paste.

SNAILS

1   Preheat oven to hot (400° F.).

2   Wash and drain **4 dozen snails** according to directions on can. Wash thoroughly **4 dozen snail shells** according to directions.

3   Put a little snail butter in the bottom of each shell. Add a snail. Fill shell with butter mixture.

4   Place shells in snail dishes or in flat baking dish, with open ends up. Sprinkle with **bread crumbs** if you wish.

5   Pour **2 tablespoons dry white wine** in bottom of each dish.

6   Bake in the hot oven for 8 minutes.

PRESENTATION

Serve piping hot in baking dishes with snail forks or cocktail forks. Use thick slices of **French bread** for mopping up extra sauce.

HARICOTS VERTS À LA LYONNAISE *(String Beans Lyonnaise)*
SERVES 4

One great thing about vegetables in France is that they are never overcooked and thus retain their color, flavor, and texture. Another great thing is cooking them with sautéed onions, which makes anything taste good and is a culinary trick that evidently originated in Lyons. Lyons is a famous gastronomic city, and I like to think that it made its reputation by the simple expedient of adding browned onions to *everything*. Cooks have done a lot worse!

butter
string beans
salt, pepper
onions
parsley
vinegar

1   Boil: **1 pound fresh string beans** in **salted** water for 12 minutes. Drain and dry well on paper towels.

2   In a skillet heat: **2 tablespoons butter.** Add: **2 medium onions, cut in thin slices.** Sauté until onions are light brown. Add: the cooked beans, **1 teaspoon salt,** and

¼ teaspoon pepper. Sauté until beans are lightly browned.

PRESENTATION

Sprinkle with: **1 tablespoon freshly chopped parsley,** and add **1 tablespoon vinegar.** Mix well and serve in a vegetable bowl.

CROQUE-MONSIEUR *(Toasted Cheese and Ham Sandwich)*

SERVES 4

I think I like the name of this famous French sandwich as much as anything about it, though it is delicious. *"Croque"* means crunch, and the sandwich is crisp and crunchy. You can cut it into small squares and serve it as a hot hors d'oeuvre, or it makes a very good little dish for lunch or light supper.

bread
butter
ham
Roquefort cheese
Gruyère cheese
egg (optional)
milk (optional)

1 Take: **8 slices of bread** and spread with **butter** on one side only.

2 Place on 4 of the slices: **1 thin slice Gruyère cheese, 1 thin slice ham,** and **1 thin slice Roquefort cheese.**

3 Close sandwiches with remaining 4 slices of bread.

4 If used for hors d'oeuvres, cut into quarters, otherwise cut into halves.

5 If you wish, you can dip sandwiches into batter made from **1 beaten egg** and **2 tablespoons milk** before sautéing.

6 Sauté until golden on both sides in hot **butter.** Serve hot.

ITALY

ITALY is surely one of the most beautiful countries in the world, a place where every vista is a feast for the eye. Time seems to have sustained it through all the ages only, I suspect, because it has been so loved by those who live there. When the orchards produce their first fruits, when the old earth yields a new crop of vegetables, Italians thank God for these fresh proofs of His bounty.

This gratitude is one of the secrets of Italian happiness, and this seasonal respect for the good things of the earth is what makes each meal in Italy a special feast. The waiter peeling a red orange from Sicily, the first little pencil-thin stalks of asparagus, rich ruby cherries, tender baby lamb, all are celebrated as they are eaten. In time with nature, never out of step, one can taste the months go by in the simplest or most elegant places to eat.

That is what a restaurant is in Italy—a place to celebrate food and a place to cherish friends. It is not an uncommon sight to see a family, or even a party of twenty or more Italians, dining out, loving one another and every mouthful of food and drink. And in every restaurant the feasting of old cronies or young couples is a pleasure to watch. Neither the meal nor the company is taken for granted. There is a positive delight in both that generates a warmth of feeling in every Italian eating place. You never see people champing their food, silent and glum as they sit across the table from one another. To eat is to live, to live is to be happy, and why not let the world know it?

Most Americans, and even many Europeans, think of Italian menus as overloaded with pasta, and it is true that the Italians are fond of their spaghetti, macaroni, *fettuccine* and dozens of related starches. Ever since

Marco Polo brought the first noodle back to Italy from China, the Italians have lavished all their inventiveness on this basic dough, twisting it into a dazzling variety of shapes and bathing it in a multitude of marvelous sauces. But Italian cooking is far more varied, more subtle than many suspect, and I learned to love it in all its guises during the many months I spent there traveling or working in movies.

One of the hallmarks of Italian cooking is, of course, herbs. Anything that springs from the earth has a special charm for the Italians—fruits, vegetables, herbs and flowers—and it is not surprising that these people are among the world's best gardeners. Their food is perfumed with oregano, rosemary, basil and fennel and these herbs give Italian cookery its distinctive aromatic quality.

Then there are the great cooking cheeses—Romano, ricotta, mozzarella and Parmesan, all of which are readily available in American markets. Grated Parmesan is sprinkled on Italian food almost as universally as salt and pepper, and with much more interesting results. Soups, meats, pastas, fish, vegetables, everything is given that extra little lift with a sprinkle of Parmesan, but the secret is that the cheese is always freshly grated from a large chunk just before it is used.

Italian cuisine varies from one part of the country to another. Northern Italy boasts the richer more continental cuisine, the south is all too well known for its heavier, spicier fare and the ever-present tomato sauce that has become a cliché of Italian cooking outside of Italy. We find all Italian food exciting, and can readily understand that when Catherine de Médicis came to queen it at the French court in the sixteenth century, her Italian chefs taught the French ones a few culinary tricks that are being practiced there to this day. We learned a few ourselves, and pass them on to you in our favorite Italian recipes in this section.

Tre Scalini has a sidewalk café
just off the Piazza Navona. You can sit
at a table outside and enjoy the
view of Bernini's fountains over an ice cream,
or go indoors and enjoy the view
of their sumptuous buffet over a dish of pasta.

Only a people who loved their pasta
could have invented so many charming shapes
for it. But the great classic dish
remains spaghetti with savory meat sauce.

P. KREDEL

TRE SCALINI

ONE of the happiest times we ever spent in Rome was on a quick visit we made there one December. The city had thrown off its summer torpor and it bustled with Christmas animation. We arrived in the early evening after two weeks in Greece and Turkey, and we were starved for Italian food, having had our fill of lamb and rice and vine leaves stuffed with Zeus knows what.

With one mind we decided that the only place for us that night was Tre Scalini, on the Piazza Navona, where we could dine to the music of Bernini's fountains. In the summertime, Tre Scalini has tables on the piazza under a flapping awning. There, cooled by the fountain-conditioned air, you can eat the superb Italian ices and ice creams for which Tre Scalini is renowned. Their specialty is an ice cream made with white Italian truffles, the recipe for which is such a jealously guarded secret that we didn't dare even hint that we might be interested in it. (It's not my favorite ice cream, anyhow.)

But that December night, surfeited with Turkish delight, we craved just good, old-fashioned Italian cooking with no nonsense. And so we ordered spaghetti with meat sauce, of all things! And it was fabulous, as only Italian pasta can be. That recipe, so much less exotic than truffled ice cream, the chef imparted to us gladly, plus several good tips on how to boil spaghetti. I suppose you could dine in Rome for a-thousand-and-one nights without exhausting the marvelous variety of foods and restaurants there. But somehow on your first night revisiting the city you return to a favorite place and a favorite dish, and are never disappointed.

Ristorante

LISTA DEL GIORNO

ZUPPE

ZUPPA ORTOLANA 200
CREMA AURORA "
TORTELLINI AL CONSOMÉ "
CAPELLINI " " "
QUADRUCCI " " "
CONSOMÉ IN TAZZA "
STRACCIATELLA "
MINESTRONE "

ASCIUTTE

CANNELLONI TRE SCALINI   35
RISOTTO E FUNGHI "
SPAGHETTI VONGOLE
FETTUCCINE AL RAG
MACC. AMATRICIA
TORTELLINI BURR
E FUNGHI   4
& POMODORI
CON RISO   4

PIATTI

POLLO ALLA ROMANA CON PEPERONI
ROAST BEEF CON SPINACI
ABBACCHIO AL FORNO CON PATATE
VITELLO ARROSTO CON FAGIOLINI
POLLO ARROSTO CON INSALATA
FRITTO MISTO ALL'ITALIANA
CERVELLO BURRO E PISELLI
CROCCHETE DI POLLO CON ZUCCHINE
ROGNONCINO AL FUNGHETTO
FEGATO ALLA VENETA
OSSOBUCO CON FUNGHI

PIATTI FREDDI

MISTO FREDDO CON GELATINA 9

GALANTINA DI POLLO " " 80

VERDURE

FAGIOLINI 300

SPINACI 300

ZUCCHINE 300
INSALATA 200
POMODORI CITRIOLI 250

DOLCI E GELATI

Tartufo Tre Scalini	3
Torta 4 Fiumi	3
Bisquit Moison	3
Dolci assortiti	3
Crema caramella	3
Torta Margherita	
Torta Zabaione	
Cassata alla Siciliana	3
Granita di Caffè con panna	3

"Tre Scalini"

Antipasti variati - Servizio al carrello S.Q.

BOLLITI		PESCE	
GALLAHCA con Risotto	800	TRAHCIA	900
		FRITTO SCAMPi SALAMARI	900
CACCIAGIONE			
		Sogliole A.L.	S.Q.

GIORNO

SPECIALITÀ BAULETTO TRE SCALINI CON FUNGHI

Pollo ALLA DIAVOLA	900
Filetto di BUE Ai FERRi	900
ENTRECOTE	750
Combatina di Vitello	850
Filetto di Tacchino con Piselli	750
SALTIMBOCCA CON FUNGHi	750
Cotoletta MiLANESE con FAGIOLiNi	750
SCALOPPE Pomodoro e FuNghi	750
MELANZANE PARMiGiAN	600

PRIMIZIE

ASPARAGi PARMiGiANA	600
PiSELLi FRESCHi	600
FuNGHi TriFoLATi	600

FRUTTA		FORMAGGI
di STAGIONE	200	Gran Servizio S. Q.
MACEDONIA	300	
FRAGOLE	500	

COPERTO L. 150   PREZZO FISSO L.

Caffé	. . L.	60
Caffè Hag	. L.	80
Nescafè	. . L.	150
Tè	. . L.	150
Camomilla	. L.	120
Zabaione (caldo) L.		350

SPAGHETTI ALLA BOLOGNESE *(Spaghetti with Meat Sauce)*

SERVES 4

The best known and best loved pasta dish in all Italy is probably this one. The city of Bologna has a gastronomic fame for more than the sausage that bears its name, and the *Ragù alla Bolognese*, this rich meat and tomato sauce, is used on many other pasta dishes throughout Italy. Every chef varies it a bit to suit himself, and this recipe has evolved slightly from the Tre Scalini original since we have been using it. Try this sauce on *conchiglie*, the little shells, sometime. They hold more of the sauce because of their shape, and you might prefer it that way.

MEAT SAUCE

spaghetti
onion
carrot
celery
tomato puree
garlic
butter
lemon
bay leaf
beef
bacon
chicken livers
dry white wine
beef stock
(see index)
Parmesan cheese
salt, pepper
olive oil
cream

1 In a heavy skillet heat: **2 tablespoons butter** and **2 tablespoons olive oil**. Add: **1 onion, finely chopped,** and cook until soft. Add: **3 rashers lean bacon, cut into small pieces, 1 carrot, chopped,** and **1 stalk celery, chopped.** Sauté over medium heat until lightly browned.

2 Add: **½ pound beef, coarsely ground,** and stir until meat is coated with fat. Add: **2 chicken livers, minced.** Stir until meat browns evenly.

3 Add: **2 tablespoons tomato puree, ½ cup dry white wine, 1 cup beef stock, 1 bay leaf,** and **1 strip lemon peel** (thin yellow skin only). Season with: **salt, freshly ground pepper,** and **1 clove garlic, crushed.**

4 Cover and simmer for 40 minutes, stirring occasionally. Remove bay leaf and lemon peel and allow to simmer uncovered until sauce thickens slightly. Just before serving stir in: **¼ cup cream** and reheat sauce. (Makes 1 pint.)

SPAGHETTI

1 In a large pot pour: **3 quarts of water.** Rub a little **olive oil** or **butter** around sides of pot above water line. This will prevent water from boiling over when you cook the spaghetti.

2 Add: **1 tablespoon salt** and bring to a rapid boil. When water has been boiling briskly, take: **1 pound spaghetti** and feed by handfuls into the boiling water. Dip one end of the spaghetti sticks into the water, and as they get soft let them coil into the pot. Never break them. Stir with a wooden spoon occasionally.

3 If you are using packaged spaghetti, cook for about 12 minutes, or according to directions on package. It should be soft but firm when you bite it. (The Italians call this *al dente*, or "to the tooth.") Homemade pasta will need less time to cook—only 5 to 7 minutes. Drain cooked spaghetti in a colander. You can keep it warm by placing colander over a pan of boiling water and covering it with a towel wrung out in warm water.

PRESENTATION

Place spaghetti on a warm platter and dot with: **4 tablespoons butter.** Sprinkle with: **4 tablespoons freshly grated Parmesan cheese.** Serve with meat sauce on the side, or in the center of the platter with the spaghetti around it. Pass a bowl of **freshly grated Parmesan cheese** with the platter.

FRITTO MISTO ALLA ROMANA *(Assorted Fried Foods Roman Style)*

SERVES 4

At Tre Scalini they serve this Roman version of a mixed grill which is really a mixed fry. On a large platter you get an assortment of bite-sized tidbits of various meats and vegetables, fried to a golden crispness. Sometimes fish and seafood are used in place of the meats. This is one of those dishes that invites the cook to improvise with all the imagination at his command—and all the foods in his refrigerator.

salt, pepper
cayenne pepper
flour
eggs
milk
cauliflower
eggplant
butter
cooking oil
veal scallops
chicken livers
veal kidneys
artichoke hearts
string beans
·ied basil or oregano
lemon
Italian watercress

BATTER

Make a batter by sifting: **2 cups flour** with **1 teaspoon salt** and **⅛ teaspoon cayenne pepper**. Combine: **4 eggs**, beaten with **1⅓ cups milk**, and blend thoroughly with dry ingredients. Add: **3 tablespoons melted butter** and mix well.

MEATS AND VEGETABLES

1 Have: **1 pound veal scallops** pounded very thin and cut into 2-inch circles. Take: **1 pound chicken livers** and cut into halves. Trim: **4 veal kidneys** of all fat and sinews and cut into small pieces.

2 Blanch: **½ pound string beans, cut** into 1-inch lengths, **8 artichoke hearts, 16 small cauliflower florets**, and **1 small eggplant, cut into slices.**

3 Sprinkle meats and blanched vegetables with **salt, coarsely ground pepper,** and **a little dried basil** or **oregano.**

4 Dip each piece in batter and fry, a few pieces at a time, in hot **cooking oil** (380° F.) until golden brown.

PRESENTATION

Serve hot on one large platter or arrange assortment of fried foods on individual plates with wedges of **lemon** and **Italian watercress.**

SPUMONI

SERVES 6

Homemade ice creams are incomparably better than most bought ones, but unless you have an ice-cream freezer you can't do them properly. Here is a recipe for spumoni from Tre Scalini that is simplicity itself. You just make a zabaglione, add whipped cream, and freeze it in a soufflé dish or individual molds. A few hours later you have a heavenly ice cream.

Marsala
eggs
sugar
almond extract
cream
almonds
marrons

1 Place a heatproof bowl in a pan of boiling water. Turn heat down till water barely simmers. In the bowl put: **½ cup Marsala, 3 egg yolks, 3 tablespoons sugar, 2 teaspoons water**, and **¼ teaspoon almond extract**. With a wire whisk beat constantly until mixture is warm and begins to thicken. Do not let water boil.

2 Remove bowl from water and whip until mixture becomes smooth and thick. Fold in: **¾ cup cream, whipped,** and mix carefully.

3 Spoon into individual cups, cover, and put in freezer for 6 hours.

PRESENTATION

Remove molds from freezer. Sprinkle with **chopped, toasted almonds** and place **½ marron** in center of each portion.

HAZELNUT ICE CREAM

SERVES 8

Tre Scalini is highly original about its ice creams and ices. This one is interesting and rich, and is good all by itself or as the filling for a mold that has been lined with a chocolate or fruit-flavored ice cream first. This hazelnut ice cream can then be put in the center of the lined mold, covered and frozen to make a beautiful bombe.

hazelnuts
milk
sugar
eggs

1 Boil: **1¼ pounds shelled hazelnuts** (1 quart) in water to cover for 1½ hours. Drain.

2 Blend nuts in electric blender, one cup at a time with a generous ½ cup milk each time, to a smooth paste. Use a total of **2¼ cups milk.**

3 Blend in electric blender: **½ cup boiling water, 1¼ cups sugar,** and **3 egg yolks.** Stir into nut paste.

4 Pour into 2 ice-cube trays and freeze. This makes a soft ice cream.

SCALOPPINE DI VITELLA ALLA PASSETTO
(Veal Scallops au Gratin)

SERVES 4

One of Rome's most fashionable restaurants is Passetto, a place that staggers you when you enter with a dazzling buffet of foods, including a whole haunch of uncooked veal. Passetto's veal may be beautiful enough to display raw, but cooked it is really superb, as witness this recipe, quick, easy and delicious.

veal scallops
flour
salt, pepper
butter
mushrooms
prosciutto ham
mozzarella cheese
brown sauce
(see index)
basil
parsley
Parmesan cheese

VEAL

1 Preheat oven to moderate (350° F.).

2 Dip: **8 thin, neatly trimmed veal scallops** into **flour** and sprinkle with **salt** and **pepper**.

3 In large skillet or shallow ovenproof dish melt: **¼ cup butter.** Place the scallops in the hot butter, one slightly overlapping the other, and cook for 3 minutes, or until lightly browned. Turn to other side. On each scallop place: **a thin slice prosciutto ham.** Cover the ham with: **a thin slice mozzarella cheese.** Top the cheese on each scallop with: **1 tablespoon brown sauce.** Sprinkle the surface of all the scallops with a mixture of: **1 teaspoon dried basil** and **2 tablespoons minced parsley.** Sprinkle with: **½ cup grated Parmesan cheese.**

4 Transfer dish to the moderate oven and bake for 10 minutes, or until cheese browns.

PRESENTATION

Serve with: **1 pound sautéed mushrooms.**

CANNELLONI ALLA PASSETTO
(Chicken Cannelloni with Cream Sauce)

SERVES 4

If you have two cups of leftover chicken, turkey or veal, invite two friends for dinner and give them this elegant specialty of Passetto. I sometimes think Mary purposely plans to have leftovers so that we can dine the following night in Roman splendor!

butter
flour
salt, white pepper
nutmeg
milk
cannelloni
(see index)
olive oil
onion
celery
carrot
parsley
cooked chicken,
turkey or veal
oregano
basil
dry white wine
tomato sauce
(see index)
cream
Parmesan cheese

SAUCE

In saucepan melt: **4 tablespoons butter.** Stir in: **4 tablespoons flour, ½ teaspoon salt, ⅛ teaspoon white pepper,** and **⅛ teaspoon nutmeg.** Add: **2 cups hot milk** and cook, stirring, until sauce is smooth and thickened. Cook over low heat for 5 minutes, stirring occasionally.

FILLING

1 In skillet heat: **2 tablespoons olive oil** and in it sauté: **3 tablespoons minced onion, 3 tablespoons finely chopped celery, 2 tablespoons finely chopped carrot,** and **1 tablespoon minced parsley** for 10 minutes, or until vegetables are tender.

2 Add: **2 cups ground or finely chopped cooked chicken, turkey** or **veal, ¾ teaspoon salt, ¼ teaspoon oregano,** ¼ **teaspoon basil, ½ teaspoon white pepper,** and ¾ **cup dry white wine.** Simmer until wine is reduced by half. Stir in ½ cup of the sauce.

CANNELLONI

1 Preheat oven to very hot (450° F.).

2 Cook: **8 cannelloni** in boiling **salted** water for 8 minutes. Drain and rinse in cold water. On each cannelloni put 2 tablespoons of the filling and roll up. Arrange 2 filled cannelloni in a **buttered** au gratin dish for each serving.

3 To remaining sauce add: **4 tablespoons tomato sauce** and **¼ cup cream.** Stir to blend. Pour ½ cup of this sauce over each serving and sprinkle with: **2 tablespoons grated Parmesan cheese.**

4 Bake in the very hot oven for 10 minutes, or until top browns.

LOMBATINA DI VITELLA ALLA PASSETTO
(Veal Chops with Mushroom Sauce)

SERVES 4

This is an especially good recipe to use if you are unable to get really fine milk-fed veal at the market. Passetto's mushroom sauce will give flavor and dash to the most ordinary veal chops, and if there is any sauce left on your plate it does wonders for a piece of Italian bread too.

olive oil
onion
carrot
celery
salt, pepper
mushrooms
tomato sauce
(see index)
prosciutto ham
capers
veal chops
flour
butter

SAUCE

1 In a small pan heat: **2 tablespoons olive oil**. In it cook: **2 tablespoons minced onion, 2 tablespoons minced carrot**, and **2 tablespoons minced celery** for 10 minutes, stirring occasionally.

2 Add: **8 medium mushrooms, minced, ½ teaspoon salt, ¼ teaspoon pepper** and cook for 5 minutes longer, stirring frequently.

3 Add: **1 cup tomato sauce, ½ cup shredded prosciutto ham, 1½ tablespoons chopped capers** and cook for 25 minutes, stirring occasionally. Makes 1½ cups sauce.

VEAL

Dip: **4 veal chops** into **flour** and sprinkle with **salt** and **pepper**. Sauté in: **⅓ cup butter** for 3 minutes on each side, or until lightly browned. Add the mushroom sauce, cover, and cook over low heat for 20 minutes.

CARCIOFI VIGNAROLA *(Garnished Artichoke Hearts)*

SERVES 4

You really have to go to Rome to discover all the delicious ways that artichokes can be prepared. On the terrace of the Casina Valadier, with its view from the Pincian Hill, we had these artichokes one afternoon. Signora Banfi, the owner, told us how to cook them, and I must say, they taste just as good at home as they did in that glamorous setting.

large artichokes
lemon
butter
lettuce
bacon
dry white wine
peas
celery
fennel
carrot
small new potatoes
tomato
salt, pepper

ARTICHOKES

1 Trim stems from: **4 large artichokes** and remove two rows of the lower outer leaves. Cut 2 inches of the leaves from the tops of the artichokes. Separate leaves, wash well, and cut out pale yellow leaves from centers. With a silver spoon, scrape out the chokes. Drop artichokes immediately into cold water acidulated with **the juice of 1 lemon**.

2 Grease a casserole large enough to hold the artichokes with: **2 tablespoons butter**.

3 Shred: **1 head lettuce** and spread it on bottom of casserole.

4 Shred: **2 strips bacon** and sprinkle pieces on top of lettuce.

5 Place artichokes on the bed of lettuce.

GARNITURE

1 Shell: **1 pound fresh peas** and fill centers of artichokes with the peas.

2 Surround artichokes with: **the heart of 1 bunch of celery, chopped, ½ head fennel, chopped (including some of the green leaves), 1 carrot sliced, 8 small new potatoes, peeled,** and **1 large ripe tomato, cut into wedges.**

3 Add: **2 cups water, 1 cup dry white wine, 2 teaspoons salt,** and **¼ teaspoon pepper**.

4 Bring liquid to a simmer, cover casserole tightly, and cook over low heat for 1¼ hours.

POLLO DISOSSATO VALADIER *(Boned Chicken Valadier)*
SERVES 6

The recipe for this delicious dish, written out for us by the chef of the Casina Valadier, begins, "Clean well a chicken and cut it on the back and take out from it every bones"! Actually, it's as easy to do as to say. With a sharp boning knife anyone can bone a chicken in fifteen minutes, and we will tell you how in this recipe.

CHICKEN

chicken
ham
salt, pepper
peppercorns
sage
onion
cloves
carrot
garlic
parsley
thyme
bay leaf
dry white wine
butter
Marsala

1 Cut off wing tips and first joints of a **5-pound roasting chicken.** Slit skin down the back and, with a sharp knife, scrape away skin and flesh from both sides, revealing shoulder and thigh joints. Cut through these joints, and continue cutting away skin and flesh around and over the breast. Lift out and discard entire carcass. Peel back and scrape away skin and flesh from wing bones and remove bones. Do the same to the thigh bones, revealing knee joints. Cut through knee joints and remove thigh bones. Continue scraping flesh and skin away from leg bones, and remove leg bones. The chicken is now boneless, with meat and skin intact. Lay it flat on a cutting board, skin side down.

2 Cut: **1½ pounds raw ham** into julienne strips. Insert several strips into legs and thighs to replace the bones. Spread remaining strips lengthwise over breast meat.

3 Sprinkle with: **½ teaspoon salt, ¼ teaspoon pepper**, and **½ teaspoon crumbled sage leaves.**

4 Fold skin of chicken around filling, tucking in wing and neck skin, and sew up. It now looks like a wingless duck. Tie it in a piece of cheesecloth, and put it in a **buttered** braising pot or casserole, with the wing and leg bones.

5 Add to casserole: **1 onion, stuck with 4 cloves, 1 carrot, sliced, 1 clove garlic, 1 teaspoon salt, 8 peppercorns, a few sprigs parsley, ¼ teaspoon thyme, 1 bay leaf, 1 cup dry white wine, and 4 cups water.** Bring liquid to a boil, cover tightly, and poach the stuffed chicken for 50 minutes.

6 Preheat oven to very hot (450° F.).

7 When chicken is tender, remove from liquid, take off cheesecloth wrapping, and place chicken in **buttered** shallow roasting pan. Spread with: **2 tablespoons butter** and bake in the very hot oven for 30 minutes, basting with pan juices every 10 minutes.

SAUCE

1 Place chicken on hot serving platter. Pour off excess fat in pan, and place pan over high heat.

2 Add: **½ cup dry white wine** and cook, scraping all the brown glaze from bottom of pan, until wine is reduced by half.

3 Add: **½ cup Marsala** and **2 tablespoons butter.** Reduce heat, and stir just until butter is melted. Add **a little salt** and **pepper**, and pour into sauce dish. Serve separately with the boned chicken.

Overlooking the blue San Marco Canal in Venice, the Terrace of the Royal Danieli offers exquisite food to match the beauty of the scene.

Osso Bucco, veal knuckles rich with marrow and meat and bathed in a full-bodied sauce, is served with *Risotto alla Milanese*, the famous saffron rice of Milan.

THE ROYAL DANIELI

THE view from the Royal Danieli Roof Terrace at dusk rivals the greatest paintings of Venice. It seems almost a sacrilege to think of food in a setting of such beauty, but the Danieli's chef is an artist himself, and you find yourself dining sumptuously here, accepting the total magnificence as though you were a Renaissance prince to the *palazzo* born.

The Hotel Danieli Royal Excelsior, to give it its full title, is in fact three palaces, one of them dating from the fourteenth century. The Terrace Restaurant is on the roof of the newest palace, built only about ten years ago. The last time we were in Venice, we stayed there for a few days in November. No tourists, constant fog and rain—the city was wonderful for cozy sightseeing. And we were made to feel really welcome in a Venice, which for those few short winter months, belongs to the Venetians.

This great hotel in the heart of Venice made us doubly welcome with its service, friendliness, and fine food. We couldn't eat on the magnificent roof as we had on former visits, because of the weather, but we enjoyed our favorite dishes almost as much downstairs.

The Danieli's cuisine borrows from every section of Italy, so when you eat here you can sample the local specialties from the top to the toe of the Italian boot. Naples, Bologna, Piedmont, Florence, Milan, Rome, Tuscany, and Venice itself are all represented in the names of various dishes. How marvelous to be able to eat all over Italy without having to leave the splendors of Venice!

Carta del Giorno

Antipasti - Hors d'Oeuvre

Hors d'oeuvre varié 700 - Prosciutto di S. Daniele 500 - Salame di Cremona 500
Salmone affumicato 1000 - Scampi Cocktail 900 - Granzeola 900 - Gamberetti 800
Coppa di frutta 400
Foie Gras de Strasbourg importato - porzione 2000 - Caviale Malossol importato - porzione 5000

Zuppe - Potage

Consommé aux Pâtes 300 - Consommé au Sherry 400 - Stracciatella alla Romana 350
Zuppa Pavese 350 - Zuppa di Verdura 300 - Minestrone all'Italiana 350
Crema di pomodoro 350 - Crema di piselli 350 - Crema Regina 400 - Potage Parmentier 300

Farinacei - Pâtes

Spaghetti alla Napoletana 500 - Vermicelli alla Marinara 500 - Fettucine alla Bolognese 500
Cannelloni alla Ligure 600 - Ravioli alla Piemontese 600 - Risotto alla Valencienne 600

Uova - Oeufs

Oeufs en Cocotte à la Crème 400 - Pochés Florentine 600 - Pochés Mornay 500
Uova fritte all'Americana 600 - Al Tegame con Salsiccia 600 - Brouillés au Jambon 600
Frittata con Carciofi 600 - Omelette alla Spagnola 500 - Con Gamberetti 800
Mozzarella in carrozza 500 - Welsh Rarebit 500 - Crostini di Prosciutto e Pomodoro 400
Crostini Provatura 400 - Toast di Sardine 500

Pesce - Poisson

Sole Meunière 1100 - Turbot Dugléré 1300 - Branzino **s. g.**
Suprème di Sogliola Serenissima 1300 - Filetto di S. Pietro Riviera 1200
Scampi alla brace **s. g.** - Frittura di Pesce alla Veneziana 1200
Scampi fritti, sauce Tartare 1500 - Aragosta alla Parigina **s. g.** - Homard Thermidor **s. g.**

Piatti di Mezzo e Arrosti - Rôtis et Grillades

Escalope alla Milanese 1000 - Piccata di Vitello al Pomodoro 1000
Costoletta di Vitello Danieli 1300 - Filet Mignon alla Brace 1600
Entrecôte Bordelaise 1300 - Hamburger-Steak 1000
Entrecôte Minute 1200 - Chateaubriand (2 p.) Sauce Bearnaise **s. g.**
Cotoletta di Agnello grillée 1000 - Costata di Maiale alla Sassi 1200
Ham Steak alla Bismarck 1000 - Fritto misto alla Lombarda 1300 - Fegato di Vitello all'Inglese
Mixed Grill all'Inglese 1300 - Pollo alla Cacciatora 1500 - Sovrana di Pollo Ducale 1200
½ Pollo di Toscana allo Spiedo e ai ferri 1200 - Piccione con Piselli 1100

Legumi - Légumes

Fagiolini al burro 300 - Carote Vichy 300 - Tomates Provençale 300
Zucchine trifolate 300 - Melanzane 300 - Spinaci in Foglia 300 - Patate 250
Insalata Verde 250 - Insalata mista 300

Dolci - Entremêts

Gâteau Danieli 350 - Torta di Frutta 300 - Crème Caramel 300 - Crêpes Normande 400
Omelette Confiture 500 - Soufflés Divers 700 - Zabaglione al Marsala 500
Macedonia di Frutta al Liquore 450 - Pere diacce Perugina 500 - Pesche alla Cardinale 500
Coppa Danieli con friandises 600 - Gelati vari 400 - Composta assortita 400
Pasticceria Francese 150 p. pièce.

Formaggi vari - Fromages variés 300

Frutta di Stagione - Fruits de Saison 300

POUR LES REPAS À PRIX FIXE VEUILLEZ VOUS ADRESSER AU MAÎTRE D'HÔTEL

20 % de supplément pour service dans l'appartement

A La Carte Service

Appetizers

Choice of appetizers 700 - Smoked Ham of St. Daniele 500 - Sausage of Cremona 500
Smoked Salmon 1000 - Scampi Cocktail 900 · Granzeola 900 - Shrimps 800 - Fruit Cocktail 400
Imported Goose liver of Strasbourg 2000 portion - Imported Malossol Caviar 5000 portion

Soup

Consommé with thin Noodles 300 - Consommé au Sherry 400
Consommé with Egg yolks & Parsley 350 - Soup with poached eggs and French fried Toast 350
Vegetable soup 300 - Vegetables & Spaghetti Soup 350 - Cream of Tomato 350
Cream of Green Peas 350 - Cream of Chicken 400 - Cream of Potatoes 300

Farinaceous

Spaghetti with Tomato Sauce & Cheese 500 - Spaghetti with Tomato & Parsley Sauce 500
Home made Noodles with Meat Sauce 500 - Ravioli Piemontese Style 600
Cannelloni 600 - Rice with Shrimps 600

Eggs and Savouries

Creamed Eggs in Tureen 400 - Poached Eggs with Spinach 600
Poached Eggs Mornay 500 - Fried Eggs on Toast with Tomato & Bacon 600
Fried Eggs with Sausage 600 - Scrambled Eggs with Ham 600 - Omelet with Artichokes 600
Omelet with Onion 500 - Omelet with Shrimps 800 - Mozzarella in Carrozza 500
elsh Rarebit 500 - Ham with Tomato on hot Toast 400 - French fried Toast with Anchovies 400
Sardines on Toast 500

Fishes

Sole done in Butter 1100 - Turbot Dugléré with cream Sauce 1300 - Sea Bass a. s.
Fillets of Sole in White Wine sauce 1300 - Fillets of St. Pietro with Vegetables 1200
Grilled Shrimps a. s. - Assorted Fried Fish Venetian style 1200
French fried Shrimps, Tartare Sauce 1500 - Lobster with Russian Salad & Mayonnaise a. s.
Homard Thermidor a. s.

Meat Dishes and Roast

Breaded Veal Steak done in Butter 1000 - Small Collops of Veal with Tomatoes 1000
Chop of Veal with Cream Sauce & Mushrooms 1300 - Grilled Fillet Mignon 1600
Sirloin beef Steak done in Butter with Red Wine Sauce 1300 - Hamburger Steak 1000
Minute Steak 1200 - Grilled Lamb Chops 1000 - Chateaubriand Bearnaise Sauce a. s.
Pork Cutlet with Sage and potatoes 1200 - Bismarck Ham Steak 1000
Mixed Grill English Style 1300 - Stewed Chicken with Tomato & Mushrooms Sauce 1500
Mixed Fried Meat in Butter 1300 - Calf's Liver English Style 1000
White of Chicken on Toast with fresh Vegetables 1200 - Broiled Chicken 1200
Pigeon with Green-peas 1100

Vegetables

Green-peas 300 - String Beans in Butter 300 - Carrots Vichy 300 - Tomatoes 300
Squash 300 - Egg-plants 300 - Spinach 300 - Potatoes 250 - Green Salad 250
Mixed Salad 300

Sweets

Gâteau Maison 350 - Fresh Fruit Tarte 300 - Cold Caramel Custard 300 - Jam Omelet 500
Pancake Normande 400 - Soufflés all styles 600 - Egg Punch with Marsala Wine 500
Fruit salad with Liquor 450 - Peach on Ice Cream with Jelly 500
DANIELI ICE CREAM CUP - SPUN SUGAR DESSERT 600 - Assorted Ice Cream 400
Compote of Stewed Fruit 400 - Choice of French Pastry 150 p. piece

Assorted Cheeses 300

Fresh Fruit of the Season 300

FOR FIXED PRICE LUNCH OR DINNER PLEASE APPLY TO THE HEAD-WAITER

20% supplement for meals served in the apartment

OSSO BUCCO ALLA MILANESE
(Veal Shinbones Braised with Vegetables)

SERVES 6

veal shinbones
flour
butter
salt, pepper
celery
carrots
rice
onion
mushrooms
sage
rosemary
tomato
white wine
lemon
parsley
anchovy
garlic

This famous specialty of Milan is one of the Royal Danieli's marvelous recipes. *Osso bucco* always makes a big hit with men, I suspect because we like the challenge of getting the meat off the bone and digging for the marrow inside. Try it next time you have an informal dinner, and you'll see what I mean.

1 Have butcher cut: **2 veal shinbones full of marrow** into 3-inch pieces, to make 6 individual servings.

2 Roll the shinbones in **flour** and sauté in: **4 tablespoons butter** over high heat until brown on all sides. Turn bones on sides to hold in marrow.

3 Add: **1 teaspoon salt, ½ teaspoon pepper, ½ cup finely chopped celery, 1 medium onion, finely chopped, ½ cup finely chopped carrots, ½ cup minced mushrooms, 1 large ripe tomato, peeled, seeded, and chopped, ½ teaspoon crum-** bled sage, and ½ teaspoon rosemary. Reduce heat, cover, and braise for 10 minutes.

4 Add: **2 cups white wine.** Cover and gently simmer for 2 hours. The liquid should barely cover the bones.

5 Just before serving stir in the **gremolada.** This consists of **the grated rind of 1 lemon, 2 tablespoons chopped parsley, 1 anchovy, mashed, and 1 clove garlic, minced.** Serve with cooked rice. *Risotto alla Milanese* is the classic accompaniment to this dish.

SCAMPI FLAMINGO *(Shrimp in Sherry Cream Sauce)*

SERVES 4

butter
onion
celery
carrot
thyme
large shrimp
cognac
cream
milk
sherry
béchamel sauce
(see index)
salt
rice
lemon

The giant Italian prawns called *scampi* are a favorite seafood there, prepared in any number of marvelous ways. We can use *scampi* recipes for the large shrimp available here and they work out very well. The Royal Danieli's recipe for *Scampi Flamingo* is one of the most elegant and successful in our repertoire, and not at all difficult, praised be the chef!

1 In skillet heat: **½ cup butter.** Add: **1 medium onion, minced, 1 stalk celery, finely chopped, 1 carrot, finely chopped, and ¼ teaspoon thyme.** Cook for 10 minutes, or until vegetables are tender and lightly browned.

2 Add: **2 pounds large shrimp in their shells** and cook for 10 minutes until most of the liquid has evaporated. Stir frequently and be careful that the vegetables do not burn.

3 Add: **¼ cup cognac,** ignite, and let the flame burn out. Remove shrimp, cool slightly, then remove shells and intestinal veins.

4 Add to skillet: **1½ cups cream, ½ cup milk, ⅓ cup sherry, and ½ cup béchamel sauce.** Simmer for 10 minutes, or until sauce is the consistency of heavy cream. Add: **½ teaspoon salt** and **1 teaspoon lemon juice.** Replace shrimp and heat for 5 minutes.

PRESENTATION
Remove shrimp to a hot serving dish. Swirl: **¼ cup butter** into sauce and strain over the shrimp. Serve with **rice pilaf.**

RISOTTO ALLA MILANESE (*Rice with Saffron and Parmesan Cheese*)

SERVES 6

The true Milanese rice is rich and golden. Butter and chicken stock give it a luxurious flavor, and saffron, used sparingly, colors it a delicate yellow. Sometimes half a cup of white wine is substituted for half a cup of the stock. The chef at the Royal Danieli only insisted that we be careful not to let the rice become too dry. We have followed his advice and find this a marvelous way to cook rice.

butter
onion
rice
chicken stock
(see index)
saffron
Parmesan cheese

1 In saucepan melt: **4 tablespoons butter.**

2 Add: **1 small onion, minced,** and cook until onion is lightly browned.

3 Add: **1½ cups rice** and stir to mix.

4 Add: **4 cups chicken stock** and bring to a rapid boil. Cover and cook over low heat for 25 minutes, stirring frequently.

5 Stir in: **¼ cup butter** and **1 teaspoon saffron** softened in **2 tablespoons chicken stock** and cook, uncovered, over low heat for 5 minutes longer.

PRESENTATION

Turn into warm serving dish and sprinkle with: **2 tablespoons freshly grated Parmesan cheese.**

FETTUCCINE ALLA BURANELLA (*Noodles with Fish and Shrimp*)

SERVES 4

Everyone makes a big to-do about *fettuccine all'Alfredo,* noodles tossed with butter, cream and Parmesan cheese, for which Alfredo was awarded an 18-carat gold fork. If we had any gold *fettuccine* forks to give away, ours would go to the chef of the Royal Danieli whose recipe is a fabulous fisherman's delight, named for one of the islands in the Venetian Lagoon.

thin egg noodles
fillets of sole
butter
dry white wine
fish stock (see index)
salt
leek
light cream
béchamel sauce
(see index)
cayenne pepper
lemon
shrimp
Parmesan cheese

1 Cook: **8 ounces thin egg noodles** in boiling **salted** water for 8 minutes. Drain, rinse, cool slightly, and stir in: **1 tablespoon butter.**

2 Cut: **4 fillets of sole** (¾ pound) into ¾-inch squares.

3 Heat in skillet: **2 tablespoons butter.** Add the fish fillets, **⅓ cup dry white wine, ½ cup fish stock, ½ teaspoon salt,** and **the white part of 1 small leek, finely chopped.** Bring liquid to a boil and simmer the fish for 3 minutes. Remove fish and cook liquid remaining in skillet until it is reduced by half.

4 Add: **1 cup light cream, ½ cup béchamel sauce, ½ teaspoon salt,** and **⅛ teaspoon cayenne pepper.** Cook, stirring occasionally, until sauce is smooth and glossy, but not too thick. Remove from heat and stir in: **1 teaspoon lemon juice.** Strain through fine sieve.

5 Poach: **½ pound shrimp** in simmering water for 5 minutes. Drain, remove shells and intestinal veins, chop and stir into fish fillets.

6 Grate: **6 tablespoons Parmesan cheese.**

7 Melt: **4 tablespoons butter.**

8 Preheat oven to hot (400° F.).

9 In bottom of a 2-quart casserole put one-quarter of the noodles. Cover noodles with one-third of the fish mixture and sprinkle with 1 tablespoon grated Parmesan cheese, one-quarter of the sauce, and 1 tablespoon of the melted butter. Repeat twice, then top with remaining noodles, add remaining sauce, sprinkle with 3 tablespoons grated Parmesan and the remaining melted butter.

10 Bake in the hot oven for 10 to 15 minutes, or until lightly browned.

Note: This may be made in advance and heated before serving. In this case, preheat oven to 350° F. and bake for 25 to 30 minutes, or until sauce is bubbling and surface is lightly browned.

BACCALÀ ALLA VICENTINA (Braised Salt Codfish)

SERVES 4

Fish and seafood abound in Venice, the city of islands. At the Royal Danieli even salt cod is made glamorous—no easy task. But this is a most interesting way of preparing what can be very dull fish indeed.

salt codfish
onions
garlic
butter
olive oil
flour
parsley
tomato paste
pine nuts
anchovy fillets
cinnamon
pepper

FISH

1 Soak: **1 pound salt codfish** in water to cover for 6 to 8 hours, or overnight, changing the water several times.

2 Cover fish with fresh cold water and bring just to a boil. Do not let boil or fish will be tough. Drain, and put fish into baking dish.

SAUCE

1 Preheat oven to very slow (275° F.).

2 Stew: **2 onions, chopped,** and **2 cloves garlic, minced,** in **¼ cup butter** with **2 tablespoons olive oil** for 10 minutes, or until onion is pale and golden.

3 Stir in: **1½ tablespoons flour, 2 tablespoons minced parsley, 2 tablespoons tomato paste,** and **1 cup water.** Heat to simmering and pour over fish in baking dish. Stir to mix.

4 Sprinkle with: **2 tablespoons pine nuts, 2 fillets of anchovies, chopped, ¼ teaspoon cinnamon,** and **freshly ground pepper.** Bake in the slow oven for 1 to 1¼ hours, or until most of the liquid is absorbed. Serve in baking dish.

ZUPPA DI PESCE ROYAL DANIELI (Fish Soup)

SERVES 6

We love all of the beautiful fish soups and stews that the Mediterranean cooks blend with such artistry. This one, from the Royal Danieli in Venice, is especially good because of the fine Italian handful of assorted herbs. All the flavors come together so smoothly it's impossible to guess what went into the kettle.

lobster
assorted fish
squid
onion
celery
vinegar
salt, pepper
large shrimp
olive oil
garlic
bay leaf
thyme
basil
parsley
dry white wine
tomato
saffron
bread

1 Plunge: **a 1½-pound lobster** into rapidly boiling water and cook for 5 minutes. Cool slightly, remove body and claw meat. Reserve both the meat and the shell.

2 Wash: **3 pounds assorted fish,** such as **a small sea bass, a small red snapper, a slice of cod** or **salmon,** and **a small trout** or **a fillet of haddock.** Cut off heads and tails and cut fish into thick slices.

3 Clean: **a ½-pound squid** (see index) and cut into slices.

4 Into saucepan put: **1 quart water, 1 onion, coarsely cut, 1 stalk celery with leaves, chopped, 2 tablespoons vinegar,** and **2 teaspoons salt.** Add: **½ pound large shrimp,** bring to a boil, and simmer for 5 minutes. Remove shrimp with slotted spoon, reserving liquid. Cool slightly, remove shells, and discard intestinal veins. Set shrimp and shells aside.

5 Add to shrimp liquid the shells of the lobster and shrimp and the fish heads and tails. Simmer for 20 minutes. Strain.

6 In large kettle heat: **¼ cup olive oil.** Add: **2 cloves garlic, minced, 1 bay leaf, crumbled, ½ teaspoon thyme, 1 teaspoon basil,** and **2 tablespoons minced parsley.** Add the shrimp, the fish and squid chunks, and sauté for 5 minutes, stirring constantly.

7 Add the fish broth, **½ cup dry white wine, ½ cup chopped, peeled tomato, ¼ teaspoon saffron, 1 teaspoon salt,** and some **freshly ground pepper.** Bring liquid to a boil, reduce heat and simmer for 10 minutes, stirring occasionally.

PRESENTATION

Serve in soup plates with **slices of bread** sautéed in **olive oil.**

RISI E BISI ALLA VENEZIANA (*Venetian Rice and Peas*)
SERVES 4

In northern Italy rice is the favorite starch, and one of the most delicious Venetian specialties is this combination of rice and peas. The rice is not cooked dry, and sometimes *risi e bisi* is almost like a very thick soup. We like the Royal Danieli's version which is just moist enough to soak up a generous sprinkling of grated Parmesan cheese.

butter
onion
bacon
celery
fresh peas
cooked ham
rice
chicken stock
(see index)
salt, pepper
Parmesan cheese

1 In heavy kettle heat: **¼ cup butter.** Add: **1 small onion, chopped, 1 slice bacon, diced,** and **1 stalk celery, chopped.** Sauté for 5 minutes, or until onion is golden and bacon is cooked.

2 Add: **2 cups fresh, shelled green peas** (2 pounds in pods) and **½ cup diced cooked ham.** Cover and braise for about 5 minutes, stirring occasionally.

3 Add: **¾ cup rice** and cook for 3 minutes, stirring to coat all the grains with the butter.

4 Add: **1¾ cups chicken stock, 1 teaspoon salt,** and **¼ teaspoon pepper.** Bring to a rapid boil, cover, turn heat low and cook very slowly for 30 minutes, or until rice is tender and the liquid is absorbed. The rice and peas should remain fairly moist.

5 Stir in: **1 tablespoon grated Parmesan cheese.** Serve hot with **additional grated Parmesan.**

POLLO ALLA CACCIATORA (*Chicken Hunter's Style with Noodles*)
SERVES 6

Every little Italian restaurant in the United States features its "chicken *cacciatora*," but it is far from being the most popular, or even the most typical, dish in Italy. At the Royal Danieli this chicken in its spicy sauce is served with noodles, as in this recipe, or with polenta, cornmeal mush, that has been cut into slices and fried in olive oil. It's good either way. The real secret of this recipe's excellence is the red wine added for the last bit of cooking. That's the master touch.

chickens
olive oil
butter
onions
green pepper
garlic
basil
salt, pepper
stewed tomatoes
dry red wine
noodles

1 Sauté: **2 chickens,** about 3 pounds each, cut into serving portions, in **4 tablespoons olive oil** and **½ cup butter** for about 10 minutes, or until golden brown on all sides.

2 Add: **2 cups finely chopped onion, 1 green pepper, chopped, 4 cloves garlic, minced, ½ teaspoon dried basil, 1½ teaspoons salt,** and **½ teaspoon pepper.** Cook for 5 minutes, or until onion is transparent.

3 Add: **1 cup stewed tomatoes** and stir to mix. Bring to a boil, cover, and cook over low heat for 20 minutes, stirring occasionally.

4 Add: **½ cup dry red wine** and simmer for 10 minutes longer.

5 While the chicken is cooking, cook: **8 ounces noodles** in a pot of rapidly boiling **salted** water for 8 to 10 minutes, or according to package directions. Drain.

PRESENTATION
Serve the chicken and sauce over the hot cooked noodles.

LASAGNE VERDI ALLA BOLOGNESE *(Green Lasagne Casserole)*
SERVES 6

You can buy uncooked *lasagne*, but it's not hard to make your own, and they do taste much better. In case you can't tell one pasta from another without a scorecard, *lasagne* are the broad, ribbon-like squares or rectangles, and when they are green it is because spinach has been added to the dough—spinach and vitamins. This casserole is a marvelous one-dish meal.

frozen chopped
spinach
eggs
flour
salt, pepper
butter
onions
celery
carrots
oregano
ground lean beef
ground loin of pork
dry white wine
tomato sauce
(see index)
milk
cream
Parmesan cheese

GREEN LASAGNE OR NOODLES
1 Cook: **1 package frozen chopped spinach** according to directions on package. Drain well, pressing out moisture with back of spoon. Chop finely and force through food mill.

2 In mixing bowl beat: **2 eggs** and **½ teaspoon salt**. Beat in the spinach puree. Beat in: about **2½ cups flour**, or enough to make a firm dough. Knead thoroughly, adding a little more flour if necessary. Cut dough into 4 pieces and let rest for 30 minutes. Then roll out one piece at a time very thinly on well **floured** board into a 12-inch square.

For *lasagne:* cut into 4-inch squares.

For noodles: cut into strips ¼ inch wide.

3 Let *lasagne* or noodles dry on towels for 1 hour. Then cook in a large quantity of boiling **salted** water for 8 minutes. Drain and rinse thoroughly. Makes about 1 pound green pasta.

MEAT SAUCE
1 In skillet heat: **¼ cup butter**. In it sauté: **2 onions, finely chopped, ½ cup finely chopped celery,** and **2 small carrots, chopped,** for 10 minutes or until onion is lightly browned. Sprinkle with: **2 teaspoons salt, ½ teaspoon pepper,** and **1 teaspoon oregano.**

2 Add: **1 pound ground lean beef, 1 pound ground loin of pork, ½ cup dry white wine,** and **6 tablespoons tomato sauce.** Simmer for 15 minutes, stirring frequently.

CREAM SAUCE
1 In saucepan melt: **½ cup butter.** Stir in: **½ cup flour, 1 teaspoon salt,** and **¼ teaspoon pepper.**

2 Add: **1 quart hot milk** and cook, stirring, until sauce is smooth and thick. Cover and cook over low heat for 5 minutes, stirring occasionally.

3 Stir in: **1 cup cream.**

PRESENTATION
1 Preheat oven to moderate (350° F.).

2 Grate enough **Parmesan cheese** to measure 1 cup.

3 In a **buttered** 9 x 13½-inch baking dish arrange a layer of *lasagne* using 6 of the cooked squares. Spread with one-third of the meat sauce, sprinkle with 2 tablespoons cheese and top with 6 more squares *lasagne.* Spread with one-third of the cream sauce and sprinkle with 2 tablespoons cheese. Repeat these layers twice more, so you have 6 layers, ending with cream sauce. Sprinkle with the remaining grated cheese.

4 Bake in the moderate oven for 15 minutes, and serve in the baking dish.

FEGATO ALLA VENEZIANA *(Calf's Liver with Onions and White Wine)*
SERVES 3

If you have trouble getting your family to eat liver as often as they should, try it Venetian style, as prepared at the Royal Danieli. It should happen to a doge, and probably did, it's that good.

onions
butter
sage
flour
salt, pepper
calf's liver
parsley
beef stock
(see index)
dry white wine

1 In large skillet sauté: **2 cups thinly sliced onions** in **½ cup butter** with **¼ teaspoon crumbled sage** for 10 minutes, or until onion is lightly browned and cooked.

2 Cut: **1 pound sliced calf's liver** into thin strips.

3 In paper bag combine: **¼ cup flour**, **½ teaspoon salt**, and **⅛ teaspoon freshly ground pepper**. Add the calf's liver and shake bag to coat the pieces with the seasoned flour. Add liver to onions and butter and cook over high heat for 5 minutes, stirring constantly.

4 Put liver on warm serving platter.

5 To pan add: **1 tablespoon minced parsley**, **3 tablespoons beef stock**, and **3 tablespoons dry white wine**. Cook for 1 minute, stirring in all the brown glaze from bottom of pan. Pour over the liver and onions and serve immediately.

ITALIAN TIPSY PUDDING

SERVES 10

You can go overboard in decorating this dessert so that you have something as colorful as an Italian festival. It is not really a pudding, and it is a good deal less tipsy than the Tower of Pisa, but it is certainly Italian in the most exuberant tutti-frutti tradition.

MADEIRA CAKE

butter
flour
eggs
sugar
Madeira or rum
cream
milk
vanilla
semisweet chocolate
confectioners' sugar
candied violets or
candied fruit

1 Preheat oven to moderate (325° F.).

2 **Butter** a 9-inch layer cake pan 2 inches deep, line with waxed paper, and **butter** the paper.

3 Melt and cool: **½ cup butter**.

4 Sift and measure: **1 cup flour**.

5 With electric beater beat: **4 eggs** and **½ cup sugar** for about 5 minutes, or until mixture is thick and takes some time to level out when the beater is withdrawn. Fold in half the flour. Fold in the melted butter. Fold in remaining flour. The best way to do this is with the hand.

6 Pour batter into prepared cake pan and bake in the moderate oven for 35 to 40 minutes, or until cake tests done. Let cool for 5 minutes, then turn cake out on rack to cool completely.

CUSTARDS

1 Heat: **2 cups cream** and **4 cups milk** to simmering.

2 In saucepan beat: **12 egg yolks** and **1 cup sugar**. Beat in: **¾ cup flour**. Add hot milk mixture and cook, stirring rapidly, until custard is smooth and thick. Cook over low heat for 5 minutes, stirring constantly. Do not let custard boil. Pour 3 cups of the custard into a bowl and stir in: **2 teaspoons vanilla**. Into remaining custard stir in: **6 ounces semisweet chocolate, melted**. Cool the custards.

PRESENTATION

Slice the cake into 3 layers about ½ inch thick. Place one layer in bottom of a handsome glass bowl about 10 inches in diameter. Sprinkle with: **¼ cup rum** or **Madeira** and pour in the vanilla custard. Cover with second cake layer, sprinkle with: **¼ cup rum** or **Madeira** and pour in the chocolate custard. Cover with third cake layer and sprinkle with: **¼ cup rum** or **Madeira**. Chill.

When ready to serve, beat: **2 cups cream** until thick and stir in: **½ cup confectioners' sugar** and **1 teaspoon vanilla**. Pipe large rosettes of the whipped cream through a fluted tube, covering the entire surface of the dessert. Garnish with **candied violets** or **chopped candied cherries, citron**, and **orange peel**.

ICE CREAM CUP ALLA DANIELI

SERVES 4

Wherever there is a topflight pastry chef in residence you will find desserts capped with clouds of spun sugar. It is one way of telling the pros from the amateurs. The stuff is very pretty, but no better to taste than the cotton candy at the circus—unless I'm suffering from an acute case of sour grapes. In any event, I would rather have whipped cream any day, so here is our version of the Royal Danieli's fruit and ice cream dessert, minus the spun sugar.

cantaloupe or melon
orange
banana
strawberries
sugar
maraschino or kirsch
vanilla ice cream
frozen raspberries
cream
confectioners' sugar

1 Combine: ½ ripe cantaloupe or melon, peeled and diced, 1 orange, peeled and sectioned, 1 banana, sliced, ½ cup sliced strawberries, 2 tablespoons sugar, and 2 tablespoons maraschino or kirsch.

2 Defrost: a 10-ounce package frozen raspberries. Empty berries and juice into container of blender and blend on high speed for 10 seconds. Strain through a fine sieve. Stir into the raspberry sauce:

1 tablespoon kirsch or maraschino.

3 Whip: ½ cup cream and stir in: 1 tablespoon confectioners' sugar.

PRESENTATION

Into large brandy snifters put ½ cup of the fruit mixture and top with a scoop of vanilla ice cream. Spoon 3 tablespoons raspberry sauce over ice cream, and top with a big dollop of whipped cream. Garnish with a big ripe strawberry.

SCAMPI AURORA *(Shrimp with Hollandaise Sauce au Gratin)*

SERVES 2

Harry's Bar in Venice is a tiny place, enormously chic, where the customers, crowded at little round tables, are fed some of the best food in Italy. Harry's can only accommodate fifty people, and the chef must have to operate out of the world's smallest kitchenette but the place, the people, and the cuisine have a style and elegance quite apart from these limitations. This is one of our favorite appetizers at Harry's Bar and it makes a very good luncheon dish too, served with a crisp green salad.

large shrimp
lemon
olive oil
hollandaise sauce
(see index)
salt, pepper

1 Peel, devein: 1 pound large shrimp.

2 Arrange the shrimp in a shallow au gratin dish.

3 Sprinkle with: juice of ½ lemon, 2 tablespoons olive oil, ½ teaspoon salt, and ¼ teaspoon pepper. Broil for 3 to

4 minutes, turn shrimp and continue to broil for 3 to 4 minutes longer.

4 Spoon over the shrimp: 1 cup warm hollandaise sauce and return to the broiler for about 2 minutes, or until top is lightly browned.

TAGLIATELLE VERDI GRATINATE AL PROSCIUTTO
(Green Noodle Casserole with Prosciutto)

SERVES 2

Another of Harry's specialties is this green noodle casserole. We have seen him use noodles as a salute to his American customers by arranging them like a flag on a large flat dish in thirteen stripes of plain noodles alternating with tomato sauce, and with a square of green noodles starred with fifty little pasta stars. A pretty sentiment, but we still prefer this casserole.

butter
flour
salt, pepper
milk
cream
green noodles
prosciutto ham
Parmesan cheese

1 In saucepan heat: **4 tablespoons butter.** Stir in: **¼ cup flour, ½ teaspoon salt,** and **⅛ teaspoon pepper.** Add: **2 cups hot milk** and cook, stirring, until sauce is smooth and thickened. Cook over low heat for 5 minutes. Stir in: **½ cup cream.**

2 Preheat oven to moderate (350° F.).

3 Cook: **6 ounces green noodles** in **3 quarts rapidly boiling water** with **1 tablespoon salt** for 8 minutes. Drain, rinse with hot water, and empty into shallow baking dish. Toss with: **2 tablespoons butter** and the cream sauce.

4 On top arrange slightly overlapping **thin slices of prosciutto ham,** using about ¼ pound in all. Sprinkle with: **¼ cup grated Parmesan cheese** and **2 tablespoons melted butter.**

5 Bake in the moderate oven for 10 minutes and serve with **additional freshly grated Parmesan.**

CONSOMMÉ STRACCIATELLA *(Raggedy Soup)*

SERVES 4

We enjoyed this consommé on the "Leonardo da Vinci" once, and when I asked the steward what "*stracciatella*" meant and he told me it meant "rags" or "tatters" we knew we had to have the recipe. Somehow the idea of serving "raggedy soup" or "tattered broth" in Mary's gold luster soup bowls is infinitely appealing! And besides, it's delicious.

eggs
semolina
Parmesan cheese
salt
nutmeg
chicken stock
(see index)

1 Beat: **2 eggs.**

2 In a bowl put: **2 rounded teaspoons semolina, 2 teaspoons grated Parmesan cheese, salt to taste,** and **a pinch of nutmeg.** Add beaten eggs and beat well together.

3 Add: **1 cup cold chicken stock** and mix well.

4 Bring to a boil: **2½ cups chicken stock.** Pour mixture into boiling stock slowly through a colander with large holes, stirring with fork or whisk so that lumps don't form.

5 Cook slowly for 10 or 15 minutes. The eggs and semolina will form little shreds or "rags" in the soup.

PRESENTATION

Serve immediately with **grated Parmesan cheese** on the side.

PASTICCIO DI POLENTA (*Cornmeal with Mushrooms*)

SERVES 4

Our old friend, cornmeal mush, is a favorite dish of north Italians under the far more exotic name of polenta. They seldom eat it mushy, but prefer to let it get cold and stiff enough to slice. Then they do any number of interesting things—fry the slices, wrap them in bacon and bake them until brown and crisp, sprinkle with cheese and butter and bake, or make this main-dish *pasticcio*—my favorite.

yellow cornmeal
salt
butter
bread crumbs
mushrooms
cream
Parmesan cheese

POLENTA

1 In top of double boiler, over direct heat, bring **1 quart water** to a boil. Add: **1¼ teaspoons salt.** Gradually let **1 cup yellow cornmeal** trickle into boiling water, stirring constantly.

2 When polenta becomes thick, place pan in bottom of double boiler. Cover and cook over hot water for 2 hours.

3 Pour into a loaf-shaped baking dish and chill overnight.

PASTICCIO

1 Preheat oven to moderate (350° F.).

2 Turn out chilled loaf of polenta and slice it in 3 horizontal layers.

3 **Butter** the baking dish and sprinkle it with: **2 tablespoons bread crumbs.**

4 Place a sliced layer of polenta on bottom of dish. Dot with: **1 tablespoon butter.** Cover with: **½ cup sliced mushroom caps** and **3 tablespoons cream.** Sprinkle with: **1 tablespoon grated Parmesan cheese.**

5 Put second slice of polenta on top. Dot with: **1 tablespoon butter.** Cover with: **½ cup sliced mushroom caps** and **3 tablespoons cream.** Sprinkle with: **1 tablespoon grated Parmesan cheese.**

6 Put last slice on top. Dot with: **1 tablespoon butter** and sprinkle with: **1 tablespoon grated Parmesan cheese.** Cover and bake 1½ hours in the moderate oven.

Note: Polenta is delicious if allowed to chill in a jelly-roll pan. When cool, turn it out and cut into 2-inch strips or squares and fry in hot fat.

MUSHROOM SOUP WITH PARMESAN CHEESE

SERVES 4

This fabulous soup was something we stumbled on quite by accident on a cold November day in Venice. It was drizzling and we stopped to warm ourselves in a tiny little restaurant. The owner recommended his mushroom soup, which didn't particularly send us, but we thought at least it would warm us. We loved it so that he dictated the recipe to us on the spot. We've made it many a time since, always with a pang for not being able to remember the name of the place where we had it first.

butter
olive oil
onion
eggs
Italian bread
garlic
mushrooms
chicken stock
(see index)
parsley
Italian vermouth
salt, pepper
Parmesan cheese
tomato paste

1 In a heavy pan melt: **1 tablespoon butter** and **1 tablespoon olive oil.** Sauté: **1 medium onion, grated,** and **1 clove garlic, split.** Let brown gently and discard garlic.

2 Stir in: **1 pound mushroom caps, sliced thin.** Sauté for 5 minutes and add: **3 tablespoons tomato paste.** Mix well and add: **3 cups chicken stock.**

3 Stir and add: **2 tablespoons Italian vermouth** (the sweet kind). Add: **½ teaspoon salt** and **a dash of pepper,** or to taste. Let simmer for 10 minutes.

GARNITURE

1 Beat together: **4 egg yolks, 2 tablespoons finely chopped parsley,** and **2½ tablespoons Parmesan cheese.**

2 Cut about 1-inch-thick slices of **Italian bread. Butter** and grill under broiler on one side only.

3 Place one slice of the bread in each soup bowl.

4 Beat egg mixture into boiling soup and serve at once poured over the bread slices. Hearty and delicious!

CROSTATA DI MELE (*Apple Tart*)
SERVES 6

This wonderful apple tart was the finale to a sumptuous lunch we had one afternoon. No one really wanted dessert, but then the waiter whisked a beautifully sugared apple tart under our noses. It was still warm and fragrant, and all of us, like hypnotized zombies, followed it with our eyes, watched the waiter cut it, let him place slices in front of us, and ate it with complete satisfaction. The recipe is notable in our collection for what is perhaps the most perfect pastry crust we know.

flour
sugar
butter
eggs
salt
lemon
apples
apricot preserve
confectioners' sugar

1 Preheat oven to hot (425° F.).

2 Sift onto pastry board: **1¼ cups flour.** Make a well in center and in the well put: **4 tablespoons sugar, 1 stick butter, sliced, 2 egg yolks, a pinch of salt,** and **the grated rind of 1 lemon.** Work the center ingredients to a paste, then knead in flour. Form dough into a ball, wrap in waxed paper, and refrigerate for at least 30 minutes.

3 On lightly **floured** board roll out 2/3 of the pastry and transfer to an 8-inch pie plate. Trim overhanging edges. Fill about 2/3 full with: **3 apples, peeled,** **cored, and thinly sliced,** spiraling the slices from center to outer edge. Spread with: **12 ounces apricot preserve.**

4 Roll out remaining pastry thinly and cut into strips ½ inch wide. Arrange 10 strips lattice-fashion over filling and trim overhanging edges. Place a strip all around edge of filling and flute this with the bottom layer of pastry.

5 Bake in the hot oven for 15 minutes. Reduce oven temperature to 350° F. and bake for 30 minutes longer. Remove from oven and sprinkle with **confectioners' sugar.** Serve warm.

MONTE BIANCO *(Chestnut Puree in Meringue Nests)*

SERVES 6

The Italian name for this dessert means "Mont Blanc" because traditionally the sweet chestnut puree is served in a tall pyramid topped with whipped cream, rather like a snowcapped mountain. We have done it more delicately in individual meringues, and when you're in the mood for something very sweet and very rich, this is it.

eggs
salt
lemon
sugar
sweet chestnut puree
strega
cream
semisweet chocolate

MERINGUE NESTS

1 Beat: **2 egg whites** and **a pinch of salt** until foamy. Add: **1 teaspoon lemon juice** and continue to beat until egg whites are stiff. Beat in gradually: **½ cup sugar** and beat until meringue is stiff and glossy.

2 Preheat oven to very slow (250° F.).

3 Line a baking sheet with waxed paper.

4 Put meringue into a pastry bag fitted with a large fluted tube and press out a spiral of meringue, about 2½ inches in diameter, to make a base for the nests. On top of the base, and around the outer edge, press out a ring of meringue and finish with a little rosette where the ends of the ring meet. Bake in the slow oven for 30 minutes. Remove from the waxed paper while still warm and moist, and place on a cake rack to finish drying.

FILLING

1 Beat: **1 cup sweet chestnut puree** with **2 tablespoons strega**.

2 Whip: **1 cup cream**.

3 Shave: **a bar of semisweet chocolate** with a sharp knife to make ½ cup of shaved chocolate.

PRESENTATION

Put a heaping tablespoon of the chestnut puree into each meringue nest and top with the unsweetened whipped cream. Garnish with shaved chocolate.

HOLLAND

For me the feast of Holland has always been celebrated in its incomparable museums. I can hardly think of eating when Rembrandt, Hals, Vermeer, Van Gogh stare down at me from their walls. But if you need any proof that the Dutch love food, you can find it in those same museums in the glorious still life paintings of de Heem and the other seventeenth- and eighteenth-century Dutch masters. These paintings are among the most wonderful celebrations of man's concern with good living ever to be recorded. I always save seeing them until the end of my museum tour as a sort of appetizer to send me out into the real world once more, hungry for real food.

Dutch food is good enough to make you forget museum feet. The Dutch are hearty, sturdy citizens who enjoy life, and one of the best ways of enjoying life is at the table. Compared with the cuisines of France, Italy or Spain, the cooking of Holland is not very influential or highly thought of. After Edam and Gouda cheese and hollandaise sauce, then what? seems to be the general attitude. Well, I would beg to differ. Dutch home cooking, which I have had an opportunity to sample, is good, solid, stick-to-the-ribs fare. I can only think of Hans Brinker coming home after a wintry afternoon's skating and tucking into a Dutch hotchpotch or a bowl of savory *snert* (the pea soup with sausage that is a national specialty). Believe me, any country that faces into the North Sea had better eat to stay warm and strong above all.

Actually Dutch housewives cook well and Dutch families eat well. When they dine out their tastes are international, judging from the food offered in most restaurants. You seldom get the typical home-cooked dishes of Holland in restaurants. But the continental or French cuisine is presented to perfection because the customers know and appreciate good food.

There is one exotic strain that runs through the cookery of the Netherlands, very much tied up with its history. The spice-laden dishes of Indonesia must be counted as a very important part of Dutch cooking. For several centuries the East Indies were under Dutch rule, and the colonizers brought back not only the condiments of the Spice Islands but many of the unusual native dishes. *Rijsttafel* (which means "rice-table"), the Indonesian rice dinner with dozens of highly seasoned side dishes, is as popular in Holland as chop suey is here. I remember visiting friends in Amsterdam, and having them telephone to have *rijsttafel* sent in much as we would order Chinese food to be delivered at the last minute here.

Another legacy from Holland's former colonies is the Dutch love of chocolate. One of the customs that I particularly like is the steaming cup of rich hot chocolate at midnight. And chocolate cakes, Dutch style, are among the very best in the world.

So though we went to Holland the first time primarily because of the art treasures in the museums, we found that as a by-product we had also accumulated some treasures for our recipe files that rank with the finest dishes we have eaten anywhere.

The Amstel Hotel sets a lavish table and its specialties are exhibited like a tempting Dutch still life against the background of the Amstel River.

"A man becomes a cook, but he is a born roaster of flesh," said Brillat-Savarin. To prove his point, here is a roast rib of veal, brown and succulent, to tantalize the appetite of all of us born eaters of roasts.

AMSTEL HOTEL

Massive and stately the ocher brick Amstel Hotel stands at the very edge of the busy Amstel River. It will soon celebrate its hundredth birthday, but you'd never guess it, the hotel has been so carefully modernized. The only give-aways about its age are its classic proportions and high ceilings and the pleasantly old-fashioned courtliness with which guests are treated. Would we could all grow old so gracefully!

The Garden Terrace of the hotel overlooks the lawns as well as the river, and is our favorite place to dine. The restaurant sets a splendid table, as do a number of others in Amsterdam. But I find that increase of appetite not only grows by what it feeds on, but is enormously stimulated by the beauty of one's surroundings. Whenever there is a possibility of dining in some quiet outdoor spot, or in a room that opens onto a lovely view, that is my choice. When the food and service are superlative too, that is the frosting on the cake. The Amstel's cuisine is continental, but when the chef turns his hand to it he can make a Dutch pea soup as good as any in the land.

Incidentally, although wines are imported into Holland, and every good restaurant has an impressive wine card, we like to drink native when we are there. Dutch gin is world famous, their beer is excellent, and their cordials and liqueurs are among the finest in the world. Dutch coffee is wonderful too—after all, they used to own Java so they had ample opportunity to master the art of making a cup of the same.

The only ingredient missing from our Amstel recipes that follow is that inspiring river view I told you about. But I think all of these dishes are good enough to be appreciated completely for their own sakes.

117

AMSTEL HOTEL

AMSTERDAM

Carte des Spécialités

Hors d'Oeuvre

Saumon Fumé à la Danoise	fls.	10.—
Huîtres de Zélande 000000 la douzaine		11.50
Champignons de Couche à la Française		5.—
Escargots à la Bourguignonne la douzaine		7.—

Potages

Crème d'Artichauts	2.50
Consommé Chasseur aux Profiteroles	3.50
Crème d'Ecrevisses à la Joinville	5.—
Consommé Moelle au Cerfeuil	3.—

Poissons et Crustacés

Truite de Rivière à la Belle Meunière	6.—
2 Filets de Sole aux Queues de Langoustines	7.50
Médaillon de Turbot à la Mornay	6.50
Scampi à l'Indienne	7.50

Viandes

Piccata de Veau	8.50
Jambon de Gueldre Chaud, Sauce Madère	7.50
Ris de Veau à la Parme	10.—
Filet Mignon Choron	10.—

Volailles

Poulet de Grain à l'Estragon	(2 pers.)	15.—
Canard Sauvage au Suc d'Ananas	(2 pers.)	15.—
Pintadeau à la Choucroute	(2 pers.)	15.—
Coco Ambarawa		8.50

Gril

Entrecote sur Gril, Beurre Maître d'Hôtel	(2 pers.)	16.50
Poulet Grillé ou Rôti à la Broche, sauce selon désir		15.—
Côte d'Agneau sur Gril		7.50
Turbot Grillé, sauce selon désir		7.50

Entremets

Sabayon Froid aux Avelines		3.50
Coupe Glace vanille au Gingembre		2.50
Charlotte Plombière	(2 pers.)	7.—
Crêpe Surprise Flambée au Kirsch	(2 pers.)	7.50

CARRÉ DE VEAU À LA DUXELLES *(Roast Stuffed Rib of Veal)*
SERVES 8

This is absolutely the best veal roast I've ever tasted. The mixture of chopped mushrooms, onions, tongue, and ham, used as a sort of mortar to cement the pre-carved meat back onto the bones, serves a brilliant double purpose. It acts as a flavorful stuffing for the veal, and it enables the roast to be pre-carved and then fitted back together again, making a grand entrance all in one beautifully browned piece when it comes to the table. The mushroom mixture, called *duxelles*, is excellent as a side dish with almost any meat, by the way. This is one of the favorite tricks picked up at the Amstel.

rib roast of veal
butter
onion
garlic
shallots
cooked smoked tongue
cooked ham
mushrooms
Madeira or port
salt, pepper
bread crumbs
Parmesan cheese

VEAL ROAST

1 Have butcher prepare **the rib section of a young milk-fed veal.** This should consist of 5 ribs on both sides of the backbone. Crack and remove short ends of ribs. The ready-to-roast ribs will weigh from 5 to 5½ pounds.

2 Preheat oven to very hot (450° F.).

3 Place roast, curved side up in shallow baking pan and roast in the very hot oven for 30 minutes. Reduce oven temperature to 325° F. and continue to cook for 1 hour.

4 While roast is cooking, prepare the *duxelles* (a kind of mushroom hash). In skillet heat: **½ cup butter** and in it cook: **2 tablespoons finely chopped onion, 2 cloves garlic, minced, and 2 shallots, minced,** for about 5 minutes. Add: **½ cup minced smoked tongue, ½ cup minced cooked ham, 1 cup finely chopped mushrooms, and ⅓ cup Madeira** and cook for 5 minutes longer, or until most of the moisture has cooked away. Stir in: **¼ teaspoon salt, some freshly ground pepper, and ½ cup dry bread crumbs.**

5 Increase oven to very hot (450° F.).

6 Remove roast from oven and place curved side up on cutting board. Slice down to the rib bones on both sides of the backbone. Then cut across rib bones, following the curve so that the fillet on each side is removed intact. Slice each fillet lengthwise into 8 thin slices. Spread ribs with a little of the *duxelles*, then replace the slices of meat with a little of the *duxelles* between each slice. Cover the roast with the remaining *duxelles* and sprinkle with: **2 tablespoons grated Parmesan cheese.** Return roast to the very hot oven and cook for 15 to 20 minutes, or until well browned.

SAUCE

Place roast on serving platter and make gravy. Put roasting pan over direct heat and add: **½ cup boiling water.** Cook, stirring in all the brown crust from bottom and sides of pan. Add: **2 tablespoons Madeira** or **port** and swirl in: **2 tablespoons butter.** Strain gravy into sauce dish and serve separately.

PRESENTATION

To serve the roast, give each person 2 of the pre-carved slices, and some of the mushroom stuffing. Pass sauce separately.

FAMOUS DUTCH GREEN PEA SOUP
SERVES 6 TO 8

You or I might consider this good, solid Dutch soup a meal in itself. But it is par for the first course for Dutch appetites which can then go merrily on to consume the rest of dinner. *Snert* is the nice, straightforward name of the soup, which is practically a national institution. It is frequently served with dark bread, and I can just see Van Gogh's "Potato Eaters" sitting around their lamplit table enjoying this same peasant fare as a change from those eternal potatoes. *Snert* is served at the Amstel Hotel as a change from the eternal elegance, I would guess.

fresh pork hock	1 Into large kettle put: **1 pound fresh pork hock and 2½ quarts water.** Bring liquid to a boil and simmer for 1¾ hours, or until meat is very tender, skimming surface of liquid as often as necessary.
split peas	
leeks	
celery root	
onions	
celery tops	
salt, pepper	2 Remove meat and add to liquid: **1 pound green split peas.** Simmer for 30 minutes, stirring frequently.
frankfurters	
	3 Add: **3 leeks, white part only,**

chopped, **1 celery root, peeled and diced, 2 medium onions, chopped, 1 cup chopped celery tops with leaves, 2½ teaspoons salt,** and **1 teaspoon coarsely ground pepper.** Simmer for 30 minutes longer.

4 Remove meat from pork hock and dice. Slice: **6 frankfurters.** Ten minutes before soup is finished cooking, add the meat and sausage. Makes about 2 quarts.

FILETS DE SOLE PIERRE LE GRAND
(Poached Fillets of Sole with Wine Sauce)
SERVES 4

Although this dish is named for Peter the Great, there's nothing at all Russian about it—not even a grain of caviar. It is a most attractive way to serve sole—each fillet has a different garnish, and they lie side by side in a shallow casserole (we use a copper one) covered with a wine sauce mixed with hollandaise and glazed under the broiler. When the fish is served, each person should take part of each of the four fillets in order to divide the four garnishes equally. Our waiter at the Amstel had the eye of a hawk when it came to share-and-share-alike on this dish, and no one could walk off with all the truffles when he was around.

Holland ham	1 Cut: **4 ounces cooked Holland ham** into thin julienne strips. Cut: **1 truffle** and the **whites of 2 hard-cooked eggs** into similar strips. Press: **yolks of 2 hard-cooked eggs** through a coarse sieve.
truffle	
eggs	
fillets of sole	
dry white wine	
salt, white pepper	2 Arrange: **4 fillets of sole** in a **buttered skillet.** Add: **½ cup water, 1 cup dry white wine, ½ teaspoon salt,** and **⅛ teaspoon white pepper.** Bring liquid to a boil, cover, and simmer fish for 8 to 10 minutes. Transfer fillets to shallow casserole or serving dish. Sprinkle one fillet with the ham, a second with the truffle, the third with hard-cooked egg white and the last with the sieved egg yolk for an attractive garnish.
butter	
flour	
milk	
cream	
hollandaise sauce (see index)	

3 Cook liquid in which fish were poached over high heat until reduced to ½ cup.

4 In saucepan melt: **2 tablespoons butter.** Stir in: **3 tablespoons flour, ½ teaspoon salt,** and **⅛ teaspoon white pepper.** Cook, stirring, for 5 minutes. Add: **1 cup hot milk** and cook, stirring rapidly, until sauce is smooth and thick. Stir in the reduced fish liquid. Stir in: **½ cup hollandaise sauce** and fold in: **½ cup whipped cream.**

5 Spoon the sauce over the fillets and place under broiler heat for about 1 minute, or until sauce is lightly browned.

121

COQ AU VIN ROUGE À L'AVERGNATE *(Chicken in Red Wine)*
SERVES 6

This is a classic French dish, and one of those things that each chef does a little differently. Basically, chicken, bacon, onions, and red wine go into the dish, but from there on you're swinging on your own. We liked this *coq au vin* from the Amstel enough to adapt it as our own favorite. The trick of adding beef stock and the masterly use of herbs sets it apart as a superior *coq au vin*.

butter
bacon
chickens
silverskin onions
garlic
mushrooms
brandy
thyme
bay leaf
salt, pepper
claret
flour
beef stock
(see index)
parsley
fresh tarragon

1 In heavy casserole heat: **¼ cup butter** and **4 slices bacon, diced.** In it brown: **3 broiler chickens, split,** on both sides.

2 Add: **24 small silverskin onions, peeled, 1 clove garlic, minced,** and **5 medium mushrooms, sliced.**

3 Add: **¼ cup brandy** and ignite.

4 When flame burns out, add: **½ teaspoon thyme, 1 bay leaf, 1 teaspoon salt, ½ teaspoon pepper,** and **1 bottle** claret. Bring to a boil, cover, and simmer for 15 minutes.

5 Stir in: **2 tablespoons flour** mixed to a paste with **2 tablespoons butter.** Add: **1 cup beef stock,** cover, and simmer for 30 minutes longer.

PRESENTATION

Just before serving, sprinkle with: **3 tablespoons chopped parsley** and **1 teaspoon minced fresh tarragon.**

ASPARAGUS DUTCH STYLE
SERVES 4

Dutch people eat only the thick white asparagus, and it has a very delicate and distinctive flavor. This recipe from the Amstel Hotel we find just as good with the plump green asparagus. Unless we are serving this for lunch or light supper, we dispense with the ham and concentrate on the asparagus, butter, and egg. But if you include the ham, this really makes a very satisfactory light meal.

asparagus
salt
eggs
Holland ham
nutmeg
butter
chicken stock
(see index)

ASPARAGUS

1 Clean and cut tough ends from: **3 pounds asparagus.** Tie in large loose bunch.

2 In a deep pan bring to a boil: **1 quart water** and **1½ teaspoons salt.** Stand asparagus bunch in boiling water, keeping tips up. Cover and let boil from 18 to 22 minutes. Asparagus should be tender but not overcooked.

3 Drain asparagus on rack and keep warm.

GARNISHES

1 Hard-cook: **4 eggs** for 10 minutes. Peel and mash them.

2 Melt: **½ pound butter.**

3 Poach: **12 to 16 thin slices of Holland ham** in **1½ cups chicken stock** over moderate heat for 20 minutes. Keep warm.

PRESENTATION

Put some mashed egg on each plate. Add 2 or 3 tablespoons of the melted butter, **a little salt,** and **a sprinkle of nutmeg.** Each person mixes this with a fork, making a thick sauce. Put slices of ham and some asparagus beside the sauce. The asparagus is eaten with the sauce, the ham without.

AMSTEL GINGER CAKE

SERVES 12

Here we have a very rich cake, made with marzipan and ginger. Holland, as a next-door neighbor to Germany, enjoys many of the German foods—in this case marzipan, or almond paste. But then the exotic spices of the Dutch colonies are another strong influence on the Dutch cuisine, and in this cake we find preserved ginger, the pungent Asiatic plant, used with the marzipan. The richness of the cake is typically Dutch—no halfway measures for them. If you're going to eat cake, may as well go whole hog.

butter
light brown sugar
salt
vanilla
flour
eggs
blanched almonds
superfine granulated
sugar
lemon
preserved ginger

1 In mixing bowl cream: ¾ cup butter. Add: ¾ cup moist light brown sugar and cream together until light and fluffy. Stir in: ¼ teaspoon salt and 1 teaspoon vanilla. Beat in: 2½ cups flour alternately with ½ cup water to make a stiff cookie dough. Wrap in waxed paper and chill for several hours or overnight.

2 In electric blender blend enough blanched almonds, ½ cup at a time, to measure 2 cups. Mix nuts with: 1¼ cups superfine granulated sugar. Beat in: 2 beaten eggs, ½ teaspoon grated lemon rind, 1 teaspoon lemon juice, and ½ cup chopped preserved ginger.

3 Preheat oven to moderate (325° F.).

4 Roll out two-thirds of the cookie dough into a large round and line a 9½-inch pie pan. Cut away overhanging dough. Spread the almond filling in pan. Roll out remaining dough and cut into a 9½-inch round. Place over filling. Fold edge of bottom dough over top dough and brush with: 1 egg, lightly beaten. Surround with a wreath of thinly sliced preserved ginger.

5 Bake in the moderate oven for 40 minutes. Cool before cutting into thin wedges. A little goes a long way!

CHICKEN AND CELERY SALAD

SERVES 4

All food in Holland is not heavy or rich. Here is a lovely cool chicken salad, different from most because of the addition of fresh herbs and apples. At Dikker and Thijs the chef prettied this up by cutting all of the salad ingredients into julienne—long thin strips. For the salad to look attractive, the strips must be uniform, and that takes a sharp eye, a sharp chef's knife, and steady fingers. It also takes large pieces of chicken rather than the usual bits and pieces of leftovers. So we usually dice ours, but if you want to equal, if not beat, the Dutch, by all means do your "chop-chop" julienne.

apples
lemon
cooked chicken
celery
onion
fresh herbs
(dill, tarragon,
or sweet basil)
cream
mayonnaise
salt, pepper
romaine lettuce
eggs
tomatoes
cooked asparagus

1 Peel and core: 2 medium apples. Dice the apples and drop pieces into cold water acidulated with 1 tablespoon lemon juice.

2 Combine: 2 cups diced cooked chicken and 2 cups sliced celery. Drain and add apples. Add: 2 teaspoons minced onion and 1 teaspoon chopped fresh dill, tarragon or sweet basil.

3 Combine: 1 cup cream, whipped, ⅔

cup mayonnaise, ⅛ teaspoon pepper, 1 teaspoon salt, and 2 teaspoons lemon juice. Pour over the salad and toss lightly. Correct seasoning with salt to taste. Chill until ready to serve.

PRESENTATION

Heap salad on bed of crisp romaine leaves and garnish with: 4 hard-cooked eggs, quartered, 2 tomatoes, cut into wedges, and 16 stalks cooked asparagus.

POULARDE DIKKER AND THIJS
(Braised Chicken with Mushrooms and Lobster)
SERVES 4

I suppose you could call this a chicken à la king, but that would be the understatement of the year. Dikker and Thijs is one of the most elegant restaurants in Amsterdam, with an equally fashionable branch in Rotterdam, and anything you eat there has been prepared with a special flourish. They serve this chicken with truffled white rice, and the sauce is unlike any cream sauce I've ever tasted. When they gave me the recipe, I understood why. All that butter that the chicken was browned in; all that wine and cream and brandy! And then, for good measure, they add a boiled lobster! It is a marvelous dish, quite unlike the creamed chicken that usually inhabits those dreary patty shells at banquets and luncheons.

lobster
chicken
butter
salt, pepper
white wine
button mushrooms
flour
cream
brandy

1 Plunge: **a 1½-pound live lobster** into boiling water and simmer for 15 minutes. Let cool in liquid.

2 In casserole melt: **½ cup butter** and in it brown: **a ready-to-cook 2½-pound frying chicken** on all sides. Sprinkle with: **1 teaspoon salt** and **¼ teaspoon pepper.**

3 Add: **1 cup white wine** and **½ pound fresh button mushrooms.** Cover and simmer for 45 minutes.

4 Remove chicken and mushrooms. To sauce remaining in pan stir in: **2 tablespoons soft butter** mixed to a paste with **2 tablespoons flour.** Cook, stirring, until sauce is slightly thickened. Stir in: **1 cup cream** and **2 tablespoons brandy.**

5 Remove meat from chicken and cut into large pieces. Cut lobster in half, crack claws and remove meat.

6 Return chicken meat and mushrooms to the sauce. Add lobster meat and heat.

FISH FILLETS ZEELAND
SERVES 4

You can't make this dish for fewer than four people and have it look effective. For this is Dikker and Thijs's imaginative and striking tribute to their countrymen who inhabit Zeeland, the low dike-protected lands that jut into the North Sea. The platter is artfully divided by dikes of fluted mashed potato—very ingenious, really—which makes sections for the sole, shrimps, oysters, and lobster tails. A clever and beautiful arrangement. It works equally well with a hot vegetable platter, by the way. Pipe dividing "dikes" with a pastry tube filled with mashed potatoes and fill the long section with asparagus, the others with tiny peas, beets, carrots, or any combination you prefer.

124

potatoes	
butter	
cream	
salt, white pepper	
fillets of sole	
dry white wine	
lemons	
mushrooms	
shrimp	
oysters	
lobster tails	
eggs	
flour	
parsley	

1 Cook: **4 medium potatoes** in **salted** water until very tender. Drain and mash. Beat in: **3 tablespoons butter** and enough **hot cream** to make fluffy potatoes that are still stiff enough to be pressed through a fluted pastry tube. Season to taste with **salt** and **white pepper.** Keep warm over simmering water.

2 Poach: **4 fillets of sole** (about 1¼ pounds) in **1 cup water** with **1 cup dry white wine, the juice of 1 lemon, ½ teaspoon salt,** and **¼ teaspoon white pepper** for 5 minutes. Remove fillets and keep warm. Boil liquid over high heat until reduced to ½ cup.

3 Heat: **1 tablespoon butter** in each of 4 small skillets. In one sauté: **8 large mushrooms** for 5 minutes. In another sauté: **8 large shrimp,** cleaned and deveined, for 5 minutes. In a third, toss: **8 freshly-opened oysters** in the hot butter for 2 minutes, or just until edges curl. In the last cook: **4 small lobster tails,** removed from shells, for 5 minutes.

4 Fill a pastry bag, fitted with a large fluted tube, with the mashed potatoes and press out fluted ribbon down the center of a large serving platter. On one side press out 3 ribbons from center to edge of platter, making 4 evenly divided compartments. Arrange oysters, shrimp, lobster tails and mushrooms in the compartments. Arrange the fillets on the other side in the long compartment. Put platter into a warm oven to keep warm.

SAUCE

In saucepan beat: **2 eggs** with **1 tablespoon flour** and **1 cup cream.** Strain the ½ cup of reduced fish liquid into the egg-cream mixture and cook, stirring rapidly, until sauce is hot and slightly thickened. Be careful not to let it boil. Stir in: **¼ teaspoon salt,** or to taste, and **1 tablespoon lemon juice.**

PRESENTATION

Pour sauce over the fish fillets only and garnish with **parsley.**

SATEH BABI (Skewered Pork)
SERVES 4

The Bali restaurant in Amsterdam is just about the last outpost of the far-flung colonial empire that once belonged to the Netherlands. Here the Dutch people may still indulge their appetites for Indonesian cookery with all the exotic spices, herbs, and condiments that come from half a world away. The Java soy sauce in this recipe is called *ketjap* in Malaya, and our ketchup, though a different kind of condiment, is named for it. This skewered pork should be served with rice and some of the other *rijsttafel* dishes to which it is a marvelous addition.

pork	
Java soy sauce	
salt, pepper	
sugar	
cooking oil	

1 Cut: **1 pound lean tender pork** into small cubes. Marinate the meat in: **⅓ cup Java soy sauce** (*ketjap benteng*) with **1 teaspoon salt, ¼ teaspoon pepper,** and **½ tablespoon sugar** for several hours, or overnight. The longer the better.

2 When ready to cook, thread the meat on short wooden sticks, using about 4 cubes on each stick. Brush with **cooking oil** and broil 2½ inches from heat for 20 minutes, turning frequently and basting with **cooking oil.**

DADAR DJAWA (Javanese Omelet)
SERVES 1

Every country does its omelets with a different twist. This Javanese omelet from the Bali is similar to the Chinese egg foo young, except that it has a bit of added oomph because of the *sambal ulek*, one of those hot pepper condiments so dear to Indonesian chefs. The Bali's menu carries this legend: "*Ulek Manis Betis*" which means "Beware the Pepper!" But this recipe does not overdo it. In fact, I'll take my eggs this way anytime. The best ever!

eggs
salt, pepper
green onions
preserved hot pepper
paste
butter

1 Beat: **3 eggs** with **¼ teaspoon salt, 1 tablespoon water, 2 green onions, chopped, a little freshly ground pepper,** and **½ teaspoon preserved red hot pepper paste (*sambal ulek*).**
2 In a 9-inch skillet heat: **2 tablespoons butter.** When butter begins to brown, add the egg mixture. Stir rapidly for a few seconds to heat egg mixture through, then cover and cook over low heat for 3 minutes, or until eggs are set on top. Turn out onto a warm plate and serve 1 omelet per person as a luncheon dish, or cut into wedges as you would a pie if you are using the omelet with *rijsttafel.*

ATJAR KETIMUN (Marinated Cucumber)
SERVES 4

No wonder Dutch beer is so good! It was developed just to cool and soothe the larynx after some of these Indonesian relishes passed by. This is a hot one, served at the Bali in tiny amounts with their meat dishes. It certainly does wonders for jaded appetites and jaded thirsts.

cucumber
salt
vinegar
sugar
onion
dried chili pepper

1 Slice: **1 large cucumber** into a glass or enamelware bowl.
2 Add: **½ teaspoon salt, ½ cup vinegar, 3 tablespoons sugar, 1 medium onion, thinly sliced,** and **1 dried chili pepper (*lombok*), finely cut.**
3 Let cucumber marinate in refrigerator for several hours. The cucumbers are very hot. Serve in small dishes with grilled pork cubes or stewed beef.

NASI GORENG (Indonesian Fried Rice)
SERVES 4

This fried rice recipe was brought from Indonesia to Holland where it became such a favorite that it is now a traditional Dutch dish. There are many variations, but in general the rice, onions and meat are fried together with spices to make a good, highly seasoned dish. Indonesian spices and condiments aren't always easy to come by, but we like this rice with curry powder and soy sauce, instead of the hotter native spices.

cooked rice
onions
butter
cooked chicken
cooked ham
corn oil
salt, pepper
soy sauce
curry powder
eggs
tomatoes

FRIED RICE

1 In a large iron skillet heat: **4 tablespoons butter** and **4 tablespoons corn oil.** Add: **2 medium onions, finely chopped,** and cook until golden. Add: **4 tablespoons cooked chicken, diced,** and **4 tablespoons cooked ham, diced.** Sauté gently for 5 minutes.

2 Add: **4 cups cold cooked rice,** mix well, and when rice is warm add: **2 teaspoons soy sauce, 1 teaspoon curry powder, salt** and **freshly ground pepper** to taste. Cook gently, stirring frequently, until mixture is heated through.

GARNISH

1 In a small bowl beat: **2 eggs** with **1 tablespoon water.**

2 In a skillet heat: **2 tablespoons butter.** Add the eggs and make a thin omelet. Turn it out on a board and cut into thin strips.

3 Slice: **2 tomatoes.**

PRESENTATION

Put the fried rice on a heated platter. Place the strips of omelet across the top, and surround with slices of tomato.

HAARLEM CELEBRATION CAKE
SERVES 10 OR 12

I don't know exactly what this cake celebrates, unless maybe it is the fact that Frans Hals lived in Haarlem and his very fine museum is there now. We had afternoon coffee with some people from the museum, and they served us this divinely chocolatey cake to sustain us on the twelve-mile drive back to Amsterdam. I drove back with all that chocolate and whipped cream sticking to my ribs and the recipe clutched in my sticky hand. Here it is, you chocolate lovers.

CAKE

eggs
superfine granulated sugar
sweet butter
lemon
unsweetened chocolate
vanilla extract
self-rising flour
milk
salt
confectioners' sugar
Dutch cocoa
cream

1 Preheat oven to moderate (350° F.).

2 Cream: **½ cup sweet butter** and **½ cup superfine granulated sugar** until mixture is light and fluffy.

3 Beat in: **grated rind of 1 lemon** and **2 eggs,** one at a time.

4 Stir in: **1½ cups unsifted self-rising flour** and **½ teaspoon salt** alternately with **½ cup milk.**

5 Stir in: **3 ounces unsweetened chocolate, melted and cooled.**

6 Turn batter into a **buttered 9-inch layer cake pan** and bake in the moderate oven for 35 minutes, or until cake tests done. Turn out on cake rack to cool.

FILLING

Cream: **½ cup sweet butter** with **½ cup confectioners' sugar** and **3 tablespoons Dutch cocoa.** Stir in: **½ teaspoon vanilla extract.**

TOPPING

1 Whip until stiff: **1½ cups heavy cream.**

2 Using a heavy knife, scrape a slab of chocolate until you have **½ cup chocolate shavings.**

PRESENTATION

Cut the cake into 2 layers. Spread the filling between the layers. Just before serving, whip the cream and frost top and sides of cake with big swirls of the cream. Sprinkle the shaved chocolate on top generously.

DAGING RUDJAK (Javanese Beef Stew)

SERVES 4

You would think that a beef stew is a beef stew, give or take a few odds and ends that may go into some and not others. But until you've thrown *kemiri* nuts, *salam*, and *laos* into your stew pot, you don't know the half of it! They do something fantastic to good old beef stew, and I can understand why men sailed over the seas to strange lands just to bring back these spices. We don't have to go that far, but I would recommend that you look in your classified phone book for the place nearest you where you can get Indonesian spices.

butter
top round of beef
onions
coconut milk
(see index)
kemiri nuts
Java laurel leaf
Java root
garlic
dried chili peppers
salt
ginger

1   In saucepan melt: **2 tablespoons butter.** In it sauté: **2 medium onions, sliced,** for 10 minutes, or until well browned.

2   Add: **1 pound top round of beef, cut into small cubes,** and cook for 5 minutes longer, or until meat loses color, stirring occasionally.

3   Add: **1½ cups coconut milk, 1 tablespoon ground *kemiri* nuts, 1 Java laurel leaf (*salam*), 1 teaspoon Java root (*laos*), 2 cloves garlic, minced, 2 dried chili peppers, 1 teaspoon salt,** and **⅛ teaspoon ginger.**

4   Bring liquid to a boil and simmer for 1½ hours, or until meat is tender. Taste occasionally and, if the stew becomes too hot, remove and discard the peppers. Serve with cooked rice.

DUTCH MEAT BALLS

SERVES 4 TO 6

We had these meat balls for lunch one day at the home of a friend in Amsterdam and I thought they were better than mere meat balls had any right to be. They are really more like beef stroganoff, but in a road company version. A very good buffet dish.

ground beef
ground veal
ground pork
onion
bread crumbs
egg
cooking oil
tomato puree
sour cream
beef stock
(see index)
salt, pepper
nutmeg

1   Mix together: **½ pound finely ground beef, ½ pound finely ground veal,** and **½ pound finely ground pork** with **1 large onion, chopped,** and **4 tablespoons fine bread crumbs.** Add: **1 beaten egg** to bind mixture. Season with: **1¼ teaspoons salt, ¼ teaspoon pepper,** and **¼ teaspoon nutmeg.**

2   Form into small balls and sauté quickly in: **2 tablespoons hot cooking oil.** Do not try to sauté too many at a time or they will not brown nicely.

3   When meat balls are all sautéed, put them all in skillet together and gradually add: **2 tablespoons tomato puree** and **1 cup beef stock.**

4   Simmer for 15 minutes.

5   Let stand for several hours or refrigerate overnight.

PRESENTATION

Just before serving, reheat but do not boil. Add: **1 cup sour cream,** stirring it in with a wire whisk.

HOLLANDSCHE BIEFSTUK (*Dutch Beefsteak*)
SERVES 4

A Flemish recipe this, and another favorite Dutch home specialty. The traditional side dish with the steak is boiled potatoes with butter and parsley. Holland grows some of the best potatoes in the world, and plain boiled potatoes, mealy and white, thirstily soaking up butter or gravy, are a real Dutch treat.

oneless sirloin steak
wine vinegar
salt, pepper
scallions or leeks
butter
beer
beef stock
(see index)
parsley
potato flour
thyme
sugar

STEAK

1 Pound and cube on both sides: **a 2-pound boneless sirloin steak**, about 1½ inches thick. Be sure the beef is tender, as it does not cook long.

2 Mix: **2 tablespoons wine vinegar** with **1 teaspoon salt** and **¼ teaspoon pepper.** Rub this mixture well into both sides of the steak. Let it stand and marinate for ½ hour.

3 In a heavy skillet brown: **¼ cup butter.** Sauté steak for 4½ minutes on each side, moving it around while it cooks.

4 Remove steak and keep warm on a hot platter.

SAUCE

1 To the butter in the pan add: **½ cup chopped scallions** or **leeks.** Cook, stirring, until they are browned. Remove and place on top of steak.

2 Stir in: **1 teaspoon potato flour, 1 cup beef stock,** and **½ cup beer.** Stir until sauce boils. Add: **½ teaspoon thyme, 1 teaspoon sugar, 2 tablespoons chopped parsley,** salt and **pepper** to taste.

PRESENTATION

The sauce is served separately in a gravy boat. The steak is carved at the table and is cut into very delicate thin slices slanting down on the bias.

HOTCHPOTCH OF CURLY KALE
SERVES 4

There are a number of hearty dishes in Holland called hotchpotch or hotchpot. They are all stews or mishmashes of various ingredients and our word "hodgepodge" derives from them. This one, made of potatoes, kale (a kind of cabbage), and sausage is a real peasant dish. It is very good, especially if you slather it with butter.

curly kale
potatoes
frankfurters
butter
salt, pepper
chicken stock
(see index)

1 Remove stems from: **3 pounds curly kale,** wash kale thoroughly, and cook in boiling **salted** water to cover for 25 minutes, or until tender.

2 Drain and chop coarsely.

3 Boil: **2 pounds potatoes,** peeled. Drain.

4 In a saucepan put: **½ pint chicken stock,** the cooked kale, **½ pound frankfurters,** and the cooked potatoes. Simmer for 15 minutes, uncovered, until stock has almost evaporated.

5 Remove frankfurters, and slice. Set aside and keep warm.

6 Mash the vegetables with: **2 tablespoons butter.** The hotchpotch should be of a creamy consistency. Add more **butter,** if you wish, and season with **salt** and **pepper** to taste.

PRESENTATION

Serve the hotchpotch on a warm platter and top it with the frankfurter slices.

FRIED CUCUMBERS
SERVES 4

We had these one night at the home of a friend in Amsterdam. They were served with the excellent Dutch herring, the kind that is sold at nearly every street corner out of a barrel, and eaten right on the street. This is a good and unusual way to use young cucumbers as a hot vegetable, with or without the herring.

cucumbers
flour
egg
sour cream
salt
chicken stock
(see index)
cooking oil
dill or parsley

BATTER
Mix: **a scant ½ cup flour** with **a pinch of salt, 1 egg, beaten,** and **8 tablespoons chicken stock.** Mix well to make a batter.

CUCUMBERS
1 Get the young, small cucumbers, allowing about 3 per person. Cut off the tips and scrub thoroughly.

2 Dip: **12 cucumbers** in the batter and drop, a few at a time, in a kettle of **hot fat** (360° F.). Fry until crisp and golden.

PRESENTATION
Serve hot with **commercial sour cream** and **a sprinkle of fresh dill** or **parsley.** These are usually eaten with boiled new potatoes, heavily buttered.

F. KREDEL

SCANDINAVIA

WE have not spent as much time as we would have wished in the Scandinavian countries. But for the little time that we were there, we felt remarkably at home. Nearly everyone we encountered spoke English and spoke it well, and there was a pleasant orderliness about the cities we visited, a friendliness about the people that made us feel comfortable and at ease. And they fed us so well!

The smorgasbord, under one name or another is universal. Even the pickiest appetite is bound to find something to please it in the dazzling array of foods set forth on these groaning tables. In Denmark, there is *smørrebrød* —literally "spread for bread." Above a thin slice of dark bread, coated with the wonderful Danish butter, you might have a small mountain of tiny shrimp, thin curls of cold meat and pickles, salads, fish, cheeses, eggs, all to be consumed with aquavit and beer. Norway's *koldt bord*, or cold table, is a fabulous buffet of similar foods. I must confess I parted company with them on one point, however, I could not face the *koldt bord* for breakfast as the Norwegians do. But there is more, much more, to Scandinavian cookery than these artistically arranged little Dagwood specials.

French influence was strong throughout Scandinavia in the eighteenth century and naturally their kitchens have not been the same since. Let a Frenchman in your kitchen and from then on meats get *flambéed*, sauces get saucier, and native foods are given a French twist. The Scandinavian cranberries, called lingonberries, are almost a mealtime habit in one form or another, but one of the most popular is the dessert made of thin pancakes with lingonberry sauce. They must surely have had a French grandfather.

Scandinavian salads are quite unlike our California ones. Greens and raw vegetables play a minor role. You might get a so-called "summer salad" of sliced radishes, onions, and cucumber, but they will be embedded in a marvelously rich cream cheese and sour cream mixture. Spicy, chopped herring makes another salad, and tiny pickled mushrooms still another. Lettuces and crisp greens, as we know them, are evidently for the rabbits. The thin, brittle Scandinavian bread, really more like a cracker, that every American dieter knows, is marvelous with these salads and supplies the crisp texture. Maybe the reason I love the bread so is that in Norway I ate their *flat brod* with a quarter-inch coating of sweet butter. Fit for the old Norse gods it was.

Also fit for the Norse gods or, at the very least, for the Vikings, are the aquavit and beer that are traditional Scandinavian drinks. Aquavit, a white firewater that comes to the table in a bottle encased in a block of ice, is poured into a tiny glass. When someone says *"Skoal!"* you say *"Skoal!"* and knock back the aquavit in one gulp. You then reach for a tidbit from the smorgasbord and pop that into your mouth as a chaser. It is amazing how much you can consume in this fashion, both liquid and solid, without feeling the effects of either.

These are a pleasure-loving yet dignified people who make a nice ceremony of eating. As a matter of fact the rules of protocol at Scandinavian dinner parties are rather awesome at first to Americans. But there is a sweetness and graciousness underlying the strict etiquette. At the end of a meal the guest of honor says a formal "thanks for the meal," and upon leaving the dining room each guest must go first to the hostess and thank her for the food. I think it is a lovely custom. And I would like to repeat my "thanks for the meal" here and now to the people in the restaurants of Scandinavia who not only fed us with a festive flourish, but who graciously gave us the recipes so that we could share their dishes with our friends at home.

In Copenhagen's Tivoli Gardens is one of the world's most delightful restaurants, the Belle Terrasse. I like the cut of their jib, Mary likes the fold of their napkins, we both admire their marvelous Danish cuisine.

As if plain roasted duck weren't enough, the Belle Terrasse goes one step further and flames the breast of their wild duck in a heavenly cognac sauce.

F.KREDEL

BELLE TERRASSE

COPENHAGEN is a lively city of fun-loving, life-loving people. The night life rivals the gaiety of Paris, and one of the most brilliant spots in the city is Tivoli. In the heart of Copenhagen, this twenty-acre plot of gardens, lakes, amusement park, cabarets, concert hall, theaters, and restaurants is unsurpassed in any city of the world. The season is short, coinciding with Copenhagen's mild long evenings from May through September. But while it lasts it is brilliant. The buildings are outlined with strings of lights, there is music in the air, and firework displays blaze against the sky.

We went there for dinner one mild evening and the Belle Terrasse was the perfect restaurant for this enchanted park. We ate on a trellised terrace overlooking the gardens, and the restaurant managed somehow to retain some of the carnival atmosphere of Tivoli without losing its own dignity or style. The gardens are brought indoors in the colorful flower arrangements that are a trademark of the Belle Terrasse, and the flowered chintz chairs are another horticultural touch.

The restaurant is one of the finest in Copenhagen, but because Scandinavian prices are relatively sensible, we dined magnificently without having to tear out traveler's checks by the handful. My steak, flamed and served with a special mustard sauce, French fried potatoes, and a salad was just a little over two dollars! I've included the recipe for it, one of our best, but you'll be hard put to duplicate the meal at Danish prices.

135

KURT E. CHRISTENSEN
PROPRIÉTAIRE
★
Maître Rôtisseur
★
Chevalier du Tastevin

CONFRÉRIE DE LA CHAINE DES RÔTISSEURS

GRILL RESTAURANT

Belle Terrasse

& *Fajance Bar*

TIVOLI

TELEFON: Minerva 1136
Gæstetelefon BYen 35808
PINEAPPLE JUICE 2/75
FRESH ORANGE JUICE 2/75
TOMATO JUICE 2/75

COCKTAILS
Dry Martini 6/50
Very dry Martini (american style) 9/00
Manhattan 7/25 (american style) 8/50

APÉRITIFS à 3/25
BELLE (brun Vermouth, Angostura
og Citron).
Aperitivo ROSSI, DUBONNET,
BYRRH, CAP CORSE,
Martini og Rossi, Ganzia, Cinzano,
brun, hvid eller tør.
Noilly Prat 4/00
tør eller sød – dry or sweet.
CARPANO PUNT-e-MES 4/50

VINS EN CARAFE
Vin blanc extra (halvtør) ¹/₁ 22/–, ¹/₂ 11/50
¹/₄ 6/25
Vin rouge extra ¹/₁ 21/–, ¹/₂ 11/25, ¹/₄ 5/85

Recommandée par:
MR. TEMPLE FIELDING
LES AUBERGES DE FRANCE
"HOLIDAY MAGAZINE"
LONDON CHOP HOUSE
LIFE MAGAZINE
(Ask for it here).

Les Specialitets Très Recommandée

☆☆☆ TOAST GRAND VEFOUR 9/25
(Smørristet toast fyldt med lækker rejestuvning, maskeret med hollandaise og glaceret – toast filled with a ragout of shrimps, glazed).

☆☆☆ EN LILLE LÆKKERBIDSKEN 12/75
(fransk gåselever, hjerteblade med fransk dressing og tomat fyldt med portvinsgele – pâté de foie gras, lettuce, french sauce and portwine-jelly).

GRUMINSKI AUX CHAMPIGNONS 9/25
(indbagte champignons, crème fraîche og kaviar – baked mushrooms, thick cream, danish caviar and lemon).

BISQUE de HOMARD 9/00
(Hummersuppe med hummerkød og ris, smagt til med cognac).

☆☆☆ ÉCREVISSES à la CARLTON 9/50
(Varme dildkogte krebsehaler serveret i en dildsauce med løse smørdampede ris crayfishtails served in a delicious dil-sauce and rice – a perfect first course).

Le Tournebroche

COQUILLE SAINT-JACQUES BRETAGNE 11/25
(Muslinger skåret i skiver dampes i hvidvin med champignons og rejer, monteres med Mornay sauce og ost, gratineres).

HOMARD ROTHSCHILD 26/50
(Friskkogt hummerkød og champignons serveret i hummerskallen i en sauce americaine, smagt til med sherry, cognac og rosenpaprika, glaceret – lobster and mushrooms served in the shell in sauce americaine, flavoured with sherry, cognac and paprika, glazed).

BROILED LIVE NORDSEA LOBSTER
at price ruling
(Grilleret hummer med smeltet smør. Dagspris).

☆☆☆ TRUITE AU BLEU OU MEUNIÈRE 8/75
BOILED or FRIED TROUT
(Bækforel kogt med løg, urter og laurbær, sauce hollandaise eller stegt i smør med persille frit, fintskårne mandler og hvide kartofler).

RISOTTO ALLA BOLOGNESE 8/75
(Risret med hønsekød, fuglelever, grønærter, piment, serveres med pikant sauce og grøn salat).

OMELET SURPRISE 9/00
(min. 2 couverts)
(Vanilleis med fyld af blandede frugter og chokolade, overhældt med likør og indbagt i piskede æggehvider – Baked Alaska).

SOUFFLÉ AU GRAND MARNIER 8/00
(min. 2 couverts)
(En let lækker æggesouffle, smagt til med Grand Marnier likør).

HORS d'OEUVRE

SALADE DE HOMARD prix du jour. TOMATE JAPONAISE 5/50 (udhulet tomat fyldt med krabbekød, maskeret med mayonnaise, hakket æg, kapers og grøn salat). OEUFS FROIDS A LA RUSSE 6/75 (²/₂ hårdkogte æg med ital. salat, caviar, ferskrøget laks i strimler og tomat). SALADE DE TOMATES 4/50. CHICKEN SALAD SPECIAL 11/00 (hønsesalat i mayonnaise, ananas, oliven, æg, kirsebær, asparges og finthakket æble). SALADE NIÇOISE 6/75 (tomat, æg, tunfisk, sardeller, kartoffelskiver, oliven, agurk, grøn salat og fransk dressing).

POTAGES & OEUFS

1) CONSOMMÉ THÉODORA 5/25 (chicken consommé with chicken meat and asparagus). 2) REAL TURTLE SOUP EN TASSE 6/75 (en kop ægte skildpaddesuppe med æggeblomme og skildpaddekød). 3) SOUPE À L'OIGNON GRATINÉE 5/00 (gratineret fransk løgsuppe – onion soup). 4) CRÈME D'ASPERGES 5/50 (flødelegeret aspargessuppe). 5) CRÈME DE CHAMPIGNONS 5/50 (flødelegeret champignonssuppe). 6) OMELETTE AUX FOIS DE VOLAILLE 6/50 (omelet med frisk hønselever sauteret i madeira). 7) OMELETTE ESPAGNOL 7/50 (omelet med hønsekød, piment og baconterninger).

POISSONS

10) SOLE BELLE MEUNIÈRE 14/50. 11) ½ HOMARD FROID MAYONNAISE (selon grosseur) – (½ cold lobster with mayonnaise sauce, at price ruling). 12) SOLE GRILLÉE 14/50. 13) FILETS DE SOLE A LA BONNE FEMME 14/50. 14) SOLE A LA RICHELIEU 17/50 (hel søtunge, stegt i friture, fyldt med en ragout af hummer, rejer og asparges – ¹/₁ sole fried in oil and stuffed with a ragout of lobster meat, shrimps and asparagus). 15) FILETS DE CARRELET MARGUERY 13/50 (dampede rødspættefileter i hvidvinssauce med muslinger, champignons og rejer, glaseret – poached filets of plaice served in whitewine sauce with mussels, shrimps and mushrooms, glazed). 16) SCAMPI FRITTI 11/75 (indbagte jomfruhummerhaler med citron og kold ravigote sauce).

ENTRÉES

20) BOMBAY CHICKEN 13/50 (en halv kogt kylling i flødesauce, smagt til med curry, tomat, paprika og andre pikante krydderier, serveres med flere garniturer og løse ris). 21) COQ AU VIN PROVENÇALE 14/50 (½ udbenet hane dampet i hvidvin, på spinatbund, perleløg med muskatnød, champignonsauce med hvidløgssmag). 22) FILET DE VEAU BEURRE MARCHAND DE VINS 14/50 (stegt kalvefilet med kold rødvinssmør, ærter, tomat, haricots verts og franske kartofler – filet of veal, cold redwine butter, garnished with vegetables). 23) WIENERSCHNITZEL 11/00 24) SUPRÊME DE VOLAILLE PERIGOURDINE 17/50 (paneret ristet kyllingebryst med Strassbourg gåseleverpostej og trøffelsauce – chicken cutlet with Strassbourg liverpaste and truffles sauce). 25) STEAK MOUTARDE 15/00 (tournedos i fransk sennepssauce, pom. frites og salat – steak served in special prepared french mustard sauce, french fried and salad).

Le demi poulet rôti à la broche 10/50

Den lækreste halve sprøde spidstegte kylling med pom. frites og salat. (Most delicious half chicken from the spit-grill, french fried and green salad).

✄ LES GRILLADES Chef rôtisseur: Monsieur Piroud

De bedes elskværdigst meddele betjeningen, om De ønsker Deres grill-ret bleu – blue – lige vendt på grill'en, nærmest rå saignant – underdone – lidt mere stegt, à point – done – godt stegt, men kødet er stadig rødt, eller bien cuit – well done – godt gennemstegt.

ENTRECÔTE MINUTE 13/50 (minute steak). TOURNEDOS 14/75 (tenderloin steak). CÔTE DE PORC 10/50 (svinecotelet stegt på grill). RUMP STEAK 14/00. T-BONE STEAK 16/50. CHATEAUBRIAND BÉARNAISE OU BORDELAISE (mindst 2 couverts) à 16/25. TWO GRILLED LAMB CUTLETS CUT DOUBLE THICK 16/00. CÔTE DE BOEUF (mindst 2 couverts) à 17/00.

Le Specialita Italiane:

30) TOURNEDO ALLA SICILIANA 15/75 (tournedos med piment, selleri, tomat concassé, oliven & pom. frites – fried tournedos served with pimentos, celery, tomato concassé, olives & french fried). 31) SPAGHETTI ALLA FIORENTINA 8/75 (spaghetti i tomatsauce med ristede champignons, fuglelever, hakkede løg, skinke og ærter, gratineret). *32) SPAGHETTI ALLA NAPOLITANA 5/50 (ital. spaghetti i en krydret tomatsauce med en anelse af hvidløg og olivenolie). *33) COSTELLETA DI VITELLA ALLA TORINO 13/75 (kalvemørbrad tilberedt med rosmarin, citron og lidt hvidløg i ægte italiensk tomatsauce med spaghetti).

Til alle italienske retter serveres reven italiensk parmesanost.

LEGUMES

40) PETITS POIS À LA BONNE FEMME 4/50 (grønærter tilberedt med bacon og løg). 41) ÉPINARD EN BRANCHE SAUTES AU BEURRE 3/50 (hel spinat sauteret i smør, tilsmagt med en anelse muskatnød). 42) CHAMPIGNONS À LA BORDELAISE 6/50 (champignons ristet i smør og olivenolie med hakket persille og charlotteløg). 43) HARICOTS VERTS SAUTÉS AU BEURRE 4/50.

FROMAGES

CASTELLO (the new surprice in Danish Cheese), DANISH BLUE, PORT SALUT ou CAMEMBERT 4/00. EMENTHALER SUISSE 4/50. GORGONZOLA 4/25 (le portion). LES FROMAGES ASSORTIES 5/50.

DESSERTS

50) GRAND CRÊPES SUZETTE AUX GRAND MARNIER ET COGNAC 9/50. 51) ICE CREAM WITH CHOCOLATE SAUCE 4/75. 52) ANANAS AU MARACHINO OU KIRCH 5/75. 53) BANANE FLAMBÉES 6/75. 54) SALADE DE FRUITS AUX LIQUEURS 5/75. 55) BANANE CHINOIS 5/75 (Banan på vanilleis, hakket ingefær, chantillycreme – banana vanillaice, ginger & creme chantilly). 56) PÊCHE CARDINALE 5/75 57) PRUNES CHANTILLY 4/75 (Cathrine blommer med chantillycreme). 58) BELLE ORANGES 7/25 (marineret appelsin, garneret med glaseret appelsinskal, flødeskum, mandler og orange likør – marinated orange, peel wheeped cream, almonds and orange liqueur).

*) Retter med hvidløg tilsmagt efter dansk smag. Ønskes meget hvidløg, bedes dette pointeret VINKORT se venligst bagsiden.

WINE LIST t. o.

SELSKABER MODTAGES INDTIL 230 COUVERTS

WILD DUCK FLAMBÉ BELLE TERRASSE *(Duck in Cognac Sauce)*
SERVES 2

Evidently the Danes enjoy hunting, and their country is rich in game. Restaurants serve partridge, pheasant, duck and, when in season, even such gamy game as roebuck and wild boar. This recipe for wild duck works just fine with domestic duck and is a nice change from the usual duck with orange, cherries, or peaches. I don't know what they do with the rest of the duck at Belle Terrasse, but at the Prices', we grill the legs and save the carcass for duck soup.

**a wild or domestic
duck
butter (optional)
cream
cognac
sour cream
chicken bouillon
cubes
sweet paprika
salt
Tabasco**

1 Preheat oven to very hot (450° F.).

2 Place **a ready-to-cook duck** on rack in roasting pan. If wild: roast for about 20 minutes, or until done to taste, basting several times with **melted butter.** If domestic: roast for 30 minutes, pour off all fat from pan, reduce oven temperature to a moderate 350° F. and continue to roast for about 30 minutes longer.

3 Mash: **the duck liver,** remove all sinews, and keep cold.

4 When duck is cooked to desired doneness, cut the 2 breast fillets off the bird and place in a skillet over low heat with the pan juices (pan juices from domestic duck should be free of fat). Add: **2 tablespoons cognac** and ignite.

5 When flame burns out, stir in: **½ cup cream** mixed with **3 tablespoons sour cream.** Add: **2 chicken bouillon cubes** and the mashed duck liver and cook, stirring, until sauce is hot. The sauce should not boil. Stir in: **½ teaspoon sweet paprika, ¼ teaspoon Tabasco,** and salt to taste.

PRESENTATION

Arrange duck breasts on hot serving platter and strain the sauce over them. Serve with potatoes sautéed in butter and with a favorite salad, if you wish.

STEAK MOUTARDE FLAMBÉ *(Flamed Mustard Steak)*
SERVES 4

We are inclined to think that nowhere else in the world is there beef the equal of ours. But in Denmark the beef raised on their rich farm and grazing lands is superlative, their dairy products without peer. In this recipe, rich Danish beef is prepared with a mustard sauce that utilizes the thick, heavy cream—both sweet and sour—for which the country is famous. By flaming the beef with cognac, all of the juices and flavorings are sealed into the meat, and all the wonderful brownings in the pan are loosened to become part of the sauce. At Belle Terrasse these steaks were served with French fried potatoes and a cool, crisp salad. An unbeatable combination.

**beef fillets
butter
salt, pepper
rosemary
sage
cognac
Dijon mustard
mild mustard
sour cream
cream
rose paprika**

1 In skillet heat: **1 tablespoon butter.** In it sauté over high heat: **4 fillets of beef,** 1½ inches thick, for 4 minutes. Turn and sprinkle with: **salt, coarsely ground pepper, ¼ teaspoon rosemary,** and **½ teaspoon crumbled sage leaves.** Cook to desired degree of doneness (4 to 5 minutes per side for rare).

2 Pour off excess fat from pan and sprinkle fillets with: **¼ cup cognac.** Ignite the cognac and when the flame burns out, transfer fillets to a warm serving platter and keep warm.

3 To skillet add: **4 teaspoons Dijon mustard, 4 teaspoons mild brown or herb-flavored mustard,** and **¼ teaspoon rose paprika.** Combine: **2 tablespoons commercial sour cream** and **½ cup cream** and stir into mustard in skillet. Cook, stirring, for 1 minute. Pour the sauce over the fillets and serve.

BELLE ORANGE
SERVES 2

We had to travel all the way to Copenhagen to find something different and delicious to do with our native California oranges. We are inclined to think of oranges for breakfast and then call it a day. To use them with precious Grand Marnier and to combine them with whipped cream in a deluxe dessert never would have occurred to us. I guess in Northern Europe, where these golden globes are an imported luxury, this dessert is even more special. We find it a lovely way to deal with oranges, especially in season, when a whole bag of them goes for thirty-nine cents.

navel oranges
sugar
Grand Marnier
cream
vanilla
almonds

1 In small saucepan combine: **1 cup sugar** and **½ cup water.** Bring to a boil and boil rapidly for 3 minutes. Set aside to cool.

2 With vegetable peeler remove: **the thin orange rind from 1 orange.** Peel: **2 navel oranges** deeply, removing all trace of the white pith. Cut through segments to core of oranges to separate meat from connecting tissue. Work over a bowl to retain the juice.

3 To the orange segments add: **2 tablespoons Grand Marnier** and 2 tablespoons of the sugar syrup. Marinate in refrigerator for 2 hours.

4 Cut the orange rind into very thin slivers about 1 inch long. Add them to the remaining syrup, return to heat, and boil rapidly for 5 minutes. Remove rind with slotted spoon to drain and cool.

5 Divide orange segments into 2 champagne glasses. Divide the peel, sprinkling it on top of the oranges. Add to each serving: **1 tablespoon Grand Marnier.** Top with **whipped cream flavored with vanilla** and sprinkle with **blanched sliced or slivered almonds.**

GURKAS NORGE *(Stuffed Cucumbers Norwegian Style)*
SERVES 6

These crisp cucumber rings with their salty filling are a good thing to serve with drinks, particularly with Bloody Marys on a hot afternoon. We learned about them at the Belle Terrasse where they were an unusual prelude to a fine dinner.

cucumbers
anchovies
dill
chives
cream cheese
sour cream
salt, pepper
lumpfish roe
lemon
parsley

1 Scrape: **6 small, unpeeled cucumbers** lengthwise with fork tines to make long grooves. Cut into 2-inch sections and hollow out seeds in center, leaving firm cucumber rings.

2 Mash: **12 anchovies** and mix well with: **1 tablespoon chopped fresh dill, 1 tablespoon chopped fresh chives,** and **6 ounces cream cheese** softened with **2 tablespoons sour cream.** Season to taste with **salt** and **freshly ground pepper.**

3 Fill cucumber rings and chill in refrigerator for several hours.

PRESENTATION

Serve with: **1 teaspoon sour cream** on top of each stuffed cucumber ring. Top cream with a little **lumpfish roe** (Scandinavian caviar). Garnish platter with **lemon wedges** and **parsley.**

CRAYFISH TAILS À LA CARLTON
SERVES 4

The Scandinavians not only eat well, they make a delightful ceremony of their meals, almost a ritual. The year is punctuated for them by a number of food festivals when special dishes are prepared—special almond-cream buns during Lent, roast goose on Martin Luther's Name Day, breads and cakes that are traditional at Christmas, ham on New Year's, and in August and September, when the delicious native crayfish are in season, a two-months' orgy of eating them. *Kräftor* are usually boiled and served in their shells with lots of fresh dill, and the empty shells are piled sky-high before the meal is over. The Belle Terrasse serves them already shelled in a wonderful rich sauce, and they make an ambrosial first course.

salt
sugar
parsley
dill
frozen Danish
crayfish tails
hollandaise sauce
(see index)
dry white wine
rice

CRAYFISH

1 In skillet boil: **1 quart water** with **1 teaspoon salt, 1 tablespoon sugar, a handful of parsley leaves, and 12 stalks of fresh dill.** Simmer for 10 minutes.

2 Add: **2 dozen (2 pounds) frozen Danish crayfish tails,** bring liquid to a boil and simmer for 5 minutes. Let the crayfish cool in the liquid. When cool enough to handle, remove meat and discard intestinal vein which runs down back. The easiest way is to slit covering on underside of tail on both sides with kitchen scissors, then peel off shells.

SAUCE

Put into small saucepan: **1 cup hollandaise sauce.** Stir in: **1 tablespoon finely chopped dill** and **½ teaspoon sugar.** Whisk the sauce over low heat until warm, then whisk in gradually: **⅓ cup dry white wine.** Be careful not to let the sauce get too hot. Pour sauce over the crayfish and serve with **cooked white rice.**

BROILED TROUT WITH CUCUMBER SALAD
SERVES 4

Fish and cucumbers, two of the most omnipresent foods in Scandinavia, here show their affinity for each other. La Belle Sole, one of the finest restaurants in Oslo, serves trout broiled to perfection with mustard and a savory butter, and to complement the piping hot dish, a cool, crisp cucumber salad. The cucumber salad, called *pressgurka*, crops up all over Scandinavia, and we have learned to love it. Mary bought one of those boards with an adjustable blade called a *mandoline* just so she could shave the cucumbers sufficiently thin to make *pressgurka* the true Scandinavian way.

cucumber
wine vinegar
sugar
salt, pepper
white pepper
trout
Dijon mustard
cooking oil
sweet butter
parsley or dill
lemons

1 Sprinkle: **4 ready-to-cook trout** with **salt** and **pepper** and spread both sides with a thin layer of **Dijon mustard,** using about 2 teaspoons per fish. Arrange trout on a **greased** broiler rack and broil about 3 inches from heat for 15 minutes, turning once and brushing frequently throughout the cooking with **oil.**

2 While fish are broiling make maître d'hôtel butter. Cream: **¼ cup sweet butter.** Beat in: **1 tablespoon minced parsley** and **the juice of 1 lemon.**

3 Arrange fish on warm serving platter and spread with the savory butter. Garnish with **lemon wedges** and serve with cucumber salad.

CUCUMBER SALAD

Peel and thinly slice: **1 large cucumber.** Put slices into a bowl or china serving dish. Sprinkle with: **½ cup wine vinegar, 2 tablespoons water, 1 tablespoon sugar, ¼ teaspoon salt, dash of white pepper,** and **2 tablespoons minced parsley** or **dill.** Chill in refrigerator for 2 hours.

FILLET OF PLAICE LA BELLE SOLE

SERVES 4

La Belle Sole is probably the finest restaurant in Norway, and it is as famous for this dish as Tour d'Argent is for its Pressed Duck. The plaice used in their recipe is a European flounder. We use flounder or sole. At La Belle Sole, the fish motif is carried through to the restaurant's decor where Neptune, mermaids, sea horses, and sole disport against a severely modern Scandinavian background. Mary knew the food was going to be wonderful the minute we walked in. Each place setting had crisp white napkins folded into elaborate fans and Mary, who was brought up on *Mrs. Beeton's Book of Household Management*, feels to this day that fine food and fancily folded napkins somehow go together. This time she was right.

lobster
flounder
butter
onion
salt, pepper
peppercorns
mussels
button mushrooms
asparagus
flour
dry white wine
tomato puree
cognac (optional)

1   Remove meat from: **a 1½ pound lobster.** Crack the shell and sauté in: **2 tablespoons butter** until shell turns red.

2   Fillet: **2 flounder** and remove skin from fillets. Add: **fish head, bones, skin, and tail** to the lobster shells. Add: **1 onion, sliced, ½ teaspoon salt, ¼ teaspoon peppercorns,** and **2 cups water.** Bring to a boil and simmer for 20 minutes. Strain the stock.

3   Slice tail meat from lobster and cook with claw meat in: **1 tablespoon butter** for 5 minutes, stirring occasionally. Set aside.

4   Steam: **1 dozen mussels** until shells open. Remove from shells. Keep warm.

5   Sauté: **8 button mushrooms** in **1 tablespoon butter** for 5 minutes, or until lightly browned. Set aside.

6   Cook: **8 short stalks asparagus** until barely tender. Drain and set aside.

7   Preheat oven to moderate (350° F.).

8   In saucepan melt: **4 tablespoons butter.** Stir in: **4 tablespoons flour** and cook for 5 minutes, stirring occasionally. Add: 1½ cups of the hot fish stock and cook, stirring, until sauce is smooth and thickened. Stir in: **⅓ cup dry white wine, 1 tablespoon tomato puree** and **salt** and **pepper** to taste. Cook over low heat for 10 minutes, stirring occasionally. If desired, stir in: **1 tablespoon cognac.**

9   Arrange fillets in a **buttered** baking pan. Cover with **buttered** brown or parchment paper and bake in the moderate oven for 10 minutes.

PRESENTATION

Transfer to warm serving platter and mask with the sauce. Garnish with the lobster slices, mussels, mushrooms and asparagus spears.

GROUSE IN CREAM

SERVES 4

La Belle Sole serves ptarmigan, a kind of wild grouse found in the mountains of Norway, in this typical Norwegian cream sauce. Game birds are usually drier than domestic fowl, and this method of braising and saucing them gets around that drawback deliciously. We are not so likely to use game birds in this country where our supply of other meats and domesticated fowls is enormous, compared with the Norwegians'. But we found that Rock Cornish game hens develop an absolutely new personality cooked à la Belle Sole. The special trick, according to Hans Larsen, owner of La Belle Sole, is to braise your bird very, very slowly in the oven, a procedure that keeps the juices in and prevents the cream from cooking away. And the lingonberries, a Scandinavian culinary trademark, are absolutely perfect with this dish.

grouse or Rock
Cornish game hens
salt, pepper
butter
lemon
cream
flour
bacon
sour cream
reserved lingonberries

1 Truss: **4 grouse** or **small Rock Cornish game hens.** Sprinkle birds with **salt** and **pepper.**

2 Preheat oven to moderate (350° F.).

3 In skillet heat: **4 tablespoons butter** and in it sauté the birds until well browned on all sides.

4 Transfer birds to suitable-size casserole and add: **3 cups cream.** Bring cream to a boil over direct heat, cover, and cook in the moderate oven for 30 minutes. Remove birds.

5 To butter and juices remaining in skillet stir in: **4 tablespoons flour.** Gradually stir in the hot cream and cook, stirring in all the brown glaze from bottom and sides of skillet, until sauce is smooth and quite thick. Cook over low heat for 20 minutes, stirring occasionally. Correct seasoning with **salt** and **pepper.**

6 Split birds and remove all bones except leg bones. Arrange boned birds in a casserole and keep warm.

7 Cook: **4 slices bacon** until crisp and golden.

8 Stir into sauce: **1 cup commercial sour cream** and **1 teaspoon lemon juice.** Heat. Strain over birds in casserole and garnish with bacon slices. Serve with **preserved lingonberries.**

WALNUT CAKE WITH MARZIPAN
SERVES 10

We generally think of Scandinavian baking in terms of their marvelous cookies, buttery coffeecakes, and the inevitable "Danish" that are wheeled around offices at coffee-break time. But here, from La Belle Sole, is a cake that is a cake. Mary, in whose department the cake baking is done, proclaims this a "perfect cake." To that I can only add, "I like what I eat" when she serves up this beautiful confection.

eggs
sugar
cake flour
strawberry jam
butter or oil
curaçao
cream
walnuts
almond paste
confectioners' sugar

1 Preheat oven to moderate (350° F.).

2 With electric beater beat: **6 eggs** and **¾ cup sugar** until mixture is very thick and takes some time to level out when beater is withdrawn. Measure **1⅓ cups cake flour.** Sift the flour and fold into the egg-sugar mixture, preferably by hand. Pour into a **greased** round layer cake pan (10 x 2 inches), lined with waxed paper, and bake in the moderate oven for 30 to 35 minutes, or until cake tests done. Cool for 4 minutes, then turn out on cake rack to cool completely. Remove waxed paper from bottom.

3 While cake is baking, beat: **1 cup almond paste** with **2 egg whites.** Beat and knead in about **4 cups confectioners' sugar,** or enough to make a firm dough. Roll out ¼ inch thick on waxed paper sprinkled with **confectioners' sugar.** Cut into a 10-inch round and transfer to cake plate.

4 Cut cake horizontally into three layers. Place bottom layer over the almond paste and spread with: **¾ cup strawberry jam.** Sprinkle all three cake layers with **curaçao,** using about ½ cup in all.

5 Beat: **3 cups cream** until stiff and beat in: **½ cup sugar.** Fold in: **¼ cup chopped walnuts** and **2 tablespoons curaçao.** Put the cake layers together with the cream mixture and frost top and sides. Decorate with **whole walnuts.**

BLOM'S BLACK POT (*Chicken and Steak in Red Wine*)
SERVES 2

Oslo is a city that has been kind to artists—there is even a park there devoted exclusively to the sculpture of one man, Gustav Vigeland, whose total output was subsidized by the state. And one of Oslo's finest restaurants is Blom's *Kunsternes* or Artists' Restaurant. Here writers and theater people gather as well as musicians, painters, sculptors and just plain epicures. Blom's started out nearly ninety years ago as a wineshop with a rather Bohemian atmosphere. The atmosphere is still jaunty, the food and wine excellent. The Black Pot is their great specialty, a chicken and beef casserole served in the individual iron pots in which it is cooked. We like to serve ours in individual earthenware casseroles, although when we make it for more than two people, we cook it in one large pot.

butter
whole chicken breast
salt, pepper
peas
string beans
cauliflower
carrot
mushrooms
flour
red wine
thyme
garlic
ham
beef fillets
asparagus
tomato
parsley

1 In skillet melt: **3 tablespoons butter** and in it brown: **2 half chicken breasts,** skin side down. Sprinkle with: **½ teaspoon salt** and **some freshly ground pepper,** turn and brown the other side.

2 Transfer chicken breasts to a 6-cup heavy iron casserole. Add: **½ cup shelled peas, ½ cup Frenched string beans, 4 cauliflower florets,** and **1 carrot, sliced.**

3 To the butter remaining in skillet add: **2 medium mushrooms, sliced,** and cook for 5 minutes. Stir in: **2 tablespoons flour** and cook for 5 minutes. Gradually stir in: **¾ cup red wine** and **1 cup water** and cook, stirring, until sauce is slightly thickened. Add **a good**

pinch of thyme and pour the sauce over chicken and vegetables in casserole. Bring to a boil over direct heat. Add: **1 clove garlic** and **1 slice ham, ⅛ inch** thick. Cover and simmer for 15 minutes.

4 Sear: **2 fillets of beef,** about 1 inch thick, in **greased** skillet or under broiler for about 1 minute on each side, or until browned. Add to casserole, placing the fillets on top of the ham. On top of the fillets put: **4 stalks asparagus** and **2 wedges tomato.** Sprinkle with **chopped parsley,** cover, and simmer for 15 minutes longer.

5 Remove garlic and serve very hot in the covered casserole.

MUTTON AND CABBAGE
SERVES 4

This simple, good dish is a Norwegian specialty that is featured on Blom's menu. Although they call it mutton, we were told by Sigfred Stephensen, the manager of the restaurant, that one-year-old lamb is most commonly used. We certainly prefer lamb to mutton, and like to serve this with Swedish flat bread and cold Danish beer by way of making a Scandinavian meal of it.

lamb
cabbage
leeks
bay leaf
salt
peppercorns
parsley
potatoes

1 Rinse: **2 pounds shoulder or breast of lamb** in hot water. Cut in large cubes.

2 Cut: **1 head cabbage** into wedges.

3 Clean and slice: **6 large leeks.**

4 Put meat into a heavy casserole with: **1 bay leaf, 2 teaspoons salt, 10 peppercorns,** and **2 cups water,** or enough to cover the meat. Bring liquid to a boil,

skim, cover and simmer for 30 minutes.

5 Put cabbage and leeks on top of meat, cover, and steam for 1 hour.

PRESENTATION
Arrange meat and vegetables in deep serving dish with liquid and sprinkle with **chopped parsley.** Serve with **boiled potatoes** on the side.

FILLET OF SOLE À LA STEPHEN
SERVES 4

Blom's does delicious things with the fish and seafood so readily available throughout Norway. This recipe for sole, shrimp, and lobster is more typical of the French influence in Scandinavian cookery than of the native dishes. We like it especially because of the sauce, one of the best in our collection. At Blom's, this dish is elegantly garnished with little crescents of puff pastry, but for home consumption we use toast triangles made from my home-baked bread.

fillets of sole
white wine
salt, white pepper
mushrooms
shrimp
lobster tails
butter
flour
eggs
cream
lemon
parsley
toast

SEAFOOD

1 Into **buttered** skillet put: **4 fillets of sole.** Add: **1 cup white wine, ½ teaspoon salt, ⅛ teaspoon white pepper, 4 medium mushrooms, 4 large shrimp, cleaned and deveined,** and **4 small lobster tails.** Bring liquid to a boil, cover, and simmer for 10 minutes.

2 Remove fillets to serving dish and garnish with mushrooms and shrimp. Remove meat from lobster tails, cut into slices and arrange on platter. Add lobster shells to skillet and cook over high heat until liquid is reduced to ½ cup.

SAUCE

In saucepan melt: **3 tablespoons butter.** Stir in: **1 tablespoon flour** and simmer for 5 minutes. Stir in: **2 egg yolks** mixed with **½ cup cream.** Strain and stir in the fish stock. Season to taste with **salt** and **white pepper** and add: **2 teaspoons lemon juice.**

PRESENTATION

Pour sauce over fish on platter, sprinkle with **chopped parsley** and garnish with **toast triangles.**

DANISH OPEN SANDWICHES

There are two things that are a "must" on your first trip to Copenhagen. You must go down to the harbor and see the "Little Mermaid," Hans Christian Andersen's fairy-tale creature cast in bronze, and you must go to Oskar Davidsen's, the restaurant of 200 sandwiches which you order from a four-foot-long menu. This is the Danish *smørrebrød* at its supreme best, and the concoctions are so imaginative that we have kept our menu to prod our ingenuity whenever sandwiches are to be made. I should explain, before listing some of them, that a Danish sandwich is a thin slice of buttered bread buried under a full-course meal. At Davidsen's when you order assorted *smørrebrød*, an enormous tray is brought to your table. On it is a basket of bread, a crock of Danish butter, a dish of mayonnaise, and an assortment of little dishes with dozens of ingredients from which you can make your own sandwiches. Following are some of their specialties served on this black bread unless otherwise specified.

Roast Beef with Bacon and Crisp Fried Onions
Buttered bread covered neatly with **1 slice rare roast beef, 1 slice crisply fried bacon,** and **¼ onion,** sliced very thin, **crisply fried.**

Cheese, Shrimps, and Mayonnaise
Buttered bread with **3 narrow strips Swiss cheese, 2 rows of tiny shrimps** between cheese strips, dots of **mayonnaise,** and **a sprig of parsley** on each row of shrimps.

Roast Veal and Cucumber

Bread spread with **mustard mayonnaise, a slice of cold roast veal,** topped with **4 thin slices marinated cucumber.**

Tartar Steak with Lumpfish

Put: **½-inch layer of raw scraped beef** on **buttered rye bread.** Surround with border of **finely minced onion.** Make depression in center of beef and fill with **lumpfish** (Danish caviar, inexpensive and good this way). Sprinkle with **grated horse-radish, chopped hard-cooked egg,** and **capers.**

Liver Paste and Ham

Roll **1 thin slice of ham** into cornucopia around **1 teaspoon liver paste.** Lay diagonally across **buttered bread** and garnish with **tiny slices of sweet pickle.**

Scrambled Egg and Smoked Salmon

Buttered white toast, topped with **hot scrambled egg** and a **strip of smoked salmon** rolled into a flower.

Tartar Steak with Small Shrimps

Put: **½-inch layer of raw scraped beef** on **buttered rye bread,** leaving margin all around. Place border of **tiny shrimp** around beef. Make depression in center of beef for **raw egg yolk.** Top with **finely minced onion** and **capers.**

Salmon Butter and Asparagus (Serves 4)

Chop: **4 ounces smoked salmon** and put through food mill with: **6 ounces soft butter.** Season with **coarsely ground pepper** and **½ teaspoon lemon juice.** Spread thickly on **bread.** Drain and dry: **canned asparagus tips.** Place one asparagus diagonally across each sandwich.

SILLSALAD (Herring Salad)
SERVES 6

Scandinavian salads are so nourishing they can be used for an entire supper, especially if there is plenty of dark bread and butter to accompany them. You come across this herring salad everywhere there, and in one version or another it is a North European mainstay. Potatoes, beets, cucumbers (pickled), salted fish — all of the winter foods of these lands that know such long dreary winters are utilized. But even in sunny California with its eternal summer, this is a delightful treat.

salt herring
potatoes
beets
cooked veal
new dill pickle
green apples
lettuce
pepper
onion
sugar
wine vinegar
cream
eggs
capers

HERRING

1 Wash: **2 large salt herring.** Cut off heads and tails, rinse under cold water, and soak overnight.

2 Drain. Remove skin and cut fillets from bones. Dry fillets and dice fine.

SALAD

1 Mix together: the diced herring, **2½ cups diced boiled potatoes, 2 cups diced boiled beets, 2 cups diced cooked veal, 1 new dill pickle,** diced, **2 large green apples,** peeled, cored, and diced, **½ onion,** chopped fine, **1 teaspoon sugar, 5 tablespoons wine vinegar, ½ teaspoon pepper,** and **½ cup cream.** Toss lightly with 2 forks. Taste for seasoning and consistency. Salad should be moist but not runny. Add another **¼ cup cream,** if necessary.

2 Cover and let chill in refrigerator for 6 hours, or overnight.

PRESENTATION

Place crisp **lettuce leaves** on a platter. Mound up chilled herring salad on it— salad will be pink because of beets. Surround with slices of: **2 hard-cooked eggs** sprinkled with: **2 tablespoons capers.** Chop the white of: **1 hard-cooked egg** and press the yolk through a sieve. Sprinkle on top of herring salad.

SUMMER SALAD
SERVES 4

chervil
radishes
mushrooms
smoked salmon
butter
Boston lettuce
tomatoes
parsley
sour cream
white vinegar
tarragon vinegar
salt, pepper
horse-radish
chives
dill

SALAD

1 Cut into 1-inch pieces: **4 slices smoked salmon.** Cut into quarters: **8 mushrooms.**

2 In a skillet lightly brown: **2 tablespoons butter.** Add the smoked salmon and the mushrooms. Sauté for 5 minutes.

3 In a large salad bowl put: **1 head Boston lettuce,** washed, dried, and torn into bite-sized pieces, **2 tomatoes,** skinned, seeded, and cut into large dice, **8 radishes,** sliced, **1 tablespoon fresh chopped chervil, 1 tablespoon fresh chopped parsley, 1 teaspoon chopped chives,** and **1 tablespoon chopped dill.**

4 Mix the cold vegetables and herbs and add the hot salmon and mushrooms.

SOUR CREAM DRESSING

Beat together: **1 cup sour cream, 2 teaspoons tarragon vinegar, 1 tablespoon white vinegar, 1 teaspoon horse-radish, ½ teaspoon salt,** and a generous sprinkle of **freshly ground pepper.**

PRESENTATION

Pour dressing over salad and mix well with fork and spoon so all ingredients are coated. Serve at once while there is still contrast between the warm salmon and mushrooms and the cold vegetables.

FISH PUDDING WITH MUSHROOM CREAM SAUCE
SERVES 4

Scandinavian fish puddings were something new to me until we had one there and fell in love with its delicate and subtle flavor. This is the family recipe of a Norwegian friend, but I will tell you a secret. At home we found that we could buy excellent fish pudding imported from Scandinavia in a tin shaped like a melon mold. All we need do is bake it, unmold it, and make the sauce for it. Here is the entire recipe, as it was given to us, in case you want to make this excellent dish from scratch.

halibut or trout
salt, white pepper
cream
eggs
fish stock (see index)
mushrooms
butter
flour
cardamom
cayenne pepper

FISH PUDDING

1 Preheat oven to slow (325° F.).

2 Put: **2¼ pounds halibut** or **trout** through meat grinder with fine blade 3 times. Beat in: **1½ cups cream** and add: **1½ teaspoons salt, ½ teaspoon cardamom,** and **a dash of cayenne pepper.**

3 Separate: **3 eggs.** Reserve yolks and beat whites until they form stiff peaks.

4 Fold egg whites into fish mixture.

5 **Butter** an 8-cup mold or casserole and fill three-fourths full with fish pudding.

6 Place in pan of boiling water, covered. Cook in slow oven for 1 hour.

SAUCE

1 In a saucepan melt: **3 tablespoons butter.** Add: **1 pound mushrooms,** chopped, and stew gently in covered saucepan for 10 minutes.

2 Add, a little at a time: **3 tablespoons flour,** stirring it in with wire whisk.

3 Add: **1½ cups hot fish stock,** stirring well. Add: **¾ cup cream, 1 teaspoon salt,** and **⅛ teaspoon white pepper,** and cook 5 minutes longer.

4 Beat: **2 egg yolks** and add to them a little of the hot sauce. Then mix egg yolks into the saucepan, stirring constantly. Cook over low heat until sauce thickens. Cover and remove from heat.

PRESENTATION

On a hot platter, unmold fish pudding. Carefully spoon some sauce over pudding and pass the rest in a sauce dish.

GRILLED GRAVAD LAX *(Grilled Marinated Salmon)*
SERVES 6

Gravad lax is a great delicacy in the Scandinavian countries. In the old days, salmon was preserved by salting and seasoning it and then putting it in a hole in the ground to "ripen." Now it is marinated in sugar, salt, pepper, and dill. Sometimes it is eaten raw after several days of this treatment, but we liked it this way. You can barbecue *gravad lax* instead of broiling it, and the effect is even better.

salmon steaks
salt, pepper
fresh dill
olive oil
parsley
butter
dry mustard
sugar
eggs
tarragon vinegar
Dijon mustard

GRAVAD LAX

1   Put in a shallow bowl: **3 pounds raw salmon steaks**, cut 1 inch thick.

2   Cover with: **½ cup salt, ¾ cup sugar, about 12 to 15 sprigs fresh dill, chopped,** and **1 teaspoon freshly ground pepper.** Rub mixture into salmon.

3   Be sure salmon is thoroughly coated with these ingredients, and then let it stand in refrigerator, weighted down by a heavy plate, for 24 to 48 hours.

4   Place fish in a very hot broiler, close to the flame, and grill only 3 minutes on each side. It should be only partly cooked —hot and tinged with brown on the outside and still cold inside.

MUSTARD SAUCE

1   Beat: **2 egg yolks.** Add: **1 tablespoon dry mustard, 1 teaspoon Dijon mustard, ½ teaspoon sugar,** and **½ teaspoon salt.** Mix well.

2   Beat in, drop by drop: **1 scant cup olive oil,** as you would do for mayonnaise. Continue beating until sauce is thick enough.

3   Beat in: **2 tablespoons tarragon vinegar.** Add: **2 tablespoons chopped dill.**

PRESENTATION

Serve salmon steaks right from the broiler. Put **a pat of very cold butter mixed with chopped dill and parsley** on top of each steak. Serve mustard sauce on the side.

AEBLEKAGE *(Danish Apple Cake)*
SERVES 6

Danish whipped cream can make almost anything taste good. It is not only marvelously rich and fresh, but Danish cooks use great artistry in decorating a cake with it. This cake made with apples, bread crumbs, and brown sugar is the perfect foil for the cream. I find it as great a temptation as Adam found Eve's original, unadorned apple— with far less penalty for eating it!

cooking apples
orange
sugar
brown sugar
vanilla
bread crumbs
butter
raspberry jam
red currant jelly
sherry
cinnamon
cream

APPLE CAKE

1   Preheat oven to moderate (350° F.).

2   Peel and core: **3 pounds cooking apples** (about 8 cups) and cut into quarters.

3   Simmer in covered saucepan with: **¼ cup water** for about 25 minutes, or until apples are soft. Mash and add: **⅔ cup sugar, the grated rind of 1 orange,** and **½ teaspoon vanilla.**

4   Mix together: **2 cups fine bread crumbs, 1 teaspoon cinnamon,** and **¼ cup brown sugar.** Brown lightly in skillet with: **2 tablespoons butter.**

5   **Butter** a round 8-inch baking dish that is 3 inches deep.

6   Alternate layers of the crumb mixture, the apple puree, and **raspberry jam,** and finish with a layer of the crumb mixture on top.

7 Using a large wooden spoon, press layers down firmly. Pour over cake: **½ cup melted butter.**

8 Bake in the moderate oven for 40 minutes, or until cake is firm.

RED CURRANT GLAZE

In a small saucepan heat: **⅔ cup red currant jelly** with **2 tablespoons sherry.** Cook, stirring with a wooden spoon, until jelly is melted and bubbling and coats spoon lightly. Let glaze cool slightly.

PRESENTATION

Cool the cake and unmold on serving plate. With a pastry brush, spread a layer of red currant glaze over top of cake. Decorate with **whipped cream.**

DANSK KAGE   (Danish Pastry)
MAKES 36 PIECES

The Danish pastry that you eat in its homeland is meltingly delicious. Danish butter being what it is, and the amount of it that goes into their coffeecakes and pastries, no wonder! This is just one short step from being puff pastry, and all the buttering and folding are what make it so light and flaky. Best of all, the strong Danish coffee is worthy of it to the last crumb.

flour
salt
sugar
active dry yeast
eggs
milk
butter
nutmeg
lemon extract
almond extract
almonds

1 Mix: **4 cups sifted flour** with **1 teaspoon salt** and **¼ cup sugar.** Mix: **1 package active dry yeast** with **¼ cup lukewarm water.** Stir until yeast is dissolved.

2 In a large warm bowl stir yeast into dry ingredients and add: **1 beaten egg, 1 cup tepid milk, ½ teaspoon nutmeg, ½ teaspoon lemon extract,** and **½ teaspoon almond extract.** Stir until smooth with wooden spoon. Dough should be soft and pliable. Remove to a **floured** board and knead until smooth.

3 Put dough in a warm **buttered** bowl. Cover with tea towel and let rise in warm place out of drafts until doubled in bulk (about 30 to 40 minutes).

4 Lightly **flour** a pastry board.

5 Roll out dough until ½ inch thick.

6 Stir: **12 ounces softened butter** in a small bowl until it is easy to spread.

7 With a spatula spread one-third of the butter over two-thirds of the surface of dough. Fold the unbuttered part of dough over once. Fold buttered part on top of it so dough is in 3 layers.

8 Roll dough into square about ¾ inch thick. Repeat buttering and folding 2 more times.

9 Place dough in **buttered** bowl, cover with towel and let stand in cold place for 30 minutes.

10 On lightly **floured** board roll out dough ¼ inch thick. Cream together: **¼ cup sugar** and **¼ cup softened butter** and spread over dough. Cut into 4-inch squares.

11 Mix: **4 ounces butter, 4 ounces sugar,** and **4 ounces ground almonds.** Place 1 teaspoon of this almond paste down the center of each square and fold over. Seal edges together and make 3 slashes in outer edge.

12 Place pastries on a **buttered** cookie sheet and let stand in cold place for 20 minutes.

13 Preheat oven to very hot (450° F.).

14 Brush pastries with **egg white,** sprinkle with mixture of **chopped almonds** and **sugar,** and bake in the very hot oven for 15 to 20 minutes, or until golden.

SCANDINAVIAN FRUIT SOUP

SERVES 8

In what part of the world do people eat soup for dessert? I could win the $64,000 question all over again with the answer to that one. Why, in Scandinavia, of course, where soups made of berries or fruits are served either hot or cold with a cream topping as the grand finale to a meal. Here is a delicious recipe for one of my favorites.

prunes
dried apricots
dried peaches
salt
butter
flour
half and half
eggs
vanilla
sugar
cornstarch
lemon
dark rum or sherry

FRUIT SOUP

1 Rinse: **1 cup prunes (pitted), 1 cup dried apricots,** and **1 cup dried peaches.** Place in deep pot and cover with: **2 quarts boiling water.** Let fruit soak overnight. Add: **the thin yellow rind of ¼ lemon, grated.**

2 Place pot over medium heat and, keeping the same water, cook fruit until it is quite soft.

3 Mix: **½ cup sugar** with **2 tablespoons cornstarch.** Blend with: **½ cup dark rum** or **sherry** to make smooth paste. Stir in a small amount of the fruit mixture, then add the paste to the fruit. Add: **a pinch of salt.** Stir to mix well and turn on heat. Cook for about 10 minutes, or until slightly thickened.

4 Serve hot or cold. We prefer it cold, topped with Swedish cream, less attractively known as Cold Dumplings.

SWEDISH CREAM

1 In a saucepan melt over medium heat: **2 tablespoons butter.** Add: **4 tablespoons flour** and stir. Add gradually, stirring constantly, **1½ cups half and half.** Continue stirring for about 20 minutes until mixture has boiled and thickened.

2 Beat until fluffy and lemon-color: **2 eggs.** Add a little of the hot mixture to eggs and blend well. Then stir eggs slowly into the hot cream mixture. Add: **1 tablespoon sugar** and **1 teaspoon vanilla.** Mix well.

PRESENTATION

Chill the fruit soup in a compote bowl. Chill the Swedish cream in an attractive sauce bowl. Pass them both together and let each person top their serving of fruit with a gob of the cream.

Note: The soup and the cream can be served independently, too. In that case you chill the Swedish cream in a mold and serve it unmolded as a separate dessert. This amount serves four.

ENGLAND

OF all the countries we have traveled in, England is for us most like a second home. Mary's family is British and she has lived in various parts of the Empire—in the days when the sun never set on it—from Canada to Shanghai to England itself. My foot first touched foreign soil when I landed in England on a student tour of Europe during my sixteenth summer. That foot has had the wanderer's itch ever since.

It was in England that I took my first crack at the theater when I was twenty-two, and it was on the London stage two months later that I won the role of Prince Albert in *Victoria Regina*, to be repeated in New York opposite Miss Helen Hayes' Victoria. I have studied in England and I have worked there numberless times over the years so, heaven knows, I've done my share of eating British.

London does not have the reputation for fine eating that Paris does, and England in general suffers even more by comparison with France. But for my money both are grossly underrated. My friend, Boris Karloff, backs me up on this one hundred percent. (Of course, being British, he might be a little prejudiced.) Yet I'm as American as blueberry pie and I love English cooking. Certainly there are some British delicacies that can't be beat in any country and I mention only a few: Scotch salmon, potted shrimp, Yorkshire pudding, roast ribs of beef, grouse, trifle, Whitstable oysters, steak and kidney pudding, and my beloved "toad," a marvelous dish of English sausage in a nest of crisp, tasty popover dough.

Pubs are as much a part of English life as Buckingham Palace, and if it ever came to a point where one or the other had to go, I'd lay my money it wouldn't be the pubs. These public houses are scattered throughout the island, and people have their local favorites. More than just a friendly neighborhood bar, the "local" takes the place of the gentlemen's club for the rank-and-file Englishman. Snacks are the order of the day in most pubs, but some serve excellent simple food.

Restaurants in London, as in any cosmopolitan center, reflect a broad cross section of international cuisines. The only country that is not so well represented is England itself. Try to find typical English dishes in a top flight London restaurant and you will be greeted by the maître d's iciest stare. Italian, Greek, German, or most usually French is what you will get, with an occasional British specialty thrown in, as a sop to the tourist trade, no doubt.

Dining at country inns is not what it was when Tom Jones was a boy. But rural England can still come up with a good meal if it is a question of local fish, cheeses, ham, or game. And something new has been added to the restaurant picture outside London. The stately homes that are open for business to paying visitors also feed them for a fee. Luncheon and tea are served, and when the food has been prepared according to old family recipes you are likely to find top-flight English home cooking instead of the usual restaurant fare.

Maybe English food is not as exciting as some of the more exotic or imaginative cuisines in the world, but then, sensible meals are served at regular hours, and one is far less likely to suffer from indigestion there than any other place on earth. That is almost recommendation enough for a country's way of eating.

The Ivy sets out a handsome array of British specialties—roast sirloin, smoked Scotch salmon, Scotch Trifle, Gooseberry Fool, and the fine English cheeses, Stilton, cheddar, and Cheshire. So who needs India?

A lordly loin of beef surrounded by a coronet of Yorkshire pudding—this is a dish to set before a king. James I knighted just such a roast. Whacking off a slice with his sword he said, "I dub thee Sir Loin!" And sirloin it's been to this day.

THE IVY

About half a century ago a restaurant was opened on London's West Street close at hand to most of the city's theaters. Its founder, bless his heart, set out to attract a theatrical clientele because he wanted to "provide a fine cuisine for cultured palates." An actress of the day inadvertently gave the restaurant its name when she told the owner she and her friends would always come to see him—"We will cling together like the ivy." Statesmen, actors, artists, and writers have clung through the years, and the list of Ivy clients reads like a *Who's Who* of British arts and politics.

The restaurant looks very English with its dark wood paneling, but the menu might have come straight from the other side of the Channel. French cuisine, we found, is as typically English in London's topflight restaurants as are the dark wood walls! You can get "native" dishes if you ask for them, and the Ivy's are beautiful. But I suspect the waiter always wonders a bit at anyone who would choose Gooseberry Fool over *Poire Cardinale*.

There are London restaurants like the Guinea and Simpson's that specialize in lordly roasts of beef. And in Soho you can find Greek, Italian, Spanish, Chinese—the gamut of nationalities. But best of all, for me, are the restaurants that specialize in fish and seafood—England is, after all, a small island surrounded by large seas teeming with good things to eat. At Wheelers, the great oyster house, Pruniers, Sheekey's, and Bentley's you can find all the delicious gifts of the sea—Whitstable oysters, whitebait, Dublin prawns, Dover sole, lobsters, and the magnificent fish from Britain's rivers. Let no one tell you that eating in England is not a gastronomic adventure. How do you suppose John Bull got so plump?

THE IVY

★ **Saumon d'Ecosse Palace 18/6**
Slice of Scotch Salmon, cooked in white wine garnished, tomato, mushrooms, asparagus tips and glazed.

Aile de Caneton d'Aylesbury Montmonrency 18/6
Roast Aylesbury Duckling, served in port wine sauce, garnished with pitted cherries.

★ **Chop de Veau à la Sassi 15/6**
Veal Chop cooked in butter, sage leaves and diced potatoes.

★ **Entrecôte Sauteé Bordelaise 16/6**
Sirloin Steak cooked in butter, served in red wine sauce, additioned marrow fat and shallots.

★ **Poulet de Grain Grand Mere 16/6**
Chicken cooked en casserole garnished button mushrooms, onions and bread snippets.

PLATS DE SAISON

| Salmon Trout | Asperges | Saumon d'Ecosse Frais |

Hors D'œuvres Caviar 30/- Foie Gras 20/- Jambon de Parme 11/6 Saumon fumé 11/
Truite fumée 9/6 Anguille fumée 10/6 Large Prawns (According to Size) 10/
Salade de Thon 8/6 Potted Shrimps 6/6 Pâté Maison 5/6 Salami de Cremona 6/
Cocktails of Lobsters 12/6 Prawns 7/6 Seafood 8/6 Escargots de Bourgogne (½ doz.) 7/
Melons (According to Season) Artichauds 7/6 Avocado ((When available) 6/6 Hors D'Oeuvres au Choix 7/
Grapefruit Cocktail 4/6

Les Potages Consommé aux Pâtes 3/- Consommé en Gelée 3/6 Petite Marmite 5/6
Tortue au Sherry 6/6 Kangaroo Tail Soup 6/6 Soupe à l'Oignon 3/
Minestrone 3/6 Crème de Tomate 3/6 Saint-Germain 3/6 à la Reine 4/6 Asperges 4/
Champignons 4/6 Bisque de Homard 6/6 Vichisoise 4/-

Les Farinages Spaghetti Napolitaine 6/6 Tagliatelli Bolognese 7/6 Raviolis Maison 8/
Nouilles Vertes au Beurre 6/6

Les Œufs Au Plat Bercy 8/6 Aux Foies de Volailles 8/6 Brouillé au Tomate 10/6
(*2 Pieces*) Poché Benedictine 9/- Washington 9/- Cocotte à la Crème (2) 7/- En Gelée (1P) 3/

L'Omelette Fines Herbes 7/6 Fromage 7/6 Champignons 8/6 Espagnole 8/6 Ivy 10/

L'Homard Americaine - Newburg - Thermidor - Bercy - Cardina

Scampis Frits 13/6 Meunière 13/6 Provençale 13/6 En Brochette 14/

Truite de Riviere Grillée 8/6 Aux Amandes 10/6 Court-Bouillon 10/

Soles de Douvres En Goujon 13/6 Frites ou Grillées 14/6 Meunière ou Caprice 15/
Bonne Femme 16/6 Veronique 16/6 Waleska 16/6 Palace 16/
D'Antin 16/6 Normande 17/6 Turbot Poche ou Grille 14/6 Saint Jacques Mornay 12/

Les Rotis Caneton (2 cvts) (45 minutes) 45/- Poulet Nouveau 35/- Poussin 16/
(*Cooked to Order*) Surrey (3 cvts) 42/6 Carré d'Agneau (4 cvts) 50/- (35 minutes

Salades Laitues 3/6 Vertes 3/6 Panachées 3/6 Tomate 3/6 Pommes 2/

Fromage Stilton 4/- Camembert 4/- Brie 4/- Gruyère 4/-
Cheddar 3/6 Gorgonzola 3/6 Hollandais 3/6

Les Fruits de Saison

ROOMS AVAILA

SPECIALITIES MAISON

Terrine de Canard Maison 8/6
Paté of Duck

Mousseline de Sole Nantua 14/6
Mousse of Sole.   Shrimp sauce.

Douvriene Monick 16/6
Dover Sole Poached in white wine sauce and garnished.

Supreme de Volaille Nelo 17/6
Breast of Chicken.   Cooked in cream and brandy.

Tournedos Dini 18/6
Tournedos.   Cavity filled and grilled, savoury sauce.

Escalope de Veau Irma 16/6
Slice of Veal and Bel Paese.   Wallet fashion, cooked in butter, Italian sauce.

Côte de Bœuf Choron (2 cvts) 42/-
Grilled rib of beef.   Luxuriously garnished, sauce choron.

Crepes Verlaine 8/6
Pancake.   Flambé in brandy and absinthe

Entrees Suprèmes de Volaille: Maryland 17/6   A la Kieff 17/6   Bergerette 17/6
Vol au Vent de Volaille à la Reine 15/6   Poussin Grand Mère 16/6
Poulet de Grain Mascotte 16/6   Ris de Veau au Madeire 15/6   Piccata de Veau au Marsala 14/6
Escalope de Veau Viennoise 14/6   Holstein 17/6   Ivy 17/6   Foie de Veau au Lard 12/6
Cervelle au Beurre Noir 12/6   Tête de Veau Gribiche 12/6   Tripe à l'Anglaise 12/6
Kebab à l'Orientale 15/6   Rognons de Veau ou d'Agneau Turbigo 12/6   Boeuf Strogonoff 15/6
Minute Diane 17/6   Côtes D'agneau Montpensier 14/6   Tournedos Rossini 22/6   Ou Rachel 18/6
Filets de Steak Forestiere 18/6   L'Entrecôte Chasseur 16/6   Demi Caneton à l'Orange 22/6

Grillades L'Entrecôte 15/6   Filets 17/6   Tournedos 17/6   Rump or Point Steak 15/6
Chateaubriand (2 cvts) 40/-   Côtes d'Agneau 12/6   Chop d'Agneau ou de Veau 15/6
Chump Chop 13/6   Rognons d'Agneau ou de Veau au Lard 12/6   Poussin Grille Ivy 16/6
Poulet Nouveau (2 cvts) 35/-   Aile 17/6   Cuisse 10/6   Gammon 12/6   Porc Chop 14/6

Buffet Froid Caneton (P/P) 18/6   Poulet Aile 17/6   Cuisse 10/6   Bœuf 12/6
Jambon 12/6   Agneau 12/6   Langue 10/6   Steak Tartare 16/6
Demi-Homard Froid ou en Mayonnaise

Legumes Petits Pois 3/6   ou à la Française 4/-   Chouxfleurs 3/6   Au gratin 4/-   Brocolis 3/6
Epinards en Branche 3/6   à la Crème 4/-   Haricots Verts 4/6   Fèves 3/6
Choux de Bruxelles 3/6   Onions Frits ou Braises 3/6   Celeris 3/6   Endives 3/6
Flageolets 3/6   Aubergines Provençale 4/6   Courgettes 4/6   Artichauds 7/6
Tomate Grillée 3/6   Champignons Grillé 5/6

Pommes Frites 2/6   Sautée 2/6   Purée à la Crème 3/-   Croquette 3/-   Parisiennes 2/6
Neige 2/6   Au Four 2/6   Nouvelles 2/6   Maître d'Hotel 3/-

Entremets Crêpes Confiture 4/6   Ou Suzette 8/6   Crème Caramel 4/-
Eclairs Café ou Chocolat (2P) 3/6   Gateaux 3/6   Mille Feuilles 4/6
Profiterolles 4/6   Compotes de Fruits 5/6   Macedoine de Fruits 6/6   Zabaglioni 5/6
Glaces Variées 3/6   Sorbet 3/6   Cassatta 5/6   Bombes Pralinées 5/6   Napolitain 5/6
Coupe Jacques 5/6   Pêche Melba 6/6   Poire Cardinale 5/6   Crème Fraîche ou Chantilly 2/6
Ananas Frais 6/6   Soufflé aux Liqueurs (2P) 15/-   En Surprise 15/-

Savouries Canapé Diane 5/6   Champignons sur Toast 5/6   Welsh Rarebit 5/6
Canapé Baron 5/6   Diable à Cheval 5/6

PRIVATE PARTIES   *Cafes 2/-*

ROAST BEEF
SERVES 6

Regardless of the reputation of English cooking in general, most Americans believe that the English know how to turn out a roast beef second to none. Perhaps it's because we romanticize the days of Merrie England when succulent joints were roasted on spits and even great kings gnawed on beef bones and ate with greasy fingers. The roast beef in England *is* superb and cooked to perfection. But I like it especially because they carve it in lovely thin slices that seem to improve its flavor and texture. Next time you order roast beef in a restaurant here, ask for it "English cut" instead of the usual thick slab and see if it doesn't taste better.

rib roast of beef
salt, pepper
garlic (optional)
onion (optional)
red wine (optional)
horse-radish
Yorkshire pudding
(see index)

MEAT

Note: A standing rib of beef makes the best roast.

1 Have your butcher cut off short ribs from: **a 2 rib roast**, weighing about 6 pounds.

2 Remove meat from refrigerator at least 3 hours before cooking. Trim off excess fat.

3 Preheat oven to very hot (525° F.).

4 Do not salt the meat before roasting as salt draws out the juices. If you wish to season the meat, rub it with **onion** or **garlic**, or insert **a few slivers of garlic** near the bone. You can rub in some **freshly ground pepper**.

5 Stand the roast, fat side up, on a rack set over a shallow roasting pan. Place in the very hot oven, then lower oven heat to moderate (350° F.) as soon as roast is in.

6 If meat is of top quality, do not baste it. There will be enough fat in the meat without pouring drippings over it.

7 Roast 16 minutes to the pound for rare, 22 minutes for medium, and 28 minutes (heaven forbid!) for well-done.

8 When roast is cooked, remove it to a hot platter and let stand 15 or 20 minutes until meat and juices set. Sprinkle with **salt** and **additional pepper**.

GRAVY

1 Pour off fat from pan. Add: **¼ cup red wine** or **water** to pan and stir to lift up solidified meat sediment. Add: **salt** to taste.

2 Cook on top of stove until gravy boils, then reduce heat and simmer for about 1 minute.

3 Strain into heated sauce boat.

PRESENTATION

Serve roast on a hot platter surrounded by **Yorkshire pudding**. Pass gravy and **prepared horse-radish**.

YORKSHIRE PUDDING
SERVES 6

In the old days, a roast beef was cooked at high heat on the oven rack with a pan on the shelf below to catch the drippings. It was in that pan that the batter for Yorkshire pudding was poured about forty minutes before the roast was done. Then the roast and the puffy brown pudding emerged from the oven together. But today we roast our beef at a much lower temperature. Better for the meat, impossible for the pudding. So now the Yorkshire pudding goes into a hot oven as soon as the roast comes out, and it cooks while the roast rests.

flour
salt
milk
eggs
beef drippings
or butter

1 Have all ingredients for batter at room temperature or pudding will not puff up properly.

2 Sift together: ⅞ cup flour and ½ teaspoon salt.

3 Add gradually: ½ cup milk, stirring all the time.

4 When smooth, beat in: 2 eggs, beaten until fluffy and pale yellow.

5 Add: ½ cup water. Beat vigorously until batter bubbles. (You can make this batter in a blender, on high speed for 15 seconds, with excellent results.)

6 Preheat oven to hot (400° F.).

7 Make this batter at least an hour before it is to be cooked. Beat it again just before baking.

8 In the hot oven heat a 9 x 10 baking dish or muffin tins. Pour about ¼ inch beef drippings or melted butter in bottom and let fat get smoking hot.

9 Pour in batter. Bake in the hot oven for 20 minutes. Reduce oven temperature to moderate (350° F.) and continue baking for 15 minutes longer.

PRESENTATION

Cut Yorkshire pudding into squares or remove individual ones from muffin tins and arrange on platter with roast beef.

DEVILED RIB BONES
SERVES 4

In a country that consumes a lot of roast beef there are bound to be a lot of rib bones leftover. And sooner or later a clever chef will think of something good to do with them. At the Ivy the Deviled Rib Bones are almost a better by-product than the original roast. They tell me that this recipe was an old club favorite, and since the ribs must be eaten with the fingers, it is possible that English clubs are a lot less stuffy than we think.

roasted rib bones
salt, pepper
bread crumbs
English mustard
cream
butter

1 Take: 4 freshly roasted rib bones. Trim them but leave a fairly generous portion of meat on the bones.

2 Sprinkle with salt and pepper.

3 Make a thin paste with: 2 tablespoons English mustard and 3 tablespoons cream.

4 Coat rib bones all around with the mustard paste.

5 Sprinkle generously with fine bread crumbs, covering bones completely.

6 Dot generously with: 3 tablespoons melted butter.

7 Place under broiler until crisp and crusty, turning to brown all sides.

PRESENTATION

Serve hot and, says the chef, "Come to terms with fingers."
Note: The chef suggests that you can follow the same procedure with a fresh unpicked capon carcass. In that case break or cut it into manageable pieces.

HARE SOUP
SERVES 6

English winters can be nasty—damp and penetratingly chill, especially in houses that lack central heating. But the Ivy's rich and heartening Hare Soup takes care of that. A people's climate most certainly affects their cuisine, and this delicious cold-weather soup must surely have been created as an antidote to winter weather.

hare legs and liver
butter
onions
leeks
carrots
ham
parsley
flour
chicken stock
(see index)
rosemary
basil
thyme
marjoram
salt, cayenne pepper
port
bread

1   Separate: **forelegs and drumsticks of 2 hare legs.** Cut the meat from the forelegs into small pieces.

2   In soup kettle heat: **4 tablespoons butter.** Add the drumsticks and meat from the forelegs, **2 onions, coarsely cut, 4 leeks, quartered, 2 carrots, sliced, 1 cup diced lean ham,** and **a few sprigs of parsley.** Cook over moderate heat for about 20 minutes, or until meat and vegetables are browned.

3   Stir in: **2 tablespoons flour** and cook for 5 minutes longer.

4   Add: **6 cups chicken stock** and bring to a boil. Simmer for 2 hours. Remove drumsticks and let cool. Add to soup: **the liver of the hare, chopped,** and cook for 10 minutes longer.

5   Blend soup in electric blender, about 2 cups at a time, until smooth and strain through a fine sieve. Return the puree to the heat. Add a cheesecloth bag containing: **¼ teaspoon each of rosemary, basil, thyme,** and **marjoram** and bring soup to a boil.

6   Stir in: **⅛ teaspoon cayenne pepper,** salt to taste, **2 tablespoons butter,** and **¼ cup port.** Keep hot over low heat.

7   Toast: **3 slices bread.** Remove crusts. **Butter** and cut into triangles.

PRESENTATION
Remove meat from drumsticks and mince. Spread each toast triangle with a little of the minced meat and put one into each soup plate. Ladle soup over the toast and serve very hot.

KEDGEREE OF SALMON
SERVES 4

The Ivy prepares this excellent Kedgeree, a sort of curried rice and fish dish that originated, I believe, in Singapore. It is still a popular dish in England, as are many of the preparations brought back in the days of the Empire. At the Ivy they used poached fresh salmon, but we have found that this Kedgeree is very good with canned salmon, too. Nice to have one rather exotic recipe that you can use in a pinch with a can of salmon from the pantry shelf.

KEDGEREE

salmon
butter
onions
salt
curry powder
rice
chicken consommé
egg
béchamel sauce
(see index)
cream

1 Flake: **a 1-pound can of salmon** or **enough poached fresh salmon** (1½ pounds) to measure **2 cups.** Set aside.

2 Preheat oven to moderate (350° F.).

3 In saucepan melt: **2 tablespoons butter** and in it sauté: **1 medium onion, chopped,** for 5 minutes. Add: **1 teaspoon salt, 1 cup rice,** and **1 can chicken consommé** plus enough **water** to measure **2 cups.** Bring liquid to a boil. Cover tightly and cook over low heat without stirring for 30 minutes. Remove cover, stir rice, and let steam for 5 minutes.

4 Mix 1 cup of the rice pilaf with 1 cup of the flaked salmon. Add: **1 hard-cooked egg, diced, ½ cup béchamel sauce,** and **salt** to taste. Make a ring of this mixture in a glass baking dish, 8 inches round and 2 inches deep. Fill center with the remainder of the flaked salmon and cover completely with the remaining rice. Dot with: **1 tablespoon butter.** Set dish in pan containing 1 inch hot water. Cover baking dish with **greased** brown paper and bake in the moderate oven for 20 minutes.

5 Serve with favorite curry sauce or the following simple curry sauce.

SIMPLE CURRY SAUCE

Sauté: **2 tablespoons minced onion** and **1 tablespoon curry powder** in **2 tablespoons butter** for 5 minutes, or until onion is transparent. Stir in: **1½ cups béchamel sauce, ½ cup cream** and cook over low heat for 10 minutes, stirring occasionally. Season to taste with **salt.**

TRIPE AND ONIONS
SERVES 6

We eat things abroad that we would never touch at home. In France and England tripe is a great delicacy, maybe because they know how to prepare it well, and I was finally tempted to try Tripe and Onions at the Ivy. It was excellent. Once you get over the unpleasant fact that tripe is the stomach tissue of a cow or ox, and can get yourself to think of it as a "variety meat" rather than offal, you're halfway to enjoying it. There is a great deal of gelatin in tripe and very little flavor. It needs long cooking and careful seasoning, but given the proper treatment, it can be very good indeed, as you will see if you try this recipe.

honeycomb tripe
Spanish onions
salt, pepper
butter
flour
cream

1 Cut: **1½ pounds honeycomb tripe** into 2-inch squares. Put them into a saucepan with: **3 large Spanish onions, sliced,** and **1 teaspoon salt.** Add: **1 quart water,** or enough to barely cover. Bring to a boil, cover, and simmer for 2 hours.

2 In saucepan melt: **6 tablespoons butter.** Stir in: **½ cup flour** and cook over low heat for 5 minutes, stirring occasionally. Strain liquid from the tripe into the butter-flour mixture and cook over high heat, stirring rapidly, until sauce is smooth and quite thick. Add the tripe and onions, **1 teaspoon salt,** or to taste, and **⅛ teaspoon pepper.** Cook over low heat for 30 minutes.

3 Just before serving the Tripe and Onions, stir in: **½ cup cream.**

BOILED LEG OF LAMB WITH CAPER SAUCE
SERVES 6

Surprisingly enough a boiled leg of lamb can be absolutely delicious. I had thought it would be a crime to do anything but roast lamb until I tried this at the Ivy. Maybe it was my English blood answering an old ancestral call, but I rather think the dish stands on its own merits. It is a more sophisticated New England Boiled Dinner made with lamb instead of beef, and the caper sauce is excellent.

leg of lamb
onions
carrots
leeks
celery
garlic
salt, peppercorns
flour
capers

LAMB

1 Put: **a 5-pound leg of lamb** into a large kettle. Add boiling water just to cover. Bring water to a boil. Cover and simmer for 30 minutes.

2 Add: **6 large onions, 6 large carrots, 6 large leeks,** and **3 hearts celery, halved.** Cover and simmer for about 30 minutes.

3 Add: **1 clove garlic, 1 tablespoon salt,** and **1 teaspoon peppercorns.** Cover and simmer for 30 minutes longer. Set kettle off heat and allow fat to float to surface.

CAPER SAUCE

Skim off: **4 tablespoons fat** from surface and combine with: **4 tablespoons flour.** Cook for 5 minutes, stirring occasionally. Add 3 cups of the hot lamb broth, **½ teaspoon salt, 4 tablespoons capers (1½ ounces)** and cook, stirring, until sauce is slightly thickened.

PRESENTATION

Arrange the leg of lamb, partially carved, on a large serving platter and place vegetables around it. Serve the caper sauce separately.

STEAMED APPLE PUDDING
SERVES 10

flour
baking powder
salt
shortening
apples
vanilla or sherry
milk
sugar
ground cloves
lemon
cornstarch
eggs
butter

If you like a typical English steamed pudding you will like this one from the Ivy. If you don't, nothing I can say will help. This is a good one, and there are times when a bland and substantial dessert is just the ticket.

PASTRY

1 Sift together into mixing bowl: **3 cups flour, 3 teaspoons double-acting baking powder,** and **1 teaspoon salt.** Cut in: **¾ cup shortening.**

2 Add, all at once: **1 cup water** and stir with a fork until all flour is moistened. Add a little more water, until dough can be gathered together.

3 Turn out on **floured** board and knead gently, about 10 kneading strokes.

APPLES

Peel and thinly slice: **6 medium-sized apples.** Mix apples with: **1 cup sugar, ½ teaspoon ground cloves, the grated rind of 1 lemon, 3 tablespoons cornstarch,** and **1 tablespoon lemon juice.**

PUDDING

1 Roll out two-thirds of the dough into a large round. Fold in quarters and transfer to a 1½-quart oven-glass mixing bowl. Line bowl with the unfolded dough and trim off overhanging edges. Fill bowl with the apples and dot with: **1 tablespoon butter.**

2 Roll out remaining pastry into a round large enough to cover apples. Place on top and seal edges of dough.

3 Tie **a floured** napkin over the top of the bowl and lower it into a large kettle containing about 2 inches simmering water. Cover and steam for 1½ hours. While the pudding steams, make the following custard sauce to serve with it.

CUSTARD SAUCE

Beat: **6 egg yolks.** Stir in: **¼ cup sugar** and **a pinch of salt.** Gradually stir in: **2 cups hot milk.** Cook over simmering, but not boiling, water for about 7 minutes, stirring occasionally, until custard coats the spoon. Flavor with **vanilla** or **sherry** to taste.

PRESENTATION

Remove from kettle, unwrap and let sit for 5 minutes. (Steamed puddings "sit," cakes "stand.") Unmold on serving platter and serve hot with custard sauce.

GRILLED ANCHOVIES
MAKES 8

Boulestin is one of the grander restaurants in London, richly decorated and dedicated, as Marcel Boulestin once said, "to the glory of true French cooking." We have always enjoyed eating there, and though the great chef died more than twenty years ago, his cuisine has been faithfully preserved. We were given some of Boulestin's original recipes, delightful one and all.

anchovy fillets in oil
parsley
garlic
olive oil (optional)
bread
butter

1 Open: **a can of anchovy fillets,** reserving the **oil.**

2 Cut anchovies into small pieces, pound in a mortar and pour their oil over them. Add: **2 tablespoons chopped parsley, ½ teaspoon minced garlic,** and a little **olive oil,** if necessary, to moisten the mixture.

3 Cut into quarters: **2 slices of 2-day-old bread,** with crusts removed. Sauté the squares in a little **butter** until toasted.

4 Spread with the anchovy mixture.

PRESENTATION

Just before serving, put a bit of **cold butter** on top of each canapé and put under the broiler to melt. Serve warm.

ROLLMOPS
SERVES 2

Boulestin's hors d'oeuvres are designed, according to the precepts of the founder, to sharpen the appetite before a meal and to help the guest pass the time while his first course is being prepared. This herring appetizer serves its double purpose admirably.

salt herring
milk
salt
mustard
thyme
bay leaves
peppercorns
ground coriander
onion
wine vinegar
cloves
garlic
cream or sour cream
(optional)

1 Wash well: **4 small salt herring** (not smoked). Soak in: **1 cup milk** for 4 hours.

2 Drain well, cut lengthwise, and remove the bones.

3 Lay the 8 fillets flat on a board. **Salt** lightly and spread each with: **¼ teaspoon mustard.**

4 Put over each: **4 peppercorns, a sprinkle of ground coriander,** and **2 very thin slices of onion.**

5 Roll up and secure with a toothpick or tie around with string.

6 Place rollmops in a shallow dish and pour over them: **1½ cups wine vinegar** which has been boiled for 5 minutes with: **1 bay leaf** and **a few leaves of thyme.** Let stand for about an hour.

7 When rollmops and vinegar are cold, transfer to a small crock or jar. Put 2 rollmops at bottom, sprinkle with **salt, a few peppercorns, a little coriander** and **2 cloves.** Continue in layers until all are used. Top with: **1 clove garlic** and **1 bay leaf.**

8 Fill crock or jar with the vinegar, cover, and store in refrigerator for 4 days. Rollmops will keep for several weeks.

PRESENTATION

Serve rollmops drained, without string or toothpick. Sometimes they are served unrolled, drained, and with a little **fresh cream** or **sour cream** poured over them.

EGG AND POTATO SALAD BOULESTIN
SERVES 4

Just a tiny bit of this salad served with a few other cold hors d'oeuvres makes a delightful appetizer before luncheon. We were advised that the best potatoes for this kind of salad are the long yellow Dutch spuds that are waxy rather than floury or mealy when cooked. Our new potatoes are similar. On the other hand you want the mealy kind for baking or mashing, so don't just buy any old potatoes—get the right ones for each recipe.

new potatoes
eggs
salt, pepper
anchovy fillet
salad oil
chervil
chives
wine vinegar

1 Boil in their skins: **1 pound yellow new potatoes.** Peel and chill.

2 Hard cook: **4 eggs.** Shell and chill.

DRESSING

1 In a wooden bowl put: **1 teaspoon salt** and **¼ teaspoon freshly ground pepper.**

2 Add: **2 tablespoons wine vinegar** and mix well to dissolve salt. Add: **5 tablespoons salad oil, 1 teaspoon chopped chervil, 1 teaspoon chopped chives,** and **1 anchovy fillet, minced.**

PRESENTATION

Remove yolks from hard-cooked eggs and pound them into dressing. Cut the whites into small pieces. Cut potatoes into thin slices. Mix well and serve thoroughly chilled.

MUSSELS WITH SAFFRON
SERVES 4

There should be a few simple but tasty and unusual hors d'oeuvres in every cook's repertoire. These mussels from Boulestin are prepared ahead of time and chilled, and they make a piquant and delicious little appetizer—not so overpowering that they ruin appetites, but delicious enough to heighten one's anticipation for what's to come.

mussels
olive oil
onion
leeks
tomatoes
salt, pepper
garlic
thyme
bay leaf
saffron
dry white wine
parsley

SAUCE

1 In a sauté pan heat: **3 tablespoons olive oil.** Add: **1 small onion, chopped,** and **2 leeks (white part only), cut in thin pieces.** Cook for a few minutes.

2 Add: **2 tomatoes, cut into pieces, ½ clove garlic, chopped, a sprig of thyme, 1 bay leaf, a pinch of saffron, 1½ cups dry white wine** (vermouth does very nicely), **1 teaspoon salt,** and **½ teaspoon coarsely crushed pepper.** Cook until liquid is reduced to about ½ cup.

MUSSELS

1 Scrub thoroughly: **20 mussels.** Scrape off any beard or barnacles and soak well to get rid of sand.

2 Add mussels to pan and cover. Shake pan occasionally and cook for 3 minutes. When mussels open keep them on slow fire for 5 minutes more.

3 Remove mussels with slotted spoon. Take them out of shells and put in a bowl.

4 Pour sauce through strainer over mussels and chill in refrigerator.

PRESENTATION
Serve mussels cold, sprinkled with **chopped parsley.**

CRÈME BRÛLÉE
SERVES 8

This rich custard with a glazed caramel top was a favorite with Chef Boulestin. He had eaten it originally at Cambridge, but the chef at Trinity College refused to oblige him with a recipe. His own seems perfectly fine to us, and I especially like the variation with macaroons which is included.

superfine sugar
eggs
cream
macaroons (optional)
butter
brown sugar

1 Preheat oven to very slow (275° F.).

2 In a mixing bowl beat: **6 egg yolks** and **¾ cup superfine sugar.** Beat for 4 minutes, or until mixture is pale yellow and thick.

3 Bring to a boil: **2¼ cups cream.**

4 While beating the egg yolks let the hot cream trickle into them. Mix well.

5 Pour mixture into saucepan. Over moderate heat stir constantly until custard thickens. Do not let it boil.

6 Pour into a **buttered** shallow baking dish. Put into very slow oven till custard is set (about 1¼ hours).

7 Remove from oven and cool. Chill in refrigerator overnight.

PRESENTATION
Sprinkle top of chilled custard with: **a ¼-inch layer of brown sugar,** put through strainer. Put baking dish in larger pan surrounded by ice. Place under hot broiler just long enough for sugar to melt and form crust. Serve at once.

Note: A very good Boulestin variation is to crumble **6 macaroons** and add them to the egg yolk and cream mixture. Make custard the same as above recipe.

SOUSED MACKEREL
SERVES 6

The names of some of the traditional English dishes are the most amusing in the whole lexicon of gastronomy. Bubble-and-Squeak, Jugged Hare, Tipsy Pudding, and this Soused Mackerel are among my favorites. English cooking may not be on so lofty a plane as French, but at least you get a few chuckles from an English cookbook. And in this case a very good fish in wine.

mackerel
Spanish onion
carrot
olive oil
thyme
bay leaf
salt, pepper
white wine
lemon

1 Clean: **2 mackerel** and remove heads and tails.

2 Preheat oven to slow (300° F.).

3 Place mackerel in a shallow oven-glass or earthenware baking dish.

4 Cover with: **1 Spanish onion, cut into thin slices, 1 carrot, thinly sliced, a pinch of thyme, 1 bay leaf, crumbled,** **¼ teaspoon pepper, ½ teaspoon salt, 1 teaspoon olive oil, 2 cups white wine, and 1 teaspoon lemon juice.**

5 Put in the slow oven and baste frequently. Bake for about 2 hours, or until vegetables are tender.

6 Let cool in the juice. Chill and serve cold as an appetizer.

TOAD-IN-THE-HOLE
SERVES 6

This is one of my favorite English treats. It is really a Yorkshire pudding sort of batter (also much like popover batter) that is baked with sausages. Absolutely marvelous! It is usually served as one large dish, but sometimes I like to make it as I would popovers, with the addition of a small, fried pork sausage in each muffin tin.

Vienna sausages
cooking oil
flour
eggs
milk
salt

SAUSAGES

1 Heat: **1 tablespoon cooking oil** in a shallow 9 x 12-inch baking tin.

2 Put in: **1 pound Vienna sausages.** Prick lightly with fork and fry for 5 minutes.

BATTER

1 Have all ingredients at room temperature. Sift into bowl: **1 scant cup flour** and **¼ teaspoon salt.**

2 Stir in: **1 cup milk.**

3 Beat until frothy: **2 eggs.** Beat into the batter. Let batter stand for 30 minutes.

TOAD

1 Preheat oven to hot (400° F.).

2 Heat baking tin with sausages and fat in the hot oven.

3 Pour batter into tin and put in the hot oven.

4 Bake for 20 minutes and reduce heat to moderate (350° F.). Bake 10 to 15 minutes longer, or until batter is browned and puffy.

PRESENTATION

Serve at once on a hot platter. The sausage "toads" will be nestled in holes in the puffy dough.

WELSH RABBIT
SERVES 4

There has been a tremendous amount of argument about whether this dish is called "rarebit" or "rabbit." We go along with those students of the language who say that originally it was a wry joke, like Scotch woodcock. The poor Welshman's rabbit was only a piece of toast under cheese sauce and the poor Scotsman's woodcock was also mere toast under an egg sauce. Some literal-minded fellow must have said, "Shucks, that ain't no rabbit, but it's a *rare bit*," and a new word and the argument were born. This is a good dish whatever you want to call it, only whatever you call it, do please make it with beer instead of with milk.

bread
cheddar cheese
butter
beer or stout
paprika
dry mustard
Worcestershire sauce
eggs
cayenne pepper

1   Remove crusts from: **4 thick slices bread.** Toast and keep warm.

2   In a double boiler, over very low heat, melt: **3 tablespoons butter.** Add: **½ pound grated cheddar cheese.**

3   Stir with a wooden spoon and add, a little at a time: **1 cup beer** or **stout** that is at room temperature or warmer. Stir continually till smooth.

4   Add: **2 beaten egg yolks.** Keep stirring and do not let the rabbit boil or simmer or it will "string" and get lumpy.

5   Season with: **½ teaspoon paprika, ½ teaspoon dry mustard** dissolved in **2 teaspoons beer** or **stout, a few grains cayenne pepper,** and **1 teaspoon Worcestershire sauce.**

PRESENTATION

When rabbit is warm and smooth, pour at once over slices of toast, each on its own plate. If you have kept stirring steadily over low heat the rabbit will be satin smooth and creamy.

BUCKINGHAM EGGS
SERVES 6

In seventeenth-century England, George Villiers, the Duke of Buckingham, cut quite a figure as a courtier and playwright. Perhaps he served these eggs at his after-theater parties—I like to think so. In any event they bear his name and they are a perfect late snack for a midnight supper.

bread
butter
anchovy paste
eggs
cheddar cheese
salt, pepper
English mustard
cream
onion (optional)
Worcestershire sauce
(optional)

1   Trim crusts from: **6 slices bread.** Toast lightly.

2   Cream together: **2 tablespoons butter, 2 tablespoons anchovy paste,** and **1 teaspoon English mustard.**

3   Spread toast with anchovy mixture and keep warm.

4   Beat **8 eggs** with: **3 tablespoons cream, ¼ teaspoon salt,** and **⅛ teaspoon pepper.** Add: **1 tablespoon finely minced onion** (optional).

5   In a skillet over low heat melt: **2½ tablespoons butter.**

6   Pour in the beaten eggs. When eggs begin to thicken, stir with wooden spoon.

7   Remove from skillet while still moist and underdone.

8   Mound up on anchovy toast. Sprinkle each with: **1 tablespoon grated cheddar cheese.** Dot with **melted butter.** Sprinkle with **a few drops Worcestershire sauce,** if desired.

PRESENTATION

Place under hot broiler until cheese melts and serve at once.

165

TRIFLE
SERVES 6

Here again is an English dish with an enchanting name. I'm always tempted to invent a likely story for how these names came to be. This one, I believe, might have come about when a Victorian housewife couldn't bear to throw out a few small cakes and cookies that were a bit on the dry side. How to use them and still not displease her lord and master? Well, she soused them in his best sherry and brandy, tried to hide them under a layer of jam and, that failing, buried them under a delicious custard. She gave the whole thing a glorious façade of whipped cream and slivered almonds. And then, when the master glowered at it and rumbled "What have we here?" she modestly said, "Oh, just a trifle, Henry, just a trifle." Some trifle!

sponge cupcakes
macaroons
sherry
brandy
confectioners' sugar
thick pastry cream
(see index)
raspberry jam
cream
blanched slivered
almonds

1 In a deep dish or bowl put: **3 sponge cupcakes** cut in half crosswise. It is better if they are a little dry. Crumble over them: **6 macaroons.**

2 Pour over the cakes: **¾ cup medium sweet sherry** and **3 tablespoons brandy.** Let soak 15 minutes.

3 Spread thickly with: **1 cup raspberry jam.**

4 Make: **1¼ cups thick pastry cream.** When it is cool, pour it over the trifle.

5 Whip: **1 cup cream.** When it is almost stiff add: **1 tablespoon sifted confectioners' sugar** and **1 teaspoon sherry.** Whip until stiff.

PRESENTATION

Cover the trifle with whipped cream and decorate with: **¼ cup blanched slivered almonds** inserted in whipped cream like a porcupine's barbs.

LANCASHIRE HOT POT
SERVES 6

It's always interesting, when you eat from country to country and pay attention to national dishes, to notice how similar specialties crop up with slightly different names in one place and another. The Dutch have a hotchpotch, the French a *hochepot*, and in England there is Lancashire Hot Pot. All of these dishes are robust meat-and-vegetable casseroles that originated in country kitchens and because of their basic goodness have infiltrated the national cuisine. This one is particularly interesting because it calls for lamb, kidneys, and oysters in a most unusual combination.

lamb or mutton
Idaho potatoes
onions
butter
mushrooms
lamb kidneys
beef stock
(see index)
flour
salt, pepper
sugar
paprika (optional)
oysters

1 Preheat oven to slow (325° F.).

2 Cut: **2 pounds lamb** or **mutton shoulder** into 1-inch cubes.

3 In a deep casserole melt: **2 tablespoons butter.**

4 Brown the meat over moderately high heat. When pieces are well browned, remove with slotted spoon and set aside.

5 Slice thinly: **3 onions** and brown in casserole. Sprinkle with: **2 teaspoons sugar** and cook until glazed.

6 Put back lamb or mutton. Season with a little **salt** and **pepper.** Lower heat.

7 Add: **2 cups hot beef stock,** thickened with **1 tablespoon flour** mixed to a smooth paste with **1 tablespoon butter.**

8 Trim fat and skin from: **3 lamb kidneys.** Cut into slices and place in a layer over meat. Season with **salt** and **pepper.**

9 Slice: **½ pound mushrooms** and place in a layer over kidneys. Season with **salt** and **pepper.**

10 Place in another layer: **12 fresh oysters.**

11 Peel: **4 Idaho potatoes** and cut into ¼-inch slices. Arrange them in overlapping circles on top of stew. Spoon up some of the stock and pour over potatoes. Sprinkle with a little **salt, pepper,** and **paprika** (optional).

12 Cover casserole tightly and place in the slow oven for 3 hours.

13 Just before serving, increase oven temperature to very hot (450° F.). Uncover casserole, baste, and allow top to brown for 10 minutes.

SALMON IN PASTRY
SERVES 4

The town of Bath in the West Country is one of England's architectural gems. It was a handsome resort in the eighteenth century when Beau Brummell made it famous, and it is still a popular watering place. One of its charming restaurants is The Hole in the Wall, a small, slightly Bohemian place that prides itself on unusual and well-prepared food served from an informal buffet. This specialty takes advantage of the really superlative salmon that is one of the joys of the British cuisine.

salmon
salt, pepper
butter
preserved ginger
flour
Dijon mustard
light cream
currants
rich pastry
(see index)
shallots
parsley
chervil
tarragon
eggs
lemon

SALMON

1 Skin and bone: **a 2- to 3-pound piece of salmon.** (It should be about 8 inches long.) You should then have 2 thick salmon fillets which you can put together again as a sandwich.

2 Season lightly with **salt** and **pepper** and let stand while you make filling.

FILLING

Make a paste of: **2 tablespoons softened butter, 2 globes of ginger in syrup, chopped,** and **1 tablespoon currants.**

HERB SAUCE

1 Mince: **2 shallots, 6 sprigs each of parsley, chervil,** and **tarragon.**

2 In a saucepan melt: **2 tablespoons butter.** Stir in: **2 tablespoons flour** and blend over low heat. Stir in slowly: **1¼ cups light cream.**

3 Stir over moderate heat until smooth. Add: **1 teaspoon Dijon mustard, ½ teaspoon salt,** and **⅛ teaspoon pepper.**

4 Stir in the herb mixture and cook gently for a few minutes.

5 Beat: **2 egg yolks.** Add a little of the hot sauce to them and mix well. Beat yolks into sauce and allow to thicken.

6 Finish with: **1 teaspoon lemon juice,** or to taste. (The salmon can stand a fairly sharp sauce.)

PRESENTATION

1 Preheat oven to hot (400° F.).

2 Make **rich pastry** in the quantity for a 2-crust pie. Roll fairly thin and large enough to wrap salmon.

3 Place 1 salmon fillet in center of pastry. Spread fish with filling. Top with the second fillet of salmon and press edges together.

4 Wrap pastry neatly around salmon, tucking ends in carefully. Avoid having pastry too thick at ends, but be sure it is completely sealed. Cut a few decorative slits in top of pastry to let steam escape. Brush with a little **melted butter.**

5 Place on a baking sheet in the hot oven and reduce temperature to moderate (350° F.).

6 Bake for 40 to 45 minutes and serve hot with the herb sauce on the side.

167

ICED LEMON SOUFFLÉ

SERVES 6

If there is one thing cooler than a cucumber it is an Iced Lemon Soufflé. This one from The Hole in the Wall is light and tangy, a lovely summertime dessert. Cold soufflés are not baked, and they rise above the rim of the soufflé dish and stay there, unlike cooked ones. It is the gelatin, egg whites, and whipped cream that enable them to hold their shape, and when you chill cold soufflés in a bowl with a waxed paper cuff, the gelatin sets so that the cuff can be removed leaving about two inches of fluffy soufflé standing firmly above the bowl. We like to decorate this soufflé with a little whipped cream, very thin lemon slices, and a few fresh mint leaves.

lemons
superfine sugar
plain gelatin
cream
eggs
fresh mint leaves

1   In small saucepan soften: **1 envelope plain gelatin** in **2 tablespoons water.** Add: **grated rind of 4 lemons, ½ cup strained lemon juice, and 1 cup superfine sugar.** Stir over low heat until gelatin is thoroughly dissolved, then chill to syrup consistency.

2   Beat: **1 cup egg whites** (7 to 8) until very stiff. Beat into the lemon-gelatin mixture. Whip: **1 cup cream** and fold into the lemon meringue until thoroughly mixed.

3   Tie a double band of waxed paper around the top of a 1-quart soufflé dish. Pour in the lemon soufflé and chill.

PRESENTATION

Remove waxed paper collar before serving. Decorate top of the soufflé with additional **whipped cream,** paper-thin slices of **lemon,** and **fresh mint leaves.**

How high is high tea?
Here in the drawing room of Woburn Abbey,
their Graces, the Duke and Duchess
of Bedford, serve a beautiful assortment
of teatime goodies on the family gold plate.

In the late afternoon
we like to entertain beside our swimming pool.
Mary's gift to me for Father's Day
was this real British high tea complete with
Raspberry Fool, Potted Shrimp,
and other friends too numerous to mention.

WOBURN ABBEY

ONE of England's stateliest homes is Woburn Abbey, residence of the Dukes of Bedford for nearly three hundred years. It was originally a monastery, but when the Abbot spoke out against King Henry VIII's marriage to Anne Boleyn, the king had him hanged for treason and gave his abbey to the more sympathetic Earl Russell. One of Russell's descendants became the first Duke of Bedford. Over the generations, the Russells have remodeled and improved Woburn, filled it with fine furniture and china, hung its walls with magnificent paintings, and stocked its park with a fascinating private zoo.

But when the present Duke of Bedford inherited it in 1953, Woburn was in a shocking state of disrepair, and there were death duties of nearly fifteen million dollars to be paid. The Duke's brilliant solution was to let Woburn save itself and it was opened to the public for an admission fee. It is now a thriving industry as well as being once again the stately home of the Duke of Bedford and his family. Lunch and tea are served in a restaurant on the grounds to hundreds of visitors each day with the Duke and his Duchess nearly always on the scene informally as host and hostess. When they entertain privately, however, tea might be served in any one of a dozen splendid state rooms.

The last time I was in London, the Duke invited me to come up to Woburn, but my movie schedule was too tight. We did get the recipes for some of the delicious Woburn tea specialties, though. And Mary surprised me, upon my return, with a sumptuous poolside tea that made me feel positively ducal myself!

TEA SCONES
MAKES 12 TO 16 SCONES

Scones and crumpets figure in every comedy of teatime manners as a sort of British status symbol. Actually they are very unpretentious tea cakes, usually baked on a griddle and far less elaborate and difficult than pastries. Scones can also be baked in the oven, as this recipe from Woburn Abbey directs. The result is a meltingly light hot bread that is delicious split, buttered, and eaten warm.

flour
salt
baking powder
butter
shortening
superfine sugar
egg
milk
sultana raisins

SCONES

1 Preheat oven to hot (425° F.).

2 Combine in mixing bowl: **2 cups flour, ½ teaspoon salt, 2½ teaspoons double-acting baking powder,** and **¼ cup superfine sugar.**

3 With pastry blender cut in: **⅓ cup shortening.** Add: **½ cup sultana raisins.**

4 Lightly beat: **1 egg** and add enough **milk** to make a total of **⅔ cup** liquid. Add liquid to dry ingredients and stir gently with a fork until dough holds together.

5 Gather dough into a ball, place on lightly **floured** board and knead gently, about 12 kneading strokes.

6 On lightly **floured** board roll dough out ¼ inch thick and cut into rounds with **floured** biscuit cutter. Place scones on a baking sheet about 1 inch apart and bake for 12 to 15 minutes.

PRESENTATION

Split scones while hot and spread with **butter.** Scones may be eaten hot or cold, but they are at their very best served fresh from the oven with the butter just melting inside them.

FRUIT CAKE
SERVES 10

A proper tea includes a great variety of things to eat from plain bread and butter to rich cakes. In the days when ladies were "at home" to friends at teatime, when calling cards, white kid gloves, and a massive silver tea service were part of the whole rigmarole, the kitchen preparations were monumental. Breads, jams, sandwiches, cheeses, raw salad vegetables, and cakes—plain, fancy, and iced—were the order of the day. The ladies ate and sipped tea with their white gloves on, and they wore their hats and veils too. I don't know how they managed, but I do know that out of deference to the white kid gloves, tea sandwiches were rolled so that no filling could ooze around the edges. And so they are to this informal day. Tea at Woburn Abbey is taken sans gloves. But there is still an impressive assortment of things to eat. This Fruit Cake, very rich, and certainly fit for a duke, is one of my favorites.

172

candied cherries
candied pineapple
light raisins
angelica
candied orange peel
almonds
flour
butter
sugar
baking powder
salt
lemon
orange
confectioners' sugar
eggs

1   In bowl combine: **1 cup halved candied cherries, 1 cup thinly sliced candied pineapple, ½ cup light raisins, 2 tablespoons chopped angelica, ¼ cup chopped candied orange peel,** and **¼ cup chopped almonds.** Add: **4 tablespoons flour** and toss to coat the fruit with the flour.

2   **Butter** an 8-inch layer cake pan and line with heavy brown paper.

3   Preheat oven to slow (300° F.).

4   Cream: **1 cup butter** and **1 cup sugar** until light.

5   Beat in: **3 eggs,** one at a time.

6   Sift together: **1½ cups flour, 1 tea-** spoon **double-acting baking powder,** and **1 teaspoon salt.** Stir into butter-egg mixture. Stir in: **1 teaspoon lemon juice** and **1 teaspoon orange juice.** Fold in fruit mixture.

7   Turn batter into prepared cake pan and bake in the slow oven for 1¾ hours. Let cool in pan, then turn out and frost top with lemon icing.

LEMON ICING

Beat: **1 cup sifted confectioners' sugar** with **2 teaspoons lemon juice** and **1 tablespoon hot water.** Beat until icing is smooth, then spread on top of cake.

CHOCOLATE LAYER CAKE
SERVES 8

There are no halfway measures about this chocolate cake. The filling is chocolate, the icing is chocolate, and so is the cake itself, which is more of a flat torte than the kind of high layer cake so familiar here. We served it to a friend recently and mentioned that the recipe came from Woburn Abbey. Our friend took his first bite of the cake, tasted it carefully, and exclaimed, "Good for old England!" And good for us too. A marvelous cake which, Mary tells me, is not at all difficult to make.

butter
sugar
vanilla extract
salt
eggs
self-rising flour
cocoa
confectioners' sugar
semisweet chocolate

CAKE

1   Preheat oven to moderate (350° F.).

2   **Grease** and **flour** two 8-inch round layer cake pans.

3   Cream together: **½ cup butter** and **½ cup sugar.** Beat in: **3 drops vanilla extract, a pinch of salt,** and **3 eggs.**

4   Sift together: **1 cup self-rising flour** and **1 tablespoon cocoa** and stir into egg mixture.

5   Stir in: **1 tablespoon hot water.**

6   Divide the batter into the prepared pans and spread evenly over bottom making a layer about ¼ inch thick. Bake in the moderate oven for 15 minutes. Remove, cool, loosen edges with knife, and turn out on cake racks.

FILLING

Cream: **¼ cup butter** and **1 cup confectioners' sugar.** Stir in: **2 ounces semisweet chocolate, melted,** and **2 drops vanilla extract.**

ICING

Put into mixing bowl: **3 ounces semisweet chocolate** and **1 tablespoon butter.** Place bowl in skillet containing simmering water. When chocolate and butter are melted, remove from heat and stir in: **1½ cups confectioners' sugar** and **2 tablespoons water.**

PRESENTATION

Put the two thin layers of cake together with the filling and swirl the chocolate icing over the top.

LEVENS HALL POACHED SALMON

SERVES 5

Up in the North Country high tea is a very different proposition from ordinary afternoon tea. It is a substantial meal served when the family has been out all day riding or shooting and has missed lunch, or if they are going out early in the evening and will miss dinner. A typical menu for this kind of tea served at Levens Hall, includes Cumberland ham or fresh salmon, a salad, gingerbread, white and brown bread with butter, a currant pasty, and Indian tea. Levens Hall in Westmorland is another of the great old English homes now open to the public. Its medieval core was once a fortified tower, dating from the fourteenth century's Border wars against the Scots. We were fascinated by the house and tales of its ghosts—a Grey Lady, a Pink Lady, a White Fawn, and a Black Dog. Though we came away without seeing any of the ghosts, we did get some Levens Hall recipes from Mrs. Bagot, wife of the present owner. This one for salmon is excellent. Cooked this way, Mrs. Bagot explains, all the oils remain in the fish "and even the horror of deep-frozen salmon is largely alleviated." At Levens Hall we had extraordinary salmon caught in the river just outside the door. But we have used this recipe at home and can testify that it is very good with bought as well as caught fish.

salmon
salt
dry mustard
sugar
flour
paprika
egg
vinegar
cream
green mayonnaise
(see index—
optional)

SALMON

A 5-pound salmon will serve 5 people.

1 Fill a kettle, large enough to accommodate **a whole salmon** (or a piece of salmon), three-quarters full of water. Add: **1 tablespoon salt** per quart of water and bring to a boil.

2 Tie salmon in cheesecloth and lower gently into the boiling water. Let water come again to a boil and boil for exactly 4 minutes, regardless of the size of the salmon. (The bigger the piece of salmon, the longer the brine takes to reach a boil for the second time.) Remove kettle from heat and let the salmon cool in the brine.

3 Remove salmon from brine, remove cheesecloth, and skin the salmon, leaving the pink flesh exposed. Place on a platter, cover, and chill.

BOILED DRESSING (Makes 1 Cup)

1 In saucepan combine: **1 teaspoon dry mustard, 1 tablespoon sugar, ½ teaspoon salt, 2 tablespoons flour, ¼ teaspoon paprika,** and **½ cup cold water.**

2 Stir in: **1 egg** beaten with **¼ cup vinegar.** Cook, stirring rapidly, until mixture is smooth and thick, being careful not to let it boil. Stir in: **¼ cup cream.** Chill.

PRESENTATION

Serve the chilled salmon with **green mayonnaise** or the boiled dressing in a separate sauce dish.

GINGERBREAD

SERVES 6

The fragrance of gingerbread is very nearly the best part of it. And we like to eat it while it is still warm, to take fullest advantage of the spicy aroma. This is the Levens Hall Gingerbread recipe, and I wouldn't be at all surprised but that the scent of it, wafting through the long halls, sets the Levens' ghosts to prowling.

butter
sugar
egg
corn syrup
dark molasses
flour
salt
ginger
baking soda

1 Preheat oven to moderate (350° F.).

2 Cream together: **½ cup butter** and **1 cup sugar.**

3 Beat in: **1 egg, 1 tablespoon corn syrup,** and **1 tablespoon dark molasses.**

4 Sift and measure: **2 cups flour.** Combine sifted flour with: **½ teaspoon salt,** and **2 teaspoons ginger.**

5 Combine: **1 teaspoon baking soda** and **¾ cup boiling water.**

6 Sift flour mixture into the butter-egg mixture alternately with the liquid, stirring until smooth after each addition.

7 Pour into a **buttered** 8-inch cake tin and bake in the moderate oven for 25 to 30 minutes. Best served warm.

CURRANT PASTY
SERVES 6

Pasties are hearty North Country pies, usually filled with meat. This one from Levens Hall has a currant filling and is especially delicious at teatime served with hard sauce —as what isn't!

flour
shortening
salt
currants
butter
sugar
lemon
hard sauce
(see index)

1 Preheat oven to hot (425° F.).

2 Measure into mixing bowl: **2 cups flour, 1 teaspoon salt,** and **¾ cup shortening.** Cut in shortening with pastry blender or 2 knives. Add: **about 6 tablespoons water** and mix lightly with a fork until all flour is moistened. With hands gather dough into a ball and divide in half, making 2 equal balls.

3 Roll out half the pastry on a lightly **floured** board and cut into a 9- or 10-inch round. Transfer to baking sheet.

4 Sprinkle pastry with: **1 cup currants,** keeping them ½ inch away from outer edge. Sprinkle currants with: **6 tablespoons sugar** and dot with: **4 tablespoons butter.** Sprinkle with: **the juice of 1 lemon.**

5 Roll out second half of the pastry and cut into a round about 1 inch larger in diameter than the bottom round. Slash center to permit steam to escape and place over filling. Tuck overhanging edges under bottom pastry and flute edge.

6 Bake in the hot oven for 15 minutes. Reduce oven temperature to 350° F. and bake for 25 to 30 minutes longer.

7 Serve with **hard sauce.**

HARD SAUCE
MAKES 1 CUP

Since British tea is nonalcoholic, a bit of rum or brandy in one of the accompanying sweets is not amiss. Tea before one of the great fireplaces at Levens Hall on a cold bleak day is a cheerful affair. And the Hard Sauce adds considerably to the cheer.

superfine sugar
butter
salt
cream
brandy
vanilla

1 Beat until soft and creamy: **4 tablespoons butter.**

2 Sift: **1 cup superfine sugar.**

3 Continue beating the butter and add the sugar, little by little.

4 Beat together until well blended.

5 Add: **a pinch of salt, ½ teaspoon vanilla,** and **2 teaspoons brandy.**

6 Beat in: **¼ cup cream.** Sauce should be very smooth.

7 Chill in a small bowl.

MELTON MOWBRAY PIE (Lancaster Pork Pie)
SERVES 12

This is one of Mary's favorite recipes, and you can see the impressive cold meat pie in the picture of our poolside tea table. It is wrapped in a napkin but the top crust with its pastry rose is exposed. That rose serves a double purpose, one practical, the other romantic. For practical purposes the rose is made to rest on top of a hole cut in the crust so that steam can escape while the pie is baking. Romantically the decoration commemorates the Wars of the Roses. A Melton Mowbray Pie is a masterpiece of jellied meat enclosed in a flaky pastry crust. Beautiful, too, for a cold buffet.

pork shoulder
veal
ham
pig's foot or veal
knuckle
celery
onions
carrots
parsley
salt, pepper
cloves
bay leaf
ginger
sage
flour
shortening or
leaf lard
egg
gelatin

MEAT

1 Remove skin, bones, fat, and sinews from: **5 pounds pork shoulder, 3 pounds lean veal,** and **1 pound raw ham.** Discard fat and put bones into a heavy kettle with: **1 pig's foot** or **1 veal knuckle,** cracked. Add: **2 stalks celery,** coarsely cut, **2 onions,** sliced, **1 large** or **2 small carrots,** sliced, **a few sprigs parsley, 1 teaspoon salt, 3 cloves, ½ bay leaf, ¼ teaspoon pepper,** and **⅛ teaspoon ginger.** Add: **1 quart water,** or enough to barely cover. Bring to a boil and skim. Cover and simmer this stock for 3 hours.

2 Cut meat into small cubes (there should be 5 pounds net lean meat) and mix with: **1 tablespoon salt, 1 teaspoon pepper,** and **¼ teaspoon sage.**

PASTRY

1 Into a bowl measure: **6 cups flour.** Stir in: **1 teaspoon salt.**

2 Bring to a boil: **1 cup less 2 tablespoons water** and **1½ cups shortening** or **leaf lard.** Boil briskly for 3 minutes. Pour into flour and stir until all flour is moistened. Let cool until cool enough to handle, then knead on **floured** board until smooth. Cover with cloth and let rest for 30 minutes.

3 Preheat oven to hot (400° F.).

4 Cut dough into three parts. Knead each part before rolling out. Roll out one part and cut into a long band 3½ inches wide. Line the sides of a 9-inch spring-form pan with the band of dough and press cut edges together firmly with fingers.

5 Roll out second part of dough into a large circle about ⅛ inch thick and cut out a round ¼ inch larger than bottom of pan. Place round in pan and seal edges of side band and bottom dough with fingers.

PIE

1 Put meat mixture into the lined pan and add: **1 cup water.**

2 Roll out last part of dough into a large circle about ⅛ inch thick and cut out a round 1¼ inches larger than diameter of pan. Place over meat. Moisten underside of overhanging dough with: **1 egg** beaten with **1 tablespoon water** (reserve rest of egg-water mixture). Tuck under the dough which lines sides of pan and flute edge. Cut out a ¾-inch hole from center of top crust. From scraps of dough, cut out about 9 petals and press these around nubbin of dough to form a rose. Set the rose in the hole. Cut out several leaves and place around the rose.

3 Brush dough, rose, and leaves with remaining egg-water mixture.

4 Bake in the hot oven for 30 minutes. Reduce oven temperature to 300° F. and cook for 2 hours longer.

5 Strain the stock from the skin and bones. Let stand until fat rises to surface. Skim off fat. Add: **1 envelope gelatin** softened in **2 tablespoons cold water** and bring to a boil, stirring. Carefully remove rose from pie and pour the hot stock into the meat. Replace the rose. Cool pie, then chill for about 4 hours.

PRESENTATION

Place spring form on a round serving dish. Run a sharp knife between crust of chilled pie and the sides of pan. Remove spring-form rim. You can wrap a napkin around sides of pastry if you wish, but you will have to remove it in order to slice the pie.

SCOTCH SHORTBREAD
MAKES 48 COOKIES

These shortbread squares are perfect with a cup of tea, and you will see them in with all the other goodies on our tea table. Mary's sister, Clay Davidson, gave us her recipe for them, and they are just about the best cookies in our collection.

confectioners' sugar
butter
vanilla
cake flour
salt
baking powder

1 Sift: ½ cup confectioners' sugar.

2 Beat: 1 cup butter until it is as soft as the sugar.

3 Continue beating and gradually add the sugar.

4 When mixture is creamy and light, add: 1 teaspoon vanilla.

5 Combine: 2 cups cake flour, ¼ teaspoon salt, and ¼ teaspoon baking powder in a separate bowl.

6 Stir into the butter-sugar mixture, blending thoroughly.

7 Preheat oven to moderate (350° F.).

8 Chill the dough.

9 Roll dough to a ¼-inch thickness.

10 Cut into squares and prick the dough all over with a fork.

11 Cover a cookie sheet with foil and place squares on it.

12 Bake for about 20 minutes. Shortbread should just begin to color.

POTTED SHRIMP
SERVES 6

A delightful spread for bread, toast, or crackers at teatime, Potted Shrimp are a delicious British invention. This recipe was given to us by Boris and Evie Karloff, who serve them at their house as a first course or with cocktails. We are inordinately fond of them (the shrimp as well as the Karloffs) and have them often at our house, too. Mary likes to make Potted Shrimp in tiny individual crocks and we serve one to each guest with crisp melba toast on the side.

butter
cooked shrimp
mace
nutmeg
salt (optional)
brown bread
melba toast
crackers
lettuce (optional)

1 Melt: ¼ pound butter until it is hot but not bubbling.

2 Add to the melted butter: ½ teaspoon mace, ¼ teaspoon nutmeg, and ½ teaspoon salt (optional).

3 Have ready: 2 cups cooked shrimp, shelled and deveined. (These are best if they are very small, as they should remain whole but you don't want the pieces to be too large.)

4 Pour a little of the melted butter over the shrimp, making certain that each shrimp is well coated with the butter.

5 Put shrimp into a large mold or small individual crocks and press down, taking care not to crush the shrimp.

6 Pour the remaining melted butter on top and chill until firm in the refrigerator. Potted shrimp will keep well for about a week.

PRESENTATION
Serve in individual crocks, or turn out of a larger mold onto a bed of shredded lettuce. Serve with slices of brown bread, melba toast, or crackers.

TEA

Probably one reason the British are such avid tea drinkers is that they brew their tea correctly and wind up with a delicious beverage. Here are the five cardinal rules of good tea making, given to me by the expert who buys all the tea for B. Altman's in New York. Following them really does make a difference, so I pass them on to you as a very helpful recipe, and perhaps the most important one of all in a chapter on high tea.

HOW TO MAKE GOOD HOT TEA

1 Bring freshly drawn cold water to a full rolling boil (reheated water has a flat taste; the air has been boiled out). Merely hot water isn't enough; only boiling water can extract all the flavor from the tea leaves.

2 Use a teapot, preheat it and dry it. A teapot holds the water temperature very high during the brewing period.

3 Add 1 teaspoonful of tea per cup, plus "one for the pot." A tea bag is equivalent to 1 teaspoon of tea.

4 Steep the tea to the strength you prefer—3 to 5 minutes. This is time needed for the essential oils to escape from the leaves. After brewing, decant into a serving pot. For weaker tea, add hot water to the cup when serving.

5 Don't judge the strength of tea by its color—delicate teas may produce a dark brew, strong teas a light brew, depending on the blend of tea.

HOW TO MAKE GOOD ICED TEA

Follow the same basic steps as above, allowing *twice* as much tea per cup: 2 teaspoons or 2 tea bags for each cup of boiling water. This allows for dilution of the tea with melting ice. You can pour the hot, fully brewed strong tea over ice and serve immediately, or make the tea in advance, let it cool, and serve as needed.

Survival of Edwardian elegance, the Food Halls at Harrods are not only the sources of feasts, they are feasts for the eye as well. Here meats and seafood are displayed as lovingly as if they were rare gems.

In Los Angeles, Farmers' Market offers a colorful panorama of subtropical bounty. Mary and I wander through this amazing maze of succulent decor knowing that somewhere we will find a little booth that sells anything we might want from anywhere under the sun.

HARRODS FOOD HALLS

Every chef, every restaurateur to whom we've ever spoken in the course of our gastronomic sight-seeing has been adamant about one thing—the quality of raw ingredients. All good cooking, they insist, begins at the markets. Probably the most glamorous markets in the world are the Food Halls at Harrods in London. This great department store is practically a national institution covering a solid square of nearly five acres, and supplying every human need from the cradle to the grave. (Baby Shop, first floor, Funeral Furnishings, fourth floor.) But it was the Food Halls on the ground floor that bowled us over. The British Museum crossed with Les Halles!

Harrods started out in 1849 as a little double-fronted grocery shop in Knightsbridge. That first little store has been swallowed up by the vast complex that is Harrods today, but its ghost lingers in the Food Halls. Salmon from the rivers of Scotland, grouse from the upland moors, English lamb and beef, Irish bacon, fish and seafood from the waters that surround the British Isles, fruits and vegetables from the Continent—all are to be found in the Food Halls, displayed like national treasures, and only top quality need apply.

Our own more rustic counterpart of Harrods Food Halls is Farmers' Market in Los Angeles. A sort of indoor-outdoor labyrinth of open stalls set up in a huge shed, Farmers' Market is a dazzling collection of all the good things to eat. Mary and I like to get there early in the morning when the dew is still on the peaches. The pleasure of that night's dinner—and sometimes even the plan—starts when we see the beautiful raw materials laid out before us, waiting for us to choose and create.

CUMBERLAND SAUCE

MAKES 2 CUPS

This is a wonderful sauce to serve with cold sliced ham or game. There has been so much said and written about French sauces that we tend to overlook the contribution of English cookery in that department. The English have always been masters at inventing sauces to go with their meats and game. Worcestershire sauce, mint sauce for lamb, and this Cumberland Sauce are just a few. When you look at the array of meats, poultry, game, and seafood in an English market, you can rest assured that most of them will be cooked fairly simply and served with one of the flavorful English sauces.

lemon
orange
glacéed cherries
port
red currant jelly
wine vinegar
prepared mustard
salt, cayenne pepper

1 Peel the thin colored rind from: **1 lemon** and **1 orange.** Be sure no bitter white peel is included. Squeeze juice from both and reserve. Shred the orange and lemon rinds and boil them in: **½ cup water** for 7 minutes.

2 Discard rinds and keep water in saucepan.

3 Add: **½ cup port, 2 tablespoons red currant jelly, 2 tablespoons wine vine-** gar, **½ teaspoon prepared mustard, ⅛ teaspoon salt, a pinch of cayenne pepper,** and the juice of the lemon and the orange.

4 Boil this mixture for 4 minutes. Set aside to cool.

5 Chop: **¼ cup glacéed cherries.** Add to sauce when it is cold.

6 Serve in a sauce dish.

CORNISH PASTIES

SERVES 6

Just as the food in a great market like Harrods Food Halls comes from all over Britain, so there are regional dishes that originate in various sections of the British Isles. The famous Cornish Pasties—little meat turnovers in a rich crust—come from Cornwall, the southwestern part of England. These are good served for a light supper, a heavy tea, or made very small as a hot hors d'oeuvre.

rich pastry
(see index)
beefsteak
potatoes
onion
veal kidneys
egg
salt, pepper
flour

PASTRY

1 Make the quantity of **rich pastry** for a 2-crust pie.

2 Roll out on lightly **floured** board to ⅛-inch thickness. Cut into 6-inch circles (about the size of a saucer). You should get 6 circles.

FILLING

1 Dice: **½ pound raw beefsteak, ¼ pound veal kidneys,** and **¼ pound potatoes.**

2 Add: **½ onion, minced, 1¼ teaspoons salt,** and **¼ teaspoon pepper.** Mix well.

PASTIES

1 Preheat oven to hot (400° F.).

2 Put one-sixth of the meat mixture in the center of each pastry circle.

3 Moisten the edges of the circle with cold water.

4 Fold each circle in half and crimp edges with a fork, being sure to seal tightly.

5 Beat: **1 egg** and brush tops of pasties with the beaten egg.

6 Place on baking sheet in the hot oven and bake for 20 minutes.

7 Reduce heat to 325° F. and continue to bake for 1 hour longer.

PRESENTATION

Serve hot and crisp. For a hot hors d'oeuvre make these exactly half as large. The small ones are delicious too as an accompaniment to a bowl of soup.

HUNTER'S PIE
SERVES 4

A good family dish this. If you want to serve lamb chops or mutton chops without having to cook them at the last minute, this is a good method for the dish can wait without being spoiled. This is an Irish recipe, as the copious use of potatoes might have told you. It is also an economical one because, thanks to those selfsame potatoes, one chop is plenty for each person.

lamb or mutton chops
potatoes
butter
salt, pepper
beef stock
(see index)
Worcestershire sauce

1 In a skillet melt: **2 tablespoons butter.** When it is hot add: **4 lamb or mutton chops,** trimmed of their fat.

2 Brown on both sides for about 6 minutes all told. Remove chops and keep warm.

3 Add to pan juices: **¾ cup beef stock.** Stir in all the brown drippings. Bring to a boil, set aside, and keep hot.

4 Preheat oven to moderate (350° F.).

5 Boil, peel, and mash: **1½ pounds potatoes** (about 3 cups).

6 Beat in: **4 tablespoons butter, 1 teaspoon salt,** and **⅛ teaspoon pepper.**

7 **Butter** an ovenproof dish and line with 1½ cups of the mashed potatoes.

8 Place the 4 chops on top. Sprinkle with a little **Worcestershire sauce.**

9 Cover with the remaining potatoes and smooth top like a pie crust.

10 Place in the moderate oven and bake for 30 minutes.

PRESENTATION
Make depression in center of pie and pour in the hot gravy. Serve at once.

MUSHROOMS IN CREAM
SERVES 4

Some English restaurants serve a delicious side dish made with field mushrooms, which undeniably give a better flavor than their cultivated cousins. Mushroom collecting can be a rather dangerous hobby, however, unless you're something of a botanist, so we recommend using the cultivated mushrooms fresh from the market. Did you know that they're loaded with vitamins and practically noncaloric? So you can cook them with butter and cream, and at least the mushrooms themselves don't add to the calorie count.

mushrooms
butter
cream
salt, pepper
bread

1 Wipe with a damp cloth: **1 pound mushrooms.** Do not peel them as the best flavor is in the skin. Cut into uniform slices.

2 In a skillet melt: **3 tablespoons butter.** When the butter just finishes foaming, add the sliced mushrooms. Toss them well for 1 minute to coat thoroughly with butter.

3 Sprinkle with: **¼ teaspoon salt** and **½ teaspoon freshly ground pepper.** (If anything, there is more pepper than you might think in the seasoning.)

4 Add: **1 cup cream** and simmer gently for 5 minutes, stirring occasionally.

PRESENTATION
Sauté: **8 bread triangles** in butter. Serve the mushrooms in a shallow casserole and stand the toast triangles around the edges with points up.

ROAST CHICKEN WITH BREAD SAUCE

SERVES 4

"A warm bird and a cold bottle," those seven words are the sum and substance of the traditional English meal popular throughout the centuries. The bird might originally have been a game bird—quail, grouse, partridge, or pheasant, or a barnyard fowl—chicken, duck, or goose—any and all of which you can find today at a fine market like Harrods. In the old days the bottle was probably malmsey, sack, or canary. Nowadays you would most likely be served Roast Chicken and a French red wine, but the unmistakable English touch would be the Bread Sauce served with the chicken.

chicken
bacon
milk
cream
mace
shallot or onion
cloves
butter
salt, pepper
chicken stock
(see index)
fresh bread crumbs
peppercorns

CHICKEN

1 Preheat oven to moderate (350° F.).

2 Wash and dry: **a roasting chicken** (about 3½ pounds). Rub cavity and skin with: **1 teaspoon salt** and **a pinch of pepper.** Spread: **1 tablespoon softened butter** over skin. Truss and place on a rack in a shallow roasting pan.

3 Roll up: **6 rashers streaky bacon** and place on rack around chicken. Place roasting pan in the moderate oven.

4 Roast for 1½ hours, basting 3 or 4 times. If the chicken browns too quickly, cover breast with foil.

5 When chicken is done, untruss and remove to a hot platter with bacon rolls. Remove rack and pour off excess fat in pan. Add: **1 cup chicken stock** and set over high heat until liquid boils. Stir well. Add **salt** and **pepper** to taste.

BREAD SAUCE

1 In a double boiler heat: **1 cup milk,** but do not let it boil. Add: **1 small onion** or **1 shallot, peeled, 2 cloves, a pinch of mace,** and **6 peppercorns.**

2 Allow liquid to simmer, not boil, for 30 minutes.

3 In a saucepan place: **½ cup fresh bread crumbs.** Strain hot milk over bread crumbs, beating with a fork. Add: **½ teaspoon salt** and **1 tablespoon butter.**

4 Cook over low heat for 20 minutes, beating frequently with fork. Add: **1 tablespoon butter** and **1 tablespoon cream.** Pour into sauce boat.

PRESENTATION

Serve chicken on platter surrounded by bacon rolls. Serve the hot gravy and hot bread sauce separately.

COLCANNON

SERVES 4

Irish bacon is almost the best in the world, and potatoes are the mainstay of the Irish diet. Combine the two in this Gaelic dish and you have something to dance a jig about. Sometimes this dish is called "stelk" or "champ." That is when it consists of potatoes and scallions boiled and then mashed with a large wooden masher. Mash, or as the Irish say, "beetle" cooked cabbage into the potatoes and you have Colcannon. The addition of Irish bacon makes it deluxe—and delish.

potatoes
scallions
milk
butter
salt, pepper
cooked cabbage
Irish bacon

1 Chop: **6 scallions** very fine. Soak in: **1 cup milk** with **1 teaspoon salt** for ½ hour. Put in a saucepan and simmer for ½ hour.

2 Boil: **6 medium potatoes, peeled,** in **salted** water to cover until tender.

3 Drain, dry, and begin to mash. When smooth, beat in the scallions and milk.

4 Add: **3 tablespoons butter** and continue beating over low heat. Add: **¼ teaspoon freshly ground pepper** and **2 cups cooked chopped cabbage.** Con-

tinue to beat or mash until light and fluffy, keeping pan over low heat.

5 In a skillet fry until crisp: **12 rashers of Irish bacon,** cut ⅛ inch thick. Drain on absorbent paper.

6 Soften: **¼ pound butter.**

PRESENTATION

Mound up the hot mashed potatoes on a hot round serving platter. With a large spoon make a well in the center of the mountain. Put the softened butter in the well—the hot potatoes will soon melt it. Stand bacon rashers against sides of mound lengthwise.

Note: In Ireland the whole family eats this from the same dish, every man for himself, which is fine if you're blood relations. If you're not, you can make individual Colcannon mountains on each person's plate, break the bacon rashers in half and stand the halves around the smaller mounds of potato.

CAESAR SALAD
SERVES 6

Fresh fruits and fresh vegetables look so tempting in Farmers' Market that they're the items we are most likely to buy on impulse. We generally stroll through the produce department with no clear-cut idea of what we want. Whatever vegetables and fruits are in season, and whichever of those are irresistibly beautiful that day—those are the ones we choose. On a day when romaine lettuce is exceptionally crisp and fresh looking you can bet we'll wind up at home with a Caesar Salad. Although several California chefs and restaurants claim it as their invention, it is really supposed to have come from that wonderfully mad border town, Tijuana, Mexico. Here is our version, devised after having watched Caesar Salads tossed beside a hundred tables north and south of the Border.

garlic
olive oil
romaine lettuce
salt, pepper
egg
anchovies (optional)
Parmesan cheese
stale bread
lemon
cayenne pepper
Tabasco
sugar
French bread
garlic butter
(see index)

1 Tear off leaves from: **2 heads romaine lettuce.** Wash well and dry thoroughly, being careful not to bruise leaves. Put in refrigerator to chill.

2 Crush: **1 clove garlic, peeled,** and let stand overnight in **1 cup olive oil.** Keep in refrigerator.

3 Trim crusts from: **4 slices stale bread** (preferably French). Cut into cubes and brown these croutons in about ¼ cup of the olive oil, which has been strained to remove garlic. Sauté over moderate heat, turning croutons to brown on all sides. Drain on paper towels and set aside.

4 In a jar add to the garlic-flavored salad oil: **a dash of cayenne pepper, a dash of Tabasco, ½ teaspoon sugar,** and **6 anchovy fillets, diced and mashed** (optional).

5 Break chilled romaine leaves in pieces and place in large bowl.

6 Sprinkle with: **1 teaspoon freshly ground pepper** and **½ teaspoon salt.**

7 Pour over the seasoned olive oil and mix thoroughly so that every leaf is well coated and shiny.

8 Boil: **1 egg** for 1 minute. Remove, crack shell, and drop into salad.

9 Squeeze: **the juice of 1 large lemon** (about 3 tablespoons) over egg and stir gently into salad. It will have a creamy appearance.

10 Taste for seasoning.

PRESENTATION

When just ready to serve, sprinkle over salad: **about ⅜ cup grated Parmesan cheese** and the croutons. Toss lightly to mix. We like to serve this with **French bread** slashed into slices, spread with **garlic butter,** and heated in the oven.

LEMON AND STRAWBERRY SURPRISE
SERVES 6

One of Mary's loveliest dinner party desserts is this Lemon and Strawberry Surprise. Lemons we have always with us in this land of citrus fruits, but during the strawberry season the market tempts us with berries of phenomenal size and perfection, and that is when this dessert appears on our menu. Here is the recipe for six. It is even more spectacular if you double the quantity and use a two-quart round bowl. If you are quite certain of your oven temperature, you can even make this in a crystal bowl, as the 225° oven is slow enough for crystal to be used safely.

eggs
cream of tartar
sugar
lemons
cream
strawberries

1 Preheat oven to very slow (225° F.).

2 Beat: **4 egg whites** with **¼ teaspoon cream of tartar** until stiff. Gradually beat in: **¾ cup sugar** and continue to beat until meringue is smooth and glossy. Empty into a round 8½ x 2-inch baking dish, making a nest about 1 inch deep with a rim about 2 inches thick. Bake in the very slow oven for 1¼ hours. Cool.

3 In top of double boiler beat: **4 egg yolks** and **½ cup sugar.** Stir in: **1 teaspoon grated lemon rind** and **6 tablespoons lemon juice.** Cook, stirring, over simmering water for about 15 minutes, or until custard is thick. Cool.

4 Beat: **1 cup cream** until stiff. Fold into the lemon custard. Pour custard into the meringue nest and chill for 24 hours.

PRESENTATION

Just before serving beat: **½ cup cream** and stir in: **2 tablespoons sugar.** Spread the whipped cream over the lemon custard and stud with: **6 large whole strawberries,** one enormous berry to mark each serving.

SPAIN

Long before we ever went to Spain, we felt that we knew it from the bold imprint it had left on the New World. We adore Mexico, we live in a Spanish style house, Mary collects Spanish tiles and wrought iron as lovingly as J. Paul Getty collects money, so we came to Spain with great expectations. We were disappointed that first trip. Modern Madrid is nothing at all like old Mexico City—it isn't even like the rest of Spain, but we didn't find that out until subsequent visits.

But there were two saving graces, two big pluses that kept our letdown from being cellar deep. One was the art of Spain—the old masters in the Prado and cathedrals and the new young painters—and the other was the food. To spend a day feasting your eyes, and then to be well fed at night leaves not too much room for discontent.

Spanish food is very different from its Mexican derivatives. Substitute garlic and olive oil for the hot peppers and lard in Mexican cookery, and right away it's a different kettle of fish. The Spaniards are very fond of saffron in their food. I thought at first that the sunny yellow color was what they were after, being a visual-minded fellow myself. Alas for my naïveté! One of our waiters kindly explained to me about saffron, "It makes much passion," but we never fully researched that theory. We did learn to love *paella*, however, which is marvelous served with a dry saffron rice.

Spain has many different cuisines, North, South, East and Central, all of them interesting. As is true in most European countries, it is the everyday fare that is most exciting and the hardest for the tourist to find outside of private homes. A few years ago I had the good fortune to be invited to several homes in Barcelona. Exquisite hospitality, marvelous eating!

Someday someone will do a sausage guide to Europe and it will give the real clue to Spanish home cooking—everything has sausage in it. It's a delightful surprise to come upon a hunk of sausage deep in the heart of a plate of white beans and rice, or hidden at the bottom of a *paella*, or served in a dozen different forms as hors d'oeuvres. Spanish sausages are sometimes to be found in our country. If you can get them, try using a bit to spice up almost any dish.

Pork, lamb and seafood share top honors in Spain with this difference: Spaniards seem to be particularly fond of eating the young of the species. Suckling pig, roasted to a crisp, is a national delicacy as is baby lamb roasted whole, or baby lamb chops that are served by the dozen. Then there are bowls of baby eels, looking like nothing so much as fish bait, and baby octopus, which round out this culinary kindergarten.

Most of these dishes are to be found in the country. The restaurants of Madrid are continental and only occasionally serve regional specialties. But wherever you dine in Spain, there is one thing you will have to get used to. Dinner is never served before 10:00 P.M. and 11:00 is really more fashionable. How do they fill the long hours between lunch time and dinner? Eating and drinking, of course. The between-meal snacks called *tapas*, a kind of spicy Spanish smorgasbord washed down with dry sherry, are just the thing to tide you over. We would often have been tempted to retire early and call it a day after gorging ourselves on *tapas*, but the thought of missing dinner in Madrid, where the resturants are interesting as well as inexpensive, kept us going until 10:00 P.M. A good thing too, because we garnered some of our favorite recipes in these Spanish restaurants.

In Madrid the two-hundred-year-old Sobrino de Botín serves Spanish specialties in a vaulted brick cellar, mellowed by time.

Our keeping-room, with its brightly patterned tiles, gives an added Spanish flavor to a dinner of Mediterranean fish soup. Nearly everything you see here—including the soup—was a do-it-yourself project.

188

SOBRINO DE BOTÍN

OST of the well-known eating places in Madrid are not very Spanish, either in atmosphere or cuisine! Horcher's, with its dark walls and red drapes, is German, the Palace Hotel is palatial, the Ritz ritzy, the Jockey (pronounced "hockey") is horsey. But the Antigua Casa Sobrino de Botín is pure Spanish from its long and grandiloquent name to its vaulted ceilings and tile decorations. The name means "Ancient House of the Nephew of Botín," and ancient is no exaggeration.

In the sixteenth century, when Madrid was scarcely more than a trading post for merchants from all over Spain, an inn stood on the spot where Botín is now. Even then the inn enjoyed a local fame for its stone oven, from which the aroma of roasted meat wafted across the marketplace. Two hundred years ago the inn was remodeled into the present restaurant, but the famous oven was not touched. Today Botín's roasted suckling pig and baby lamb are considered to be the best in all Spain, no mean distinction in a land where these are the national specialties. The chef has something to do with it, but the real secret is in the ancient stone oven, still faced with its original tiles.

Botín is a favorite hangout for bullfighters. The upstairs restaurant has cheerful whitewashed walls, dark beams and blue-and-white tile decorations. But we are inclined to agree with the bullfighters who prefer to gather downstairs in the room that was formerly a wine cellar. Emilio Gonzalez, the owner, wrote out the recipes that we asked for, and they are among our most cherished souvenirs of Spain. When we serve them in our own tile-walled keeping-room, these dishes look and taste authentically Spanish.

191

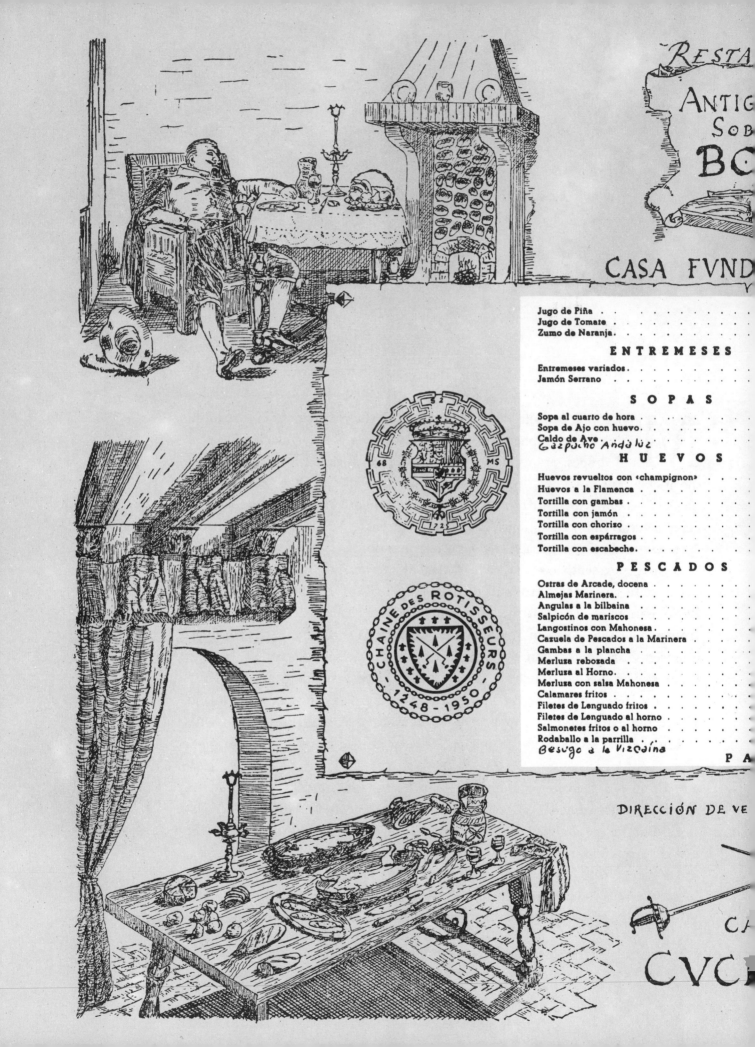

RESTA

ANTIG
SOB
BO

CASA FVND

Jugo de Piña . . . .
Jugo de Tomate . . . .
Zumo de Naranja. . . . .

ENTREMESES

Entremeses variados. . . . . . .
Jamón Serrano . . . .

SOPAS

Sopa al cuarto de hora . . . . .
Sopa de Ajo con huevo. . . . . .
Caldo de Ave. . . . .
Gazpacho Andaluz

HUEVOS

Huevos revueltos con «champignon» . .
Huevos a la Flamenca . . . . . .
Tortilla con gambas . . . . . .
Tortilla con jamón . . . . . .
Tortilla con chorizo . . . . . .
Tortilla con espárragos . . . . .
Tortilla con escabeche . . . . .

PESCADOS

Ostras de Arcade, docena . . . . .
Almejas Marinera. . . . .
Angulas a la bilbaina . . . . . .
Salpicón de mariscos . . . . . .
Langostinos con Mahonesa . . . . .
Cazuela de Pescados a la Marinera . .
Gambas a la plancha . . . . . .
Merluza rebosada . . . .
Merluza al Horno. . . . .
Merluza con salsa Mahonesa . . . .
Calamares fritos . . . .
Filetes de Lenguado fritos . . . .
Filetes de Lenguado al horno . . .
Salmonetes fritos o al horno . . .
Rodaballo a la parrilla . . . . .
Besugo a la Vizcaína

PA

DIRECCIÓN DE VE

CH

CVC

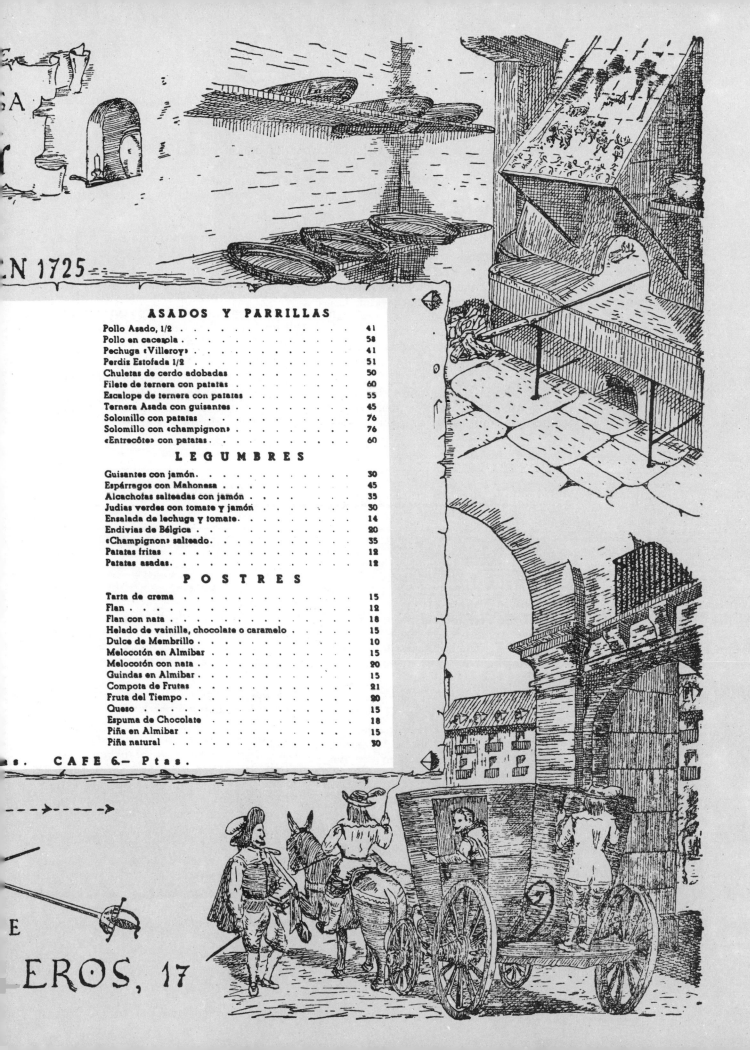

EN 1725

ASADOS Y PARRILLAS

Pollo Asado, 1/2	41
Pollo en cacerola	58
Pechuga «Villeroy»	41
Perdiz Estofada 1/2	51
Chuletas de cerdo adobadas . . .	50
Filete de ternera con patatas . . .	60
Escalope de ternera con patatas . .	55
Ternera Asada con guisantes . . .	45
Solomillo con patatas	76
Solomillo con «champignon» . .	76
«Entrecôte» con patatas	60

LEGUMBRES

Guisantes con jamón.	30
Espárragos con Mahonesa . . .	45
Alcachofas salteadas con jamón . .	35
Judias verdes con tomate y jamón	30
Ensalada de lechuga y tomate. . .	14
Endivias de Bélgica	20
«Champignon» salteado. . . .	35
Patatas fritas	12
Patatas asadas.	12

POSTRES

Tarta de crema	15
Flan	12
Flan con nata	18
Helado de vainilla, chocolate o caramelo	15
Dulce de Membrillo	10
Melocotón en Almibar	15
Melocotón con nata	20
Guindas en Almibar	15
Compota de Frutas	21
Fruta del Tiempo	20
Queso	15
Espuma de Chocolate	18
Piña en Almibar	15
Piña natural	30

s. CAFE 6.— Ptas.

EROS, 17

GAZPACHO ANDALUZ (*Andalusian Cold Soup*)

SERVES 4 TO 6

Gazpacho originated in Andalusia, the colorful southern section of Spain. This is a very hot, very poor, but very gay part of the country. Their soup, served icy cold, is refreshing and energizing on the hottest day, and Botín's recipe is the classic Andalusian one. For the best flavor, you must be sure to use very ripe tomatoes, otherwise the taste falls flat.

bread
very ripe tomatoes
red or green pepper
cucumbers
olive oil
garlic
wine vinegar
salt
ground cumin
butter (optional)

GAZPACHO

Into a mixing bowl put: **6 thin slices bread, diced, 3 very ripe tomatoes, chopped, 1 cucumber, chopped, 3 tablespoons olive oil**, and **1 quart water**. Let soak for 1 hour, then puree in food mill or blend, half at a time, on high speed in an electric blender for 8 seconds. Strain through a coarse sieve into a large soup bowl.

Add: **2 cloves garlic, minced, 2 tablespoons wine vinegar, 2 teaspoons salt, 1 teaspoon ground cumin**, and **4 ice cubes**.

Chill in refrigerator for at least half an hour.

PRESENTATION

In separate small dishes put: **1 red** or **green pepper, diced, 1 large ripe tomato, diced, 1 small cucumber, diced**, and **2 slices bread, diced**. If desired, the bread cubes may be browned in **butter**.

Serve the *gazpacho* in well chilled bowls. Let each person help himself to the diced garnishes in the small dishes, sprinkling some of each into his soup bowl.

BESUGO A LA VIZCAÍNA (*Sea Bream Biscay Style*)

SERVES 4

Some of the best food in Spain is found in the Basque country on the Bay of Biscay. Baby eels, octopus and other fish specialties are famous there. At Botín for this recipe they use sea bream, a delicate European fish that is not available here. But we find that red snapper or striped bass make very good substitutes.

red snapper or
striped bass
salt, pepper
lemon
olive oil
bread crumbs
garlic
parsley
small new potatoes
watercress

FISH

1 Preheat oven to very hot (450° F.).
2 Clean and scale: **1 red snapper** or **striped bass**, weighing about 2 pounds. Wash carefully, being sure to remove all blood clots from the inside. Dry on paper towels. Sprinkle inside and out with: **1 teaspoon salt** and let drain on dish, setting dish at a slight incline to allow water to run off.
3 Make 6 parallel slits deep down to the bone on one side of the fish and in each insert **a thin slice of lemon**.
4 Mix: **4 tablespoons olive oil, 2 tablespoons fresh bread crumbs, 1 teaspoon minced garlic** (less if you do not share the Spanish enthusiasm for garlic), **1 tablespoon chopped parsley**, and **⅛ teaspoon freshly ground pepper**.
5 Spread half of this mixture on the bottom of a shallow oval baking dish about 15 inches long (in Spain these earthenware dishes are called *besugueras*). Place the fish in the dish, lemon side up, and spread with remaining oil-garlic mixture.
6 Bake fish for 25 to 30 minutes, basting several times with juices in the pan.

PRESENTATION

Sprinkle fish with **lemon juice**. Serve very hot in the baking dish. Garnish with **small boiled new potatoes** and **watercress**.

194

ROAST PORK CASTILIAN STYLE

SERVES 12

This is Botín's famous recipe for *cochinillo asado*, roast suckling pig, which we prefer to do with fresh ham for several reasons. In the first place neither of us could bear to cook or to eat a three-week-old piglet—no matter how you slice it, it has the look of an infant and that appalls us. And even for those who are not so squeamish, suckling pig is a seasonal dish and rarely available. Botín also prepared four-week-old baby lamb in this same fashion. Again, not for us, but a leg of lamb is very good "Castilian style," roasted for thirteen minutes per pound altogether instead of the longer time necessary for pork.

fresh ham
butter or shortening
bay leaves
garlic
dry thyme
salt
parsley
onion
lemon
white wine
sweet paprika

1 Preheat oven to moderate (350° F.).

2 Score the skin and fat of **a fresh ham** weighing from 12 to 14 pounds. Place in a shallow roasting pan (in Spain they use an oval earthenware one) and rub the skin with: **4 tablespoons butter** or **shortening.**

3 Mix: **3 bay leaves, crumbled, 3 cloves garlic, minced, ½ teaspoon dry thyme, 2 tablespoons chopped parsley,** and **3 tablespoons minced onion.** Sprinkle mix-

ture over meat.

4 Sprinkle meat with: **juice of 1 lemon, ⅓ cup white wine, 2 tablespoons sweet paprika,** and **2 teaspoons salt.**

5 Roast the meat for 1½ hours. Remove fat that has accumulated in pan.

6 Add to pan: **⅓ cup white wine** and **1 cup water.** Continue to roast for 3½ to 4½ hours longer, or a total of 25 minutes per pound, basting every half hour with the liquid in the pan.

MEDITERRANEAN FISH SOUP

SERVES 6

In the South of France this soup is called bouillabaisse, and all along the European shores of the Mediterranean you will find versions of it. This Spanish recipe comes from Señor Charles Cortés, the owner of the Jockey, and we like it because it is not too complicated to make and it has a heavenly flavor.

jumbo shrimp
mussels
cherrystone clams
striped bass
thyme
bay leaf
salt, pepper
peppercorns
olive oil
carrot
leeks
garlic
tomato
saffron
French bread

SEAFOOD

1 Wash: **6 jumbo shrimp.** Remove shells and intestinal vein that runs down the back. Set shrimp aside, save shells.

2 Fillet: **a 2-pound striped bass** and cut the meat into 6 thick slices.

3 Scrub: **12 mussels** carefully. Wash: **12 cherrystone clams.** Set aside.

4 Wash head and bones of bass and put into saucepan with the shrimp shells and **2 quarts water.**

5 Add: **¼ teaspoon thyme, 1 bay leaf, ¼ teaspoon peppercorns,** and **½ teaspoon salt.** Bring to a boil and simmer for 15 minutes.

SOUP

1 Heat in kettle: **¼ cup olive oil.** Add: **1 carrot, finely chopped,** and **2 leeks, finely chopped** (white part only). Cook over low heat for 10 minutes until slightly browned, stirring occasionally.

2 Add: **2 cloves garlic, minced,** and **1 small tomato, peeled and chopped,** and cook for 5 minutes longer, stirring occasionally. Strain the hot stock from fish bones and shrimp shells into the kettle and add: **¼ teaspoon saffron.** Bring to a rapid boil.

3 Add the sliced bass fillets, cover, and cook for 10 minutes.

4 Add the cleaned shrimp, cover, and simmer for 5 minutes.

5 Add the 12 mussels and 12 cherry-stone clams. Cover and cook for 5 minutes, or until clams and mussels have opened.

PRESENTATION

Correct seasoning with **salt** and **freshly ground pepper** and serve from large tureen. Ladle into individual soup plates, dividing fish and seafood equally among them, with open mussels and clams on top. Serve with hot crusty **French bread**.

ROCK CORNISH GAME HENS WITH GRAPES
SERVES 2 OR 4

Also from the Jockey comes this continental recipe. Originally we were served pheasant with grapes, but that is a rare bird at the Prices' so we follow the Jockey's excellent directions using game hens instead. Should a pheasant happen to come your way, try cooking it according to this recipe. It can't fail to be superb since even this road company version with game hens is extraordinary.

Rock Cornish game hens
salt, pepper
bacon
bread
butter
lemon
cognac
cream
scallions
light seedless grapes
port
cayenne pepper
watercress

GAME HENS

1 Preheat oven to moderate (350° F.).

2 Sprinkle **2 Rock Cornish game hens** with **salt** and **pepper** and arrange in a well **buttered** shallow roasting pan. Cover each with: **3 half slices bacon.** Roast in the moderate oven for 50 minutes, basting several times with juices in pan. (If you are roasting a pheasant, 30 or 35 minutes will suffice as it should be rare.)

3 Trim: **2 slices bread**, cut into triangles, and sauté in **2 tablespoons hot butter** until golden on both sides. Drain on absorbent paper.

4 Remove hens from oven, cut in half and arrange each half on a triangle of fried bread on a hot serving platter. Keep warm.

SAUCE

1 Put roasting pan over direct heat. To liquid in pan add: **½ cup cognac** and cook until cognac is reduced by half. Add: **½ cup cream** and boil until sauce is reduced to a creamy consistency.

2 In small saucepan heat: **1 tablespoon butter.** Add: **2 scallions, finely chopped,** and sauté for 2 minutes. Add: **1 can (8¼ ounces) light seedless grapes, drained,** and **½ cup port.** Heat and ignite wine. Stir until flame burns out.

3 Strain the cream gravy from roasting pan into wine and grape sauce, correct seasoning with **salt, a dash of cayenne pepper,** and **1 teaspoon lemon juice.**

PRESENTATION

On warm platter each half game hen is resting on a toast triangle. Pour sauce over hens and garnish, if desired, with **watercress.**

CANTÁBRIC SOLE RITZ (Stuffed Sole Ritz)
SERVES 4

The Ritz in Madrid is one of the splendid old aristocratic hotels of Europe. Its Terrace restaurant, set in a garden around a Moorish pool, is a delightful place for lunch if you want to eat leisurely and well. This sole, though it is named for a place near the northern coast of Spain, is not so much Spanish in style as it is continental, and quite typical of the Ritz cuisine. In other words delicious!

FISH

soles
butter
shallots
mushrooms
button mushrooms
bread crumbs
chives or green
onion tops
eggs
salt, white pepper

Have your fish market fillet **4 small soles,** weighing 12 ounces each, leaving the white skin on one fillet, but removing the black skin from the other on each fish. Wash the soles, sprinkle with **salt** and **white pepper,** and set aside.

FILLING

1   In a small skillet heat: **2 ounces butter.**

2   Add: **½ cup minced shallots** and cook for 2 minutes without letting them brown.

3   Add: **½ cup minced mushrooms (2 medium ones)** and cook over low heat, stirring occasionally, for 5 minutes or until most of the moisture has evaporated. Cool.

4   In mixing bowl combine: **2 cups fine fresh bread crumbs (4 slices),** the shallot-mushroom mixture, **⅓ cup minced**

chives or green onion tops, **4 ounces soft butter, 3 egg yolks, ½ teaspoon salt,** and **⅛ teaspoon white pepper.**

CANTÁBRIC SOLE

Preheat oven to moderately hot (375° F.).

1   Arrange the fillets that have the white skin, skin side down in a shallow **buttered** casserole. Spread each fillet with one-fourth of the filling. Cover with the skinless fillets.

2   Slice: **4 button mushrooms** and arrange an overlapping row of slices down center of each stuffed fish.

3   Dot with: **2 ounces butter** and bake in the moderately hot oven for 20 minutes, basting twice with butter in the pan.

4   Sprinkle with: **2 tablespoons bread crumbs** about 5 minutes before serving, baste again, and complete the cooking.

CHICKEN PEPITORIA *(Spicy Chicken Fricassee)*

SERVES 6

chicken
carrot
onions
cloves
leeks
thyme
bay leaf
parsley
lemon
eggs
salt, peppercorns
olive oil
sweet red pepper
saffron
butter
flour
sherry
blanched toasted
almonds

CHICKEN

1   In a large pot put: **a 5-pound roasting chicken,** ready-to-cook and trussed. Place it breast down.

2   Add: **1 carrot, peeled, 2 whole onions,** each stuck with **3 cloves, 3 leeks** (white part only), **½ teaspoon thyme, 1 bay leaf, 4 sprigs parsley, 2 teaspoons salt,** and **1 teaspoon crushed peppercorns.**

3   Add: **4 quarts water** and bring to a boil. Cover and poach the chicken for 1¼ to 1½ hours, or until just tender.

4   Remove chicken and cut into serving portions: 2 wings, 2 drumsticks, 2 thighs, and 6 pieces of breast. Put the parts into a saucepan and cover with a little of the warm stock. Skim fat from surface of remaining stock. Return remains of carcass to the pot and cook over high heat until stock is reduced to about 1 quart.

SAUCE

1   In large skillet heat: **½ cup olive oil.**

2   Add: **1 cup finely chopped sweet red pepper (1 large one), 2 cups minced onion (4 medium ones)** and cook over moderate heat for 5 minutes.

3   Soak: **½ teaspoon saffron** in **2 tablespoons chicken stock** for 5 minutes. Add to skillet. Add the reduced stock and simmer for 20 minutes.

4   In a small skillet heat: **6 tablespoons butter** and add: **8 tablespoons flour.** Cook over high heat, stirring constantly, until roux becomes color of light brown sugar. Stir into large skillet and cook, stirring, until sauce is thickened.

5   Add: the pieces of cooked chicken, **½ cup blanched toasted almonds,** slivered, and **1 teaspoon salt,** or to taste.

PRESENTATION

Just before serving stir in: **½ cup sherry,** and if desired **a squeeze of lemon juice.** Turn into serving dish and garnish with **2 hard-cooked eggs, coarsely chopped,** and some **chopped parsley.**

PORK CUTLETS ESCORIAL

SERVES 4

The vast white Palace Hotel in Madrid has one of the best restaurants in the city and their recipe for pork cutlets is one of the most interesting in our collection. The sauce is a fabulous combination of intriguing flavors, and yet this dish can be prepared quickly and with a minimum of fuss. Why they named such a delightful concoction after the Escorial, Philip II's gloomy old palace and monastery, I can't even begin to guess. Maybe they just wanted to indicate that this dish is tremendous, as is the Escorial.

PORK CUTLETS

pork cutlets
Dijon mustard
salt, pepper
butter
flour
mustard fruits
dry white wine
cream
brown sauce
(see index)
large stuffed olives
glacéed chestnuts

1 Rub: **4 pork cutlets** with **1 teaspoon Dijon mustard** each, and sprinkle with a little **salt** and some **freshly ground pepper.**

2 In a skillet heat: **2 tablespoons butter** and in it sauté the pork cutlets for 5 minutes on each side, or until brown. Reduce heat and cook slowly for 5 minutes longer. Transfer cutlets to warm dish and keep warm.

SAUCE

1 Discard all but 1 tablespoon drippings in pan.

2 Add to pan: **1 tablespoon flour** and cook, stirring, for 1 minute.

3 Add: **1 cup dry white wine**, bring to

rapid boil and boil briskly, stirring constantly, for 2 minutes.

4 Stir in: **½ cup cream, 3 tablespoons brown sauce, 8 large stuffed olives, finely chopped**, and **4 glacéed chestnuts.**

5 Return pork cutlets to sauce and simmer for 3 minutes.

6 In a small pan heat: **6 tablespoons finely chopped mustard fruits** in their **syrup.**

PRESENTATION

Transfer cutlets to warm serving dish, cover with sauce and top each cutlet with a **glacéed chestnut.** Drain the chopped mustard fruits and sprinkle on top.

PAELLA "GOOD FRIEND"
(Chicken and Rice with Almonds, Olives, and Mushrooms)

SERVES 6

The Palace Hotel serves this chicken and rice dish, really an *arroz con pollo*, under the name of *paella* "Good Friend." The implication is that for a good friend you don't have to go to the trouble of the more elaborate *paella*, but Mary and I hold quite the opposite philosophy.

olive oil
chicken
salt, pepper
small onions
garlic
rice
dry white wine
chicken stock
(see index)
oregano
blanched salted
almonds
stuffed olives
mushrooms
butter

1 Preheat oven to moderate (325° F.).

2 Heat in large kettle: **½ cup olive oil.**

3 Add: **a 3½-pound chicken**, cut into serving portions, and sprinkle with: **2 teaspoons salt** and **½ teaspoon pepper.** Cook in the moderate oven, uncovered, for 15 minutes.

4 Add: **6 small onions, peeled**, and continue to cook for 45 minutes.

5 Add: **2 cloves garlic, minced**, and **2½ cups raw rice.** Mix well.

6 Add: **1 cup dry white wine** and **3**

cups **chicken stock**, cover, and cook for 45 minutes longer. Correct seasoning with **salt** and **pepper.**

7 Sprinkle with: **1 teaspoon oregano, 3½ ounces blanched salted almonds**, and **¾ cup chopped stuffed olives.** Add: **2 cups chicken stock** to make the mixture juicy. Keep hot in oven.

8 Sauté: **12 medium mushrooms, quartered**, in **4 tablespoons butter** for 5 minutes. Sprinkle on top of the *paella* and serve hot with a tossed green salad.

PAELLA A LA VALENCIANA (*Paella Valencia Style*)

SERVES 6

Chicken, rice and seafood cooked together equals *paella*, and there are as many ways to cook it as there are to skin a cat. The *paella* of Valencia is supposed to be the best and though we have never had it in that city, I would bet that it isn't one whit better than this magnificent one from the Palace Hotel.

lobster
cherrystone clams
mussels
olive oil
chicken
veal
lean pork
garlic
saffron
asparagus tips (fresh or canned)
onion
salt, pepper
ripe tomatoes
rice
sweet red pepper
frozen peas
frozen artichoke hearts
crab meat
pimiento

SEAFOOD

Remove meat from: **a 1½-pound lobster.** Scrub: **6 cherrystone clams** and **6 mussels.** Pick over: **½ pound crabmeat.**

MEAT

Cut into parts: **1 frying chicken.** Dice: **¼ pound veal** and **¼ pound lean pork.**

PAELLA

1 In a heavy deep skillet heat: **¼ cup olive oil.**

2 Add chicken, veal, and pork. Cook until chicken pieces are browned on all sides.

3 Add: **1 clove garlic,** minced, and **1 onion,** finely chopped. Cook, stirring, until onion is transparent.

4 Add: **2 teaspoons salt, ¼ teaspoon freshly ground pepper,** and **2 ripe tomatoes** (1 pound), peeled and chopped. Cover and cook for 10 minutes longer.

5 Add: **2 cups rice** and **4 cups water.** Stir to combine.

6 Add: **1 sweet red pepper,** chopped, **1 package frozen peas,** and **1 package frozen artichoke hearts.** Cover and cook over low heat for about 20 minutes.

7 Mash in mortar: **1 clove garlic** and **1 teaspoon saffron** and add to *paella.* With large spoon turn rice from top to bottom to mix well.

8 Add the crabmeat and the lobster meat, cover, and cook for 10 to 15 minutes longer.

GARNISH

Meanwhile, put mussels and clams in a heavy pot with **½ cup water.** Cover and bring to a lively boil over high heat. Cook for 2 minutes, or until shells open. Cook: **12 asparagus tips** until tender in boiling **salted** water (or heat **canned asparagus**).

PRESENTATION

Arrange rice mixture in shallow *paella* dish or large shallow casserole. Place open mussels and clams in their shells on top of rice and garnish with the asparagus tips and **strips of pimiento.**

CRÊPES SIR HOLDEN

SERVES 6

The traditional dessert of Spain (and of most countries with a Spanish heritage) is *flan*, a caramel custard. We have included our favorite recipe for it in our collection of Mexican recipes. But this dessert from Horcher's, while not traditionally Spanish, is a great one and we'd rather have it than custard any day.

butter
sugar
curaçao
vanilla ice cream
whipped cream
strawberries
maraschino or framboise
kirsch
crepes with sugar (see index)
almonds

Make 6 French crepes with sugar.

SAUCE

1 In the pan of a chafing dish or in a large skillet melt: **½ cup butter.**

2 Add: **2 tablespoons sugar** and **3 tablespoons curaçao.** Heat to boiling.

3 Add: **1 pint strawberries,** hulled and halved. Heat, stirring.

4 Add: **¼ cup maraschino** or **framboise** and **¼ cup kirsch.** Set aflame.

PRESENTATION

Put **a scoop of vanilla ice cream** on a cold serving plate. Dip **a crepe** into the sauce in the skillet, turning to coat both sides, and place it over the ice cream. Top with strawberries and sauce. Finish with **a dab of whipped cream** and **a sprinkling of toasted slivered or crushed almonds.**

LOBSTER TITUS

SERVES 4

The first time we ever went to Horcher's we arrived far too early — a little before ten o'clock — and the place was empty. So to pass the time until the proper Spanish dinner hour rolled around, I ordered a shrimp cocktail. Never had I tasted anything so marvelous! I had two of them while waiting for the restaurant to fill up (I filled up first, I must confess) and for dinner to be served. Here is Otto Horcher's recipe for Lobster Titus with the same remarkable sauce that I enjoyed with the shrimp. We use it for any kind of seafood cocktail.

fresh pineapple
boiled lobster
wine vinegar
dry mustard
eggs
celery
horse-radish
lemon
chives
parsley
shallots
salt, pepper
olive oil
cognac
chili sauce

LOBSTER

Cut: **4 thin slices fresh pineapple.**
Cover each slice with: **¼ pound boiled lobster,** cut into chunks.
Pour the following special cocktail sauce over all.

COCKTAIL SAUCE

In a bowl put: **2 tablespoons wine vinegar, 1 teaspoon dry mustard, 2 egg yolks, 1 tablespoon minced celery, 1 tablespoon horse-radish, 2 teaspoons chopped chives, 2 teaspoons chopped parsley, 1 tablespoon chopped shallots, ½ teaspoon salt,** and **½ teaspoon pepper.**
Beat until smooth and light.
Beat in: **4 ounces olive oil** and mix well.
Add: **2 ounces cognac** and **2 ounces chili sauce,** mixing well.
Add: **juice of ½ lemon** and mix thoroughly.
Chill in the refrigerator and serve over this lobster cocktail, or shrimp or crabmeat cocktail.

CONSOMMÉ FARLEY

SERVES 1

Although Madrid is the home of *consommé à la madrilène,* there is a far better consommé served at Horcher's that has achieved local fame. Named for Jim Farley, this is one of the great specialties of Horcher's. When you order it there, a rare-grilled fillet of beef is brought to the table where the juice is extracted by means of a meat press. At home we use our blender with a lesser cut of beef, such as a slice of bottom round, with the same superb result.

fillet of beef
beef stock
(see index)
egg
cream
salt, pepper
sherry

1 For each serving, grill or sauté: **a 6-ounce fillet of beef** for 5 minutes on each side, or until well browned but rare.

2 Cut warm fillet into small cubes and put into container of electric blender.

3 Add: **¾ cup hot beef stock,** cover, and blend on high speed for 45 seconds.

4 Strain through a fine sieve, pressing juices out of pureed beef with the back of a wooden spoon. Put liquid into a small saucepan and heat.

5 Beat: **1 egg yolk** and **½ cup cream.** Gradually beat in the hot liquid. Return the mixture to the saucepan and cook, stirring rapidly, for 2 minutes, being careful that it does not boil.

6 Add: **¼ teaspoon salt** and some **freshly ground pepper.** Add: **2 tablespoons good sherry** and cook, stirring, for 30 seconds longer.

PRESENTATION

Pour into consommé cup and serve hot.

EL GRAN FROU FROU (*Fondue Bourguignonne*)

SERVES 4

We are very fond of some of the recipes we picked up in Barcelona. At a restaurant called the Soley we had something they called *El Gran Frou Frou* that we had always had before in Switzerland under the name of Burgundy fondue. Call it what you will, it's great fun on a cold night. Everyone sits around a low table and each person is armed with a long fork. A deep pot of hot fat sizzles over a warmer in the center of the table. A platter heaped with cubes of raw beef tenderloin and individual dishes of assorted sauces complete the service. Each guest impales a cube of beef on his fork and lets it sputter in the fat till it's done to his liking. Then he dips it into the sauce of his choice. A perfect meal for do-it-yourselfers and rugged individualists — which most of our friends seem to be.

beef
peanut oil
butter
onion
garlic
fresh ginger root
curry powder
brown sugar
flour
salt
chicken stock
(see index)
béchamel sauce
(see index)
cayenne pepper
hot Hungarian
paprika
eggs
olive oil
lemon
pepper
tarragon vinegar
dry white wine
shallots
tarragon
peppercorns
cream

FONDUE

1 Cut: **2 pounds very tender beef, preferably tenderloin,** into 1-inch cubes.

2 Make: mild curry sauce, hot paprika sauce, garlic sauce and sauce *béarnaise*.

3 Put: **2 cups peanut oil** and **2 cups butter** in a deep earthenware, enamel, cast-iron, or copper pot over Sterno or alcohol lamp. The mixture of oil and butter should be sizzling hot. It will spatter unless the pot is quite deep.

PRESENTATION

Each person has a long 2-pronged fork with wooden handle. Spear a piece of meat, put it in the hot oil and let it brown; about 2 minutes for rare. Dip in individual dishes of one or more of the following savory sauces.

MILD CURRY SAUCE

1 In a saucepan sauté: **½ medium onion, chopped, 1 small clove garlic, minced,** and a **1-inch piece of fresh ginger root, slivered,** in **1 tablespoon butter** for about 10 minutes, or until onion is lightly browned.

2 Stir in: **½ tablespoon curry powder** and **½ teaspoon brown sugar** and cook, stirring, for 1 minute.

3 Stir in: **1½ tablespoons flour** and **¼ teaspoon salt.** Gradually add: **1 cup chicken stock** and cook, stirring, until sauce is thickened. Cook over low heat for 10 minutes, stirring frequently. Strain into small sauce dish and serve either hot or cold.

HOT PAPRIKA SAUCE

In saucepan heat: **1 cup béchamel sauce.** Stir in about **1 tablespoon hot Hungarian paprika** to taste. The sauce should be quite pink.

GARLIC SAUCE (see index for sauce *aïoli* or below)

1 Mash: **4 large cloves garlic** with **2 egg yolks.**

2 Add: **1 cup olive oil,** drop by drop, until sauce is the consistency of mayonnaise. Stir in: **1 teaspoon lemon juice, ¾ teaspoon salt,** and **¼ teaspoon coarsely ground black pepper.**

BÉARNAISE SAUCE (see index or below)

1 In small saucepan combine: **¼ cup tarragon vinegar, ¼ cup dry white wine, 2 shallots, chopped, 1 sprig fresh tarragon,** and **4 peppercorns, crushed.** Bring to a boil and cook over the high heat until liquid is reduced to 1 tablespoon. Cool and strain liquid into a china bowl.

2 Add: **3 egg yolks** and **½ tablespoon cream.** Set bowl into a pan of hot, but not boiling water, and stir with a wire whisk until sauce is creamy. Gradually whisk in: **½ cup melted butter,** being careful not to include the milky sediment which settles to the bottom. Continue beating until sauce is thickened. Season to taste with **salt** and **cayenne pepper.** Chop the tarragon leaves and add. Add the chopped shallots.

ALMEJAS A LA MARINERA (*Clams Mariner's Style*)

SERVES 4

Almost every Latin country has its version of various kinds of seafood mariner's style. This Spanish recipe for clams is hot and zesty, guaranteed to make a flamenco dancer, if not a bullfighter, out of the mildest of men.

clams
olive oil
onion
garlic
bread crumbs
dry white wine
lemon
bay leaf
tomato
paprika
parsley
salt
cayenne pepper
hot dry red pepper

1 Wash and scrub thoroughly: **2 pounds large clams.** Change the water about 3 times to remove all sand.

2 Place clams in a covered saucepan with **1 cup water** over high heat. When water boils and clams open, remove from heat and set aside.

3 In a skillet heat: **2 teaspoons olive oil.** Sauté: **1 onion, chopped finely, 1 clove garlic, chopped finely, 1 very ripe tomato, peeled, seeded, and chopped,** and **several small pieces of hot, dry red pepper** (in Spain this is called *guindilla*).

4 When onion turns a golden brown, add: **½ cup fine bread crumbs,** the liquid from the steamed clams, **½ cup dry white wine, 1 teaspoon lemon juice, 1 bay leaf, 1 teaspoon paprika, 1 teaspoon salt,** and **a dash of cayenne pepper.** Bring to a boil.

5 Add clams to sauce and simmer for 8 to 10 minutes.

PRESENTATION

Before serving, remove bay leaf. Put clams and sauce in a large casserole and sprinkle with: **1 tablespoon freshly chopped parsley.** Serve in large shallow soup bowls.

CREMA DE MALAGA (*Malaga Cream*)

SERVES 6

At the private homes where I was entertained in Barcelona, we had some of the most delightful frothy desserts. They were ideal after the spicy Spanish food and I begged recipes for several of them from my hostesses. Some of them bear a resemblance to zabaglione, all of them are simple little last-minute concoctions. And in Spain they were generally followed by a glass of dark, sweet dessert sherry. *Ole!*

eggs
Malaga
sugar
cinnamon

1 In top of double saucepan beat: **12 egg yolks** and **6 tablespoons sugar.** (Save the 12 whites for an angel food cake.)

2 Add: **¾ cup Malaga** and **1 teaspoon cinnamon.**

3 Place saucepan over hot, but not boiling water, and beat constantly with a rotary beater or wire whisk until mixture is thick and foamy.

PRESENTATION

Spoon into parfait glasses and serve at once.

SABOYAN DE NARANJA (*Orange Zabaglione*)

SERVES 6

This frothy dessert is lighter and more delicate than a traditional zabaglione. Actually it's closer to our Southern syllabub than to the popular Italian dessert of egg yolks, sugar and wine.

sugar
eggs
oranges
lemon
milk

1 In top of double saucepan put: ¼ cup sugar and 4 egg yolks.

2 Add: 1 cup orange juice and juice of ½ lemon.

3 Place saucepan over hot, but not boiling water, and beat constantly with a rotary beater or wire whisk until mixture is warm and frothy.

4 Beat: 1 egg and 1 cup milk and grad-

ually add to the egg yolk mixture, beating constantly.

5 Continue beating for about 15 minutes, or until mixture becomes a creamy froth that does not separate upon standing.

PRESENTATION

Spoon while hot into *coupe* glasses or punch glasses and serve at once.

SORBETE DE CAFÉ (Coffee Sherbet)

SERVES 4

We are great coffee drinkers and take it hot or iced, with caffeine or without — it's that rich brown taste we love. Here's a simple little Spanish dessert that combines after-dinner coffee and brandy in one deliciously cooling concoction. No freezer should be without it.

coffee
sugar
Benedictine

1 Make: 4 cups double-strength coffee.

2 Add: 4 teaspoons sugar and chill.

3 Stir in: 2 tablespoons Benedictine. Pour into freezer tray and freeze for about 1 hour, or until mixture is mushy but not solid.

4 Beat with rotary beater, or blend, 1 cup at a time, in an electric beater.

PRESENTATION

Spoon into sherbet glasses and serve immediately.

FLAN SOUFFLÉ AL MIEL (Soufflé Custard with Honey)

SERVES 6

This dessert is not the classic *flan*, which is baked. It is a very easy, double-boiler custard sweetened with honey, but the Spanish touch comes with the orange liqueur that flavors the whipped cream, and the crunchy pistachios that are the perfect finishing touch.

eggs
honey
cream
Grand Marnier
pistachio nuts

1 Separate: 4 eggs. Set aside whites and put 4 yolks in top of double boiler.

2 Add: ½ cup honey, strained, and ¼ cup cream. Beat well and let chill.

3 Set top of double boiler over simmering water and stir with wire whisk until thick.

4 Beat the 4 egg whites until they form stiff peaks. Fold in quickly to the cus-

tard. Let chill in refrigerator for several hours.

5 Whip: ¾ cup cream until stiff, and mix in: 2 teaspoons Grand Marnier.

PRESENTATION

Serve in parfait glasses topped with the flavored whipped cream. Sprinkle chopped pistachio nuts over the cream.

PEPITAS A LA CURRY *(Curried Pumpkin Seeds)*

MAKES 2 CUPS

These are wonderful to nibble on with cocktails, and far better than the commercially salted *pepitas* that you get in jars and tins. You can buy the plain, hulled pumpkin seeds in health stores and prepare them according to this recipe, happy in the thought that they're so good for you!

curry powder
garlic
salt
lime
pumpkin seeds
butter

1   In a saucepan mix: ¼ cup curry powder, ¼ cup warm water, 1 clove garlic, finely minced, 1 teaspoon salt, and the juice of 1 lime. When smoothly blended, add: 1 cup water and heat, stirring constantly, until liquid simmers.

2   Add: 2 cups plain, hulled pumpkin seeds and simmer, do not boil, for 5 minutes. Drain. (You can save curry mixture in a screw-top glass jar and use again, adding another cup of water when you do.)

3   Preheat oven to very slow (225° F.).

4   Spread pumpkin seeds on a cookie sheet, dot with butter and sprinkle with salt. Toast in very slow oven until crisp.

MEXICO

Eating in Mexico can be heaven or hell, depending not so much on your indiscretions as on your discretion. Mexicans apparently have tough stomachs and a little valve in the top of their heads to let off steam. Between their 90-proof tequila and their hot peppers and chili, you can literally blow your top, if you want to, South of the Border. But you don't have to. Mexican cooking covers a broad range of styles, each of them stemming from a country that helped to shape Mexican culture.

Basically the cuisine, like the country itself, is Indian. Since the days of the Mayas and the Aztecs, the Indians' staple food has been corn, and corn is what you get today in a multitude of forms. Their tortilla is a pancake made from ground corn, and it is the bread, the soul, the everything of a Mexican meal.

Tortillas are available almost everywhere now and, steamed from their frozen cellophane security, they can't be beat either as a wrapping for the food at hand or simply by themselves, just oozing with melted butter. When we serve a Mexican meal, we like to have a basket full of tortillas which we keep moist and hot in a warm, slightly damp napkin. The bread of every country is a major part of the meal, and shouldn't be overlooked.

Spain and France have left their mark on Mexican cookery, too. There are chicken and rice dishes that remind one of Spanish *paella*, and *flan*, that favorite Latin-American dessert, is just a version of French caramel custard.

We want to give you some of the red-hot Mexican dishes, but we also think you may like the Spanish and French sides of Mexican cooking and some of the gentler native dishes. Mexico City, which incidentally is the oldest city in this hemisphere, abounds in good restaurants of all kinds, and it was hard to decide which one was our favorite.

There's the famous House of Tiles, Sanborn's, at the entrance to the old part of Mexico City. That's fun for breakfast or lunch when they serve delicious crepes (see the index for our recipe) filled with strawberry jam and snowed with powdered sugar. All the Mexican restaurants are glamorous; one serves you on solid silver plates that are purposely far too heavy to steal for souvenirs. Another, out in St. Angel, is in a converted seventeenth-century house, St. Angel's Inn. Still another features marimba bands so loud that they aid the digestion supersonically.

Mexico has its regional cookery too, and we've included some of the local dishes from other parts of the country, although the restaurant whose meal we've chosen to recreate is in Mexico City. Maybe we have a special leaning toward things Mexican—our house abounds with art and objects brought, carried, dragged across the border, and our recipe file bulges with an exotic array of dishes with that special Mexican oomph. I'm sure you'll agree, when you've tried them, that some of the most flavorful cooking in the world is done right next door, by our neighbors to the south.

At the Rivoli in Mexico City a gala dinner is served with great elegance. Although the food was Mexican the atmosphere was continental.

In our den an old Franklin stove blazes cheerfully, surrounded by an array of Pueblo candlesticks. The Spanish rug, a fourteenth-century Tarascan dog and a bowl of *guacamole* make for a merry Mexican cocktail hour.

THE RIVOLI

ARY and I have a sentimental attachment to the Rivoli, where on two previous collecting trips, we spent two delightful New Year's Eves. It is a restaurant that is fairly new as places go in this six-hundred-year-old city, having been founded in 1954. The Rivoli's host is Dario Borzani who came to Mexico from Hungary after a long and successful stopover in the United States.

He has given the Rivoli a continental air—the food is French and Viennese with a Mexican accent—and you eat to the strains of quiet dinner music in this land of uninhibited marimba bands. In place of the ever-present Mexican pottery, Dario collects antique china, and occasionally he permits one of his prize pieces to grace the dining table of an old customer. He let us feast our eyes on a beautiful tureen the last time we were there.

But the real feast was the food. Knowing of my long love affair with the Mayan ruins of Yucatán, Dario served us a main course called Chicken Chichén Itzá, complete with the red and black spices that you can get only in Yucatán. The result was unusual and delicious, but in all honesty I must confess that eating Chicken Chichén Itzá wasn't a patch on the experience of seeing the real Chichén Itzá in the moonlight many years ago.

Nevertheless it's one of our favorite recipes, maybe because we had such fun working out a seasoning that tasted like the Yucatán specialty but was available everywhere. We have each portion brought to the table, wrapped in the leaf it was cooked in. Each guest unfolds his leaf, and immediately the spicy smell of Mexico wafts through the room. It's the cheapest, quickest way I know to get back there, at least with your senses.

RESTAURANT  RIVOLI

HAMBURGO 123   MEXICO, D. F.   TEL. 25-68-62

ENTREMESES:

COCTELES: Ostiones   Camarones   Aguacate   LANGOSTINOS   Frutas   Mariscos

Langosta   Aguacate relleno Maryland   Salmón Ahumado   Caviar Ruso   DELICES SUECOS

ENTREMES DE LA CASA   CHAUDFROIX "RIVOLI", SALSA CUMBERLAND   Sesos a la vinagreta

Mousse de Arenque a la Rusa   Melón   Jamón ahumado   Huevos con anchoas

MELON A LA MARSELLESA   Ostiones meuniere   Tostado Rouenesa   Tostado a la Suiza

ENSALADA DE POLLO A LA VILLEROY   Ensalada de pescado a la Vasco

SOPAS:

Consomé Juliana   Sopa de legumbres   Madrileña   Sopa de cebolla   Sopa de papas   Crema de Espárragos

Vichissoise   BISQUE DE OSTIONES   BISQUE DE LANGOSTA   CREMA DE POLLO A LA REYNA   Crema St. Germain

PEQUEÑOS Y HUEVOS:

Huevos poches Florentine   Omelette Chasseur   Huevos cocotte Rouenesa

Huevos revueltos con riñones   OMELETTE REALE O CARDINAL   SOUFFLE DE QUESO FAVORITE

Rizotto con hígados de pollo   SOUFFLE DE LANGOSTA MONTE CARLO   Spaghetti Boloñesa ó Fetuchini

Champiñones a la Ritz   VOL AU VENT TOULOUSIENNE

PESCADOS y MARISCOS:

HUACHINANGO FLAMEADO CON HIERBAS   SOLE DE DOVER A LA "RIVOLI"   CAMARONES AL VERMOUTH

CREPAS DE MARISCOS A LA AMERICANA   LANGOSTINOS FLAMEADOS AL PERNOD, ESTILO RIVOLI

Langosta al Whisky ó Thermidor   TIMBALE CASIMIR A LA INDIANA   MARISCOS SAN TROPEZ FLAMEADOS AL BOURBON

Filete de Robalo Florentina   Filete de Sole a la parrilla con salsa mostaza

POLLOS Y AVES:

Coq al Riesling   POLLO CHICHEN-ITZA   Pechuga de pollo a la Kiev   COQ AL VINO BLANCO PARISIENNE

Pechuga de pollo Verónica   POLLITO RELLENO DEL REY   Pollo curry Indian   Pato a la naranja

PATO A LA TROPICAL (2) O.A.   ROUENESA A LA PRENSA (2) O.A.   FAISAN A L'ANCIENNE. O. A. (2)

CARNES:

EL STEAK DEL CHEF   FILETE MIGNON GILBERTO   STEAK A LA PIMIENTA   FONDUE BOURGUIÑONA

Steak Tártara   Carne asada   STEAK DIANA   TOURNEDOS ENRIQUE IV   Chateaubriand salsa bearnesa (2)

Goulash   TOURNEDOS ALFONSO XIII   FILETE ENCROUTE DUQUE DE BORGOÑA (2)   Mixed grill con salsa curry

Steak a la Julieta   Jamón con salsa Madera   RIÑONES FLAMEADOS AL ARMAÑAC   BROCHETA CASA

Sesos Rivoli   Milanesa Liegoise   Bitotchkis

POSTRES:

Carlotta Malakoff   Pastel de queso   Omelette con mermelada   Sopa Inglesa   Pastel Vienesa

SOUFFLE AL LICOR   SOUFFLE AL CHOCOLATE   Crepas Rivoli   Crepas Suzette

Piña flameada al Kirsch   Pastel de chocolate Vienesa   CEREZAS O DURAZNOS FLAMEADOS AL LICOR

Profiteroles   Mousse de chocolate   Helados   Copa Helena   Duraznos Melba

Ensalada de frutas   Café   Té   Expreso

PINEAPPLE MONTE CARLO

SERVES 4

Our first course at the Rivoli was charmingly served in a whole pineapple that had fresh flowers twined in its top. We thought it was an original way to present the eternal fruit cup, but we had underestimated the Rivoli's ingenuity. A seafood cocktail with a marvelous sauce and some chunks of fruit mixed with it was the surprise awaiting us inside the pineapple shell. This has become a favorite first course *chez* Price, and the combination of fresh fruit and *fruits de mer* ("fruits of the sea" is so much more poetic than "seafood") is always a smash success.

whole pineapple
apples
tarragon
parsley
Cointreau
port
mayonnaise
catsup
lobster tails or
shrimp

SEAFOOD COCKTAIL

1   Cut into small dice: **2 pounds lobster tails, boiled and shelled, or 2 pounds shrimp, boiled, shelled and deveined.** Chill.

2   Cut top off of **1 medium pineapple** and set aside. Scoop out meat of pineapple, dice it, and put it in salad bowl.

3   Peel and core: **2 apples,** dice them, add to pineapple, and chill.

4   Add lobster meat or shrimp to fruit.

5   Add: **1 tablespoon chopped tarragon** and **1 tablespoon chopped parsley.**

SAUCE

In a small bowl put: **3 tablespoons mayonnaise, 6 tablespoons catsup, ¼ ounce Cointreau, and ¼ ounce port.** Mix gently and pour over seafood-fruit mixture.

PRESENTATION

Mix seafood cocktail and sauce gently with wooden spoon to moisten completely. Fill scooped out pineapple with mixture and cover with pineapple top. Decorate with a few fresh flowers tucked or twined in the leaves. Serve pineapple on a small tray and let each person help himself with a serving spoon.

CHICKEN CHICHÉN ITZÁ (*Chicken Cooked In Leaves*)

SERVES 4

This exotic dish depends for its effect on its spicy sauce and the manner of its preparation. At the Rivoli the chicken and sauce are sealed in a large banana leaf, tied with string, and heated for about ten minutes in hot deep fat. We do it a little differently at home. Mary gets ti leaves (pronounced like tea leaves) at the florist's when she can. Otherwise we use aluminum foil or parchment paper for wrapping the chicken. And we prefer putting the wrapped meat in the oven instead of in hot fat. Also, we substitute a mixture of oregano and cumin for the Yucatán spice called *achiote* which is not available here. The end product tastes typically Mexican and we consider it one of our more triumphant experiments. Fun to serve, too.

chicken
butter
cooking oil
tomatoes
onion
garlic
oregano
ground cumin
flour
rice
salt, pepper
ti leaves, foil, or
parchment paper

CHICKEN

1   Cut into quarters: **1 frying chicken.** (You may use **4 chicken parts** or **2 broilers, halved,** if you prefer.)

2   Combine in a paper bag: **½ cup flour, 1 teaspoon salt,** and **¼ teaspoon pepper,** shaking the chicken pieces in this mixture until they are well coated.

3   In a skillet heat: **2 tablespoons butter** and sauté chicken pieces until golden on both sides. Cover and cook over low heat for 20 minutes. Set aside to cool.

SAUCE

1   In skillet heat: **1 tablespoon butter** and **1 tablespoon cooking oil.**

2   In the hot fat sauté: **3 large ripe tomatoes, chopped, 1 small onion, chopped,** and **3 cloves garlic, chopped.** Cook for 3 minutes or until onion is wilted.

3   Sprinkle with: **1 tablespoon oregano** and **1 tablespoon cumin.** Cover and cook over moderate heat for 10 minutes. Uncover and simmer 10 minutes longer.

211

4 Empty sauce into container of electric blender and blend on high speed for 20 seconds or puree in food mill. This makes 2 cups sauce or enough for 8 servings. Cool, and freeze any extra sauce.

PRESENTATION

1 Preheat oven to moderate (350° F.).
2 Place each piece of chicken in center of a square of heavy-duty aluminum foil. Or arrange 3 large ti leaves so that centers overlap, making a 6-pointed star, and place a piece of chicken in center.

3 Beat: ¼ **cup butter** into 1 cup of the tomato sauce.

4 Cover each portion of chicken with ¼ cup of sauce. Fold chicken in foil or ti leaves and tie at the top. Place packages in baking pan and bake in the moderate oven for 20 minutes.

5 Place chicken packages on individual serving plates that have been heated, and let each person open his own. Serve with boiled **rice**.

SOUP ANGLAISE *(Cake with Custard Cream)*
SERVES 8

The Italians call a cake with fruit and custard cream *zuppa Inglese*, English soup, and every so often this odd sounding dessert crops up on foreign menus. Its name will always be a mystery to me because there is nothing the least bit soupy about this marvelous dish. The beauty that we had at the Rivoli is more like a baked Alaska with trimmings and I heartily recommend it as a finale to a very gala dinner.

Génoise (see index)
cantaloupe
papaya
oranges
apples
pineapple
lemon
salt
confectioners' sugar
maraschino cherries
(optional)
sugar
kirsch
milk
vanilla bean
flour
cornstarch
eggs

CAKE

Make a 9-inch *Génoise* layer and when it is cool, cut into two slices. Set aside.

FRUIT

1 Make a mixture of fresh fruits by combining a variety of them such as **finely diced cantaloupe, papaya, orange sections, diced apple, diced pineapple** to make 1 quart finely diced fruit.
2 Sprinkle with: ¼ **cup sugar** and **2 tablespoons kirsch**. Mix well and chill until ready to use.

VANILLA CUSTARD CREAM

1 Heat to boiling: **2 cups milk** and a **1-inch stick vanilla bean**.
2 In saucepan combine: ⅓ **cup flour, 1 teaspoon cornstarch, ½ cup sugar,** and **4 egg yolks** (reserve whites for meringue).
3 Gradually stir in the hot milk with a wooden spoon or wire whisk and cook over low heat, stirring rapidly from sides and across bottom of pan, for about 3 minutes, or until custard is as thick as mayonnaise. Cool. To cool more rapidly,

set saucepan into bowl of cracked ice. Stir occasionally as custard cools.

MERINGUE

1 Preheat oven to very hot (450° F.).
2 Beat until frothy: **4 egg whites** and a **pinch of salt**. Add: ½ **teaspoon lemon juice** and continue to beat until egg whites are very stiff but not dry. Beat in: **1 cup sugar**, 1 tablespoon at a time, and continue to beat until meringue is stiff and glossy.

PRESENTATION

Place 1 slice of *Génoise* in a 9-inch heat-proof container from 2 to 2½ inches deep. Choose something attractive enough to bring to the table. Pour the diced fruit and juice over the cake and cover with the second slice of *Génoise*. Sprinkle with: **2 tablespoons kirsch**. Pour the custard cream over the cake and cover with a thick layer of meringue. Sprinkle with: **1 tablespoon confectioners' sugar** and, if desired, garnish with **fresh sliced fruit** and **maraschino cherries**. Brown in the very hot oven for 4 minutes.

CEVICHE *(Marinated Fish)*

SERVES 8

If anyone had told me that in Mexico I would not only eat raw fish but I'd like it, I'd have eaten my Mexican hat. But it's true. We had a marvelous *ceviche* in Acapulco, made of sawfish that had been marinated for a day or so. Sawfish is native to the Caribbean, and is closely related to the ray or skate, which you can get here only when the deep-sea fishermen have brought in a catch. Otherwise halibut, which is a firm white-fleshed fish with good flavor, can be used just as well. This is an excellent appetizer or first course, especially in summer, as there's no cooking involved.

halibut fillets
lemons
onions
green olives
green chilies
tomatoes
parsley
tomato puree
tomato juice
salt
Worcestershire sauce
Tabasco

FISH

Cut into cubes: **2 pounds halibut fillets.** Marinate in: **2 cups lemon juice** in refrigerator for 6 hours.

MARINADE

In a bowl mix: **2 cups chopped onion, ½ cup tomato puree, ½ cup tomato juice, 1 tablespoon salt, 16 green olives, chopped, 2 tablespoons Worcestershire sauce, 1 teaspoon Tabasco, 2 small green chilies, chopped, 3 firm tomatoes, peeled, seeded, and chopped,** and **2 tablespoons chopped parsley.**

After 6 hours, remove fish from refrigerator, pour off 1 cup of the lemon juice and add the above sauce to the fish and remaining lemon juice. Mix well and let stand in refrigerator overnight.

GUACAMOLE *(Avocado Spread)*

MAKES 2 CUPS

Elaborate canapés have been the ruination of more dinner parties than bad cooks in the kitchen ever have. We're against pre-stuffing our guests, and prefer to serve cocktails with a simple dip and crackers that are crisp but without too strong a taste of their own—English biscuits or plain matzoth are perfect. A strongly flavored *guacamole,* which we learned about in Mexico, goes well with our philosophy, our crackers, and above all with our Mexican den where we gather for a pre-dinner drink.

avocados
onion
green chili
Worcestershire sauce
(optional)
ground coriander
salt
garlic
tomato
mayonnaise
lemon
cayenne pepper
(optional)

1   Peel and seed: **2 large avocados.** Save the seeds. Mash avocados with a fork.

2   Add: **3 tablespoons lemon juice, 1 small onion, chopped fine, 1 small green chili, chopped fine, ⅛ teaspoon ground coriander, salt to taste, ½ clove garlic, minced, 3 tablespoons mayonnaise, 1 tomato, peeled, seeded, and chopped, 1 teaspoon Worcestershire sauce (optional),** and **a dash of cayenne pepper (optional).**

3   Leave the avocado seeds in mixture until ready to serve, and they will prevent discoloration. If you like a very smooth *guacamole,* remove the seeds and put mixture into blender container and blend on high speed for about 8 seconds before you are ready to serve it.

PRESENTATION

Serve in a small bowl—Mexican if you have one—with crackers or corn crisps or raw vegetables.

CHILIES POBLANOS RELLENOS *(Stuffed Green Peppers)*

SERVES 4 OR 6

Hot or sweet, a chili is nothing more nor less than a pepper. But what a profusion of them you find in Mexico! Long ones, short ones, fat ones, small ones, green, pale yellow, red, terra cotta—they are a delight to the eye with their varied shapes and colors. And to the palate as well—if you have a strong one. The little chili called *piquin* is small but mighty hot. The large green chili known as *poblano* is milder, and red pimientos are sweet. All have their place in Mexican cookery. Chilies *poblanos* can be bought in cans in many cities of the United States. Or, if you cannot find fresh ones, the long, pale green Italian peppers can be used in place of fresh *poblanos* in many recipes.

chilies *poblanos*
cooking oil
onion
garlic
ground pork
ground beef
potato
salt, pepper
raisins
blanched slivered
almonds
tomato puree
eggs
flour
sour cream

CHILIES

Roast: **12 chilies *poblanos*** (or use them canned) on a rack placed over direct flame, turning frequently, until skins are charred. Wrap in towel for 15 minutes, then remove skins. Slit on one side only and rinse out seeds. Drain on absorbent paper. For milder chilies, soak in warm **salt** water for 15 minutes, then drain.

FILLING

1 Heat: **2 tablespoons cooking oil** and in it sauté: **½ medium onion, finely chopped,** and **1 clove garlic, minced,** for 5 minutes.

2 Add: **½ pound ground pork, ½ pound ground beef, 1 small potato,** diced, **2 teaspoons salt, ¼ teaspoon coarsely ground pepper, ¼ cup raisins,** and **¼ cup blanched slivered almonds.** Cook for 10 minutes, stirring frequently.

3 Stir in: **1 cup tomato puree** and simmer for 15 minutes longer. Cool.

STUFFED CHILIES

1 Separate: **6 eggs.** Beat yolks until thick and pale in color. Beat whites until stiff. Fold egg yolks lightly into egg whites.

2 Stuff chilies with meat mixture and roll in **flour.** Dip in beaten eggs and fry in **hot deep fat** (365° F.) until lightly browned, turning once. Drain on absorbent paper. Serve with **sour cream.**

QUESO RELLENO DE CHIAPAS *(Stuffed Cheese)*

SERVES 6

This is a specialty of the state of Chiapas, and the recipe was given to me by a dark-eyed, raven-haired beauty from Southern Mexico. It is made there with Chiapas cheese, a red-coated cannonball that resembles Edam or Gouda. In Mexico they remove the red casing, hollow out the cheese ball and fill it with a meat stuffing, wrap the whole thing in a cloth and steam it for about an hour. It is delicious, but when we tried it at home with an Edam cheese it not only collapsed, but we found that Edam, when cooked, tastes like it smells—an old cow pasture. Still the *Queso Relleno* had been marvelous in Chiapas, and that dark-eyed girl. . . . Now we do it with cheddar cheese lining a casserole, using the same delicious filling and sauce from the Chiapas recipe, and the result is every bit as good as our recollection of the original.

214

cooked pork
onion
green pepper
canned stewed
tomatoes
fresh coriander
garlic
cooking oil
tomato juice
flour
butter
olives
raisins
salt, pepper
eggs
cheddar cheese
capers
beef stock
(see index)

STUFFED CHEESE

1 Grind together: **1 pound lean cooked pork, ½ medium onion, ½ green pepper, 1 stewed tomato, 3 sprigs fresh coriander,** and **3 cloves garlic.**

2 In skillet heat: **1 tablespoon cooking oil.** Add meat mixture and cook over low heat for 15 minutes, stirring occasionally.

3 Add: **1 cup tomato juice, 8 olives, pitted, 1 tablespoon raisins, 1 teaspoon salt,** and **¼ teaspoon pepper.** Remove from heat and stir in: **chopped whites of 4 hard-cooked eggs.**

4 Preheat oven to moderate (350° F.).

5 Slice thinly: **1 pound aged cheddar cheese.**

6 Line a 6-cup casserole with sliced cheese, using about half of it. Fill with meat mixture and top with remaining slices of cheese. Bake in the moderate oven for 30 minutes.

SAUCE

1 While casserole is baking make the following sauce. Chop: **tomatoes from a 1-pound 12-ounce can of tomatoes.** In saucepan heat: **1 tablespoon cooking oil** and in it sauté the tomatoes, **¼ green pepper, chopped,** and **2 tablespoons chopped onion** for 5 minutes.

2 Add: **2 tablespoons raisins, 2 tablespoons chopped capers,** and **3 cups beef stock.** Bring to a boil and simmer for 20 minutes. Strain, pressing vegetables through sieve.

3 In small skillet heat: **2 tablespoons butter.** Stir in: **4 tablespoons flour** and cook, stirring, until this roux bubbles. Stir into the strained sauce and simmer for 10 minutes longer, or until slightly thickened. Serve with the meat and cheese casserole.

FLAN *(Baked Custard)*

SERVES 6 TO 8

The rich custard dessert called *flan* is one of the specialties of Spanish-American cooking, served throughout Mexico, South America, and the Caribbean. This recipe, which was given to us by the amiable Mexican cook of some friends in Cuernavaca, produces one of the best custards ever, and is the one we use most often.

sugar
blanched almonds
condensed milk
cream
eggs

CUSTARD

1 Measure: **3 tablespoons sugar** into an 8-inch layer cake pan. Place over heat and stir constantly until the sugar melts and turns a dark caramel color. Let cool until caramel hardens.

2 Preheat oven to moderate (325° F.).

3 Into container of electric blender put: **3 ounces blanched almonds.** Blend on high speed for 3 seconds. Leave nuts in container.

4 Add: **1⅓ cups condensed milk, ¾ cup cream, 3 whole eggs** and **3 egg yolks.**

Stir to mix, then blend on high speed for 8 to 10 seconds.

5 Empty into caramelized pan, set pan in larger pan containing about ½ inch hot water, and bake for 45 minutes, or until set.

6 Cool and place in refrigerator. Do not remove from pan until the following day.

PRESENTATION

Invert onto chilled platter. There is no trick to this; it slips out easily. If desired, garnish with **whipped cream.**

215

MONTEZUMA PIE

SERVES 4

This is a sort of Mexican pizza which is named for the last of the Aztec emperors. When Cortés and the Spaniards conquered Mexico, they took over many of the strange new foods as well as a wealth of gold and silver. Peppers, corn, chocolate, and sweet potatoes were introduced to Europe as a result of the Mexican conquest. Probably even in Montezuma's time the Aztec women made the flat corn cakes called tortillas. They are still a staple of Mexican cookery, a sort of instant bread that the people fold around cooked beans or chili and eat like sandwiches. In this recipe the tortillas are used in place of a pie crust for the tomato, pepper, meat, and cheese pie. We like to serve this with a tossed salad and a glass of cold beer.

cooking oil
tortillas
tomatoes
onion
salt
chilies *poblanos*
cooked chicken
or pork
cream
cheddar cheese

1 Preheat oven to moderately hot (375° F.).

2 In small skillet heat: **1 cup cooking oil** to 360° F. and in it fry **6 tortillas**, one at a time, for about 8 seconds on each side. Do not let them get crisp. Drain on absorbent paper and cut into quarters.

3 In large skillet heat: **2 tablespoons cooking oil** and in it cook: **3 medium tomatoes, chopped,** and **1 medium onion, chopped,** for 20 minutes. Stir in: **½ teaspoon salt** and set aside.

4 Roast: **3 chilies *poblanos*** on rack over charcoal or gas flame, turning frequently, until skin is charred. Wrap in a towel and let steam for 15 minutes, then remove skin, stem, and seeds. Cut chilies into strips. (Canned chilies *poblanos* may be used instead.)

5 In an 8-inch **greased** pie plate arrange a layer of tortillas, using half, and cover with half the tomato-onion mixture, and **1 cup diced cooked chicken** or **pork**. Top with a layer of the chili strips and add: **½ cup cream.** Sprinkle with: **¼ cup grated cheddar cheese.** Top with remaining tortillas, cover with remaining tomato-onion mixture, add: **½ cup cream,** and sprinkle with: **¼ cup shredded cheddar cheese.**

6 Bake in the moderately hot oven for 15 to 20 minutes.

PRESENTATION

Serve hot, in the pie plate, and cut into wedges as you would with pizza.

SOPA POBLANO *(Chili Poblano Soup)*

SERVES 4

Corn and chilies of every variety are the mainstays of Mexican cookery. This hearty soup, a sort of Mexican minestrone, is made with both, as you might expect, but it is the unexpected ingredients that make it so good.

cooking oil
lean pork
onion
corn
salt
Parmesan cheese
chili *poblano*
zucchini
tomato puree
chicken stock
(see index)
avocado

SOUP

1 In saucepan heat: **1 tablespoon cooking oil.**

2 Add: **¼ pound lean pork, cut into small cubes,** and sauté over medium heat until pork is browned, stirring frequently.

3 Add: **½ medium onion, chopped, kernels scraped from 1 ear fresh corn,** **1 chili *poblano*, thinly sliced, 1 small zucchini, thinly sliced, 3 tablespoons tomato puree,** and **1 quart chicken stock.** Simmer for 20 minutes, or until vegetables are tender.

PRESENTATION

Just before serving, add: **salt to taste, 1 ripe avocado, peeled, seeded, and diced,** and **¼ cup grated Parmesan cheese.**

ELOTE CON CREMA A LA MEXICANA (*Mexican Creamed Corn*)

SERVES 4

Creamed corn is usually a rather pallid dish, but we found that this Mexican version was flavorful and interesting. When we had it there, it was made with a semisoft sheep cheese that came from the district of Chihuahua, unavailable in this country. Swiss or Muenster cheese are good substitutes.

corn
butter
onion
garlic
chilies *poblanos*
salt
Swiss or Muenster cheese
sour cream

1   In a skillet melt: **4 tablespoons butter.**

2   Add: **1 medium onion, chopped** (4 tablespoons), and **1 clove garlic, minced.** Sauté until onion is lightly browned.

3   Add: **the kernels cut from 8 ears of fresh corn, 4 chilies *poblanos*, thinly sliced, ½ teaspoon salt,** and **¾ cup diced** Swiss or **Muenster cheese.**

4   Cover with a towel and cook over low heat, stirring occasionally, for 30 minutes.

PRESENTATION

Serve the corn with a bowl of **sour cream** on the side. A generous spoonful on top of each portion is delicious.

ASOPAO DE POLLO (*Chicken and Rice*)

SERVES 8

Not all of our treasured Mexican recipes come from Mexico. This one comes from our favorite restaurant in Puerto Rico, La Mallorquina in Old San Juan. Oddly enough, we have also eaten it in Mexico where it is called *Asopao Puertorriqueño.* The common Spanish heritage is especially apparent in the cooking of the Caribbean and Latin-American countries, and they seem to trade recipes back and forth. We do too.

chickens
garlic
salt, pepper
oregano
lemon
olive oil
ham
onion
tomato
tomato puree
rice
canned peas
jar of asparagus tips
pimientos
green pepper

Have **2 frying chickens** cut into serving pieces, or use **8 chicken parts.**

1   Combine: **2 cloves garlic, minced, 2 teaspoons salt, 1 teaspoon oregano, 1 teaspoon pepper,** and **the juice of ½ lemon.** Rub into the chicken parts and let stand at room temperature for 1 hour.

2   Heat in large saucepan: **½ cup olive oil.** Add: **½ cup finely diced ham** and sauté for 5 minutes. Add: **1 green pepper, seeded and diced, 1 large onion, thinly sliced, 1 tomato, cut into wedges,** and **1 cup tomato puree.** Cook for 5 minutes longer. Add chicken parts and cook for 3 minutes on each side.

3   Add: **2 cups rice, 8 cups water, 2 teaspoons salt,** and **the liquid from a 1-pound can of peas.** Bring to a boil and cook rapidly, uncovered, for 15 minutes. Stir well and cook for 5 minutes longer. Lower heat, cover, and cook for 15 minutes. Stir in: **half the can of peas,** correct seasoning, and cook for 5 minutes.

4   In a separate pan, heat the remaining **peas** and the contents of **a 13-ounce jar of asparagus tips.**

PRESENTATION

Ladle the rice and chicken mixture into a large casserole. Garnish the center with remaining peas. Arrange the asparagus tips on top, radiating from the peas in the center. Take pimientos from a 4-ounce can and cut them into halves. Place **pimiento halves** between asparagus tips.

Note: You can make a delicious lobster and shrimp *asopao* by substituting for the chicken 1 pound of shrimp and 1 large lobster cut into 1-inch chunks. Omit the seasoning for the chicken, and simply add the raw shelled shrimp and raw lobster chunks to the rice mixture. Everything else remains the same, but the seafood gives the dish a completely different character.

LANGOSTA A LA MALLORQUINA *(Soufflé-Topped Lobster)*

SERVES 2

We had this marvelous lobster at La Mallorquina in Puerto Rico, and though it certainly isn't typical of the cooking in that part of the world, it is such an attractive and appetizing way to serve lobster, we pass it on to you.

lobster
olive oil
butter
sherry
cream
flour
salt
cayenne pepper
cooked shrimp
eggs
parsley
pimiento

1 Plunge **a 2-pound live lobster** into boiling water. Cover and simmer for 15 minutes. Drain and cut in half. Remove meat from tail section and cut into large medallions. Remove claw meat, keeping it whole if possible. Reserve shells.

2 Preheat oven to hot (400° F.).

3 Heat in skillet: **2 tablespoons olive oil** and **2 tablespoons butter.** Add the lobster meat and cook, stirring, until heated.

4 Add: **4 tablespoons sherry** and cook, stirring, until sherry is reduced by half. Stir in: **1 cup cream** and heat. Stir in: **2 tablespoons flour** mixed to a smooth paste with **2 tablespoons soft butter.** Season to taste with **salt** and **cayenne pepper.** Cook over low heat for 5 minutes, stirring occasionally. Drain ½ cup of the sauce into a mixing bowl.

5 Set lobster shells into shallow baking dish. Divide lobster and remaining sauce between the lobster shells. Sprinkle each with: **¼ cup finely chopped cooked shrimp.**

6 Beat: **2 egg yolks** and stir into sauce in mixing bowl. Beat: **2 egg whites** until stiff and fold into the yolk mixture. Spread this soufflé mixture over the lobster meat and bake in the hot oven for 12 minutes. Garnish each serving with **a sprig of parsley** and **two crossed strips of pimiento.**

BLACK BEAN SOUP

SERVES 8 TO 12

The Mallorquina restaurant in Puerto Rico gave us the best recipe for Mexican Black Bean Soup in our collection. Having tried the ones we brought back from Mexico, our vote goes to this one from Puerto Rico which tastes marvelous and is not hard to make. We were told to use a small bunch of Mexican tea called *"epazote,"* and Mary puzzled over that for a while, until someone at Farmers' Market explained that it was "long sour leaves." *Epazote* turned out to be sorrel, and this favorite Mexican Black Bean Soup has that in common with the lovely *Potage Tour d'Argent* that is one of our prize French recipes.

chicken stock
(see index—optional)
black beans
salt, pepper
sour cream
onion
sorrel
cooking oil or
meat drippings

1 Wash: **1 pound black beans.** Put them into a large kettle with **3 quarts water** and let soak overnight.

2 Next day, bring beans to a boil in the same water with: **3 teaspoons salt** and **1 teaspoon pepper.** Simmer for 2 hours, or until beans are very tender, adding more water if necessary. Blend 2 cups at a time of beans and liquid in electric blender until smooth and strain through a fine sieve. This will make about 7 cups thick puree, depending on the amount of liquid that has evaporated during the cooking.

3 In skillet cook: **1 large onion, minced,** in ½ **cup cooking oil** or **meat drippings**

218

for 15 minutes, or until onion is tender and golden. Tie together the stalks of **10 leaves of fresh sorrel** (sour grass), add to the onions and let stand for about 10 minutes, stirring occasionally, until leaves are wilted and flavor is extracted. Remove sorrel.

4 Add onions and oil to puree. Thin to desired consistency with **water** or **stock** and correct seasoning with **salt** and **pepper**. Heat and serve with **sour cream.**

Note: If fresh sorrel is not available, add to puree along with the cooked onion, 1 jar (1 pint 8 ounces) *schav* and 2 tablespoons red wine vinegar.

SOPA DE AJO *(Garlic Soup)*

SERVES 6

This recipe is a triumph of experiments over experience. The first time I had this soup in San Juan at La Mallorquina, I was nearly overpowered and so were my traveling companions. But I was assured that garlic soup was a great delicacy and I'd be missing something if I didn't have it in my repertoire. So I took the recipe and we tried it this way and that way. Suddenly, a marvelous concoction! Garlic soup! The trick is that your garlic must be absolutely fresh, and you sauté it very gently—don't burn it. An easy and truly delicious soup.

garlic
olive oil
eggs
salt
beef stock
(see index)

1 Chop finely: **8 cloves garlic.** Sauté in: ¼ **cup olive oil** until lightly browned.
2 Add: **1 quart beef stock** and **1 teaspoon salt.** Bring to a rapid boil.

PRESENTATION
Break **a fresh egg** into each heated soup plate. Strain the hot soup over the raw egg and serve immediately.

ALMOJABANAS *(Rice Meal Crullers)*

MAKES 30

At the Dorado Beach Hotel in Puerto Rico we had these very good, typically Spanish-American crullers. They tasted much like our hot corn bread, and I couldn't have been more surprised to find out that rice meal and cheese went into the batter, not corn at all. An interesting hot bread to serve with Mexican or Puerto Rican food.

flour
rice meal*
baking powder
salt
milk
eggs
butter
cheddar cheese
Parmesan cheese
cooking oil

1 Combine: ½ **cup flour** and ¼ **cup water** and let stand for 2 hours.
2 Mix: **1 cup rice meal***, **2 teaspoons double-acting baking powder,** and ½ **teaspoon salt.** Sift into flour mixture.
3 Add: **4 eggs,** one at a time, beating vigorously after each addition.
4 Add: **4 tablespoons melted butter, 1 cup shredded cheddar cheese,** ¼ **cup grated Parmesan cheese,** and mix well.

5 Stir in: ¼ **cup milk.**
6 Drop by half tablespoons into **hot deep fat** (360° F.) and fry for 3 minutes, turning once. Drain on absorbent paper. Serve hot.

* To make rice meal in an electric blender, put **1 cup raw rice** into container. Cover and blend on high speed for 2 minutes. Sift and discard any particles which do not go through sieve.

EL PESCADOR (*Seafood and Rice Casserole*)

SERVES 4

The Puerto Rican chef who specializes in native dishes at the Dorado Beach Hotel gave us this recipe which he assured us is a typical dish of his homeland. I believe that there are certain local herbs that they throw in for good measure, but we find we do very nicely without them, there are so many flavorful ingredients as it is.

rice
butter
saffron
cooked peas
pimiento
salt pork
oregano
ham
green pepper
onion
garlic
mushroom
tomato
salt, pepper
canned beef gravy
shrimp
lobster
brandy

SPANISH RICE

1   In a saucepan melt: **3 tablespoons butter.** Add: **1 cup rice** and sauté lightly, stirring with a wooden spoon, until rice is coated with butter and slightly golden. Add: **2 cups boiling water** and stir well. Add: **½ teaspoon saffron** dissolved in ¼ cup hot water, mixing thoroughly. Cover pan tightly and cook over low heat for 25 minutes.

2   Add: **¼ cup cooked green peas** and **2 strips of pimiento, chopped.** Set aside and keep warm.

SAUCE

1   In a skillet fry: **3 ounces salt pork, finely diced,** and **2 ounces ham, finely diced.**

2   When the meat is brown add: **1 small onion, minced, 1 clove garlic, mashed, 1**
mushroom, chopped, 1 small green pepper, seeded and chopped, ¼ teaspoon dried oregano, ½ ripe tomato, peeled, seeded, and chopped, 1 cup canned beef gravy, salt and pepper to taste. Let sauce come to boil, cover, and set aside.

SEAFOOD

1   In another skillet melt: **2 tablespoons butter** and sauté: **16 shrimp** that have been shelled and deveined and **the meat of 1 lobster** that has been removed from shell and cut into chunks. Cook for 10 minutes.

2   Flame with: **¼ cup brandy.**

PRESENTATION

Mix rice, sauce, and seafood together. Let it come to a boil and serve in a deep casserole.

BREASTS OF CHICKEN TROPICAL

SERVES 6

At the Dorado Beach Hotel in Puerto Rico, there is a fine version of chicken served in a shell—this one uses coconut shells. It takes a little practice to cut a coconut neatly in half, but it is often possible to have it done for you at the market, and the result is unusual enough to be well worth the effort.

chicken breasts
cantaloupe
honeydew melon
papaya
cream
butter
paprika
salt, pepper
sherry
coconuts
brown sauce
(see index)
flour

COCONUTS

Cut in half: **3 coconuts.** Make coconut milk from contents (see index). Remove most of coconut meat, grate it, and set aside. Reserve the 6 half shells and heat them in hot water.

CHICKEN

1   Have your butcher bone: **3 large**
chicken breasts, making 6 half breasts.

2   Shake breasts in a paper bag with: **½ cup flour, 1½ teaspoons salt, ¼ teaspoon pepper,** and **½ teaspoon paprika.**

3   In a large skillet heat: **2 ounces butter.** Sauté the chicken breasts until lightly browned.

4   Add: melon balls made from **1 honeydew melon, 1 cantaloupe,** and **1 papaya.**

220

5 Add: ¼ cup sherry and 2 table-spoons of the coconut milk.

6 Remove melon balls with a slotted spoon and set aside. Add to sauce: 1 cup brown sauce, 3 tablespoons cream, and the rest of the coconut milk.

7 Let simmer until chicken breasts are tender.

8 Remove chicken and swirl into sauce: 1 tablespoon butter.

PRESENTATION

Put a portion of chicken breast in each of the 6 coconut shells. Fill almost full with sauce, garnish with the melon balls and top with shredded coconut.

ARROZ CON DULCE (Coconut Rice Pudding)

SERVES 6

The last time we were in Puerto Rico, I had this coconut-rice dessert at the Dorado Beach Hotel and was delighted to get the recipe to bring home. With a young child in the family, rice pudding is apt to crop up on the home menus every so often and this is a delightful and different way to prepare it. Our Mary Victoria loves it.

rice
fresh coconut
sugar
salt
cinnamon
raisins

1 In saucepan combine: ½ cup rice, 1 teaspoon salt, and 2 cups water. Bring to a boil and boil rapidly for 15 minutes.

2 While rice is cooking, open a large coconut by giving it sharp glancing blows with a hammer at opposite end from the eyes. Drain water from inside coconut and reserve. Remove flesh from shell. Peel and grate enough to measure 1 cup and set aside. Dice enough of the remaining coconut to measure 2 cups. Put into container of an electric blender. Add the coconut water and enough boiling water to make a total of 2¼ cups liquid. Cover and blend on high speed for 1 minute. Strain through a fine sieve, pressing out as much of the coconut

milk as is possible with the back of a wooden spoon.

3 Add to rice: ¼ cup sugar, 2 cups of the coconut milk, and ¼ teaspoon cinnamon. Cover and cook over simmering water for 1 hour, stirring occasionally. Remove from heat.

4 In small saucepan combine: the shredded coconut, 1 cup sugar, and ½ cup water. Bring to a boil and cook rapidly, for about 15 minutes, or until most of the liquid has cooked into the coconut, being careful that it does not burn.

5 Stir the candied coconut and ½ cup raisins into the rice pudding. Serve warm or chilled.

CHICKEN IN PINEAPPLE

SERVES 1

One of our friends in Puerto Rico served this very rich, beautiful, semitropical con-coction at lunch time, and we have done so occasionally at home. The table looks most attractive with the real pineapple shells ready and waiting. It is surprising how well they hold the heat if they have been kept in very hot water for about ten minutes. And the pineapple flavor subtly creeps into the chicken and sauce.

small pineapple
cooked chicken
button mushrooms
shallots
butter
slivered almonds
sherry
cream
supreme sauce
(see index)
egg
salt, white pepper
shredded coconut

1 For each person to be served take: **1 small, ripe pineapple.** Cut off top and set aside. With a sharp knife cut out pineapple meat, leaving shell about 1 inch thick. Save fruit to be used some other time.

2 Dice: **½ cup white meat of cooked chicken** and **8 fresh button mushrooms.**

3 In a saucepan heat: **2 tablespoons butter.** Simmer diced chicken, mushrooms, and **4 chopped shallots** lightly in the butter.

4 Add: **2 tablespoons sherry** and **½ cup cream.** Allow sauce to reduce slowly for 5 minutes. Add: **½ cup supreme sauce.** Mix: **1 egg yolk** with **1 table-spoon cream** and add a little of the warm sauce, mixing well.

5 Add the warm egg-cream mixture to the saucepan gradually, beating with a whisk. Season with: **½ teaspoon salt** and **a dash of white pepper.** Do not allow chicken and cream sauce to boil.

6 Preheat pineapple shell by immersing it in hot water for 10 minutes.

PRESENTATION

Place chicken mixture inside the pineapple. Top with **slivered almonds** and **shredded coconut** and cover with pineapple top. Serve with wild or steamed rice, in a separate bowl.

UNITED STATES

M ARLENE DIETRICH once said that if she heard an American man rave about a meal, she knew he must have eaten a steak. A lot of Europeans believe this to be true of us—and they are not altogether mistaken. We do have marvelous beef here, and a slab of sirloin, broiled simply, is hard to beat as an all-time favorite.

But if you visit almost every sizable town and city in this country, as I have had to do, you will find a variety in their restaurants that is absolutely staggering. There are always a few good steak-and-chop houses in every city, but you can also eat Chinese, French, Italian, German or Scandinavian food in most big cities. And in a metropolis like New York the restaurant listing in the telephone book has *forty* different national categories, from Algerian to West Indian with stopovers at nearly every country in the alphabet in between.

You can go on a round-the-world eating binge in this country without leaving your city limits. As a matter of fact, I once took my son Barrett and a gaggle of his young friends, piled them into the station wagon, and off we went for a global tour of Los Angeles. We covered the Orient, the South Pacific, Spain and Mexico with time off for a kosher dill pickle and an American hot dog. We could have gone on to do France, Germany and Scandinavia. We could have, that is, if Daddy had been made of cast iron —and money.

Aside from this wealth of international cuisine, America boasts its own treasures of regional cookery to offer the gourmet. The South has its special way with crisp fried chicken, Virginia ham, hot breads, and my favorite starch, hominy grits. New England's no-nonsense foods include the satisfying boiled dinner, baked beans, Indian pudding, and the freshest fish and seafood served with purest simplicity. The Middle West is proud of its steaks and summertime corn-on-the-cob. The Southwest sets out the hearty fare of the wide open spaces—beef and sparerib barbecues, the spicy Mexican tamales and chili con carne. Around New Orleans the Mexican influence gives way to the more elegant and subtle creole cuisine. On the West Coast, Polynesia and the Orient are well represented. California salads achieve the status of culinary specialties to be served as a separate course. And the seafood of this coast—Olympia oysters, abalone, sand dabs, Dungeness crab—proves the Pacific is terrific for gastronomes as well as surfers.

We have to admit that much as we like to travel, to eat strange and new foods, to sip our aperitif and eavesdrop visually on the wonderful world of people all over the globe—still here at home we can eat superbly too. And because of the very melting-pot nature of our country we can eat just about any kind of food we have a fancy for at the moment.

As we said at the beginning of this book, "gourmet" doesn't necessarily mean grand or fancy or even expensive. It is just the know-how that all good cooks have and all appreciative eaters recognize. And you can't tell us that after a trip to foreign parts, after sampling all the delights of world-famous cooking, the good old American hot dog and hamburger aren't among the most treasured delicacies a returned traveler can ask for. So we salute the United States as a treasure trove of good eating—the only place in the world for us where we can enjoy international cuisine and home cooking at one and the same time.

Where but in New York could you find a bit of India blooming exotically in the basement of a smart hotel? The Pierre Grill features authentic Indian curry with all the trimmings.

The Huastecan figure in our hall looms over Mary's "sixteen-boy" curry. Props borrowed from many friends make a spectacular array of curry accessories—enough to require sixteen girls to clean up afterwards!

F. KREDEL

PIERRE GRILL

NEW YORK is one of those few cities in the world where it seems to me no one ever eats at home. Every restaurant is full, and since there is such a variety of great and good ones, maybe that explains why New Yorkers eat out so much—they can never hope to try them all otherwise. Mary and I both lived in the Big City in our theater days, and we ate around a good deal. But now when we come to New York for a spree or to work, we really cover the restaurants, revisiting old favorites and adding a few new ones to our collection. Two quick lunches we never miss—oyster stew at Grand Central Station's Oyster Bar, and Chock Full O'Nuts' cream cheese and nut sandwiches on almost any corner. Ah, gourmets!

But when we want a relaxed lunch and one of the best curries this side of Bombay, we head for the Pierre Grill. The Pierre Hotel has had a reputation for good food since its founding some forty years ago when the great Escoffier was brought over from France to supervise the cuisine. In the Grill, an informal and friendly room, they make a specialty—more than that, a ceremony—of curries prepared by an East Indian chef. Reaj Ali rules over his own kitchen, then sends his fragrant curries out into the Grill in an exotic wagon which wouldn't look amiss perched on top of an elephant. But the Pierre settles for two East Indian boys in native costume who wheel the curry wagon to your table. They serve you the curry of your choice, and sprinkle a selection of condiments over it. Mary and I usually go for the whole works—from Bombay duck to grated orange rind. And we have found curry an exciting and colorful meal to serve at our own buffet suppers at home.

Hotel Pierre

Reaj Ali suggests:

THE CURRIES OF THE DAY

East Indian Beef Curry	East Indian Chicken Curry
with Condiments	with Condiments
Tossed Green Salad	Tossed Green Salad
$3.50	$3.50

Michelob on Draught
Stein .65   Glass .50

with Your Dinner:
Carafe of Imported Red or White Wine 1.25

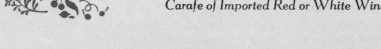

From the Broiler

Chateaubriand (for 2) 15.00   Double Steak (for 2) 15.00
Chopped Steak 3.10   Sirloin Steak 7.25   Filet Mignon 6.75
Minute Steak 6.25   Loin Lamb Chop 3.50   Half Chicken 3.00
Rib Lamb Chop 3.95   Royal Squab 4.25   Half Guinea Hen 4.00
Squab Chicken 3.50   Broiled Lobster 6.00

Cold Buffet

Cold Rib of Beef 5.25   Assorted Cold Meat 3.25   Salmon Parisienne 3.75
Galantine of Capon 3.25   York Ham 3.25   Lobster Mayonnaise (Half) 3.25
Veal and Ham Pie 3.00   Tongue à l'Ecarlate 2.85   Crab Flakes Ravigotte 3.75

Salads

Sliced Tomato 1.00   Lettuce 1.00   Caesar 2.50   Bibb Lettuce 1.35
Romaine 1.00   Vegetable 2.00   Mixed Greens 1.00   Endive 1.20

Vegetables

Fresh Asparagus Hollandaise 3.00   Spinach in Cream .95   Baby Carrots 1.00
New String Beans .90   Mushrooms on Toast 1.40   Broccoli Hollandaise 1.20
Celery with Marrow 1.10   Cauliflower au Gratin .90
Potatoes: Boiled .70   Mashed .75   French Fried .75   Baked Idaho .75

Desserts

Lemon Meringue Pie .80   Soufflé Pudding Pierre .75
Timbale of Fruits Florida .95   Nectarine Glacé Marquise 1.25
Parfait Pierre .95   Coupe Caruso 1.00
Green Apple Pie .80   French Pastry .80
Baked Apple .75   Cheese Cake Pierre 1.00   Petits Pots de Crème Assortis .80
Ice Creams: Vanilla, Coffee, Chocolate, Strawberry, Pistachio, Butter Pecan .95
Ices: Lemon, Orange, Raspberry .95

Roquefort .95   Bel Paese .95   Port du Salut .85   Bleu .80
Swiss Gruyère .95   Camembert .80   Liederkranz .75

Demi-Tasse .40   Coffee .55   Tea, Plain or with Lemon .55
Cream Portion .15   Milk .45

Couvert 35c.

CHICKEN CURRY
SERVES 6

These curry recipes come from Reaj Ali, the Moslem chef of the Pierre's East Indian kitchen. According to him a curry is not really a curry unless you use coconut milk in it. It does improve the flavor, and we have found that with an electric blender coconut milk is easy to come by—once you have your coconut, that is! You can make a meat curry of this recipe simply by substituting three pounds diced raw beef, lamb, or veal for the chicken.

cooking oil or butter
garlic
onions
canned tomatoes
bay leaf
cinnamon
cloves
chickens
salt, pepper
curry powder
cumin
coriander
paprika
coconut milk
(see index)

CHICKEN
Remove the meat from: **2 tender frying chickens**, each about 2½ pounds (or use **5 pounds of chicken parts**). A boning knife is a big help in cutting the raw meat from the bones, and you might ask your butcher to order the proper kind for you. Remove the chicken skin and cut meat into bite-sized pieces. The skin, bones, necks, backs, and wings may be used to make chicken stock.

CURRY
1 In a heavy saucepan heat: **½ cup cooking oil** or **butter.**

2 Add: **4 cloves garlic, chopped, 4 medium onions, chopped,** and sauté for 5 minutes, or until vegetables are golden.

3 Add: **2 whole canned tomatoes, chopped, 1 bay leaf, 1 teaspoon cinnamon,** and **6 cloves.** Cover and cook for 5 minutes.

4 Add the chicken meat and cook over high heat for 10 minutes, shaking pan occasionally, until most of the liquid in pan has steamed off. Reduce heat.

5 Add: **2 teaspoons salt, 2 tablespoons curry powder, 1 teaspoon pepper, 1 teaspoon cumin, 1 teaspoon coriander,** and **1 tablespoon paprika.** Stir to mix the spices with the chicken meat, being careful not to let the spices burn.

6 Add: **3 to 4 cups water,** or enough to cover chicken meat. Bring to a boil and simmer for 35 minutes.

7 Before serving add: **½ cup fresh coconut milk** and heat gently.

PRESENTATION
The best part of curry is its presentation. It is always served with a rice, and with an assortment of condiments, each in a separate bowl or dish. This curry is served with Baked Saffron Rice, the recipe for which follows, and this suggested selection of condiments.

CURRY CONDIMENTS
chopped peanuts   Bombay duck
grated coconut   grated orange rind
candied ginger   white raisins
chopped fresh parsley   nutmeg
chutney   chopped hard-cooked eggs

BAKED SAFFRON RICE
SERVES 6

rice
saffron
butter
onion
garlic (optional)

1 Soak: **½ teaspoon saffron** in **1 cup cold water** for about 2 hours.

2 Preheat oven to hot (400° F.).

3 In heavy casserole melt: **½ cup butter.**

4 Add: **1 onion, chopped, 1 clove garlic, chopped** (optional), and cook for 3 minutes, or until onion is soft.

5 Add: **2 cups raw rice** and stir until rice is well coated with butter.

6 Add the saffron and water and bring to a boil. Cover tightly and bake in hot oven for 10 minutes. Remove cover and stir to mix thoroughly.

7 Add: **2 cups boiling water,** cover, and continue to bake for 15 minutes.

8 Turn off heat, fluff rice with 2 forks, and keep warm until ready to serve.

EAST INDIAN FISH CURRY
SERVES 6

This is an interesting curry to make when you don't want to use meat, poultry, or shellfish. You can use sole, halibut, or flounder fillets—almost any firm-fleshed fish will do—and the varied curry condiments will transform your dish into something festive and exotic.

cooking oil
fish fillets
onions
tomato puree
curry powder
paprika
salt, pepper

1 In a heavy saucepan heat: **½ cup cooking oil.**

2 Add: **4 onions, chopped, 2 tablespoons curry powder, 1 teaspoon paprika, 1½ tablespoons salt,** and **1 teaspoon pepper.** Cook until browned.

3 Add: **¾ cup tomato puree.**

4 Cook until almost dry, stirring constantly to prevent burning.

5 When almost dry, add: **3 to 4 cups hot water.**

6 Boil about 20 minutes.

7 Add to sauce: **3 pounds fish fillets,** cut into pieces, and cook slowly until tender (about 15 minutes).

8 Do not stir after adding fish.

PRESENTATION
Serve fish curry on a bed of saffron rice with curry condiments.

SOUFFLÉ PUDDING PIERRE
SERVES 12

This cross between a custard and a soufflé makes a light and delectable dessert served with a hot fruit sauce. It is one of those little nothings that can be whipped up quickly and still has that extra flourish when you serve it.

SOUFFLÉ PUDDING

flour
butter
sugar
milk
sherry (optional)
lemons
salt
eggs
strawberries
red currant jelly

1 Preheat the oven to moderately hot (370° F.).

2 Heat in a saucepan: **1 pint milk** with **a pinch of salt.**

3 Cream together: **6 tablespoons flour, 6 tablespoons butter,** and **6 tablespoons sugar.**

4 When the milk boils, add this mixture and stir well for ½ minute. Remove from fire and cool slightly.

5 Separate: **6 eggs.** Add the yolks to the mixture in the saucepan. Mix well.

6 Add: **the grated rind of 2 lemons.**

7 Beat the egg whites until firm. Add them to mixture gently with a spoon.

8 Put in individual molds which have been **greased** and **sugared** (about 12 molds). Put molds in pan of hot water and bake in the moderately hot oven for about 30 minutes.

SAUCE

1 In a saucepan melt: **¾ cup red currant jelly** and **¼ cup sherry** (optional).

2 Add to the warm liquid: **1½ cups sliced strawberries** and **a squeeze of lemon juice.**

PRESENTATION
Unmold each soufflé pudding in a hot dish. Serve with hot strawberry sauce.

BUTTERFLY STEAK HONG KONG
SERVES 2

Sometimes when life in a big American city gets too jazzy, too brassy, too urban to bear for another minute, its citizens long to escape to some mythical South Sea Island. When that happens those who are really loaded with loot can book a flight on the next Pacific jet. Those who are only fairly flush settle for booking a table at Trader Vic's. In New York you walk off the sidewalk of East 58th Street and stumble into a shadowy Polynesian world dreamed up by a decorator in love with bamboo, wicker, fish net, votive lights, and the arts and crafts of the Outer Marquesas. Never mind all that. The food at Trader Vic's is marvelous, and would taste just as good at an unromantic Automat. Their Butterfly Steak with a hot sauce is particularly good, and a fine chafing-dish recipe for a small dinner at home.

STEAK

boneless sirloin steak
salt, pepper
monosodium glutamate
Dijon mustard
chili sauce
Worcestershire sauce
bottled steak sauce
beef bouillon cube
cognac

1 Trim the fat from: **a 12-ounce boneless sirloin steak**, about 1 inch thick. With a sharp knife cut it almost in half horizontally.

2 Open it up and spread it flat, so that it resembles a butterfly with open wings.

3 Pound to flatten it a little and sprinkle with: **½ teaspoon monosodium glutamate.** Rub: **¼ teaspoon freshly ground pepper** and **1 tablespoon cognac** into meat and let stand about 15 minutes.

4 Place under hot broiler or on grill, and cook 3 minutes per side for rare.

5 Place on hot platter and keep warm.

SAUCE

1 In the top of a chafing dish put: **1 teaspoon Worcestershire sauce, 1 teaspoon Dijon mustard, ¾ cup boiling water** in which **1 beef bouillon cube** has been dissolved, **½ teaspoon salt, a dash of pepper,** a dash of bottled steak sauce, and **a dash of chili sauce.** Stir and cook until sauce bubbles.

2 Put steak in chafing dish and spoon sauce over it. Heat: **1 jigger of cognac** and pour, flaming, over the steak.

STRAWBERRIES PUIWA
SERVES 4

You couldn't really duplicate any of Trader Vic's oriental or Polynesian dishes at home. That's why it's such fun to eat that kind of food out. But here is a very good dessert served there that depends more upon your neighborhood liquor store than on your kitchen equipment. It is dessert, coffee, and after-dinner liqueur all in one delicious package. As for its Polynesian name? It probably means potted strawberries.

strawberries
cream
coffee ice cream
babas au rhum
Cointreau
cognac
Grand Marnier

1 Clean and hull: **1 pint strawberries.** Set aside 4 berries. Place the rest of the strawberries in a bowl and pour over them: **3 tablespoons Cointreau, 3 tablespoons cognac,** and **1 tablespoon Grand Marnier.** Stir gently and let stand 1 hour.

2 Add to berries and liqueurs: **2 cups whipped cream.** Fold all together gently with a rubber spatula.

3 Put: **4 scoops of coffee ice cream**

(1 pint) into mixture.

PRESENTATION

1 Cut: **2 *babas au rhum*** in half horizontally.

2 Place each half, cut side up, on a dessert plate. Put a scoop of ice cream coated with the strawberry mixture on top of each piece of cake. Top with additional sauce and place a strawberry in the center of each dessert.

LANGOUSTINE MIMOSA
SERVES 5

These little *langoustines* make a wonderful hot appetizer. Although this is a recipe we got at Trader Vic's, we like to serve this dish with French bread. When you eat *Langoustine* Mimosa in the South Sea's atmosphere of the restaurant, you can almost believe you are in Tahiti where France and Polynesia meet and blend.

butter
fine bread crumbs
garlic
shallots
monosodium
glutamate
parsley
Worcestershire sauce
Tabasco
frozen *langoustines*
dry white wine

BUTTER

Cream together: ½ pound softened butter, ¾ cup fine bread crumbs, ½ clove garlic, minced very fine, ½ tablespoon chopped shallots, ½ teaspoon monosodium glutamate, ½ tablespoon chopped parsley, a dash Worcestershire sauce, and a dash Tabasco. Set aside.

LANGOUSTINES

1 Preheat oven to hot (425° F.).

2 Defrost: **25 langoustines.** Dry them well.

3 In a skillet melt: **2 tablespoons butter.**

4 Lightly sauté the *langoustines* in the butter.

5 Add: **¾ cup dry white wine** and cook until wine is reduced by half.

6 Place *langoustines* and wine sauce in shallow baking dish. (If you wish to make individual servings, use 5 small baking dishes and put 5 *langoustines* and some sauce in each.)

7 Dot with the special butter (about 1½ tablespoons per serving).

8 Bake in the hot oven for 4 minutes, or until butter has browned a bit.

PRESENTATION

Serve in the baking dish (or dishes) as a hot appetizer. If you wish, you can sprinkle a little more **fresh parsley** on the *langoustines* just before bringing them to the table.

CHINESE ROAST PORK
SERVES 4

There is one oriental dish we *can* do at home that measures up very well to the restaurant version, and that is the roast pork served in thin finger-length strips for an appetizer. It is a recipe I was given many years ago at the House of Chan, one of the oldest and best Cantonese restaurants in New York, located in the theater district. We like the pork either hot or cold, with a little soy sauce or mustard.

pork tenderloin
brown sugar
salt, pepper
soy sauce
cinnamon
sherry or rice wine
monosodium
glutamate

1 Wipe off with damp cloth: **2 pounds boneless pork tenderloin.** (You could use boned shoulder of pork, but tenderloin is better.) Cut into two strips lengthwise.

2 In a bowl mix: **2 tablespoons sherry or rice wine, 1½ teaspoons salt, ½ teaspoon monosodium glutamate, 2 tablespoons soy sauce, ½ teaspoon cinnamon,** and **2 tablespoons brown sugar.**

3 Rub seasoning mixture thoroughly into 2 strips of pork. Put them in a shallow bowl with rest of seasoning, cover, and keep in refrigerator for 3 hours.

4 Remove pork strips from bowl and allow to drain.

5 Broil under very hot broiler, turning frequently, for 1 hour. Baste with any of seasoning mixture that is left.

PRESENTATION

When thoroughly cooked remove to a board and let stand 15 minutes. With a very sharp knife cut in thin slices ¼ or even ⅛ inch thick. Serve hot or cold, with small bowls of mustard and of soy sauce to dip the slices in, if you wish.

LUNG HA FOO YOUNG (*Lobster Omelet*)
SERVES 4

The Chinese omelet called egg foo young is an easy dish to do at home, and wonderful for using up any bits of leftover seafood, chicken, pork, or veal. The Chinese vegetables that come in cans, available at almost every supermarket, enable you to make something delicious with just a few eggs and a small quantity of meat. Frying them in peanut oil seems to help give them that authentic flavor and texture.

OMELET

lobster meat
bamboo shoots
water chestnuts
scallions
cornstarch
canned mushrooms
salt, white pepper
monosodium glutamate
eggs
peanut oil
soy sauce

1 Mix together: **¾ cup boiled lobster meat, shredded** (if you are using other meats instead, dice them), **¼ cup bamboo shoots, sliced thin, ¼ cup water chestnuts, sliced thin, 3 scallions, chopped fine, ¼ cup canned mushrooms, sliced thin, 1 teaspoon salt, ¼ teaspoon white pepper,** and **½ teaspoon monosodium glutamate.**

2 Beat well: **6 eggs.**

3 In a heavy skillet heat: **½ cup peanut oil.** When it is quite hot, mix eggs and vegetables thoroughly.

4 Take one ladle full of mixture and pour into oil. Flatten it into a cake about 6 or 7 inches across. When it is slightly brown on the bottom turn and brown the other side. Remove and keep warm.

5 Repeat procedure 3 more times, or until the mixture has all been used.

SAUCE

Take: **½ cup water.** Mix: **2 tablespoons cornstarch** with a small amount of the water to make a smooth paste. Gradually add the remainder of the water, **1 tablespoon soy sauce, a pinch of monosodium glutamate** and stir over medium heat until sauce thickens.

PRESENTATION

Pour a ribbon of sauce down center of each foo young pattie and serve hot.

At Christmas time, Lüchow's old-fashioned charm is at its best. The giant tree glitters and host Jan Mitchell spreads his arms wide in a gesture of welcome to his lavish board.

Light as an eiderdown and almost as large, this German pancake comes to the table on a cloud of fragrance, in a blaze of glory.

234

LÜCHOW'S

WHEN New York was young and Fourteenth Street was the city's center of music and theater, Lüchow's was its mahogany monument to good living. Fourteenth Street has decayed over the past eighty years, but Lüchow's Old-World *gemütlichkeit* has simply grown mellower and richer. To dine there is to go back in time to an era when meals were leisurely and plentiful, and waiters really cared.

Lüchow's is one of the best German restaurants in the world. I once went there, newly arrived from the West Coast and starving for shellfish. My dinner consisted of nothing but crustaceans and my elderly waiter was in a state of shock until I ordered dessert—a flaming German pancake with applesauce. Then, somewhat revitalized, he offered me the following suggestion, "Fy don't you chust eat at the Fulton Street Fish Market undt come here for dessert?" Thoroughly chastened, I apologized and made a reservation for the next night, asking him to order my dinner for me. Needless to say, it was great—a cavalcade of all the German specialties that Lüchow's does so well, accompanied by a giant seidel of Würzburger beer. I had to walk all the way back to 52nd Street and Madison to shake it down.

At Christmas time the board really groans at Lüchow's. Then the largest indoor tree in the city blazes with lights, the orchestra plays Christmas carols, and the diners feast on oxtail soup, boiled carp, roast goose with chestnut stuffing, and plum pudding. Well, Christmas comes but once a year. Our special delights at Lüchow's go on forever, and we thank owner Jan Mitchell and his chef for enabling us to cook them at home when we're three thousand miles away from Fourteenth Street.

Lüchow's
RESTAURANT

VICTOR HERBERT

ENRICO CARUSO

LILLIAN RUSSELL

JULIA MARLOWE

THE GOURMET'S
RENDEZVOUS
Since 1882

110-112 East 14th Street
New York

PADEREWSKI

DIAMOND JIM BRADY

FRESH CHICKEN LIVERS SAUTE WITH APPLE RINGS 2.45
Tasty Chicken Livers Sautéed in Dry Sherry Wine
with Apple Rings, Smothered Onions
and Mashed in Cream Potatoes

DREI MIGNONS A LA BERLINER 6.00
Three Delicious Filets — Pork, Beef and Veal
that are delicately Sautéed in Sweet Butter and
served with Stuffed Fresh Artichoke
and Mushroom Caps

NATUR SCHNITZEL MIT IMPORTIERTEN STEINPILZEN 3.95
A Generous Portion of Sautéed Veal Steak with
Imported Cèpes, Crisp Pan Roast Potato

SCHWARZWÄLDER PFIFFERLINGE 2.35
A Rare Delicacy —
Imported Black Forest Mushrooms,
Sautéed in Butter, and served in a
Delicate Dill Sauce, with Boiled Potato

FILET MIGNON OF PRIME BEEF 6.00
A Prime Cut of Blue Ribbon Beef,
Carefully broiled to your order,
served with Salad in Bowl, French Dressing

BREAST OF CAPON A LA LÜCHOW 3.50
Flavorful Breast of Capon garnished with
Sautéed Sliced Fresh Mushrooms,
Wild Rice and Buttered Garden Fresh Peas

LÜCHOW'S

BEEF BOURGEOISE 4.25
Tender Boiled Beef which is baked
in Vegetable Jardinière or Winekraut
and served with a
Burgundy Wine Sauce with
Whipped in Cream Potatoes

PRIME SIRLOIN STEAK, ONE POUND 6.50
The finest Prime Beef,
Grilled to your exact order
and served with Salad in Bowl,
French Dressing

Cocktails

exander, Gin	1.00
exander, Brandy	1.25
cardi	.90
onx	.90
ampagne, Imported	1.25
ver Club	1.00
bonnet	.90
nd Prix Cocktail	.90
k Rose	.90
how's Special	.95
ANHATTAN	.90
URBON MANHATTAN	1.05
RTINI-GIBSON	.90
RTINI, Extra Dry	.95
DKA MARTINI	1.00
DKA MARTINI, xtra Dry	1.10
D FASHIONED, RYE	.90
D FASHIONED, SCOTCH	1.00
nge Blossom	.90
k Lady	1.00
o Roy	1.05
e Car	1.25
ger	1.25
iskey Sour	1.00
rbon Sour	1.10
ndy Sour	1.20
tch Sour	1.10

Long Drinks

ret Punch	.80
a Libre	1.00
Fizz or Rickey	.90
with Tonic	1.00
er's Planters Punch	1.10
n Collins	1.00
er or Golden Fizz	1.00
al Fizz	1.05
Gin Fizz or Rickey	.90
Collins	1.00

APPETIZERS

IMPORTED LARGE GRAIN BELUGA MALOSSOL CAVIAR 6.00   Tidbits Mixed 2.25
IMPORTED PATE DE FOIE GRAS 3.50   *Filet von Marinierten Heringen .75*
Smoked Eel .85   Crabflake Cocktail 2.00   Imported Norwegian Brislings .90
LÜCHOW'S Special Appetizer 3.00   Fresh Dill Herring, Red Onions .75
Schlemmerschnitte 3.75   *Hering Salat .75*   Apple or Tomato Juice .40
Crabflakes Ravigotte 2.50   Head Cheese, Vinaigrette .80   Imported French Sardines 1.50
Filet of Iceland Maatjes Herring .85   Shrimp Cocktail 1.50   Chopped Chicken Livers .80
Ochsenmaul Salat .80   Herring Filet, Mustard Sauce .75
Bismarck Herring .70   Lobster Cocktail 2.25   Herring Filet, Wine Sauce .75

CLAMS AND OYSTERS IN SEASON

Cherrystone Clams 1.00   Little Neck Clams 1.00   Cape Cod Oysters 1.00
Blue Point Oysters 1.00   Fried Oysters or Clams, Cole Slaw, Tartar Sauce 2.25

RELISHES

Celery .75   Ripe Olives .75   Stuffed Celery .85
Queen Olives .65   Radishes .50   Dill Pickle .30   Pickled Mushrooms .85
Imported Indian Chutney .75   Celery and Olives 1.50

SOUPS

Soup du Jour .50   Consommé du Jour .50   *Kraft Suppe .75*   Chicken Broth, Rice .65
Home Made Noodle Soup .50   French Onion Soup au Gratin en Marmite .85

FISH AND SEAFOOD (to order)

Filet of Sea Bass Sauté with Seedless Grapes, Boiled Potato 3.00
Boiled or Broiled Kennebec Salmon, Cucumber Salad, Boiled Potato 3.50
Broiled Pompano Maitre d'Hotel, Creamed Potatoes 4.00
Lobster Curried with Rice and Chutney, or à la Newburg with Toast, Chafing Dish (for 1) 4.75
Broiled Swordfish, Potato 2.50; Jardinière 2.95
Frog's Legs Fried with Tartar Sauce or Sauté Meunière, Mixed Salad 3.00
Crabflakes Creamed, Sherry Sauce, Glazed on Toast 3.50
Fried Filet of Sole, Tartar Sauce, Potato Salad 2.95
Lobster Thermidor, Allumette Potatoes 4.50   Halibut Steak, Broiled, Parsley Potatoes 2.65
State of Maine Lobster, Broiled, French Fried Potatoes, from 4.25 up
Fried Long Island Scallops, Tartar Sauce, Cole Slaw 3.25
Whole Imported English Sole Sauté Meunière, Mixed Salad, Boiled Potato 3.50 up
Fresh Jumbo Shrimps, sautéed in Dill Butter, Rice Pilaff 3.25

ENTREES

(Dishes marked with * are Ready to Serve)
Calf's Liver Steak, Smothered Onions, Mashed Potatoes 3.25; with Bacon 3.75
Filet of Veal Goulash à la Minute en Casserole, Rice 3.50
Calf's Sweetbreads Broiled, Potatoes 2.50; Bouquetière 3.00
Hamburger Steak, Smothered Onions, Mashed Potatoes 2.75
Home Made Bratwurst, Sauerkraut, Mashed Potatoes 1.75
Two Broiled Lamb Chops 3.75   Chicken Fricassée with Rice 2.75; White Meat Only 3.25
*Boiled Plate of Beef with Horseradish Sauce, Bouillon Potatoes 3.75
Sauerbraten und Kartoffel Klösse 3.25; with Red Cabbage 3.65
Corned Pig's Knuckles, Sauerkraut, Mashed Potatoes 2.50   Two Pork Chops Broiled 2.75
Chicken à la King, White Meat, Chafing Dish (for 1) Toast 3.50
Veal Chop Nature 2.85   Wiener Schnitzel 3.25; à la Holstein 3.50
Hamburger Steak à la LÜCHOW, Mashed Potatoes 2.75; Garni 3.00
Broiled Half Chicken with Boiled Potato and Mixed Salad 3.00
Tyrolian Alps Ragout 4.25   Filet of Veal with Kidney en Casserole Jardinière 3.85

PANCAKE DESSERTS

Golden Brown thin Lüchow Pancake 1.00   Lüchow Apple Pancake 1.25
Lüchow's Pancake with Huckleberries 1.40
Lüchow's Pancake with Imported Swedish Lingonberries 1.75
with Flaming Jamaica Rum .85 extra; with Flaming Kirsch .90 extra
Kaiserschmarrn: A Favorite of Emperor Franz Josef of Austria —
Sliced Viennese Pancake with Raisins, Cinammon and Apple Sauce 1.75

Bread and Butter or Toast .15

LÜCHOW'S GERMAN PANCAKE
MAKES 8 LARGE PANCAKES

At Lüchow's when you order a German pancake for dessert you get a small floor show from the waiter and captain. A pancake measuring about a foot and a half in diameter, delicately browned and hot, is brought to the serving table where the captain goes to work on it with fruit, sugar, cinnamon, and flaming liqueur. These enormous pancakes are made in the kitchen in a large, long-handled, iron frying pan. Few homes are equipped with a pan that size, but many have a twelve-inch crepe or *flambé* pan that is part of a chafing dish. This may be used successfully to produce a *pfannkuchen* not quite, but almost, as large as those made at Lüchow's and equally spectacular.

eggs
flour
salt
sugar
lingonberries
powdered cinnamon
confectioners' sugar
lemon
butter
Jamaica rum or kirsch
(optional)
milk

PANCAKE

1 In mixing bowl beat: **6 large eggs.**

2 Beat in: **1½ cups sifted flour** (1¼ cups unsifted), **¼ teaspoon salt,** and **1 tablespoon sugar.**

3 Gradually add: **2 cups milk** and continue to beat for several minutes. The batter should be thin and smooth. Pour batter into pitcher or large glass measure and let stand for 30 minutes. Makes 1 quart of batter.

4 In large crepe pan melt: **1 tablespoon butter** over medium heat.

5 When butter begins to turn golden, pour in about ½ cup of the batter. Quickly swirl pan to coat bottom with a large thin flat pancake. Cook until pancake is brown, then turn with a large pancake turner and cook until pancake is brown on other side. Slip onto hot platter.

PRESENTATION

1 While batter is standing, heat: **a jar (14¾ ounces) imported lingonberries.**

2 Set on tray on table the hot lingonberries, a shaker of powdered cinnamon, a shaker of confectioners' sugar, and a cut lemon.

3 Carry pancake to table, unrolled. Sprinkle thickly with **confectioners' sugar, cinnamon,** and **the juice of ½ lemon.** Spread with the hot lingonberries, and roll the pancake like a jelly roll.

4 Sprinkle with more **sugar** and **cinnamon.**

5 If desired, sprinkle with: **¼ cup Jamaica rum** or **kirsch** and ignite.

6 Cut each rolled pancake in half for 2 servings. (We know people who can down a whole one with ease. Namely me.)

Note: You can substitute huckleberry jam, cooked apples, or even hot chocolate sauce for the lingonberries, and this is still delicious.

This batter also makes excellent small crepes, about 8 6-inch crepes per cup of batter. It keeps for a week refrigerated.

APPLE PANCAKE
EACH PANCAKE SERVES 2

German pancake
batter (see index)
butter
apples
sugar
cinnamon

PANCAKE

1 Make pancake batter. Any batter you do not use can be stored in closed container in refrigerator.

2 In a large frying pan melt: **2 tablespoons butter** and coat bottom and sides.

3 Pour into pan: **3 tablespoons batter,** or enough for very thin coating. Tilt pan to spread batter evenly and bake for about 1 minute.

4 Cover pancake with **sliced raw apple** (about 1 apple per pancake).

5 Pour: **3 tablespoons batter** over apple. Turn cake when browned on bottom and brown other side.

PRESENTATION

Turn apple pancake out on hot platter and fold over like an omelet or roll loosely. Dash with **sugar** and **cinnamon.** Cut in half to serve 2.

240

KAISERSCHMARRN *(Emperor's Omelet)*
EACH OMELET (OR PANCAKE) SERVES 2 OR 3

The same pancake batter is used for one other specialty of Lüchow's, *Kaiserschmarrn.* A nice way of serving a smaller amount to each person.

PANCAKE

German pancake batter (see index)
raisins
butter
sugar
cinnamon

1 Make pancake batter. Any batter you do not use can be stored in closed container in refrigerator.
2 In large frying pan melt: **2 tablespoons butter** and coat bottom and sides.
3 Add: **½ cup blanched raisins.**
4 Pour into pan: **3 tablespoons batter** and tilt to spread evenly.
5 Fry on both sides till golden brown.

PRESENTATION
On a hot platter, roll up pancake. Cut with fork and spoon (do not use knife) into 1½-inch pieces. Dash with **sugar** and **cinnamon** and serve.

SCHNITZEL À LA LÜCHOW *(Veal Cutlets à la Lüchow)*
SERVES 4

Timing is important in this "short order" recipe, for the veal must be hot and the eggs cooked until just set and still creamy. It is a delicious and attractive dish to toss together at the last minute, and if you have your stock prepared and your vegetables ready to cook, you can turn it out very quickly.

eggs
chives
salt, pepper
mushrooms
asparagus
veal cutlets
butter
beef stock
(see index)
flour

EGG MIXTURE
1 Beat: **6 eggs.**
2 Stir in: **1 tablespoon chopped chives, 1 teaspoon salt,** and **¼ teaspoon pepper.** Set aside.
3 Wash and slice: **10 medium-sized fresh mushrooms** (¾ pound).

VEAL
1 With a damp cloth wipe: **4 6-ounce veal cutlets,** about ¼ inch thick. Pound with side of heavy knife or cleaver, between pieces of waxed paper, until very thin. (Or you can have your butcher do this for you.)
2 In a large skillet heat: **4 tablespoons butter** and cook cutlets in it for about 1 minute on each side, or until nicely browned. Remove to warm serving dish and keep warm.

SAUCE
Add to pan: **1 cup beef stock** and cook over high heat until liquid is reduced to ½ cup. Swirl in: **1 teaspoon butter** mixed to a smooth paste with: **1 teaspoon flour** to slightly thicken sauce. Keep hot.

PRESENTATION
1 In another skillet heat: **4 tablespoons butter** and in it sauté the mushrooms for 3 minutes, stirring constantly. Add egg mixture and cook over moderate heat, stirring constantly from sides and bottom of pan with a wooden spoon, until eggs are barely set.
2 Cook: **16 stalks fresh asparagus** and keep hot.
3 Spoon the eggs over the cutlets. Streak each serving with a band of the hot gravy and garnish platter with asparagus.

LÜCHOW'S SAUERBRATEN MIT KARTOFFEL KLÖSSE
(Pot Roast with Potato Dumplings)
SERVES 8

This sauerbraten is probably one of Lüchow's most famous specialties, and justly so. Jan Mitchell gave us the recipe, and when we tell people it takes five days to make pot roast the Lüchow way, they are terribly impressed. Actually four of the five days are carefree ones for the cook—the meat is just marinating quietly in the refrigerator. On the fifth day you cook it and eat it, and on the sixth and seventh days, if you've planned well, you have the best leftovers in the world.

MEAT

round steak
salt, pepper
onions
carrot
celery
cloves
peppercorns
bay leaves
kidney fat
butter
flour
sugar
gingersnaps
red wine vinegar

1 Wipe: **a 3-pound round steak**, from 2½ to 3 inches thick, with a damp cloth. Sprinkle with: **1 tablespoon salt** and **½ teaspoon pepper**. Place meat in an earthenware, glass, or enamelware bowl or deep dish.

2 Add to meat: **2 onions, sliced, 1 carrot, sliced, 1 stalk celery, chopped, 4 cloves, 4 peppercorns, ½ cup red wine vinegar, 2 bay leaves**, and **3½ cups water**, or enough to cover meat. Cover container and refrigerate for 4 days.

3 On the fifth day, remove container from refrigerator. Drain meat and pat dry with paper towels. Strain and reserve the liquid or marinade.

4 In heavy casserole or Dutch oven heat: **2 tablespoons kidney fat** and **1 tablespoon butter**. Add round steak and cook over high heat until well browned. Turn and brown other side. Add the marinade, bring to a boil, cover, and cook over low heat at just the simmering point for 3 hours.

GRAVY

1 In small skillet melt: **3 tablespoons butter**. Stir in: **3 tablespoons flour** and **1 tablespoon sugar** and cook, stirring, until this roux becomes a good dark color, about the color of dark brown sugar. Add to simmering meat liquid, cover, and continue to simmer for 1 hour longer. Remove meat to warm serving platter.

2 Add to gravy: **5 gingersnaps, crushed** (or pulverized for 3 seconds in an electric blender at high speed). Cook, stirring, until sauce is smooth and thickened. Strain into sauce boat and serve with the meat and potato dumplings.

PRESENTATION

To serve, slice meat slantwise as you would corned beef or pastrami, pour some of the gravy over it, and surround platter with potato dumplings. To reheat, heat some of the gravy to simmering. Add slices of meat and cook without letting the sauce boil, until meat is heated through.

KARTOFFEL KLÖSSE *(Potato Dumplings)*
MAKES 16 DUMPLINGS

potatoes
salt, pepper
eggs
cornstarch
farina
nutmeg
bread
butter
flour

1 Peel: **3 pounds potatoes** (9 medium). Cook in boiling **salted** water for about 30 minutes, or until soft enough to mash. Drain and mash thoroughly.

2 Beat in: **3 egg yolks, beaten, 3 tablespoons cornstarch, 3 tablespoons raw farina, ½ teaspoon pepper, 1 teaspoon salt**, and **¼ teaspoon grated nutmeg**.

3 Dice: **2 slices white bread**. Sauté in: **2 tablespoons hot butter** until golden brown. Drain croutons on a paper towel.

4 Shape the potato mixture into dumplings about the size of a golf ball, with a few croutons in the center of each. Roll each dumpling lightly in **flour**.

5 In a large skillet bring **1½ quarts salted water** to a rapid boil. Reduce heat to simmer and gently lower dumplings into the water. Cover skillet and poach dumplings for 15 to 20 minutes without allowing the water to boil.

PRESENTATION
Remove cooked dumplings with slotted spoon and serve hot around platter of sauerbraten.

To reheat, leftover dumplings may be cut in half and sautéed in butter to serve with leftover sauerbraten and sauce.

COLD SAUERBRATEN À LA MODE IN ASPIC
SERVES 4 TO 6

Leftover sauerbraten is nothing to sneeze at when it is reheated in its own gravy. But you can also make an elegant cold dish with it by putting the meat in an aspic, as they do at Lüchow's.

sauerbraten
Madeira
gelatin
beef stock
(see index)
vegetables

1 Measure **3 cups beef stock** and heat to boiling. Moisten: **2 tablespoons gelatin** in **¼ cup cold stock** and stir into hot liquid. Add: **1 cup Madeira.**

2 Stir until gelatin is completely dissolved and let stand until cool and slightly thickened. Makes 1 quart aspic.

3 Rinse out a 1-quart mold or loaf tin. Pour about: **½ inch thickened aspic** in bottom. Chill for 10 minutes. Place over layer of aspic: **1 pound leftover sauer-**braten, cut into thin, even slices. Have slices overlap. Cover with a layer of slightly thickened aspic and chill for 10 minutes. Place on top: **slices of cooked carrots, a few cooked peas, asparagus tips,** or other cooked vegetables for decoration and cover with 1 inch of aspic. Chill in refrigerator until ready to use.

PRESENTATION
Unmold on a platter and decorate with **cold cooked** or **raw vegetables.**

KÖNIGSBERGER KLOPS (*Meat Balls with Caper and Sardellen Sauce*)
SERVES 4

This excellent recipe from Lüchow's illustrates why their food enjoys such a reputation. The unusual addition of lemon peel and lemon juice to the meat balls, and a mashed sardine added to the sauce, lifts this dish right out of the ordinary. It's an economy meal with a flair.

ground veal
ground fat pork
butter
bread
lemon
eggs
salt, pepper
Worcestershire sauce
beef stock
(see index)
parsley
flour
skinless, boneless
sardine
capers
onion
noodles
bread crumbs

MEAT BALLS
1 Combine: **1½ pounds raw ground veal, ¼ pound ground fat pork,** and **2 tablespoons melted butter.**

2 Soak: **2 slices bread** in water until soft. Squeeze out water and add bread to meat.

3 Sauté: **2 tablespoons grated onion** in **1 tablespoon butter** until golden. Add to meat mixture.

4 Add: **½ teaspoon grated lemon peel, 3 eggs,** beaten, **½ teaspoon pepper, 1 teaspoon salt, 1 tablespoon lemon juice, 1 teaspoon Worcestershire sauce,** and **2 tablespoons chopped parsley.** Mix thoroughly and shape into 12 large balls.

(The best way to mix ground meat with other ingredients is with the hand.)

5 In a large skillet put: **5 cups beef stock.** Bring to a boil. Lower meat balls gently into the liquid, cover, and simmer for 10 minutes. Turn balls with slotted spoon, cover, and simmer for 10 minutes longer. Remove balls from stock to warm dish and strain stock into saucepan.

SAUCE
1 Combine: **5 tablespoons soft butter** with **5 tablespoons flour** to make a smooth roux. Gradually stir the roux into the hot stock and cook, stirring, until gravy is slightly thickened.

2 Stir in: **1 tablespoon butter** mashed with: **1 small skinless, boneless sardine.**

3 Stir in: **2 tablespoons chopped capers** and **2 tablespoons chopped parsley.**

PRESENTATION
1 Brown: **½ cup fresh bread crumbs** in **1 tablespoon butter.**

2 Pour the gravy over the meat balls. Sprinkle with the browned bread crumbs, and serve as they do at Lüchow's with **boiled noodles.**

CHICKEN LIVERS SAUTÉED WITH APPLES AND ONION RINGS
SERVES 2

One of Lüchow's most popular dishes, this is a marvelous way to serve chicken livers. The combination of liver, apple, and onion is so outstanding that I don't even mind dirtying the three pans necessary for their proper preparation.

chicken livers
salt
paprika
flour
sherry
butter
Spanish onion
cooking apple
sugar

LIVERS

1   Rinse and drain: **12 chicken livers**. If very large, cut in half. Season lightly with: **½ teaspoon salt** and **¼ teaspoon paprika**. Sprinkle lightly with **flour**.

2   In a skillet heat: **2 tablespoons butter**. Cook livers gently until browned on all sides. Remove livers.

3   Add to pan: **¼ cup sherry**. Stir to lift glaze, and bring to boil. Turn off heat and put back livers.

ONION

1   Slice: **½ Spanish onion** in rings.

2   In a small pan heat: **1 tablespoon butter** and cook onion rings until they are golden and translucent. Arrange on top of livers.

APPLE

1   Peel and core: **1 cooking apple**. Cut 4 slices about ½ inch thick.

2   In a third pan heat: **1 tablespoon butter**. Cook apple slices gently and sprinkle them with: **2 tablespoons sugar** to give them a glaze and good flavor. After 5 minutes, remove apple slices and place on top of liver and onions.

HERRING IN DILL SAUCE
SERVES 8 OR MORE

This is one of the most famous old specialties of Lüchow's, going back to the time of August Lüchow. The Herring in Dill Sauce had been a favorite snack of King Frederick Augustus III of Saxony, invented by his chef, one Oscar Hofmann. Lüchow was entertained by the king, admired his cuisine, and asked for permission to walk off with his chef. The story is that the king gave his consent, and that's how Oscar Hofmann came to Lüchow's. A perfect illustration of H. H. Munro's line: "He was a good cook, as cooks go; and as cooks go, he went."

fresh herrings
salt, pepper
white pepper
mustard
olive oil
wine vinegar
lemon
dill
whole allspice
sugar
red onions

HERRING

Clean: **8 fresh herrings** (there are 6 to the pound). Remove skin and cut fillets from bones. Discard bones. Rinse fillets under cold water, pat dry, and sprinkle with: **2 teaspoons salt**.

SAUCE

1   Combine: **1 cup mustard** with **1 cup olive oil**. Beat smoothly until mixture has consistency of mayonnaise.

2   Beat in gradually: **4 tablespoons wine vinegar**. Beat well and add: **the juice of 1 lemon, 1 cup coarsely chopped fresh dill, ½ tablespoon coarsely ground pepper, ¼ tablespoon white pepper, ½** tablespoon salt, ½ tablespoon whole allspice, and **2 tablespoons sugar**. If sauce is too thick, thin with a little water or vinegar.

PRESENTATION

In a deep platter or dish lay the 16 herring fillets. Pour mixture over them and let stand, covered, in refrigerator for 3 or 4 days, or until fish is well flavored with sauce. Serve garnished with **thinly sliced red onion rings**, overlapping, and **a sprig of fresh dill**.

Note: We have used this recipe for large sardines, drained of their oil, and marinated for just 24 hours. They are delicious! Almost better than herring.

BEEF STEAK TARTAR
SERVES 4

One of the pleasantest ways I know of to lose weight is to go on a raw meat binge for a few days. Prepared the way Lüchow's does it, raw beef is satisfying and energizing and it does trim you down. At Lüchow's, they use fillet of beef, but since it is being ground anyhow, I find round steak just as good.

beef (round or
fillet)
bread
eggs
sardines
capers
butter or margarine

1 Remove all fat from: **2 pounds of fillet of beef** or **round steak**. Grind meat fine.

2 Toast: **4 slices of bread** and spread with **butter** or **margarine**. Trim off crusts but serve slices whole.

3 Arrange ½ pound ground beef on each slice of toast. Put: **1 raw egg** on top of each serving.

4 Garnish each with: **2 sardines** and **½ tablespoon capers**.

SCHLEMMERSCHNITTE *(Raw Meat Lucullus)*
SERVES 4

For really deluxe tartar steak, this Lüchow recipe has no peer. It costs $3.75 an order there and is a remarkably expensive way to diet. But if you want to eat it for pure pleasure, why then it's worth every penny.

fillet of beef
bread
black caviar
onion
butter

1 Remove all fat from: **2 pounds fillet of beef**. (No use economizing with round steak on this shoot-the-works recipe.) Grind meat fine.

2 Toast: **4 slices of bread** and spread with **butter**.

3 Arrange ½ pound ground beef on each slice of toast. Put: **1 tablespoon black caviar** (fresh, if possible) on top of each serving.

4 Put: **1½ tablespoons finely chopped onion** in a little side dish and let each person sprinkle a bit on their steak if they wish. An after-dinner mint cures all.

SAURE LEBER *(Calf's Liver in Wine)*
SERVES 4

Lüchow's calf's liver is always done to perfection. I think, in the first place, they must use only very fresh liver from young milk-fed calves. Then—and this is the secret of tender liver instead of old shoe soles—they cook it for *only three minutes*. The onions and wine help, too.

calf's liver
Chablis
onion
brown gravy
(see index)
salt, pepper
butter
flour

1 In a skillet heat: **2 tablespoons butter.** Over medium heat sauté: **1 medium onion, diced very fine.**

2 When onion pieces are very soft add: **1 pound calf's liver, thinly sliced** (8 thin slices), and lightly **floured.**

3 Sauté liver for 3 minutes (1½ minutes each side). **Salt** and **pepper** lightly.

4 Add: **½ cup Chablis**, stir well. Add: **½ cup brown gravy** and let sauce come to boil. Serve piping hot, at once.

PRESENTATION
Serve the liver, onions, and gravy with boiled, buttered noodles, home fried potatoes, or rice.

DREI MIGNONS À LA BERLINER *(Three Fillets Berlin Style)*
SERVES 4

This is a marvelous dish for anyone who can't make up his mind—beef, pork, or veal? You get just a small, delightful sample of each. Served at home *Drei Mignons* makes a spectacular platter if you march everyone's portion in a row, hemmed in by the stuffed artichoke garnish.

pork fillets
beef fillets
veal fillets
butter
wild rice
cooked artichoke
bottoms
hollandaise sauce
(see index)
chicken stock
(see index)
mushrooms
nutmeg
onions
salt, pepper
sherry
béchamel sauce
(see index)
Parmesan cheese

WILD RICE

1 Wash: **1 cup wild rice.** Drain and dry thoroughly.

2 In a heavy skillet heat: **2 tablespoons butter.** Sauté: **½ cup minced onion.** When onion is golden, stir in wild rice. Cook over medium heat, stirring gently, for 3 or 4 minutes.

3 Add: **2 cups boiling chicken stock.** Cover and turn down heat to low. Cook without stirring for 30 minutes, or until all stock is absorbed.

4 Add to the cooked wild rice: **1 cup béchamel sauce, ½ cup minced, sautéed mushrooms,** and **½ teaspoon nutmeg.** Reheat and stuff into: **8 cooked artichoke bottoms.**

FILLETS *(Mignons)*

1 Wipe with a damp cloth: **4 fillets of pork, 4 fillets of veal,** and **4 fillets of beef,** weighing 3 ounces each. Pound and shape them into fairly even circles.

2 Season lightly with: **1 teaspoon salt** and **¼ teaspoon pepper.**

3 Take 3 skillets. Put: **3 tablespoons butter** in each. Sauté veal and pork fillets in separate skillets, cooking until they are tender and a golden brown.

4 Remove veal and pork fillets to a warm platter. In the veal skillet sauté: **12 mushroom caps.** Set aside and add to skillet: **1 cup chicken stock.** Cook over high heat for 2 or 3 minutes, stirring carefully. Add: **2 tablespoons sherry.** Cook and stir rapidly for 2 minutes.

5 Sauté beef fillets in their skillet last. Cook 3 minutes per side for rare. Remove to the warm platter.

GARNITURE

1 Preheat the oven to moderately hot (375° F.).

2 Place the 8 stuffed artichoke bottoms in a **buttered** baking dish. Cover each with: **2 tablespoons hollandaise sauce** and **a sprinkle of grated Parmesan cheese.** Bake in the moderately hot oven until lightly browned, about 15 minutes.

PRESENTATION

If you serve this from a large platter, arrange each portion in a row across platter. Each should have 1 pork, 1 veal, and 1 beef fillet topped with a mushroom cap. Place a stuffed artichoke bottom at both ends of each row. Pour the sherry sauce over the meat and mushroom caps.

NUSSTORTE *(Hazelnut Torte)*
SERVES 8 TO 12

Anyone who goes to Lüchow's on a diet is out of their mind. The management thoughtfully keeps a scale at the front door, but it dates from the old days when customers proudly weighed themselves to see how much they had managed to *gain* after a Lüchow feast. This old-time German torte dates from those happy times, and is a great favorite today, even with figure-conscious actors and actresses.

hazelnuts
sweet butter
cake flour
flour
sugar
eggs
cream
vanilla
confectioners' sugar

HAZELNUTS

1 Preheat oven to very hot (450° F.).

2 In a cake pan spread: **¾ pound or 3 cups hazelnuts** in one layer. Toast in very hot oven for 15 minutes, shaking pan occasionally to turn nuts so they toast evenly on all sides.

3 Spill nuts onto a clean towel and rub briskly between palms of hands to remove skins. Pick out nuts, discarding skins, and put through a nut grater or into electric blender, 1 cup at a time, at high speed for 3 seconds.

CAKE (Génoise)

1 Reduce oven to moderate (325° F.).

2 **Butter** and **flour** an 8-inch spring-form pan, 3 inches high.

3 Melt: **½ cup sweet butter** and cool it.

4 Sift and measure: **1½ cups cake flour** (be sure to measure after sifting).

5 Beat together: **¾ cup sugar** and **6 large eggs** (at room temperature).

The beating of the eggs is the secret of the success of this cake, the famous *Génoise*. Use an electric beater and beat at top speed for 5 to 8 minutes, until the mixture is as thick as a beaten meringue and holds soft peaks when beater is withdrawn.

6 Carefully fold in: **¾ cup cake flour**, then the ½ cup melted butter, being careful not to include the milky sediment which settles to bottom of pan, then the remaining **¾ cup cake flour**.

The best way, actually the *only* way, to mix this properly is with the hand, turning the frothy batter over and over with the palm until thoroughly mixed.

7 Fold in: **1 teaspoon vanilla.**

8 Pour batter carefully into prepared pan and bake in the moderate oven for 45 to 50 minutes, or until cake tester comes out clean. Run spatula around cake to loosen it from edge of pan, remove sides of pan, and cool cake on rack. When cool, remove from bottom of pan and slice into 3 layers with a serrated knife.

FILLING

1 Whip until stiff: **2 cups cream.**

2 Fold in: **½ cup sugar, 2½ cups ground hazelnuts**, and **1 teaspoon vanilla.**

GLAZE

Beat together: **2¼ cups unsifted confectioners' sugar** and **3 tablespoons water** to make a thin glaze.

PRESENTATION

Place bottom layer of cake on a rack over waxed paper. Put the three layers of cake together with whipped cream-hazelnut filling between each layer. Pour the glaze on top of cake. It will flow slowly over sides, leaving a translucent glaze on top. Quickly run a spatula around sides of cake, spreading glaze as smoothly as possible, and letting excess run through cake rack. Sprinkle sides and top with remaining: **½ cup ground toasted hazelnuts.**

Refrigerate the cake for several hours before cutting it.

KRAFT SUPPE *(Beef Soup with Marrow)*
SERVES 8

This excellent soup is served at Lüchow's in a large silver cup from which it is poured, steaming and fragrant, into a soup bowl. I had never realized, when eating it at the restaurant, that the marrow was raw. Actually the soup is so hot when it is poured, that the marrow poaches a little. In any case, it tastes so good, forget that you know it isn't cooked and enjoy this delicacy.

beef short ribs
salt, pepper
leek
celery
carrots
butter
cloves
potato
chives
bay leaf
onion
beef marrow
parsley
dill

1 In bottom of heavy soup pot brown: **1½ pounds beef short ribs** in **1 tablespoon butter.** Cover meat with: **3 quarts water** and bring to a boil. Turn heat down to simmer and skim the top for about 5 minutes until all scum is removed.

2 Add: **1 teaspoon salt, ½ teaspoon pepper, 1 leek, 1 stalk celery, 1½ carrots, diced, 1 onion** stuck with **2 cloves, 1 bay leaf, 2 sprigs parsley, 2 sprigs dill.**

3 Bring to boil. Lower heat, cover, and simmer for 1½ hours. Add: **½ potato, diced,** and cook 1 hour longer.

4 Skim off all fat from top.

PRESENTATION

Remove meat and cut into small pieces. Remove pieces of carrot and potato and set aside. Strain soup and put back meat, carrots, and potato. Reheat to boiling. Serve with: **2 small slices raw beef marrow** garnished with **chopped chives** in each soup bowl.

MUSHROOMS IN SOUR CREAM
SERVES 6

Lüchow's makes a specialty of the marvelous wild mushrooms that grow in European forests—*Schwarzwälder pfifferlinge* and *steinpilzen* to name two of them. We have wild mushrooms here too, but if you can't tell the poisonous ones from the nonpoisonous without eating them first, better do as we do and play it safe with cultivated mushrooms.

mushrooms
butter
onion
salt, pepper
flour
sour cream
meat extract
parsley

MUSHROOMS

1 Wash: **2 pounds fresh mushrooms.** Dry them and break off stems. Slice in quarters.

2 In a skillet heat: **3 tablespoons butter.** When butter stops foaming, add the mushrooms. Sauté for 2 minutes. Add: **1 teaspoon salt** and **¼ teaspoon pepper.**

3 Add: **1 medium-sized onion,** peeled. Lower heat, cover pan, and cook gently for 15 to 20 minutes. Remove onion.

4 Sprinkle on mushrooms: **1 tablespoon flour.** Stir gently. Stir in: **½ teaspoon meat extract.** When it is completely melted add: **1 cup commercial sour cream.** Stir well and heat for a few minutes but do not let mixture boil.

PRESENTATION

Sprinkle with: **1 tablespoon chopped fresh parsley** just before serving.

Portrait of three Vincents—Sardi, Sr., Price, and Sardi, Jr. This is New York's most famous theatrical restaurant, and the Sardis' well-fed customers include nearly every stage luminary of our time.

Boccone Dolce, Sweet Mouthful, is the name of Sardi's Italian icebox cake. No actor, having tasted it, could fail to speak his speech trippingly on the tongue and in honeyed tones at that.

KREDEL

SARDI'S

THE NAME Sardi's means theater as much as it does good food. Every actor who has ever played in a New York show knows the opening-night ceremony of waiting at Sardi's for the early morning newspaper reviews. Thumbs up or thumbs down? While the cast and producer await the verdict they can try to calm their butterflies with Sardi's wonderful food. Believe me, the food must be superlative to be a distraction at a time like that!

In the old days, Vincent Sardi, Sr. was a legendary benefactor of broke and hungry actors. I wasn't broke when I first went to Sardi's, thank God, but I was lonely. Because of the welcome I received I can claim a regular three-times-a-week attendance at Sardi's during the three-year run of *Victoria Regina* in which I appeared with Helen Hayes, and many repeats thereafter.

Closing-night parties are another tradition at Sardi's. But at any time, from lunch through the small hours of the morning, you are likely to see a galaxy of Broadway stars eating at Sardi's. And those you don't see in the flesh adorn the walls in the seven hundred or so Gard caricatures that are part of Sardi's fame. Gard himself selected his subjects, and his rogues' gallery is known as "Gard's Chosen People." I am proud to be one of them, portrayed in 1949 as the bearded, evil Mr. Manningham of *Angel Street*.

Over the years I have developed a special fondness for certain Sardi dishes. Vincent Sardi, Jr., who now operates both the original restaurant and the newer Sardi's East, carries on his father's tradition of kindness to actors. He gave this actor—and now cookbooker—the recipes for these favorite dishes, so my gratitude continues unto the second generation.

Hors d'Oeuvres
(75c. Additional Charge for Hors d'Oeuvres Served as a Main Course)

Alaska King Crab Meat Cocktail 1.75
Blue Point Oyster Cocktail 1.00
Heart of Artichoke, Vinaigrette 1.50
Pate de Foie Gras, Strasbourg 3.25
Marinated Herring 1.25

V-8 Juice 50
Sliced Italian Salami 1.35
Tomato Juice 50
Cannelloni Appetizer 1.50

Shrimp Cocktail 1.50
Lobster Cocktail 2.35
Avocado Pear and Prosciutto 1.75
Fresh Beluga Caviar 6.00 p.p.
Pineapple Juice 50

Relishes

Hearts of Celery and Green Olives 75
Stuffed Celery 1.00
Pickled Black Walnuts 50

Radishes 50

Ripe Olives 50
Carrot Sticks 50
Major Grey's Chutney 50

Soupes
(75c. Additional Charge for Soupes Served as a Main Course)

Beef Bouillon on the Rocks 75
Vegetable Soup 75

Chicken Broth 75
Split Pea Soup 75

Green Turtle Amontillado 1.25
Onion Soup au Gratin 1.00

Grillades

Minute Steak 5.75   Sirloin Steak (for one) 6.85   (for two) 13.75   Chateaubriand (for two) 13.75
Planked Double Sirloin Steak with Vegetable and Potatoes (for two or more) .... 8.75 per Person
Filet Mignon 6.85   Broiled Half Chicken 3.00   Lamb Kidney and Bacon 3.00
Sliced Calf's Liver and Bacon 3.50   Broiled Ham Steak, Pineapple 3.25
Lamb Chops (2) 3.75   French Lamb Chops (2) 3.75
Double English Lamb Chop with Lamb Kidney, Bacon and Currant Jelly (25 Minutes) ... 4.25
Broiled Mushrooms 3.00   (Side dish with Steaks, etc.) 1.25   Chopped Sirloin Steak 3.25
Broiled Maine Lobster with Drawn Butter and Potatoes (Price according to size)
Roast Prime Ribs of Beef au Jus, Baked Idaho Potato 4.85   with Rib 5.25
(Sauce Bearnaise or Garlic Butter 50c. per Person)   (Sauce Maison 25c. per Person)

Pomme de Terre

Mashed Potatoes 65   French Fried Potatoes 65   Boiled Potatoes 65   Home Fried Potatoes 75
Baked Potatoes 65   with Chives and Sour Cream 90   Hashed Browned Potatoes 75   Au Gratin 75

Salades

Avocado Pear and Grapefruit 1.50   Mixed Greens 75   Romaine 75
Escarole 75   Heart of Palm, Vinaigrette 1.50   Combination Salad 1.00
French Endive 1.25   Spinach with Bacon 1.25   Cresson 75   Avocado Pear Salad 1.25
Sliced Tomato 75   Hearts of Lettuce 75

(75c. Additional Charge for Above Salades Served as a Main Course)

Crab Meat Salad 3.75   Fruit Salad 2.75   Lobster Salad 4.25

Chicken Salad 3.25   Shrimp Salad 3.50

Felix Dressing 25   *Lorenzo Dressing 25*   *Cheese Dressing 50*

We will gladly furnish a receipt upon request for expenditures made while dining at Sardi's.

Hors d'Oeuvres and Potages du Jour
(75c. Additional Charge for Hors d'Oeuvres Served as a Main Course)

Bismarck Herring 1.25
Cape Cod Oyster Cocktail 1.10
Sliced Italian Salami 1.25
Beluga Caviar 6.00 p.p.
Seafood Cocktail 2.50   Crab Meat Cocktail 1.75
Cream of Tomato Soup aux Croutons 75   Cold Vichyssoise 75
Consomme with Rice 75

Cherrystone or Little Neck Clam Cocktail 1.00
Supreme of Grapefruit 75
Escargotte Bourguignonne 1.75
Smoked Brook Trout with Horseradish Sauce 1.75
Half Cantaloupe 75
Vegetable Soup 75
Minestrone a la Milanese 75

Poissons

BROILED SWORDFISH STEAK Maitre d'Hotel with French Fried Potatoes 3.50
FRIED DEEP SEA SCALLOPS with Tartar Sauce and Cole Slaw 3.00
FROG'S LEGS SAUTE aux Pignoli with Stewed Tomatoes 3.75
SHAD ROE SAUTE aux Amandines with Pomme Vapeur 3.75
BROILED FILET OF RED SNAPPERS Colbert with Saratoga Chips 3.75
FRESH SALMON AU GRATIN with Garden Peas 3.25

Plats de Resistance

BAKED OLD FASHIONED CHICKEN POT PIE with Oysters a la Golden 3.75
BREAST OF PHEASANT au Porto Wine Sauce, Garni with Wild Rice 6.00
SPAGHETTI WITH MEAT BALLS en Casserole 2.75
YANKEE POT ROAST OF BEEF aux Legume Glace en Casserole 3.25
ROAST PRIME RIBS OF BEEF AU JUS with Baked Idaho Potato 4.85
GRILLED BROCHETTE OF SPRING LAMB with Rice a la Grecque 3.85
ROAST WHOLE ROCK CORNISH GAME HEN Veronique with Wild Rice and Garden Peas 4.75
BREADED VEAL CUTLET SAUTE au Beurre with Green Noodles 3.75
ROAST HALF L. I. DUCKLING BIGARADE with Lima Beans 4.00
HALF SPRING CHICKEN SAUTE PRINTANIERE en Casserole 3.50
BROILED HAM STEAK with Candied Sweet Potato 3.25

Legumes

Fresh Asparagus Hollandaise 1.50   Egg Plant au Parmesan 1.25   Wild Rice 1.25   Braised Celery 1.00
Corn Saute 75   Plain Spinach 75   Vegetable Dinner 2.75
Heart of Artichoke, Hollandaise 1.50   Petits Pois 80   Creamed Spinach 85
Buttered Carrots 75   Buttered String Beans 75   Broiled Tomato 80   Stewed Tomatoes 75
Broccoli, Hollandaise or Butter Sauce 1.25   Spinach and Mushrooms Saute au Beurre 1.00

Desserts
(Additional Charge for Desserts and Beverages Served as a Main Course)

Banana Cream Pie 75
Old Fashion Strawberry Shortcake 1.00
Danish or French Pastry 75   Apple Pie 75
Fresh Strawberries with Sour Cream 1.50   Snow Ball, Chocolate Sauce 90
French Cheese Cake 75   Coupe au Cherise 90   Moka Parfait 90   Baked Apple 75   Bisquit Tortoni 75
Frozen Cake, Zabaione Sauce 85   Baked Alaska (for 2) 3.50   Crepes Suzette (for 2) 4.00
Orange Sherbet or Lemon Ice or Vanilla, Chocolate, Butter Pecan, Strawberry or Chocolate Ice Cream with Cookies 75
Rice Pudding 75   Jello 75   Plain Cake 75   Raisin Cake 75   Caramel Custard 75

Fresh Stewed Rhubarb 75
Boccone Dolce 85
Lemon Sherbet with Creme de Menthe 1.25
Peach Melba 90

Assorted Imported Cheese with Crackers 80c. per Portion   with Fresh Pear or Apple 25c. Additional
ORDERS ACCEPTED IN ADVANCE FOR SPECIAL CAKES AND PASTRIES

Beverages

Pot of Coffee 40   Pot of Tea 40   Milk 40   Florentine Coffee 40   Neapolitan Coffee 40
Buttermilk 40   Pot of Sanka 40   Pot of Postum 40   Iced Coffee or Tea 40

B. & B. 50c. p.p.   Saturday, March 28, 1964

Private Dining Rooms Are Available for Luncheon, Cocktails, Dinner and After-Theatre Functions.

BOCCONE DOLCE (*Sweet Mouthful*)
SERVES 8

This is actually an icebox cake, the like of which I've never tasted anywhere but at Sardi's. The combination of strawberries and bittersweet chocolate in a meringue-and-whipped cream cake is enough to send you right out of this world!

eggs
salt
cream of tartar
sugar
semisweet chocolate
cream
strawberries

MERINGUE LAYERS

1 Preheat oven to very slow (250° F.).

2 Beat until stiff: **4 egg whites, a pinch of salt,** and **¼ teaspoon cream of tartar.**

3 Gradually beat in: **1 cup sugar** and continue to beat until the meringue is stiff and glossy.

4 Line baking sheets with waxed paper, and on the paper trace 3 circles, each 8 inches in diameter. Spread the meringue evenly over the circles, about ¼ inch thick, and bake in the very slow oven for 20 to 25 minutes, or until meringue is pale gold but still pliable.

5 Remove from oven and carefully peel waxed paper from bottom. Put on cake racks to dry.

FILLING

1 Melt over hot water: **6 ounces semisweet chocolate pieces** and **3 tablespoons water.**

2 Whip: **3 cups cream** until stiff. Gradually add: **⅓ cup sugar** and beat until very stiff.

3 Slice: **1 pint fresh strawberries.**

PRESENTATION

Place a meringue layer on serving plate and spread with a thin coating of melted chocolate. Then spread a layer about ¾ inch thick of the whipped cream and top this with a layer of the sliced strawberries. Put a second layer of meringue on top, spread with chocolate, another layer of the whipped cream and sliced strawberries, then top with third layer of meringue. Frost sides smoothly with remaining whipped cream. Decorate top meringue layer in an informal pattern, using remaining melted chocolate squeezed through a pastry cone with a tiny round opening. Or you may decorate with **whole ripe strawberries.** Refrigerate for 2 hours before serving.

LONDON BROIL
SERVES 4

London broil, which is served at all too few restaurants, is my favorite standby at Sardi's. Much leaner than steak, it makes a hearty yet nonfattening lunch or dinner.

top round of beef
cooking oil
salt, pepper
butter
red wine (optional)
consommé (optional)

BEEF

Sardi's uses a prime beef top round, cut at least 2½ inches thick. A **2-pound piece of beef,** cut for London broil, should measure 3 inches wide and 8 inches long.

1 Brush the meat with **cooking oil,** place on broiler pan, and sprinkle with **salt** and **pepper.**

2 Broil for 10 minutes, turn and broil for 10 to 15 minutes longer, or until done to taste. (This is for rare.)

3 Place on hot serving platter.

PRESENTATION

1 To juices in dripping pan add: **½ cup water, red wine,** or **consommé.** Cook, stirring in brown glaze in pan. Add: **1 tablespoon butter** and stir until butter is melted. Correct seasoning.

2 Carve the meat crosswise on a slant in thin slices and serve with the pan gravy in a separate gravy boat.

HOT SHRIMP À LA SARDI
SERVES 2

This is the most special of Sardi's first courses, a dish that is their own invention and for which Vincent not only gave me the recipe, but a small cooking lesson into the bargain. He wanted to be sure that my version of his dish had no ad-lib flourishes thrown in by me, and all I can say is that I'm glad Vincent Sardi doesn't write plays. The poor actors would really have to stick to the script, down to the very last crossed "t" and dotted "i"!

Sardi's meat sauce
(see index)
shrimp
butter
dry white wine
garlic
bread

1   Make Sardi's meat sauce. (The recipe will make 6 cups, but you can freeze what you don't use for the shrimp.)

2   Preheat oven to hot (400° F.).

SHRIMP

Poach: **12 medium shrimp** in simmering water for 5 minutes. Drain and remove shells and dark vein running down backs. Set aside.

SAUCE

Heat: **1 cup Sardi's meat sauce** and **½ cup dry white wine.** Stir in: **1 clove garlic, minced.**

PRESENTATION

1   Trim the crusts from: **2 slices bread** and cut into triangle halves. Sauté until golden in: **1 tablespoon butter** to which has been added: **½ teaspoon minced garlic.**

2   Take 2 individual au gratin dishes. Place 6 cooked shrimp in each and cover with hot sauce. Arrange 2 garlic croutons like wings in center of dish and heat in hot oven for 10 minutes, or until sauce is very hot and bubbly. Serve immediately.

FROGS' LEGS POLONAISE
SERVES 2

If you like frogs' legs, you will like the delicate and simple way they are prepared at Sardi's. No overwhelming garlic, a light hand with the seasonings, and a sauce that is just right for this crispy sautéed delicacy. They are usually served with boiled new potatoes.

frogs' legs
light cream
flour
butter
paprika
salt
egg
parsley
lemon

FROGS' LEGS

1   Pour in a bowl: **¼ cup light cream.** Dip in it: **8 small frogs' legs.** Dip them in **flour** and coat evenly.

2   In a skillet heat: **3 tablespoons butter.** Sauté the frogs' legs for about 10 minutes, browning on both sides. Sprinkle with: **¼ teaspoon salt.**

3   Remove from heat and keep warm, uncovered, so frogs' legs stay crisp.

SAUCE

Pour off used butter and add to skillet: **3 tablespoons butter, 1 hard-cooked egg, riced, 1 tablespoon chopped parsley,** and **½ teaspoon lemon juice.** Cook over high heat for 1 minute.

PRESENTATION

Pour the hot sauce over frogs' legs. Decorate platter with: **2 slices lemon,** dipped in **chopped parsley** and **paprika.**

ÉMINCÉ OF CHICKEN TETRAZZINI AU GRATIN
(Chicken and Spaghetti Casserole)
SERVES 6

This chicken and spaghetti dish was invented for the opera star Luisa Tetrazzini, who lived and sang in the days when calories *really* didn't count. Sardi's version of chicken Tetrazzini is especially good because their interesting sauce adds that little something special to it. We like this same recipe made with a pound of sautéed chicken livers in place of the cooked chicken sometimes. Try it both ways and see if it isn't something to sing about.

butter
mushrooms
cooked chicken
sherry
supreme sauce
(see index)
hollandaise sauce
(see index)
cooked spaghetti
Parmesan cheese
light cream
salt, white pepper

1 In a skillet melt: **¼ cup butter.** Sauté in it: **1 cup sliced mushrooms** for about 5 minutes.

2 Add: **3 cups diced cooked chicken** and shake well to distribute chicken and mushrooms evenly.

3 Add: **¼ cup sherry,** stir, and cook 5 minutes.

4 Add: **1 cup supreme sauce,** stir well, and add: **½ cup hot light cream.** Mix all thoroughly.

5 Simmer slowly for 5 minutes, and stir occasionally, so sauce does not scorch. Do not let it boil. Taste for seasoning and add: **½ to 1 teaspoon salt,** if necessary, and **⅛ teaspoon white pepper.**

PRESENTATION

Take an 8-cup **buttered** casserole or 6 individual **buttered** baking dishes. Cover the bottoms with: **3 cups cooked spaghetti** (see directions on package). Fill with hot chicken and sauce, and top the large casserole with: **¾ cup hollandaise** or top each individual portion with: **2 tablespoons hollandaise.** Sprinkle with: **¼ cup grated Parmesan cheese** and brown lightly under broiler.

ASPARAGUS VINAIGRETTE
SERVES 6

This is an excellent cold vegetable to use instead of a salad. It is also an interesting way to serve leftover asparagus, than which there is nothing limper and sadder looking when you open your refrigerator door. The vinaigrette sauce perks it right up, and does well by cold boiled artichokes and salads, too.

cooked asparagus
dill pickle
onion
capers
olive oil
dry mustard
(optional)
parsley
pimiento
egg
salt
wine vinegar
lemon (optional)

ASPARAGUS

Cook asparagus according to directions in recipe for Asparagus Milanese. Although you can use leftover asparagus very nicely, the vegetable is firmer if you have boiled and chilled it especially for this dish. Allow 8 to 10 spears of asparagus per serving, with about 2 tablespoons of sauce.

SAUCE VINAIGRETTE
(Makes ¾ Cup)

1 Place in a screw-top jar the following ingredients: **½ dill pickle,** finely chopped, **1 tablespoon finely chopped onion, 1 teaspoon capers,** finely chopped, **1 teaspoon salt, ¼ teaspoon dry mustard** (optional), **2 tablespoons wine vinegar, 1 teaspoon lemon juice** (optional), and **½ cup olive oil.**

2 Put top on jar and shake vigorously for about ½ minute, or until all ingredients are well blended.

3 Remove jar top and add: **1 tablespoon finely chopped parsley, 1 tablespoon finely chopped pimiento,** and **1 teaspoon finely chopped hard-cooked egg white.**

4 Stir well and pour over asparagus.

ASPARAGUS MILANESE
SERVES 4

An ideal luncheon dish, this, and for all its simplicity, one which I've never seen served anywhere but at Sardi's. I used to pop in on matinee days and order Asparagus Milanese which happily combined breakfast and lunch and carried me through an afternoon performance in fine fettle.

ASPARAGUS

asparagus
eggs
butter
Parmesan cheese
salt

1 Cut off the tough ends from: **2 pounds asparagus.**

2 With a vegetable knife scrape off the tough outer skin and any scales on the spear below the tip.

3 Wash in a large bowl of cold water, being careful to remove all sand.

4 Tie in bunches of about 12 medium spears each.

5 In a large pot bring to a rapid boil: **6 quarts water** and **3 tablespoons salt.** Gently lower asparagus bundles into boiling water so that they lie flat.

6 When water boils again, reduce heat and allow to boil slowly 14 minutes, uncovered.

7 Remove asparagus bunches carefully, supporting at ends and tips. Remove strings and drain asparagus on a folded towel.

PRESENTATION

Put 8 spears of the asparagus on each warm plate. Cover with: **2 fried eggs.** Pour over each portion: **2 tablespoons brown melted butter** and sprinkle with: **1 tablespoon grated Parmesan cheese.**

CANNELLONI AU GRATIN WITH SARDI SAUCE
SERVES 6

At Sardi's, a delicate mixture of chicken and spinach is rolled, first in a crepe, then in a cooked *cannelloni* rectangle. The first time I tried this recipe at home I started from scratch, even with the meat sauce. It seemed that I was cooking for three days only to wind up with Sardi's *cannelloni*, which I can have in ten minutes anytime I go there. Now life is simpler. The meat sauce comes out of the freezer, and we use *either* the crepes or the *cannelloni*, not both. Easier and less fattening.

French crepes
without sugar
(see index)
or
cannelloni
(see this recipe)
eggs
flour
butter
chicken stock
(see index)
salt, white pepper
cheddar cheese
Sardi's meat sauce
(see index)
light cream
cooked chicken
cooked spinach
Parmesan cheese

CANNELLONI

1 In mixing bowl beat: **3 eggs.**

2 Gradually beat in: **1½ cups flour,** ½ cup at a time, to make a sticky paste. Turn paste out onto a pastry board sprinkled with: **½ cup flour** and knead in as much of this additional flour as necessary to make a firm, smooth dough. Divide dough in half, cover with a towel, and let rest for 30 minutes.

3 Roll out *cannelloni* paste, half at a time, on **floured** board. Roll very thin and cut into rectangles about 6 x 4 inches.

Place on towel to dry for a few hours or overnight.

4 Cook the *cannelloni* in rapidly boiling **salted** water for 5 minutes. Drain and cover with cold water. Set aside.

CANNELLONI SAUCE

1 In saucepan heat: **4 tablespoons butter** until melted.

2 Stir in: **5 tablespoons flour.**

3 Add: **1½ cups hot chicken stock** and cook, stirring rapidly, until sauce is smooth and thickened. Cook over low

257

heat for 5 minutes. Add **salt** and **white pepper** to taste.

4 Stir in: **¾ cup ground cheddar cheese** and stir until cheese is melted.

5 Stir in: **1 cup Sardi's meat sauce** and **½ cup light cream.** Keep hot.

FILLING

1 Grind: **2 cups chopped cooked chicken** and **½ cup chopped cooked spinach.** Put mixture into saucepan.

2 Stir in: **¼ cup grated Parmesan cheese** and **¾ cup chicken stock.** Cook over low heat, stirring occasionally, for 20 minutes. Remove from heat and cool.

PRESENTATION

1 Preheat oven to very hot (450° F.).

2 Spread each crepe or *cannelloni* with about 3 tablespoons of the chicken mixture and roll up. Place 2 per person in individual baking dishes. Cover each 2 with ½ cup *cannelloni* sauce. Sprinkle each with: **1 tablespoon grated Parmesan cheese,** and bake in very hot oven for 10 minutes. Serve at once.

SARDI'S MEAT SAUCE
MAKES 6 CUPS

This meat sauce is excellent just as it is, served on spaghetti or any of the pastas. But mixed with other ingredients it becomes a base for other Sardi specials. When we make a batch, the kitchen smells like Italian heaven. We like to store the delicious sauce in the freezer and have it on hand for whenever we're in a Sardi mood.

ground beef
ground veal
sage
oregano
salt, pepper
onion
mushrooms
garlic
canned tomatoes
tomato puree
tomato paste

1 Preheat oven to moderate (350° F.).

2 Mix: **1 pound ground beef** and **¼ pound ground veal.** Spread meat in a baking pan and cook in the moderate oven for 20 minutes. Stir and continue to cook for 10 minutes longer.

3 In a saucepan combine: **¼ teaspoon sage, ¼ teaspoon oregano, 1 tablespoon salt, ½ teaspoon pepper, 1 onion, ground, ¼ pound mushrooms, ground (4 medium),** and **3 cloves garlic, ground.** Heat, stirring, on top of stove.

4 Spread over meat and continue to cook in oven for 15 minutes longer.

5 Remove meat mixture from oven and transfer to a large saucepan.

6 Add: **4 cups canned tomatoes, 1 cup tomato puree,** and **½ cup tomato paste.** Mix well, bring to a boil, and simmer for 1¼ hours. Correct seasoning with **salt,** cool, and store in refrigerator, where it will keep for at least a week, or in freezer. Reheat when needed.

At The Four Seasons you dine in luxury beside a quiet pool
with New York as a backdrop beyond the tall windows.
The hors d'oeuvre wagon offers
just a small sample of what is to come.

A dinner party at our house is illuminated by Mary's candelabra
made out of old lamp parts and secondhand brass turnings.
The lazy Susan is weighed down with our collection of mercury
glass, loaded with flowers. The napkins are folded
like water lilies around copper luster bowls and metal cups
from India. In this scrumptious setting we serve
as a first course the simplest of dishes—Vermont Cheese Soup.

THE FOUR SEASONS

I F THERE IS one restaurant that epitomizes New York today it is The Four Seasons. Sophisticated, urbane, expensive, its stark geometry reflects that city of skyscrapers. Nature is permitted to intrude, as it does on the city itself, in seasonal plantings that scarcely affect the austere architecture. New Yorkers who dine at The Four Seasons know which season has arrived by the plants in the window baskets. Who needs a calendar?

Perfectionists down to the last tiny detail, the management of the restaurant have planned a cuisine that is seasonal too. The menu changes four times a year and in this day of frozen foods that are monotonously available all year 'round, it's fun to get the fresh things only in season and only at their very best. Vegetables, usually the dullest part of restaurant meals, are a special treat at The Four Seasons. They use only young tiny ones, and you select them not from the menu but from a basket that is brought to your table. Baby peas, asparagus, beans, carrots are arranged like a rustic still life, and the ones you choose are then prepared to order for you. Desserts are wheeled over to each table on a special dessert wagon, and hors d'oeuvres are yours to choose from an iced wagon that displays them like a work of art.

The Four Seasons has a pretty stupendous real work of art too—Picasso's original stage curtain, painted for the ballet, *The Three-Cornered Hat*. In scale with the generous proportions of this restaurant, the Picasso measures a heroic twenty feet by twenty-two feet! On top of all this, I hasten to add, the food is good—delicious and unusual.

Dinner at

ICED BROCHETTE OF SHRIMP 2.25   PERIWINKLES *Mignonette* 1.65
Small Clams with Green Onions and TRUFFLES 1.65
YOUNG SALMON OR STURGEON, *Our Smokehouse* 2.95
SUMMER *Hors d'Oeuvre, A Sampling* 2.50
LOBSTER CHUNKS *with Sorrel* 3.25   A TUREEN OF AUGUST *Fruit* .95
Ham Mousse in Whole Peach, VIRGINIA 1.50

Hot Appetizers

Crisped Shrimp Filled with MUSTARD FRUITS 1.95
CALF'S BRAINS *en Brioche* 1.85   BEEF MARROW *in Bouillon or Cream* 1.85
Field Mushrooms and PROSCIUTTO EN CROUSTADE 2.25
THE FOUR SEASONS *Mousse of Trout* 2.50
SNAILS *in Their Shells,* BURGUNDIAN STYLE 1.85

Cream Cressonière 1.10   AN AUGUST *Vegetable Potage* 1.10
Consommé Royale 1.25
COLD: *Beet and Onion Madrilène* .95   *Gazpacho* 1.25

Sea and Fresh Water Fish

Planked Silver SALMON STEAK 5.50   RED CURRY OF ROCKFISH, *Mango Rice* 4.85
Broiled MAINE LOBSTER 6.50; *Filled with* CRABMEAT 7.85   *The* CLASSIC *Truite au Bleu* 5.50
Poached LOBSTER *in Court-Boullion* 6.75   *Summer Sole,* FOUR SEASONS 4.95

SOFT SHELL CRABS, *Amandine* 5.50   VEAL CHOPS *Sautéed, Grand'mère* 5.75
WHOLE BABY CHICKEN, *Smitane Sauce, Wild Rice* 5.50

A Variety of Seasonals

CALF'S LIVER AND PROSCIUTTO, *Venetian Style* 5.25   RARE FILET STROGONOFF 6.50
ROAST RACK OF LAMB *Persillé with Robust Herbs, for Two* 14.00
Braised SQUAB, *Farci Suprême* 6.50   *Atelier of* TWO QUAIL 6.75

BROILED OVER CHARCOAL ✻
Amish Ham Steak, Apricot Dumpling 4.85   *Calf's Liver-*THICK, *Sage Butter* 5.25
✻ ✻ ✻ ✻ ✻ ✻ ✻
Sirloin VINTNERS STYLE 7.75   SKILLET STEAK *with Smothered Onions* 7.50
Beefsteak SCANDINAVIAN 7.75   *Filet of Beef* POIVRE, *Flambé* 8.00
Butterfly Steak Paillard, FOUR SEASONS 6.75
SPIT ROASTED WITH HERBS ✻
FARMHOUSE DUCKLING, *Brandied Apricots, for Two* 13.00
BROCHETTE OF MARINATED LAMB, *Turkish Pilaff* 5.25

Summer Salads
✻ ✻ ✻ ✻ ✻ ✻ ✻

Bouillabaisse Salad 4.75   *Mousse of Gaspé Salmon* 5.65
JULEP OF CRABMEAT *in Sweet Pepperoni* 5.50   *Buffet of Sliced Meats,* DUTCH POTATO SALAD 5.85
AS A DINNER ACCOMPANIMENT ✻
COOKED CARROTS, *Sweet and Sour* 1.25   *Beefsteak Tomato,* CARVED AT TABLE 1.25
Beets and RIPE OLIVE .85   *Early Summer Greens* 1.25
OUR FIELD GREENS ARE SELECTED EACH MORNING AND WILL VARY DAILY

SEASONAL GATHERINGS MAY BE VIEWED IN THEIR BASKETS   ZUCCHINI *with Walnuts* .95
Leaf Spinach, ELIZABETH .95   BOUQUET PLATTER, *per Person* 1.50
MANGETOUTS 1.25   *Cracked Wheat, Forestiére* .95
✻ ✻ ✻ ✻
POTATOES: *French Fried* .95   *Roesti* .95   *Mashed in Cream* .95

The Four Seasons

Cold Appetizers

THE NEW AMSTERDAM HERRING, *Pommes Vapeur* 2.25   *Todays Melon* .95
Tidewater BLUE CRAB *Lump* 2.95   SMOKED NATIVE BROOK TROUT, *Spiced Cream* 2.65
SUMMER COUNTRY TERRINE 2.25   *Cherrystones in* PEPPER VINAIGRETTE 1.50
PROSCIUTTO *with Ripe Figs or Melon* 2.75   *Caviar, per Serving* 7.50
Little Neck or Cherrystone Clams 1.50   MOUSSE *of Chicken Livers* 2.25
Egg in TARRAGON ASPIC, *Strasbourg Toast* 1.75   VITTELLO TONNATO — PICCOLO 1.75

LOBSTER QUICHE, *Savory* 1.50
Smoked SALMON SOUFFLÉ, *Onion Sauce* 2.65
Mussels in POTS 2.25   *Tiny Shrimps in Shoyu — French Fried* 2.50
CRÊPES OF CRABMEAT, *Imperial* 2.45
Our Coquille Saint-Jacques 2.25

Soups and Broths

Chicken Cream with NEW OATS 1.35   *Double Consommé with Sorrel* 1.25
Onion Soup with PORT, *Gratinée* 1.25
Black Cherry Soup 1.25   *Watercress* VICHYSSOISE 1.10

BARQUETTE OF FLOUNDER *with Glazed Fruits* 4.95   *Crabmeat Casanova* FLAMBÉ 5.75
Sea Bass—GRILLED 4.65   LOBSTER AROMATIC *Prepared Tableside* 6.50
Frog's Legs PROVENÇALE *or Sautéed with Moselle* 5.25

This Evening's Entrees

ROAST SIRLOIN OF BEEF, *Tomato Provençale* 6.50
LAMB STEAK IN SUSU CURRY, *Mango Rice* 5.85

CRISPED DUCKLING *with Peaches, Sauce Cassis* 5.95   MEADOW VEAL CUTLET *with Morels* 5.75
Baby Pheasant in Golden Sauce—NUTTED WILD RICE 6.25
Sweetbreads in Mustard Crumbs, DIABLOTINE 5.50

Steaks, Chops, and Birds

* * * * * * *
Jersey Poularde 4.50   *Three French Lamb Chops* 5.95
* * * * * * *
SIRLOIN STEAK *or* FILET MIGNON *Served for One* 7.50; *for Two* 15.00
Côte de Boeuf, Bordelaise, for Two 18.00   *Entrecôte à la Moëlle* 7.75
Twin Tournedos with WOODLAND MUSHROOMS 7.00
* * * * * * *
Baby Lamb: ROASTED EPAULET, *for Two* 11.00; OREGANO ROASTED LEG, *for Three* 17.00
THE HEART OF THE PRIME RIB 5.50

* AS A MAIN COURSE
LOBSTER AND SHRIMP *in Zucchini, Sauce Vincent* 6.00   AVOCADO *with Scallops Seviche* 5.25
ROAST CHICKEN, *Green Bean Salad* 5.75   BEEF IN BURGUNDY ASPIC 4.75
* * * * * * *
NASTURTIUM *Leaves* 1.50   WILTED SPINACH *and Bacon* 1.35
Raw Mushrooms, MALABAR DRESSING 1.75
Salad Dressing with Roquefort or Feta Cheese .50 *additional*

Vegetables and Potatoes

The YOUNGEST CARROTS *in Butter* 1.25   BEIGNETS VARIES 1.35   ONIONS *in Onions* .95
BROCCOLI FLOWERS, *Hollandaise* 1.95   LANCASTER *Corn Kernels, Tableside* 1.50
Wild Rice 1.65   SOUFFLÉ OF SPINACH, *for Two* 3.85
* * * *
New Potatoes .95   *Baked in Jacket* .95

VERMONT CHEESE SOUP
SERVES 4

I like to try restaurant dishes that sound a little offbeat, and Vermont Cheese Soup on The Four Seasons' menu sounded rather far out. It turned out to be a delicious winter soup created by Chef Albert Stockli, and no doubt a reflection of his Swiss background where cheese is melted into any number of hot dishes.

chicken stock
(see index)
leek
celery
onion
cornstarch
sharp cheddar cheese
salt, white pepper
nutmeg
egg
cream
dry white wine

1 Heat to boiling: **3 cups chicken stock.** Add: **1 leek, chopped** (white part only), **1 stalk celery, chopped,** and **½ medium onion, chopped.**

2 Simmer soup for 45 minutes. Strain into clean saucepan.

3 Mix: **2 tablespoons cornstarch** with **2 tablespoons cold water,** stir into soup, and cook until it is slightly thickened.

4 Add: **1 cup shredded sharp cheddar cheese,** firmly packed, and cook, stirring, until cheese is melted.

5 Stir in: **⅛ teaspoon white pepper, ⅛ teaspoon nutmeg,** and **salt,** if necessary. (This will depend upon the saltiness of your cheese. It varies.)

PRESENTATION

1 Combine: **1 egg yolk** with **½ cup cream.** Mix together well and stir in ½ cup of the hot soup. Add this mixture to the soup, stirring rapidly, and cook for 2 minutes, being careful that it does not boil.

2 Just before serving add: **¼ cup dry white wine.** It does wonders for the final flavor of the cheese.

CARROT VICHYSSOISE
SERVES 4 TO 6

When I first saw this soup on the menu of The Four Seasons, I was perplexed by its name. It was either carrot soup or vichyssoise, but how could it be both? Then I ordered it, found it superb, and when Chef Albert Stockli gave me the recipe, I discovered that this Luther Burbank of the kitchen had grafted carrots onto the well-known vichyssoise and come up with something far more original and delicious.

potatoes
carrots
leek
chicken stock
(see index)
salt, white pepper
cream

SOUP

1 Into a saucepan put: **2 cups peeled, diced potatoes, 1¼ cups sliced carrots, 1 leek, sliced** (white part only), and **3 cups chicken stock.** Bring to a boil and simmer for 25 minutes, or until vegetables are tender.

2 In an electric blender puree half the vegetables and liquid at a time for 30 seconds on high speed. (Or you can puree with a food mill.) Empty into mixing bowl or pitcher.

3 Stir in: **a pinch of white pepper, 1 teaspoon salt,** and **1 cup cream.**

PRESENTATION

Serve in chilled bowls, icy cold, with a topping of **shredded raw carrot.**

CRISPED SHRIMP WITH MUSTARD FRUIT
SERVES 4 OR 8

This is an exotic dish, more suitable as an unusual appetizer than as a main dish. For an appetizer, two large shrimp per serving are plenty. But if you plan to use this as a main course, count on at least four per person. At The Four Seasons, preserved fruits from Cremona, Italy, are used. That is the town of the great violin makers, but now they have another string to their bow. The Cremona mustard fruits are glacéed apricots, pears, cherries, tangerines, figs, citrons, plums, and peaches, preserved in a heavy syrup flavored with mustard. If you cannot find them in a specialty market, use assorted fruits with their peel, preserved in heavy syrup, and add a tablespoon of spicy mustard.

fruits in mustard
syrup
shrimp or prawns
salt
lemon or vinegar
butter
eggs
flour
milk
cream
Dijon mustard
baking powder
cooking oil

SHRIMP

1 Drain: **1 pint fruits in mustard syrup.** Chop fruits finely, almost to a paste. This will measure about 1¾ cups.

2 Poach: **16 large shrimp** or **prawns** in **salted** water to cover, with **1 tablespoon lemon juice** or **vinegar.** Simmer without letting water boil for 5 minutes.

3 Drain and remove shells, leaving tail intact. Split deeply down the back and remove dark vein. Stuff the shrimp or prawns with the chopped fruit, using from ¾ to 1 cup in all. Set aside.

SAUCE

1 In saucepan melt: **2 tablespoons butter.** Stir in: **3 tablespoons flour** and cook, stirring, until mixture bubbles.

2 Remove from heat and add: **1 cup hot milk.** Return saucepan to heat and stir vigorously for about 1 minute, or until sauce is smooth and thickened. Cover. Cook on low heat for 5 to 10 minutes.

3 Stir in: **1 cup cream, 1 tablespoon Dijon mustard, ½ teaspoon salt,** or to taste, and the remaining chopped fruit. Keep hot.

BATTER

1 Sift and measure: **1½ cups flour.** Stir in: **1½ teaspoons baking powder** and **½ teaspoon salt.**

2 Combine: **2 eggs, beaten,** and **1 cup milk.** Add to dry ingredients gradually and mix to make a thick batter. Strain if lumpy.

PRESENTATION

Roll stuffed shrimp or prawns in **flour,** dip each into batter, holding by the tail, and fry in deep **cooking oil** heated to 390° F. until golden brown and crisp. Drain on absorbent paper and serve hot with the mustard fruit sauce and additional **Dijon mustard.**

MEDALLIONS OF BREADED VEAL IN PARMESAN AND GRATED LEMON ZEST
SERVES 4

The food at The Four Seasons is not elaborate, but it is served beautifully and there is always some small imaginative touch that lifts it above the average and makes it different. When we eat out it is those little differences that we are alert to—simple tricks that we can do at home to make something special of an ordinary dish. This recipe is a perfect case in point. Everybody does breaded veal scallops—but not like this.

veal scallops
fine bread crumbs
Parmesan cheese
flour
parsley
lemons
cooking oil
eggs
salt, pepper

1 Pound very thin: **8 veal scallops.** Dredge them in **flour** and pat them between your palms to give them a thin, even dusting of flour.

2 In a small bowl mix: **1½ cups fine bread crumbs, 1 cup finely grated Parmesan cheese, the grated yellow rind of 2½ lemons, 1 teaspoon salt,** and **⅛ teaspoon pepper.**

3 In another bowl beat: **2 small eggs.**

4 Dip each floured veal scallop in egg, then in bread crumb mixture.

5 In a large skillet heat: **3 ounces cooking oil.** Sauté veal scallops until golden brown on both sides.

PRESENTATION

Serve veal scallops with garnish of **parsley** and **lemon wedges.**

CALF'S LIVER WITH AVOCADO
SERVES 6

Here is an unusual way to serve calf's liver, typical of The Four Seasons' inventiveness with everyday foods. It doesn't have to be nightingales' tongues or quails' tails to qualify for their elegant bill of fare.

calf's liver
avocados
lemons
flour
thyme
beef stock
(see index)
butter
salt, pepper

1 Mix together: **½ cup flour, 1 teaspoon salt,** and **¼ teaspoon pepper.**

2 Peel and cut into thin slices: **6 avocados.** Sprinkle with **lemon juice.**

3 Rinse and dry thoroughly: **12 slices of calf's liver,** cut very thin. Remove any membranes or veins.

4 Dip slices of liver and avocado into the seasoned flour, and pat between your palms to give them a thin, even dusting.

5 Heat in a heavy skillet: **2 ounces butter.** When it has stopped foaming, sauté very quickly the slices of liver and

avocado. Do a few at a time as they will not brown properly if your skillet is too crowded. Keep them warm.

6 Arrange sautéed liver and avocado in alternating slices on a hot platter and keep warm.

SAUCE

1 Empty skillet and put in: **8 ounces butter.** Heat until butter browns. Then add: **the juice of 3 lemons, ½ cup beef stock,** and **½ teaspoon thyme.**

2 Stir quickly to mix. When sauce is hot, pour over liver and avocado and serve.

BOEUF À LA BOURGUIGNONNE (*Beef Stew Burgundy Style*)
SERVES 6

Probably the most illustrious restaurant in the United States is Le Pavillon in New York. Its owner and guiding genius is Henri Soulé, a perfectionist who caters to a clientele with cultivated palates and unlimited bank accounts. A magnificent dinner for two, with distinguished wines appropriate to each course, could carry a price tag of seventy dollars or so. But it is the quality and not the cash that one should consider when thinking of the Pavillon's cuisine. M. Soulé himself, though a connoisseur of the epicurean delicacies that made his restaurant famous, is reported to like nothing better than a good country beef stew when dining at home. And though he is considered one of the foremost experts on caviar, he can exercise that same discernment on hot dogs— there is a roadside stand near his country home that gets his frequent patronage because their frankfurters *are* delicious. This is M. Soulé's recipe for his favorite beef stew.

beef kidney fat
(suet)
salt pork or bacon
beef
salt, pepper
onions
carrots
shallots
butter
lemon
flour
garlic
red Burgundy
beef stock
(see index)
parsley
celery
bay leaf
thyme
mushrooms

STEW

1 Preheat oven to moderate (350° F.).

2 In a pan heat: **1 tablespoon beef kidney fat** (suet).

3 Add: **1 cup diced salt pork** or **bacon** and sauté until golden brown. Remove from pan and set aside.

4 Season: **3 pounds lean beef,** cut into medium-sized pieces, with **1 tablespoon salt** and **¼ teaspoon pepper.** Sauté the beef, **12 to 15 small onions,** and **6 medium carrots, cut in pieces,** until golden brown.

5 Drain off fat and add: **2 shallots, chopped, 1 clove garlic, crushed,** and **2 tablespoons flour.** Mix well with a wooden spoon and let stand in moderate oven for a few minutes until flour becomes golden brown.

6 Remove pan from oven and add: **1 pint red Burgundy** and **1 cup beef stock.** Be sure meat is covered with liquid.

7 Tie up in cheesecloth: **3 sprigs parsley, 2 stalks celery, 1 bay leaf,** and

a pinch of **thyme.** Add this **faggot** or *bouquet garni* to beef and wine. Bring to a boil and cook slowly over low heat for 2 hours, or until meat is well done. If the stew has cooked slowly, the sauce should be of a medium consistency. But if it cooked too quickly, the sauce is apt to be thick. In that case, skim the fat from the top and add a little **stock.**

8 Sauté: **½ pound medium-sized or small fresh mushrooms in 2 tablespoons butter.** Cook over high heat for 3 minutes, add: **1 teaspoon lemon juice, ⅛ teaspoon salt, a dash of pepper,** and cook 2 minutes longer.

PRESENTATION

1 Remove meat, carrots, onions, pork, and mushrooms to serving dish and keep hot.

2 Correct seasoning in sauce by adding **salt** and **pepper** to taste.

3 Rub sauce through sieve, bring to a boil and pour over meat and vegetables. Serve with boiled potatoes or noodles.

POULARDE PAVILLON *(Chicken in Champagne Sauce)*
SERVES 4

chicken
salt
butter
dry French
champagne
cream
shallots
mushrooms
parsley
bay leaves
thyme

CHICKEN

1 Preheat oven to moderate (350° F.).

2 Season: **a 3-pound chicken** with **1 teaspoon salt.** Truss it and place in a small casserole with: **2 tablespoons butter** and **2 cups dry French champagne.**

3 Cook in the moderate oven about 45 minutes. Baste every 8 minutes and turn until the chicken is an even golden brown on all sides.

4 Remove chicken, cut off string, and keep chicken warm on hot platter.

SAUCE

1 Add to juices in the casserole: **4 cups cream, 3 shallots, chopped fine, 4 mush-

rooms, crushed by rolling with rolling pin** (the chef's directions said to "roll with a bottle"), **1 sprig parsley, chopped, 2 bay leaves,** and **a pinch of thyme.**

2 Simmer on top of stove until sauce has reduced to two-thirds the original amount. Strain through a fine sieve into a clean saucepan.

3 Place over medium heat and swirl in: **2 tablespoons butter.** Add: **6 ounces** (a glass) **dry French champagne.**

PRESENTATION

Spoon some of the sauce over the chicken, serve the rest separately. At Pavillon the chicken is brought to the table whole and carved there by the captain.

POMME DE TERRE MACAIRE *(Sautéed Baked Potato)*
SERVES 1

Reportedly potatoes baked and then hashed browned in this manner are the favorites of the Pavillon's Henri Soulé himself. It is a simple recipe but—you *must* use Idaho potatoes, *break* them in half when they are baked, use good butter and lots of it, sauté extremely slowly—in short, follow the directions to the letter. No improvising.

Idaho potato
butter
salt, pepper

1 Preheat oven to moderately hot (375° F.).

2 Bake: **1 large Idaho potato** in the moderately hot oven for approximately 1 hour.

3 Break potato in half and scoop out the pulp with a fork. Mash into pulp: **1 tablespoon butter** and **salt** and **pepper** to taste. Mash until smooth.

4 In a heavy skillet melt: **1 tablespoon butter**. Put the potato pulp into the skillet and spread in a flat cake. It is best when it is at least 1 inch thick. Sauté very, very slowly until it is golden brown on both sides. Serve in wedges like a *quiche Lorraine.*

SALADE GAULOISE *(Mushroom, Truffle and Tongue Salad)*
SERVES 4

This most unusual salad was served at the Pavillon with a cold stuffed chicken in aspic. Subtle, delicate, only the soupçon of lemon juice and the slightly sour taste of the cream gave the dressing its tang. This is the perfect salad to serve with any dish that could be overpowered with a more robust combination of greens and dressing.

celery
truffles
mushrooms
cooked tongue
sour cream
paprika
lemon
light cream
salt, pepper

1 In salad bowl combine: **1 heart of celery** or **4 large tender stalks**, thinly sliced, **2 truffles**, cut into julienne strips, **4 medium-sized fresh mushrooms**, thinly sliced, and **¼ pound (8 slices) cooked tongue**, cut into julienne strips.

2 In small mixing bowl combine: **1 cup commercial sour cream**, **½ teaspoon paprika**, **1 teaspoon lemon juice**, **½ teaspoon salt**, **⅛ teaspoon pepper**, and **¼ cup light cream**. Pour the dressing over salad and toss lightly.

Under the flickering gaslights of Gage and Tollner's, steaks, chops, and succulent seafood have been served with plain perfection for more than eighty-five years. The waiter in the foreground has done some of the serving for fifty-nine years, as his sleeve emblems testify.

Here in our kitchen, filled with the clutter of Mary's collections of everything one could use for cooking, we have laid out the makings of our favorite mixed grill. The pot-and-pan rack was made to Mary's design and mounted on a butcher-block table bought from a secondhand restaurant supply store. The coffee urn was discovered in a country antique shop, painted green. The Tiffany shades I found for a favorite Christmas present. This is how our kitchen grows!

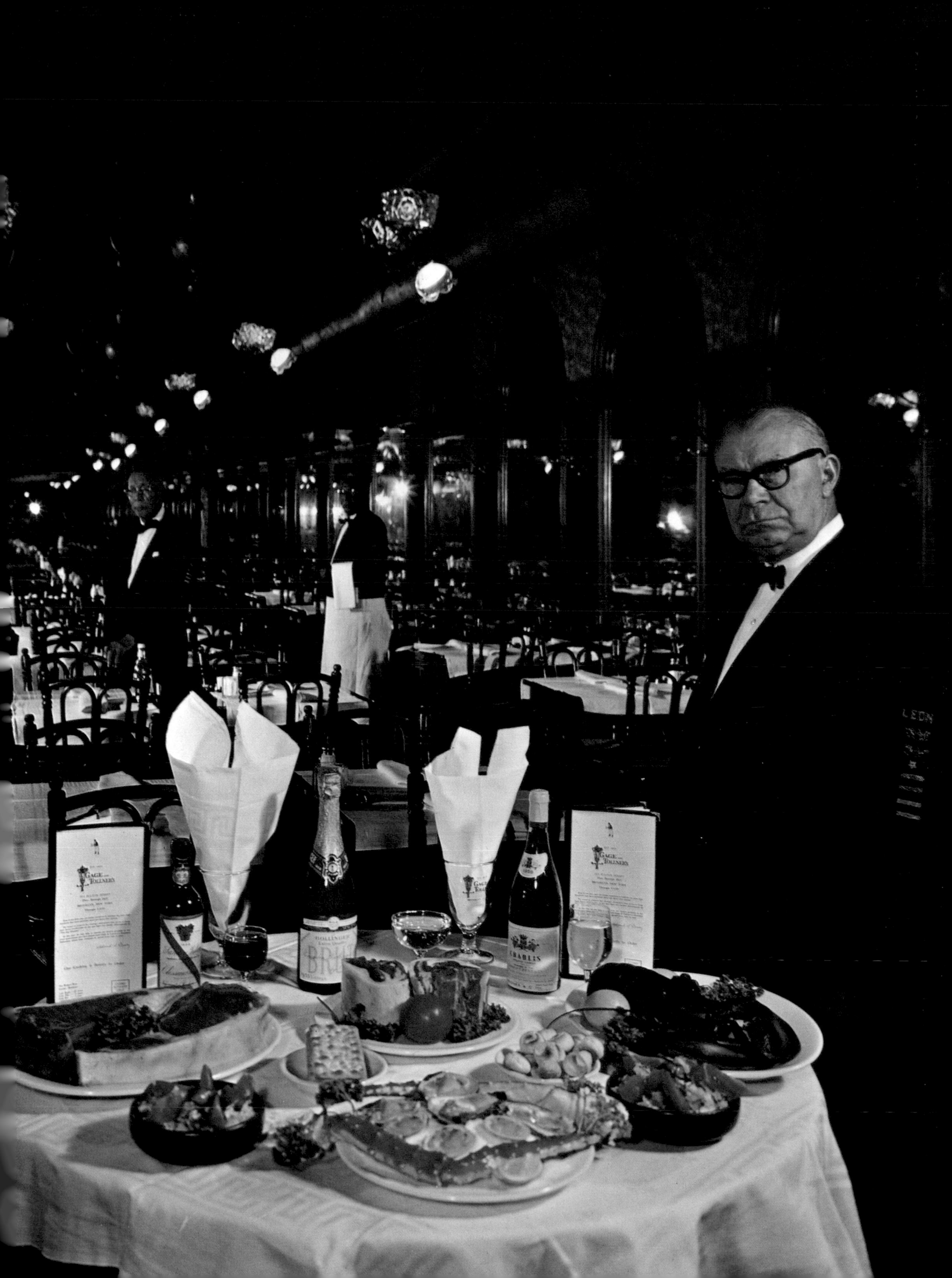
CHABLIS
LEON

GAGE AND TOLLNER'S

KREDEL

Now THAT the Dodgers no longer play ball in Brooklyn, Manhattanites have lost one of their most powerful incentives for crossing the Brooklyn Bridge. There is another, however. For those who like their steaks and chops broiled to a tee, or some of the finest seafood on the Eastern seaboard, this venerable chop-and-chowder house with its Gay Nineties' atmosphere is a powerful magnet.

We lunched at Gage and Tollner's once when my art collection was being shown in Brooklyn, and to walk through its brown-pillared entrance was to be transported to an older, more leisurely time. The rows of cut-glass chandeliers, mirrored walls lined with dark red brocade, and hat hooks large enough to accommodate the tall toppers of the horse-and-buggy era—all are preserved today just as they were. Even the waiters are old retainers, and they wear on their sleeves the insignia of their service: a gold eagle, 25 years; a gold star, 5 years; a gold bar, 1 year. Almost the youngest men working at Gage and Tollner's now are Edward and Thomas Dewey who inherited the eighty-five-year-old restaurant from their father.

I asked Edward Dewey if his chef would give us some of his recipes, and back in the kitchen I discovered part of the secret of Gage and Tollner's distinctive broilings. They have a special anthracite broiler, having found that hard coal burns without fumes and consequently doesn't obscure the real flavor of meat or seafood as charcoal does. That's not anything we can adopt at home, but some of Gage and Tollner's recipes we have used with pleasure. For the anthracite product, we just have to cross the Brooklyn Bridge whenever we're in New York.

EST. 1879

GAGE AND TOLLNER'S

372 FULTON STREET
(Near Borough Hall)

BROOKLYN, NEW YORK

TRiangle 5-5181

Now in our 85th year, we pledge ourselves to maintain the same high standards that have prevailed since our doors first opened.

We intend to preserve the nostalgic atmosphere that serves to bring back found recollections of the gas light era, known affectionately as "The Gay Nineties."

At this time, we also wish to express our sincere gratitude to the many good friends who have helped make Gage & Tollner's a Brooklyn Institution, whose fame continues to spread from year to year.

Edward S. Dewey

Our Cooking is Strictly to Order

Our Waiters Wear
Service Emblems

Gold Eagle — 25 years
Gold Star — 5 years
Gold Bar — 1 year

CLOSED
SUNDAYS
ONLY

Relishes

Olives	25	Chow Chow	35
Celery	35	Stuffed Celery	75
Chutney	50		

Appetizers — Cocktails

Chilled Tomato, Clam, Veg. Juice	40	Lobster Cocktail	2.75
Fresh Fruit Cup	80	Soft Clam Belly Appetizer	1.25
Crabmeat Cocktail	1.90	Little Neck or Cherry Stone Clam Cocktail	1.00
Shrimp Cocktail	1.85	Blue Point or Large Oyster Cocktail	1.25
Seafood Cocktail	2.25		

American Wines by the Glass 60c.

Soups — Bisques

	Cup	Plate		Cup	Plate
Cream of Chicken or Tomato	50	60	Green Turtle Soup	75	85
Clam Soup or Clam Broth	50	60		Cup	Bowl
Chicken Broth with Rice	50	60	Soft Clam Bisque	70	1.60
Clam Chowder	50	60	Lobster Bisque	1.60	3.25
Soft Clam Soup	60	70	Clam Bisque	70	1.60
			Oyster Bisque	85	1.80

Large or Blue Point Oysters

Cocktail	1.25	Milk Broil	2.25
Steamed	2.25	Cream Broil	2.50
Stew	2.25	Crumb Broil	2.25
Milk Stew	2.25	Celery Broil	2.50
Cream Stew	2.35	Celery Cream Broil	2.75
Fry	2.25	Seasoned Broil	2.30
Chicago Fry	2.30	Broil on Toast	2.30
Baltimore Fry	2.25	Shell Roast	2.50
Seasoned Fry	2.25	Shell Roast (Casino)	2.75
Crumb Fry	2.25	Pan Roast	2.25
Broil	2.25	En Brochette	2.75
Chicago Broil	2.30	Creamed	2.50
Baltimore Broil	2.25	Patties	2.75

Little Neck or Cherry Stone Clams

Cocktail	1.00	Milk Broil	2.10
Pan Roast	2.00	Cream Broil	2.20
Stew	2.00	Celery Broil	2.10
Milk Stew	2.00	Chicago Broil	2.10
Cream Stew	2.10	Seasoned Broil	2.10
Boston Stew	2.00	Steamed	2.00
Fry	2.00	Fricasseed	2.00
Seasoned Fry	2.10	Fritters	2.00
Shell Roast	2.00	Patties	2.50
Chicago Fry	2.10	Creamed	2.30
Broil	2.00	Shell Roast (Casino)	2.75

One portion served for two, 50¢ extra
Half portion, 25¢ extra

Soft Clams

Milk Stew	2.40	Chicago	2.50
Cream Stew	2.50	Baltimore Broil	2.50
Fry	2.50	Milk Broil	2.50
Seasoned Fry	2.50	Belly Broil	2.50
Pan Roast	2.50	Celery Broil	2.60
Dewey Pan Roast	2.60	Cream Broil	2.60
Broil	2.50	Shell Roast	2.60
Steamed	2.50	Celery Cream Broil	2.60
Fritters	2.50	Shell Roast (Casino)	2.75
Duxbury Stew	2.50	A la Newburg	2.75
Fricasseed	2.50		

Steaks, Chops, Other Meats

Sirloin Steak for 2	11.00	Single English Mutton	
Single Sirloin Steak	6.00	Chop with Sausage	
Filet Mignon	5.75	and Kidney	3.35
Tenderloin	5.50	Calf's Liver and Bacon	
Minute Steak	4.00	or Onions	2.75
Chopped Tenderloin Steak		Broiled Ham Steak	2.75
with Mushroom Caps	3.00	Lamb Kidneys,	
Loin Lamb Chops (2)	4.00	En Brochette	2.25
Loin Lamb Chops with		Plain	2.00
Sausage and Kidney	4.35	Lamb Kidneys, Saute with	
Single English Mutton		Mushrooms in Gravy	2.25
Chop	3.00	Sausages	2.25

Chicken

Fried with Bacon and		Broiled or Fried	2.50
Corn Fritters	3.00	Patties	2.50
A la Maryland with Bacon		Chicken Livers Saute with	
and Corn Fritters		Mushrooms in Gravy	2.50
(Cream Sauce)	3.00	Chicken Livers	
A la King	2.75	en Brochette	2.25
Chicken Sandwich	1.25	Club Sandwich	1.50

Fish (In Season)

Bluefish Boned	2.50	Salmon Steak	2.75
Brook Trout	2.50	Sea Bass	2.50
Eels	2.25	Striped Bass Boned	2.50
Filet of Sole	2.25	Fried Seafood Comb.	3.00
Halibut Steak	2.50	Seafood a la Newburg	4.00
Frog Legs	3.75	Smelts	2.50
Red Snapper	2.50	Seafood au Gratin	3.75
Lemon Sole	2.50	Seafood Salad	3.75
Whale Steak with French Fried Onion Rings			2.50

Lobsters

Cream Stew	3.50	Deviled	4.50
Patties	4.50	Salad	4.50
Croquettes	4.50	Thermidor	4.50
Stewed	4.50	A la Newburg	5.00
Creamed	4.50	Fried	5.50
Small Broiled or Boiled, Hot or Cold			3.25
Large Broiled or Boiled, Hot or Cold			
A la Maryland with Bacon and Corn Fritters (Cream Sauce)			
Broiled Australian Lobster Tails			4.00

Bacon served with above orders, 40¢ extra

American Wines by the Glass 60c.

Scallops

Stew	2.50	A la Newburg	3.75
Milk Stew	2.50	Baltimore Broil	3.25
Cream Stew	2.75	Broil, half and half	3.25
Fry	3.00	Seasoned Broil	3.25
Seasoned Fry	3.00	Milk Broil	3.25
Fry, half and half	3.00	Cream Broil	3.50
Chicago Fry	3.25	Celery Broil	3.50
Broil	3.25	Celery Cream Broil	3.75
Fricasseed	3.25	Chicago Broil	3.50
En Brochette	3.50	Bisque	3.25

Shrimp

Cocktail	1.85	A la Newburg	3.25
Fried	2.75	Curried (with Rice)	3.25
Creole (with Rice)	3.00	Au Gratin	3.00
		Salad	2.75

Crabmeat

Cocktail	1.90	Virginia	3.25
Au Gratin	3.25	A la Dewey	3.35
Creamed in Shell	3.50	A la Newburg	3.75
Creamed on Toast	3.25	Salad	3.35
Deviled	3.35		
Alaskan King Crab Legs			3.75

COMPLETE WINE LIST ON REQUEST

Eggs, Omelettes

Scrambled	1.20	Omelette, Plain	1.20
Poached on Toast	1.20	" Spanish	1.60
Bacon and Eggs	1.75	" Mushroom	1.60
Ham and Eggs	2.25	" Chicken	1.65
Shirred Eggs, Dewey	1.35	" Chicken	
Shirred Eggs with		Liver	2.00
Mushrooms	1.60	" Cheese	1.70
Shirred Eggs with		" Ham	2.00
Sausage or Kidneys	2.00		

Welsh Rabbits

Long Island	1.90	Golden Buck	2.00
Welsh	1.80	Yorkshire Buck	2.10

Toast

Dry	10	Buttered	15
Cream Toast	75	Milk Toast	50

One portion served for two, 50¢ extra

Half portion, 25¢ extra

Bacon served with above orders, 40¢ extra

MIXED GRILL
SERVES 2

There is certainly an art to grilling meat properly, and at Gage and Tollner's the art has been practiced to perfection. When you order a steak or mutton chop combination (their equivalent of a mixed grill), the meat is brought for your inspection on its way to the broiler. Steaks and chops are about two inches thick, firm, bright red, and beautifully marbled. You can't broil an inferior piece of meat and get good results. Broil thicker cuts of meat farther away from the heat than thinner ones, and quickly sear a thick steak or chop on both sides to retain the juices before broiling at a more moderate heat. Always salt broiled meats after cooking, or the salt will draw out valuable juices. Brush meat with butter or oil before broiling to keep it from sticking and to prevent its drying out. And now, on to the Mixed Grill.

lamb chops
lamb kidneys
mushrooms
butter
tomato
salt, pepper
white sausages
(bratwurst)
Canadian or regular
bacon
parsley or watercress
cooking oil

MIXED GRILL

1 Have: **2 loin lamb chops** cut about 2 inches thick. Trim off any excess fat. Wipe with a damp cloth.

2 Trim the white membrane and fat from: **2 lamb kidneys.** Slice them almost in two, but without separating the pieces. Lay them flat.

3 Wash and remove stems from: **4 large mushrooms.** Brush caps with **melted butter** (save stems in refrigerator to use for soup or sauce some other time). Set aside.

4 Cut in half: **1 large tomato.** Brush with **melted butter** and sprinkle with **salt** and **pepper.**

5 Set out: **2 large white sausages** (bratwurst) and **2 slices Canadian** or **regular bacon.**

6 Heat broiler and **oil** broiler rack. Grill the chops close to the heat to sear on both sides. Then add the sausages, tomato, bacon and grill about 6 inches from heat. Remove tomato as soon as it is done, turn sausages to keep from burning, and remove them and the bacon when they are done. Broil chops about 5 minutes on each side for rare. **Salt** each side after it is cooked. When little drops of red juice appear on surface of second side, chops are cooked sufficiently.

7 The kidneys and mushrooms can be sautéed in: **2 tablespoons butter** in a skillet if they are too small to broil without falling through grids of broiler rack. In that case, don't butter mushrooms.

PRESENTATION
Arrange on each heated plate 1 lamb chop, 1 kidney, 1 sausage, ½ tomato, 1 slice bacon, and 2 mushroom caps. Garnish with **parsley** or **watercress.**

CRABMEAT VIRGINIA
SERVES 1

When I got these recipes at Gage and Tollner's, I couldn't believe my eyes. "You mean those terrific things we ate for lunch—this is all there is to preparing them?" Well not quite, they explained. The quality of the raw ingredients was very, very important. Take this recipe. Not any old crabmeat at all would do. It had to be fresh, it had to come from Maryland, it had to be "lump," by which was meant in lumps about robin's-egg size. And the very best butter. And lemon juice, freshly squeezed at the very moment you use it. It is called Crabmeat Virginia because this is the way it is prepared in Virginia—even though the crab itself comes from Maryland.

lump crabmeat
butter
lemon
parsley

1 Preheat oven to hot (400° F.).

2 In a shallow ovenproof dish place: **6 ounces of fresh Maryland lump crabmeat**, carefully picked over and free of cartilage or shell.

3 Dot with: **3 tablespoons butter** and sprinkle with: **1½ tablespoons freshly** squeezed lemon juice.

4 Bake in the hot oven for 8 minutes, or until golden brown.

PRESENTATION

Serve in individual ramekin in which crabmeat was baked, garnished with **a lemon wedge** and **fresh parsley.**

CHICKEN LIVERS EN BROCHETTE
SERVES 1 OR 2

These were delicious broiled under Gage and Tollner's anthracite flame, but I must say they were every bit as good done on my new barbecue broiler, so maybe it's the recipe that's responsible.

chicken livers
bacon
toast
butter
parsley

1 In a shallow pan put: **10 small chicken livers.** Brush them with a little **melted butter** and broil on both sides until partially cooked.

2 Set aside to cool.

3 Put: **4 slices of bacon** in boiling water for 2 minutes. Drain, and cut into thirds.

4 On a skewer thread a piece of bacon and a chicken liver alternately until all are used.

5 Broil again, turning frequently until evenly browned.

PRESENTATION

This serves two people as an appetizer, one person as a main course. Serve on **toast points** that have been brushed with **butter.** Garnish with **parsley.**

LOBSTER BISQUE DEWEY
SERVES 2

This makes a most delectable curtain raiser for a fine dinner. Usually lobster bisque is made from lobster cooked in stock, and the soup is pureed before being served. But this delicious soup is the result of cooking lobster meat in butter and then adding cream. Rich, delicious, and tasting of pure essence of lobster.

lobster
butter
flour
sherry (optional)
paprika
cream
light cream
salt
cayenne pepper

1 Split: **a small live lobster.** Remove the meat and mince it. (You should have about 4 ounces.)

2 In saucepan melt: **2 tablespoons butter.** Add the lobster meat and cook over moderate heat for 3 minutes, stirring constantly so lobster won't burn.

3 Stir in: **1 tablespoon flour.** Add: **½ cup cream, ½ cup light cream, ¼ teaspoon salt,** and **a dash cayenne pepper.**

4 Cook, stirring constantly, until soup is slightly thickened and very hot. Divide into bouillon cups and sprinkle with **paprika.** A dash of **sherry** may be added.

GEORGIA SALAD
SERVES 4

This is Gage and Tollner's most popular salad, a crisp slaw served with their own spicy French dressing. It is excellent with broiled meats or seafood.

white cabbage
eggs
lettuce
garlic
salt, pepper
olive oil
wine vinegar
catsup
dry mustard
paprika
sugar

FRENCH DRESSING (Makes 1 Pint)

1 Mince and mash: **1 clove garlic.** Add: **1 teaspoon salt, ¼ teaspoon freshly ground pepper, ¼ teaspoon dry mustard, ½ teaspoon paprika,** and **½ teaspoon sugar.** Mix with a fork.

2 Add: **⅔ cup wine vinegar** and stir well to dissolve dry ingredients.

3 Add: **⅓ cup catsup** and **1 cup olive oil.** Pour into screw-top jar and shake

dressing vigorously to blend.

SALAD

1 Shred finely: **½ head firm white cabbage.** Chop into small pieces. Combine with ¼ cup French dressing, or enough to moisten cabbage.

2 Firmly press cabbage salad into 4 cups or small molds. Invert on bed of **lettuce** and garnish each individual salad with: **½ hard-cooked egg, cut into quarters.**

GRILLED TOMATOES
SERVES 2

This dish isn't going to taste any better than the tomatoes you use for it. Never think that because you are going to cook them anyhow, partially ripe tomatoes will do. They must be ripe to have flavor and they must have flavor or they add nothing to your dish. So be sure to use good ripe ones when they are in season.

tomatoes
egg
milk
fine cracker meal
butter
parsley

1 Cut off tops and bottoms from: **3 medium tomatoes.** Cut in half through their "equator."

2 Beat together: **1 egg** and **2 tablespoons milk.**

3 Dip tomato halves in egg-milk mix-

ture and dredge in **fine cracker meal.**

4 Broil on rack about 4 inches from flame until browned on both sides.

5 Brush with **melted butter** and top each tomato half with **a small "flower" of parsley.**

HASHED BROWNED POTATOES
SERVES 4

The simplest things are often the most wonderful, and some of the most marvelous things you can eat are by the same token the simplest—an egg, a slice of good bread, a potato. We did nip-ups over these Hashed Browned Potatoes as they were served at Gage and Tollner's. And by golly there is a trick or two to making this seemingly simple dish. Follow the directions exactly for best results.

Maine potatoes
cooking oil or butter
salt

Buy the proper kind of potato for boiling. A white potato that stays firm when cooked, like the Maine potato, is best.

1 In a saucepan put: **4 potatoes in their jackets.** Cover with cold water and bring to a boil. Boil until just done when tested, about 30 minutes.

2 Remove and cool. Chill in refrigerator. When cold, peel and chop coarsely.

3 In a heavy skillet melt: **3 tablespoons cooking oil** or **butter** over high heat.

4 Add potatoes to cover one half of skillet and sprinkle with: **½ teaspoon salt.**

5 When crisply browned, turn to other half of skillet with spatula, keeping potatoes in one piece. Potatoes should be crisp and brown on both sides and soft in the middle.

RICE CUSTARD
SERVES 6

Gage and Tollner's serves only the plainest desserts. After gorging on broiled oysters, crabmeat, a whole lobster, or an enormous steak or mixed grill, no one would be able to tackle anything very rich. This Rice Custard has an old-fashioned wholesomeness that is quite in keeping with the restaurant's atmosphere, and it makes a nice light dessert when your appetite has been surfeited.

rice
milk
eggs
raisins
sugar
vanilla extract
salt
cinnamon

1 Preheat oven to moderate (350° F.).

2 In a large saucepan put: **1 quart milk** and **¼ cup rice.** Bring to boil and simmer until rice is tender, about 30 minutes. Remove from heat.

3 Beat together: **2 eggs, ¼ cup sugar, ½ teaspoon vanilla extract, a pinch of salt,** and **¼ cup raisins.**

4 Slowly stir egg mixture into rice,

bring to boil, and cook 5 minutes, stirring constantly.

5 Ladle mixture into custard cups.

6 Sprinkle tops with cinnamon-sugar made of: **1 tablespoon cinnamon** mixed with **¼ cup sugar.**

7 Bake in the moderate oven 10 to 15 minutes, until custard is set.

8 Refrigerate when cool.

FILET MIGNON CAESAR AUGUSTUS
SERVES 4

At the other end of the spectrum from Gage and Tollner's simple excellence is the elaborate and rococo cuisine of New York's Forum of the Twelve Caesars. The two restaurants are as different from each other as the Gay Nineties were from Imperial Rome. This recipe for Filet Mignon is relatively restrained for the Forum's cuisine and, if you want to do something a little different, is a most interesting way to serve beef fillets for a change.

fillets of beef
pâté de foie gras
butter
salt, pepper
watercress

1 Wipe: **4 12-ounce fillets of beef** with a damp cloth.

2 Press a 2-inch cookie cutter into top of each fillet, cutting about halfway through. Take a sharp, pointed knife and cut out circle made by cookie cutter.

3 Place in each indentation: **a 1-ounce slice of canned pâté de foie gras.**

4 Cover with cutout circle of fillet and press into place.

5 Sprinkle each fillet with a little **freshly ground pepper.**

6 Brush with **melted butter.**

7 Broil to your taste and sprinkle with **salt** after fillets are cooked.

8 Serve with a garnish of **watercress.**

PUREE OF MUSHROOMS WITH BRAISED CELERY
SERVES 6

This is a delicious vegetable garnish for almost any meat or poultry dish. I must confess it does not look particularly beautiful, at least when we make it, but this is one dish where the flavor is far more important than the appearance.

mushrooms
salt, pepper
white pepper
nutmeg
cream
celery
chicken stock
(see index)
butter

MUSHROOM PUREE

1 Mince: **1 pound very fresh mushrooms.**

2 Put minced mushrooms into a saucepan and cook over low heat for 10 minutes, or until most of the moisture in the mushrooms has cooked away, stirring occasionally.

3 Sprinkle with: **¾ teaspoon salt, ⅛ teaspoon pepper,** and **a pinch of nutmeg.** Add: **1 cup cream** and cook over low heat for 20 minutes, stirring fre-

quently. Serve hot over braised celery.

BRAISED CELERY

1 Remove thick outer leaves from: **2 hearts of celery.** Cut remaining hearts lengthwise into 4 sections each.

2 Arrange celery in a heatproof casserole and add: **1 cup good chicken stock** and **3 tablespoons soft butter.** Sprinkle with: **½ teaspoon salt** and **⅛ teaspoon white pepper.** Bring liquid to a boil, cover, and braise over low heat for 45 minutes, or until tender.

Thanksgiving at the Wayside Inn is authentically Early American. In the Colonial kitchen with its open hearth and ancient utensils, a modern chef carves the turkey which is surrounded by traditional New England provender.

Thanksgiving dinner at our house is eaten at our great round table set festively for the occasion. We serve from the buffet under a favorite painting that is—to put it mildly—modern. Better, we believe, than having an ancestor, real or purchased, peering over your shoulder at every mouthful.

WAYSIDE INN

Let the board groan, let the belly bulge, let our hearts be thankful—lest we forget what our ancestors went through to achieve that first Thanksgiving. The fullness of our fields and fruit trees, of our dairies and hatcheries load the table, and this is a day for family and friends to make welcome the stranger.

The Wayside Inn has been offering a tranquil and hospitable welcome to strangers for 276 years. It stands on a winding country road in South Sudbury, about twenty miles west of Boston, and was immortalized by Longfellow in his *Tales of a Wayside Inn*. Thanksgiving dinner as served in the old Colonial kitchen of the inn follows the New England tradition, and I am grateful that we're reminded of our heritage—a bountiful one as you can see—every autumn.

Clear across the country in California, Mary and I start our Thanksgiving preparation early. We search our marvelous markets for all the decorative fruits we can find—colored corn, the comical shapes of gourds and squash, amethyst cabbage, jade artichokes, ruby apples and tomatoes, weirdly twisted peppers, red and green. The great round table is the pride of our eating lives. It evolved from an old garden table cut round and added to over the years. The fighting cocks, carved by self-taught artists on a Caribbean isle, ride the lazy Susan like carrousel figures. The family waits—all's ready, get set, go!

So, if your mouth is watering and I hope it is, join us in my favorite, strictly nonsectarian grace—"So much thou givest us, O Lord, grant us one thing more—truly grateful hearts."

LONGFELLOW'S

1683
D.H. 1686   E.H. 1746
A.How 1796
L.H. 1830

"As Ancient is this Hostelry
As any in the Land may be,
Built in the Old Colonial day,

When Men lived in a Grander
With ampler Hospitality...
LONGFELLOW

Wayside Inn

SOUTH SUDBURY, MASSACHUSET

1683

LONGFELLOW'S

Wayside Inn

SOUTH SUDBURY, MASS.

Thanksgiving Day 1963

FRESH PRESSED SWEET APPLE CIDER

FRESH FRUIT CUP WITH MARASCHINO   LOUISIANA SHRIMP COCKTAIL   .75

TOMATO JUICE COCKTAIL   CRANBERRY SHRUB

ONION SOUP, WITH CROUTON   CREAM OF CHICKEN SOUP

CELERY HEARTS, RADISHES, OLIVES

COTTAGE CHEESE AND CHIVES

Roast Stuffed Massachusetts Turkey   4.00

GIBLET GRAVY   WAYSIDE BREAD STUFFING

CRANBERRY SAUCE

Roast Stuffed Massachusetts Duckling   4.50

ORANGE SAUCE   CORN BREAD STUFFING

Roast Prime Ribs of Beef, Yorkshire Pudding   4.75

WHIPPED POTATOES   CANDIED SWEET POTATOES

BUTTERNUT SQUASH   CREAMED ONIONS   BUTTERED GREEN PEAS

CHIFFONADE SALAD   MOLDED FRUIT JELLO SALAD

— May We Recommend A Bottle of Fine Wine with Your Dinner —

HOT MINCE PIE   PUMPKIN PIE   BLACK CHERRY CHIFFON PIE

DEEP DISH APPLE PIE, SPICED WHIPPED CREAM

BAKED INDIAN PUDDING and ICE CREAM   CHOCOLATE CAKE with FUDGE SAUCE

INDIVIDUAL CHEESE AND CRACKERS   ICE CREAM   SHERBET

COFFEE   TEA   SANKA   MILK

MIXED NUTS   FRESH FRUIT   MINTS

*The rolls and muffins are made daily in our own Kitchen from flour and meal stone
ground at The Wayside Grist Mill operated by Pepperidge Farm Inc. Rolls and muffins
may be purchased as well as the stone ground flour and meal, in our Gift Shop.*

Mass. Old Age Tax of 5% on all meals over 1.00

OPEN DAILY ALL YEAR AROUND

ROAST TURKEY WAYSIDE INN
SERVES 8

Everyone has his own favorite turkey recipe, but we are partial to this one from the Wayside Inn which celebrates traditional Thanksgivings close to the scene of the original one. "Fresh-killed turkeys are best for flavor and moistness," the chef told us, though he admitted that good quality frozen ones would do in a pinch. Long, slow cooking and frequent basting result in a beautifully browned bird with succulent flesh. The Wayside Inn's stuffing using home-baked bread and homemade sausage has an old-fashioned excellence hard to duplicate with store-bought ingredients.

turkey
salt, pepper
Wayside stuffing
butter
bacon
onions
cloves
celery
carrots
bay leaves
parsley
thyme
flour
cooked ham
cooked chicken
Wayside country
sausage (see index)
day-old bread
eggs
sage
mace
marjoram
chicken stock
(see index)

TURKEY

1 Preheat oven to moderate (325° F.).
2 Rub inside of a ready-to-cook **12-pound turkey** with: **1 teaspoon salt** and **¼ teaspoon pepper**. Stuff body and neck cavities with: **Wayside stuffing**. Truss legs and wings close to body. Rub skin with: **½ cup butter** and sprinkle with: **1 teaspoon salt** and **a little pepper**. Place breast up in shallow roasting pan and arrange: **2 slices bacon** over the breast.
3 To roasting pan add: **2 cups water, 1 onion stuck with 3 cloves, 1 stalk celery, 2 carrots, 2 bay leaves, 5 sprigs parsley,** and **½ teaspoon thyme**.
4 Cook turkey in the moderate oven for 10 to 20 minutes per pound (3½ to 4 hours), or until it is a rich even brown, basting every 30 minutes with drippings in pan.
5 Place turkey on large heated platter and serve with giblet gravy.

GIBLET GRAVY

While turkey is cooking, simmer: **the turkey giblets, neck** and **wing tips** in **1 quart water** for 2 hours. When turkey is arranged on serving platter, strain liquid in roasting pan and let fat rise to surface. Return 6 tablespoons fat to baking pan. Stir in: **6 tablespoons flour** and cook for 5 minutes, stirring in all the brown bits from bottom and sides of pan. Stir in: **3 cups combined stock** from giblets and liquid from roasting pan (degreased) and cook, stirring, until gravy is thickened and smooth. Add the chopped giblets.

WAYSIDE BREAD STUFFING (Makes About 8 Cups)

1 In skillet melt: **½ cup butter**. Add: **2 onions, chopped, 2 stalks celery, chopped,** and cook over low heat for 10 minutes.
2 Add: **1 cup finely diced cooked ham, 1 cup finely diced cooked chicken meat, ½ cup Wayside country sausage** and cook for 5 minutes longer, stirring occasionally.
3 Pour mixture over: **6 cups day-old bread crumbs** in large mixing bowl. Add: **4 eggs, lightly beaten, 1 teaspoon crumbled sage, ¼ teaspoon pepper, ¼ teaspoon thyme, ¼ teaspoon mace, ¼ teaspoon marjoram,** and **1 teaspoon salt**. Mix lightly and stir in: **½ cup chicken stock** to moisten.

WAYSIDE COUNTRY SAUSAGE
MAKES 1 POUND

You can buy very good pork sausage, it is true, but there is a special satisfaction in making your own. This is the Wayside Inn's easy recipe for their excellent country sausage, good fried for breakfast or for the stuffing in your Thanksgiving turkey.

pork shoulder	1 Trim the excess fat from: **1 pound pork shoulder.** Grind the pork through the fine blade of a meat grinder.	spoon thyme, **¼ teaspoon dry mustard,** and **1 teaspoon crumbled sage.**
salt, pepper		
dry mustard		3 Shape into patties and pan fry or broil
thyme	2 Combine the ground pork with: **1 teaspoon salt, ½ teaspoon pepper, 1 tea-**	slowly for about 15 minutes, or until well browned on both sides.
sage		

STEAMED BOSTON BROWN BREAD
MAKES TWO 1-POUND LOAVES

It's a rare thing these days to be served homemade bread, and rarer still to have that bread made from stone-ground flour. One of the historic buildings that belongs to the Wayside Inn is The Old Grist Mill where wheat, rye, corn, and buckwheat are ground today between stones powered by a creaking waterwheel. The breads, rolls, and griddle cakes served at the Inn are superlative, and I recommend using stone-ground products, if you can get them, when you follow these recipes.

cornmeal	1 Combine: **1 cup cornmeal, 1 cup rye flour, 1 cup graham flour,** and **1 teaspoon salt.**	4 Place molds on rack in kettle. Add boiling water to come halfway up around sides of molds. Cover and steam for 3 hours. Keep water in kettle boiling, and add more as needed to keep water at proper level.
rye flour		
graham flour		
salt	2 Dissolve: **1 teaspoon baking soda** in **1 tablespoon water** and stir into: **½ cup molasses.** Stir molasses into: **2 cups sour milk.** Then stir the liquid into the dry ingredients.	
baking soda		
molasses		5 Preheat oven to moderate (325° F.).
sour milk		6 Unmold loaves and bake in the moderate oven for 10 to 15 minutes to dry.
raisins	3 Mix: **1 cup raisins** with **2 tablespoons all-purpose flour** and add to batter. Mix thoroughly and divide into 2 **greased** 1-quart molds with tight covers.	*Note:* Steamed brown bread should never be cut with a knife: it should be sliced with a string.
butter		
all-purpose flour		

CORNMEAL MUFFINS
MAKES 16 MUFFINS

If you stay overnight in one of the charming Colonial guest rooms of the Wayside Inn, you will wake up to the kind of morning our ancestors must have known. No Indians lurk behind the trees, but there is bird song and the fresh New England green of fields and woods. And the smell of good things cooking for breakfast, like the following muffins and griddle cakes.

cornmeal	1 Preheat oven to hot (400° F.).	eggs, well beaten, and **1½ tablespoons melted butter.**
flour	2 Mix and sift: **1 cup cornmeal, 2 cups flour, 1½ tablespoons baking powder, 1 teaspoon salt,** and **¼ cup sugar.**	
baking powder		
milk		4 Bake in **buttered** muffin pans in the hot oven for about 25 minutes.
salt		
sugar	3 Gradually beat in: **1½ cups milk, 2**	5 Remove from pans and serve warm.
butter		
eggs		

285

BUCKWHEAT GRIDDLE CAKES
MAKES 15 GRIDDLE CAKES

buckwheat flour
baking powder
flour
eggs
salt
milk
butter

1 Sift together: **1 cup buckwheat flour, 3 teaspoons baking powder, ¼ cup flour, and ¾ teaspoon salt.**

2 To **1¾ cups milk** add: **2 tablespoons melted butter** and **2 eggs, well beaten.**

3 Combine with dry ingredients and beat well.

4 Slightly **butter** a hot griddle and bake cakes, turning once when underside is browned. Serve at once.

WHOLE WHEAT BREAD
MAKES TWO 1-POUND LOAVES

If we ate bread like this all the time, we wouldn't have to worry so much about vitamins. The Wayside Inn's loaves have a marvelous nut-brown color and flavor, and they make the best toast ever.

yeast
all-purpose flour
milk
shortening
molasses
sugar
salt
whole wheat flour

1 Soften: **1 cake yeast** or **1 package active dry yeast** in **1 cup lukewarm water.** Stir in: **about 2 cups all-purpose flour** to make a thick batter. Beat until smooth. Cover and let stand in a warm place overnight.

2 Next day scald: **1 cup milk** with **3 tablespoons shortening, 2 tablespoons molasses, 1 tablespoon sugar, and 2½ teaspoons salt.** Cool to lukewarm.

3 Stir down the yeast sponge and combine with the milk mixture. Beat in: **4 cups sifted whole wheat flour,** or enough to make a stiff dough. Turn dough out on lightly **floured** board and knead until smooth. Divide into 2 equal portions. Cover with a towel and let rest for 10 minutes. Then shape into loaves and put into **greased** 1-pound loaf pans. Brush tops with **melted shortening,** cover, and let rise for about 1½ hours, or until double in bulk.

4 Preheat oven to hot (400° F.).

5 Bake loaves for 45 to 50 minutes in the hot oven, or until brown.

BANANA PANCAKE FLAMBÉ STONEHENGE
SERVES 2

The United States can boast its fair share of lovely country inns. Some of them are historic, some are truly rural, others are sophisticatedly rustic. By and large they all set a fine table. Stonehenge, near Ridgefield, Connecticut, is a white New England farmhouse famous for its elegant cuisine. This unusual luncheon entrée can hardly be called country fare, but it is delightful to be eating *flambéed* bananas while looking out over rolling hills and a placid pond.

bananas
butter
crepes (see index)
bacon
banana liqueur

1 Make: **8 crepes** and set aside.

2 Peel and split lengthwise: **4 bananas.**

3 In a skillet heat: **2 tablespoons butter.** When it sizzles, put the banana halves in for 3 minutes. Turn to coat with butter and remove them.

4 Lay out the 8 crepes on a board. Roll a banana half in each. Place in a skillet or chafing dish. Garnish each crepe with: **a strip of crisp cooked bacon.**

5 Heat: **½ cup banana liqueur** and pour, flaming, over the banana pancakes.

PRESENTATION

Serve each person 4 banana-filled crepes with a little of the liquid from the pan.

COCOTTE OF GUINEA HEN WITH BRANDY SAUCE
SERVES 2

On the North Shore of Long Island the Beau Séjour is more like a country estate than an inn. It was founded at the turn of the century by a French chef who had worked in New York. The local seafood is a great specialty, but so too are the dishes so dear to the hearts of French chefs. Our favorite is this beautiful guinea hen, served in the oval cocotte or casserole in which it was cooked.

guinea hen
salt, pepper
thyme
butter
corn oil
cornstarch
chicken stock
(see index)
chicken bouillon
cube
garlic
red currant jelly
cream (sweet or
sour)
brandy
red wine

GUINEA HEN

1 Preheat oven to moderately hot (375° F.).

2 Take: **an oven-ready guinea hen.** Rub it lightly inside and out with: **1 teaspoon salt** and **⅛ teaspoon pepper.** Place inside cavity: **1 leaf thyme.** Truss the guinea hen and brush with **melted butter** and a little **corn oil.**

3 Place bird on its back in shallow roasting pan in the moderately hot oven. After 10 minutes baste with a little **melted butter** and **corn oil** and turn on its side. Repeat in 10 minutes, turning on other side. Baste and turn every 10 minutes. In 30 minutes the bird should be golden brown.

4 Reduce oven heat to slow (300° F.).

5 Transfer guinea hen to small oval cocotte or casserole with tight-fitting cover.

6 Add: **1 tablespoon butter** and **½ cup chicken stock.** Cover and place in slow oven for 20 minutes.

SAUCE

1 Pour off all cooking fat from roasting pan, being careful not to lose the brown drippings.

2 Place over medium heat and add: **¼ cup red wine.** Stir to lift drippings. Add: **¾ cup chicken stock, 1 chicken bouillon cube, 1 tablespoon butter, a pinch of thyme, 1 clove garlic, 1 tablespoon red currant jelly,** and **1 tablespoon sweet** or **sour cream.** Stir well to blend and bring to a boil.

3 If sauce needs thickening dissolve: **1 tablespoon cornstarch** in **½ cup water.** Add to the sauce little by little, stirring constantly. Stop when sauce is thick enough.

PRESENTATION

Strain sauce over guinea hen in casserole. Sprinkle: **1 ounce brandy** over all and serve piping hot.

FILET DE BOEUF CRÉMAILLÈRE (*Roast Fillet of Beef*)
SERVES 6

La Crémaillère-à-la-Campagne in Banksville, New York, is most like the great country dining places in France. Yes, expensive too. Here is their superb recipe for fillet of beef, unsurpassably marvelous. This is expensive even at home, but if you do splurge you may as well do justice to this luxury roast. The Crémaillère's recipe calls for larding the fillet—introducing long, thin strips of pork fat into the meat with a larding needle. This is an excellent gambit of French chefs when dealing with dry or inferior cuts, but may be gilding the lily where a fillet of beef is concerned. I should say you could suit yourself about whether to lard or not to lard.

fillet of beef
larding pork
butter
carrots
onion
truffle
salt, white pepper
celery salt
garlic
Calvados
Madeira
canned beef gravy
tomato paste

FILLET

1 Preheat oven to very hot (500° F.).

2 Wipe with a damp cloth: **a 5-pound fillet of beef.**

3 Soak: **10 small strips larding pork** in **3 tablespoons Calvados** (apple brandy) for 5 minutes. Reserve the Calvados. With a larding needle insert pork fat strips from one narrow end of roast through to the other end.

4 Rub roast well with: **1 teaspoon celery salt, ½ teaspoon salt,** and **¼ teaspoon white pepper.**

5 Roll meat lengthwise and tie with white string every 2 inches.

6 In a roasting pan melt: **½ cup butter.** Roll fillet in butter and roast in the very hot oven for 35 minutes. Baste and turn meat every 10 minutes.

7 Remove fillet to a warm platter.

SAUCE

1 Pour fat from roasting pan. Put in: **2 carrots, sliced, 1 onion, sliced,** and **1 clove garlic, chopped.** Put back in oven for 8 minutes, or until onion browns. Do not let it burn.

2 Remove pan from oven and set over burner on top of stove. Add the 3 tablespoons Calvados. Stir well to lift pan drippings. Stir in: **1 cup canned beef gravy, 1 teaspoon tomato paste,** and **½ cup Madeira.**

3 Bring to boil, reduce heat, and simmer for 10 minutes, stirring. Strain sauce and add: **1 large truffle, chopped.**

PRESENTATION

Cut string from fillet of beef. Serve on warm platter, cut into ½-inch slices. Serve sauce on side.

In the Men's Bar at Locke-Ober's their famous Lobster Savannah, all three glorious pounds of it, is set before a hungry diner. This is one of the continental specialties of Boston's venerable restaurant.

New England Boiled Dinner is, for us, the epitome of honest excellence. Here, cooked according to Locke-Ober's recipe, is our boiled dinner, hearty and colorful, fresh from the steaming pot.

LOCKE-OBER'S

ONCE upon my college days, the Men's Bar at Locke-Ober's was the scene of revelries on the night of the Yale-Harvard game. Every other year The Game is played in Boston, and on the big night tradition is tossed to the winds and women are permitted to enter the Men's Bar. As I recall it, there is a painting of a large, coy nude at one end of the bar, and if Harvard has lost, her rosy flesh is draped with a black scarf. Fortunately this pretty sentiment occurs often enough to protect the sensibilities of the ladies present.

I had come a long way from St. Louis to New Haven, and Boston's Yankee cuisine was new to me. There is no better place I could have chosen for an introduction to it than Locke-Ober's. The restaurant is more than eighty years old, and the original mahogany bar and silver steam dishes date from 1886 when they graced Ober's elegant Restaurant Parisien. In those days Ober's neighbor and rival was Frank Locke, who ran a hearty pub specializing in strong booze and New England dishes. Eventually the restaurants combined, and to this day the menu is a schizophrenic mishmash of continental specialties and homespun Yankee goodies, all prepared to perfection.

I guess I lean toward the Locke side of the restaurant, even to enjoying the cocktail invented there—the Ward Eight. Named for one of Boston's more colorful political wards, the Ward Eight was concocted one election eve as a toast to the success of the candidates. It is a whiskey sour with grenadine added to give it the proper pink glow of optimism. I recommend that you scan the Locke-Ober menu on the next page, and then launch into some of their prize recipes with a similar glow of anticipation.

291

LOCKE-OBER CAFÉ
EST·1875

LUNCHEON

Appetizers

Fruit Cup 60	V-8 Cocktail 30	Crabmeat Cocktail 1.85
Cranberry Juice 30	Hearts of Palm 85	Hearts of Artichokes 85
Tomato Juice 30	Shrimp Cocktail 1.85	Seafood Cocktail 2.25
Clam Juice 30	Hors d'Oeuvres, Varies 1.90	Eggs, Fisherman 1.85

Oysters and Clams

Oyster Cocktail 1.50	Baked Oysters, Ballard 1.65	Little Neck Clam Cocktail 90
Baked Oysters, Winter Place 1.65	Baked Oysters, Rockefeller 1.90	Cherrystone Cocktail 90
Baked Oysters, Gino 2.00	Oyster Stew 1.50	Baked Clams, Gino 1.85
Fried Oysters (6) 1.25	with Cream 1.85	Baked Clams, Casino 1.50
Fried Oysters (12) 2.00		

Soups

New England Fish Chowder 45-85

Cup of Consomme 30	Cup of Green Split Pea 30
Cup of Hot Essence of Chicken 30	Cup of Cream of Tomato 40
Cup of Fresh Vegetable Soup 30	Cup of Hot or Cold Vichyssoise 40

Fish

Fresh Eastern Swordfish Saute Meuniere, Chiffonade Salad 2.75
Broiled Finnan Haddie, Maitre d'Hotel, Mixed Green Salad 2.20
Boiled, Broiled or Baked Chicken Lobster (1¼ lb.), Drawn Butter 4.25
Broiled Cape Scallops and Bacon, French Fried Potatoes 3.00
Fried Cape Scallops, French Fried Potatoes 2.75

Entrees

Petite Tenderloin Steak, Sauce Bordelaise, Parisienne Potatoes, Mixed Green Salad 4.25
Broiled Fresh Mushrooms on Toast 1.75   a la Sam Ward 2.00
Chicken a la Maryland, Bacon, Candied Sweet Potato 1.95
Emince of Milk-Fed Veal Hunter Style en Casserole, Rice Pilaff 2.10
Broiled Ground Prime Sirloin, Sauce Bordelaise,
Parisienne Potato, Mixed Green Salad 2.20
Poached Eggs, St. Jacques, Cream Cape Scallops, Asparagus Spears Mornay 1.90

A LA CARTE

Meats and Poultry

Club Sirloin Steak (Boston Cut) 6.25	Brochette of Tenderloin, Bordelaise 4.00
Filet Mignon of Beef, Mirabeau 6.00	Calf's Liver and Bacon 3.25
Broiled Fresh Honeycomb Tripe 2.00	with Mustard Sauce 2.25
Wiener Schnitzel 3.25	Wiener Schnitzel à la Holstein 3.50
Frog's Legs, Provencale 3.75	Breast of Duck, Sliced Orange, Sauce Bigarade 3.50
Broiled Lamb Chops (2) 4.00	Breast of Chicken Sauté (Under Glass) Richmond 3.00

Fish

Brook Trout Saute Meuniere (1) 1.75 (2) 3.25	Curry of Shrimps on Curried Rice 3.25
Planked Fillet of Lake Trout, Winter Place 3.50	
Casserole of Shrimps and Lobster à l'Americaine 4.75	Fresh Lobster Stew 4.50
Baked Stuffed Jumbo Shrimps, Sauce Diable 4.00	Fresh Lobster Newburg 4.75
Coquille of Lobster Savannah 5.00	Baked Lobster Savannah 10.00

Vegetables and Potatoes

Buttered Carrots 40 in Cream 50		Spinach — Plain 30 in Cream 40
String Beans 50	Green Peas 40 Stuffed Tomato 75	Stuffed Pepper 75
Delmonico Potatoes 50	Lyonnaise Potatoes 45	Julienne Potatoes 40

Salads

Fresh Lobster 4.50	Chicken 2.25	Chiffonade 50-90
Seafood 3.00	Tunafish 1.85	Watercress 75
Crabmeat 3.00	Egg 1.00	Hearts of Lettuce 40
Jumbo Shrimp 3.00	Kentucky Bibb Lettuce 80	Fresh Fruit 1.75

Roquefort Cheese Dressing (60c extra)   Russian Dressing (40c extra)

Desserts

Fresh Strawberries with Cream 80		Strawberry Shortcake 90
Butterscotch Walnut Sundae 80	Baked Indian Pudding with Ice Cream 60	
Rhubarb Pie 30	Pies a la Mode 75	Half Grapefruit 60
Lemon Meringue Pie 40	Lillian Russell 90	Grapefruit, Delmonico 65
Cheese Cake 50	French Macaroons 40	Melon in Season 60
Apple Pie 30	Sultana Roll, Claret Sc. 65	Frozen Pudding 45
with Cheese 40	Spumoni 65	Lemon Sherbet 45
Locke-Ober's Vanilla, Chocolate or Coffee Ice Cream 45		Macaroons 40 Eclair 35

Fudge or Butterscotch Sauce 15c extra

Cheese

Camembert 30	Imported Cheddar 40	Imported Roquefort 75
Liederkranz 30	Cream Cheese with	Port-du-Salut 65
Cream 30	Bar-le-Duc 45	Bel Paese 65
	Imported Swiss 50	

Beverages

Coffee (pot) 35	Sanka 25	Milk 20
Demi Tasse 25	Tea (pot) 25	Iced Tea 20
Café Frappe 30		Iced Coffee 30

Bread and Butter 20

One Order Served for Two 50c extra   MASSACHUSETTS MEALS TAX 5%

Private Room Charge 25c per person

Friday, March 6, 1964

NEW ENGLAND BOILED DINNER
SERVES 8

The honest goodness of this dish depends entirely on the quality of the meat used. When Mr. Little, the president of Locke-Ober's, gave me their recipes he could not be emphatic enough about the importance of using quality ingredients in all of them. In a dish like this one, where nothing is fancied up, it is more than important—it is imperative that the meat and the vegetables be the very best.

corned brisket of
beef
beets
potatoes
carrots
cabbage
silverskin onions
mustard (optional)
horse-radish
(optional)

BOILED DINNER

1 Buy: **4 pounds New England style heavy steer corned brisket.** Wipe with damp cloth and tie with white string to make a compact piece.

2 Place brisket in large, heavy pot and cover with cold water. Bring water to boil and simmer for 3½ hours, or until brisket is tender, adding more water if necessary to keep brisket covered at all times with the cooking liquid.

3 An hour before brisket is cooked, put: **8 small beets** into a saucepan. Cover with boiling water and boil for 1 hour. Peel while hot and keep hot.

4 45 minutes before brisket is cooked, put: **8 medium-sized potatoes, peeled,** into a saucepan. Cover with hot water and boil for 45 minutes, or until tender. Drain and keep hot.

5 20 minutes before brisket is cooked, add to liquid in pot: **4 large carrots, peeled and halved,** and **16 small silverskin onions, peeled.** Continue to cook the brisket with the vegetables.

PRESENTATION

1 Remove the brisket from pot, drain, and place in center of large, heated platter. Cut off string. To liquid and vegetables in the pot add: **8 wedges of cabbage** (1 large head). Cover and simmer for 15 minutes.

2 Surround the brisket with the cabbage wedges, onions, carrots, potatoes, and beets.

3 To serve: Slice the meat in thin, slantwise slices across the grain. Place a wedge of cooked cabbage in the center of each individual plate, place slices of hot brisket over it, and surround with the other cooked vegetables. If desired, serve with **mustard** and **horse-radish.**

COQUILLE OF LOBSTER SAVANNAH
SERVES 4 FOR ENTRÉE; 6 FOR FIRST COURSE

This is Locke-Ober's most famous specialty. Their regular Lobster Savannah is a gargantuan three-pound lobster, its huge shells heaped high with chunks of Maine lobster in a rich cream sauce. But for more delicate appetites they serve a smaller portion in *coquilles*, scallop shells. We like to make several pints of béchamel sauce at a time to freeze in one-cup containers. Then when a recipe like this one comes along, the basic preparation for the sauce is right at hand and the rest goes quickly.

béchamel sauce
(see index)
butter
green pepper
mushrooms
sherry
paprika
lobster meat
cream
pimientos
Parmesan cheese
cooked green peas

1   In saucepan melt: **1½ tablespoons butter** over moderate heat.

2   Add: **1 large green pepper, cut into large dice**, and **4 large mushrooms, cut into large dice**. Toss the vegetables in the butter, cover, and cook over moderate heat for 5 minutes.

3   Preheat oven to hot (400° F.).

4   Add to vegetable mixture: **½ cup sherry, 1 teaspoon paprika** and cook, uncovered, over high heat until sherry is reduced by half, about 5 minutes.

5   Add: **1 pound fresh lobster meat, diced, 1¼ cups béchamel sauce**, and **¼ cup cream**. Stir to mix lobster and sauce and heat to boiling.

6   Stir in: **a 4-ounce can pimientos, cut into large dice.**

PRESENTATION

Divide mixture into 4 large, or 6 medium, scallop shells or au gratin dishes. Sprinkle each with: **1 tablespoon grated Parmesan cheese**, and bake in the hot oven for 10 minutes. Serve with **cooked green peas.**

CAPE COD SCALLOPS SAUTÉ MEUNIÈRE
SERVES **4**

New England seafood is without peer, and when you have a fresh Maine lobster or Cape Cod scallops to work with, the simpler the preparation the better for letting their own true taste come through. No amount of fancy seasoning can beat it. If you are lucky enough to live where fresh scallops (pronounced "skulps" by the Down Easters) are available, this Locke-Ober recipe is one to treasure.

scallops
butter
cooking oil
lemon
parsley
flour

SCALLOPS

1   Wash and drain: **3 pounds fresh Cape Cod scallops** (the small ones) and dry in a kitchen towel.

2   Dredge in **flour** and shake vigorously to remove all excess flour.

3   In a heavy iron skillet heat **cooking oil** ¼ inch deep. When it is almost smoking hot add half of the scallops. Let them brown lightly for about 5 minutes.

4   Remove from pan with slotted spoon, drain on paper towels, and keep warm.

5   Add more **cooking oil** to the pan to maintain ¼-inch depth, and heat almost

to smoking. Brown remaining scallops.

6   Remove and drain scallops.

SAUCE

1   Pour off all fat from pan and add: **¼ pound butter**. Heat butter until it turns a light brown.

2   Remove from stove at once and add: **the juice of ½ large lemon** and **2 teaspoons finely chopped parsley.**

PRESENTATION

Put browned scallops on warm platter or in oval copper casserole. Pour hot butter sauce over them and serve with a garnish of **parsley** and **lemon wedges.**

295

OYSTERS À LA GINO
SERVES 1

This is a very quick recipe to make, if you have a supply of béchamel sauce in your refrigerator or freezer. It was invented by the chef at Locke-Ober's in collaboration with the restaurant's president, who occasionally likes to try his hand in the kitchen. A typically masculine appetizer, it is eaten with gusto by the businessmen who patronize Locke-Ober's at lunch time, and we have found it a splendid first course when the balance of the dinner is light.

bacon
garlic
lump crabmeat
béchamel sauce
(see index)
cream
Madeira
bread crumbs
olive oil
rock or kosher salt
oysters
lemon

1 Preheat oven to moderately hot (375° F.).

2 Mince: **1 strip raw bacon** and **½ clove garlic.** Sauté in a hot skillet until bacon is crisp. Drain off fat and mix with: **½ cup fresh lump crabmeat.**

3 In a saucepan combine: **¼ cup béchamel sauce, 1 tablespoon cream,** and **3 tablespoons Madeira.** Stir and bring to a quick boil.

4 Stir in the crabmeat mixture, reduce heat, and cook for 2 minutes.

5 Mix: **½ clove garlic, minced, 2 tablespoons fresh bread crumbs,** and **1 tablespoon olive oil.**

PRESENTATION

1 Cover an ovenproof plate with a layer of **rock** or **kosher salt,** and in it bed: **6 large, opened oysters on the half shell** (Locke-Ober's uses Cape Cod oysters).

2 Put a generous mound of the crabmeat mixture on each oyster, sprinkle each with some of the bread crumbs, and top each oyster with: **a 1½-inch square of raw bacon.** Bake in the moderately hot oven for 15 to 18 minutes, or until bacon is crisp and crumb topping is browned. Serve at once with **lemon wedges.**

NEW ENGLAND CLAM CHOWDER
SERVES 8

This is the true, the authentic clam chowder invented and relished by seagoing New Englanders, and a favorite there for generations. There is something called Manhattan Clam Chowder, made with tomatoes and therefore a ruddy color, but your proper Bostonian will have nothing to do with that aberrant form. Locke-Ober's recipe is for the pale cream-colored soup to which you may add a dusting of paprika for color, no more. As far as flavor is concerned, it doesn't even need that.

chowder clams
celery
onions
garlic
bay leaf
parsley
potatoes
salt pork
leek
flour
light cream
butter
paprika (optional)

CHOWDER

1 Wash and scrub: **12 chowder clams** or **quahogs** and put them in a large kettle.

2 Add: **2 stalks celery, diced, 1 medium onion, diced, 1 clove garlic, minced, 1 small bay leaf, a small bunch parsley stems,** and **1½ quarts cold water.** Bring water to a boil, cover pot, and simmer the clams for 10 minutes.

3 Remove clams, discard shells, and strain the stock through a fine strainer into a large saucepan.

4 Add: **1 cup diced raw potatoes** and simmer for 15 minutes, or until potatoes are tender.

5 Peel back the outer sheath from the soft inner belly of the clams and cut

away connecting cord. Dice the bellies, and mince the tough outer sheaths. Cover with a little of the hot stock and set aside.

6 In another kettle put: **2 ounces salt pork, minced, 1 small onion, minced, 1 stalk celery, finely sliced,** and **1 leek, chopped.** Cook over low heat for 15 minutes, or until vegetables are tender and the salt pork is rendered.

7 Sprinkle with: **3 tablespoons flour,** stir to mix, then stir in the hot stock and potatoes. Simmer for 15 minutes longer.

PRESENTATION

Just before serving stir in the clams, **1 tablespoon butter,** and **1 cup hot light cream.** Sprinkle lightly with **paprika** (optional). This is usually served with pilot crackers or oyster crackers.

LOBSTER BISQUE
SERVES 4

This is unlike the French bisques which are made with a white-wine fish stock and have a good jolt of cognac added just before serving. But for a straightforward lobster soup, this recipe from Locke-Ober's is excellent.

fish heads, bones
and trimmings
onions
parsley
peppercorns
lemon
dry white wine
cooking oil
chicken lobster
celery
carrot
garlic
flour
paprika
tomato puree
salt, pepper
cream
butter

FISH STOCK

Into a kettle put: **2 pounds fish heads, bones,** and **trimmings, 1 onion, thinly sliced, 6 sprigs parsley, ¼ teaspoon peppercorns, 1 teaspoon lemon juice, 1 cup dry white wine,** and **2½ quarts cold water.** Bring liquid to a boil and boil for 30 minutes. Strain. This makes 2 quarts stock. Use half for this recipe, and freeze the rest for another time.

BISQUE

1 In a large pot heat: **¼ cup cooking oil** to the smoking point.

2 Cut: **a live chicken lobster** in half (or ask your fish man to do this for you). Detach and crack claws. Cut body into 2 or 4 sections. Add the lobster pieces to the hot oil and cook over high heat, stirring, until lobster shells turn pink.

3 Add: **1 stalk celery, diced, ½ medium onion, chopped, ½ large carrot, chopped,** and **1 small clove garlic.** Continue to cook, stirring occasionally, until vegetables are lightly browned.

4 Stir in: **½ cup flour** and cook, stirring, until well blended.

5 Add: **1 teaspoon paprika, 1½ tablespoons tomato puree, ½ teaspoon pepper,** and **½ teaspoon salt.**

6 Gradually stir in 1 quart of the hot fish stock and cook, stirring, until soup boils. Reduce heat to very low, cover, and cook slowly for 2 hours.

PRESENTATION

Strain soup and add: **3 tablespoons butter** to prevent a crust from forming on top. Remove lobster meat from body and claws and dice. When ready to serve mix soup with: **1 cup cream.** Heat and serve with some of the diced lobster meat in each serving.

BAKED INDIAN PUDDING
SERVES 8

Located in the bustle of Boston's market district, Durgin-Park has been dispensing plain but plentiful food since 1742. You eat at one of several long tables in a large noisy room, and the portions are stupefyingly enormous. But if you like the specialties of New England, as I do, you'll be delighted with Durgin-Park. The traditional Indian Pudding is surprisingly delicious here. Some people feel we would be wise to give this pudding back to the Indians, but when it is well prepared it can be very good in a homey, Early American way. It is soft and it does separate somewhat (Fannie Farmer says it's supposed to), but the long, slow baking gives the spices a chance to fuse into a mellow symphony of flavor.

milk
yellow cornmeal
dark molasses
sugar
cinnamon
ground ginger
butter
salt
baking soda
eggs
cream (optional)
ground cloves

PUDDING

1 Preheat oven to hot (425° F.).

2 Mix together: **1 cup yellow cornmeal, ¼ cup sugar, ¼ teaspoon salt, ¼ teaspoon baking soda, 2 eggs, beaten, ½ cup dark molasses, 4 tablespoons softened butter, ½ teaspoon cinnamon, ¼ teaspoon ground ginger, and ¼ teaspoon ground cloves.**

3 Beat mixture well and add: **3 cups hot milk.** Mix well and pour into a buttered 2-quart baking dish or casserole pretty enough to serve from.

4 Put in the hot oven until mixture boils. Then reduce oven heat to very slow (225° F.).

5 Stir in: **3 cups hot milk** and bake the Indian Pudding slowly for 5 hours.

PRESENTATION

Let pudding stand for about 30 minutes to set. Serve warm with **whipped cream** and a sprinkling of **ground ginger.**

A banquet at the Virginia Museum of Fine Arts takes on added splendor from its setting in the Medieval Hall. Here, after dining by candlelight and surrounded by objects of art, I was invested with the Order of the Collectors' Circle.

What artistry there can be in the simplest things! A salad of crisp, fresh greens was one of the banquet courses, and we choose a similar one here to illustrate the beauty of simplicity. Aesthetically, too, a dinner of herbs can be better than a stalled ox or fatted calf.

VIRGINIA MUSEUM
OF FINE ARTS

IN AMERICA many non-culinary organizations pride themselves on serving great food. The Virginia Museum of Fine Arts honored us and our collection in 1964 with a magnificent gourmet banquet held in the Medieval Hall of the museum itself. Here indeed was a museum housing all the arts. The wonderfully equipped little theater was rehearsing a new play; collections of furniture, decorative arts, Fabergé jewelry and fine paintings gleamed and gloried all around.

Ladies and gentlemen in dinner dress and wearing their badges of the Order of the Collectors' Circle looked their best and deserved the best, which was served promptly and piping hot by the highly efficient staff. I have sat through too many a tepid banquet, in places that should know better, not to appreciate fine service when it comes along. It is a very important part of dining well, and all too often neglected.

But the South is still concerned with all the gentle arts of living and the graceful traditions of a bygone day. During dinner, seated at the long table in the Medieval Hall where heraldic banners hung overhead and a knight in armor was spotlighted before a great tapestry, we drank toasts. Formal toasts they were, drunk in vintage wines—to the President of the United States, to the Governor of Virginia, to Her Majesty the Queen. The menu was the inspiration of Mary Tyler Cheek, wife of the museum's brilliant director, Leslie Cheek, Jr. The whole evening was a work of art and a great pleasure, as all art should be.

Mr. Vincent Price

The Collectors' Circle

of the

Virginia Museum of Fine Arts

presents a Dinner in honor of

MR. VINCENT PRICE

Collector and Thespian

at the

Museum Building in Richmond

on Saturday, March 14th, 1964

at 7 o'clock

THE EVENTS

RECEPTION
in the Theatre Gallery
(Before Dinner)

Mr. and Mrs. Vincent Price
Guests of Honor

*

TOASTS
in the Medieval Hall
(During Dinner)

The President of the United States
proposed by the President of the Museum

The Governor of Virginia
proposed by the Director of the Museum

Her Majesty the Queen
proposed by the Steward of the Circle

PROGRAM
in the Medieval Hall
(After Dinner)

REMARKS
Mr. Joseph Bryan, III
President of the Circle

INVESTITURE
Order of the Collectors' Circle
Mr. Paul Mellon
COMMANDER, 1963

Mr. Vincent Price
COMMANDER, 1964

RESPONSE
Mr. Vincent Price
Collector and Thespian

THE MENU

In the Theatre Gallery
(7 p.m.)

HORS D'OEUVRES

APERITIFS

*

In the Medieval Hall
(8 p.m.)

CONSOMMÉ AU CÉLERI
CROÛTONS
Chablis, Les Preuses

·

POUSSINS ZIZANIE
TURBAN D'ARTICHAUTS ET PETITS POIS
TRANCHES D'ORANGES GRILLÉES
PETITS PAINS
Chateau Margaux, 1957

SALADE DE CRESSON
FROMAGES VARIÉS
BISCUITS D'OR

·

MOUSSE D'ABRICOT
PETITS FOURS DE DENTELLE
Veuve Clicquot, Brut

·

DEMI TASSE
LIQUEURS

*

In the Members' Suite
(10 p.m.)

EVENING REFRESHMENTS

Piano Music
by Mr. George Ryall

MIXED GREEN SALAD
SERVES 6

This is a simple green salad with a classic French dressing. We like to mix our salad greens for color, taste, and texture. The curly escarole, dark green romaine, and pale cucumber slices are a good combination here. For the dressing, you must experiment until you find the oil and the vinegar that suit you best, but these proportions are the tried and true ones.

romaine lettuce
escarole
salt, pepper
dry mustard
lemon
cucumbers
olive oil
red wine vinegar
garlic
bread (optional)

SALAD

1 Wash: **1 head romaine** and **1 head escarole.** Shake well to get rid of excess moisture. Break off leaves and dry separately in kitchen towel. Put dry leaves in salad bowl that has been rubbed with: **a clove of garlic.**

2 Wash: **2 cucumbers.** Cut off tips. Score deeply with tines of a fork to make lengthwise grooves in skin. Cut cucumbers in fairly thin slices. The edges will be fluted. Mix cucumber slices with salad greens.

DRESSING

Combine: **3 tablespoons olive oil, 1 table-** spoon red wine vinegar, the juice of ¼ lemon, ¼ teaspoon salt, ¼ teaspoon dry mustard, and **some freshly ground pepper.** Mix well.

CROUTONS (Optional)

Cut: **2 slices bread** in cubes. Sauté over medium heat in: **2 tablespoons hot olive oil** with **1 small clove garlic** until bread cubes are golden on all sides. Drain on absorbent paper.

PRESENTATION

When you are ready to serve, stir the dressing vigorously and pour over the salad. Sprinkle with the toasted croutons (optional) and toss lightly.

VEGETABLE BOUILLON
SERVES 6

There are two good reasons for beginning a banquet or dinner party with bouillon: it is light but flavorful, and it can make an attractive table setting served in handsome cups. We like this one from the Virginia Museum's feast, because when we keep beef stock in the freezer we can make this elegant first course in about twenty minutes.

beef stock
(see index)
celery
green onions
radishes
carrot
salt, pepper
lemon

1 Bring to a boil: **4 cups good beef stock.** Turn heat to low.

2 Add: **2 tablespoons minced celery leaves, 4 green onions, thinly sliced, 4 radishes, thinly sliced, 2 stalks celery, thinly sliced,** and **1 medium carrot, cut** into julienne strips. Simmer for 15 minutes, covered.

3 Add a little **salt** and **freshly ground pepper,** or to taste (the seasoning will depend upon your original beef stock), and **1 teaspoon lemon juice.** Serve in bouillon cups.

RING MOLD OF PEAS WITH ARTICHOKE HEARTS
SERVES 8

Food should delight the eye as well as the taste buds, and naturally when you dine in an art museum that is especially apt to happen. The two shades of green made this vegetable mold a picture, and the recipe itself is delicious. The grated onion does something marvelous to the puree of peas.

flour
butter
light cream
fresh green peas
salt
onion
eggs
soda cracker crumbs
cooked artichoke
hearts
parsley

1 Shell: **2 pounds green peas** and cook in **salted** water to cover for 20 minutes, or until peas are tender. With slotted spoon transfer peas to container of an electric blender. Add ½ cup of the pea liquid, cover and blend on high speed for 20 seconds, stopping to stir down if necessary. Strain through a coarse sieve. This should make 2 cups fresh pea puree.

2 **Butter** a 6-cup ring mold. Cover bottom of mold with a band of waxed paper and **butter** the paper.

3 In saucepan melt: **2 tablespoons butter.** Stir in: **2 tablespoons flour** and cook, stirring, for 2 minutes. Stir in: **½ cup hot light cream** and cook, stirring, until sauce is smooth and thick. Stir in: **1 teaspoon grated onion, 1 teaspoon salt** and let mixture cool slightly.

4 Stir in: **4 egg yolks** and **½ cup fine soda cracker crumbs.** Fold in the pea puree.

5 Preheat oven to moderate (350° F.).

6 Beat: **4 egg whites** until stiff but not dry and fold into the pea mixture. Fold lightly but thoroughly. Pour the mixture into the prepared ring mold and bake in the moderate oven for 40 minutes, or until set.

PRESENTATION
Remove ring from oven and let stand for a few minutes. Unmold on heated platter and remove waxed paper from bottom. Fill center with **buttered cooked artichoke hearts** and sprinkle with **chopped parsley.**

SPOON BREAD WITH VIRGINIA HAM
SERVES 6

Spoon bread is a little like a heavy soufflé made with cornmeal. The real old-fashioned spoon bread was made without leavening, but nowadays many recipes suggest using baking powder to help puff it up. I like this recipe which, like a man who wears both belt and suspenders, keeps the spoon bread up both ways.

white cornmeal
milk
salt
eggs
Virginia ham
butter
baking powder

1 Preheat oven to moderate (350° F.).

2 Heat just to boiling point: **2 cups milk.**

3 Sift together: **1 cup white cornmeal** and **1 teaspoon salt.** Add to the scalded milk slowly, stirring constantly. Cook over low heat and stir until thick.

4 Remove from heat and cool cornmeal mixture to lukewarm.

5 In a skillet heat: **2 tablespoons butter.** Sauté in it: **½ cup finely chopped Virginia ham.** Add ham and butter to the

cornmeal mixture.

6 In a large bowl beat well: **3 eggs.** Add the cornmeal mixture slowly to eggs. Add: **2 cups milk** and mix gently.

7 Sprinkle: **2 teaspoons baking powder** over top of batter and stir in rapidly.

8 Pour batter into **buttered** 10-inch casserole or soufflé dish.

9 Bake in the moderate oven for about 1 hour, or until spoon bread puffs and browns slightly. Serve at once.

GAME HENS WITH WILD RICE AND ORANGE SAUCE
SERVES 4

At the Virginia Museum, we were served squab chickens, undoubtedly raised locally. Since they are not always available we have used this recipe with Rock Cornish game hens which make excellent individual servings.

GAME HENS

Rock Cornish
game hens
salt, pepper
butter
oranges
Grand Marnier
chicken stock
(see index)
flour
wild rice
walnuts

1 Preheat oven to moderate (350° F.).
2 Spread: **4 Rock Cornish game hens** with **½ cup butter.** Sprinkle with **salt** and **pepper.** Arrange in a shallow roasting pan and bake in the moderate oven for 50 to 60 minutes, turning the birds and basting frequently with pan juices.
3 Remove birds to warm serving platter and keep warm.

SAUCE

1 Remove: **the thin orange rind** from **1 orange** with a vegetable peeler and cut rind into very fine shreds. Cover orange shreds with water, bring to a boil, and simmer for 10 minutes. Drain and set aside.
2 With a sharp knife, peel: **2 oranges,** removing all rind and every trace of the bitter white covering. Cut oranges into sections, free of connecting membranes, and add to shredded rind.

3 Pour off excess butter in roasting pan. Add: **4 tablespoons Grand Marnier** and ignite. When flame burns out stir in: **1 cup chicken stock** and cook, stirring in all the brown glaze from bottom and sides of pan. Stir in: **1 tablespoon flour** mixed to a paste with **1 tablespoon soft butter** and cook, stirring, until sauce is slightly thickened.

4 Add the shredded orange rind and orange sections and simmer for 2 minutes.

WILD RICE

Toss: **2 cups hot cooked wild rice** (cook according to package directions) with **½ cup chopped walnuts, ¼ cup soft butter,** and **salt** and **pepper** to taste.

PRESENTATION

Put the wild rice around edges of platter with the game hens in the center. Spoon the orange sauce over the hens and pass any extra sauce in a gravy boat.

APRICOT MOUSSE
SERVES 6

The Virginia Museum wisely chose a light fruit dessert served with thin, crisp cookies as a finale to their dinner. You can make this same dessert using dried prunes or dried peaches in place of the apricots. Its charm is in its frothy texture and good fruit flavor, and if you serve it in little porcelain *pot de crème* cups, this Apricot Mousse is as delightful to look at as it is to taste.

dried apricots
sugar
lemon
cream

1 In small saucepan combine: **1½ cups dried apricots, 1 cup water, ½ cup sugar,** and **1 thin strip yellow lemon rind.** Bring to a boil, cover, and simmer for 20 minutes. Cool.

2 Blend apricots and juice in an electric blender on high speed for 20 seconds, stopping to stir down if necessary.
3 Fold apricot puree into: **1 cup cream, whipped.** Spoon into sherbet glasses or *pot de crème* cups and chill.

306

OATMEAL LACE COOKIES
MAKES ABOUT 48 COOKIES

They have a way with breads, muffins, cookies, and other baked goods in the South. Light, deft hands and a pride in the ladylike accomplishments must be responsible for this regional talent. And then they dote on old family recipes, and the South has countless old families to supply them. Here's the recipe for the delightful cookies that were served with dessert at the Virginia Museum. If you want to be fancy, you can roll them around the handle of a wooden spoon while they're still warm and soft. The rolled cookies can be served plain or filled with whipped cream.

quick-cooking oatmeal
dark brown sugar
egg
vanilla
salt
butter

1 Preheat oven to moderate (350° F.).
2 Put through the fine blade of a meat grinder: **1 cup quick-cooking oatmeal.**
3 Add to the oatmeal flour: **1½ cups dark brown sugar, firmly packed, 1 egg, beaten, 1 teaspoon vanilla, ½ teaspoon salt, and 1½ cups melted butter.** Mix well until you have a thick dark brown batter.
4 Drop by half teaspoonfuls on **buttered** cookie sheet, 2 or 3 inches apart—the cookies spread into large, thin circles while baking.
5 Bake for 12 minutes in the moderate oven. Remove cookies with spatula while they are still warm. As soon as they cool, they harden and will stick. If that happens, put them back in warm oven for a few seconds until they are soft enough to remove. Store in closed cookie jar.

ELFO'S SPECIAL (*Buttered Spaghetti with Shrimp and Mushrooms*)
SERVES 2

Just to prove that all is not magnolia and old lace cookies in the South, here are a couple of recipes I collected last time I was in Memphis, Tennessee, at a very good restaurant called Grisanti's. As the name would suggest, the specialties are Italian, but gentled down a bit as a result of a sojourn in southern U.S.A. In southern Italy, the herbs and seasonings would have been far more exuberant. Still, Elfo's Special is very special indeed.

thin spaghetti
salt, pepper
butter
garlic
jumbo shrimp
mushrooms
Romano cheese
monosodium
glutamate

SPAGHETTI

1 Cook: **4 ounces thin spaghetti** in rapidly boiling **salted** water for 10 minutes. ("Use long fork to stir spaghetti so it won't wed," were the chef's romantic directions!) Drain, rinse with cold water, and set aside.
2 Heat in large skillet: **½ cup butter.**
3 Add: **1 small clove garlic, minced, 4 jumbo raw shrimp, diced, and 3 large mushrooms, diced.** Cook slowly in the hot butter for 5 minutes.

4 Add the spaghetti to the skillet. Sprinkle with: **3 tablespoons grated Romano cheese, ½ teaspoon salt, a little freshly ground pepper, and ½ teaspoon monosodium glutamate.** Using a large spoon, turn spaghetti over from edge of skillet to center, being careful not to cut it. Continue until spaghetti is very hot, but do not let the butter brown.

PRESENTATION
Turn out onto warm serving dish and serve with **grated Romano cheese.**

307

SPINACH AND EGGS GRISANTI
SERVES 2

This is a delightfully different way to serve bacon and eggs, and a marvelously painless way to eat spinach. It makes a very good luncheon dish served with hot popovers or fresh brioche, for example. Just one word of advice: the dish improves in proportion to the amount of liquid you press out of the spinach, so trust in Grisanti's—but keep your spinach dry.

frozen chopped
spinach
olive oil
bacon
garlic
eggs
salt, pepper
monosodium
glutamate
Parmesan cheese

SPINACH

1 Cook: **1 package (10 ounces) frozen chopped spinach** according to package directions. Drain thoroughly, pressing out as much of the liquid as possible.

2 Sauté: **2 slices bacon** until crisp. Drain on absorbent paper.

3 Heat in skillet: **3 tablespoons olive oil** with **1 small clove garlic, minced.** Cook until garlic is golden brown. Add: the spinach, **¼ teaspoon salt, ⅛ teaspoon pepper,** and **¼ teaspoon monosodium glutamate** and mix. Spread the spinach mixture over bottom of skillet and sprinkle with: **1 tablespoon freshly grated Parmesan cheese.** Cook, turning spinach over until very hot.

4 Break in: **2 fresh eggs** and keep turning the spinach until eggs are cooked. Crumble and add the crisp bacon, stirring to mix.

PRESENTATION

Drain off any excess oil from skillet. Turn spinach onto warm serving platter and sprinkle with: **2 tablespoons grated Parmesan cheese.**

In Philadelphia, cradle of our country's independence, Bookbinder's bountiful menu reminds us of the abundance that this land enjoys.

Bookbinder's famous Snapper Soup is made from a huge snapping turtle. The recipe should really begin, "First catch your turtle."

OLD ORIGINAL BOOKBINDER'S

BOOKBINDER's is a Philadelphia institution. In a city more famous for its historical monuments than for its eating establishments, this restaurant ranks high on both counts. Its food is as good as any in the United States, and its own history goes back an impressive hundred years. Bookbinder's still occupies its original red brick building near the docks of the Delaware River.

The waterfront location was chosen by Samuel Bookbinder, not because of the historic neighborhood, however, but because the ships that docked nearby brought the choicest foods, spices, teas, and liquors from all over the world. And lobsters, shad, oysters, clams — the wealth of marvelous seafood from the Eastern shores — all were brought to market at Bookbinder's door. To this day seafood is still the great specialty there.

The last time I was in Philadelphia, I was taken to lunch at Bookbinder's by Curtis Ruddle of National Publishing Co., the company that is manufacturing this book, and he told me a charming story about the place. It seems that about fifty years ago two immigrant boys from Austria landed on the docks near the restaurant. They knew very little English — only enough to ask for a job in their trade which was binding books. Lo and behold! The first sign that caught their eye said "Bookbinder's," so they headed for it and asked for jobs. They were immediately offered a golden opportunity — to wash dishes. When they made it clear that they were really, literally bookbinders, they were sent up the street to National Publishing, and there they are to this day. Both had an active part in binding this very book.

APPETIZERS

JUMBO SHRIMP COCKTAIL	1.50
Fat selected shrimp flown in from Gulf of Mexico	
CRAB MEAT COCKTAIL	2.00
LOBSTER COCKTAIL	2.50
TOMATO JUICE COCKTAIL	35
MRS. BOOKBINDER'S FAMOUS MARINATED HERRING IN SOUR CREAM	1.25

OYSTERS + CLAMS

Fresh as the morning paper—and washed within an inch of their lives!

STEAMED CLAMS . . . (BASKET)	2.75
SERVICE FOR 2	3.25
LITTLE NECK CLAMS (½ Dozen)	1.15
CHERRYSTONE CLAMS (½ Dozen)	1.25
CLAM STEW 1.50 WITH CREAM	1.75
BLUE POINT OYSTERS (½ Dozen)	1.50
MEDIUM SALT OYSTERS (½ Dozen)	1.75
LARGE SALT OYSTERS (½ Dozen)	2.00
BROILED OYSTERS (½ Dozen)	2.00
BARBECUED OYSTERS (½ Dozen)	2.00
OYSTERS A LA ROCKEFELLER	2.00
OYSTER STEW 1.50 WITH CREAM	1.75

SOUPS

SNAPPER SOUP A LA BOOKBINDER
(Laced with sherry)

BOWL	1.00	CUP	75

CLAM CHOWDER A LA BOOKBINDER

BOWL	90	CUP	60
CLAM BROTH		CUP	35

SEAFOOD SALADS

Freshness makes the difference!

CRAB SALAD—4.50 SHRIMP SALAD—4.50	
LOBSTER SALAD . . (according to size desired)	
COLD SEAFOOD PLATTER	4.75

SEAFOOD PLATTERS

Includes Salad, Baked or French Fried
Potatoes, Cole Slaw
Rolls and Butter

GENUINE LONG ISLAND SCALLOPS, Broiled or Fried	4.00
CRAB MEAT AU GRATIN	4.25
FRIED SHRIMP	3.75
SHRIMP A LA NEWBURG	4.50
STEAMED OR SAUTED CRAB MEAT	4.25
DEVILED CRAB A LA BOOKBINDER	4.00
OYSTER PLATTER	3.75
SHRIMP LAMAZE	4.25

FISH PLATTERS

Includes Salad, Baked or French Fried
Potatoes, Cole Slaw
Rolls and Butter

JUMBO FROG'S LEGS SAUTE	4.75
BROILED SWORDFISH	4.25
BROILED BLUEFISH	3.85
FILET OF FLOUNDER	4.00
BROILED MACKEREL	3.85
BROILED KENNEBEC SALMON	4.25
CHARCOAL BROILED FINNAN HADDIE	4.25

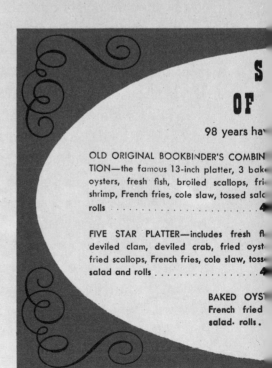

S
OF

98 years ha

OLD ORIGINAL BOOKBINDER'S COMBIN
TION—the famous 13-inch platter, 3 bake
oysters, fresh fish, broiled scallops, fri
shrimp, French fries, cole slaw, tossed sala
rolls 4

FIVE STAR PLATTER—includes fresh fi
deviled clam, deviled crab, fried oyst
fried scallops, French fries, cole slaw, toss
salad and rolls 4

BAKED OYST
French fried
salad. rolls .

1865 — *Ninety nine years at the same addr*

BOOKBINDER'S ·············

LOBSTER

The only good lobster is a *live* lobster. Rushed by air from Nova Scotia waters right to our own lobster tanks.
Our world-famous specialty
Includes Salad, Baked or French Fried Potatoes, Cole Slaw Rolls and Butter

CHICKEN LOBSTER (1¼ lbs.)	4.25
MEDIUM LOBSTER (2½ to 3 lbs.)	7.75
JUMBO LOBSTER (3 to 3½ lbs.)	8.75
EXTRA JUMBO LOBSTER (over 3½ lbs.) (serves 2)	11.00

Our chefs "gild the lily" with these delicacies

LOBSTER THERMIDOR	4.75
LOBSTER NEWBURG	4.75
LOBSTER STEW	4.25

DESSERTS

Created fresh daily by our own chefs

PIE, PER PORTION (Choice varies Daily)	35
FRESH STRAWBERRY SHORTCAKE	75
FRENCH PASTRIES	50
MELONS, IN SEASON	75
BOOKBINDER'S OWN RICE PUDDING	50
ICE CREAM	50
FRESH FRUIT SHERBET	35
JELLO	35

BEVERAGES

COFFEE	25
TEA	25
MILK	25

(additional coffee no charge)

MEATS —from the Charcoal Broiler

Includes Salad, Baked or French Fried Potatoes, Cole Slaw, Rolls and Butter

BROILED CHOPPED SIRLOIN, ONIONS	4.00
HALF BROILED OR FRIED CHICKEN, DISJOINTED	4.00
BREADED VEAL CUTLET, Tomato Sauce	3.85
FRESH CALVES LIVER AND ONIONS	4.25
ROAST PRIME RIBS OF BEEF	5.00
BROILED LAMB CHOPS (3 Double Chops)	5.00
(2) Double Chops	4.50
U. S. PRIME 10 oz. SIRLOIN MINUTE STEAK	4.00
U. S. PRIME KANSAS SIRLOIN STEAK (18 oz.)	6.50
U. S. PRIME FILET MIGNON	6.00
French Fried Onions (Portion for Two)	2.00

CHEESE

served with toasted crackers

ROQUEFORT	50
LIEDERKRANZ	50
CAMEMBERT	50
LIMBURGER	50
AMERICAN, CREAM OR SWISS	35

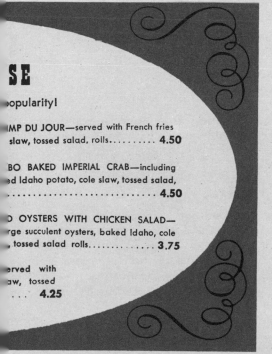

...SE

...opularity!

...MP DU JOUR—served with French fries
...slaw, tossed salad, rolls.......... 4.50

...BO BAKED IMPERIAL CRAB—including
...ed Idaho potato, cole slaw, tossed salad,
.... 4.50

...D OYSTERS WITH CHICKEN SALAD—
...rge succulent oysters, baked Idaho, cole
..., tossed salad rolls.............. 3.75

...erved with
...aw, tossed
... 4.25

**TO SEND A FRIEND
FROM OUR GIFT SHOP**

**Old Original Bookbinder's
Soups and Sauces**

Snapper Soup, Clam Chowder, Clam Bisque,
Red Clam Sauce, White Clam Sauce,
Omelette Sauce, Lentil Soup
New England Clam Chowder
Chicken Noodle Soup

**Souvenir Lobster Bibs
Our Special Blend Coffee
Our Own French Dressing**
and many specially selected gift items

5 *Walnut Street, Philadelphia, Pa.* — **1964**

BOOKBINDER'S SNAPPER SOUP
SERVES 12

The dish for which Old Original Bookbinder's is most famous is their Snapper Soup, made from five-pound snapping turtles. These creatures are not the most commonplace things to find in a market, but with persistence you can sometimes line up a fish store that can get one for you. If not, you can make a sort of "mock snapper" soup using a red snapper. Cook the skin, head, and bones of the fish with some of the flesh for an hour and a half. Dice about a cup and a half of the snapper fillets and add them to the soup for the last half hour. With either the mock or the authentic snapper soup, the snapper is that you serve a beaker of sherry with the soup, and each person laces his own portion with the wine.

frozen snapper
bay leaf
beef stock
(see index)
carrots
celery
Tabasco
beef extract
eggs
sherry
onions
marjoram
salt, pepper
tomato puree
flour
lemons
butter
garlic

1　In a large soup kettle cook: **a 5-pound frozen snapper** in **3 quarts water**. Cook in its shell for 1½ hours.

2　When meat is tender, remove snapper from pot and let it cool. Pick snapper meat from shell, keep warm, and set aside.

3　Put shell back in snapper stock with: **3 tablespoons beef extract, 3 quarts beef stock, 2 carrots, chopped, 2 stalks celery, chopped, 3 onions, chopped, ½ teaspoon marjoram, salt** and **pepper** to taste, **2 cups tomato puree, a dash of Tabasco, 1 bay leaf,** and **2 cloves garlic, minced.**

4　Simmer for 30 minutes and strain. Mix: **½ cup melted butter** with **1½ cups flour** and beat into soup until smooth.

5　Cut snapper meat into small pieces and add to soup.

6　Chop: **3 hard-cooked eggs** and add to soup.

7　Stir in: **1 cup sherry** and **2 lemons, halved and thinly sliced** (you should have 24 half slices). Let soup simmer for ½ hour.

PRESENTATION

Serve soup in a tureen. Into each soup bowl ladle some of the snapper meat, 2 half slices of lemon, and some soup. Pass a small pitcher or beaker of **sherry** and let each person add some to his own taste.

BOOKBINDER'S SEAFOOD COCKTAIL SAUCE
SERVES 2

The big, meaty shrimp from the Gulf of Mexico, crabmeat from Maryland and Virginia, Chincoteague long salt oysters—all are served at Bookbinder's with this special cocktail sauce. It is good and hot, and just a little of it sets off the fresh seafood to perfection.

mayonnaise
chili sauce
lemon
horse-radish
mustard
Tabasco (optional)

COCKTAIL SAUCE

1　Mix: **1 tablespoon mayonnaise** with **3 tablespoons chili sauce, 3 teaspoons lemon juice, 1 teaspoon prepared horse-radish,** and **1 teaspoon prepared mustard.**

2　Combine and taste. If you like your sauce hotter, add: **2 drops Tabasco.**

3　Cover and chill well in refrigerator.

PRESENTATION

Do not serve seafood in sauce. Pass sauce in separate dish and let each person help himself or, best of all, serve it in small individual containers so that each piece of seafood can be dipped into it as it is eaten. Otherwise seafood absorbs flavor of sauce and loses its own taste.

DEVILED CRAB
SERVES 8

Seafood has been the mainstay of Bookbinder's reputation for all the years of its history. The restaurant is almost on the riverfront of one of the world's great ports, and the Eastern seacoast, from Nova Scotia to Florida, ships delicacies to its door. Naturally, when there is such an abundance of fine fresh seafood, much of it is served just plain for its very excellence is enough. But there are also some interesting seafood recipes that Bookbinder's John Taxin gave me, good to know for those of us who *don't* have the Delaware River right at our back door. This Deviled Crab is delicious, but it isn't necessary to use the finest back-fin crabmeat.

green pepper
onions
celery
pimiento
salt, pepper
dry mustard
thyme
Worcestershire sauce
butter
flour
milk
lump crabmeat
eggs
Tabasco
fine cracker crumbs
cooking oil

1 In saucepan melt: **¾ cup butter.** In it stew: **½ green pepper, minced, 1 cup minced onion, 1 stalk celery, minced,** and **½ pimiento, minced,** for 20 minutes, or until onion is soft. Add: **1 teaspoon salt, ½ teaspoon pepper, 1 teaspoon thyme, 1 teaspoon dry mustard, 1 tablespoon Worcestershire sauce,** and **a few drops Tabasco.**

2 Stir in: **1 cup flour** and cook over low heat for 20 minutes longer, stirring occasionally.

3 Add: **2 cups hot milk** and cook, stirring, until mixture is the consistency of heavy paste. Stir in: **2 pounds lump crabmeat,** that has been carefully picked over.

Remove from heat and cool.

4 Form crabmeat mixture into cakes, using about ½ cup per cake. Refrigerate until ready to cook.

5 Preheat oven to moderate (350° F.).

6 Heat **cooking oil** about 1 inch deep in deep skillet to 360° F. Dust the cakes with **flour,** dip in a mixture of: **2 eggs,** lightly beaten with **¼ cup milk,** then roll in **fine cracker crumbs.** Lower gently into the hot shortening and deep fry for about 4 minutes on each side, or until brown. Drain on absorbent paper.

7 Bake in the moderate oven for 15 minutes, or until very hot all the way through. Makes 16 cakes.

SHRIMP DU JOUR
SERVES 6

This popular shrimp dish is on Bookbinder's menu every day. We like it served with a salad for a light but satisfying dinner. But we also serve it as a hot appetizer in small individual ramekins. In that case this recipe is enough for twelve.

shrimp
butter
Worcestershire sauce
bread crumbs
garlic
parsley
chives
salt, pepper
Parmesan cheese

1 Shell: **5 pounds medium-sized shrimp.** Clean, devein, and dry them. (You should have about 80 shrimp.)

2 In a skillet heat: **4 tablespoons butter.** Add shrimp and cook over high heat until shrimp turn bright pink (about 2 minutes—do not overcook or they will become tough).

3 Add: **2 teaspoons Worcestershire sauce, 1 clove garlic, finely chopped, ¼ cup chopped parsley, ¼ cup chopped**

chives, 1 scant teaspoon salt, and ¼ teaspoon pepper. Mix well and place in a single layer in a large **buttered** baking dish, or in individual **buttered** baking dishes.

4 Sprinkle with: **¼ cup fine dry bread crumbs** and **¼ cup grated Parmesan cheese.**

5 Pour evenly over the top: **¼ pound melted butter.**

6 Put under hot broiler to brown.

BAKED WHOLE SEA BASS
SERVES 10

There is no more beautiful sight than a planked baked fish, beautifully browned, surrounded by colorful vegetables within a frame of duchess potatoes. You could serve the same things in separate dishes and they would look ordinary. Put them all together on a plank and they spell "PICTURE." See our picture of Bookbinder's restaurant and you'll know what I mean.

sea bass
salt, pepper
cayenne pepper
butter
nutmeg
cooked vegetables
bacon
lemons
parsley
cream
potatoes
eggs

FISH

1 Preheat oven to moderately hot (375° F.).

2 Have: **a 5-pound sea bass** boned for baking. (Allow about ½ pound of fish per serving.) Remove head and tail if you wish.

3 Clean fish and rub insides with: **1½ teaspoons salt, ¼ teaspoon pepper,** and **1 teaspoon lemon juice.**

4 Place fish on its side in a **buttered** baking dish. Brush with a little **melted butter** and lay: **1 strip bacon** over top of fish.

5 Bake in the moderately hot oven from 1 to 1½ hours, or until fish flakes easily with a fork. Time varies with size of fish. Baste every 10 minutes so flesh does not dry out.

DUCHESS POTATOES

1 Cook: **2 pounds peeled potatoes** in simmering **salted** water to cover, with lid on pot. Cook for 30 minutes, or until soft but not soggy.

2 Drain and dry potatoes by shaking pan over heat.

3 Put potatoes in food mill or through a coarse sieve.

4 Beat until smooth, adding: **2 tablespoons butter, 2 tablespoons cream, 1 teaspoon salt, a dash of cayenne pepper, ⅛ teaspoon nutmeg,** and **2 eggs plus 2 egg yolks, beaten until light and pale.** Beat hard until potato mixture is fluffy.

PRESENTATION

Place cooked fish on a large plank. Spoon over it any of its cooking juices. Lay a row of **lemon slices** along top. Sprinkle with **chopped parsley.** Put **buttered cooked vegetables** around fish. You can use carrots, peas, turnips, string beans, pieces of cauliflower, or whatever you choose. Make a border of duchess potatoes around the edge of plank. This is most attractive piped through a pastry tube. Just before serving, pop under hot broiler to slightly brown the potatoes.

LOBSTER CANTONESE
SERVES 4

Personally I like my lobster plain boiled or broiled. But if you have only two lobsters and you want to serve four people, what do you do? You serve them Bookbinder's Lobster Cantonese, very, very good to eat and besides, it stretches the amount wonderfully well.

lobsters
ground pork
garlic
salt, pepper
chicken stock
(see index)
egg
cornstarch
soy sauce
sherry
rice
bay leaf
thyme
peppercorns

LOBSTER

1 In a large pot put: **3 quarts water, 1 bay leaf, a pinch of thyme, 3 teaspoons salt,** and **3 peppercorns.** When water comes to a vigorous boil, put in: **2 live lobsters,** weighing from 2 to 2½ pounds each. Cook about 20 minutes, and let lobsters cool in the liquid.

2 Remove lobsters. Cut off claws, crack and remove meat. Split lobsters in half and loosen meat. Remove intestinal vein and the sac near the head. Chop lobster halves, with shells, into serving pieces (about 3 or 4 per half).

CANTONESE SAUCE

1 In a heavy skillet brown quickly: ½ **pound ground pork.** When it is brown, add: **1 cup chicken stock, 1 clove garlic, minced,** the lobster pieces and claw meat, **1 teaspoon salt,** and ⅛ **teaspoon pepper.** Cover tightly and cook 5 minutes.

2 Blend together: **1 egg, beaten, 2 tablespoons cornstarch** dissolved in ¼ cup water, **2 teaspoons soy sauce,** and ¼ **cup good sherry.**

3 Stir into the lobster mixture and continue to cook, stirring constantly, until mixture is piping hot.

PRESENTATION

Serve the Lobster Cantonese on a bed of **hot boiled rice.**

CHEESECAKE
SERVES 10

This is one of the best cheesecakes I've ever had anywhere. Its recipe has long been a secret at Bookbinder's where it is their most popular dessert, and they were loath to divulge it. I'm glad they finally have, as it is delicious and, if you have an electric beater, not at all difficult. Beautiful with or without the strawberries.

butter
graham cracker
crumbs
cream cheese
sugar
light cream
eggs
flour
vanilla
salt
strawberries
(optional)
red currant glaze
(see index—optional)

1 Grease an 8-inch spring-form cake pan thickly with: **1½ tablespoons butter.** Turn the form on its side, put in a few **graham cracker crumbs** and shake so they stick to the sides. Keep turning the form and adding more crumbs as needed. When sides are well coated, shake a light coating of crumbs onto the bottom (about ½ cup crumbs in all). Put spring form in freezer for 30 minutes, or refrigerate for 2 hours.

2 Preheat oven to slow (300° F.).

3 In bowl of electric beater put: **12 ounces soft cream cheese, ¾ cup sugar, 4 egg yolks, 2 tablespoons flour, 1½ teaspoons vanilla,** and ½ **teaspoon salt.** Beat thoroughly until mixture is smooth. Turn speed to lowest and gradually pour in: **2 cups scalded light cream.**

4 Beat: **4 egg whites** until stiff but not dry. Add to cream cheese mixture and fold in lightly but thoroughly. Pour mixture into the prepared pan, set pan in a shallow pan containing 1 inch hot water, and bake in the slow oven for 1½ hours. Refrigerate for at least 6 hours before serving.

Note: You may, if you wish, cover the top of the cake with a layer of **fresh strawberries** after it is removed from the spring form. Wash and hull them. Dry thoroughly. Stand with pointed ends up, as close together as possible. With a pastry brush, paint with **red currant glaze.**

GRILLED TIDBIT
SERVES 6

The Warwick Hotel's Coach Room is another favorite eating place in Philadelphia. I don't usually like the idea of filling up on canapés before a meal, but we had this excellent tidbit when we had cocktails at the Warwick once, and we've served it occasionally with great success.

sardines
onion
lemon
salt, pepper
bacon

FILLING

1 Drain the oil from: **a can of sardines.** Put sardines in a bowl and mash well with a fork.

2 Add: **1 tablespoon minced onion, ¼ teaspoon salt, ⅛ teaspoon pepper,** and **½ teaspoon lemon juice.** Mix well.

TIDBITS

1 Lay out on a board: **12 large slices bacon.** Spread each one with the sardine mixture.

2 Roll bacon slices up like jelly rolls.

3 Place on broiler rack, open ends down, and broil until crisp. Serve hot.

CHICKEN AND VIRGINIA HAM SHORTCAKE
SERVES 6

This recipe from the Warwick Hotel in Philadelphia has a bit of the Old South about it. It is a rich but delicious concoction served on a slice of toasted corn bread. For a shortcut, you can buy corn muffin mix and bake it in a loaf mold, picking up the recipe from that point.

Virginia ham
butter
cooked chicken
cream
eggs
salt, pepper
sugar
milk
nutmeg
white wine
white cornmeal
flour
bacon fat
baking powder
Parmesan cheese

CORN BREAD

1 Preheat oven to hot (425° F.).

2 Mix: **1½ cups white cornmeal** with **½ cup flour.** Stir in: **1 beaten egg** and **3 tablespoons bacon fat.** Add: **¾ teaspoon salt, 2 tablespoons sugar,** and **2 teaspoons double-acting baking powder.**

3 Stir in: **¾ cup milk.** Put batter into hot **buttered** 9 x 9-inch pan and bake in the hot oven for 30 minutes.

CHICKEN AND HAM

1 In a skillet heat: **4 tablespoons butter.** Add: **6 thin slices Virginia ham** and cook gently for 5 minutes. Remove ham and keep warm.

2 To the ham gravy add: **3 cups minced cooked chicken** (the meat from 1 small chicken). Let it simmer for 10 minutes. Season with: **1 teaspoon salt, ⅛ teaspoon pepper,** and **a dash of nutmeg.**

3 Add: **¼ cup white wine.** Mix well and simmer for 5 minutes more.

4 Add: **1 cup cream** mixed with **3 beaten egg yolks.** Stir constantly to blend without curdling.

PRESENTATION

When corn bread is cool, cut into thick slices. Toast them in oven. Place a slice of Virginia ham on each corn bread slice. Top with the chicken mixture. Sprinkle each with: **1 tablespoon grated Parmesan cheese,** brown under hot broiler, and serve at once.

New Orleans grillwork serves a useful function in Antoine's wine cellar. I was a privileged customer even to be permitted to gaze longingly through the bars at the bottled treasure within.

Under the Mission cross on the fireplace our houseman, Harry Mullen, ladles *Café Brûlot* for our guests. This enormous living room was Mary's greatest challenge— like trying to make Grand Central cozy. After-dinner coffee around the fireplace achieves an intimacy, thanks to the paintings and objects that are so personal a part of our lives.

318

ANTOINE'S

MY mother and father dined here on their honeymoon in 1894, and seventy years later Roy Alciatore, the direct descendant of founder Antoine Alciatore, served this direct descendant a gorgeous meal. Even for non-honeymooners, dining at Antoine's is a romantic experience. Located in the French Quarter of New Orleans, the restaurant is housed in an old building festooned with iron grille balconies. Inside there are a number of small dining rooms, intimate and warm and very turn-of-the-century with their red walls and gilded chandeliers.

Host Roy Alciatore knows and cares deeply about fine food and wines —Antoine's cellar is reputed to be one of the best in this country — and the meals he serves are a masterful blending of the two. For example, the meal he produced for us began with an aperitif of chilled Chablis Cassis. Sipping it, I became aware once again of how roughly we Americans bruise our taste buds with hard liquor, almost as though we dreaded the meal to come. Whiskey and cocktails seem to anesthetize the palate and make it impervious to anything, good or bad, that follows. If you know you're going to have a superlative dinner, try Antoine's aperitif sometime instead of a stronger drink and see how much more subtly you can savor all the delicate nuances of flavor in each dish.

New Orleans, which is known for jazz, the Mardi Gras and good eating, all of which we have sampled at one time or another, can become heavy sledding for the fun-loving gourmet. But the rewards for collectors of fine recipes such as we are, more than compensate for the wear and tear.

ANTOINE'S

1840 CENTENNIAL 1940

Restaurant Antoine

Fondé En 1840

Le service chez Antoine exclusivement à la carte

Minimum $3.00 par personne

NOUS RECOMMANDONS

Huîtres en coquille à la Rockefeller (notre création) 1.25

Les Escargots à la Bourguignonne 1.50   Les Escargots à la Bordelaise 2.50

Huîtres nature .90 — Huîtres à la Foch 1.25 — Canapé Balthazar 1.00

Huîtres Thermidor 1.25 — Huîtres bonne femme 1.00 — Canapé St. Antoine 1.25

Huîtres à la Ellis 1.25 — Huîtres bourguignonne 1.00 — Canapé Rothschild 1.25

Caviar sur canapé 1.75 — Anchois sur canapé 1.00 — Ecrevisses sous cloche 1.25

Crevettes à la marinière 1.25 — Avocat crabmeat Garibaldi 1.25 — Ecrevisses à la marinière 1.25

Crevettes à la Richman 1.25 — Avocat Garibaldi 1.10 — Ecrevisses cardinal 1.25

Crevettes cardinal 1.25 — Cocktail aux crevettes 1.00

Crevettes rémoulade 1.25 — Cocktail aux crabes 1.25

Pâté de foie gras à la gelée (importé) 2.00

Champignons sous cloche 1.25 — Champignons sur toste 1.00

Lump crabmeat ravigote 1.50 — Crabmeat au gratin 1.25

Crabes St. Pierre 1.25

POTAGES

Gombo Créole .75 — Potage tortue au sherry .75

Bisque d'écrevisses cardinal .90

Consommé chaud au vermicelle .60 — Consommé froid en tasse .60

Vichyssoise .75 — Soupe à l'oignon gratinée (30 minutes) .75

POISSONS

Filet de truite meunière 2.25 — Filet de truite amandine 2.50

Filet de truite à la Marguery 2.25 — Filet de truite florentine 2.00

Filet de truite au vin blanc 2.50 — Filet de sole Colbert 2.25

Pompano grillé 3.00 — *Pompano* en papillote 3.00

Pompano Pontchartrain 3.50 — *Pompano* amandine 3.25

Pompano à la marinière 3.00 — Crevettes à la Créole 2.25

Langouste Thermidor 2.75 — Langouste grillé 2.25

Langouste sauté 2.25

Bouillabaisse à la Marseillaise (commander d'avance) 3.50

Crabes (*Busters*) grillés 2.25 — Crabes (*Busters*) amandine 3.00

Crabes mous frits 2.50 — Crabes mous amandine 2.75

Salade de crabmeat 2.50 — Salade de crevette 2.00

Crabmeat au gratin (main dish) 2.50 — Crabmeat ravigote (main dish) 2.50

Crabmeat marinière (main dish) 2.50 — Crabmeat sauté (main dish) 2.25

OEUFS

Omelette nature 1.00 — Omelette aux crevettes 2.00

Omelette espagnole 1.50 — Omelette au fromage 1.50

Omelette au crabmeat 2.50 — Oeuf Sardou 1.50

Oeufs Benedict 1.25 — (2) Oeuf St. Denis 1.50

Oeuf froid Balthazar 1.25 — Oeuf Coquelin 1.25

Oeuf à la florentine 1.25 — Oeuf Coolidge 1.25

Oeufs aux tomates St. Antoine 1.25 — Oeuf à la tripe 1.25

ENTRÉES

Poulet à la parisienne 2.50 — Poulet sauté demi-bordelaise 2.50

Poulet grillé 2.00 — Poulet à la creole 2.50

Poulet aux champignons 2.75 — Poulet sauce Rochambeau 2.75

Poulet en cocotte (30 minutes) 2.50 — Poulet chantecler (30 minutes) 3.00

Pigeonneaux sauce paradis 4.50 — Pigeonneaux grillés 4.00

Faison sous cloche 5.25 — Dinde sauce Rochambeau 2.75

Antoine's

Depuis Plus De 100 Ans.

CAFÉ BRÛLOT DIABOLIQUE
SERVES 4

New Orleans is famous for two drinks, the Sazerac, a lethal bourbon and Pernod cocktail, and *café brûlot*, a flaming after-dinner coffee with cognac. The *café brûlot* is traditionally served in special cups, tall and slim and with handles in the shape of red devils. It is most dramatic served in the drawing room, with the lights turned down while the cognac flames hellishly. Actually all that happens is that most of the alcohol burns out of the cognac and by the time the coffee is added all you get is the marvelous flavor.

CAFÉ BRÛLOT

sugar cubes
cloves
stick cinnamon
lemon
coffee
French cognac

1 Make: **4 cups strong black coffee.**

2 In a fire-resistant bowl put: **8 sugar cubes, 8 whole cloves, a 1-inch piece stick cinnamon,** and **the thin yellow peel of ½ lemon.**

3 Heat in small pan: **6 ounces French cognac.** Pour over ingredients in bowl. Ignite cognac and stir it around with other ingredients until sugar is melted and all flavors are blended (about a minute or so). Don't let cognac burn away completely.

4 Pour the 4 cups hot coffee into the flaming bowl.

5 Stir around until the fire goes out.

PRESENTATION

There is a special ladle that has a strainer to strain out the spices. If you do not have one, use an ordinary ladle, being careful to fill it only with the liquid. Have the *brûlot* cups, or demitasse cups, standing near the bowl. Ladle the coffee into them and serve black.

CHABLIS CASSIS
SERVES 1

Our luncheon at Antoine's on a recent trip to New Orleans was memorable for the wines as well as the food. In order not to blunt our taste for either, we had this most delightful aperitif and I pass it on to you as a perfect substitute for that pre-dinner cocktail. It whets the appetite without dulling the palate.

crème de cassis
French Chablis

1 In a large Burgundy-style glass place: **1 tablespoon crème de cassis.** (This is a currant syrup produced in Dijon, France. A little of it goes a long way, but it is a remarkable addition to dry white wines or vermouth.)

2 Fill glass half full of well-chilled **French Chablis** (a dry, white Burgundy wine. Mr. Alciatore was emphatic about using only a French Chablis. Other domestic white Burgundies might be good, but the so-called Chablis wines that do not come from that section of France are not up to his standards).

3 This drink must be served icy cold, but it should not have ice in it. Chill your wine and the glasses before serving.

BREAST OF PHEASANT SOUS CLOCHE
SERVES 4

At Antoine's they serve this elegant dish under a glass bell or dome, which keeps it hot and appetizingly visible. These glass bells are available at any restaurant supply store and are not very expensive. On the other hand, the pheasant is. Brillat-Savarin says that a fresh pheasant is not as good as a good chicken. He recommends hanging pheasant in its plumage for at least eight days and then plucking and preparing it when it is a little high. That, however, is a matter of taste, and it is possible to strike a happy medium. This is Mr. Alciatore's recipe for pheasant, but I see no reason why breast of duck or even chicken or half a game hen could not be substituted for it, if you wish.

pheasants
brown sauce
(see index)
truffles
Madeira
bread
salt, pepper
butter
lemon

PHEASANT

1 Preheat oven to moderate (350° F.).

2 Rub the cavities and skin of: **2 ready-to-cook pheasants** with the cut side of ½ lemon. Season inside and out with **salt** and **pepper**.

3 In a heavy pan melt: **4 tablespoons butter.** Brown the birds on all sides.

4 Place pan in the moderate oven. Baste birds with pan juices every 10 minutes and roast about 30 minutes for average-sized pheasants. Remove and keep warm.

SAUCE

In a saucepan heat: **2½ cups brown sauce.** Let it simmer until it has reduced about one-quarter. Add: **¼ cup Madeira** and **2 tablespoons minced truffles.** Season to taste with **salt** and **pepper.**

PRESENTATION

1 Cut into rounds: **4 slices bread** and toast them.

2 Sauté: **the 2 pheasant livers** gently in **2 tablespoons butter.** Mash well and spread liver and butter on the toast rounds.

3 Carve pheasants so you have 4 breasts. (I don't know what Mr. Alciatore did with the rest of our pheasants, but at home we have the most elegant snacks the next day!)

4 Place a roasted breast of pheasant on each round of toast. Cover with the sauce and place glass bell over each dish. Serve at once. At Antoine's, the wine served with this was a Côte de Beaune-Villages 1955, a magnificent Burgundy.

OYSTERS À LA FOCH
SERVES 4

This dish was created in honor of France's Marshal Foch when he visited New Orleans and Antoine's in 1921. As they say in vaudeville, he's a hard man to follow, but we couldn't have been treated any more lavishly than the Marshal was. With his oysters we drank a great white Burgundy, Bâtard-Montrachet 1961. We can't always duplicate the wine at home, but if the brown sauce and tomato sauce have been made in advance or stored in the freezer, this dish doesn't take long to put together and is topflight.

oysters
flour
cooking oil
salt
brown sauce
(see index)
tomato sauce
(see index)
hollandaise sauce
(see index)
Worcestershire sauce
bread
pâté de foie gras
lemon
parsley

1 Wash: **24 raw oysters** to remove shell and sand. Drain on paper towels.

2 Drop oysters into a paper bag containing a little **flour** and shake bag to coat oysters evenly. Remove oysters and shake off excess flour.

3 Fry in: **2 inches hot deep cooking oil** (365° F.) for about 1½ minutes, or until crisp. Drain on absorbent paper and keep warm. Sprinkle with a little **salt**.

4 In saucepan combine: **1 cup brown sauce, ¼ cup tomato sauce,** and **1 teaspoon Worcestershire sauce** and heat.

PRESENTATION

1 Toast: **4 slices bread,** trim off crusts, and spread with a layer of **pâté de foie gras.**

2 For each serving, place a slice of the toast on a warm serving dish. Arrange oysters on the toast.

3 Remove simmering sauce from heat, add: **½ cup hollandaise sauce,** and beat briskly until combined. Cover the oysters with this sauce and sprinkle with a little **minced parsley.** Serve immediately with **a wedge of lemon** on each plate.

BELGIAN ENDIVE SALAD
SERVES 4

Belgian endive is a great delicacy and a salad of plain endive with a simple dressing is just what is needed when the rest of the meal is fairly rich. At Antoine's we were served the following classic salad, but I will also give you my favorite recipe for a winter salad made of endive and beet which can be eaten as a dish by itself.

endives
olive oil
wine vinegar
salt, pepper
Dijon mustard

SALAD

1 Break off the leaves from: **4 heads of endive.** Wash in cold water, shake out, and dry thoroughly in a clean towel. Refrigerate until you are ready to use.

2 Place the dry, chilled leaves in a wooden salad bowl. Season with dressing immediately before serving.

DRESSING

1 Mix: **4 tablespoons olive oil** with **1 tablespoon wine vinegar.** Add: **½ teaspoon salt, ⅛ teaspoon freshly ground pepper,** and **a dash of Dijon mustard.**

2 Beat with a fork and pour over endive leaves. Toss gently so each leaf is shiny and coated with dressing.

ENDIVE AND BEET SALAD
SERVES 4

endives
cooked beet
parsley
olive oil
wine vinegar
tarragon
chervil
salt, pepper

SALAD

1 Wash: **4 heads of endive,** keeping them whole. Shake well and dry thoroughly in a towel.

2 Cut endives in quarters lengthwise and then into pieces about 2 inches long.

3 Put endive spears in wooden salad bowl. Add: **1 cooked beet, cut in very thin slices.** Sprinkle with: **2 teaspoons finely chopped parsley, 2 teaspoons finely chopped tarragon,** and **2 teaspoons finely**

chopped chervil. (If you can't get all of these herbs, at least use the parsley.)

PRESENTATION

Just before serving, sprinkle salad with: **½ teaspoon salt** and **⅛ teaspoon freshly ground pepper.** Pour over it: **3 tablespoons olive oil,** mixing well to coat all the salad. Add: **1½ tablespoons wine vinegar** and mix to blend all thoroughly. This can be done at the table.

OMELETTE NORVÉGIENNE (Baked Alaska Omelet)
SERVES 8

This dessert at Antoine's was a thing of beauty. It came to our table a golden brown oval with fanciful decorations piped on it through a pastry tube — birds, flowers, and my name written in sugar icing like a birthday child's. We don't even attempt the decorations at home, but the rest of the dessert is easy and fun to do, and it is an impressive dish to set before our guests.

pound cake
eggs
salt
lemon
confectioners' sugar
vanilla ice cream

Make or buy: **a 1-pound pound cake.** This is available frozen. If homemade, bake in a small loaf pan, 7½ x 3½ x 2 inches high.

MERINGUE

1 Beat until frothy: **4 egg whites** and **a pinch of salt.**

2 Add: **½ teaspoon lemon juice** and continue to beat until egg whites are stiff.

3 Gradually beat in: **1 cup confectioners' sugar** and continue to beat until the meringue is thick and glossy.

PRESENTATION

1 Preheat oven to hot (425° F.).

2 Cut a ¾-inch thick slice from bottom of pound cake and place on an oval stainless steel platter.

3 Cover cake with **scoops of vanilla ice cream,** using about 1 quart ice cream in all.

4 Slice remaining cake into three thin layers. Place one layer on top of ice cream. Cut a second layer in half lengthwise and press one-half against each lengthwise side of ice cream. Cut third layer in half crosswise and place at ends of ice cream, completely enclosing the ice cream with cake. Trim end pieces neatly to fit.

5 Completely cover top and sides of cake with a 1-inch layer of meringue. Swirl remaining meringue on top of cake lavishly. Bake in the hot oven for 6 to 8 minutes, or until meringue is lightly browned.

OYSTER VELOUTÉ (Cream of Oyster Soup)
SERVES 4

The Esplanade of The Royal Orleans is a hotel dining room that lives up to the gastronomic excellence of New Orleans. The last time we dined there, I was taken back to the magnificent kitchens and permitted to taste and watch and learn while Chef Lacan patiently taught me some of his fine preparations. This cream of oyster soup is a beauty, and the whole trick is in *simmering*, not boiling, the fresh oysters for just one minute. They remain tender and delicate then, and that final dash of Tabasco adds the necessary pizzazz.

oysters
butter
flour
cream
Tabasco

1 Open: **2 dozen fresh oysters,** being careful to retain all the liquor (2 cups).

2 Put oysters and liquor into a saucepan and add: **1 cup water.** Bring liquid to a simmer and cook until edges of oysters curl, about 1 minute.

3 In saucepan melt: **5 tablespoons butter.** Stir in: **6 tablespoons flour.** Gradually stir in the hot oyster liquor and cook, stirring, until sauce is smooth and thick. Cook over very low heat for 30 minutes, stirring occasionally.

4 Heat to simmering: **1 cup cream.** Add the hot cream and the oysters to the sauce and season with: **¼ teaspoon Tabasco,** or to taste.

327

STUFFED EGGPLANT
SERVES 2

Galatoire's is another well-known New Orleans restaurant. Located on Bourbon Street where sleazy nightclubs and dilapidated buildings hem it in, Galatoire's is a narrow strip of respectability in a tough neighborhood. Still, the line of patrons waiting for tables sometimes stretches right up Bourbon Street, which shows you the lengths to which gourmets will go. We liked this unusual eggplant dish last time we lunched at Galatoire's.

eggplant
bread crumbs
butter
Parmesan cheese
scallions
parsley
lump crabmeat
or shrimp
salt, pepper

EGGPLANT

1 Boil: **1 medium eggplant (1¼ pounds)** in water for 20 minutes. Drain and when cool enough to handle, cut lengthwise and carefully remove pulp, leaving a shell ¼ inch thick. Chop the pulp and reserve. Arrange the shells in a shallow baking dish.

2 Preheat oven to hot (400° F.).

STUFFING

1 Brown: **½ cup bread crumbs in 1 tablespoon butter.** Mix with: **2 tablespoons grated Parmesan cheese.**

2 In a skillet melt: **4 tablespoons butter.**

3 Add: **2 large scallions (including tender part of the green stalks),** chopped, **2 tablespoons chopped parsley,** and sauté for 2 minutes.

4 Add: **½ pound fresh lump crabmeat** or **diced raw shrimp** and cook, stirring, for 3 minutes longer.

5 Add the eggplant pulp and sprinkle with: **¼ teaspoon salt** and **¼ teaspoon pepper.** Mix, cover, and cook over low heat for 5 minutes.

PRESENTATION

1 Pile this filling into the eggplant shells. Sprinkle with the bread crumb-cheese mixture and dot each portion with: **1 teaspoon butter.**

2 Bake in the hot oven for 20 minutes. Serve piping hot.

A breakfast of French toast and pancakes on the Super Chief is a perfect way to start the day. Between orange juice and coffee we travel through a good fifty miles of scenic America—and hundreds of scrumptious calories.

The library is my favorite room in anybody's house— a wonder world of books to suit each person's taste. We like to take an informal breakfast in ours, with popovers and coffee for early morning guests.

SANTA FE SUPER CHIEF

When Mary and I sat down to write this cookbook, we both laughed about one thing. The greatest breakfasts that either of us could remember ever having eaten were served in a railroad dining car. And what, you may ask, is so gourmet about that? All I can say is, "Plenty!"

Mornings should be bright and crisp and immaculate as the new day, holding promise of new adventures. The dining car of the Super Chief, with its gleaming silver, white napery and the colorful Western landscape rolling past the window, is all those things. Besides, it smells deliciously of breakfast. The aroma of coffee and bacon greet you at the door, as do the white-coated waiters whose gentle solicitude is just what you need to start the day right.

At home, breakfast is light and informal and we often have early guests who drop by to work on one project or another with us. Then it's my turn to cook up a basket of my favorite popovers and brew a large pot of coffee which we serve in the library-workroom. Our library is filled with fun things —a portrait above the fireplace by Lee Hankey, a much neglected English impressionist, which cost $100 on Madison Avenue a couple of years ago; a coffin bench converted into a coffee table (where the popovers now rest in peace); a sofa from the Salvation Army; a carved wooden figure from Africa; and napkins from linen sales all over the country, dyed lovely colors by Mary. Breakfast in this cheerful room gives even the hardest, longest day a bright send-off. And a breakfast that is made from any of the recipes in the following section is guaranteed to do the same for you.

South Rim Grand Canyon of Ariz

To serve you better and expedite service, waiters are NOT permitted to serve orders given orally. Please write your order.

A la Carte

FAMOUS SUPER CHIEF BREAKFAST ENTREES

Kippered Herring on Toast 1.10; with Scrambled Eggs 1.45

Calf's Liver Saute with Rasher of Bacon 1.65

Grilled French Lamb Chop au Cresson 1.45

Browned Corned Beef Hash 1.50; with Poached Egg 1.85

OLD FASHIONED HOT BREADS AND CAKES

Griddle Cakes with Maple Syrup 1.00; with Bacon 1.60

Buckwheat Cakes with Little Pig Sausages 1.60

French Toast with Apple Sauce or Currant Jelly 1.00

BREADS

Hot Bran or Corn Muffins 25; with Jam or Marmalade 40

Dry Toast, Whole Wheat or Raisin 25; with Jam or Marmalade 40

BEVERAGES

Coffee, per pot 40 *Tea, per pot 40* *Postum, per pot 30*

Cocoa or Chocolate, per pot 40 *Milk 25*

Instant Sanka Coffee, pot 40

2-64 ♤ 13583

Saccharin available on request.

Sodium - Free salt substitute available on request.

Santa Fe Dining Car *Fred Harvey Service*

FRENCH TOAST SANTA FE
SERVES 2

The Santa Fe Railway bills this as "The French Toast with the Most" and they tell me that of the million breakfasts served in their dining cars last year, their French toast topped the popularity poll. See for yourselves why that should be.

bread
eggs
cream
salt
nutmeg
maple syrup
cooking oil
confectioners' sugar

1 Preheat oven to hot (400° F.).

2 Use bread that is a little dry—2 or 3 days old.

3 Cut: **3 slices of bread,** ¾ inch thick. Trim crusts and cut across diagonally to make 6 triangles.

4 In a bowl beat: **2 eggs** until light and frothy. Add: **½ cup cream, a pinch of salt,** and **a dash of nutmeg.**

5 Soak bread, a few pieces at a time, so that they absorb egg-cream mixture thoroughly.

6 In skillet heat: **¼ cup cooking oil.**

7 Fry bread on both sides to a golden color.

8 Remove bread from pan and drain on paper towel to absorb any excess grease.

9 Place on baking sheet and allow to puff up in the hot oven for 3 to 5 minutes.

PRESENTATION

On heated plates put 3 triangles of French toast per portion. Sprinkle with **confectioners' sugar** and serve with **maple syrup.** For variations you can also serve with applesauce, currant jelly, honey, jam, or cinnamon sugar.

HARVEY GIRL SPECIAL LITTLE THIN ORANGE PANCAKES
MAKES ABOUT 36 PANCAKES

In the days of the Old West when the railroads were new, Fred Harvey's station restaurants were one of the few links with the more civilized ways of the eastern United States. The Harvey Girls, as his waitresses were known, are part of the folklore of the West, many of them marrying miners and prospectors who struck it rich and made grand ladies of the erstwhile hash-slingers. There are still Harvey Girls in the station restaurants, and their pancakes are served on the Santa Fe diners as well as in the restaurants. Those girls really can cook!

oranges
packaged
pancake mix
bacon
butter
maple syrup
or honey

1 Grate: **the thin orange rind** from ½ **orange.**

2 Squeeze the juice from: **2 or 3 oranges.** You will need 1 cup.

3 Peel and section: **½ orange,** being careful to remove all of the bitter white skin and membranes. Do this over a bowl to catch the juice. Dice the sections and put them in bowl. You should have ¼ cup.

4 Combine: **1 cup packaged pancake mix** with the cup of orange juice, the grated orange rind, and the ¼ cup diced orange sections.

5 Heat a griddle and put a little **butter** on it. Use 1 tablespoon batter for each pancake.

PRESENTATION

The pancakes will be about 2¾ inches in diameter. We serve 6 to each person with **maple syrup** or **honey** on the side, and a platter of **crisp bacon** to go with them.

RANCH EGGS
SERVES 6

For a hearty breakfast, Ranch Eggs are substantial and they lend themselves to attractive service because they are so colorful. This is a particularly good dish to arrange for buffet breakfasts as it can be kept warm and the platter looks beautiful.

bacon
onions
green peppers
tomatoes
butter
garlic
salt, pepper
white pepper
eggs
cream
chives
bread

PEPPER AND TOMATO SAUCE

1 In a large skillet sauté: **6 slices bacon.** When crisp, remove and drain.

2 In 4 tablespoons of the bacon fat, sauté gently: **4 green peppers, seeded and cut into thin slices,** and **2 large onions, peeled and sliced thin.**

3 When vegetables are soft add: **4 tomatoes, skinned, seeded, and quartered, 1 clove garlic, minced, ½ teaspoon salt,** and **¼ teaspoon pepper.**

4 Cook gently, and when all vegetables are very soft, mash them a little with a fork. Set aside and keep warm.

EGGS

1 Beat: **12 eggs** with **½ cup cream.**

2 In a skillet heat: **4 tablespoons butter.** Turn heat to low and add the egg-cream mixture.

3 Stir over low heat until eggs are just set but not dry. Add **salt** and **white pepper** to taste.

PRESENTATION

1 Toast: **6 slices bread,** without crusts. **Butter** lightly and cut into small triangles.

2 Mound up scrambled eggs in center of warm platter. Sprinkle with **chopped chives.** Crumble the bacon and sprinkle over the eggs. Arrange the pepper and tomato sauce in a border around eggs. Place the toast triangles around outside edge of platter.

BUTTERMILK WAFFLES
SERVES 4

Waffle irons are so attractive nowadays that it is fun to have them right at the table. They're intelligent, besides, and turn out perfect waffles, let you know when they are ready, and some even turn themselves off quietly without disturbing anyone. Have an earthenware bowl filled with batter and a ladle the right size for each waffle. Mary presides over the iron as though she were pouring at a tea party, and everyone loves getting their waffle after watching it bake.

buttermilk
eggs
butter
sugar
salt
baking soda
baking powder
maple syrup
cornmeal
flour

1 Beat until light and thick: **2 egg yolks.** Add: **1½ cups buttermilk.**

2 Sift and measure: **1 cup flour.** Sift again with: **1 tablespoon cornmeal, 1 teaspoon baking powder, ½ teaspoon baking soda, ½ teaspoon salt,** and **½ teaspoon sugar.**

3 Add the buttermilk-egg mixture to the dry ingredients and mix well.

4 Add: **2 tablespoons cool melted butter.**

5 Beat: **2 egg whites** until stiff and fold into waffle batter gently. *Note:* If you like your waffles soft, add a little more **buttermilk.** This batter makes them crisp.

6 Spread a little firm **butter** on waffle iron and heat it well before baking the waffles. Serve with **softened whipped butter** and **maple syrup.**

POACHED EGGS HARLEQUIN
SERVES 4

This is a good dish for brunch, or what the Harvey people call their Sunday English Breakfast. Everything can be made in advance except for the poached eggs. Then it is just a matter of minutes to put the whole thing together and keep it warm in a chafing dish or a hot server on the buffet. The black-and-red harlequin garnish is an attractive touch.

mushrooms
butter
shallots
flour
cream
cooked chicken
sherry
salt, white pepper
eggs
bread
cooked asparagus
pimiento
black olives
vinegar

CHICKEN SAUCE

1 In a heavy saucepan melt: **4 tablespoons butter.**

2 Sauté: **1 cup finely chopped mushrooms** until nearly done (about 3 minutes). Add: **1 tablespoon finely chopped shallots** and cook a few minutes longer.

3 Blend in: **3 tablespoons flour.** Add: **1¼ cups cream** and cook, stirring constantly, until smooth and thick (about 5 minutes).

4 Add: **1 cup finely chopped cooked chicken** and **¼ cup sherry.** Season with **salt** and **white pepper** to taste. Remove from heat and cover.

POACHED EGGS

Note: Unless you can be sure that your eggs are very fresh, you will have trouble poaching them in the usual way. To play it safe, first put them into simmering water for 10 seconds in their shells, then proceed.

1 Heat to simmering: **1 quart water** and **1 tablespoon vinegar.** (Water should be 2 inches deep.)

2 Stir water to make a small whirlpool. Break: **1 egg** and let it drop gently into center of whirlpool of simmering water. Poach for 4 minutes, or until white is set. Remove with slotted spoon and keep warm in bowl of warm water. Continue until you have poached **4 eggs.**

PRESENTATION

1 Toast: **4 slices of bread** and trim into large rounds.

2 Place a poached egg on each piece of toast. Cover with hot chicken sauce.

3 Garnish each serving with: **4 cooked asparagus spears.** Place: **1 strip pimiento** and **½ pitted black olive** on top of each serving for harlequin garnish.

BLUEBERRY MUFFINS LA POSADA
MAKES 18 MUFFINS

These are the blueberry muffins served on the Santa Fe diners and a specialty of La Posada Hotel in Winslow, Arizona, one of the Fred Harvey hotels in the Southwest. Too few of us have time for homemade hot breads in the morning, and I think it is a shame. But we can at least serve them for more leisurely weekend breakfasts.

sugar
butter
eggs
milk
flour
baking powder
salt
blueberries

1 Preheat oven to hot (400° F.).

2 Cream together: **⅔ cup sugar** and **⅓ cup softened butter.**

3 Add: **2 eggs, well beaten.** Mix thoroughly with sugar and butter.

4 Sift and measure: **2 cups flour.** Sift again with: **2 teaspoons double-acting baking powder** and **½ teaspoon salt.** Add alternately, little by little, with: **⅔ cup milk** to the creamed ingredients.

5 Carefully fold in: **1 cup blueberries.**

6 Grease muffin pans with **butter,** fill half full, and bake in the hot oven for 20 minutes. Serve warm.

SOPAIPILLAS *(Fried Puffs)*
MAKES 24 PUFFS

These are crisp, fried puffs, excellent served in place of bread, particularly with Mexican food. *Sopaipillas* are traditional with Mexican chocolate at four in the afternoon, or accompanying coffee and *chango* (cream cheese with guava jelly and guava husks) for a dessert or a snack any time of day. This is a recipe from Fred Harvey's La Fonda in Santa Fe given to us for our collection by the railway people.

dry yeast
milk
sugar
salt
butter
egg
flour
cooking oil

1   Into mixing bowl put: **¼ cup luke-warm water** (110° F.).
2   Sprinkle in: **1 package active dry yeast** and let stand until yeast is softened.
3   In saucepan combine: **¾ cup milk, 6 tablespoons sugar,** and **1 teaspoon salt.** Bring to a boil, remove from heat and stir in: **2 tablespoons butter.** Let cool to lukewarm, then stir into yeast mixture.
4   Stir in: **1 beaten egg.**
5   Gradually beat in: **3 cups flour.** When dough becomes too thick to beat, work in the last ½ cup flour with your hand to make a dough which is soft, but not sticky. It should not be stiff.

6   Cover dough with a towel and let rise for 1½ hours. Punch down, turn out on lightly **floured** pastry board, and knead briefly until dough is smooth. Cover and let rest for 10 minutes.
7   Then roll out dough about ¼ inch thick into a 12-inch square and cut into 24 strips, each 2 x 3 inches.
8   Heat in saucepan: **2 inches cooking oil** to 350° F.
9   Add the strips of dough, a few at a time, and deep fry for 3 minutes, or until golden brown, turning once when puffed and browned on the underside.

CORN STICKS
MAKES ABOUT 24 STICKS

These are a delicious breakfast treat and I especially like them made in a **corn-stick** pan, though you can do them in regular muffin pans just as well. If you can get the water-ground cornmeal, the Corn Sticks will be crisper and more flavorful.

white cornmeal
eggs
milk
butter
salt
bacon (optional)

1   Preheat oven to hot (425° F.).
2   Sift together: **1½ cups white cornmeal** and **1 teaspoon salt.**
3   Stirring constantly, pour over the cornmeal and salt: **1½ cups boiling water.** Mix well and let the mixture cool to lukewarm.
4   Add: **1 tablespoon melted butter.**
5   Beat in, one at a time: **3 eggs.**
6   Stir in: **1½ cups milk.**
7   If you like bacon in your muffins, fry until crisp: **6 slices bacon.** Drain and crumble. Add crisp bacon bits to batter.
8   **Butter** a corn-stick or muffin pan. Heat pan in oven and pour batter into hot pan.
9   Bake in the hot oven until brown (about 25 minutes).

PRESENTATION

Let corn sticks cool slightly, remove from pan and serve warm, wrapped in a fresh white napkin.

LA FONDA PUDDING
SERVES 8

From the Harvey La Fonda in Santa Fe, New Mexico, comes this pudding-cake, also served in the dining cars. It is sweet and light and makes a nice dessert for family dinners. Using graham cracker crumbs instead of flour is a great idea.

eggs
sugar
graham crackers
butter
vanilla
walnuts
baking powder
salt
cream (optional)

1 Preheat oven to moderate (350° F.).

2 Separate: **4 eggs.** Beat the yolks until light and pale.

3 Gradually beat in: **¾ cup sugar** and continue to beat until mixture is thick.

4 Fold in: **1 cup finely crushed graham crackers** (12 double crackers), **½ cup chopped walnuts, 1 teaspoon double-acting baking powder, ⅛ teaspoon salt,** and **1 teaspoon vanilla.**

5 Beat until stiff the **4 egg whites.** Gradually beat in: **¼ cup sugar** to make a thick, glossy meringue.

6 Add half the meringue to the egg yolk mixture and beat until well blended. Add remaining meringue and fold in lightly.

7 **Butter** an 8 x 8 x 2-inch cake pan. Pour the very stiff batter into pan. Bake in the moderate oven for 45 minutes.

PRESENTATION
Cool pudding-cake in pan for 10 minutes. Then turn out of pan. Cut into squares and serve warm topped with **whipped cream** and additional **chopped walnuts,** if you wish.

Behind the elegant dining rooms of the Whitehall Club we get to the heart of the matter—the kitchen. It is here that the reputation of every great restaurant is made, and here that we find, like hidden treasure, the secrets of fine cooking.

The Whitehall Club's luscious Chocolate Roll hits the spot, though our photographer's dart missed the creamy bull's-eye. We don't really recommend playing games with this heavenly dessert—just make it and eat it and thank the Mexican Indians for discovering chocolate.

338

THE WHITEHALL CLUB

Cʜɪᴄᴀɢᴏ has been a long time living down the label pinned on it by Carl Sandburg—"Hog Butcher for the World." The stockyards aren't what they used to be, but meats and steaks are still superlative in this town, and a new dimension has been added gastronomically. There are now many wonderful restaurants here with fantastically varied cuisines, a few of them so popular that they have become private clubs in order to limit the crowds.

The best, I would say, is The Whitehall Club, one of the few American restaurants ever mentioned in that Who's Who of French gastronomy, the *Guide Michelin*. Elegantly paneled, and decorated with an antique wallpaper like the one used in Sacher's in Vienna, the room manages to seem private and intimate even when it is jammed. The host-owners are the Keller brothers, Sidney and Will, men of many enterprises, but with none so close to their hearts as this excellent eating club. They and their staff not only love good food, they love sharing its secrets with other interested gastronomes.

Aside from some marvelous recipes, the Whitehall staff also gave me a few good cooking tips, which I happily pass on to you. Their chef's big secret is to use shallots in everything requiring garlic or onion, except for salad. Don't overdo any flavor — use herbs and spices sparingly to let the flavor of the original food come through. And don't overcook, or again you will lose the flavor of the original. Their recipe for good cooking? Two cups care, one heaping teaspoonful of imagination and generous dashes of subtlety. Result? Some of the most delicious food we've ever eaten anywhere.

DINNER

THE WHITEHALL CLUB

Appetizers Cocktails

Gray Perles of Fresh Beluga Caviar (when available) 6.50

Foie Gras Strasburgeois 5.00   Canelloni, Quo Vadis 1.25

Pate de foie Maison 1.75   Our Own Marinated Herrings 1.00

Imported Prosciutto with Melon in Season 2.25   Broiled Grapefruit .75

Alaskan King Crab Legs, Mustard Mayonnaise 2.00

Scampi Meuniere 2.00   Fresh Fruit Cocktail 1.50

Shrimp Cocktail, Sauce Maison 1.50   Fresh Lump Crab Meat Cocktail 1.75

Baked Crabmeat, Deauville 2.00   Cherrystone Clams 1.00

Escargots Bourguignonne 2.00

Baked Crabmeat, Hampton 2.00   Shrimps Provencale 2.00

Blue Points in Half Shell 1.50   Escargots Saute Bordelaise 2.00

Broiled Langoustines, Sauce Choron 2.00

Baked Oysters, Rockefeller or Bourguignonne 2.00

Soups

Consomme Double .65   Chicken Broth .65   Petite Marmite, Henry IV 1.00   Baked Onion Soup Parisienne .75   Green Turtle Xeres 1.50

Vichyssoise, Cold .65   Madrilene (Jelly) .65   French Crayfish Bisque 1.25

Chicken and Crab Gumbo WHITEHALL 1.50

Sea & Stream

Whole Dover Sole, Grilled Hoteliere 4.00   Turbot, Saute Belle Meuniere 4.00   Grilled Lake Superior Jumbo Whitefish 3.75

Whole Broiled Maine Lobster 6.50   Crab Meat Louise 4.25   Frog Legs Meuniere or Provencale 4.25

Baked Lobster, Thermidor or Mornay 6.50   Shrimps Curry, Madras 4.00   Split and Boned Colorado Brook Trout Amandine 3.75

Long Island Pearl Scallops, Saute Meuniere 4.25

Entrees

Veal Kidney Saute, Bruxelloise 3.75   Scaloppine of Veal, Au Marsala 3.75   Rock Cornish Game Hen, WHITEHALL 4.00

Sliced Beef Tenderloin Pepper Steak, Cantonese 5.50   Steak Diane (prepared at table) 6.50   Tournedos of Beef Rossini 6.25

Saute Calf's Liver and Bacon 4.00   Calf's Sweetbreads, Perigourdine 3.75   Long Island Duckling Bigarade, Wild Rice 4.50

Our Special Corned Beef Hash WHITEHALL with Poached Egg 3.75   Rack of Spring Lamb Persillade (for two, 45 minutes) 9.00

Supreme of Chicken, A La Kiev 3.75   Royal Squab, Wild Rice 4.00   Double Breast of Chicken, Saute Mascotte 4.00

From the Charcoal Broiler

Prime Sirloin 6.25   Prime Double Sirloin 12.50   Minute Steak 5.25   Filet Mignon 6.25

Steak Au Poivre Flambe, Au Cognac 7.00   Chateaubriand (for two) 12.50   French Lamb Chops 4.25

Chopped Sirloin 3.75   Calf's Liver Steak 4.00   Calf's Sweetbreads 3.75   Half Spring Chicken 3.50

At your request the above grillades will be accompanied by Perigourdine or Mushroom Sauce

(Bearnaise Sauce .75 Extra)

Vegetables

French String Beans .75   Petit Pois Bonne Femme .75   Baby Carrots .75   Golden Kernel Corn .75

Spinach, Leaf or Creamed .75   Broccoli Hollandaise 1.50   Fried Onion Rings .75

Braised Belgian Endives 1.50   Large, White French Asparagus, Melted Butter or Hollandaise 2.00

POTATOES: Hashed Brown .60   French Fried .60   Lyonnaise .60   Baked Idaho .50   Au Gratin .60   Cottage Fried .75

Salads

Chicken 3.25; White Meat 3.75   Shrimp 3.75   Fresh Crab Meat 4.00

WHITEHALL Salad 1.50   Chef 1.50   Belgian Endive 1.50   Hearts of Lettuce .75   Romaine .75

Kentucky Limestone Lettuce 1.25   Avocado 1.25   Mixed Green .75

Large White French Asparagus, Vinaigrette 2.00   Hearts of Palm 1.50   Sliced Tomato .75   Caesar Salad 1.75

At your request Salads will be served with French Club, Sour Cream, Thousand Island or Lorenzo Dressing

Russian Dressing .75   Roquefort Dressing .75

Desserts

Strawberries, Romanoff 2.25   Assorted Ice Creams .70   Fresh Pineapple au Kirsch 1.25   Snowball 1.00

Sherbets .70   Parfaits .75   Coupe Angele 1.00   Peach Melba 1.00   Cherries Jubilee 2.00

Profiterolles au Famous WHITEHALL Chocolat 1.00   Crepe Suzette 2.25   Gateau du Jour .75   Pear Helene 1.00   Zabaglione 1.75

Whitehall Special Hot Caramel or Chocolate Fudge Sundae 1.00   Whitehall Special Chocolate Ice Cream .70

Fruits Frais Au Porto 1.50

CHEESE: Liederkranz, Camembert, Swiss Gruyere, Roquefort, Cream Cheese, Tilsiter with Toasted Crackers, per portion .75

Patience is a virtue—So is culinary art—Please, your indulgence!

Special Blend Whitehall Coffee Pot .50   Demi Tasse .25   Sanka .40   Postum .40   Expresso .60

Orange Pekoe Tea .40   Coffee Diable 2.25   Grade "A" Milk .35   Cocoa or Chocolate .60

Cigars & Cigarettes

WHITEHALL CHOCOLATE ROLL
SERVES 8

We have never had this dessert brought to the table without it eliciting a chorus of rapturous sighs — followed by a chorus of calorie-conscious groans. Once in a while everybody should splurge on a good, rich dessert, even if it means doing penance in the gymnasium the next day. I can't think of anything more worth the pounds and the penance than this velvety brown Chocolate Roll. If you make it at Christmas time, you can put the chocolate topping on to simulate a tree trunk. Then you will have the classic *Bûche de Noël*, or yule log cake with which the French traditionally celebrate their Christmas season.

eggs
sugar
vanilla extract
cocoa
flour
butter
cream
dark sweet chocolate
coffee liqueur

CAKE

1 Preheat oven to moderate (350° F.).

2 **Butter** a baking sheet 11 x 16 inches, line with waxed paper, and **butter** the waxed paper.

3 Separate: **4 eggs.**

4 Beat the egg yolks with: **½ cup sugar** and **½ teaspoon vanilla extract** until eggs are thick and pale in color.

5 Combine: **3 tablespoons cocoa** and **¾ cup sifted flour.** Stir into egg yolk mixture. Beat the egg whites until stiff and fold into the batter. Fold in: **2 tablespoons melted butter.**

6 Spread the batter on the prepared baking sheet and bake in the moderate oven for 15 minutes. Remove from oven and let cool for 5 minutes. Turn out on a clean towel, remove waxed paper from bottom and roll lengthwise in the towel. Let cool for about 20 minutes.

FILLING

Bring: **⅔ cup cream** and **2 tablespoons butter** to a rapid boil. Add: **10 ounces dark sweet chocolate, cut into pieces,** and stir until chocolate is melted and mixture is smooth. Cool. Beat vigorously (use electric beater if possible). Add: **2 ounces coffee liqueur** and continue to beat until filling is thick.

TOPPING

Whip: **1 cup cream** and stir in: **3 ounces dark sweet chocolate, melted and slightly cooled,** and **1 ounce coffee liqueur.** Mix thoroughly but gently.

PRESENTATION

Unroll cake, spread with filling and roll again. Place on a long serving board. Swirl the topping over top and sides of the roll and sprinkle generously with **shaved chocolate.**

PETITE MARMITE HENRY IV *(Clear Soup with Meat and Vegetables)*
SERVES 8

You can almost make a meal out of The Whitehall Club's wonderful consommé, if you cut the meat and chicken breasts into larger slices, and if you cook several marrow bones in the soup pot. Then you spread the marrow on toasted French bread, have a good-sized portion of beef and chicken in the soup, all the vegetables, and there you are—dinner. This famous French soup takes its name from the *marmite*, a tall earthenware stockpot in which soups and stews are always cooked in France.

shin of beef
chicken
salt, pepper
turnip
celery
leeks
carrots
onion
French bread

1 Put into large kettle: **2 pounds shin of beef, without fat, 1 frying chicken, cut into parts, with giblets, 3 quarts water, 3 teaspoons salt,** and **¾ teaspoon pepper.** Bring to a boil and skim off the foam that rises to the surface. Reduce heat and simmer for 3 hours, skimming as often as necessary.

2 Remove soup from heat. Take out meat and chicken. Cut meat and breast of the chicken into fine julienne strips. (Save the rest of the chicken to use some other time.) Strain the broth through a sieve lined with cheesecloth into a clean kettle.

3 Add: **1 stalk celery, 4 carrots, 2 leeks,** and **1 medium turnip,** all cut into thin julienne strips about 2 inches long. Add: **1 medium onion, thinly sliced.** Bring to a boil. Correct the seasoning with **salt** and **pepper** to taste and simmer for 15 minutes.

4 Add the julienne of meat and chicken and simmer for 2 minutes longer.

PRESENTATION

Serve in large bowls with some of each kind of meat and vegetables in each one. Pass **hot French bread** to eat with the *Petite Marmite.*

BREAST OF CHICKEN AU CHAMPAGNE
SERVES 4

The Whitehall Club serves this delicious chicken and when they gave me the recipe, they told me there were just two important instructions they would add to it. It is a simple dish and to make it perfectly, first buy fresh breasts, and second, use *only* French champagne. You can buy a 6½-ounce bottle, and the difference in quality and flavor, they believe, makes all the difference in your finished dish. We did exactly as we were told, and it was superb!

chicken breasts
flour
salt, pepper
milk (optional)
butter
mushrooms
cream
French champagne

CHICKEN BREASTS

1 Buy fresh breasts, 1 single breast of capon or 1 whole double breast of a 2-pound broiler per person.

2 Remove skin and bones from: **4 single breasts of capon** or **4 double breasts of chicken.** Place boned breasts between 2 pieces of waxed paper and pound with a heavy cleaver until slightly flattened.

3 Mix: **¼ cup flour, 1 teaspoon salt,** and **½ teaspoon pepper.** Roll the chicken breasts in this mixture. Pat them to shake off excess flour.

4 Heat in large skillet: **½ cup butter.** Cook chicken breasts in the hot butter over low heat until lightly browned on both sides.

5 Add: **½ pound mushrooms, sliced,** cover, and cook for 10 minutes. Drain off any excess butter.

6 Add: **1 cup cream** and simmer over low heat for 10 minutes.

7 Transfer breasts to a warm serving platter.

SAUCE

Add to liquid in skillet: **¼ cup French champagne.** Bring to a rapid boil and cook until sauce is reduced to a creamy consistency. If sauce becomes too thick, add a little **milk.**

PRESENTATION

Spoon sauce over the chicken breasts. Garnish the platter with: **4 large mushroom caps** that have been sautéed in a little **butter.**

STEAK DIANE
SERVES 4

Usually in Chicago you are brought enormous, thick steaks that all but come to the table wearing the blue ribbon of the steer that they were part of. So for a change it was pleasant to be served a steak that had been pounded thin and was cooked quickly at the table in a chafing dish. The Whitehall Club's maître d'hôtel did the steaks and their sauce so deftly and rapidly, I couldn't wait to get home and try it myself. It really does go 1-2-3, and tastes marvelous.

sirloin steaks
butter
shallots
Worcestershire sauce
salt, pepper
parsley

1 Put: **4 sirloin steaks,** each about 6 ounces, between pieces of waxed paper and pound to a ⅓-inch thickness.

2 Heat in small saucepan: **2 tablespoons butter.**

3 Add: **4 tablespoons finely chopped shallots** and cook until shallots are lightly browned. Add: **2 tablespoons Worcestershire sauce** and heat to bubbling. Keep the sauce hot.

4 Heat in 12-inch skillet or chafing dish: **6 tablespoons butter.** When it begins to brown, add steaks and cook for 3 minutes. Turn and cook for 2 to 3 minutes longer, or until done to taste. Transfer to a serving dish and sprinkle with **salt** and a generous amount of **freshly ground pepper.**

PRESENTATION
Spread the shallot sauce over the steaks and sprinkle with **chopped parsley.**

COTTAGE FRIED POTATOES
SERVES 4

There are hundreds of recipes for fried potatoes of one kind or another, but very few of them tempt me—either to eat or to cook. But these potatoes from The Whitehall Club were exceptional. Follow the recipe exactly—it is careful and loving attention to detail that makes this so good when it is prepared properly.

Idaho potatoes
butter
salt, pepper
cooking oil

1 Peel: **3 medium-sized Idaho potatoes.**

2 Cut them into slices ⅛ inch thick (which is pretty thin).

3 DO NOT WASH THEM. (This was important enough for the chef to write out in capital letters for me.)

4 Take slice by slice and lay them at the bottom of a cold, heavy skillet, starting from the center. Do them in circles with each slice overlapping the other.

5 Melt in a saucepan: **¾ cup butter, cut into pieces.** When butter has melted, spoon off the foam, pour carefully into a cup leaving the thick, cloudy residue at bottom of pan. What you have in the cup is clarified butter. Add to it: **¼ cup cooking oil.** (The butter will get hot without browning or burning as a result of adding the oil.)

6 Pour the butter and oil over the potatoes and cook over medium heat for 10 minutes.

7 The slices will all be sticking to each other and will be brown on the bottom. Turn them over with a spatula as you would a large pancake, being careful not to break the circle.

8 Cook for another 10 minutes. When each side looks crisp and golden brown, drain all the fat from the pan.

PRESENTATION
Turn out on a hot round platter. Sprinkle a little **salt** and **pepper** on top of the potatoes and serve.

STEAK AU POIVRE (*Black Pepper Steak*)
SERVES 4

If you think, as I do, that black pepper and rare beef make beautiful music together, then you will like this steak recipe too. We learned it in Chicago from friends who had brought it back from France—people in this stockyard city must be especially alert to new ways of preparing beef. This one is a winner.

sirloin steak
peppercorns
dry white wine
brandy (optional)
butter
cooking oil
watercress

1 Wipe with a damp cloth: **a 1¼-inch sirloin steak** (3 pounds). Dry carefully.

2 Coarsely crush: **2 tablespoons peppercorns.** (Use a mortar and pestle or a wooden bowl and a potato masher.)

3 Pound crushed pepper into both sides of the steak, smacking it in with flat side of a cleaver or the potato masher. Steak should be quite thickly covered. Let stand for 2 hours.

4 In a heavy skillet heat: **1 tablespoon butter** and **1 teaspoon cooking oil.** (This mixture can get hotter without burning than butter alone.)

5 Over high heat sear steak quickly on both sides. Cook 5 minutes on each side.

6 Remove steak to a hot platter.

7 Stir into pan: **⅔ cup dry white wine** and **1 tablespoon brandy** (optional). Boil wine rapidly for 2 minutes, scraping up brown meat drippings at bottom of pan.

8 Remove from heat and swirl in: **2 tablespoons butter.**

PRESENTATION

Strain the sauce over the steak (or don't strain it if you want the loose bits of pepper too) and garnish with **watercress.**

CHEESE BLINTZES
SERVES 4

In every large city there are restaurants devoted to Jewish cooking either the meat or the dairy kind, and some of my favorite foods are the dairy dishes made with cheese and sour cream. There was one such restaurant in Chicago's Loop many years ago, that has since gone out of business, where I got this recipe for Cheese Blintzes. They make a delightful lunch, and I like to put a spoonful of cherry preserve on the very last one I eat, turning it into dessert.

flour
eggs
salt
butter
cottage cheese
sugar
vanilla extract
nutmeg
sour cream
milk

PANCAKES (Blintzes)

1 Beat: **3 eggs** and add: **1½ cups milk.**

2 In a bowl put: **1 cup sifted flour, ¼ teaspoon salt,** and **2 teaspoons sugar.**

3 Add the milk-egg mixture to the dry ingredients and beat until smooth. Add: **1 teaspoon melted butter.** Let stand 30 minutes.

4 Heat a 7-inch skillet and grease with a little **butter.**

5 Pour in enough batter to thinly cover the bottom. Tilt pan to spread the thin coating of batter.

6 Bake until underside is browned. Turn out, browned side up, on a clean towel. Stack pancakes until you have made them all (about 16).

FILLING

Mix together: **2 cups cottage cheese, drained** (put in large sieve and press out any liquid with back of wooden spoon), **2 egg yolks, 2 tablespoons sugar, ¼ teaspoon vanilla extract, ¼ teaspoon nutmeg,** and **½ teaspoon salt.**

PRESENTATION

1 Place 1 tablespoon of the cheese filling in the center of the browned side of each pancake (or blintze). Fold ends in, then roll up.

2 Heat in a skillet: **2 tablespoons butter.** Brown the blintzes in it on all sides.

3 Serve hot and crisp with **sour cream** spooned on top.

SOUFFLÉ ROTHSCHILD *(Soufflé with Glacéed Fruits)*
SERVES 4

This soufflé proves that a dessert does not have to be fancy to be elegant. If it was good enough for the Rothschilds it should certainly do for us! However, a soufflé large enough to serve more than eight people is apt not to *souffle* properly. The Whitehall Club chef advises that unless you have the equipment and a large enough oven to make several at the same time, it is best to make this dessert only for four or for eight. (For eight you just double this recipe and use a three-quart dish with a cuff of waxed paper tied around it.)

milk
sugar
butter
cognac
flour
eggs
vanilla extract
mixed glacéed fruits

1 Preheat oven to hot (400° F.).

2 In a saucepan combine: **2 cups milk, ½ cup sugar,** and **¼ cup butter.**

3 Bring to a rapid boil. Remove from heat and add: **½ cup flour.** Stir in thoroughly, return to heat, and cook, stirring rapidly, until mixture is smooth and thick. Remove from heat.

4 Stir in, one at a time: **6 egg yolks.** Beat well after each addition.

5 Soak: **⅔ cup chopped glacéed fruits** in **¼ cup cognac** for ½ hour.

6 Drain fruits and set aside. Reserve the cognac.

7 Beat into the soufflé mixture: **3 drops vanilla extract** and the cognac.

8 Beat: **6 egg whites** until stiff but not dry. Fold into the egg yolk mixture.

9 Pour one-third of the soufflé mixture into a 2-quart soufflé dish. Sprinkle half of the glacéed fruits on top. Pour in half of the remaining soufflé mixture, cover with the rest of the glacéed fruits, then add the last of the soufflé mixture. Your dish should be only about four-fifths full.

10 Put dish into the hot oven. Immediately reduce oven temperature to moderately hot (375° F.) and bake for 35 to 40 minutes.

PRESENTATION
Wrap a clean white napkin around soufflé dish and serve immediately. It is delicious as it is, or with The Whitehall Club's Zabaglione Sauce (see below).

Note: Here are The Whitehall Club's additional rules and comments about soufflé making, which we found encouraging and helpful:
"This soufflé is ideal for the busy housewife. It is simple and it works. The main ingredients can be cooked in advance. Fifty minutes before dessert time, she will only have to mix the stiff whites of eggs and bake. But this recipe would be incomplete if we do not add that to make a good pastry, one must follow the instructions carefully. A sauce can be corrected after having been made, but not a pastry. Another element is the oven. In many homes the stove thermostat is not working properly or, as in gas ovens, air goes out from one side of the oven and this draft pulls the soufflé to one side so it must be turned a couple of times. Know your oven well and if the first try is not successful, do not give up."

ZABAGLIONE SAUCE *(Egg and Wine Sauce)*
SERVES 4

At The Whitehall Club this sauce is served with the dessert soufflé, but it can also be served in cups as an excellent dessert by itself. In that case you would have to double the quantity. This is one of the best zabagliones I have ever tasted, and according to the chef, the secret of its success is simply that it must be brought to the boiling point but *must not boil* or it will curdle. Simple enough!

eggs
sherry
sugar
vanilla extract
cream
Grand Marnier

1 Into a round-bottomed china or stainless steel bowl put: **3 egg yolks, 3 tablespoons sugar, 2 tablespoons sherry,** and **2 drops vanilla extract.**

2 Place bowl in a skillet containing simmering water and cook, beating constantly with a wire whisk or a rotary beater, until mixture is very thick. Remove from heat and let sauce cool.

3 Whip: **½ cup cream** until stiff.

4 Fold in the egg mixture and **2 tablespoons Grand Marnier.**

PRESENTATION

Spoon into sherbet glasses and serve at once while still warm.

PUMP ROOM CHICKEN HASH
SERVES 4

The Pump Room in Chicago's Ambassador East Hotel has long been one of the favorite ports of call for visiting celebrities. The first banquette is usually reserved for any theatrical people currently playing the Second City, and many of the dishes on the menu are named for stars. Amid all the elegance of eighteenth-century England, the flaming swords, and plumed coffee boys, my preference is for the Pump Room's plain Chicken Hash. Especially good for a late evening snack.

cooked chicken
celery
salt, white pepper
paprika
Madeira
frozen patty shells
supreme sauce
(see index)
eggs
cream
canned chicken
consommé
Escoffier sauce
parsley

1 Bake: **4 frozen patty shells** according to directions on package.

2 In a saucepan heat: **2 cups canned chicken consommé.** Add: **½ cup diced celery** and **1 cup minced cooked chicken.** Simmer for 30 minutes.

3 In another saucepan heat: **1 cup supreme sauce.** Add: **2 tablespoons cream, 2 ounces Escoffier sauce, salt** to taste, and **¼ teaspoon white pepper.** Simmer for 5 minutes and add: **3 tablespoons Madeira.** Stir well.

4 Strain the chicken and celery from the consommé. Stir chicken and celery into the sauce.

5 Beat well: **2 egg yolks** with **1 teaspoon cream.** Add a little of the hot sauce. Add egg yolk mixture to the sauce and blend well. Cook over low heat until thickened.

PRESENTATION

Fill patty shells with chicken hash. Sprinkle with **paprika** and top with a little **chopped parsley.**

FLAMING SHASHLIK (*Lamb on a Skewer*)
SERVES 6

Typical of the Pump Room's blazing cuisine is this shashlik which comes to the table there on a flaming sword that would put Excalibur to shame. Omit the razzle-dazzle and you still have a delicious recipe for lamb broiled on a skewer, which is exactly how we do it at home.

leg of lamb
red Burgundy
onions
bay leaves
Worcestershire sauce
chili sauce
catsup
piccalilli
honey
horse-radish
chutney
garlic
bread crumbs
cooking oil
salt, pepper
mushrooms
green peppers
tomatoes

MARINADE

Combine in a crock or bowl: **2 cups red Burgundy, ½ cup minced onion, 2 bay leaves, 1 tablespoon Worcestershire sauce, 1 clove garlic, crushed, 1 teaspoon salt, and ¼ teaspoon freshly ground pepper.**

LAMB

1 Cut into 1½-inch cubes: **2 pounds lamb** cut from the leg.

2 Marinate lamb cubes for 48 hours, turning them occasionally.

3 Remove meat from marinade, roll in **bread crumbs**, and thread on skewers, alternating meat with: **a mushroom cap, a wedge of tomato, a piece of green pepper,** and **a slice of onion.**

4 Sprinkle with **cooking oil** and broil under high heat for 20 minutes, or until well browned, turning frequently. (You can cook this on a barbecue grill too with excellent results.)

HOT SHASHLIK SAUCE
(Makes About 3 Cups)

1 In a saucepan combine: **2 cups chili sauce, 1 cup catsup, 1 tablespoon piccalilli, 1 tablespoon honey, 1 tablespoon horse-radish,** and **1 tablespoon chopped chutney.**

2 Mix well and cook over low heat, stirring constantly, for 10 minutes.

PRESENTATION

With a fork, push off contents of skewers so shashlik lies in neat rows on a warm platter. Serve with the hot shashlik sauce and, if you wish, saffron rice.

COUPE GERTRUDE LAWRENCE
(Ice Cream with Chocolate Rum Sauce)
SERVES 4

There is a plaque commemorating the late Gertrude Lawrence on one of the banquettes in the Pump Room, and this dessert still bears her name. The sauce is very much in the tradition of the Pump Room's cuisine—it is an interesting combination of flavors, and it flames, almost a prerequisite for appearing on their menu.

vanilla ice cream
orange
Jamaica rum
salt
semisweet chocolate
brown sugar
cream

CHOCOLATE SAUCE (Makes 1 Cup)

In a saucepan put: **4 squares semisweet chocolate, broken into small pieces, 1 cup brown sugar, ⅔ cup cream,** and **a pinch of salt.** Stir over low heat until chocolate is melted and sauce thickens. (Extra sauce will keep in jar in refrigerator for several weeks.)

PRESENTATION

Put: **a scoop of vanilla ice cream** into each of 4 bowls or *coupe* glasses. In a chafing dish put: **3 tablespoons grated orange rind.** Stir in pan to heat, then add: **4 tablespoons Jamaica rum** and ignite. While flame is burning add 4 tablespoons of the chocolate sauce. Pour over ice cream and serve.

349

RIS DE VEAU À LA CRÈME (Sweetbreads in Cream)

SERVES 6

One of the more popular Chicago restaurants is The Red Carpet which has a reputation for serving unusual food in a rather theatrical setting. Their recipe for sweetbreads is very good, and the sauce is made very easily by just adding wine and cream to the pan in which the meat was sautéed. Another advantage to this dish is that it need not be served immediately. A thin film of cream or melted butter over the top of the sauce will keep it from forming a skin, and you simply reheat the sauce in the pan for a few minutes before serving.

SWEETBREADS

bacon
onion
sweetbreads
mushrooms
lemon
dry white wine
cream
flour
salt, pepper
parsley
butter (optional)

1 Soak in a bowl of ice water: **3 pairs fresh sweetbreads** (about 3 pounds) for 2 hours. Change water several times.

2 Place sweetbreads in a saucepan with: **4 cups water, 1 teaspoon salt,** and **1 tablespoon lemon juice.**

3 Let water barely simmer for 15 minutes. Remove sweetbreads and plunge them at once into cold water.

4 Cut each pair of sweetbreads apart and remove the little tube that connected them. Carefully remove membrane that covers sweetbreads. Place the six sweetbread halves on a board and cover with large flat dish or baking sheet topped with a weight. Leave for several hours to flatten the sweetbreads and give them a firm attractive shape.

5 **Flour** sweetbreads lightly. Sprinkle with a little **freshly ground pepper.**

6 In a large skillet sauté: **¼ pound bacon, chopped.** When bacon fat is hot, add: **2 tablespoons chopped onion.**

When onion is soft, add the sweetbreads and sauté for 3 minutes on each side until brown.

7 Remove the sweetbreads, bacon, and onions from skillet and add: **½ cup sliced mushrooms.** Sauté for 4 minutes, shaking the pan vigorously.

SAUCE

1 Remove the mushrooms and stir into pan slowly: **½ cup dry white wine.** Stir to de-glaze pan.

2 Add: **1 cup cream** and stir to mix with wine. Add the mushrooms, onions, bacon, and sweetbreads and leave on low heat for 15 minutes. Taste for seasoning. (If sauce needs additional thickening, stir in a roux of **1 teaspoon soft butter** mixed with **1 teaspoon flour.**)

PRESENTATION

Lay the sweetbreads on a warm platter and spoon the sauce over them. Sprinkle with: **1 tablespoon minced parsley.**

ESCALOPE DE VEAU MARSEILLAIS
(Veal Scallops with Crabmeat)

SERVES 6

Sometimes when you dine at a restaurant you come across strange combinations of food that ordinarily you would never try. So it was with this veal and crabmeat dish from The Red Carpet. Once in a while when we are feeling rather experimental this is the kind of recipe it's fun to do. You can make the *béarnaise* sauce in a blender (see index), or use the recipe given here.

veal scallops
crabmeat
canned beef bouillon
Madeira
cooked asparagus tips
eggs
salt, pepper
tarragon vinegar
shallots
white wine
butter
cooking oil
dried tarragon
flour

VEAL

1 Pound: **12 veal scallops** to a thickness of ¼ inch. Dry well and dust very lightly with **flour.**

2 Sauté a few pieces at a time in: **2 tablespoons butter** and **1 tablespoon cooking oil** over moderately high heat for 4 minutes on each side. Remove veal and keep warm.

3 When all the veal is sautéed, pour off fat and add: **2 tablespoons butter, ¼ cup Madeira** and **⅔ cup canned beef bouillon.** Boil over high heat and reduce liquid to ½ cup.

4 Lower heat, add the veal, and simmer for 10 minutes.

BÉARNAISE SAUCE
(Makes About 2 Cups)

1 Simmer: **2 tablespoons chopped shallots** in **½ cup tarragon vinegar** until partially cooked.

2 Add: **½ cup white wine** and cook until liquid is reduced to one-third of original amount.

3 In a heatproof bowl beat: **6 egg yolks** until thick. Strain the vinegar-wine mixture and beat into the eggs.

4 Put bowl in pan of simmering water and beat until mixture thickens. Add, drop by drop: **1 cup melted butter,** beating all the time.

5 Taste for seasoning and add a little **salt** and **pepper,** if necessary. Finish with **2 tablespoons dried tarragon leaves.**

PRESENTATION

Arrange the veal scallops on a warm platter. Place: **1 lump warmed crabmeat** on each veal scallop. Cover each with 2 tablespoons of the *béarnaise* sauce and garnish with: **24 cooked asparagus tips.**

HAITIAN LOBSTER
SERVES 6

Here's an exotic specialty of The Red Carpet that makes a very different first course. The list of ingredients goes from here to eternity but don't let that frighten you. Practically the only thing you have to do is mix about three-fourths of them together for the Caribbee sauce, and deep fry your lobster tails.

rock lobster tails
mayonnaise
chives
garlic
cooking oil
bread crumbs
almonds
sour cream
parsley
lemons
anchovy paste
onion
English mustard
tarragon
Tabasco

LOBSTER TAILS

1 Split lengthwise: **6 rock lobster tails.** Remove meat from shells in 1 piece.

2 Mix together: **1 cup mayonnaise, 1 teaspoon chopped chives,** and **⅛ teaspoon crushed garlic.**

3 Roll lobster pieces in above mixture. Then roll them in: **2 cups bread crumbs** mixed with **½ cup chopped almonds.**

4 Deep fry in hot **cooking oil** (370° F.).

CARIBBEE SAUCE

Mix together: **1 cup mayonnaise, ½ cup commercial sour cream, ¼ cup chopped parsley, 1 tablespoon lemon juice, 1 teaspoon anchovy paste, ½ teaspoon grated onion, ¼ teaspoon English mustard, ¼ teaspoon chopped tarragon, ½ clove garlic, crushed,** and **a dash of Tabasco.**

PRESENTATION

Drain the fried lobster on paper towels. Arrange them on warm platter garnished with **lemon wedges** and **parsley.** Serve the Caribbee sauce in a separate sauce dish.

MARINATED BEEF SLICES
SERVES 2

Out on South Halsted Street, right in Chicago's famous (or infamous, if you're a vegetarian) stockyards, is the Stock Yard Inn, a restaurant that, naturally, specializes in meat. We were taken there for steaks, but a steak is a steak is a steak is a steak, to paraphrase Gertrude Stein, while a brand-new recipe is a joy forever. This one is most unusual, and a delicious way to use up leftover steak—although we think it good enough for summer lunches to justify making it from scratch.

boneless sirloin steak
onion
salt, pepper
sour cream
lemon
lettuce
paprika
rye bread
butter

MARINATED BEEF

1 Broil or sauté: **a 1-pound boneless sirloin steak.**

2 Cut meat into julienne strips. **Salt** and **pepper** to taste.

3 Cut: **1 onion** into very thin slices. Place onion slices over the meat.

4 Sprinkle: **2 tablespoons lemon juice** over meat and onions and mix well.

5 Let stand for ½ hour. Then add: **1 cup commercial sour cream** and mix together. Chill in refrigerator.

PRESENTATION

Place **a crisp lettuce leaf** on each plate. Put half the marinated beef on each lettuce leaf and sprinkle lightly with **paprika** before serving. We like this with **buttered rye toast,** sliced very thin.

This colorful Hawaiian cookout at the Hotel Hana-Maui is my idea of a wonderful way to give a dinner party. No shoes, no ties, no chairs, no silverware. Just lots of good food and lovely native girls to serve it with a smile.

Baked Opakapaka is our favorite specialty of the luau, prepared according to the hotel's own recipe. Now you can make one that will be just as good, but whether or not you serve it with poi, as the Hawaiians do, we leave to your discretion.

HOTEL HANA-MAUI

EVERYONE dreams of an island paradise where the bounties of nature hang within easy reach, and if you're too lazy to reach for them, a sloe-eyed siren awaits your slightest wish. The Hana-Maui comes pretty close to the picture . . . any closer and I'd still be there!

Here on the island of Maui, not yet invaded by tourists, is one of the earliest sugarcane plantations in the islands. The hotel was built on part of the plantation, and it maintains many of the graceful and gracious ways of old Hawaii. The luau is the traditional Hawaiian party-feast, and we've been lucky over the years to attend several genuine ones. The setting is always romantic with vistas of palms and misty mountains, and the sea whispering at your feet or beating a soft background rhythm for the lovely island songs.

While the idea of eating raw fish, poi, or suckling pig may give you a qualm or two, you really owe it to yourself to let go and when in Hawaii be a Hawaiian. The islands are a melting pot—no, a blend—of so many cultures you can scarcely tell what's original Hawaiian and what is Chinese, Japanese, or Philippine. But it is all part of the picture, and even the poi and seaweed begin to taste good if you let yourself melt into the pot. Blend!

Making a luau at home isn't easy, especially if you go whole hog (or whole suckling pig) and insist on digging your own *imu*, as the barbecue pit is called. But you can have fun trying some of the dishes and adding an exotic touch to your menus. If not a whole Hawaiian menu, then one course or an hors d'oeuvre will spark a dinner. One word of warning: It can't all be achieved with a can of pineapple and a dash of soy sauce.

355

HOTEL *Hana-Maui*

HAWAIIAN ISLANDS

HAWAIIAN LUAU - HANA-MAUI

PUPUS OR HORS d'OEUVRES
CRAB PUFFS
TERIYAKI SKEWERS
SESAME CHICKEN SKEWERS
FRANKFURT SOYA SKEWERS

TROPICAL FRUITS OKOLEHAO
KINILAU FISH
LOMI LOMI SALMON

KALUA PIG

POLYNESIAN COCONUT DUCKLING, SERVED IN
HALF PINEAPPLE SHELL

CRAB HALEAKALA, SERVED IN HALF AVOCADO

CHICKEN AND LONG RICE, SERVED IN COCONUT SHELL

WHOLE PLANKED OPAKAPAKA, BAKED IN COCONUT SAUCE
SERVED ON BED OF SAVORY RICE AND ASSORTED FRUITS

POI
SWEET POTATOES, BAKED IN IMU
LUAU
CANDIED PAPAYA
STUFFED BREADFRUIT
BAKED BANANAS
SAVORY RICE

HAUPIA (COCONUT PUDDING)
LILIKOI (PASSION FRUIT) CHIFFON PIE
PINEAPPLE MERINGUE PIE

BANANAS
HALF PAPAYAS
PINEAPPLE BOATS
FRUIT SALAD

HANAHO RUM PUNCH
HAWAIIAN FRUIT PUNCH

BAKED OPAKAPAKA (*Planked Fish with Coconut Sauce*)
SERVES 4

When we make this dish, the closest we can come to opakapaka is red snapper, which is a lot easier to spell, besides. At the Hana-Maui they use a coarse Hawaiian rock salt to rub into the fish. It is much like the kosher salt we get here. With those two substitutions, the rest is clear sailing for this most attractive and delicious fish course in the luau.

red snapper
coconut cream
(see index)
kosher salt
sherry
cooked rice
lemon
grapefruit
orange
papaya
pineapple
green seedless grapes

1 Preheat oven to moderate (350° F.).

2 Rub: **a 4- to 5-pound red snapper** with **kosher salt.**

3 Place fish in a shallow baking dish and pour over it: **1 cup coconut cream.** Bake in the moderate oven for 20 to 25 minutes and add: **2 tablespoons sherry.**

4 Bake 20 minutes longer, basting frequently with pan juices. When fish flakes easily with a fork it is cooked.

PRESENTATION

When fish is done, remove it carefully to a plank. Border it with **cooked rice,** garnish with **lemon slices, grapefruit** and **orange sections, pineapple** and **papaya slices,** and **green seedless grapes.**

TERIYAKI STEAK SKEWERS
SERVES 4

It takes six hours for the pièce de résistance of the luau—roast pig—to cook. In the interim there is a good deal of jollity over a *very* long cocktail hour. This is probably what has made Hawaiian *pupus*, their hors d'oeuvres, so inspired. At the Hana-Maui they serve a number of meats and marinades with little bamboo skewers. Guests are furnished with small, table-sized charcoal burners called hibachis on which they can barbecue their own appetizers. Hibachis are available in this country and can be used indoors as well as outdoors to brighten up any cocktail gathering.

sirloin tip
soy sauce
garlic
root ginger
sugar
monosodium
glutamate

TERIYAKI MARINADE

Mix in a bowl: **1 cup soy sauce, 2 cloves garlic, crushed, 2 inches root ginger, crushed, 1 teaspoon monosodium glutamate,** and **¼ cup sugar.**

STEAK

1 Wipe with a damp cloth: **1½ pounds sirloin tip.** Slice the raw beef into thin strips.

2 Put 1 strip of the beef on each bamboo skewer.

3 Put all the prepared skewers in a shallow dish with one end of skewer resting on the rim of dish.

4 Pour the marinade over the meat and let stand for 30 minutes.

PRESENTATION

Place the skewers of steak on a platter. Pour the marinade into a small bowl for dipping. Let your guests broil their marinated steak themselves on the hibachi. They may dip the broiled steak into the sauce if they wish.

FRANKFURTER SKEWERS
SERVES 4

The Hana-Maui serves these charming little skewered frankfurters that look like miniature shish kebabs to give variety to the do-it-yourself barbecuers. The platter can be
made most attractive, as the marinating and preparation of the skewers is done in
advance in the kitchen. If you are an artful platter arranger, you'll find that these raw
materials give you plenty of scope for your talents.

cocktail frankfurters
Teriyaki marinade
(see index)
button mushrooms
cherry tomatoes
green peppers

1 Marinate: **16 small cocktail frankfurters** in the **marinade** for 30 minutes.
2 Remove them and thread on each
bamboo skewer in this order: **1 button
mushroom, 1 frankfurter, 1 cherry
tomato,** and **1 piece of green pepper.**

3 Arrange prepared skewers on a
serving platter.

PRESENTATION

Serve with bowl of the marinade and let
each guest broil his own skewer to taste.

SKEWERED CHICKEN IN SESAME SOY SAUCE
SERVES 4

This appetizer, to be broiled on a hibachi, is great if you have any leftover cooked
chicken or turkey. And the sauce is sensational to use on raw chicken before broiling it,
if you want something a little exotic for a change.

cooked chicken
pineapple
apples
soy sauce
garlic
sugar
wine vinegar
sherry
sesame oil
lemon

SKEWERED CHICKEN
1 Cut into cubes: **about 1½ cups
boned cooked chicken.**
2 Put on each skewer: **1 chunk pineapple, 1 cube chicken, 1 cube raw apple**
dipped in **lemon juice,** and repeat again.
3 Marinate in sesame soy sauce for 15
minutes, remove, and drain.

SESAME SOY SAUCE
Mix in a bowl: **½ cup soy sauce, ½ cup**

water, **1 clove garlic, crushed, ½ tablespoon sugar, ¼ cup wine vinegar, ¼
cup sherry, ½ large apple, finely grated,**
and **3 drops sesame oil.**

PRESENTATION

Arrange prepared skewers on a platter
with a bowl of sesame soy sauce. Let
your guests broil their own on the hibachi and use the sauce as a dip, if
they wish.

KINILAU *(Marinated Fish)*
SERVES 4

There are dozens of little appetizers and side dishes served at a luau. The appetizers,
called *pupus*, are a delicious department of Hawaiian cookery, and many of them can
be traced to the original homelands of present-day Hawaiians. This Kinilau, for
example, is a Hawaiian-Filipino dish, and it makes a very good appetizer.

red snapper
onion
celery
tomatoes
lime or lemon
white wine vinegar
soy sauce
Worcestershire sauce
monosodium
glutamate

1 Fillet and skin: **a 1½-pound red snapper.** Cut the flesh into cubes and put into a crock or glass bowl.

2 Add: **1 medium onion, chopped, 3 tender inner stalks of celery with leaves, chopped, 1 large beefsteak tomato or 2 medium, ripe tomatoes, chopped, 2 tablespoons fresh lime or lemon juice, 2 tablespoons white wine vinegar, ½ cup soy sauce, 1 teaspoon Worcestershire sauce, and 1½ teaspoons monosodium glutamate.**

3 Mix and marinate in refrigerator for at least 2 hours before serving.

CRAB PUFFS
MAKES 36 PUFFS

If you have a store that deals in oriental foods, this recipe from the Hana-Maui is a cinch. They now sell packages of frozen Chinese Won Ton Pi squares, the little squares of noodle dough that resemble Italian ravioli or Jewish *kreplach*. (Gastronomically we're getting more one-worldly every day!) Once you have the squares, the filling is easy, and the finished product simply terrific.

frozen Won Ton Pi
squares
cream cheese
canned crabmeat
soft bread crumbs
sesame oil
monosodium
glutamate
peanut oil
Chinese mustard

1 Defrost: **1 package frozen Won Ton Pi squares.**

2 Combine: **8 ounces cream cheese, 1 can (7½ ounces) crabmeat, 2 tablespoons soft bread crumbs, 2 drops sesame oil, and ½ teaspoon monosodium glutamate.**

3 In a skillet heat: **1 inch peanut oil** to 370° F.

4 Put 1 teaspoon of the filling into the center of each Won Ton Pi square. Fold over one corner to center. Moisten other corners and fold into center, one by one. Press edges of folds to seal.

5 Deep fry for about 3 minutes, or until lightly browned and puffed, turning after 1½ minutes.

PRESENTATION
Drain the crab puffs on absorbent paper and serve hot with a small dish of **Chinese mustard.**

CRAB HALEAKALA (*Avocados Stuffed with Hot Crabmeat*)
SERVES 6

The Hana-Maui carefully explained to me that this delicious concoction was their own recipe "for American tastes." In other words, it wasn't Filipino, Chinese, Japanese, or Polynesian. It was simply Stateside. Well, their exotic recipes are superb, and I'm happy that travelers eating this American dish will feel that our taste is pretty wonderful too.

butter
button mushrooms
celery
cooked crabmeat
water chestnuts
avocados
lemon
cream
Dijon mustard
Worcestershire sauce
sugar

1 Preheat oven to hot (400° F.).

2 In skillet heat: **2 tablespoons butter.**

3 Add: **⅓ cup sliced button mushrooms** and **¾ cup chopped celery.** Cook for about 5 minutes, stirring occasionally.

4 Add: **1 pound diced cooked crabmeat** and **¾ cup sliced water chestnuts** (a 5-ounce can). Cook, stirring, until ingredients are well mixed. Cover and cook over low heat for a few minutes.

5 Halve lengthwise: **3 ripe avocados.** Discard seeds and rub cut surface with **lemon juice.** Put into a shallow dish containing ½ inch hot water and heat in the hot oven for 10 minutes.

6 In saucepan combine: **3 tablespoons**

Tabasco
hollandaise sauce
(see index)
lime
salt
brandy
parsley
almonds

butter, 1 cup cream, 1 tablespoon Dijon mustard, 1 teaspoon Worcestershire sauce, ½ teaspoon sugar, 3 drops Tabasco, and 1 cup hollandaise sauce. Heat to almost boiling, stirring constantly. Stir in: the juice of ½ lime and salt to taste.

7 Add the crabmeat mixture and ½ cup

blanched toasted almonds. Mix well.

8 Stir in: 1 tablespoon brandy and 2 tablespoons chopped parsley.

PRESENTATION

Remove avocados to serving dish, fill with the hot crab mixture, and top with more blanched toasted almonds.

POLYNESIAN COCONUT DUCKLING
SERVES 4

You don't go to a luau to eat roast duckling the way mother used to make it (unless mother was Polynesian). And the Hana-Maui's duckling is like nothing you've ever tasted, I'll bet. Experimentalists will love it, as will curry aficionados. When you want to cook something that is really different, this is your recipe. All can be prepared way in advance, and fifteen minutes in the oven readies this beautiful dish for the table.

coconuts
coconut milk
(see index)
duckling
butter
pineapples
papaya
garlic
onions
fresh ginger root
curry powder
flour
chutney
salt

1 Crack open: 2 coconuts.

2 Toast: 1 cup shredded coconut and set aside.

3 Make: 1 quart coconut milk and let stand for 1 hour.

4 Cut the 2 leg and thigh pieces, and each side of the breast from: a ready-to-cook duckling, weighing about 5 pounds. This makes 4 serving pieces. Trim the pieces of all excess fat.

5 In large skillet heat: 4 tablespoons butter and in it sauté the duckling pieces over moderate heat until lightly browned on both sides. Add: 1 cup water, cover, and simmer for 1 hour, or until tender.

6 Halve lengthwise: 2 small pineapples and remove meat carefully, leaving a shell about ½ inch thick. Discard hard core and dice the pineapple meat. Set diced pineapple and shells aside.

7 Peel: 1 small papaya. Discard seeds and slice meat. Set aside.

8 In saucepan melt: 2 tablespoons butter and in it cook: 2 cloves garlic, minced, 2 onions, chopped, and a 2-inch piece of fresh ginger root, peeled and

chopped, for about 20 minutes, or until onion is tender and golden.

9 Stir in: 1 tablespoon curry powder and cook, stirring, for 1 minute.

10 Stir in: 5 tablespoons flour.

11 Skim the cream from the top of the coconut milk and stir the remaining 1½ cups milk into the curry mixture. Add: 1 teaspoon salt and cook over low heat for 15 minutes, stirring occasionally. Blend in electric blender on high speed for 15 seconds, or puree in a food mill. Return to saucepan and stir in coconut cream. Heat, but do not let boil or the coconut cream will curdle.

12 Preheat oven to moderate (350° F.).

PRESENTATION

In each half pineapple shell, put a layer of sliced papaya and top with a layer of diced pineapple. Cover with 2 tablespoons of the curry sauce and heat in the moderate oven for 15 minutes. Place a piece of duck in each pineapple shell and cover with curry sauce. Sprinkle with the toasted coconut and serve with a small dish of chutney.

CHICKEN AND LONG RICE
SERVES 6

This is a kind of Hawaiian chop suey and a marvelous dish for a buffet or casserole supper. I see no reason why a one-dish meal, made in advance with a minimum of bother, needs to taste like a shortcut to Dullsville. Next time you want to toss together a chicken-and-rice casserole, try this one and thank the Hana-Maui for a delicious new treat.

chicken
chicken stock
(see index)
onions
peanut oil
garlic
fresh ginger root
salt, pepper
monosodium
glutamate
Patna rice
bamboo shoots
butter (optional)
green onions
soy sauce

Remove flesh from: **a 5-pound uncooked chicken** and discard skin. Use bones and wings for chicken stock. Cut meat into bite-sized pieces.

1 In skillet heat: **¼ cup peanut oil.**

2 Add: **2 medium onions, chopped, 2 cloves garlic, chopped,** and **a 2-inch piece of fresh ginger root, peeled and chopped.** Sauté for about 10 minutes, or until onions are soft and golden.

3 Add: the chicken meat, **1 quart chicken stock, 2 cups water, ½ teaspoon salt, ¼ teaspoon pepper,** and **1 teaspoon monosodium glutamate.** Bring to a boil, cover, and simmer for 30 minutes.

4 Stir in: **2 cups Patna rice.** Cover tightly and cook over low heat for 30 minutes longer, stirring occasionally.

5 Sauté: **1 can (8½ ounces) bamboo shoots, sliced,** in **1 tablespoon peanut oil** or **butter** until lightly browned.

PRESENTATION
Turn chicken and rice into a serving casserole, top with the bamboo shoots, and sprinkle with **chopped green onions.** Serve with **soy sauce.**

STUFFED ROAST BREADFRUIT
SERVES 3 TO 4

At certain times of the year imported breadfruit is available in Puerto Rican and Spanish markets, but at all times the canned product is readily obtained. At the Hana-Maui, the fresh breadfruit is baked until tender. A lid is cut from the top and the core discarded. Then the flesh is mashed with other ingredients, returned to the breadfruit shell, covered with the lid, and reheated. It is served in the breadfruit. This is our "canned" interpretation of the recipe from the Hana-Maui.

butter
bacon
onions
canned breadfruit
parsley
beef extract
allspice
cream

1 Preheat oven to moderate (350° F.).

2 Cook: **6 slices bacon, cut into strips,** until crisp. Drain bacon on absorbent paper and pour off all but 1 tablespoon of the drippings remaining in the pan.

3 Add to drippings: **¾ cup minced onion** and sauté for 5 minutes, or until onion is transparent.

4 Heat: **2 cans (1 pound each) breadfruit** in liquid from can. Drain and put the breadfruit through a ricer. Beat thoroughly in a large bowl.

5 Beat in: the pieces of crisp bacon, sautéed onion, **½ cup minced parsley, 1 teaspoon beef extract, ½ teaspoon allspice,** and **¼ cup hot cream.**

PRESENTATION
Spoon the mashed and seasoned breadfruit into a small **buttered** casserole, cover, and bake in the moderate oven for 20 minutes. Serve hot.

CANDIED PAPAYA
SERVES 4

Some of the side dishes at a luau are better than the main course—like supporting players who steal the show from the star. One of my favorites is this Candied Papaya—yes, even with the marshmallow, which horrifies me on sweet potatoes. This is yummy.

papaya
butter
salt
brown sugar
lemon
brandy
marshmallows

1 Preheat oven to moderately hot (375° F.).

2 Cut: **a large ripe papaya** in half lengthwise. Discard seeds and cut again lengthwise. Place the quarters in a **buttered** baking pan.

3 Combine: **¼ teaspoon salt, 1 tablespoon brown sugar, 1 tablespoon soft** butter, **1 teaspoon lemon juice, and 1 teaspoon brandy.**

PRESENTATION
Put a rounded teaspoon of the sweet mixture in the center of each quarter papaya and top each with **a large marshmallow.** Bake in the moderately hot oven for 30 minutes.

BAKED BANANAS
SERVES 4

Crisp roast pork or ham takes well to a garnish of cooked fruit. Instead of the usual applesauce with the former or pineapple slices with the latter, follow the Hana-Maui's luau menu and try this very good banana recipe.

bananas
orange
brown sugar
butter
cinnamon

1 Preheat oven to moderate (350° F.).

2 Peel: **4 bananas,** not too ripe. Cut them in half lengthwise.

3 **Butter** a shallow baking dish and lay the banana halves in it side by side.

4 Mix well: **the juice of ½ orange, 2** tablespoons brown sugar, and **½ teaspoon cinnamon.**

5 Sprinkle mixture over bananas.

6 Dot generously with: **1½ tablespoons butter.**

7 Bake in the moderate oven for 1 hour.

BANANA NUT BREAD
MAKES 1 LARGE LOAF

This bread—really almost a coffeecake—is good sliced thin and toasted. We use it to make one of my favorite sandwiches too. Just spread some whipped cream cheese on one slice, top with another, and nectar and ambrosia couldn't taste any better. ·

butter
sugar
eggs
all-purpose flour
baking soda
salt
bananas
walnuts

1 Preheat oven to moderate (350° F.).

2 Cream together until light: **½ cup butter** and **1 cup sugar.**

3 Beat in: **2 eggs.**

4 Sift together: **2 cups all-purpose flour, 1 teaspoon baking soda, and ½ teaspoon salt.** Stir into butter-sugar mixture, blending well.

5 Stir in: **1 cup mashed ripe banana** and **½ cup chopped walnuts.**

6 Spoon batter into a well **buttered** 2-pound bread tin (9½ x 5½ x 2¾) and bake in the moderate oven for 1 hour, or until loaf tests done.

7 Cool for 5 minutes, then turn out on rack to cool completely.

PINEAPPLE NUT BREAD
MAKES TWO 1-POUND LOAVES

For a dedicated bread baker like me, it is always a happy day when a great new recipe comes along. This one from the Hana-Maui is most unusual, most delicious. It is really more like a coffeecake, and we like to serve it in thin slices with a cup of coffee at almost any hour of the day or night. The second loaf goes in the freezer for some future time.

flour
baking powder
baking soda
salt
macadamia nuts
butter
light brown sugar
eggs
canned crushed
pineapple
sugar
cinnamon

1 Preheat oven to moderate (350° F.).

2 **Butter** two 1-pound loaf pans.

3 Sift: **about 1 pound flour** and measure **3½ cups.**

4 Sift together: the measured flour, **4 teaspoons double-acting baking powder, ½ teaspoon baking soda,** and **1 teaspoon salt.**

5 Stir in: **1½ cups coarsely chopped macadamia nuts.**

6 In mixing bowl cream: **6 tablespoons soft butter** and **1½ cups light brown sugar, firmly packed.** Beat in: **2 eggs** and continue to beat until mixture is smooth.

7 Stir in half the flour-nut mixture.

8 Stir in: **2 cups canned crushed pineapple, including juice.**

9 Stir in the remaining flour-nut mixture, and stir until well blended. Divide batter into the prepared pans.

10 Combine: **4 tablespoons sugar** and **1 teaspoon cinnamon.** Sprinkle half the sugar-cinnamon mixture over batter in each pan and bake in the moderate oven for 50 to 60 minutes, or until bread tests done. Let cool for 5 minutes, then turn out on cake rack to cool.

PINEAPPLE MERINGUE PIE
SERVES 6

They say you've never really tasted pineapple until you've eaten it in Hawaii. It has a fragrance, a sweetness, and a juiciness that the fruit shipped abroad never quite attains. This beautiful pie which we had at the Hana-Maui was made, naturally, from fresh pineapple, but we find we get better results at home using the canned crushed pineapple.

canned crushed
pineapple
cornstarch
lemon
sugar
vanilla
butter
eggs
salt
baked pie shell
(see index)

PIE

1 Bake: **a 9-inch pie shell.**

2 In a saucepan put: **2 cups canned crushed pineapple,** drained of its juice, **1 tablespoon cornstarch, 3 tablespoons sugar, 1 teaspoon lemon juice,** and **1 tablespoon butter.** Cook, stirring frequently, until thick.

3 Separate: **2 eggs.** Beat yolks lightly. Pour a little of the pineapple mixture over the yolks, beat, and stir into the saucepan.

4 Cook mixture over low heat, stirring constantly, for 1 minute, or until yolks have cooked a little and thickened.

5 Let this custard cool, then pour it into the baked pie shell.

6 Preheat oven to slow (325° F.).

MERINGUE

1 Beat until frothy: **3 egg whites** with **⅛ teaspoon salt.**

2 Add: **⅓ cup sugar,** 1 tablespoon at a time, beating constantly. Add: **½ teaspoon vanilla.** Beat until stiff and glossy.

PRESENTATION

Spread meringue over pineapple custard and bake in the slow oven for 15 to 20 minutes, or until meringue is delicately browned. Let pie cool before serving.

PASSION FRUIT CHIFFON PIE
SERVES 6

Hawaii with its semitropical climate has superb fruits, picked when they are lush and ripe and served almost fresh from the tree. Mangoes, papayas, passion fruit have a more intense flavor there because they have not been picked green and allowed to ripen far from their native sun. Hawaiian desserts use these glorious fruits to best advantage. We have to duplicate this delicious pie from the Hana-Maui with the canned passion fruit juice available here, but even so it makes a very good dessert.

eggs
sugar
salt
passion fruit juice
cream
gelatin
lemon
baked pie shell
(see index)

1 Bake: **a 9-inch pie shell** and let it cool in the pie plate.

2 Separate: **4 eggs.** Beat yolks until thick and pale.

3 Beat into the yolks: **½ cup sugar, ½ teaspoon salt,** and **½ cup passion fruit juice.**

4 Soften: **1 tablespoon unflavored gelatin** in **¼ cup cold water.** Add to egg yolk mixture.

5 Cook over low heat, stirring constantly, until mixture thickens and gelatin is dissolved.

6 Add to mixture: **1 teaspoon grated lemon rind.**

7 Cool mixture in refrigerator until slightly congealed.

8 Beat the 4 egg whites until frothy. Add: **¼ cup sugar** and beat until stiff.

9 Fold egg yolk mixture into the stiffly beaten egg whites.

10 Pour into the baked pie shell and chill until firm.

PRESENTATION

Whip: **½ cup cream** until stiff. Decorate top of pie and serve well chilled.

KALUA PIG (Pig Roasted in Pit)
SERVES 75 TO 100

The Hana-Maui's chef wrote out for us complete instructions on how to roast a pig Hawaiian style—in a hole in the ground. He even told us exactly how to dig the hole. We hasten to explain that we have never tested this recipe, but for those of you who are curious about how it is done, or who may even long to dig a barbecue pit in your own backyard, here are an expert's instructions word for word.

shovel
wood
rocks
banana tree leaves
ti leaves
potato bag
gunny sacks
kerosene
matches
chicken wire
whole pig
Hawaiian rock salt

"We buy a whole pig and have the head on which is used later for display on our buffet table. The chef rubs the pig with Hawaiian rock salt before taking it to the Imu. An Imu is a pit, dug in the ground, about 2 feet deep and up to 6 feet in diameter. When the hole is dug, the dried wood is placed into this with hickory wood forming the top layer, just like a camp fire. A thick wooden pole is then placed in the center and lava stones are built around so that the wood is completely covered by the rocks. The wood pole is then removed and a potato bag is pushed down into the hole left by the pole. If possible push the bag all the way down so it is touching the wood. Next, pour kerosene onto the bag, saturating it well and light it. There should be enough wood in the Imu to keep a fire burning for about 1½-2 hours as the stones have to be glowing hot before the pig is added.

The shoulders of the pig have been cut wide open in the kitchen to allow one hot stone to be placed inside each shoulder. The back legs must be deeply cut crisscross from the outside to allow the heat to penetrate, this is done in the kitchen. At least four hot stones are to be placed inside the belly at the side of the pit.

Banana tree leaves are placed on top of the rest of the hot lava rocks in the Imu. Over the bananas leaves a layer of washed ti leaves is placed and the pig is placed on top of these leaves. The pig is then covered by more clean ti leaves and banana leaves on top of that. Then the Imu is completely covered in with soaked wet gunny sacks. To finish off, the soil which was scooped out to dig the pit, is piled over the top of the wet sacks. This is being done to make sure no leakage of steam or heat will be possible. For a 150 lb. pig we allow 6 hours of Imu cooking.

Before placing the pig in the Imu and after filling it with hot stones, we "wrap" it into chicken wire, which will make it easier, after it is cooked, to remove from the pit. When the pig has been in the Imu 6 hours we take it out and roll it out off the chicken wire onto a wooden board for carving."

HANAHO (*"Come again!" Rum Punch*)
SERVES 1

In case you've been wondering what people find to drink as they sit around waiting for the luau's star attraction, this is it. At least at the Hana-Maui this is it—their very own trademarked rum punch, served usually in a coconut or pineapple shell. *"Hanaho,"* they tell me, means "Come again," but I've never been able to figure out if it means to come again to the Hana-Maui or to come again on the rum punch. You couldn't lose either way.

light rum
pineapple juice
lime
pineapple (optional)
crushed ice
dark rum
maraschino cherry
orange

1 Put into a cocktail shaker or an electric blender: **1¼ ounces light rum, 2¼ ounces pineapple juice** (the Hana-Maui uses fresh juice but canned juice is good too), **the juice of ½ lime,** and **½ cup crushed ice.**

2 Shake well, or if you are using a blender, cover and blend on high. speed for about 10 seconds to mix thoroughly.

PRESENTATION
Pour into 14-ounce zombie glass or hollowed pineapple shell. Top with: **¾ ounce dark rum** and decorate with: **a maraschino cherry** and an **orange slice** on a pick.

Colors are more intense under the desert sky,
and judging by this lunch for two
at The Racquet Club, so are appetites.
The menu: *Gazpacho*, Special Salad,
Aspic of Breast of Chicken, Dungeness Crab,
and Cheesecake with Fruit.
A large finger bowl is at your feet.

When we lunch in our garden, Mary has
some favorite props. A wondrous,
giant clam shell heaped with cracked crab,
a bronze art nouveau head filled
with flowers, and a towering totem pole
that once stood on John Barrymore's hillside,
all are visual aids to happy eating.

THE RACQUET CLUB

WHEN our Southern California neighbors say they're going to spend the weekend in the desert, they generally mean that blooming oasis, Palm Springs. And Palm Springs for most of the motion picture crowd means The Racquet Club. Charlie Farrell and Ralph Bellamy built a few tennis courts out in the middle of the sand about thirty years ago, and now look at it! These days tennis is just a small part of The Racquet Club, though a lot of people who never set foot on the courts amble about carrying a tennis racquet for posh.

At lunch time the athletes take a quick splash in the pool and then tuck into some of the club's superb food. The chef is French, but some of the greatest dishes here are salads, West Coast seafood, and monumental sandwiches. Cheesecake at the Racquet Club is a must—you can have it for dessert and watch the bikini-clad starlets posing for the pinup kind.

One of the great advantages of Southern California living is the informal outdoor life. There is a great deal of relaxed poolside or back-yard lounging, and a whole new way of eating to go with it. Everything tastes especially delicious under a balmy blue sky, and crisp, cold foods with a little extra zip in their seasoning offset the blandness of the atmosphere.

We have favorite little nooks and corners on our grounds that we use like separate outdoor rooms. Bloody Marys and cracked crab served on the terrace below our towering totem pole seem to us to taste and look better there than anywhere else in the house. So for a gourmet touch to your luncheon recipes, just add a dash of fresh air, and glaze under a sunny sky.

369

THE RACQUET CLUB
PALM SPRINGS

menu

appetizers

Fresh Beluga Caviar on Ice, Per Oz.	5.00
Shrimp, Crab or Lobster Cocktail	1.50
Fresh Fruits Cup Supreme	1.00
Chilled Fruit Juice . . . .40 Large	.75
Nova Scotia Smoked Salmon	1.50
Marinated Filet of Herring in Sour Cream	1.00
Pate of Chicken Livers	1.00
Escargots a la Bourguignonne	1.75

soups

Potage or Consomme du Jour

Cold Vichyssoise   Jellied Madrilene

Borscht with Sour Cream

entrees

Price of Entree Includes Hors d'oeuvres, Soup, Salad and Vegetables du Jour

Calf's Sweetbread Chasseur 4.25
Braised in White Wine Sauce with Onions and Mushrooms

Veal Cutlet Parmigiana 4.50
With Mozzarella Cheese and Spaghetti a' l' Italienne

Coquilles St. Jacques 4.25
Baby Scallops and Fresh Mushrooms in White Wine Cream Sauce, Glace in the Shell

Tournedos Rossini 5.50
Garnis with Broiled Tomato, Truffles and Pate de Foie

Shish Ke Bab a la Turque 4.50
With Pilaf and Broiled Tomato

Broiled Australian Lobster Tails . . . 5.00
Drawn Butter

Double French Cut Lamb Chops . . . 4.75
Mint Jelly

New York Cut Prime Sirloin Steak . . . 6.25

Broiled Half Spring Chicken 4.00
Crab Apple

Roast Long Island Duckling, Montmorency . . . 4.75

Roast Prime Rib of Beef, au jus 5.00

Filet of Pompano, Veronique . . . 4.75
Poached in White Wine with Seedless Grapes

Double Entrecote or Chateaubriand Bouquetiere . . 15.00
(Minimum Serving for Two Persons)

salads

Salad du Jour   Mixed Green Salad

Caesar Salad for Two   3.00
Choice of Dressings

desserts

Racquet Club Pie	.60	Peach Melba	.75
Ice Cream Snowball	1.00	Ice Cream or Sherbet	.50
Pear Charlotte	.75	Pie or Cake	.60
Creamy Cheese Cake	.75	French Pastry	.75
Parfait	1.00	Fresh Fruits in Season	.75

Ice Cream Meringue Glacee au Kirsh 1.50

Dessert Flambe, Minimum Serving for Two . . . 4.00

Tray of International Cheeses 1.50

Beverages 25

Luncheon
ALA CARTE

Appetizers

KING CRABMEAT COCKTAIL	1.50
JUMBO SHRIMP COCKTAIL	1.50
PACIFIC LOBSTER COCKTAIL	1.50
MARINATED HERRING	.85
CHOPPED CHICKEN LIVERS	.85
SUPREME OF FRESH FRUIT	.85
CHOICE OF JUICES............Regular	.40
Large	.75

Soup

	CUP	BOWL
DU JOUR	.35	.50
VICHYSSOISE	.50	.75
JELLIED MADRILENE	.40	.65
JELLIED CONSOMME	.40	.65
COLD BORSCHT with Sour Cream	.50	.75

TODAY — OUR CHEF SUGGESTS

Cold Gaspacho en supréme

Cracked Crab on ice served with mustard mayonnaise and crisp tossed salad, Racquet Club dressing

or

Aspic of Poulet garnished with celeriac, carrots, Jacamas salads and stuffed cherry tomato

Cheese Cake aux Fruits

Desserts

FRENCH PASTRY	.50
ASSORTED PIES	.40
CHEESE CAKE	.50
LAYER CAKE	.45
ICE CREAM or SHERBET	.40
PARFAITS	.75
SNOWBALL	.75
MERINGUE GLACE	.75
FRUITE COMPOTE	.75

Beverages

COFFEE or TEA	.25
SANKA or POSTUM	.35
MILK or BUTTERMILK	.25
MALT or MILK SHAKE	.75

All Cakes, Pies, Pastries, Rolls and Muffins Baked on the Premises

---

Sandwiches

Imported Danish Ham	1.25
Smoked Beef Tongue	1.25
Kosher Salami on Rye	1.25
Sliced White Meat of Turkey	1.50
Imported Swiss Cheese	1.25
Grilled or Toasted American Cheese	1.25
Sliced Brisket of Corned Beef on Rye, Cole Slaw	1.50
Smoked Salmon and Cream Cheese on Pumpernickel, Sliced Onion	1.50
Bacon and Tomato Slices on Toast	1.25
Imported Ham and Swiss Cheese on Rye, Dill Pickles	1.75
Peanut Butter and Jelly	1.25

Sloppy Moe
Gobs of Very Thin Sliced Imported Swiss Cheese and Danish Ham on Rye Bread, Cole Slaw, Pickles and Olives 1.75

Club House
Sliced Turkey, Bacon and Tomato, on Double Decked Toast 2.00

Racquet Club Special Hamburger
Half Pound Ground Round on a Toasted Bun, French Fried Potatoes, Sliced Tomato and Onion, Pickles and Olives 1.50

Danish Open Faced Sandwich Plate
Sliced Ham, Turkey and Roast Beef with Potato Salad 2.50

Tenderloin or Sirloin Steak
on Toast with French Fried Potatoes and Sliced Tomatoes, Dill Pickles 3.75

Salads and Cold Buffet

Farrell's Delight
Chopped Lettuce with Diced Avocado, Bacon, Tomato and Blue Cheese with Special Perrymead Pear Vinegar Dressing 2.35

Pineapple Boat
Half of Fresh Hawaiian Pineapple Filled with Cottage Cheese or Sherbet and Bartlett Pear Halves 2.35

Palm Springs Salad
Sliced Avocado, Fresh Dates, Fresh Orange and Grapefruit Sections, Crystalized Ginger, Date Nut Bread 2.35

Salad Princess
Tomato Filled with Chicken Salad, Asparagus Spears 2.35

Lobster, Crabmeat or Shrimp Louie
Garni 2.85

Cottage Cheese
with Assorted Fruit, Date Nut Bread 1.85

Fresh Fruit
with Cottage Cheese, Banana and Date Nut Bread 2.25

Chef's Salad Bowl
Tossed Greens with Julienne of Ham, Turkey and Imported Swiss Cheese, Hard Cooked Egg, Asparagus Tips and Tomato Wedges, Choice of Dressing 1.95

Imported Sardine Plate
Choice of Brisling or Boneless and Skinless Sardines with Tomato Wedges, Hard Cooked Egg, Cole Slaw and Olives 2.00

Prime Ribs of Beef
with Sliced Tomato, Cole Slaw and Dill Pickle 2.95

Tossed Crisp Greens
or Hearts of Romaine, Choice of Dressing .... .85

---

the racquet club   palm springs, california

DUNGENESS CRAB WITH MUSTARD MAYONNAISE
SERVES 4

This is one of the great specialties of The Racquet Club, and is quite wonderful there with their mustard mayonnaise, or indeed almost anywhere on the West Coast. The frozen Dungeness crabs that you get in other parts of the country are not as good, unfortunately. Most seafood is undeniably best eaten near its native waters. And any kind of large crab, which the eater must pick out of its shell, is best consumed out-of-doors, preferably near a swimming pool or other large body of water in which you can rinse yourself off afterward. Messy but delicious!

Dungeness crabs
salt, pepper
peppercorns
lemons
carrots
onion
parsley
dry mustard
thyme
bay leaves
eggs
salad oil
olive oil
Dijon mustard

DUNGENESS CRABS

1 Fill a pot large enough to accommodate 4 Dungeness crabs with water. Add: **2 teaspoons salt, the juice of 1 lemon, 2 carrots, sliced, 1 onion, sliced, 5 sprigs parsley, ½ teaspoon cracked peppercorns, 1 teaspoon thyme, and 2 bay leaves.** Bring water to a boil and simmer for 20 minutes.

2 Cook: **4 Dungeness crabs,** weighing from 1¼ to 1½ pounds each, in this court-bouillon for 15 minutes. Let cool in the liquid.

3 Hold a crab in both hands and lift off the top shell or carapace. Wash the carapace, scrubbing with a stiff brush, and reserve. Reserve the milky yellow substance from body of crabs.

4 Hold a crab in both hands and break in middle. Then, beginning with small legs, break legs and body into sections, leaving body portions attached to legs. Crack each leg segment with nutcracker.

5 Put crab in refrigerator to chill for 30 minutes.

MUSTARD MAYONNAISE
(Makes About 1¼ Cups)

Make mayonnaise in the regular way or in an electric blender (see index) using the following proportions: **2 egg yolks, ½ cup salad oil and ½ cup olive oil, mixed, 1½ tablespoons lemon juice, ½ teaspoon dry mustard, 1 teaspoon Dijon mustard, ½ teaspoon salt, and ¼ teaspoon pepper.** When mayonnaise is homogenized, stir in the **milky substance from the crabs.**

PRESENTATION

On a large chilled platter, arrange the crab sections and legs of the 4 crabs. In the center, place a clean carapace (top shell) filled with the mustard mayonnaise. You may serve these individually or all on one enormous platter.

KING CRAB LEGS SAUTÉ GRENOBLOISE
(King Crab Legs with Lemon Butter)
SERVES 4

This is an excellent recipe for king crab legs. The Racquet Club's French chef serves them with a sauce made from *beurre noisette*, butter that has been lightly browned to the color of a hazelnut. He then adds chopped parsley, the chopped flesh of a lemon, and capers. This is evidently the sauce used in Grenoble, high in the French Alps, where the marvelous mountain trout are served. It would be a fine addition to any kind of sautéed or broiled fish, I should think. And imagine getting such a lesson in French cooking right in our own California desert!

frozen king crab legs
light cream
flour
cooking oil
butter
parsley
lemon
capers
potatoes

1 Defrost: **4 king crab legs.** With kitchen scissors, slit the shells and remove the meat. Cut meat into sections about 4 inches long.

2 Put into a bowl, cover with: **1 cup light cream,** and let soak for 15 minutes. Drain and pat dry with paper towels. Roll in **flour.**

3 In skillet heat: **2 tablespoons cooking oil.** When very hot add crab legs and sauté for about 2 minutes, or until lightly browned on all sides. Arrange on a hot serving platter and keep warm.

4 In small skillet heat: **4 tablespoons butter.** The moment it begins to turn color swirl in: **2 tablespoons chopped parsley, 1 lemon, completely peeled and chopped,** and **1 tablespoon chopped capers.** Remove from heat.

PRESENTATION

Pour the hot butter mixture over the crab legs and serve hot with **parsley potatoes,** if you wish.

RACQUET CLUB GAZPACHO
SERVES 6

This is quite different from the Spanish *gazpacho* that we had at Botín, and is a good recipe to use when tomatoes are not at their peak. Instead of depending upon ripe fresh tomatoes for flavor, the Italian-style canned tomatoes are used as the basis of this cold soup, and they are good whatever the season.

cucumbers
green peppers
radishes
onions
canned Italian-style
tomatoes
canned consommé
olive oil
lemons
fresh dill
croutons (optional)
tomatoes
salt, pepper

1 Chop very fine: **3 cucumbers, peeled and seeded, 3 green peppers, seeded, 3 onions, 8 radishes,** and **4 ripe tomatoes, peeled and seeded.**

2 Strain: **2 8-ounce cans Italian-style tomatoes.** Chop the tomatoes and add to the vegetables with the juice.

3 Add: **4 cups canned consommé, 2 tablespoons olive oil,** the juice of **2 lemons, 2 teaspoons salt, ½ teaspoon pepper,** and **3 sprigs fresh dill, chopped.**

4 Mix well and chill thoroughly before serving. (This soup can be served hot.)

PRESENTATION

Served cold, the *gazpacho* should be poured into chilled soup plates with an ice cube placed in the center of each. It is nice to sprinkle some small crisp **croutons** on top of each serving just before bringing soup to the table.

CURRIED CHICKEN SALAD
SERVES 4 TO 6

cooked chicken
apple
pineapple
white raisins
dates
chutney
coconut
salt

Half a poached 5-pound chicken is sufficient for this quantity of salad.

1 In mixing bowl combine: **2 cups diced cooked chicken** (use the dark meat for this, reserving the breast for slicing), **1 apple, peeled and diced, 1 cup diced fresh pineapple, ¼ cup white raisins, ⅓ cup cut dates, 2 tablespoons chopped chutney** (including the syrup), and **½ cup shredded fresh coconut.**

2 Sprinkle with: **½ teaspoon salt.**

3 Simmer: **1 tablespoon good curry powder** in **2 tablespoons chicken consommé** for 2 minutes, stirring to a smooth paste.

curry powder
canned chicken
consommé
mayonnaise
(see index)
lettuce

4 Add curry paste to: **1 cup good homemade mayonnaise** and stir into the salad mixture.

PRESENTATION

Pile the salad onto a chilled serving plate on a bed of **crisp lettuce leaves** and garnish with **thinly sliced breast of chicken** and some **chopped ginger from jar of chutney**. Sprinkle with: **½ cup shredded fresh coconut**.

Individual servings of this salad are attractive served in half a coconut shell.

PANNEQUETS AU FROMAGE D'EMMENTHAL
(Little Pancakes Filled with Cheese)
SERVES 4

This heavenly Racquet Club specialty is richer than Croesus, but who cares? Once in a great while it's fun to climb on cloud seven gastronomically, and this is a great way to do it. Especially when the active outdoor life gives you an opportunity to work off some pounds. The cheese filling for these little pancakes is worth knowing about by itself. It is really an excellent Swiss fondue—grated cheese melted in white wine, seasoned with freshly ground pepper and kirsch. The Emmenthal cheese called for in this recipe is a hard cheese similar to Gruyère but creamier and less salty. Serve the fondue sometime as they do in Switzerland, with small squares of lightly toasted bread that you dip into the sauce on long forks. Drop your piece of bread in the cheese and you buy the next round of drinks. Quite a game.

flour
salt, pepper
egg
milk
butter
dry white wine
Emmenthal cheese
cornstarch
kirsch
hollandaise sauce
(see index)
cream

CREPES (Makes 12 Crepes)

1 Sift into bowl: **½ cup flour** and **a pinch of salt**.

2 Combine: **1 large egg, lightly beaten,** and **1 cup milk**. Strain into flour mixture and mix until batter is smooth.

3 To cook the crepes, heat a small frying pan, from 5 to 6 inches in diameter, until very hot. The crepes must cook quickly or they will be tough.

4 Put: **½ teaspoon butter** in pan and swirl pan to coat bottom and sides. As soon as butter begins to brown, pour in about 2 tablespoons of the batter and swirl pan in a circular motion to spread batter evenly and thinly to the edge.

5 Cook the crepe for about 1 minute, or until set and brown on underside; turn with spatula and cook for 20 or 30 seconds, or until second side browns. Turn out on towel to cool.

CHEESE FILLING (Fondue)

1 In saucepan heat: **½ cup dry white wine** but do not boil.

2 Stir in: **2 cups shredded Emmenthal cheese** (8 ounces) and continue to stir until cheese is smooth and creamy.

3 Stir in: **2 teaspoons cornstarch** dissolved in **1 tablespoon kirsch** and continue to stir until the fondue simmers.

4 Sprinkle with **freshly ground pepper**. Keep warm over hot water, or cool and reheat. Makes 1 cup fondue.

SAUCE

1 Make: **hollandaise sauce**. Measure ¾ cup and fold in: **¼ cup cream, whipped**.

2 Preheat oven to very hot (450° F.).

PRESENTATION

Spread each crepe with about 1½ tablespoons of the fondue. Roll up and arrange in a **buttered** au gratin dish large enough to hold all 12 crepes, or in individual **buttered** baking dishes. Bake in the very hot oven for 4 to 5 minutes, or until hot. Remove from oven. Spoon sauce over the crepes and run under broiler for 30 to 60 seconds, or until sauce is lightly browned.

Note: This dish is as rich as it is delicious. It serves 4 for luncheon or for a hot entrée. As an appetizer, serve only 1 or 2 crepes per person.

RACQUET CLUB SPICED VINEGAR
MAKES 1 CUP

This is a delicious piquant vinegar which The Racquet Club uses as a base for their famous French dressing and as a flavoring for mayonnaise dressings. The recipe for their dressing has always been top secret and is, like the Coca-Cola formula, one of those precious bits of paper locked away in a safe whose combination is known only to two living souls. We wheedled the ingredients out of the chef and a few clues as to the procedure. Then I locked myself in our kitchen and experimented madly for a few days. This seems to be it, and if it isn't exactly, it's so good that I'll challenge Charlie Farrell to a tossed salad at twenty paces, their formula against mine.

pear vinegar
can of anchovies
lemon
sauce Robert
Worcestershire sauce
fresh horse-radish
salt, pepper
celery salt
onion salt
garlic salt
dry mustard
pickling spices
olive oil

1 Into bowl or jar measure: **¾ cup pear vinegar.** (Use white wine vinegar if you cannot get the other.)

2 Add: **2 tablespoons anchovy oil, 2 tablespoons lemon juice, 2 teaspoons sauce Robert, 2 teaspoons Worcestershire sauce, 1 tablespoon grated fresh horse-radish, 1 teaspoon salt, ¼ teaspoon pepper,** and **⅛ teaspoon each celery salt, onion salt, garlic salt,** and **dry mustard.** Mix well.

3 Add: **2 tablespoons pickling spices,** tied in a cheescloth bag. Remove after 2 days.

4 Cover bowl or jar and let stand at room temperature for 4 days. Then strain and store in refrigerator. Use 1 part of the spiced vinegar to 3 parts **olive oil** for a French dressing with a tossed salad.

CHARLES FARRELL SALAD
SERVES 4

We're all great salad eaters in California and everyone has his favorite. Charles Farrell, because he runs The Racquet Club, is one up on the rest of us—he can have his name on his. It's a good one, though, and I'm glad to have a chance to pass it on to you.

pear vinegar
salad oil
lemon
salt, pepper
lettuce
bacon
Roquefort cheese
tomatoes
avocados

1 In a wooden bowl place: **1 medium head lettuce, finely chopped.**

2 Arrange the following 4 ingredients on top of the lettuce in separate wedge-shaped sections: **8 slices crisp bacon, crumbled, ¼ pound Roquefort cheese, broken into bits, 3 medium tomatoes, peeled, seeded, and diced,** and **2 avocados, peeled, seeded, and diced.**

PRESENTATION
This salad bowl is handsome for a buffet,

as the red, brown, white, and pale green sections make a striking design. For this reason, the salad is not tossed beforehand. It is dressed at the table with: **2 parts salad oil, 1 part pear vinegar, a little lemon juice, salt** and **freshly ground pepper** to taste. If you can't mix a dressing by eye in that way, measure out ingredients to make ½ cupful, but don't use quite all of it—unless you like drowned salad.

375

SLOPPY MOE SANDWICH
SERVES I

The Racquet Club's sandwiches are distinctive, to say the least. After all, you could do as well at the corner drugstore if all you wanted was a regular ham-and-Swiss on rye. But a Sloppy Moe, one of the club's most popular concoctions, is just that with a difference. That difference is the special trick we always look for in restaurants, the original and delicious twist that makes even a ham-and-Swiss a treat.

rye bread
imported Swiss cheese
Danish ham
butter or mayonnaise
dill pickle
cabbage
green pepper
salad oil
Racquet Club spiced
vinegar (see index)
salt, pepper

SANDWICH

1　From a loaf of **fresh rye bread** cut: **2 thin slices.**

2　Spread with **softened butter** or a little **mayonnaise.**

3　Use imported Swiss cheese. Cut thin shavings from a large solid piece. Use about **⅛ pound Swiss cheese shavings,** so thin you can almost see through them (and I don't mean the holes).

4　Use about **5 paper-thin slices of Danish ham.**

5　Alternate cheese and ham layers, building sandwich up high and light.

6　Top with second slice of bread and cut in half diagonally.

COLESLAW

1　Shred very fine: **1 cup raw cabbage.** Soak it in ice water in refrigerator for 1 hour.

2　Drain and dry well.

3　Cut: **4 very thin slices green pepper.** Remove seeds and cut pepper into 2-inch lengths. Mix with slaw.

4　Toss with: **1 teaspoon Racquet Club spiced vinegar, 1 tablespoon salad oil, salt** and **pepper** to taste.

PRESENTATION

Serve sandwich on large oval plate garnished with thin fingers of **dill pickle** and a mound of coleslaw.

In Scandia's comfortable Lounge, the mood
is mellow after a fine dinner. Friendships
ripen and business deals blossom in the warmth
of well-fed conviviality.

There is artistry in the intricate pattern
of a cabbage and in the simplicity of
this Scandinavian dish called *Kaaldolmer.*
No need for embellishments
when the forms of Nature are so handsome.

SCANDIA

Los Angeles is not the restaurant capital of the world by a long shot. Most people who live here eat at home and restaurants come and go. But the few really good ones survive, and they have become, for the residents of this city, what a good restaurant should be—a home away from home with somebody else doing the cooking.

Scandia is one of our world favorites. Located on that flamboyantly magic mile of Sunset Boulevard known as the Strip, the restaurant is staid and dignified. Kenneth Hansen, the proprietor, is one of the great chefs of our time, and though he no longer does the actual cooking, he knows how it should be done and sees that it is. For all that the restaurant specializes in Mr. Hansen's native Danish food, it is not too heavy on the *smørrebrød* treatment that can be such a bore when it is compulsory. Scandia's chefs specialize in the very best foods given their regional accents with subtlety. It's always amazing to me how the addition of one or two flavors can transport a dish to another world of taste. Here it's dill, cucumbers, lingonberries, and a slightly different combination of vegetables, and your taste buds light up like the northern lights! I guess the aquavits help, too.

The restaurant has three separate dining rooms, plus the new glass-enclosed La Belle Terrasse, named for the restaurant in Copenhagen. Our favorite, though, is the Lounge, famous for its high-backed, huge leather chairs and soft lighting. The room is comfortable and Mr. Hansen's welcome warm enough to make you delighted to wait for a table. I daresay more Hollywood business is transacted at Scandia than in the studios. The food is so good you don't care about the small print in the contracts.

"VELKOMMEN TILBORDS!"

HORS D'OEUVRES

Our individual "COLD CABARET" served at your table and consisting of all the delicacies for which the smörgåsbord is famous. Served for no less than 2 persons, per person 4.75

Smörgås Bricka, *for two or more,* per person 1.85

Shrimp Cocktail ...... 1.65   Lobster Cocktail 1.75

Avocado Cocktail, Russian Dressing 1.35

Marinated Herring .... .95

Iceland Matjes Herring, Sour Cream................. 1.00

Danish Liver Pate................................. .85

Herring Filets in Cherry Heering................. 1.50

Herring Filets in Sherry 1.25

Assorted Herring Appetizer (Silde Anretning), per person 1.75

Gravlaks with Dill Sauce........................ 1.85
The great Salmon of the north cured in the old Viking manner.

Shrimps in Dill 1.75
Mediterranean Shrimps cooked with aquavit and dill.

Louisiana Oysters on the Half Shell................. 2.00

Cherrystone Clams on the Half Shell................. 1.85

Cracked Fresh Dunguenes Crab *(in season)* 2.25

Fresh Smoked Baltic Salmon *(in season)*............. 2.75
"Via S.A.S. over the Pole."

Papaya with Crab, illumine......................... 1.85

Iranian Smoked Sturgeon.... 2.25   on Smörgås.... 1.85

The Cured Ham with Golden-Ripe Melon.............. 1.85

SKÅL!

APPETIZERS THE HOT DELIGHTS

Viking Plättar 2.00
Miniature pancakes flavored with aquavit and served with sour cream and Danish caviar.

The Coquille 1.85
Small Norwegian lobster tails, white wine sauce, peeled stoned grapes.

The Crepe 1.85
Tender pancake wrapped around tiny coral-pink Shrimps in Dill and Hollandaise, glaced under fire.

The Great Hamlets Dagger.......................... 2.00
Tiny lobster tails deviled and broiled on the skewer, served with an ice-cold sauce made with caviar and aquavit.

The Mushrooms with Deviled Crab 1.85
Tender crabmeat cooked with shallots and mustard and stuffed in mushroom caps.

The Mushrooms with Snails 1.85
Tender vineyard snails cooked in mushroom caps with garlic and walnut butter.

THE SHELLS:

Oysters 1.85
Baked in their shell with a fine herb puree, seasoned with aquavit.

Clams 1.85
Minced and Cooked with Butter, Garlic and Shallots and White Wine, Stuffed in Their Own Shells and Baked.

AQUAVIT SERVED ICE COLD WITH BEER

Aalborg	.85	Tuborg Bottle	.85
O.P. Anderson's	.85	Carlsberg Bottle	.85
Kron-Brännvinn	.85	Olympia Bottle	.60
Löitens	.85	Schlitz Bottle	.65
Tuborg or Carlsberg Draft	.75	Budweiser Bottle	.65

FISH AND SHELLFISH

Danish Sole, *Specialty of the House* 4.25
Cooked in chablis, stuffed with coral pink shrimps in lobster sauce, glaced with white wine sauce.

Danish Plaice (Rödspätter) 3.85
The flounder of the North Sea breaded and sauteed in butter. Sauce Remoulade a part.

The Danish Trout................................. 4.25
Filets of the pink steelhead sauted with tiny lobster tails and peeled grapes.

The Virgin-Lobster Tails........................... 4.00
Tiny Norwegian lobster tails breaded in fresh crumbs and fried with fresh parsley and sauce remoulade.

Broiled Fresh Lake Superior Whitefish (Boned) 4.25
With Cucumbers in Sour Cream

SALADS

Scandia Salad 1.35

Ice-Cold Sliced Tomatoes .... .85

Avocado Salad 1.00

Heart of Iced Lettuce......................... .85

Caesar Salad Bowl *for two* 2.00

Cold Green Asparagus, Vinaigrette............ 1.25

Large French Asparagus, Hot or Cold,
    Vinaigrette............................... 1.50

Our Special Salad Bowl *with Crisp Mixed Greens
    and French Dressing*...................... .95
    with Danish Bleu Dressing................ 1.20

Imported Belgian Endives 1.50

Wilted Bib Lettuce............................ 1.25

Wilted Spinach Salad......................... 1.25

For appetizers only—additional service charge added

VEGETABLES

Fresh Tender Broccoli........................ .8
    with Hollandaise......................... 1.2
Freshly Cooked Green Asparagus............. .9
    with Hollandaise......................... 1.2
Lyonnaise, Hashed Brown Potatoes............ .7
Souffle Potatoes............................. 1.5
Au Gratin Potatoes, Cottage Fried or
    Anna Potatoes............................ .7
Puree of Fresh Peas.......................... .9
Carrots Vichy................................ .9
Creamed Spinach 9

SOUPS

Swedish Pea Soup............................ .6
Curried Turtle 8
Vichysoisse 6
Suedoise 6
Gazpacho 6

STEAKS AND CHOPS

Our Regular Cuts of U.S.D.A. Prime Beef

New York Cut Sirloin	6.25
Tenderloin Steak	5.50
Filet Mignon	5.75
Two Double French Lamb Chops	4.50
Double Porterhouse Steak	13.50
A Special Tournedo, Bearnaise	4.75
Top Sirloin Steak	4.75
Sirloin Steak a la Minute—(Husets Specialitet)	5.25

Above served with large baked or French Fried Potatoes.

PLANKED STEAKS

Special cuts of Sirloin or Tenderloin *(for two or more persons, charcoal-broiled and finished on Oak Plank with potato border and many kinds of vegetables, served with fresh mushrooms and bearnaise sauce, per person* 7.00

Planked Chopped Sirloin Steak with Mushroom Sauce 4.00
Served as above

Chateau-Briand for 2—Potatoes Souffle	13.50
Bordelaise Sauce	.75
Sauce Bearnaise	.75
French Fried Onions	.75

SCANDIA SPECIALTIES

alvfilet Oskar	4.85

(Veal cutlet saute, garnished with asparagus tips, crablegs, sauce bearnaise)

öf Med Lög	4.85

(Tenderloin steak with onions fried in butter)

iff Lindström	3.25

(Chopped sirloin steak mixed with chopped beets, onions and capers, topped with fried egg)

ansk Hakke Böf	3.00

(Chopped sirloin fried in butter, smothered in fried onion sauce)

älldolmar	3.75

(The tender leaves of white cabbage filled with a veal and pork stuffing with ... Braised in the Swedish manner and served with cucumber salad and Lingon.)

Spring Chicken Saute, Louise	3.75

(Unjointed, sauteed in butter with shallot and fresh mushrooms, finished with fresh cream and a dash of old sherry)

Tournedos Theodora	5.25

(Two small filet mignons garnished with gooseliver, bouquets of fresh vegetables, sauce madeira)

Lammesaddel *for 2 or more*	per person 4.50

(Young filet of lamb, roasted and prepared in the Scandia way, carved and served at your table)

"Viking Sword" *(Served for no less than 2 persons)* per person	6.00

(Large Brochette of Broiled Breast of Turkey, small Chateau-Briand, center of a Smoked Pork Chop, Tomatoes and Mushrooms, served on a Flaming Sword with many kinds of vegetables and Sauce Bearnaise)

DESSERTS

eese Cake	.75
plecake with Whipped Cream	.75
dgröd med Flöde	.60
nish Rum Pudding	.65
enska Plättar med Lingon	1.00
nish Pancakes with Strawberry Jam	1.00
land Pancakes	1.65
ne-made Ice Cream and Sherbets	.45
ked Alaska, for 2	2.50
ffles for 2 or more, per person	1.75
orted Pastries	.75

VERAGES

of Tea or Coffee	.35
mitasse	.25
resso	.50
	.25

VELBEKOMME!"

MAY WE SUGGEST...

TODAYS SPECIALS

KAALDOLMER (Cabbage Leaves Stuffed with Meat)
SERVES 6

The idea of cooking leaves stuffed with meat and rice must be an ancient one. In Greece and Turkey they wrap pieces of lamb in vine leaves; throughout central Europe, Russia, and in Scandinavia, cabbage leaves are plumply upholstered with well-seasoned tidbits. All of these dishes have a long tradition, and the reason must be that they are convenient and good. Scandia's *Kaaldolmer* are light and savory and can be prepared in advance and reheated in their sauce just before serving. One cabbage roll per person makes an unusual and delicious first course, if you want to do something really different.

cabbage
rice
milk
ground pork
ground veal
salt, white pepper
eggs
onion
canned beef
consommé
molasses
cornstarch
potatoes
string beans
butter
lingonberries

1 Cut the core from: a **large cabbage** and cook in **salted** water for 15 minutes. Drain, cool slightly, and remove 24 large outer leaves.

2 Simmer: **2 tablespoons rice** in **2 cups milk** for 40 minutes. Cool.

3 Mix: **½ pound ground pork, ½ pound ground veal,** and **1 teaspoon salt.** Gradually beat in: **5 egg whites,** one at a time, beating vigorously after each addition. Slowly beat in the rice mixture to make a smooth creamy filling. (Use an electric beater if possible.) Stir in: **¼ teaspoon ground white pepper** and **1 medium onion,** minced.

4 Preheat the oven to moderately hot (375° F.).

5 Cut the heavy thick part of the stalks from the cabbage leaves. Take one leaf at a time and overlap slightly to close up the opening. Put a tablespoon of the meat filling on each leaf. Roll leaf over once, turn sides over filling, then roll to end of leaf, completely enclosing the filling. Arrange rolls in a **buttered** baking pan (9 x 12½ inches). Add: **1 can (10½ ounces) beef consommé** and spread each roll with: **½ teaspoon molasses.** Bake in the moderately hot oven for 30 minutes. Turn each roll and bake for 30 minutes longer.

6 Arrange rolls side by side in a warm serving casserole.

SAUCE

Stir into liquid remaining in pan: **½ teaspoon cornstarch** mixed with **1 tablespoon water.** Cook over direct heat, stirring, for 2 minutes. Pour the sauce over the cabbage rolls.

PRESENTATION

Serve with **mashed potatoes, buttered string beans,** and **cooked lingonberries** in separate bowls.

COLD CUCUMBER SOUP
SERVES 6

Many of Scandia's best dishes are authentically Swedish or Danish. This delectable Cold Cucumber Soup is one of their most popular, and is a good example of how the cooking of other lands has infiltrated our own cuisine. If you go to a dinner party in Los Angeles and are served an excellent cucumber soup, you can bet that your host and hostess probably had it first at Scandia. This is Ken Hansen's recipe with all the little touches that make for excellence—cooking the cucumber and leek in butter, not water, adding lemon juice and fresh dill or mint at the last, chilling the soup cups—these are the little things that make a big difference.

cucumbers
butter
leek
bay leaf
flour
chicken stock
(see index)
salt, pepper
cream
lemon
fresh dill or mint
sour cream

SOUP

1 Peel: **2 cucumbers** and sauté gently in: **2 tablespoons butter** with **1 leek, sliced** (white part only), and **1 bay leaf** for 20 minutes, or until tender but not browned.

2 Stir in: **1 tablespoon flour.**

3 Add: **3 cups chicken stock** and **1 teaspoon salt** and simmer for 30 minutes. Put mixture through a food mill or blend half at a time in an electric blender and strain through a fine sieve. Chill.

4 Add: **1 cucumber, peeled, seeded, and grated, 1 cup cream,** and **the juice of ½ lemon.**

5 Stir in: **1 teaspoon finely chopped fresh dill** or **mint.** Correct seasoning with **salt** and **pepper.**

6 Chill in refrigerator for at least another 30 minutes, so soup will be icy cold when served.

PRESENTATION

Serve in chilled cups with a dab of **sour cream** on top of each serving.

COQUILLE MAISON (Scallop Shells with Baby Lobster Tails)
SERVES 2

This seafood dish from Scandia is absolutely marvelous! The sauce is exquisite, and best of all it is a very easy recipe. You can make the hollandaise sauce according to directions in the blender chapter of this book or if you don't own a blender, you can make the Scandia hollandaise in this recipe. The final result is superb either way.

butter
frozen baby
lobster tails
shallots
white wine
cream
lemon
Tabasco
Worcestershire sauce
salt, white pepper
cayenne pepper
monosodium
glutamate
flour
eggs
seedless grapes
chives

LOBSTER TAILS

1 Defrost and shell: **16 Icelandic baby lobster tails.**

2 In a heavy skillet heat: **1 tablespoon butter.** Add the shelled baby lobster tails and cook, stirring, for 1 minute.

3 Add: **1 teaspoon chopped shallots** and cook, stirring, for 30 seconds longer.

4 Add: **½ cup white wine, ¼ cup cream, 1 tablespoon lemon juice, 6 drops Tabasco, 6 drops Worcestershire sauce, a pinch of salt,** and **½ teaspoon monosodium glutamate.** Heat to simmering.

5 Combine: **2 tablespoons softened butter** and **2 teaspoons flour.** Stir into sauce and simmer for 2 minutes.

6 Transfer the lobster tails to 2 *coquille* shells or au gratin dishes, using a slotted spoon. Add to each dish: **6 seedless grapes, peeled.**

7 Add to sauce: **1 teaspoon chopped chives.** Stir in: **2 tablespoons hollandaise sauce.** Fold in: **2 tablespoons whipped cream** carefully and gently.

HOLLANDAISE SAUCE (Makes 1 Cup)

If you do not make the blender hollandaise, here is Scandia's recipe for theirs.

1 In a saucepan melt: **½ pound butter** and let it cool to lukewarm.

2 In a small heatproof bowl put: **3 egg yolks** mixed with **2 tablespoons water.**

3 Place the bowl in a shallow pan of simmering, but not boiling, water. Beat eggs with a whisk until thick.

4 Remove from heat and add the butter gradually in small quantities, beating constantly. Pour butter carefully, being sure to leave sediment in bottom of butter pan.

5 Season with **salt** and **white pepper** to taste. Add: **a pinch of cayenne pepper** and **¼ teaspoon lemon juice.**

6 Keep hollandaise sauce lukewarm as it curdles at higher temperatures.

PRESENTATION

Divide lobster sauce into the two dishes and brown 1 minute under hot broiler.

KALVFILET OSKAR *(Veal Cutlets with Crab Legs)*
SERVES 6

There are all kinds of romantic stories about who invented this dish, with credit going sometimes to Sweden's King Oskar, sometimes to Oscar of the Waldorf, and sometimes to any chef or maître d'hôtel who is telling it—especially if his name is Oskar or Oscar. Well, take the *Kalvfilet* and let the credit go, is my feeling. It is one of Scandia's best dishes and a cinch to do at home.

veal cutlets
flour
butter
salt, pepper
cooked asparagus tips
cooked crab legs
chicken stock
(see index)
béarnaise sauce
(see index)

1 Have your butcher cut: **6 veal cutlets**, ¼ inch thick, preferably from the top sirloin.

2 Flatten each cutlet lightly on both sides with a heavy cleaver.

3 Sprinkle with: **1 teaspoon salt** and **½ teaspoon pepper. Flour** cutlets lightly and evenly.

4 In a skillet over moderately high heat, melt: **2 tablespoons butter.** When butter stops foaming, sauté cutlets 2 at a time (don't crowd them in skillet). Turn the cutlets twice on each side so they get golden brown without burning. Add more **butter**, if necessary.

5 Keep veal cutlets warm on heated platter while preparing pan juices.

6 Pour into skillet: **2½ tablespoons chicken stock.** Turn heat up and reduce stock slightly.

PRESENTATION

1 On top of each cutlet place: **4 cooked asparagus tips** and **5 cooked crab legs,** slightly warmed in **butter.**

2 Pour pan juices over cutlets. Top each with: **2 tablespoons** *béarnaise* **sauce** and serve hot.

CREPES TIVOLI *(Cream-Filled Crepes with Fruit Sauce)*
SERVES 6

eggs
flour
sugar
salt
lemon
light cream
butter
frozen strawberries
frozen raspberries
cornstarch
thick pastry
cream (see index)
cream
walnuts
hazelnuts
kirsch
brandy
fresh strawberries

Scandia specializes in fabulous desserts, usually some combination of crepes and fruit, sauced or covered with meringue and flamed at the table. Terribly rich, terribly pretty, and fantastically good. They bring the filled crepes to the table beautifully arranged on a large silver platter, heat the sauce in a chafing dish, and flame the whole stupendous works right there. At home the host can perform this simple feat at the sideboard before his admiring guests.

CREPES *(With Sugar)*

1 Beat: **3 eggs, ½ cup flour, 1 tablespoon sugar, a pinch of salt,** and **the grated rind of 1 lemon.** Gradually stir in: **1½ cups light cream** and **6 tablespoons melted butter.** Let batter rest for 30 minutes.

2 Make 12 crepes, 6 to 7 inches in diameter. Heat crepe or omelet pan over high heat. Add: **¼ teaspoon butter** and swirl pan to coat bottom with butter. Pour in about 2 tablespoons crepe batter. Immediately swirl pan to coat bottom with a thin film. Let cook until brown on underside. Turn carefully with a spatula and let brown on the other side. Cool on a clean towel. Cover with a second towel to keep the crepes moist. They may be stacked, with waxed paper in between, and stored in refrigerator or freezer.

FRUIT SAUCE

1 Defrost: **a 10-ounce package frozen strawberries** and **a 10-ounce package frozen raspberries.** Press through a food mill or blend in an electric blender to a puree, then strain through a fine sieve.

2 Heat sauce to simmering in saucepan and stir in: **½ teaspoon cornstarch** mixed with **1 tablespoon water.** Cook, stirring, for 1 minute. Keep hot.

FILLING

Combine: **½ cup thick pastry cream, ½ cup cream, whipped, 3 tablespoons chopped walnuts, 1 tablespoon chopped hazelnuts,** and **2 tablespoons kirsch.**

PRESENTATION

Put a tablespoon of the filling on each crepe, roll up, and arrange on a serving dish. Take sauce to table in chafing dish and heat to simmering. Add: **¼ cup each of brandy** and **kirsch.** Ignite and stir until the flame dies out. Add: **1 pint fresh strawberries, washed, hulled, and split, if large,** and heat briefly. Pour the sauce over the crepes. Serve two crepes per person.

BREASTS OF GUINEA HEN SMITANE
SERVES 4

For more than thirty years Perino's has been one of the finest restaurants in Los Angeles. Many others have come and gone in that time, and public fancy has veered like a weather vane first toward one place, then another. But Perino's quiet elegance and good food have created a solid reputation in a fickle city. This recipe for breasts of guinea hen in sour cream sauce is one of their most delicious.

breasts of guinea hen
onions
butter
salt, pepper
dry white wine
sour cream
wild rice

GUINEA HENS

1 Preheat oven to moderate (350° F.).

2 Season lightly: **4 breasts of guinea hen** with **salt** and **pepper.**

3 In a skillet melt: **⅔ cup butter.** Sauté gently: **2 cups finely chopped onion** until transparent and pale gold.

4 Put breasts of guinea hen in shallow baking pan. Pour onions and butter over them and bake, uncovered, in the moderate oven for 25 minutes, basting frequently. Remove and keep warm.

SAUCE

1 Strain onions from butter with a fine sieve. Discard butter.

2 In a saucepan heat: **6 ounces dry white wine** and the onions. Let it reduce by one-third.

3 Lower heat and gradually stir in: **2 cups sour cream.** Blend all carefully but do not let sour cream cook.

PRESENTATION

Pour hot sour cream sauce over guinea hen breasts and serve with **wild rice.**

VEAL CUTLETS CORDON BLEU
SERVES 6

One of Perino's great specialties is this "sandwich" of thin veal slices with a ham-and-cheese filling. The whole thing gets breaded and sautéed and can be served with or without a tomato sauce. You can make up the veal "sandwiches" in advance and have them breaded and ready to sauté at the last minute. Alex Perino serves his on a large silver tray with green asparagus tips in the center and the browned cutlets and red tomato sauce all around.

veal scallops
Swiss cheese
Virginia ham
flour
asparagus tips
lemons
eggs
bread crumbs
butter
salt, pepper
tomato sauce (see index—optional)
cooking oil

1 Flatten: **12 veal scallops** with the side of a cleaver. Pound them on both sides until they are ¼ inch thick.

2 Sprinkle with **salt** and **pepper**.

3 Lay the veal slices out flat. Put: **1 thin slice Swiss cheese** and **1 thin slice Virginia ham** on each of 6 veal scallops.

4 Cover with remaining 6 scallops. Pound or press edges together to seal in filling.

5 Beat: **3 eggs.** Put: **¾ cup fine bread crumbs** in a bowl.

6 Dip each veal "sandwich" in **flour,** then in the beaten eggs, and finally in the fine bread crumbs.

7 In a large skillet heat: **3 tablespoons butter** and **1 tablespoon cooking oil.** Sauté the breaded veal "sandwiches" over moderately high heat for about 4 minutes on each side, or until golden brown.

PRESENTATION

Serve on a warm platter with hot **buttered asparagus tips** and **lemon wedges.** Or if you want to serve this Italian style, serve with a **tomato sauce.** Sardi's Meat Sauce or the meat sauce for *Spaghetti alla Bolognese* are both excellent.

No one will go hungry—or thirsty—at the Blue Fox. In this wine cellar, festooned with good things to eat and drink, private parties are served some of the most fabulous food in San Francisco. Do you suppose the little fox peering down at all this luxury is thinking "sour grapes"?

Fishermen's Wharf in San Francisco is heaped with the bounty of the sea. Raw shrimp they have a-plenty, but only a fine recipe can transform them into this delectable *Scampi alla Livornese*.

BLUE FOX

ONE OF THE finest restaurants in a city of great eating places, the Blue Fox on San Francisco's Merchant Street is a champion among champions. To an out-of-towner its location is exotic to say the least. The sign of the Blue Fox hangs above a dingy alley not very far from San Francisco's fabled Chinatown, in the shadow of the city morgue. Pay all that no heed, however. The restaurant itself is lavishly decorated—Mary tells me even the powder room was a dream of Italian marble and 24-carat gold swan fixtures—and the food is beyond compare.

The main dining rooms upstairs are conventionally attractive. But if you are lucky enough to attend a large dinner party, as we were, you may dine in the remarkable wine cellar. Mario Mondin and Piero Fassio, owners of the Blue Fox, have turned their wine cellar into an Italian fantasy with clusters of grapes, salamis, prosciutto hams, and straw-covered Chianti bottles hanging from the ceiling. This room is booked in advance for large private parties, and guests had better not get obstreperous. The walls are lined with hundreds of bottles of fine wines, and I shudder to think of what the breakage could amount to!

Fascinating as the decor is, it is the food that we remember most fondly. The Blue Fox's cuisine is international, but Italian specialties predominate. Their chef does beautiful things with *scampi* and tortellini, but one of his most spectacularly delicious inventions is a boned baby pheasant baked in clay. We don't get up to San Francisco nearly as often as we'd like, but between trips we can turn to our recipe file and cook up a batch of our favorite Bay City dishes. Pretty foxy!

A La Carte

Appetizers

*Limestone Lettuce, French Dressing   2.25

*Fresh Artichokes Vinaigrette	1.00	Imported "Beluga" Caviar (for two)	5.00
*Peperoni Don Salvatore	1.00	Prosciutto e Melone	2.00
*Scampi alla Livornese	2.25	Caesar Salad	2.50
*Veal Tonne	1.75	Tossed Green Salad, Crab or Shrimp	2.25
Shrimp Cocktail Supreme	1.75	Heart of Romaine, Roquefort Dressing	2.00
Crab Legs Cocktail	2.00	Tossed Green Salad	1.75
Fresh Crab (when in season)	2.25	Escargot Bourguignonne	2.00
Belgian Endive	2.50		

Soups

Soup du Jour	.75
Chicken Broth	.75
Tortellini al Brodo	1.25
Green Turtle Soup Tureen	1.75

Pastes

*Tortellini alla Veneziana	2.00
*Pasta del Giorno alla Napoletana	1.50
*Gnocchi Verdi alla Fiorentina	2.00

Broiler

Medallion of Tenderloin wrapped with bacon avec Champignons   6.00

*Filet, Madera Wine Sauce	7.00	Chateaubriand Richelieu (for two)	15.50
New York Cut (Sirloin of Beef)	7.00	Double New York Cut (for two)	15.00
Filet Mignon Monte Carlo	7.00	Double French Lamb Chops	6.00

Oven

*Long Island Duckling Flambé aux Cerises Noir (for two)	13.50
*Fagianino alla creta (Baby boneless Pheasant baked in clay —stuffed with Risotto of Wild Rice)	6.50
Boneless Royal Squab ver jus	6.00
Rack of Lamb Parisienne (for two)	14.00

Sauces

Hollandaise (for two)	1.25	Béarnaise (for two)	1.50	French Bordelaise (for two)	1.50

Saute

*Scaloppine Dorate con Tortellini	6.00	*Sweetbreads Saute Fiorentina	4.50
*Cotoletta Imbottita alla Palatina	6.00	*Frog Legs Saute alla Piero	4.75
*Stuffed Boneless Roulade of Capon	5.00	Filet of Rex Sole Almondine	4.50
*Breast of Capon alla Mario	5.50	Filet of Pompano Farci en papillote	5.00

Desserts, Fruit, Coffee

*Crema Fritta, Flambé	1.00	Camembert Cheese	.60
*Banana Fritter	1.00	Monterey Jack	.60
*Zabaione al Marsala (for two)	3.00	Cherry Jubilee	2.00
*Zuppa Inglese	1.25	Ice Cream or Sherbet	.60
		Baked Alaska Flambé (for two)	5.00

Crêpes Suzette (for two)   6.00

Caffé Diablo	2.00	Coffee	.40	Sanka	.35
Caffé Espresso	.60	Demi Tasse	.30	Tea	.40

Blue Fox

Soup du Jour   — or —   Pasta del Giorno

Entrees

*Stuffed Boneless Roulade of Capon	5.75
*Coq au Vin Blanc	5.50
*Breast of Capon alla Mario	6.50
*Long Island Duckling Flambé au Cerises Noir (for two)	14.50
Boneless Royal Squab Ver-Jus	7.00
*Sweetbreads Saute Florentine	5.50
*Frog Legs Saute alla Piero	5.75
*Broiled Brazilian Lobster Tail Provencale	6.00
*Boneless Filet of Sturgeon, Fricandeau	6.50
Filet of Rex Sole Almondine	5.75
*Filet of Pompano Farci en papillote	6.50
*Cotoletta Imbottita alla Palatina	6.75
Scaloppine of Veal con Marsala	5.75
Medallion of Tenderloin wrapped with bacon avec Champignons	7.50
New York Cut (Sirloin of Beef)	8.00
Filet Mignon Monte Carlo	8.00
Double New York Cut (for two)	17.00
Double French Lamb Chops	7.00

Desserts

Banana Fritters with Whipped Cream   Crema Fritta   Sherbet   Ice Cream

Monterey Jack   Demi Tasse

After 10:30 P.M. Service a la Carte Only

SCAMPI ALLA LIVORNESE
SERVES 4 FOR APPETIZER

The large prawns that are native to Italian waters are prepared in many different ways in different parts of Italy. In this country Italian chefs make-do very nicely with large shrimp in place of their homeland's *scampi*, but their recipes remain authentically Italian. At the Blue Fox we especially like the *scampi* (or large shrimp) cooked as they are in Leghorn, one of Italy's great seaports. Delicate and subtle.

large shrimp
milk
cooking oil
flour
garlic (optional)
shallots (optional)
salt, pepper
sweet white wine
butter
lemon
parsley

SCAMPI

1 Remove shells from: **12 large raw shrimp.** Remove intestinal vein running down backs. With a small sharp knife, make 3 cuts from tail halfway to head, giving the shrimp 4 "tails."

2 Put shrimp in a bowl, cover with **milk,** and soak for 10 to 15 minutes.

3 In deep skillet or pan heat: **1½ inches cooking oil** to 350° F.

4 Drain shrimp, dry on paper towels, and dredge in **flour** seasoned with **salt** and **pepper.**

5 Fry a few shrimp at a time in the hot deep fat for about 2 minutes, or until lightly browned. Remove and drain on absorbent paper. Keep warm.

SAUCE

1 In a 12-inch skillet put: **2 cups sweet white wine** (a sauterne is good). If you wish, you may add: **1 tablespoon chopped shallots** or **½ teaspoon minced garlic.**

2 Bring to a boil and cook until wine is reduced to 1 cup. Add the shrimp and boil briskly for 1 minute.

3 Add: **4 ounces softened butter** and toss the butter with the wine and shrimp until the sauce is creamy and smooth. Do not cook sauce after butter has melted or it will separate. Remove from heat immediately.

PRESENTATION

Serve at once with **lemon wedges** and **parsley.**

PEPERONI DON SALVATORE
SERVES 4

Green peppers baked and served cold with a spicy dressing make a delicious first course or side dish. This is one of the recipes we especially like from the Blue Fox, an Italian specialty that peps up any meal.

green peppers
olive oil
red wine vinegar
salt, pepper
sugar
paprika
lemon
Worcestershire sauce
garlic
anchovy fillets

PEPPERS

1 Preheat oven to very hot (450° F.).

2 Wash: **4 large green peppers.** Place on baking sheet and bake in the very hot oven for 20 minutes, or until skins blister.

3 Remove, cool slightly, then peel. Cut in half, discarding stems and seeds, and place flat on a serving platter.

DRESSING

1 Combine: **8 tablespoons olive oil, 3** tablespoons red wine vinegar, ¼ teaspoon salt, ⅛ teaspoon pepper, ⅓ teaspoon sugar, ⅓ teaspoon paprika, 1 teaspoon lemon juice, and a dash of Worcestershire sauce.

2 In mortar mash: **1 clove garlic** and **2 flat fillets of anchovies.** Stir into dressing.

PRESENTATION

Pour dressing over peppers and marinate for 15 minutes. Put in refrigerator for several hours and serve chilled.

ROCK CORNISH GAME HENS IN CLAY
SERVES 4

At the Blue Fox we were served baby pheasant baked in clay, and it was a memorable dish. When we got back to Los Angeles Mary couldn't rest until she had tracked down a sculptors' supply store that carried the proper clay. It is a moist, ready-to-use ceramic clay especially prepared for the kitchen, great fun to use, and cooking with it is not just a chichi trick. We use Rock Cornish game hens, and the little birds turn out tender, moist, and marvelously flavorful. This is far and away the best method of cooking them that I've ever tried.

wild rice
salt, pepper
butter
prosciutto ham
paprika
Rock Cornish
game hens
sage
truffle
cooking oil
ceramic clay

1 Wash: **1 cup wild rice.** Place in a saucepan. Cover the rice to one inch above it with boiling water and let cool. Drain and repeat three times. Drain, cover a fifth time with boiling water, add: **1 teaspoon salt,** and simmer for 5 minutes. Drain and stir in: **4 tablespoons butter, ½ cup shredded prosciutto ham, 1 truffle, minced, salt** and **pepper** to taste. Cool.

2 Mix: **4 tablespoons softened butter** and **1 teaspoon paprika.**

3 Stuff: **4 ready-to-cook Rock Cornish game hens** with the wild rice. Rub each bird with 1 tablespoon of the paprika butter and sprinkle with **salt, pepper,** and a little **crumbled sage.** (The paprika will give the cooked birds a lovely color.)

4 Place each bird on a square of lightly **oiled** heavy-duty aluminum foil, wrap birds to completely cover and seal edges.

5 Preheat oven to moderate (350° F.).

6 Cut: **10 pounds ceramic clay** into 4 pieces. Roll out one piece at a time into a 10-inch square.

7 Place foil-wrapped bird in center and enclose bird in clay, working with the hands to mold a smooth surface to resemble a flat-bottomed football. (If you want to make the clay wrapping more attractive or amusing, you can sculpt it imaginatively into the shape of a bird, or etch feathers or a design into it. The possibilities are limitless!)

8 Place clay-wrapped birds on a baking sheet and bake for 1½ to 2 hours in the moderate oven.

PRESENTATION
Serve birds in the clay. Crack off clay with a hammer and carefully remove and unwrap birds. Lift birds out of foil and serve with the natural juices. Reheat remaining **wild rice** and serve separately.

ZUCCHINI SOUFFLÉ
SERVES 4

Even vegetables can be a treat at a really fine restaurant. The Blue Fox makes this delectable soufflé with zucchini, and suddenly summer squash becomes an epicure's delight. Any fresh vegetable should be cooked at the very last minute, so the idea of serving a vegetable soufflé need not present a greater problem in timing than an ordinary preparation. In this recipe you can have your zucchini mixture cooked in advance, and then it is just a matter of beating and adding the eggs and baking the soufflé about half an hour before you want to serve it. And you will have something well worth serving.

zucchini
butter
garlic
scallions
salt, pepper
pimientos
sauterne
lemon
nutmeg
parsley
eggs
Parmesan cheese

SOUFFLÉ

1 **Butter** a 2-quart deep baking or soufflé dish and chill it.

2 Wash: **1 pound small zucchini.** Discard tops and a thin slice from bottom of each, and cut into strips the thickness of a pencil and about 1 inch long.

3 In a 10-inch skillet melt: **4 table-spoons butter.** In it cook: **1 clove garlic, minced,** and **3 scallions, finely chopped,** for 3 minutes. Add the zucchini and cook for 2 minutes longer, tossing the zucchini to coat each piece with butter.

4 Add: **⅔ cup sauterne, the juice of ½ lemon, ⅛ teaspoon nutmeg, 1 table-spoon chopped parsley, ½ teaspoon salt,** and **a dash of pepper.**

5 Cook over high heat for 15 minutes, stirring occasionally, until most of the liquid has cooked away and the zucchini is tender but firm.

6 Stir in: **2 pimientos, finely chopped.** Set aside to cool.

7 Preheat oven to hot (400° F.).

8 Separate: **6 eggs.**

9 Add to the yolks: **2 tablespoons grated Parmesan cheese** and beat until the egg yolks and cheese are blended and creamy. Stir in zucchini mixture.

10 Beat the egg whites until stiff and fold into zucchini mixture with a wooden spoon.

11 Pour into prepared baking dish and bake in the hot oven for 25 minutes, or until set and puffy.

PRESENTATION

Wrap a clean napkin around baking dish and serve the soufflé at once.

GNOCCHI (Potato and Cheese Dumplings)
SERVES 4

When you are tired of the usual potatoes, rice, or other starches, *gnocchi* are an excellent and easy variant. These, from the Blue Fox, are good served as a main course for luncheon or supper, or as an accompaniment to a roast. We like them especially served with almost any veal dish.

Idaho potatoes
flour
butter
eggs
salt, pepper
nutmeg
spinach puree
(see index)
Parmesan cheese

1 Peel and quarter: **4 Idaho potatoes** (about 1 pound). Boil until tender, drain, and dry well.

2 Put the cooked potatoes through a ricer and set aside. (There will be about 2 cups.)

3 In a saucepan put: **1 cup water, 6 tablespoons butter, 1 teaspoon salt, ¼ teaspoon pepper,** and **2 pinches nutmeg.**

4 Bring to a boil, remove from heat, then stir in quickly: **1 cup flour.** Stir rapidly with wooden spoon until mixture leaves sides of pan and forms a ball.

5 Put into electric mixer or mixing bowl and beat in, one at a time: **3 eggs.**

6 Add: **½ cup grated Parmesan cheese.**

7 Beat in the 2 cups mashed potato and **6 tablespoons spinach puree.**

8 Mix all ingredients to a smooth paste.

On a lightly **floured** board, roll a table-spoonful at a time with the palm of your hand to form a small dumpling.

9 Drop dumplings gently into pan of simmering **salted** water and let them cook, uncovered, for about 15 minutes, or until they swell and are firm. Don't boil water or *gnocchi* will disintegrate.

10 Remove *gnocchi* with slotted spoon. Drain on paper towels.

11 Place *gnocchi* in shallow **buttered** baking dish. Brush with: **2 tablespoons melted butter.** Sprinkle with: **½ cup grated Parmesan cheese.**

PRESENTATION

Just before serving, put baking dish under broiler (about 5 inches from heat) until *gnocchi* are slightly browned.

TORTELLINI PALERMITANA
SERVES 4

One of the oldest restaurants in San Francisco is Ernie's on Montgomery Street. It is lavishly Victorian in decor and aromatically Italian in cuisine. One of their most popular dishes is this first course of tortellini, a miniature snail-shaped pasta similar to ravioli, and a happy change from the more commonplace Italian starches.

butter
garlic
onions
tomatoes
tomato paste
flour
beef stock
(see index)
thyme
bay leaf
salt, pepper
mushrooms
frozen tortellini
Parmesan cheese

SAUCE

1 In saucepan heat: **2 tablespoons butter.**

2 Add: **1 clove garlic, minced, 2 medium onions, chopped,** and cook over moderate heat for 5 minutes, or until onions are transparent.

3 Add: **4 ripe tomatoes, peeled and chopped, 1 tablespoon tomato paste, 1 tablespoon flour, 1 cup beef stock, ¼ teaspoon thyme, ½ bay leaf, 1 teaspoon salt,** and **½ teaspoon pepper.** Stir to mix well, bring to a boil, and simmer for 15 minutes, stirring occasionally.

4 Stir in: **2 medium mushrooms, minced,** and cook for 5 minutes longer. Keep hot.

TORTELLINI

1 Preheat oven to very hot (450° F.).

2 Cook: **8 dozen (or 2 packages) frozen tortellini** in rapidly boiling **salted** water for 10 minutes. Drain and rinse in hot water.

3 In shallow baking dish heat: **2 tablespoons butter.** Add the cooked and drained tortellini and cook over moderate heat, stirring to coat them with the butter, for 3 minutes.

PRESENTATION

Pour the tomato sauce over the tortellini. Add: **2 tablespoons freshly grated Parmesan cheese** and stir gently to mix. Top with: **1 tablespoon butter,** cut into small pieces. Sprinkle with: **2 tablespoons grated Parmesan cheese** and bake in the hot oven for 10 minutes. Serve very hot.

BREAST OF CAPON AU WHISKEY
SERVES 4

breasts of capon
butter
bourbon
salt, white pepper
mushrooms
cream
flour

CAPON

1 Split in half lengthwise: **2 whole capon breasts.**

2 In a 10-inch skillet heat: **6 tablespoons butter.** Place the capon breasts skin down in the hot butter and cook over low heat for 8 minutes, or until golden. Turn and cook for 8 minutes longer.

3 Add: **6 tablespoons bourbon.** Cover tightly and cook over low heat for 15 minutes.

SAUCE

1 Add to skillet: **1 teaspoon salt, ¼** teaspoon white pepper, **4 medium mushrooms, thinly sliced,** and **2 cups cream.** Bring cream to a rapid boil.

2 Remove breasts and keep warm.

3 Boil the cream vigorously for 5 minutes. Stir in: **1 teaspoon flour** mixed to a paste with **1 teaspoon butter,** and boil for 3 minutes longer, stirring frequently.

4 Return capon breasts to the thickened sauce to reheat but do not boil anymore.

PRESENTATION

Serve capon breasts in the sauce with rice or boiled potatoes on the side.

TEMPURA *(Batter-Fried Tidbits)*
SERVES 4

You can find almost any kind of oriental cookery in West Coast restaurants. So many of the people from the other side of the Pacific have settled here that, not surprisingly, a number of them have opened restaurants specializing in their native foods. Up in Portland, Oregon, there is an excellent Japanese restaurant called the Bush Garden. We especially liked their *Tempura*, bits of food dipped in a thin batter, fried in deep fat, and eaten hot and crisp as soon as they are cooked.

shrimp
scallops
lobster tail
string beans
green pepper
flour
eggs
cooking oil
clam juice
sake
soy sauce
white radishes
ground ginger
sugar
coarse salt
(optional)

TEMPURA

Note: You can use almost any raw fish, seafood, and vegetables, cut into pieces. We like this combination.

Shell: **16 raw shrimp**, leaving tails on. Remove vein from back. Cut into slices: **8 scallops**. Remove meat from: **1 lobster tail** and cut crosswise into slices. Remove ends from: **16 young string beans**. Remove seeds from: **1 green pepper** and cut pepper into neat squares.

BATTER

Sift twice and measure: **1¼ cups flour**. Beat: **2 egg yolks** with **1 cup water**. Add flour to liquid gradually, stirring lightly with chopsticks or fork. Batter should not be completely blended, a little flour should remain on top.

TEMPURA SAUCE

Mix: **¾ cup clam juice**, **¼ cup soy sauce**, **¼ cup sake** (Japanese rice wine), and **½ teaspoon sugar**. Pour into 4 small bowls. Just before serving grate: **2 tablespoons white radish** and divide into the bowls. Sprinkle into each bowl: **⅛ teaspoon ground ginger**.

PRESENTATION

1 Heat: **1 quart cooking oil** to 370° F. Use a fat thermometer, as an even temperature is necessary for well-fried *tempura*. Fry only a few pieces at a time.

2 Dip shrimp into batter, holding by the tail. Drop carefully into the hot fat. When lightly browned, remove and drain on absorbent paper. Dip fish and vegetables into batter using chopsticks or tongs. Drop carefully into hot fat and remove when lightly browned, drain, and serve.

3 Serve freshly fried *tempura* on a cloth napkin on platter. Serve with small bowls of the *tempura* sauce and a bowl of **coarse salt**, if you wish.

Let's go out to the ball game!
Here we are at Chavez Ravine with Martha
and Cleveland Amory, dear friends,
avid baseball fans, and prodigious stowers-away
of popcorn, peanuts, soft drinks, and
that *specialité de le* ball park—*le* hot dog.

Here, in all its glory, is
the great American hot dog. Originally
a sausage invented in Frankfurt,
the hot dog is now as American as blueberry pie,
and under the proper circumstances it can be
one of the gourmet treats of the national larder.

CHAVEZ RAVINE

NO HOT DOG ever tastes as good as the ones at the ball park. It is a question of being just the right thing at the right time and place. At that particular moment when the crack of a bat signals a hit, and the white uniforms move gracefully against the green outfield, at that very moment a hawker stumbles up your aisle and your wife taps you on the arm and asks you to buy her a hot dog. You miss the play, but you gain the world. Even at that critical moment, there is nothing more soul-satisfying than the first succulent bite into the juicy frankfurter. Whether you slather your hot dog with mustard, relish, and onions, or eat it purist style with just a delicate dab of mustard, it is, in that brief time, the perfect food.

So we have included Chavez Ravine, the Los Angeles Dodgers' magnificent new ball park, among our favorite eating places in the world. If you stop to consider that the average restaurant does well to feed 500 people in a day, a ball park which accommodates tens of thousands at each game, all of whom drink or eat something as the innings roll by, is certainly in the food business in a big way. Beside the vendors in white who bring the mountains of food and drink to Mahomet, Mahomet can go to the mountains.

I get more exercise than the third baseman, climbing up and down the stairs and ramps to the stands under the stadium where nourishment is for sale. I must say that I don't see any special kitchen magic going on there to account for the heavenly taste of the baseball hot dog. No use to ask *those* short-order chefs what their secrets are! Instead we have included in this section a potpourri of our own favorite hot dog, hamburger, and general short-order recipes with our special tricks and touches for glamorizing them.

STUFFED FRANKFURTERS
SERVES 4

At the ballgame you have to take your frankfurter straight, but at other hot dog emporia in Los Angeles, the variety is infinite. Frankfurters have an affinity for so many different foods that you can combine them endlessly and come up with something delicious and different every time. This is an especially happy combination.

frankfurters
butter
onions
mustard
sharp cheese
bacon
frankfurter rolls

1 Cut a lengthwise slit in: **4 uncooked frankfurters.**

2 Slice thinly: **2 medium onions.** Sauté slices in: **1 tablespoon butter** until golden brown.

3 Fill frankfurter slits with the sautéed onion.

4 Cut: **2 slices sharp cheese** into long strips. Place 2 of the cheese strips into each frankfurter.

5 Wind: **1 strip bacon** in a spiral around each frankfurter. Secure with toothpicks.

6 Broil on a rack 5 inches from heat, turning several times, until cheese has melted and bacon and frankfurters are brown.

PRESENTATION

Remove toothpicks and serve in **lightly toasted frankfurter rolls** with **mustard.**

WESTERN FRANKS
SERVES 6

These frankfurters are cooked in a hot sauce, and are good served in their sauce and eaten with a fork and knife. But if you feel, as I do, that hot dogs taste better eaten in the hand, you can put some of the sauce in the roll with the frank—and serve extra napkins.

frankfurters
pineapple juice
chili sauce
dried bell peppers
English mustard
wine vinegar
garlic salt
soy sauce
molasses
onion
frankfurter rolls

SAUCE

1 In a large skillet combine: **1 cup pineapple juice, ½ cup chili sauce, 1 tablespoon dried bell peppers, ½ teaspoon English mustard, 2 tablespoons wine vinegar, ½ teaspoon garlic salt, 2 tablespoons soy sauce, 1 tablespoon molasses,** and **2 tablespoons minced, sautéed onion.**

2 Stir to mix well and simmer for 20 minutes.

FRANKFURTERS

1 Preheat oven to moderate (350° F.).

2 Cut shallow diagonal slashes across: **6 large frankfurters.**

3 Put them in a baking pan and cover with the sauce.

4 Bake in the moderate oven, uncovered, for 40 minutes. Baste with the sauce several times.

PRESENTATION

Place frankfurters in **heated rolls** with a few spoonfuls of sauce spread over each.

BARBECUED DOUBLE HAMBURGERS
SERVES 4

A Sunday evening barbecue, especially if there are youngsters around, is bound to be wildly successful if you just grill plain frankfurters and hamburgers with no fancy stuff. But your adult customers are more inclined to appreciate this fare if it is grilled with a difference. Here are a few tricks for sparking up hamburgers.

ground beef
salt, pepper
Roquefort cheese
liver pâté
poultry dressing
hamburger rolls
butter

1 Divide: **1 pound freshly ground beef** (round, top sirloin, or chuck) into 8 patties.

2 Top 4 of the patties with: **1 slice Roquefort cheese.** Cover each with a second hamburger patty and press edges together to seal.

3 Grill about 4 minutes on each side if you like your hamburgers quite rare.

Season with **salt** and **pepper** after they are cooked.

4 Follow the above procedure, substituting: **2 tablespoons liver pâté** or **2 tablespoons of your favorite poultry dressing, cooked,** in place of the cheese filling as variations on this theme.

5 Serve on **toasted buttered hamburger rolls.**

BOSTON BAKED BEANS
SERVES 5

Frankfurters and baked beans were made for each other. Sometimes in the West and Southwest you'll find chili and hot dogs mated, but I prefer Boston Baked Beans with my franks. This is an authentic Boston recipe for the genuine article. But canned baked beans doctored with brown sugar, catsup, mustard, onions, and bacon and baked slowly for an hour and a half are not a bad substitute. For those of you who want to know what the real thing tastes like, here is the recipe for Boston's traditional Saturday evening baked beans.

California pea beans
baking soda
salt pork
onion
sugar
molasses
dry mustard
salt, pepper

1 Wash: **1 pound California pea beans.** Cover the beans with cold water and soak overnight. (Boston housewives start this on Friday.)

2 In the morning, drain beans, place in saucepan with cold water to cover, and add: **½ teaspoon baking soda.** Boil for 10 minutes.

3 Drain in colander and rinse with cold water.

4 Preheat oven to very slow (280° F.).

5 Cut the rind from: **½ pound salt pork.** Cut rind into 1-inch squares. Cut salt pork in half.

6 Place in a 1-quart casserole or bean

pot half of the pork and rind, the drained beans, and **½ onion, peeled.** Top with the rest of the salt pork.

7 Combine: **¼ cup sugar, ⅓ cup molasses, 1 teaspoon dry mustard, 2 teaspoons salt, ¼ teaspoon pepper,** and **½ cup hot water.** Mix thoroughly and pour about one-fourth of this mixture over beans.

8 Place beans in the very slow oven and bake, covered, for 5 hours. About every 1½ hours add another bit of the basting mixture.

9 When beans have cooked for 5 hours, remove cover and let them bake one more hour so top gets browned.

WILTED SPINACH SALAD
SERVES 4

We barbecue in what we call our keeping-room, a place which Thoreau describes in *Walden* as having "all the attractions of a house." This is where we live, and mighty attractive living it is, too. The television is mounted on an old butcher block, and the indoor barbecue grill is Mary's handiwork, a surprise for me while I was away on a lecture tour. Until I had this barbecue I never realized what a lot of difference grilling can mean to almost all meat and poultry, but especially to steak. We serve ours with grilled mushrooms and this Wilted Spinach Salad with bacon dressing.

young spinach
green onions
salad oil
garlic
bacon
sugar
tarragon vinegar
red wine vinegar
egg
salt, pepper

SPINACH

1 Cut roots and tough stems from: **1 pound young spinach.** Wash thoroughly in cold water, being careful to remove all sand. Drain, shake out all moisture, and blot dry with paper towels. Tear leaves into bite-sized pieces.

2 Mince: **6 green onions.** Mix with spinach leaves in large wooden bowl.

3 Mash: **½ clove garlic.** Cover with: **1 tablespoon salad oil.** Let stand for about 30 minutes. Discard the garlic. Trickle the tablespoon of garlic oil over the spinach and let stand.

BACON DRESSING

1 Sauté: **3 slices bacon** until crisp. Re-move from pan and drain on absorbent paper. Reserve bacon fat.

2 Beat together: **1 egg, 1 tablespoon sugar, 1 tablespoon tarragon vinegar,** and **1 tablespoon red wine vinegar.**

3 Pour slowly into warm bacon fat, stirring constantly, until mixture has thickened slightly. Season with **salt** and **pepper** to taste. (It will not need much salt.)

4 Pour over the spinach mixture and toss well.

PRESENTATION

Crumble bacon strips and sprinkle over salad. Serve immediately.

A two-and-a-half-inch steak sizzles on our indoor barbecue while grilled mushrooms and a spinach salad wait on the side. The food is easier to do than this room was—most of the decor is Mary's handiwork and one of the reasons Edward R. Murrow called our house "the largest do-it-yourself project in America."

"Props" as theatrical people call the objects that decorate a set, are a major concern in our lives. We glean them from our travels and incorporate them into our lives and onto our tables. Here is a luncheon setting in our Moroccan room. The dessert of rich, rich *pot de crème* and brandy snaps, delicious in itself, is glamorized by the objects that surround it.

SPECIALTIES
OF OUR HOUSE

ATING at home can become far too taken for granted when actually it should always be a very special occasion. The grab-a-bite-on-the-run routine so many of us live with in this fast-paced nation not only spoils our digestion but deprives us of the pleasure and relaxation afforded by good food and interesting people. In this chapter we've tried to bring together some of the special dishes we prepare, some of the things we do to make our meals more fun and interesting (napkins folded in attractive shapes, wines carefully selected—even for informal outdoor dining) so that home can rival the most exciting restaurant in the world.

By this time you have seen the pictures of the way we serve food in our house. It cannot have escaped your attention that the Prices eat all over the place, indoors and out, in any number of nooks and corners, though even, upon occasion, in the dining room. There's no reason why you should be stuck eating in the same place in your home any more than you should have to eat the same food at each meal, use the same herbs, or make the same salad dressing. If you have gone to the trouble of making different parts of your house and garden attractive, why not use them for yourselves and even for guests when you serve luncheon, cocktails, or an odd-hour snack?

The point of all this is to make meals fun for ourselves and our family and friends. We know a lot of people with plenty of this world's goods and even more with little. Too often the ones with little think they can't compete with the ones with a lot, while the latter think plenty tastes good just because there's plenty of it. The ones we enjoy seeing and dining with are the ones who do plenty with what they have. The riches of the kitchen are

405

stored in the heart and mind and imagination of the cook. The riches of your house lie in your ability to use every square foot of it with inspiration and charm for the pleasure of yourselves and others.

And speaking of others, we owe a debt of gratitude to some of our friends and helpers who have contributed their prize recipes to our collection over the years. In some cases the specialties of their houses have become specialties of ours. Mrs. Blanche Sundheim, Mrs. Lona Salkow, Patricia Altman, and Olean Dick and Freda Tanner, who occasionally help us when we entertain, will all find their treasured specialties included with ours.

For a treasury contains treasures—not money necessarily but those objects, memories, creations that people treasure because they are the best of their experience. Here in this book Mary and I have stored up for you many of the treasures of our lives, borrowed, bestowed and occasionally even stolen from all over the world. They have been an open sesame for us into the wonderful world of good eating.

CHAMPIGNONS GRILLÉS MARIE VICTOIRE
(Broiled Mushrooms Mary Victoria)
SERVES 6

I love mushrooms raw, or almost raw. The most elegant ones I have ever eaten were uncooked, stuffed with Steak Tartar that was in turn filled with caviar. I disgraced myself! We like to serve these broiled mushrooms with barbecued steak, and because they're pretty glamorous too, I've named them after our baby daughter.

mushrooms
butter
shallots
seasoned salt
pepper

1 Scrub lightly: **18 large brown mushrooms.** Remove stems and save them to use in stocks or sauces.

2 In a large iron-handled skillet melt: **2 tablespoons butter.**

3 Place mushroom caps, tops down, in the butter.

4 Blend: **3 tablespoons softened butter** with **1 teaspoon finely chopped shallots, ½ teaspoon seasoned salt,** and **¼ teaspoon freshly ground pepper.**

5 Fill mushroom caps with the butter mixture.

6 Broil about 6 inches from heat for about 5 minutes, watching carefully. Turn off broiler and allow mushrooms to sizzle for 5 minutes more.

PRESENTATION
Baste mushrooms with any juice in pan. Serve without spilling contents of caps.

Note: We like these with hamburgers as well as steaks. But one of my favorite treats is broiled mushrooms with canned hominy that has been heated and had a well dented into the center, filled with melted butter and a good sprinkling of white pepper. Marvelous!

POT DE CRÈME CHOCOLAT *(Individual Chocolate Mousse)*

SERVES 8

I suppose you could serve this chocolate dessert in oven-glass custard cups and it wouldn't make any difference to its deliciousness. But this is a specialty of our house not only because the flavor is so good, but also because it can be served with great charm in little *pot de crème* cups. In the picture on page 404 you can see an illustration of our philosophy of dining at home. Almost everything on that table and in that room has a special, personal meaning for us and we like to think that our guests enjoy sharing them with us. The pottery head we use as a wine cooler came from Sicily, the coffee cups from New England. Mary bought the Limoges *pot de crèmes* in France, the green glass dishes at a rummage sale, and the shells came from every beach and beachcomber type restaurant we've been to. Mary made the floor from eight different remnants of tile bought from a tile company that was going out of business. The table is plaster and once graced a movie set. I painted it to match the chairs which may or may not be old Mallorcan ones. In the background are bits and pieces from our collection of primitive art, a painting by Man Ray, and a window blind made of toy parts strung together by my inventive wife. The lighting fixtures made of Tiffany glass shades we found almost one at a time up and down the Southern California coast. Put them all together and what have you got? A most exciting setting for a very good but very simple dish—our *Pot de Crème Chocolat*.

semisweet
chocolate bits
instant coffee
eggs
almonds
light rum
cream
sugar
coffee liqueur

1 In the top of a double boiler heat: **½ pound semisweet chocolate bits, 5 table-spoons cold water,** and **1 tablespoon instant coffee.**

2 Separate: **5 eggs.** Beat the yolks into the melted chocolate mixture.

3 Beat in: **2 tablespoons light rum** and allow mixture to cool slightly.

4 In a separate bowl beat the 5 egg whites to soft peaks. Fold them gently into the chocolate mixture.

5 Pour into 8 *pot de crème* cups with lids (or any small cups that you can cover) and refrigerate 24 hours before serving.

PRESENTATION

Whip: **½ cup cream** until thick. Add: **2 teaspoons sugar, 2 teaspoons ground almonds, 2 teaspoons coffee liqueur** and continue whipping until cream is stiff enough to hold its shape. Serve with the *pot de crème* allowing each guest to spoon some on top of their portion, if they wish. Serve with brandy snaps.

BRANDY SNAPS

MAKES 30 SNAPS

butter
sugar
dark brown sugar
molasses
flour
brandy
ginger
orange
cinnamon

1 Preheat oven to slow (300° F.).

2 In a saucepan melt: **¾ cup butter.** Add: **½ cup sugar, ¼ cup dark brown sugar, ½ cup molasses, ⅜ teaspoon ginger, ¾ teaspoon grated orange rind,** and **¾ teaspoon cinnamon.** Stir over low heat until thoroughly blended and the sugars are liquefied.

3 Off the heat add: **1½ cups flour.** Mix in smoothly with wire whisk. Add: **1 tablespoon brandy.**

4 Drop by tablespoonfuls, several inches apart, on an unbuttered cookie sheet. (The cookies will spread as they bake and will become thin and crisp.)

5 Put in the slow oven and bake for about 10 to 12 minutes, or until brandy snaps are golden brown.

6 Let stand out of oven for a minute, then carefully remove with spatula and place on a flat surface to cool. Keep in covered jar or tin.

HOUSE BREAD

MAKES 1 LARGE OR 2 SMALL LOAVES

In the high-flying jangle of my professional rounds, I've found that two things can get me back to earthbound composure—gardening and bread making. The latter has become one of the great joys of my life. If you ever need to deodorize, perfume, or freshen the air at home, just bake a loaf of bread. It's really great fun and very exciting; the staff of life is no shillelagh but a highly sensitive wand with which to conduct an orchestra of delights. Fresh homemade bread is the greatest of gourmet treats. It makes all boughten breads seem tasteless and all meals far more satisfying. I prefer to bake yeast breads, perhaps because yeast has something in common with females in general and actresses in particular—temperament. However, given every consideration, they'll both rise to the occasion. Here are a few favorites of mine which are easy to make. This House Bread is very close to real French bread in flavor and texture. We serve it sometimes spread with garlic butter and sprinkled with chopped parsley and chives. Perfect with Dungeness crab, mustard mayonnaise and an Italian Soave white wine.

active dry yeast
powdered ginger
salt
sugar
flour
butter
cornmeal

1 Measure and pour in large bowl: **2 cups lukewarm water** (110° F.). Sprinkle: **1 package active dry yeast** over water and stir until dissolved.

2 Add and mix well: **½ teaspoon powdered ginger, 2 teaspoons salt, 1 tablespoon sugar,** and **2 cups sifted flour.** Beat with wooden spoon until smooth. Then add: **about 3 cups sifted flour.**

3 On a **floured** board, knead until dough is smooth and elastic (about 8 minutes), adding more **flour** if necessary. Dough should be stiff.

4 Cover hands with **softened butter** and pat dough into a greased ball. Put in a large bowl, cover with a towel, and let rise in warm, draftless place for about 1 hour, or until double in bulk.

5 Break rise in dough by punching down. Turn out on lightly **floured** board. Shape into 1 large long loaf or 2 smaller ones.

6 Lightly **butter** a cookie sheet and dust with **cornmeal.**

7 Place loaf or loaves on sheet and brush tops with cold water. With scissors make 3 or 4 diagonal slashes across top of loaf or loaves. Let rise again until double in bulk (about 1 hour).

8 Preheat oven to very hot (450° F.).

9 For a good crust put pan of boiling water on bottom of oven and brush each loaf with **melted butter.**

10 Bake in the very hot oven for 7 minutes, then reduce oven heat to moderate (350° F.) and bake for 35 minutes longer.

11 Cool bread on cake rack.

HERB BREAD

MAKES 2 LARGE LOAVES

This Herb Bread has a flavor all its own, and though it is savory rather than sweet, it has such character that it is good eaten alone like a piece of cake.

1 In a bowl combine: **½ cup lukewarm water, 1 teaspoon sugar, ¼ teaspoon powdered ginger,** and **2 packages active dry yeast.** Let stand in a warm place until mixture bubbles nicely.

2 In a large bowl stir together: **2 cups lukewarm water, 2 tablespoons sugar, 3 cups flour,** and **3 teaspoons powdered chicken stock** dissolved in **½ cup warm water.** Mix thoroughly.

sugar
active dry yeast
powdered ginger
flour
powdered
chicken stock
thyme
summer savory
rosemary
butter or margarine
egg (optional)

3   Add the yeast mixture and beat well.

4   Add: **1 teaspoon thyme, 1 teaspoon summer savory, 1 teaspoon rosemary, ½ cup softened butter** or **margarine,** and **4 cups flour.**

5   Stir dough until it comes away clean from sides of bowl.

6   Spread: **½ cup flour** on pastry board. Turn out dough and knead thoroughly, using a little more **flour** if necessary to make a smooth elastic dough.

7   Return to bowl, spread top of dough with **melted butter.** Cover bowl with towel and let rise in warm, draftless place until double in bulk (about 1 hour).

8   Punch down dough and turn it out on lightly **floured** board. Knead a little.

Divide in half and shape each half into a loaf. Put each into a well **buttered** loaf pan, brush top with **melted butter,** cover with towel, and let rise until double in bulk and dough comes up to tops of pans (about 1 hour).

9   Preheat oven to moderate (350° F.).

10   Bake in the moderate oven for about 50 minutes, or until tops are brown and loaves have a hollow ring when you rap on them with your knuckle.

11   For a glazed crust, place pan of boiling water on bottom of oven and brush tops of loaves with a mixture of: **1 beaten egg yolk** thinned with **1 teaspoon water** 5 minutes before end of baking period.

12   Cool on wire rack.

FRIDAY CHICKEN
SERVES 6

This chicken recipe got its name because it was always made on Friday—cooking and baking day—and then was eaten cold over the weekend. The seasoned stuffing is placed between the skin and the meat instead of in the cavity, giving you a well-flavored bird, a crisp brown skin, and moist, tender meat. Though we continue to call it Friday Chicken, we usually prefer to use capon, especially if we want enough to last the weekend. Incidentally, this is one of the best things we take for lunch or dinner in our mobile home, and we had it in the picture on page 50.

capon
bread
parsley
eggs
salt, pepper
thyme or sage
onion
butter

1   Loosen the skin of: **a ready-to-cook 7-pound capon** by inserting the hand over the breast meat and down around the thighs, carefully tearing any connecting tissue.

2   Cut crusts from: **5 slices white bread.** Sprinkle with: **½ cup water** and let soak for 3 minutes. Squeeze out excess moisture and mix the bread with: **½ cup finely chopped parsley, 4 eggs, lightly beaten, 1 teaspoon salt, ¼ teaspoon pepper, 1 teaspoon thyme** or **crumbled sage leaves,** and **1 small onion, grated.**

3   Preheat oven to moderately hot (375° F.).

4   Stuff the dressing between the skin and meat of the capon, over the breast, forcing it into the leg pockets. Place capon, breast up, on a rack in a shallow roasting pan. Spread with: **½ cup soft butter** and sprinkle with: **1 teaspoon salt** and **¼ teaspoon pepper.** Roast in the moderately hot oven for 45 minutes, basting frequently. Reduce oven temperature to 350° F. and cook for 1 hour longer, basting every 20 minutes. Turn capon over on its breast and cook for 15 minutes longer to brown the back. Serve hot or at room temperature.

FILLETS OF SOLE IN CREAM ASPIC
SERVES 6

Because we live in a semitropical climate, a number of our specialties are cold foods that we can serve on a hot night. Fillets of Sole in Cream Aspic is a wonderfully good and attractive warm-weather dish, different enough to be tempting, and as cool for the cook as it is for the diners.

soles
butter
dry white wine
cream
salt, cayenne pepper
gelatin
fresh tarragon

1 Preheat oven to moderate (350° F.).

2 Fillet: **6 medium soles**, reserving heads, bones, and skin. Cut each fillet in half lengthwise, roll like tiny fat jelly rolls and secure with wooden picks. Arrange the fillets in a well **buttered** oven-proof casserole. Dot with: **1 tablespoon butter** and sprinkle with: **3 tablespoons cream.** Bake in the moderate oven for 15 minutes. Remove fillets to a shallow serving dish.

3 To the casserole add: **the fish heads,** bones, and **skin.** Add: **6 tablespoons butter** and **1½ cups dry white wine.** Return to oven and cook for 40 minutes. Place casserole over direct heat. Stir in: **1 envelope gelatin** softened in **2 tablespoons water, 6 tablespoons cream, ¼ teaspoon salt,** or to taste, and **a dash of cayenne pepper.** Bring to a boil, then strain through a fine sieve over the fillets. Cool, then chill for 3 hours before serving. When the cream aspic is almost set, garnish with **tarragon leaves.**

JELLIED MADRILENE SALAD WITH EGG SALAD DRESSING
SERVES 6

In Scandinavia we learned to like soup for dessert—Fruit Soup—and in California soup sometimes becomes a salad—Jellied Madrilene Salad. Since our salads are frequently served as a first course, this kills two birds with one recipe. It is most attractive prepared in individual ring molds, the red aspic making a striking contrast with the Egg Salad Dressing in the middle and the cucumbers, watercress and lemon wedges that surround it.

canned consommé
madrilene
basil
chives
thyme
gelatin
tomato juice
green onions
seasoned salt
salt, pepper
monosodium glutamate
Tabasco
lemons
cucumbers
green pepper
water chestnuts
watercress
eggs
vinegar
salad oil
mayonnaise
garlic powder
prepared mustard

1 Heat: **3 cups canned consommé madrilene** with **½ teaspoon basil** and **½ teaspoon thyme.**

2 Soften: **2 envelopes plain gelatin** in **½ cup tomato juice.** Add to the hot madrilene. Add: **⅓ cup minced green onions.** Remove from heat and season with: **½ teaspoon seasoned salt, ¼ teaspoon salt, ¼ teaspoon monosodium glutamate,** and **a dash of pepper.**

3 Stir in: **4 drops Tabasco** and **2 tablespoons lemon juice.**

4 Chill until mixture begins to thicken.

5 Fold in: **1½ cups finely diced cucumber, ¼ cup finely diced green pepper,** and **¼ cup sliced water chestnuts.** Turn into 6 individual molds or into a 6-cup ring mold. Chill until firm. Unmold onto salad plate, or plates, and garnish with **sliced cucumbers, watercress** and **lemon wedges.** Serve with egg salad dressing.

EGG SALAD DRESSING
(Makes 1½ cups)

Slowly beat: **¼ cup vinegar** into **½ cup salad oil.** Stir in: **½ cup mayonnaise** and blend well. Season with: **¼ teaspoon salt, ¼ teaspoon garlic powder,** and **1½ teaspoons prepared mustard.** Stir in: **2 hard-cooked eggs,** finely chopped, and **3 tablespoons chopped chives.**

410

CHICKEN SWEET AND HOT
SERVES 4

This is one of Mary's specialties, something she tosses together while tiling a wall or framing a few paintings. (That three-hour marinating break is just great for cooks with several other projects going!) It has marvelous flavor, aroma, and color and couldn't be better if Mary stood over a hot stove all day to prepare it.

butter
Worcestershire sauce
garlic
red currant jelly
Dijon mustard
oranges
powdered ginger
Tabasco
chicken
farfel pilaf
(see index)

1 In saucepan combine: ½ cup butter, ¼ cup Worcestershire sauce, 1 large clove garlic, minced, ½ cup red currant jelly, 1 tablespoon Dijon mustard, 1 cup orange juice, 1 teaspoon powdered ginger, and 3 dashes Tabasco. Heat, stirring, until jelly is melted and sauce is smooth. Cool.

2 Put: 1 chicken, quartered, into a baking dish. Pour sauce over and let marinate for 2 or 3 hours.

3 Preheat oven to moderate (350° F.).

4 Cover chicken and cook in the moderate oven for 1 hour. Uncover, increase oven temperature to hot (400° F.), and baste frequently until chicken is an even dark brown.

5 Serve with farfel cooked as a pilaf.

STUFFED SMOKED HAM
SERVES 12

When we have a buffet dinner this is the baked ham recipe we like to use. Because the ham has been boned, carving is a simple matter. And for a buffet eye appeal is most important, so this fruit studded beauty, resting on a handsome platter, usually steals the show. Most of the work is done the day before, and the Stuffed Smoked Ham, decked out in its party garnish, only needs to be put in the oven an hour and a quarter before we serve it.

mixed dried fruit
white raisins
pecans
canned pineapple
chunks
re-cooked boned ham
cloves
light brown sugar
sherry
oranges
canned
sliced pineapple
canned apricots
candied cherries
honey
red currant jelly
port

1 Empty into a saucepan: an 11-ounce package of mixed dried fruits. Cover with boiling water and simmer for 10 minutes. Cool in liquid, drain and chop.

2 Preheat oven to hot (400° F.).

3 Mix the chopped fruit with: 1 can (1-pound 12-ounces) pineapple chunks, drained (reserve juice), 1 cup white raisins, and ½ cup chopped pecans. Stuff the fruit mixture into the cavity of: an 8-pound pre-cooked boned ham. Fasten with skewers, stud with about 30 cloves and spread with: 1 cup light brown sugar.

4 Put the stuffed ham in a roasting pan and add: 1 cup sherry, 1 cup orange juice, 1 cup pineapple juice, and 1 cup water. Cover with roaster cover or with heavy-duty aluminum foil and bake in the hot oven for 45 minutes.

5 Reduce oven temperature to slow (325° F.).

6 Remove ham from oven and decorate with: 8 slices canned pineapple, 8 canned apricot halves, and 8 candied cherries, fastening the garnish in place with wooden picks.

7 Spread garnish with: ½ cup honey and put ham back in the slow oven for 1¼ hours, basting frequently.

8 Transfer ham to serving platter. Skim fat from liquid in pan and stir in: ½ cup red currant jelly and ½ cup port. Bring to a boil, then strain into sauce dish. Serve separately with the ham.

Note: If desired the ham may be refrigerated after it is garnished and cooked later or the next day. If cold, bake in a moderate oven (350° F.) for 1¼ hours.

STUFFED CROWN ROAST OF VEAL
SERVES 12

One of the prettiest sights in the world is a crown roast as it is being carried into the dining room. If there was any doubt in anyone's mind (the flowers, the candles, the wine might be taken for granted) the appearance of a crown roast makes the festive occasion official. I guess we're all kids at heart, and we all cherish some notion of what constitutes party food. This is it for me.

crown roast of veal
seasoned salt
paprika
ginger
butter
onion
garlic
green pepper
celery
cooked rice
potato
toast
canned oysters
poultry seasoning
salt, pepper

VEAL
1 Preheat oven to very hot (450° F.).
2 Sprinkle: **a 12-rib crown roast of veal** (about 6 pounds) with: **1 teaspoon seasoned salt, ½ teaspoon pepper, ½ teaspoon paprika,** and **¼ teaspoon ginger.** Place in a shallow baking pan and roast in the very hot oven for 45 minutes.

STUFFING
1 In saucepan heat: **½ cup butter.** Add: **1 medium onion, chopped, 2 cloves garlic, minced, 1 small green pepper, chopped,** and **2 stalks celery, chopped.** Cook over low heat for 10 minutes. Add vegetables and butter to: **2 cups cooked rice, 1 large potato, grated,** and **4 slices dry toast, crumbled.** Add: **1 can (7 ounces) oysters with liquid, 1 teaspoon poultry seasoning, 1 teaspoon**

salt, and **½ teaspoon pepper** and mix lightly to keep stuffing fluffy.
2 Remove roast from oven. Tie a band of heavy-duty aluminum foil around the ribs and fill the crown with the stuffing.
3 Reduce oven temperature to moderate (350° F.).
4 Return roast to the moderate oven and cook for 1½ hours longer, or a total cooking time of 23 minutes per pound, depending on size of roast.

PRESENTATION
Remove aluminum foil and place roast on a large round platter. Cap the tip of each rib bone with a paper frill (we like the ones made of gold foil). Carve between each rib without removing slices, and let each guest serve himself with a slice and some of the stuffing.

OLD-FASHIONED BREAD PUDDING
SERVES 6

You can't eat fancy food all the time without becoming surfeited. When we return from a trip, having eaten high off the gourmet hog for weeks, our first meal at home usually reflects our craving for simplicity again. Lamb chops, a baked potato, and spinach taste ambrosial after feasting too long on real ambrosia. And this Old-Fashioned Bread Pudding gets us right down to earth after too many high-flying soufflés.

dark brown sugar
bread
raisins
butter
milk
eggs
salt
vanilla

1 Measure into top of a double saucepan: **1 cup dark brown sugar.**
2 Butter: **3 slices bread,** using **2 tablespoons butter** for the 3 slices. Dice the bread and sprinkle over the brown sugar in saucepan.
3 Add: **1 cup raisins.**

4 Beat: **3 eggs, 2 cups milk, ⅛ teaspoon salt,** and **1 teaspoon vanilla.** Pour over bread. Do not stir. Place over simmering water and cook for 1 hour. The brown sugar will form a sauce.
5 Serve warm or cold. Turn out onto serving plate to serve.

FARFEL PILAF *(Baked Egg Barley)*
SERVES 6

Farfel or egg barley is a specialty of Jewish cookery and can be bought packaged like any other noodle product. It is frequently cooked in soup, but we like it prepared pilaf style, especially when served with chicken that has a good gravy or sauce.

farfel
butter
salt
onion (optional)
chicken stock
(see index)

1 Preheat oven to moderate (350° F.).

2 In a skillet heat: **2 tablespoons butter.** Add, if you wish: **¼ cup finely chopped onion.** Cook over moderate heat until golden brown.

3 Add: **2 cups raw farfel.** Stir to coat with butter. Cook until lightly browned.

4 Place in a casserole and cover with: **3 cups boiling chicken stock.** Stir well and bake in the moderate oven for about 1 hour, or until liquid has nearly evaporated. Farfel should be soft and in separate tiny "beads." Fluff with 2 forks and serve hot.

ICED TEA
MAKES 1 QUART

An American from my home town is usually credited with the invention of iced tea at the St. Louis World's Fair in 1904. A hot summer and tough competition from the beer vendors prompted one concessionaire to pour his hot tea over chunks of ice, and a new drink was created. In California we serve our tea iced even for high tea—an idea to shock a true Britisher, but this brew that I make is so different even they might condone it—or fail to recognize it altogether!

mint tea
jasmine tea
black tea
green tea
stick cinnamon
cloves
mint
lemon or orange

1 Blend in a can or canister: **2 tablespoons each mint tea, jasmine tea, black tea, green tea, 2 sticks cinnamon, broken up,** and **10 cloves.**

2 Put 10 teaspoons of the tea mixture into a preheated teapot. Pour over: **1 quart boiling water.** Let steep for 4 minutes. Stir, strain into container and chill.

PRESENTATION
Serve in ice-filled glasses. Have: **a sprig of fresh mint** and **1 slice of lemon** or **orange** in each glass. (This is a good hot tea mixture, too. For hot tea use half the quantity of tea leaves.)

ICED COFFEE
SERVES 6

We serve Iced Coffee in heavy ceramic goblets, gold-lustered by Mary. It is my own most unorthodox concoction, and friends always ask about it expecting some exotic recipe involving freshly ground Colombian beans and goodness knows what in the way of brewing and flavoring. Now the secret is out. This is all there is to it.

decaffeinated
instant coffee
saccharin tablets
milk
ground cloves or
cinnamon

1 Dissolve: **6 heaping teaspoons decaffeinated instant coffee** in **1 cup boiling water.** Add: **9 saccharin tablets** and stir until they dissolve.

2 Let stand until cool. Add: **1 quart cold milk, ¼ teaspoon ground cloves** or **cinnamon.**

3 Serve straight or over ice.

DIANA TORTE
SERVES 8

A homemade ice-cream cake is really impressive. This one is rich, handsome, and easy to make—all the attributes of eligibility in a bachelor, and not hard to take in a dessert either. You can vary the torte with different combinations of ice cream—chocolate and pistachio, chocolate and raspberry ice, vanilla and coffee are all good. But our favorite is the chocolate and coffee in the following recipe.

macaroons
chocolate ice cream
coffee ice cream
chocolate sauce
English toffee
chocolate fudge sauce
(optional)
cooking oil

1 **Oil** an 8-inch spring form.

2 Crush: **14 macaroons** and spread on bottom of the spring form.

3 Slightly soften: **1 quart chocolate ice cream.** Spread on top of crushed macaroons. Dribble: **2 tablespoons chocolate sauce** over the ice cream.

4 Crush: **14 macaroons** and spread on top of ice cream layer.

5 Slightly soften: **1 quart coffee ice cream** and spread on top of second layer of macaroons. Dribble: **2 tablespoons**

chocolate sauce over the ice cream.

6 Crush: **14 pieces English toffee** and spread on top.

7 Place torte in freezer for 4 or 5 hours, or until hard.

PRESENTATION
Remove torte from spring form and put on round serving platter. Leave at room temperature for about 30 minutes before slicing and serving. Pass a bowl of **chocolate fudge sauce** with the torte, if you wish to really indulge your guests.

SUNSHINE CAKE WITH CHOCOLATE ALMOND FROSTING
SERVES 10 TO 12

Every cook should have a few simple but glamorous dessert recipes that can be used when the rest of the party menu has taken a good deal of special preparation. This one is a beauty, needing only a sunshine cake, two giant chocolate bars and whipped cream, and it works just as well with a bought cake if there is no time for baking.

sunshine cake
giant milk chocolate
almond bars
cream

CAKE
Make: **a 9-egg sunshine cake** or buy: **a 9-inch sunshine cake** (usually made in a tube pan). Cut it in half horizontally.

FROSTING
1 Melt: **2 giant milk chocolate almond bars** in the top of a double boiler.
2 Whip until stiff: **3 cups cream.**
3 Fold it into the melted chocolate.

PRESENTATION
On a round cake plate place bottom half of cake, cut side up. Spread chocolate almond frosting on top about 1 inch thick. Gently place top half of cake on frosting. Spread rest of the frosting thickly on sides and top of cake. Refrigerate for 4 hours (or 6 to 7 hours in humid summer weather). Serve proudly.

414

DARK MOCHA CAKE
SERVES 8

On baking days our large kitchen table comfortably allows us to work together separately. My department is the bread baking side, Mary's the more glamorous cake bakery. It's a good partnership, because though I supply the necessary bread and butter, life's a lot more fun trimmed up with an occasional piece of Mary's cake. This Dark Mocha Cake is one of her triumphs.

CAKE

bitter chocolate
milk
sugar
eggs
butter
light brown sugar
baking soda
salt
rum
vanilla
cake flour
instant coffee
confectioners' sugar

1 In saucepan combine: **5 ounces bitter chocolate, cubed,** and **½ cup milk.** Stir over low heat until chocolate is melted and mixture is smooth. Stir in: **1 cup sugar** and **1 egg yolk.** Cook, stirring constantly, for 3 minutes, or until custard is thick and smooth. Cool.

2 Preheat oven to moderately hot (375° F.).

3 Cream: **½ cup butter** until soft. Gradually add: **1 cup light brown sugar** and cream together until mixture is light and smooth. Beat in: **2 egg yolks,** one at a time.

4 Sift and measure: **2 cups cake flour.** Resift flour with: **1 teaspoon baking soda** and **½ teaspoon salt.** Add to butter mixture in three parts, alternately with: **¼ cup water** mixed with **½ cup milk** and **1 teaspoon vanilla.** Stir in custard.

5 Beat: **3 egg whites** until stiff, but not dry and fold into cake batter. Divide batter into 2 **buttered** 9-inch layer cake pans and bake in the moderately hot oven for 25 to 30 minutes, or until layers test done.

6 Turn cakes out onto racks to cool, then put together with French coffee icing. Frost top lavishly, or frost top and sides smoothly with remaining icing.

FRENCH COFFEE ICING

1 Beat: **1 cup butter** until soft.

2 Beat in: **¼ teaspoon salt** and **2 tablespoons instant coffee** dissolved in **4 tablespoons boiling water.**

3 Gradually beat in: **2½ cups unsifted confectioners' sugar.** Beat for 2 minutes. Add: **1 teaspoon rum,** let stand for 5 minutes, then beat again.

SHERBET CASTLE
SERVES 8

As you undoubtedly noticed in the pictures of our kitchen, we also collect copper molds. One of our most spectacular company desserts, and one with infinite variations, consists of layers of different fruit sherbets refrozen in our own molds and served surrounded with a combination of fruits. Figuring that a quart of sherbet will serve four or five generously, we select molds according to the number of guests we plan to have. On page 432 you will see one version of this Sherbet Castle, large enough to serve ten and made in three different molds and then stacked. The recipe below is for a two-quart mold filled in layers, but you can invent your own design and shape.

raspberry ice
lemon ice
lime ice
orange ice
grapes
cherries
canned peaches
canned pears
kirsch

1 Fill a tall 2-quart mold with alternating layers of varied ices, using **1 pint of each flavor.** (This is pretty, too, if the layers are narrow, giving you a multicolored striped castle when you unmold.)

2 Put in freezer for 4 hours. Unmold and return to freezer until serving time.

3 Prepare: **½ pound grapes, ½ pound cherries, 8 canned peaches,** and **8**

canned pears (or any variety of fresh fruits and berries) in separate containers, sprinkling each with a little **kirsch.** Let stand for about 1 hour.

PRESENTATION

Place unmolded Sherbet Castle in center of attractive round serving dish. Place fruit decoratively around base of castle. Serve with small pitcher of **kirsch.**

A WORD ABOUT WINE

Wines are another specialty of our house. If you order wine with your dinner in a restaurant it is a fairly (or unfairly!) expensive proposition, but you can serve a good wine at home for as little as $1.50 or $2.00 a bottle. And there is no great trick to it, really. The best way to learn about wines is to sample many different kinds and find out which ones suit you best. Our very good California and New York wines come in half bottles and it's great fun to stock up on them and do your own taste testing.

For a beginning all you need to remember is four basic words—RED and WHITE, DRY and SWEET. As a general rule, red wines are served with meat, white wines with fish. But you can compromise happily with a pink, or rosé, which goes with either. (Champagne and other sparkling wines go with everything, too.) The reds are served at room temperature, the whites and sparkling wines chilled. Dry wines have less sugar than sweet wines and are best served during the main part of the meal while sweet wines go well with dessert. As for vintage years, forget them when buying California wines—the weather is so consistent from year to year that the crop is always good. For French wines the great years were 1955, 1959, and 1961, but that does not mean that you cannot find very good wines produced in the other years. It is more important to remember that white and rosé wines should be drunk fairly young, while red ones are better at least four years after the vintage, and they improve with age.

You don't need a lot of fancy glassware for serving wine. A plain, uncolored, tulip-shaped glass on a stem can be used for all your wines. The bowl should be large enough to hold at least two ounces of wine when half full—it is never filled much beyond the halfway point. And that's about all there is to it. All the mumbo jumbo and rigmarole are not one bit necessary for the true enjoyment of wine drinking—after all, people have been enjoying the fermented juice of the grape since way back in Biblical times without making an involved production of it, and we can too. So, to your health!

BLOODY MARY
SERVES 4

We like to serve Bloody Marys before lunch, especially in the summer when my Mary and our sun-loving friends melt around the swimming pool. I retire with my drink to the fern garden where the cool greens make a lovely background for the orange-red Bloody Mary, and I can sip it while contemplating a new fern frond unfurling. (Try saying *that* after one of *these!*)

vodka
Tabasco
Worcestershire sauce
lemons
sugar
salt, pepper
monosodium glutamate
canned vegetable juice

1 In a large pitcher mix: **6 jiggers vodka, 6 drops Tabasco, 6 dashes Worcestershire sauce, 6 tablespoons lemon juice, ½ teaspoon salt, 1 teaspoon freshly ground pepper, ¼ teaspoon monosodium glutamate, 2 teaspoons sugar, and 2 medium cans vegetable juice.**

2 Stir well and pour into glasses over ice. *Note:* Our Bloody Marys are hot and sweet-sour and they show their fist!

NAPKIN FOLDING

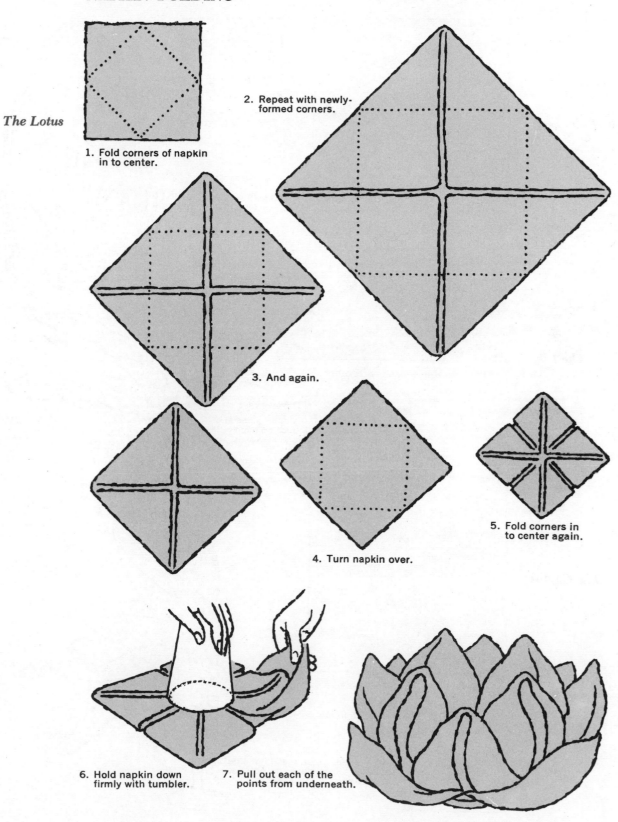

The Lotus

1. Fold corners of napkin in to center.

2. Repeat with newly-formed corners.

3. And again.

4. Turn napkin over.

5. Fold corners in to center again.

6. Hold napkin down firmly with tumbler.

7. Pull out each of the points from underneath.

NAPKIN FOLDING

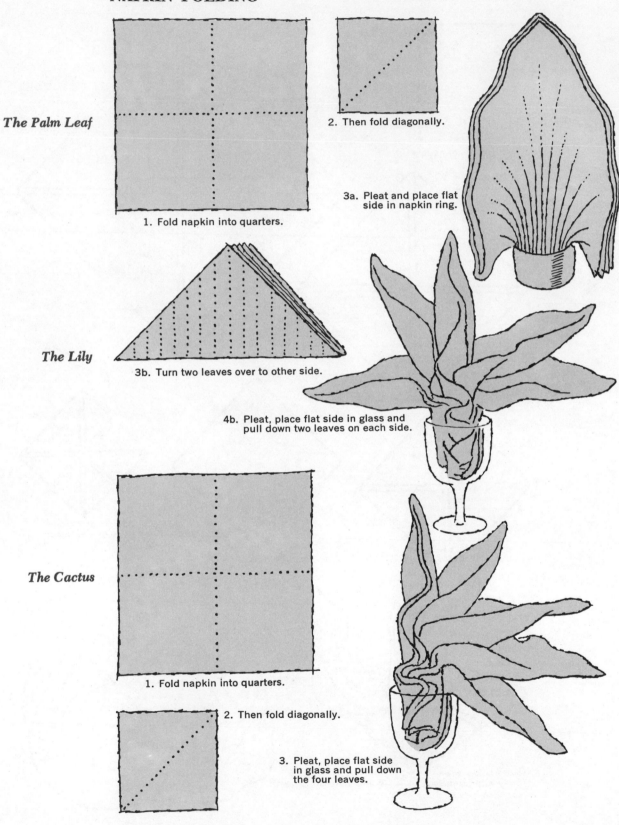

The Palm Leaf

1. Fold napkin into quarters.

2. Then fold diagonally.

3a. Pleat and place flat side in napkin ring.

The Lily

3b. Turn two leaves over to other side.

4b. Pleat, place flat side in glass and pull down two leaves on each side.

The Cactus

1. Fold napkin into quarters.

2. Then fold diagonally.

3. Pleat, place flat side in glass and pull down the four leaves.

NAPKIN FOLDING

The Mitre

1. Fold napkin into thirds.

2. Fold ends in to center.

3. Fold two diagonally opposite corners in to center.

4. Fold in half diagonally.

5. Tuck left corner into pleat.

6. Turn over and repeat with right corner.

7. Open up.

NAPKIN FOLDING

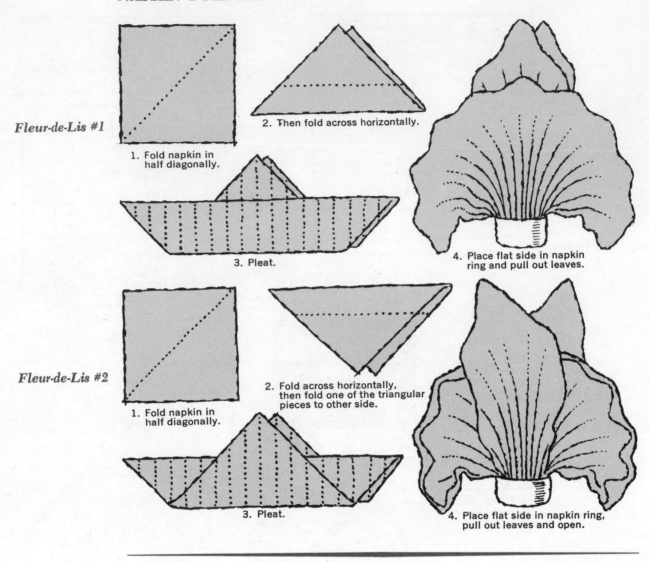

Fleur-de-Lis #1

1. Fold napkin in half diagonally.

2. Then fold across horizontally.

3. Pleat.

4. Place flat side in napkin ring and pull out leaves.

Fleur-de-Lis #2

1. Fold napkin in half diagonally.

2. Fold across horizontally, then fold one of the triangular pieces to other side.

3. Pleat.

4. Place flat side in napkin ring, pull out leaves and open.

The magic of a blender gives us home churned butter in five minutes. A crock of fresh butter and a loaf of newly baked bread are, when all is said and done, the best gourmet foods in the world.

Simple as A B C are all the fine French sauces when you make them in a blender. Béchamel, brown and tomato sauces—even mayonnaise are whirled to a velvety perfection at the mere flick of a switch.

BLENDER MAGIC

THE electric blender has come a long way since its original purpose in life—making frozen daiquiris. Today it is an essential electric appliance in any good cook's kitchen. We wouldn't be without one and, in fact, now find ourselves *with* two, a four-cup and a five-cup model. Even restaurant chefs, including the dyed-in-the-wool French masters, are giving it a nod as this magical machine is beginning to invade the kitchens of hotels and restaurants of the world. The men in the tall white bonnets no longer high-hat the electric blender, and even they are forced to admit that it can produce superior sauces, soups, dips, mousses, and frothy desserts with less effort than the long, hand-blended or sieved methods.

In this section are some of the blender recipes that we make most frequently in our home. They include the basic sauces which we keep in constant supply for the preparation of many of our treasured recipes. In addition, never a day goes by that we do not use our blender to make bread crumbs (break up slices of dried or fresh bread, blend on high speed for 4 seconds), grate cheese, chop nuts, puree vegetables or fruit, or make one of those instant desserts from fruit juice, gelatin, and crushed ice.

But for me the blender is a special joy since I learned to churn butter with it. For someone who delights in baking bread it is a real thrill to be able to offer sweet, freshly churned butter to go with the home-baked loaves. And our own herb butters and garlic butter are superb used on broiled fish or meats, or spread between slices of French bread that will be heated in the oven. Strangely enough it took this modern convenience to bring back the good old days of homemade preparations to our kitchen.

BÉCHAMEL SAUCE *(Basic Thick White Sauce)*
MAKES I PINT

butter
salt, white pepper
flour
milk

1 Into container of an electric blender put: **¼ cup softened butter, 1 teaspoon salt, 6 tablespoons flour, ¼ teaspoon white pepper,** and **2 cups hot milk.** Cover container and turn motor on low speed. When blades have reached full momentum, switch motor to high and blend for 30 seconds.

2 Pour sauce into double boiler and cook over simmering water for 15 minutes, stirring occasionally.
Medium White Sauce: Make as above, using only **4 tablespoons flour.**
Thin White Sauce: Make as above, using only **2 tablespoons butter** and **2 tablespoons flour.**

CREAM SAUCE
MAKES 3 CUPS

Make Thick White Sauce. When cooked, stir in: **1 cup cream** and heat through.

MORNAY SAUCE
MAKES 2½ CUPS

Make Medium White Sauce, adding to container along with the hot milk: **4 tablespoons diced Gruyère cheese** and **4 tablespoons grated Parmesan cheese.**

Cook over simmering water for 15 minutes, stirring occasionally. Stir in gradually: **2 tablespoons butter.**

CHICKEN VELOUTÉ
MAKES 2½ CUPS

butter
flour
salt, white pepper
cream
chicken stock
(see index)

1 Into container of an electric blender put: **4 tablespoons butter, 6 tablespoons flour, ½ teaspoon salt, ¼ teaspoon white pepper, ½ cup cream,** and **2 cups hot chicken stock.** Cover container and turn motor on low speed. When blades have reached full momentum, switch motor to high speed and blend for 30 seconds.

2 Pour into double boiler and cook over simmering water for 15 minutes, stirring occasionally.

Supreme Sauce: To 1 cup hot Chicken *Velouté* stir in: **¼ cup cream.**

Fish Velouté: Make as above, using **fish stock** instead of chicken stock.

MAYONNAISE
MAKES I ¼ CUPS

egg
dry mustard
salt
vinegar
salad oil

1 Measure: **1 cup salad oil.**
2 Into container of an electric blender put: **1 egg, ½ teaspoon dry mustard, ½ teaspoon salt, 2 tablespoons vinegar,** and **¼ cup of the salad oil.**
3 Cover container and turn motor on

low speed. *Immediately* uncover container and pour in remaining oil in a steady stream, taking no longer than 15 seconds total blending time from turning on motor. Switch blender to high speed and blend for 5 seconds.

GREEN MAYONNAISE
MAKES 1¼ CUPS

garlic
fresh dill
chives or green
onion tops
egg
salt
dry mustard
wine vinegar
salad oil

1 Measure: **1 cup salad oil.**
2 Into container of an electric blender put: **½ small clove garlic, 1 tablespoon fresh dill, 1 tablespoon chopped chives or green onion tops, 1 egg, ½ teaspoon salt, 1 teaspoon dry mustard, 2 tablespoons wine vinegar,** and **¼ cup of the**

salad oil. Cover container and turn motor on low speed. *Immediately* remove cover and pour in remaining oil in a steady stream, taking no longer than 15 seconds total blending time from turning on motor. Switch blender to high speed and blend for 5 seconds.

AÏOLI SAUCE
MAKES 1¼ CUPS

blender mayonnaise
lemon
garlic

1 Make: **blender mayonnaise** using **lemon juice** in place of the vinegar.

2 Add: **4 cloves garlic,** stir to combine, cover container and blend on high speed for 10 seconds.

RAVIGOTE SAUCE
MAKES 1½ CUPS

blender mayonnaise
capers
parsley
garlic
onion
white wine
lemon
egg

1 Make: **blender mayonnaise** and leave in container.
2 In saucepan combine: **2 tablespoons capers, 2 tablespoons parsley clusters, 1 clove garlic, 2 tablespoons chopped onion, ¼ cup white wine,** and **1 tablespoon lemon juice.** Bring ingredients to a boil and simmer for 15 minutes.

3 Pour cooked mixture into container. Stir to combine, cover, and blend on high speed for 3 seconds. Turn off motor, stir, and blend again for 5 seconds.

4 Add: **1 hard-cooked egg** and push it down into the blades. Cover and blend for just 2 seconds.

BROWN SAUCE
MAKES 1 QUART

butter
flour
brown stock
(see index)
dry white wine
carrot
onion
salt, pepper
leek
garlic
tomato puree
thyme
bay leaf
sherry or Madeira

1 In heavy skillet melt: **½ cup butter.**
2 Add: **8 tablespoons flour** and cook until a good dark brown, the color of dark brown sugar.
3 Add: **4 cups brown stock** and bring to a boil.
4 Into container of an electric blender put: **1 cup dry white wine, 1 carrot, sliced, 1 medium onion, coarsely cut, the white part of 1 leek, quartered,** and **1 clove garlic.** Cover and blend on high speed for 5 seconds, or until vegetables are chopped. Add vegetables and liquid to skillet and bring to a boil.

5 Add: **2 tablespoons tomato puree, ½ teaspoon thyme,** and **1 large bay leaf.** Simmer for 30 minutes, stirring occasionally. Skim off the fat that rises to surface.
6 Blend 2 cups at a time in container of electric blender until smooth. Correct seasoning of sauce with a little **salt** and **pepper** and stir in: **½ cup sherry or Madeira.**
Note: In blending thin sauces, it is best to begin on low speed with container covered. When the blades have gained full momentum, switch motor to high. This technique prevents any surge of the sauce out of the container.

TOMATO SAUCE

MAKES 3 QUARTS

salt pork
butter
flour
carrot
onion
chicken stock
(see index)
bay leaf
thyme
tomatoes
salt, pepper
garlic

1   Sauté: **5 tablespoons diced salt pork** in **2 tablespoons butter** until salt pork is rendered and crisp.

2   Stir in: **5 tablespoons flour** and cook until flour begins to brown.

3   Into container of an electric blender put: **1 carrot, coarsely cut, 1 medium onion, coarsely cut, 1 clove garlic,** and **1 cup chicken stock.** Cover and blend on high speed for 5 seconds, or until vegetables are chopped. Empty vegetables and liquid into flour mixture and stir.

4   Add: **1 bay leaf, ¼ teaspoon thyme, 5 pounds ripe tomatoes, quartered (or 2 quarts canned tomatoes),** and **3 cups chicken stock.** Bring to a boil, stirring, cover and cook over low heat for 1½ hours.

5   Blend 2 cups at a time in the electric blender and return to heat. Correct seasoning with: **1 teaspoon salt** and **½ teaspoon pepper,** or to taste, and stir in: **2 tablespoons butter.**

HOLLANDAISE SAUCE

MAKES 1¼ CUPS

eggs
butter
lemon
salt
Tabasco

1   In small saucepan heat: **1 cup butter** until very hot, but not brown.

2   Into container of an electric blender put: **4 egg yolks, 2 tablespoons lemon juice, ¼ teaspoon salt,** and **¼ teaspoon Tabasco.** Cover container and turn motor on low speed. Immediately remove cover and pour in the hot butter in a steady stream. When all butter is added, turn off motor.

3   Serve immediately or keep warm by setting container into a saucepan containing 2 inches hot water. If the sauce becomes too thick to pour when ready to use, return container to blender, add: **1 tablespoon hot water,** and blend briefly.

AURORIAN SAUCE

MAKES ABOUT 3 CUPS

blender hollandaise
blender mayonnaise
cream

1   Make: **blender hollandaise** and pour into small bowl.

2   When cool fold in: **½ cup blender mayonnaise** and **1 cup whipped cream.**

3   Chill and serve cold with cold fish, chicken, or vegetable mousses.

BÉARNAISE SAUCE

MAKES 1½ CUPS

blender hollandaise
white wine
tarragon vinegar
tarragon
shallots
pepper

1   Make: **blender hollandaise** and leave in container.

2   In small saucepan combine: **¼ cup white wine, 2 tablespoons tarragon vinegar, 2 teaspoons chopped fresh tarragon (or 1 teaspoon dried tarragon), 1 tablespoon chopped shallots,** and **¼ teaspoon freshly ground pepper.** Bring liquid to a boil and cook rapidly until liquid is reduced to about 2 tablespoons, or less.

3   Pour remaining liquid and seasonings into container, stir to blend, cover and blend on high speed for 8 seconds.

SWEET BUTTER
MAKES 6 OUNCES; OR ¾ CUP

cream

1 Into container of an electric blender put: **1 cup cream**. (Cream that has been refrigerated for a couple of days turns to butter faster than fresh cream.)

2 Cover and turn motor on high speed. Remove cover and blend until cream is whipped.

3 Add: **½ cup water** and **2 cracked ice cubes**. Cover and blend on high speed for 1 to 2 minutes. The time depends on the age of the cream. The water increases the amount of liquid in the container so that when the butter particles form they rise above the blades. The ice chills the butter so that it is fairly firm.

4 Pour butter particles and liquid into a small sieve to drain. Knead butter with back of a wooden spoon. Spoon into small crock, cover tightly, and chill.

Garlic Butter: Add: **1 clove garlic** along with the water and ice cubes.

Herb Butter: Add: **2 tablespoons chopped fresh herb** along with the water and ice cubes.

WATERCRESS BUTTER
MAKES 1 CUP

blender butter
watercress
lemon
salt, pepper

1 Into container of an electric blender put: **¾ cup softened butter, the leaves from ½ bunch watercress, 1 tablespoon lemon juice**, and **salt** and **pepper** to taste (don't season strongly).

2 Cover and blend on high speed for 30 seconds, stopping to stir down as often as necessary.

CHEESE DIP
MAKES 3 CUPS

cream cheese
beer
aged cheddar cheese
garlic

1 Into container of an electric blender put: **8 ounces softened cream cheese** and **½ cup beer**. Cover and blend on high speed for 20 seconds.

2 Add: **¼ cup beer, 8 ounces aged cheddar cheese, diced**, and **1 clove garlic**. Cover and blend for 20 seconds, or until smooth, stopping to stir down if necessary. Empty into bowl and chill.

TAHEENI *(Lebanese Cocktail Dip)*
MAKES ABOUT 1½ CUPS

cooked eggplant
lemon
olive oil
garlic
salt
sesame seeds
parsley

1 Into container of an electric blender put: **1 cup cooked, mashed eggplant, 3 tablespoons lemon juice, 3 tablespoons olive oil, 1 large clove garlic**, and **1 teaspoon salt**. Cover and blend on high speed for 1 minute, or until creamy, stopping to stir down if necessary.

2 Pour into serving bowl and sprinkle surface with: **1 tablespoon sesame seeds** and **2 tablespoons finely chopped parsley**.

3 Chill and serve with raw vegetables, leaves of romaine lettuce, or crackers.

BORSCHT *(Cold Beet Soup)*

SERVES 4 TO 6

canned beets
canned beef bouillon
lemon
sour cream
salt, white pepper
dill or chives
(optional)
onion

1 Into container of electric blender put: **1 cup canned beets, diced, 1 cup beet juice, 1 cup canned beef bouillon, undiluted, the thin yellow rind of ½ lemon, 2 teaspoons lemon juice, ½ small onion, ½ teaspoon salt, ¼ teaspoon white pepper, and 1 cup sour cream.** Cover and blend on high speed for 15 seconds. Add, while blending, enough crushed ice to bring liquid to top of container.

2 Chill until icy cold and serve with additional **sour cream** and a sprinkling of **chopped fresh dill** or **chives**, if you wish.

QUICK SENEGALESE *(Cold Curried Chicken Soup)*

SERVES 4

canned cream of
chicken soup
curry powder
milk
cream
chives

1 Into container of an electric blender put: **1 can (10½ ounces) cream of chicken soup, 1 teaspoon curry powder, and ½ cup milk.** Cover and blend on high speed for 15 seconds.

2 Add: **½ cup cream** and **1 cup crushed ice.** Cover and blend for 10 seconds longer, or until ice and soup are blended. Serve garnished with a generous sprinkling of **chopped chives.**

VICHYSSOISE *(Cold Potato Soup)*

SERVES 6

onion
canned chicken
broth
salt, white pepper
cooked potatoes
cream
chives
milk (optional)

1 Into container of an electric blender put: **½ small onion, ½ teaspoon salt, ¼ teaspoon white pepper, 1½ cups diced cooked potatoes, and 2 cups canned chicken broth.** Cover and blend on high speed for 8 seconds.

2 Add: **½ cup cream** and **1 cup crushed ice,** cover, and blend for 10 seconds longer. Thin to desired consistency with **milk** or **cream** and serve garnished with **chopped chives.**

CURRIED LIMA BEAN SOUP

SERVES 6

frozen baby lima
beans
butter
curry powder
green onions
salt, pepper
tarragon
parsley
cream
canned chicken
broth
chives

1 Cook: **1 package (10 ounces) frozen baby lima beans** with **2 tablespoons butter, ⅓ cup sliced green onions, and 1 teaspoon curry powder** until beans are soft (about 15 or 20 minutes).

2 Empty beans and liquid into container of an electric blender and add: **½ teaspoon salt, ⅛ teaspoon pepper, ½ teaspoon dry tarragon, 4 sprigs parsley,** and **½ cup cream.** Cover and turn motor on low speed. As soon as blades have reached full momentum, switch motor to high speed and blend for 20 seconds, or until smooth.

3 Pour into saucepan and add: **1 can (13¼ ounces) chicken broth.** Heat over simmering water and serve each portion garnished with **chopped chives.**

FISH FORCEMEAT

MAKES 1 POUND

This recipe should not be attempted in anything except a high quality electric blender with a powerful motor. In any blender, care should be taken not to overwork the motor. Stop blending and stir down as often as necessary.

fish fillets
egg
cream
salt, white pepper
nutmeg

1 Put: **½ pound raw fish fillets, free of skin and bones**, into freezing compartment for about 30 minutes, or until a few ice crystals form, but do not let them freeze. Cut the fish into small strips.

2 Into container of an electric blender put: **1 egg white**, half the fish strips, **½ teaspoon salt, ¼ teaspoon white pepper, and ⅛ teaspoon nutmeg.** Cover and turn motor on high speed. Remove cover and, while still blending, drop in remaining fish strips. Turn off motor and stir mixture with rubber spatula. Continue to blend until fish is smoothly ground.

3 Add: **1 cup cream** and stir to blend. Cover and turn motor on high speed. When vortex ceases to form in the mixture, remove cover and, with a thin rubber spatula or bottle scraper, work the top of the mixture, pulling it from sides of container to center. This will introduce air and the mixture will continue to blend. Turn off motor as soon as the forcemeat is creamy and smooth.

4 Keep cold in refrigerator until ready to use in a recipe.

Chicken Forcemeat: Use **raw white meat of chicken** in place of the fish.

BLUE CHEESE SALAD DRESSING
MAKES 3 CUPS

vinegar or lemons
salad oil
olive oil
salt, pepper
dry mustard
blue cheese
garlic (optional)

1 Into container of an electric blender put: **½ cup cider or wine vinegar** or **lemon juice, 1½ cups salad oil** (part olive oil), **1 teaspoon salt, ¼ teaspoon coarsely ground pepper, 1 teaspoon dry mustard, 1 cup crumbled blue cheese,** and **½ small clove garlic** (optional). Cover and blend on low speed for 5 seconds. Switch motor to high speed and blend for 10 seconds longer.

2 Pour into jar, cover, and store in refrigerator.

INSTANT FRUIT MOUSSE
SERVES 6

gelatin
sugar
frozen fruit
concentrate

1 Into container of an electric blender put: **⅔ cup hot water** and **2 envelopes plain gelatin.** Cover and blend on high speed for 30 seconds.

2 Add: **½ cup sugar.** Cover and blend on high speed for 5 seconds to dissolve the sugar.

3 Add: **6 ounces (1 can) partially de-** frosted **fruit concentrate** and **2 cups crushed ice** (or enough to fill container). Cover and blend on high speed for about 20 seconds, or until ice is thoroughly blended into fruit mixture.

4 Spoon immediately into serving dishes. If not quite set, it will set by the time you can carry it to the table.

COCONUT MILK AND CREAM

whole fresh coconut

Coconut Milk: Into container of electric blender put: **½ cup diced fresh coconut meat** and **1 cup water.** Blend on high speed for 30 seconds. Strain into a bowl, pressing coconut with back of a wooden spoon to extract all the milk. Makes 1 cup coconut milk. Repeat 3 more times to use all the coconut meat and make 1 quart milk.

Coconut Cream: Let the milk stand for 1 hour, or until cream rises to surface. Skim off cream.

Note: 1 quart coconut milk will make 2½ cups cream and 1½ cups milk.

CHOCOLATE BUTTER CREAM
MAKES 1½ CUPS

semisweet chocolate
pieces
coffee
butter
eggs
dark rum or brandy

1 Into container of an electric blender put: **1 package (6 ounces) semisweet chocolate pieces** and **⅓ cup hot coffee.** Cover and blend on high speed for 20 seconds, or until smooth.

2 Add: **4 egg yolks** and **2 tablespoons dark rum** or **brandy.** Cover and turn motor on high speed. With motor on, uncover, and drop in piece by piece:

1 stick slightly softened butter. If vortex ceases to form, break surface of mixture with a rubber spatula, being careful not to dip too deeply into the blades. In very warm weather it may be necessary to chill the cream before spreading over a cake. This is enough cream to fill and frost an 8-inch layer cake.

PAVÉ AU CHOCOLAT (*Molded Chocolate Pudding*)
SERVES 8

chocolate butter cream
cognac
ladyfingers
cream

1 Make **blender chocolate butter cream.**
2 Line bottom of a small spring-form pan with waxed paper. Combine: **2 tablespoons cognac** and **½ cup cold water.** Dip: **2 packages (5 ounces) ladyfingers** into liquid, one piece at a time, and arrange a layer in bottom of the pan.
3 Spread ladyfingers with half the

chocolate cream and cover with second layer of moistened ladyfingers. Top with remaining cream and cover with moistened ladyfingers.

4 Chill for 2 hours. Unmold on serving platter and decorate with rosettes of **whipped cream.**

PRALINE POWDER
MAKES ABOUT ¾ CUP

cooking oil
sugar
cream of tartar
blanched almonds

1 In saucepan combine: **¾ cup sugar, ¼ cup water, ¼ teaspoon cream of tartar,** and **½ cup blanched almonds.** Cook without stirring until mixture is color of dark molasses. Pour onto **oiled cookie sheet** and let cool.
2 Detach the praline from sheet with

pancake turner and break into pieces. Blend half at a time in container of an electric blender for about 20 seconds, or until ground to a fine powder.

3 Store in refrigerator in a tightly closed container.

The makings for a flavorful brown stock are laid out on the chopping board. Just add water, cook long and gently to extract all the goodness, and store in the freezer as a long-term investment in fine cooking.

Some people build castles in the air, but we build Sherbet Castles in the freezer. A lovely way to prepare and keep a party dessert until time to garnish and serve it. You'll find the recipe on page 415.

FROZEN ASSETS

Sauces are the basis of most cuisines, and stocks are the foundation of many of the most important sauces as well as of soups and stews. The richer the stock, the better the flavor of the dish to which it is added, and it is long slow cooking that is the secret of extracting the flavor from the bones and vegetables used to make the stock. Mary and I much prefer to use our own homemade stocks rather than the canned kind, so about every month we plan to spend a day making basic stocks. These we freeze in one-or two-cup containers with wide mouths, so that the frozen stock may be easily removed by rotating the container under hot water for a few minutes.

Part of the stock and the basic sauces, we freeze in ice cube trays and, when frozen, remove them and pack them into moisture-vaporproof bags. These are a great convenience when a recipe calls for a few tablespoons of a basic ingredient. We take a few of the frozen cubes of stock or sauce out of the bag, put them in a measuring cup and set the cup into a pan of simmering water. We estimate two to three tablespoons of stock or sauce per ice cube, depending on the size of the tray and the number of dividers in it.

We keep a constant supply of béchamel, chicken and fish *velouté*, brown, tomato, and hollandaise sauces in our freezer. The recipes for these are found in the chapter on Blender Magic. In addition to these essential sauces, we also keep in the freezer pots of roux and clarified butter. We spoon out of the pots as much as needed and return the pots to the freezer.

Mary and I try hard to make our freezer really work for us in the daily preparation of our favorite dishes, in the testing of new ones that we constantly collect on our travels, and for miraculously transforming us from cook and maître d'hôtel to host and hostess when we entertain. We don't use our freezer as a storage vault for dibs and dabs or leftovers, for prepared frozen dinners, or for huge quantities of frozen fruits, vegetables, meat, fish, or poultry. Rather, we prepare dishes a day or two in advance of entertaining, and freeze them. Some we cook and freeze; others are frozen uncooked, ready to cook or to bake. We seldom make two portions of any dish. We double or triple the recipe and freeze what we don't need for a quick meal the following week. It's just as easy to make stews, ragouts, and chowders for twelve as for six, and just as easy to bake four cakes or pies as one.

Most soups, stews, ragouts, casseroles, sauced fish, poultry, and seafood freeze well. We don't freeze vegetables that cook quickly, or sautéed fish and other dishes that are easy to prepare. Those foods that we avoid freezing for the simple reason that they don't freeze well are: hard-cooked eggs, custards, mayonnaise and mayonnaise sauces, salad greens, and raw vegetables.

Mary and I both love to make bread and biscuits. Often we make up a large batch of sweet yeast dough and have fun shaping it into a variety of breakfast breads, tea buns, sweet tea cakes, Swedish coffee rings, kuchen and stollen. We freeze these after they are baked. They defrost quickly—in about fifteen minutes—but we prefer them hot, so we reheat them in a moderate oven (350° F.) for ten to fifteen minutes.

Cakes we also freeze after baking, but only the layers, for we prefer to fill and frost the layers on the afternoon or evening of the day the cake is to be served. Pies, on the other hand, we freeze unbaked. We lift them out of their pie plates when frozen, wrap them, and return to the freezer. In this way we only need to have a few pie plates on hand.

We form cookie dough into long rolls or bricks, wrap and freeze them unbaked. We slice the frozen dough, place the slices on baking sheets and bake when needed. For drop cookie dough, we drop it by the teaspoonful on a baking sheet as if we were going to bake the cookies. When frozen we take them off the sheets and pack them in freezer bags. We bake them directly from the frozen state, adding a couple of minutes baking time to get them nice and brown.

We also keep a constant supply of good ice creams and sherbets in our freezer, and we are never without a quart of our favorite French chocolate ice cream. You'll find the recipe in this chapter. Just try it once, and you're lost forever! And now, on to our treasure trove of frozen assets.

ROUX

butter
flour

For the roux, we let ½ cup butter soften at room temperature, then mix this to a smooth paste with: 1 cup flour. The butter absorbs the flour and we end up with 1⅛ cups roux. This we freeze in a small pot or bowl, covered with aluminum foil. When a recipe specifies to "stir in 1 tablespoon flour mixed to a smooth paste with 1 tablespoon butter," we simply stir in 1 rounded tablespoon of our frozen roux.

CLARIFIED BUTTER

butter

Clarified butter is another of our frozen conveniences. It's great for sautéing fish and chicken. The food doesn't stick to the pan, for clarified butter doesn't burn as easily as regular butter; it has a higher burning point.

Melt: 1 pound butter over low heat. Skim off foam from surface and pour the clear oil carefully off the milky sediment which settles to the bottom of the saucepan. Pour into crock or bowl. Cool, cover, and freeze.

CHICKEN STOCK (White Stock or Fonds Blanc)
MAKES 3 QUARTS LIGHTLY SALTED STOCK

chicken
veal knuckle bones
carrots
onion
cloves
peppercorns
salt
celery
parsley
bay leaf
thyme

1 Into large kettle put: a 5-pound roasting or stewing chicken, ready to cook, 1 pound veal knuckle bones, cracked, 2 carrots, coarsely cut, 1 onion stuck with 3 cloves, 6 peppercorns, 2 teaspoons salt, 1 stalk celery with leaves, coarsely cut, 4 sprigs parsley, 1 bay leaf, ¼ teaspoon thyme, and 5 quarts cold water.

Bring water to a boil, reduce heat, and simmer for 3 hours.
2 Remove chicken and use for chicken salad or some other purpose.
3 Boil the stock rapidly for 30 minutes, then strain through a sieve lined with cheesecloth. Cool and skim fat from surface. Pour into containers and freeze.

BROWN STOCK (Fonds Brun)
MAKES 3 QUARTS

beef shin
veal knuckles
ham
cooking oil
carrots
onions
celery
garlic
parsley
thyme
bay leaves
salt
peppercorns

1 Preheat oven to very hot (475° F.).
2 Spread in flat baking pan: 2 pounds beef shin, cubed, 3 pounds veal knuckle, cubed, and ¼ pound lean raw ham, diced. Sprinkle with: 2 tablespoons cooking oil and bake in the very hot oven for 45 minutes, stirring occasionally.
3 Add: 3 carrots, sliced, 2 onions, sliced, 2 stalks celery, sliced, and 3 cloves garlic, and bake 15 minutes more.
4 Transfer meat and vegetables to a large soup kettle. Rinse baking pan with: 2 cups water and add to kettle. Add: 4½ quarts water, a bouquet garni of parsley, ½ teaspoon thyme, and 2 large bay leaves, 1 teaspoon crushed peppercorns, and 2 teaspoons salt.

5 Bring water to a boil and skim well. Reduce heat and simmer for 3 hours. Cool, remove fat from surface, and strain through a fine sieve lined with cheesecloth. Pour into containers and freeze.

FISH STOCK *(Fonds de Poisson Blanc)*

MAKES ABOUT 2 QUARTS

fish bones and
trimmings
onions
parsley
peppercorns
salt
lemon

1 Into large kettle put: **2½ quarts water, 2 pounds bones and trimmings of white-fleshed fish, 2 onions, sliced, 5 sprigs parsley, ¼ teaspoon peppercorns, 1 teaspoon salt**, and **the juice of ½ lemon.** Bring liquid to a boil, skim surface, and simmer for 30 minutes.

2 Strain stock through a sieve lined with cheesecloth. Cool and freeze.

YEAST BREAD

MAKES 4 LOAVES, 4 DOZEN ROLLS, OR 4 COFFEE RINGS

active dry yeast
milk
sugar
salt
shortening
flour

1 Soften: **2 packages active dry yeast** in **½ cup lukewarm water.**

2 Scald: **2 cups milk** and pour into a large mixing bowl. Add: **4 tablespoons sugar, 4 teaspoons salt, 4 tablespoons shortening**, and **1½ cups lukewarm water.** Cool to lukewarm.

3 Stir in: **2 cups flour.** Add the softened yeast. Then add: **4 cups flour** and beat with a wooden spoon until batter is smooth and elastic.

4 Add more **flour** (about **6 cups**) to make a dough that is light but does not stick to the hands, beating it in until the beating gets rough, then working it in with the hands.

5 Turn dough out on a lightly **floured** board, cover and let rest for 10 minutes, then knead until dough is smooth. Shape dough into a ball and put it in a lightly **greased** bowl. Brush surface of the dough with **melted shortening**, cover, and let rise until double in bulk, about 2 hours.

6 Punch dough down and divide into 4 equal portions. Shape each part into a smooth ball, cover, and let rest for 10 minutes.

7 Shape each part into a loaf, put loaves in **greased** bread pans (3½ x 7½ x 2¾ deep), cover and let rise for about 1½ hours, or until sides of dough reach top of the pans and the center is well rounded above it.

8 Bake in a preheated 400° F. oven for 50 minutes.

FRENCH BREAD

Note: Make recipe for Yeast Bread.

Shape the dough into long thin loaves. With kitchen scissors make gashes on top of the loaves about 3 inches apart and 1½ inches deep. Place loaves several inches apart on a **greased** baking sheet and let rise until double in bulk.

Brush tops with **slightly beaten egg white** and bake in a preheated 425° F. oven for 40 minutes. If desired, brush again with **egg white** and sprinkle with **poppy** or **sesame seeds.** Return to the oven for 10 minutes longer, or until seeds are brown.

FOUR DIFFERENT LOAVES

Note: Make recipe for Yeast Bread.

After all flour is added, divide yeast dough into four equal portions.

Nut Bread: Into one portion knead: **1 cup coarsely chopped nuts.**

Date Bread: Into one portion knead: **1 cup cut-up dates.**

Cracked Wheat Bread: Into one portion knead: **2 tablespoons honey** and **1 cup cracked wheat.**

Rye Molasses Bread: Into one portion knead: **2 tablespoons molasses, 2 tablespoons dark corn syrup,** and about **¾ cup rye flour. Raisins** and **chopped nuts** may also be added.

Bake as in Yeast Bread recipe.

SWEET DOUGH AND COFFEE RINGS

Note: Make recipe for Yeast Bread.

After the first rising, work into dough with the hands: **2 eggs, lightly beaten, ¼ cup melted butter, ½ cup sugar,** and **from ¾ to 1 cup all-purpose flour,** or enough to make a firm dough that does not stick to the hands. Knead and let rise until double in bulk, about 1½ hours. Punch down, divide into sweet rolls, coffeecakes, or rings, and let rise again before baking on a **greased** baking sheet in a preheated 400° F. oven.

Pan Rolls: Place balls of sweet dough almost touching in **buttered** deep-sided square pan. Cover and let rise in a warm place until double in bulk. Bake in a preheated 425° F. oven for about 15 minutes, or until lightly browned.

Dinner Rolls: Form sweet dough into cylindrical shapes with tapered ends. Place 1 inch apart on lightly **greased** baking sheet, let rise and bake in a preheated 425° F. oven for about 15 minutes, or until lightly browned.

Swedish Tea Ring: When sweet dough is light, punch down and let rest for 10 minutes. Divide into four portions. Roll out one portion on lightly **floured** board into a rectangle about ½ inch thick and 8 inches wide. Brush with **melted butter,** sprinkle with **brown sugar, cinnamon,** and **raisins,** and roll up like a jelly roll, sealing the edge. Place on **greased** baking sheet, sealed edge down. Moisten ends slightly and join securely to form a ring. With kitchen scissors, make deep slantwise cuts in the ring about 2/3 through and at intervals of 1 inch. Turn each slice partly on its side to make a petal-like ring. Brush lightly with **melted butter,** cover, and let rise for about 45 minutes, or until double in bulk. Bake in a preheated 350° F. oven for 30 minutes. Remove from oven and, while still warm, frost with: **1 cup confectioners' sugar** mixed to a paste with **2 to 3 tablespoons light cream.** Sprinkle with **chopped nuts** and decorate with **bits of candied fruit.**

Dutch Apple Cake: When sweet dough is light, punch down and let rest for 10 minutes. Divide into four portions. Pat out one portion into a round to fit a **greased** 8-inch layer cake pan. Brush surface with **melted butter.** Cover and let rise until double in bulk. Pare and core: **2 tart apples.** Slice apples ⅛ inch thick and arrange in spiral formation on top of the dough. Sprinkle with: **2 table-**

spoons sugar mixed with ½ teaspoon nutmeg. Dot with: 1 tablespoon butter and let rise for 15 minutes longer. Cover with buttered paper and bake in a preheated 375° F. oven for 30 minutes. Remove paper and bake for 10 minutes longer.

Hungarian Coffeecake: When sweet dough is light, punch down and let rest for 10 minutes. Divide into four portions. Break one portion into pieces the size of walnuts and form into balls. Dip balls in: ½ cup melted butter and roll in a mixture of: ¾ cup brown sugar, 1 teaspoon cinnamon, and ½ cup finely chopped nuts. Place a layer of the balls lightly in a greased 9-inch tube pan and sprinkle with raisins. Add another layer of balls and sprinkle with more raisins. Cover with a towel and let rise for about 1 hour, or until double in bulk. Bake in a preheated 375° F. oven for 35 minutes, or until lightly browned.

RICH PASTRY

MAKES 6 TWO-CRUST PIES OR 12 PIE SHELLS

flour
salt
shortening

1 In large mixing bowl combine: 12 cups all-purpose flour and 2 tablespoons salt.

2 Add: 6 cups shortening. With a pastry blender cut in shortening until mixture is mealy.

3 Sprinkle: 2¼ to 2½ cups water over the mixture, ½ cup at a time, and mix lightly with a fork until all flour is moistened. With hands gather dough into a ball and divide into 12 portions.

Two-Crust Pie: Roll out one portion of dough into a circle ⅛ inch thick and about 1½ inches larger in diameter than pie plate. Plates may be either 8 or 9 inches in diameter and, if you can roll out pastry very thinly, you can even use a 10-inch plate. Gently fit circle into pie plate and neatly trim off all overhanging edges.

Put in desired filling.

Roll out another portion of dough ⅛ inch thick and fold in half. Cut several slits for steam to escape. Unfold and place on filled pie. Trim off edges, leaving ½ inch overhanging. Fold edge of top pastry under edge of lower pastry. Flute edge. Freeze pie, then remove from pie plate and wrap. Label kind of pie, date frozen, and diameter, so you'll know what size pie plate you need when you want to bake it.

One-Crust Shell: Roll out one portion of dough into a circle ⅛ inch thick and about 2 inches larger in diameter than pie plate. Fit circle loosely into pie plate and trim off edges, leaving ½ inch overhanging. Fold overhanging edge back and under. Build up a fluted edge. Prick bottom and sides of pastry with a fork and freeze. Or bake in a preheated 425° F. oven for 12 to 15 minutes, or until golden brown. Cool, wrap and freeze.

Apple Pie Filling: Combine: 5 cups sliced tart apples with ¾ cup sugar, 2 tablespoons cornstarch, a pinch of salt, and ½ teaspoon cinnamon, nutmeg, allspice, or favorite combination of spices. Fill pie and dot with: 1 tablespoon butter. Bake in a preheated 400° F. oven for 45 minutes if defrosted, 55 minutes if baked from frozen state.

Blueberry Pie Filling: Pick over: 1 quart blueberries and combine with: 1 cup sugar, 3 tablespoons cornstarch, a pinch of salt, and ¼ teaspoon nutmeg or cardamom. Fill pie and dot with: 1 tablespoon butter. Bake in a preheated 400° F. oven for 45 minutes if defrosted, 60 minutes if baked from frozen state.

Strawberry-Rhubarb Filling: Combine: **2 cups sliced fresh strawberries, 2 cups cut fresh rhubarb, 1 cup sugar, 3 tablespoons cornstarch,** and **⅛ teaspoon salt.** Fill pie and dot with: **1 tablespoon butter.** Bake in a preheated 400° F. oven for 40 minutes if defrosted, 55 minutes if baked from frozen state.

Cherry Pie Filling: In saucepan combine: **1 quart sour cherries, pitted, with their juice, 1 cup sugar, ⅛ teaspoon salt,** and **3 tablespoons cornstarch.** Bring to a boil and simmer until juice is thickened. Pour into pastry lined pie plate and dot with: **1 tablespoon butter.** Cover with upper pastry. Bake in a preheated 400° F. oven for 45 minutes if defrosted, 60 minutes if baked from frozen state.

Lemon Meringue Pie: In saucepan combine: **1 cup sugar, ¼ teaspoon salt, 4 tablespoons flour,** and **3 tablespoons cornstarch.** Gradually stir in: **2 cups water.** Cook, stirring, until mixture is smooth and thickened. Separate: **3 eggs.** Freeze the whites. Beat yolks lightly with a little of the hot mixture. Stir into saucepan and cook, stirring, for 3 minutes longer. Remove from heat and stir in: **¼ cup lemon juice** (or to taste), **the grated rind of 1 lemon,** and **1 tablespoon butter.** Pour into baked pastry shell. Cool, wrap and freeze. Defrost and top with a 3-egg white meringue. Brown in a preheated hot oven (425° F.) for 5 to 6 minutes.

Meringue: Beat: **3 egg whites** until frothy. Add: **a pinch of salt, ¼ teaspoon cream of tartar** and continue to beat until stiff but not dry. Beat in: **2 tablespoons sugar** for each egg white and beat until meringue is stiff and glossy. Swirl onto top of pie.

BREAKFAST BREADS
MAKES FOUR 8-INCH SQUARE BREADS

**flour
baking powder
salt
sugar
shortening or butter
milk
eggs**

1 In mixing bowl combine: **8 cups sifted all-purpose flour, 4 tablespoons double-acting baking powder, 1 tablespoon salt,** and **2 cups sugar.**

2 Beat: **3 cups milk** and **4 eggs.**

3 Stir liquid into flour mixture to make a lumpy batter.

4 Stir in: **2 cups melted shortening** or **butter.**

5 Divide batter into 4 **greased** 8-inch square baking pans and bake in a preheated 375° F. oven for 25 to 30 minutes, or until breads test done. Remove from pans to cool on racks. When cool, wrap and freeze. Reheat in a moderate 350° F. oven for 10 to 15 minutes. Serve warm.

Cinnamon Nut Bread: Sprinkle the batter in one of the pans with: **½ cup brown sugar** mixed with **½ cup chopped nut meats** and **1 teaspoon cinnamon.**

Streusel Bread: Sprinkle the batter in one of the pans with: **½ cup brown sugar** mixed with **1 teaspoon cinnamon, 2 tablespoons flour, 2 tablespoons butter,** and **½ cup chopped nut meats.**

Cranberry Bread: Bring to a boil: **2 cups whole cranberries, ⅔ cup sugar, a pinch of salt, 2 tablespoons grated orange rind,** and **2 tablespoons orange juice.** Simmer for 5 minutes. Turn mixture into bottom of a **greased** 8-inch square cake pan. Pour one-quarter of the breakfast bread batter over the cranberries and bake. Turn out, cranberry side up, to cool.

Apple Bread: Generously **butter** a 9-inch square cake pan. Sprinkle bottom with: **½ cup sugar** and **¼ teaspoon nutmeg.** Cover with: **2 cups sliced apples.** Pour one-quarter of the breakfast bread batter over the apples and bake. Turn out, apple side up, to cool.

SALLY LUNN BREAD

MAKES 2 LOAVES

milk
butter
sugar
salt
eggs
flour
active dry yeast

1 Scald: **1 cup milk.** Add: **½ cup butter, 2 tablespoons sugar,** and **2 teaspoons salt.** Stir until butter is melted. Cool to lukewarm.

2 Soften: **1 envelope active dry yeast** in **½ cup lukewarm water.** Add to milk mixture. Beat in: **2 cups flour.** Stir in: **2 eggs, lightly beaten.** Add: **3 cups flour** and beat until batter is smooth and elastic. Work in: **1 cup flour** with hands to make a dough that is soft but not sticky. Cover and let rise in a warm place for 1½ hours, or until double in bulk.

3 Punch down dough and turn out on a lightly **floured** board. Knead until dough is smooth and elastic. Cut into 2 equal portions. Form each portion into a loaf and put into **greased** bread pans 4½ x 8½ x 2½ inches deep. Cover and let rise for about 1 hour, or until dough is well rounded above tops of pans.

4 Preheat oven to hot (425° F.).

5 Bake loaves in the hot oven for 30 minutes, or until lightly browned. Remove from pans to racks and cool. Serve warm with **butter** and **jam.** Delicious when sliced and toasted.

RICH BISCUITS

MAKES 4 DOZEN 2½-INCH BISCUITS

flour
baking powder
salt
shortening
milk

1 In large mixing bowl combine: **8 cups all-purpose flour, 3 tablespoons double-acting baking powder,** and **1 tablespoon salt.**

2 With pastry blender cut in: **2 cups shortening** until shortening is cut into small particles.

3 Add: **3 cups milk** and stir with a two-tined fork until all the dough holds together. Gather dough into a ball and cut into 4 equal portions. Knead each portion on lightly **floured** board, about 15 kneading strokes.

4 Roll out ½ inch thick and cut into rounds with a **floured** biscuit cutter. Place rounds on a baking sheet about 1 inch apart.

5 Bake in a preheated 425° F. oven for 12 to 15 minutes, or until lightly browned. Split, butter, and serve warm. Or cool, wrap and freeze. Reheat on baking sheet in moderate 350° F. oven for 12 minutes.

Cheese Knots: Roll out one-fourth of the dough into a rectangle ¼ inch thick and sprinkle with: **½ cup shredded cheddar cheese.** Fold rectangle in half and roll out again ¼ inch thick and about 6 inches wide. Cut crosswise into ½-inch strips. Tie each strip into a loose knot and place 1 inch apart on a baking sheet. Sprinkle lightly with **cayenne pepper** and bake in a preheated 425° F. oven for 10 minutes. Cool, wrap and freeze. Marvelous to serve with soups or salads.

Fruit Turnovers: Roll out one-fourth of the dough ¼ inch thick and cut into 4-inch squares. Place **chopped fruit** (fresh, canned or frozen) on half of each square. Dot with **butter** and sprinkle with **sugar.** Fold over to make triangles and seal. Bake in a preheated 425° F. oven for 15 to 18 minutes. If desired, serve with a fruit sauce.

Honey Buns: Cream together: **½ cup honey** and **¼ cup butter.** Spread the mixture thinly on bottom of a baking pan. Roll out one-fourth of the dough ¼ inch thick and spread with **melted butter, brown sugar, cinnamon,** and **raisins** or **nuts.** Roll like a jelly roll and slice into 1-inch thick pieces. Arrange pieces in the prepared pan. Bake in a preheated 425° F. oven for 15 minutes. Remove from pan immediately.

Jam Biscuits: Roll out one-fourth of the dough and cut into biscuits. Place rounds on ungreased baking sheet and make a deep depression in center top of each biscuit. Fill depressions with **jam** or **marmalade** and bake as usual.

DROP COOKIES
MAKES 8 DOZEN TWO-INCH DROP COOKIES

butter
sugar
eggs
flour
salt
cream of tartar
baking soda
milk
vanilla

1 Cream: **1 cup butter** and **1½ cups sugar**. Beat in: **2 eggs**, one at a time.

2 Combine: **3½ cups flour, ¼ teaspoon salt, 1 teaspoon cream of tartar,** and **1 teaspoon baking soda**. Stir the dry ingredients into the butter mixture alternately with: **1 cup milk** and **1 teaspoon vanilla**.

3 Divide dough into four equal parts. Leave one part plain or stir in: **1 teaspoon cinnamon, ½ teaspoon ginger,** and **½ teaspoon nutmeg** if you want to make spice drops.

4 To one part add: **1 cup chopped nuts, chopped dates,** or **seedless raisins.**

5 To one part add: **1 package (6 ounces) semisweet chocolate pieces.**

6 To one part add: **1 square unsweetened chocolate, melted,** and **½ teaspoon cinnamon.**

7 Drop batter onto **greased** baking sheets, keeping them about 1 inch apart. Bake or freeze.

8 To bake: Put in a preheated 375° F. oven for 12 minutes if defrosted, 15 minutes if baked from frozen state.

BROWN AND WHITE COOKIES
MAKES 8 DOZEN TWO-INCH COOKIES

butter
sugar
flour
salt
vanilla
cocoa

1 Cream together: **2 cups butter** and **1 cup sugar**. Stir in: **1 teaspoon salt** and **1 tablespoon vanilla**. Stir in: **about 4 cups flour**, or enough to make a stiff dough.

2 Cut dough in half. Work: **2 tablespoons cocoa** into one half.

3 Shape half the vanilla dough and half the cocoa dough into long rolls about 1 inch thick and cut each roll in half crosswise. Place one chocolate and one vanilla roll close together on waxed paper. Place second vanilla roll on top of chocolate, and second chocolate roll on top of vanilla roll. Press together firmly. Wrap in waxed paper and chill for several hours, or freeze until needed.

4 Roll out remaining vanilla and chocolate doughs about ¼ inch thick. Cut each dough into 4 oblongs of identical size. Stack oblongs one on top of the other, alternating colors. Press stack together firmly. Wrap in waxed paper and chill for several hours, or freeze until needed.

5 To bake: Slice refrigerated or frozen dough into slices ¼ inch thick. Arrange slices on **greased** baking sheets, about 1 inch apart. Bake in a preheated 350° F. oven for 8 to 12 minutes.

FRENCH CHOCOLATE ICE CREAM
MAKES 1 QUART

sugar
semisweet chocolate
pieces
eggs
cream

1 In small saucepan combine: **¼ cup sugar** and **⅓ cup water**. Bring to a boil and boil rapidly for 3 minutes.

2 Into blender container put: **1 package (6 ounces) semisweet chocolate pieces**. Add the hot syrup, cover, and blend on high speed for 20 seconds, or until chocolate sauce is smooth.

3 Add: **3 egg yolks**. Stir to combine, cover, and blend for 10 seconds.

4 Fold chocolate mixture into: **1½ cups cream, whipped**. Spoon into refrigerator tray, cover with waxed paper, and freeze for 2 to 3 hours. This needs no stirring and will not form ice crystals no matter how long you store it in your freezer.

441

INDEX

A

Aeblekage, 146
Aïoli Sauce, 425
Almejas a la Marinera, 202
Almojabanas, 219
Amstel Ginger Cake, 123
Anchovies, Grilled, 161
Andalusian Cold Soup, 194
APPETIZERS:
  Avocado Spread, 213
  Burgundian Snails, 83
  Ceviche, 213
  Cheese and Bacon Tart, 45
  Cheese Dip, 427
  Chilies Poblanos Rellenos, 214
  Cold Pike Pâté, 57
  Cornish Pasties, 182
  Crab Puffs, 360
  Crisped Shrimp with Mustard Fruit, 265
  Escargots Bourguignonne, 83
  Frankfurter Skewers, 359
  Grilled Anchovies, 161
  Grilled Tidbit, 317
  Guacamole, 213
  Gurkas Norge, 138
  Herring in Dill Sauce, 244
  Kaaldolmer, 382
  Kinilau (Marinated Fish), 359
  Langoustine Mimosa, 233
  Marinated Fish, 213
  Mussels with Saffron, 163
  Oysters à la Gino, 296
  Peperoni Don Salvatore, 392
  Pineapple Monte Carlo, 211
  Potted Shrimp, 177
  Quiche Lorraine, 45
  Rollmops, 162
  Shrimp à la Sardi, Hot, 255
  Skewered Chicken in Sesame Soy Sauce, 359
  Soused Mackerel, 164
  Stuffed Cucumbers Norwegian Style, 138
  Stuffed Green Peppers, 214
  Taheeni, 427
  Tempura, 396
  Teriyaki Steak Skewers, 358
  Terrine de Ris de Veau, La, 59
  Terrine of Sweetbreads, 59
APPLE(S):
  Bread, 439
  Cake, Danish, 146
  Cake, Dutch, 437
  Pancake, 240
  Pie Filling, 438
  Pudding, Steamed, 160
  Tart, 111
  and Truffle Salad, 53
Apricot Mousse, 306
Arroz con Dulce, 221
Artichoke Hearts, Garnished, 95
Asopao de Pollo, 217
ASPARAGUS:
  Dutch Style, 122
  Milanese, 257
  Vinaigrette, 256
Aspic, Chicken, 53
Aspic, Fish, 58

Atjar Ketimun, 126
Aurorian Sauce, 426
Avocado Spread, 213
Avocados Stuffed with Hot Crabmeat, 360

B

Baccalà alla Vicentina, 104
Bacon Dressing, 402
Baked Alaska Omelet, 327
Baked Custard, 215
BANANA(S):
  Baked, 363
  Nut Bread, 363
  Pancake Flambé Stonehenge, 286
Barley, Baked Egg, 413
Bass, Baked Whole Sea, 316
BATTER:
  for Deep Frying, 93, 265, 396
  for Pancakes, 240
  for Vegetables, 130
Batter-Fried Tidbits, 396
Bean Soup, 68
Bean Soup, Black, 218
Beans, Boston Baked, 401
Beans Lyonnaise, String, 83
Béarnaise Sauce, 201, 351; blender, 426
Béchamel Sauce, 424
BEEF:
  Fillets with Madeira and Truffle Sauce, 47
  Roast, 156
  Roast Fillet of, 288
  Slices, Marinated, 352
  Soup with Marrow, 247
  Steak Tartar, 245
  Stew Burgundy Style, 266
  Stew, Javanese, 128
Beefsteak, Dutch, 129
Beet Soup, Cold, 428
Belle Orange, 138
Besugo a la Vizcáina, 194
BEVERAGES:
  Bloody Mary, 416
  Café Brûlot Diabolique, 324
  Chablis Cassis, 324
  Hanaho ("Come Again!" Rum Punch), 366
  Iced Coffee, 413
  Iced Tea, 413
  Tea, Hot or Iced, How to Make, 178
BISCUITS:
  Cheese Knots, 440
  Fruit Turnovers, 440
  Honey Buns, 440
  Jam, 440
  Rich, 440
Black Bean Soup, 218
Blintzes, Cheese, 346
Blom's Black Pot, 142
Bloody Mary, 416
Blue Cheese Salad Dressing, 429
Blueberry Muffins La Posada, 336
Blueberry Pie Filling, 438
Boccone Dolce, 254
Boeuf à la Bourguignonne, 266
Boeuf Crémaillère, Filet de, 288
Boiled Dinner, New England, 294
Boiled Dressing, 174
Bookbinder's Seafood Cocktail Sauce, 314

INDEX

Bookbinder's Snapper Soup, 314
Borscht, 428
Boston Baked Beans, 401
Boston Brown Bread, Steamed, 285
Bouillon, Vegetable, 304
Brandy Sauce, 287
Brandy Snaps, 407
Bread Crumbs, 423
BREAD(s): see also Biscuits; Muffins
  Apple, 439
  Banana Nut, 363
  Cinnamon Nut, 439
  Coffee Ring, 437
  Corn, 318
  Corn Sticks, 337
  Cracked Wheat, 437
  Cranberry, 439
  Date, 437
  Dinner Rolls, 437
  Dutch Apple Cake, 437
  French, 436
  French Toast Santa Fe, 334
  Gingerbread, 174
  Herb, 408
  House, 408
  Hungarian Coffeecake, 438
  Nut, 437
  Pan Rolls, 437
  Pineapple Nut, 364
  Pudding, Old-Fashioned, 412
  Rye Molasses, 437
  Sally Lunn, 440
  Sauce, 184
  Sopaipillas (Fried Puffs), 337
  Spoon, with Virginia Ham, 305
  Steamed Boston Brown, 285
  Streusel, 439
  Stuffing, 284
  Swedish Tea Ring, 437
  Sweet, 437
  Tea Scones, 172
  Whole Wheat, 286
  Yeast, 436
Breadfruit, Stuffed Roast, 362
Breakfast Bread, 439
Breast of Capon au Whiskey, 395
Breast of Chicken au Champagne, 344
Breast of Pheasant Sous Cloche, 325
Breasts of Chicken Tropical, 220
Breasts of Guinea Hen, Smitane, 385
Brochet, Pâté de, 57
Brochet au Volnay, 78
Brochette des Corsaires, 35
Brown Sauce, 425
Brown Stock, 435
Brown and White Cookies, 441
Buckingham Eggs, 165
Buckwheat Griddle Cakes, 286
BUTTER(s):
  Clarified, 435
  Crayfish, 57
  Cream, 34
  Cream, Chocolate, 430
  Garlic, 427
  Herb, 427
  Sauce, 78
  Snail, 83

BUTTER(s): (continued)
  Sweet, Made in Blender, 427
  Watercress, 427
Butterfly Steak Hong Kong, 232
Buttermilk Waffles, 335

C

Cabbage Leaves Stuffed with Meat, 382
Cabbage and Mutton, 142
Caesar Salad, 185
Café Brûlot Diabolique, 324
CAKE(s):
  Amstel Ginger, 123
  Cheese, 317
  Chocolate Layer, 173
  with Custard Cream, 212
  Danish Apple, 146
  Dark Mocha, 415
  Dutch Apple, 437
  Fruit, 172
  Génoise, 247
  Glaze for, 247
  Haarlem Celebration, 127
  Hungarian Coffee, 438
  Madeira, 107
  Marjolaine, 33
  Meringue-Nut, 33
  Orange Liqueur, 61
  Sunshine with Chocolate Almond
    Frosting, 414
  Walnut, with Marzipan, 141
CALF'S LIVER:
  with Avocado, 266
  with Onions and White Wine, 106
  in Wine, 245
Canard, Dodine de, 59
Caneton Tour d'Argent, 71
CANNELLONI:
  Chicken with Cream Sauce, 94
  au Gratin with Sardi Sauce, 257
  alla Passetto, 94
Cantábric Sole Ritz, 196
Cantonese Sauce, 317
Caper Sauce, 160
Capon au Whiskey, Breast of, 395
Carciofi Vignarola, 95
Caribbee Sauce, 351
Carré de Veau à la Duxelles, 120
Carrot Vichyssoise, 264
Casserolettes de Filets de Sole Lasserre, 44
Celery, Braised, 278
Ceviche, 213
Chablis Cassis, 324
Champignons Grillés Marie Victoire, 406
Charles Farrell Salad, 375
CHEESE:
  and Bacon Tart, 45
  Blintzes, 346
  Cake, 317
  Dip, 427
  Ham Sandwich, Toasted, 84
  Knots, 440
  Shrimps, and Mayonnaise Sandwich, 143
  Soup, Vermont, 264
  Stuffed, 214
Cherry Pie Filling, 439
Chestnut Puree in Meringue Nests, 112

INDEX

CHICKEN: see also Game Hens; Poultry Dishes
 with Bread Sauce, Roast, 184
 Breast of, au Champagne, 344
 Breasts in Aspic, Garland of, 53
 Breasts of, Tropical, 220
 Cannelloni with Cream Sauce, 94
 and Celery Salad, 123
 in Champagne Sauce, 267
 Chichén Itzá, 211
 Cooked in Leaves, 211
 Curry, 230
 with Curry Sauce, 54
 Forcemeat, 53; blender, 429
 Fricassee, Spicy, 197
 Friday, 409
 Hash, Pump Room, 348
 How to Bone, 96
 Hunter's Style with Noodles, 105
 Livers en Brochette, 275
 Livers Sautéed with Apples and Onion
  Rings, 244
 and Long Rice, 362
 with Mushrooms and Lobster, Braised, 124
 with Onions, Bacon, and Mushrooms,
  Ragout of, 54
 Paella, "Good Friend," 198
 Pepitoria, 197
 in Pineapple, 221
 Pyramide, 32
 in Red Wine, 122
 and Rice, 217
 and Rice with Almonds, Olives, and
  Mushrooms, 198
 Salad, Curried, 373
 Sauce, 336
 in Sesame Soy Sauce, Skewered, 359
 and Spaghetti Casserole, 256
 and Steak in Red Wine, 142
 Stock, 435
 Sweet and Hot, 411
 Tetrazzini au Gratin, Émincé of, 256
 Valadier, Boned, 96
 Velouté Sauce, 424
 and Virginia Ham Shortcake, 318
 with White Wine Sauce in Paper, 70
Chili Poblano Soup, 216
Chilies Poblanos Rellenos, 214
Chinese Roast Pork, 233
CHOCOLATE:
 Almond Frosting, 414
 Butter Cream, 430
 Cups, 38
 Filling and Topping, 343
 Ice Cream, French, 441
 Icing and Filling, 173
 Layer Cake, 173
 Mousse, Individual, 407
 Pudding, Molded, 430
 Roll, Whitehall, 343
 Rum Sauce, 349
 Wafers, 34
Chowder, New England Clam, 296
Cinnamon Nut Bread, 439
Clam Chowder, New England, 296
Clams Mariner's Style, 202
Clarified Butter, 435
Clear Soup with Meat and Vegetables, 343
Cocktail Sauce, 200

Cocktail Sauce, Bookbinder's Seafood, 314
Coconut Milk and Cream, 429
Coconut Rice Pudding, 221
Codfish, Braised Salt, 104
Coeur à la Crème, 60
COFFEE:
 Iced, 413
 Icing, French, 415
 Rings, 437
 Sherbet, 203
Coffeecake, Hungarian, 438
Colcannon, 184
Coleslaw, 376
Consommé Farley, 200
Consommé Stracciatella, 109
COOKIES:
 Brandy Snaps, 407
 Brown and White, 441
 Drop, 441
 Oatmeal Lace, 307
 Scotch Shortbread, 177
Coq au Vin Rouge à l'Avergnate, 122
Coquelet à la Moutarde, Le, 55
Coquille of Lobster Savannah, 294
Coquille Maison, 383
Coquilles St. Jacques Baumanière, 80
Corn Bread, 318
Corn, Mexican Creamed, 217
Corn Sticks, 337
Cornish Pasties, 182
Cornmeal Muffins, 285
Cornmeal with Mushrooms, 110
Coupe Gertrude Lawrence, 349
Coupe Glacée Baumanière, 81
CRAB:
 Deviled, 315
 Haleakala, 360
 Legs Sauté Grenobloise, 372
 with Mustard Mayonnaise, Dungeness, 372
 Puffs, 360
Crabmeat, Virginia, 274
Cracked Wheat Bread, 437
Cranberry Bread, 439
CRAYFISH:
 Butter, 57
 Tails à la Carlton, 139
 Tails with Sauce Nantua, 56
CREAM:
 Cheese Hearts, 60
 Pastry, Thick, 79
 Pastry, Thin (Vanilla Custard), 212
 Sauce, 80, 106; blender, 424
 Swedish, 148
Crema de Malaga, 202
Crème Brûlée, 163
Crêpes Sir Holden, 199
Crepes (with Sugar), 240, 384
Crepes (without Sugar), 374
Crepes Tivoli (Cream-Filled with Fruit
 Sauce), 384
Croque-Monsieur, 84
Crostata di Mele, 111
Croustade de Barbue Lagrene, 68
Croutons, 304
Crown Roast of Veal, Stuffed, 412
Crullers, Rice Meal, 219

INDEX

CUCUMBER(S):
  Fried, 130
  Marinated, 126
  Norwegian Style, Stuffed, 138
  Salad, 139
  Soup, Cold, 382
Cumberland Sauce, 182
Currant Pasty, 175
Curried Chicken Salad, 373
Curried Lima Bean Soup, 428
CURRY:
  Chicken, 230
  East Indian Fish, 231
  Sauce, 55
  Sauce, Mild, 201
  Sauce, Simple, 159
Custard, Baked, 215
Custard Cream, Vanilla, 212
Custard, Rice, 277
Custard Sauce, 161
Custards, 107

D

Dadar Djawa, 126
Daging Rudjak, 128
DANISH:
  Apple Cake, 146
  Open Sandwiches, 143
  Pastry, 147
Dansk Kage, 147
Date Bread, 437
DESSERTS:
  Aeblekage, 146
  Amstel Ginger Cake, 123
  Apple Pancake, 240
  Apple Pie, 438
  Apple Tart, 111
  Apricot Mousse, 306
  Arroz con Dulce, 221
  Baked Alaska Omelet, 327
  Baked Custard, 215
  Baked Indian Pudding, 298
  Banana Pancake Flambé Stonehenge, 286
  Belle Orange, 138
  Blueberry Pie, 438
  Boccone Dolce, 254
  Cake with Custard Cream, 212
  Cheesecake, 317
  Cherry Pie, 439
  Chestnut Puree in Meringue Nests, 112
  Coconut Rice Pudding, 221
  Coeur à la Crème, 60
  Coffee Sherbet, 203
  Coupe Gertrude Lawrence, 349
  Coupe Glacée Baumanière, 81
  Cream Cheese Hearts, 60
  Crema de Malaga, 202
  Crème Brûlée, 163
  Crêpes Sir Holden, 199
  Crepes Tivoli (Cream-Filled with Fruit Sauce), 384
  Crostata di Mele, 111
  Currant Pasty, 175
  Danish Apple Cake, 146
  Danish Pastry, 147
  Dansk Kage, 147
  Dark Mocha Cake, 415

DESSERT(S): (continued)
  Diana Torte, 414
  Emperor's Omelet, 241
  Flaming Soufflé Pancakes, 45
  Flan, 215
  Flan Soufflé al Miel, 203
  French Chocolate Ice Cream, 441
  Fruit Cake, 172
  Gâteau Grand Marnier, 61
  Gingerbread, 174
  Grand Marnier Soufflé, 72
  Haarlem Celebration Cake, 127
  Hazelnut Ice Cream, 93
  Hazelnut Torte, 246
  Ice Cream with Chestnuts and Chocolate Sauce, 81
  Ice Cream with Chocolate Rum Sauce, 349
  Ice Cream Cup alla Danieli, 108
  Ice Cream Cups, 38
  Iced Lemon Soufflé, 168
  Individual Chocolate Mousse, 407
  Instant Fruit Mousse, 429
  Italian Tipsy Pudding, 107
  Kaiserschmarrn, 241
  La Fonda Pudding, 338
  Lemon Meringue Pie, 439
  Lemon and Strawberry Surprise, 186
  Little Pancakes Filled with Cheese, 374
  Lüchow's German Pancake, 240
  Malaga Cream, 202
  Monte Bianco, 112
  Nusstorte, 246
  Old-Fashioned Bread Pudding, 412
  Omelette Norvégienne, 327
  Orange Liqueur Cake, 61
  Orange Zabaglione, 202
  Pannequets au Fromage d'Emmenthal, 374
  Pannequets Soufflés Flambés, 45
  Passion Fruit Chiffon Pie, 365
  Pavé au Chocolat, 430
  Pineapple Meringue Pie, 364
  Pot de Crème Chocolat, 407
  Raspberry Tart, 79
  Rice Custard, 277
  Saboyan de Naranja, 202
  Sherbet Castle, 415
  Sorbete de Café, 203
  Soufflé Custard with Honey, 203
  Soufflé au Grand Marnier, 72
  Soufflé Pudding Pierre, 231
  Soufflé Rothschild (with Glacéed Fruits), 347
  Soup Anglaise, 212
  Spumoni, 93
  Steamed Apple Pudding, 160
  Strawberry-Rhubarb Pie, 439
  Strawberries Puiwa, 232
  Sunshine Cake with Chocolate Almond Frosting, 414
  Sweet Mouthful, 254
  Tarte aux Framboises, 79
  Trifle, 166
  Walnut Cake with Marzipan, 141
  Whitehall Chocolate Roll, 343
Deviled Crab, 315
Deviled Rib Bones, 157
Diana Torte, 414
Dip, Cheese, 427

445

INDEX

Dip, Lebanese Cocktail, 427
Dodine de Canard, 59
Drei Mignons à la Berliner, 246
DRESSING(S):
  Bacon, 402
  for Baked Peppers, 392
  for Belgian Endive, 326
  Blue Cheese Salad, 429
  Boiled, 174
  for Egg and Potato Salad, 162
  Egg Salad, 410
  French, 276
  Salad, 304
  Sour Cream, 145
  Spiced Vinegar, Racquet Club, 375
  Vinaigrette, 256
Drop Cookies, 441
Duchess Potatoes, 316
DUCK:
  Boned Stuffed, 59
  in Cognac Sauce, 137
  Flambé Belle Terrasse, Wild, 137
  Frederic's Pressed, 71
Duckling, Polynesian Coconut, 361
Dumplings Embassy, Fish, 47
Dumplings, Potato, 242
Dungeness Crab with Mustard Mayonnaise, 372
DUTCH:
  Apple Cake, 437
  Asparagus, 122
  Beefsteak, 129
  Green Pea Soup, 120
  Meat Balls, 128

E
East Indian Fish Curry, 231
EGG(S):
  Barley, Baked, 413
  Buckingham, 165
  Harlequin, Poached, 336
  How to Poach, 336
  and Potato Salad Boulestin, 162
  Ranch, 335
  Salad Dressing, 410
  Scrambled and Smoked Salmon
    Sandwich, 144
  and Spinach Grisanti, 308
  and Wine Sauce, 347
Eggplant, Stuffed (with Crabmeat), 328
El Gran Frou Frou, 201
Elfo's Special, 307
Elote Con Crema a la Mexicana, 217
El Pescador, 220
Emperor's Omelet, 241
Endive and Beet Salad, 326
Endive Salad, Belgian, 326
Escalope de Veau Marseillais, 350
Escargots Bourguignonne, 83

F
Farfel Pilaf, 413
Fegato alla Veneziana, 106
Fettuccine alla Buranella, 103
FILLET(S):
  Filet de Boeuf Crémaillère, 288
  Filet Mignon Caesar Augustus, 277
  Filets de Sole Cardinal, 70
  Filets de Sole Pierre Le Grand, 121

FILLET(S): (continued)
  Filets de Sole au Vermouth, 81
  Fillet of Beef, Roast, 288
  Fillet of Plaice La Belle Sole, 140
  Fillet of Sole à la Stephen, 143
  Fillet of Veal with Mushrooms, 44
  Fillets Berlin Style, Three, 246
  Fillets of Lamb with Onion Sauce, 69
  Fillets of Sole with Crayfish, 70
  Fillets of Sole in Cream Aspic, 410
  Fillets of Sole with Vermouth Sauce, 81
  Fillets of Sole with Wine Sauce,
    Poached, 121
  Fillets Zeeland, Fish, 124
FILLING: see also Stuffing
  for Cheese Blintzes, 346
  for Chilies, 214
  for Chocolate Layer Cake, 173
  Chocolate for Whitehall Roll, 343
FISH:
  Aspic, 58
  Curry, East Indian, 231
  Dumplings Embassy, 47
  Fillets Zeeland, 124
  Forcemeat, 58, 70; blender, 428
  Marinated, 213, 359
  Pudding with Mushroom Cream Sauce, 145
  with Soufflé Sauce, 68
  Soup, 104
  Stock, 57, 297, 436
  Velouté, 424
  with Wine Sauce, Baked Stuffed, 34
FISH DISHES:
  Almejas a la Marinera, 202
  Assorted Seafood on Skewers, 35
  Avocados Stuffed with Hot Crabmeat, 360
  Baccalà alla Vicentina, 104
  Baked Opakapaka, 358
  Baked Stuffed Fish with Wine Sauce, 34
  Baked Whole Sea Bass, 316
  Besugo a la Vizcaína, 194
  Braised Salt Codfish, 104
  Brochet au Volnay, 78
  Broiled Trout with Cucumber Salad, 139
  Burgundian Snails, 83
  Cantábric Sole Ritz, 196
  Cape Cod Scallops Sauté Meunière, 295
  Casserolettes de Filets de Sole Lasserre, 44
  Ceviche, 213
  Clams, Mariner's Style, 202
  Cold Pike Pâté, 57
  Coquille of Lobster Savannah, 294
  Coquille Maison, 383
  Coquilles St. Jacques Baumanière, 80
  Crab Haleakala, 360
  Crabmeat Virginia, 274
  Crayfish Tails à la Carlton, 139
  Crayfish Tails with Sauce Nantua, 56
  Crisped Shrimp with Mustard Fruit, 265
  Croustade de Barbue Lagrene, 68
  Deviled Crab, 315
  Dumplings Embassy, 47
  Dungeness Crab with Mustard
    Mayonnaise, 372
  East Indian Fish Curry, 231
  Elfo's Special, 307
  Escargots Bourguignonne, 83
  Filets de Sole Cardinal, 70

FISH DISHES: (continued)
  Filets de Sole Pierre Le Grand, 121
  Filets de Sole au Vermouth, 81
  Fillets of Plaice La Belle Sole, 140
  Fillet of Sole à la Stephen, 143
  Fillets of Sole with Crayfish, 70
  Fillets of Sole in Cream Aspic, 410
  Fillets of Sole with Vermouth Sauce, 81
  Fillets of Sole with Wine Sauce,
    Poached, 121
  Fillets Zeeland, 124
  Frogs' Legs Polonaise, 255
  Gratin de Queues d'Écrevisses, 56
  Gravad Lax, Grilled, 146
  Grilled Marinated Salmon, 146
  Haitian Lobster, 351
  Herring in Dill Sauce, 244
  Kedgeree of Salmon, 158
  Kinilau, 359
  Langosta a la Mallorquina, 218
  Langoustine Mimosa, 233
  Levens Hall Poached Salmon, 174
  Little Pastry Casseroles of Fillet of Sole, 44
  Lobster Cantonese, 316
  Lobster Omelet, 234
  Lobster Titus, 200
  Mackerel, Soused, 164
  Marinated Fish, 213, 359
  Moules à la Normande, 82
  Mussels in Cream, 82
  Mussels with Saffron, 163
  Noodles with Fish and Shrimp, 103
  Oysters à la Foch, 325
  Oysters à la Gino, 296
  Pâté de Brochet, 57
  Pike in Red Wine, 78
  Planked Fish with Coconut Sauce, 358
  Pudding with Mushroom Cream Sauce, 145
  Quenelles Ambassade, 47
  Salmon in Pastry, 167
  Sauté de Scupions à la Niçoise, 36
  Scallop Shells with Baby Lobster Tails, 383
  Scallops in Cream Sauce, 80
  Scampi Aurora, 108
  Scampi Flamingo, 102
  Scampi alla Livornese, 392
  Sea Bream Biscay Style, 194
  Shrimp with Hollandaise Sauce au
    Gratin, 108
  Shrimp du Jour, 315
  Shrimp à la Sardi, Hot, 255
  Shrimp in Sherry Cream Sauce, 102
  Soufflé-Topped Lobster, 218
  Soup, Mediterranean Fish, 195
  Spaghetti with Shrimp and Mushrooms,
    Buttered, 307
  Squid with Tomato and Anchovies, 36
  Stuffed Sole Poached in Meursault, 56
  Stuffed Sole Ritz, 196
  Stuffed Trout, Fernand Point, 32
  Truite Farcie Fernand Point, 32
Flan, 215
Flan Soufflé al Miel, 203
FONDS:
  Blanc, 435
  Brun, 435
  de Poisson Blanc, 436
Fondue Bourguignonne, 201

Fondue, Cheese, 374
Fondue de Poulet Papa Bergerand, La, 54
FORCEMEAT:
  Chicken, 53; blender, 429
  Fish, 58, 70; blender, 428
  Pork, 59
  Pork-Veal, 60
Frankfurter Skewers, 359
Frankfurters, Stuffed, 400
Franks, Western, 400
FRENCH:
  Bread, 436
  Chocolate Ice Cream, 441
  Coffee Icing, 415
  Dressing, 276
  Toast, Santa Fe, 334
Friday Chicken, 409
Fried Foods, Roman Style, Assorted, 92
Fritto Misto alla Romana, 92
Frogs' Legs Polonaise, 255
FRUIT:
  Cake, 172
  Mousse, Instant, 429
  Sauce, 385
  Soup, Scandinavian, 148
  Turnovers, 440

G

GAME HENS:
  in Clay, 393
  with Grapes, 196
  with Mustard, Roast, 55
  with Sauce Diable, Boned Stuffed, 36
  with Wild Rice and Orange Sauce, 306
Garlic Sauce, 201
Garlic Soup, 219
Gâteau Grand Marnier, 61
Gâteau Marjolaine, 33
Gazpacho Andaluz, 194
Gazpacho, Racquet Club, 373
Génoise, 247
Georgia Salad, 276
Giblet Gravy, 284
Gingerbread, 174
Ginger Cake, Amstel, 123
Glaze for Cake, 247
Glaze, Red Currant, 147
Gnocchi, 394
Gourmandise Brillat-Savarin, 44
Grand Marnier Soufflé, 72
Grand Succès Réserve, Le, 38
Gratin de Queues d'Écrevisses, 56
Gratin Savoyard, Le, 61
Gravad Lax, Grilled, 146
Gravy, Giblet, 284
Gravy, Roast Beef, 156
Green Peppers, Baked, 392
Green Peppers, Stuffed, 214
Green Salad, Mixed, 304
Griddle Cakes, Buckwheat, 286.
Grouse in Cream, 140
Guacamole, 213
Guindilla, 202
Guinea Hen Smitane, Breasts of, 385
Guinea Hen with Brandy Sauce,
    Cocotte of, 287
Guirlande de Suprêmes en Gelée, 53
Gurkas Norge, 138

INDEX

447

INDEX

H

Haarlem Celebration Cake, 127
Haitian Lobster, 351
HAM:
   with Chablis, Braised, 58
   and Cheese Sandwich, Toasted, 84
   and Liver Paste Sandwich, 144
   with Parsley, Jellied, 78
   Stock, 78
   Stuffed Smoked, 411
   Virginia, and Chicken Shortcake, 318
Hamburgers, Barbecued Double, 401
Hanaho (Rum Punch), 366
Hard Sauce, 175
Hare Soup, 158
Haricots Verts à la Lyonnaise, 83
Hash, Pump Room Chicken, 348
Hazelnut Ice Cream, 93
Hazelnut Torte, 246
Herb Bread, 408
Herb Sauce, 167
Herring in Dill Sauce, 244
Herring Salad, 144
Hollandaise Sauce, 57, 383; blender, 426
Hollandsche Biefstuk, 129
Honey Buns, 440
Hot Pot, Lancashire, 166
Hotchpotch of Curly Kale, 129
House Bread, 408
HOW TO:
   Bone a Chicken, 96
   Make Tea, Hot or Iced, 178
   Poach Eggs, 336
Hungarian Coffeecake, 438
Hunter's Pie, 183

I

ICE CREAM:
   with Chestnuts and Chocolate Sauce, 81
   with Chocolate Rum Sauce, 349
   Cup alla Danieli, 108
   Cups, 38
   French Chocolate, 441
   Hazelnut, 93
   Spumoni, 93
ICING:
   Chocolate, 173, 343
   Chocolate Almond, 414
   French Coffee, 415
   Glaze, 247
   Glaze, Red Currant, 147
   Lemon, 173
Indian Pudding, Baked, 298
Indonesian Fried Rice, 126
Italian Tipsy Pudding, 107

J

Jam Biscuits, 440
Jambon Chaud à la Chablisienne, Le, 58
Jambon Persillé à la Bourguignonne, 78
Javanese Beef Stew, 128
Javanese Omelet, 126
Jellied Madrilene Salad with Egg Salad
   Dressing, 410

K

Kaaldolmer, 382
Kaiserschmarrn, 241
Kale, Hotchpotch of Curly, 129
Kalua Pig, 365
Kalvfilet Oskar, 384
Kartoffel Klösse, 242
Kedgeree of Salmon, 158
Kidneys, Veal, 80
King Crab Legs Sauté Grenobloise, 372
Kinilau, 359
Königsberger Klops, 243
Kraft Suppe, 247

L

La Fonda Pudding, 338
LAMB: see also Mixed Grill
   with Caper Sauce, Boiled Leg of, 160
   on a Skewer, 348
   with Onion Sauce, Fillets of, 69
Lancashire Hot Pot, 166
Lancaster Pork Pie, 176
Langosta a la Mallorquina, 218
Langoustine Mimosa, 233
LASAGNE:
   Casserole, Green, 106
   How to Make, 106
   Verdi alla Bolognese, 106
Lebanese Cocktail Dip, 427
LEMON:
   Icing, 173
   Meringue Pie, 439
   Soufflé, Iced, 168
   and Strawberry Surprise, 186
Levens Hall Poached Salmon, 174
Lima Bean Soup, Curried, 428
LIVER:
   Calf's, with Avocado, 266
   Calf's, with Onions and White Wine, 106
   Calf's, in Wine, 245
Liver Paste and Ham Sandwich, 144
Livers, Chicken, en Brochette, 275
Livers, Chicken, Sautéed with Apples and
   Onion Rings, 244
LOBSTER:
   Bisque, 297
   Bisque Dewey, 275
   Cantonese, 316
   Haitian, 351
   Omelet, 234
   Savannah, Coquille of, 294
   Soufflé-Topped, 218
   Titus, 200
Lombatina di Vitella alla Passetto, 95
London Broil, 254
Loup Réserve Beaulieu, 34
Lüchow's German Pancake, 240
Lüchow's Sauerbraten mit Kartoffel Klösse, 242
Lung Ha Foo Young, 234

M

Mackerel, Soused, 164
Madeira Cake, 107
Madeira Sauce, 47, 69, 325
Malaga Cream, 202

INDEX

Marinade for Fish, 213, 360
Marinade for Lamb, 349
Marinade for Teriyaki Steak, 358
Marinated Fish, 213, 359
Marjolaine Cake, 33
Mayonnaise blender, 424
Mayonnaise, Green, 425
Mayonnaise, Mustard, 372
MEAT:
  Balls with Caper and Sardellen Sauce, 243
  Balls, Dutch, 128
  Lucullus, Raw, 245
  Sauce for Lasagne, 106
  Sauce, Sardi's, 258
  Sauce for Spaghetti, 92
  and Vegetables, Fried Roman Style, 92
MEAT DISHES:
  Barbecued Double Hamburgers, 401
  Beef Fillets with Madeira and Truffle Sauce, 47
  Beef Steak Tartar, 245
  Beef Stew Burgundy Style, 266
  Boeuf à la Bourguignonne, 266
  Braised Ham with Chablis, 58
  Butterfly Steak Hong Kong, 232
  Cabbage Leaves Stuffed with Meat, 382
  Calf's Liver with Avocado, 266
  Calf's Liver with Onions and White Wine, 106
  Calf's Liver in Wine, 245
  Carré de Veau à la Duxelles, 120
  Chinese Roast Pork, 233
  Cornish Pasties, 182
  Daging Rudjak, 128
  Deviled Rib Bones, 157
  Drei Mignons à la Berliner, 246
  Dutch Beefsteak, 129
  Dutch Meat Balls, 128
  Escalope de Veau Marseillais, 350
  Fegato alla Veneziana, 106
  Filet de Boeuf Crémaillère, 288
  Filet Mignon Caesar Augustus, 277
  Fillet of Veal with Mushrooms, 44
  Fillets Berlin Style, Three, 246
  Fillets of Lamb with Onion Sauce, 69
  Flamed Mustard Steak, 137
  Flaming Shashlik, 348
  Gourmandise Brillat-Savarin, 44
  Green Lasagne Casserole, 106
  Green Noodle Casserole with Prosciutto, 109
  Hollandsche Biefstuk, 129
  Hunter's Pie, 183
  Jambon Chaud à la Chablisienne, Le, 58
  Jambon Persillé à la Bourguignonne, 78
  Javanese Beef Stew, 128
  Jellied Ham with Parsley, 78
  Kaaldolmer, 382
  Kalua Pig, 365
  Kalvfilet Oskar, 384
  Königsberger Klops, 243
  Lamb with Caper Sauce, Boiled Leg of, 160
  Lamb on a Skewer, 348
  Lancashire Hot Pot, 166
  Lancaster Pork Pie, 176
  Lasagne Verdi alla Bolognese, 106
  Lombatina di Vitella alla Passetto, 95
  London Broil, 254

MEAT DISHES: (continued)
  Lüchow's Sauerbraten mit Kartoffel Klösse, 242
  Marinated Beef Slices, 352
  Meat Balls with Caper and Sardellen Sauce, 243
  Meat and Vegetables, Fried Roman Style, 92
  Medallions of Breaded Veal in Parmesan and Grated Lemon Zest, 265
  Melton Mowbray Pie, 176
  Mixed Grill, 274
  Mutton and Cabbage, 142
  New England Boiled Dinner, 294
  Osso Bucco alla Milanese, 102
  Pig Roasted in Pit, 365
  Pork Cutlets Escorial, 198
  Pot Roast with Potato Dumplings, 242
  Raw Meat Lucullus, 245
  Ris de Veau à la Crème, 350
  Roast Beef, 156
  Roast Fillet of Beef, 288
  Roast Pork Castilian Style, 195
  Roast Stuffed Rib of Veal, 120
  Rognons de Veau, 80
  Sateh Babi, 125
  Sauerbraten à la Mode in Aspic, Cold, 243
  Saure Leber, 245
  Sausage, Wayside Country, 284
  Scaloppine di Vitella alla Passetto, 94
  Schlemmerschnitte, 245
  Schnitzel à la Lüchow, 241
  Skewered Pork, 125
  Steak Chevillot, 79
  Steak and Chicken in Red Wine, 142
  Steak Diane, 345
  Steak Moutarde Flambé, 137
  Steak au Poivre, 346
  Stuffed Crown Roast of Veal, 412
  Stuffed Frankfurters, 400
  Stuffed Smoked Ham, 411
  Sweetbreads in Cream, 350
  Tagliatelle Verdi Gratinate al Prosciutto, 109
  Terrine de Ris de Veau, La, 59
  Terrine of Sweetbreads, 59
  Toad-in-the-Hole, 164
  Tripe and Onions, 159
  Veal Chops with Mushroom Sauce, 95
  Veal Cutlets Cordon Bleu, 386
  Veal Cutlets with Crab Legs, 384
  Veal Cutlets à la Lüchow, 241
  Veal Kidneys, 80
  Veal with Mushrooms, Fillet of, 44
  Veal Scallops with Crabmeat, 350
  Veal Scallops au Gratin, 94
  Veal Shinbones Braised with Vegetables, 102
  Western Franks, 400
Mediterranean Fish Soup, 195
Melton Mowbray Pie, 176
Meringue, 212, 327, 438
Meringue Nests, 112
Meringue-Nut Cake, 33
Mexican Creamed Corn, 217
Mignons à la Berliner, Drei, 246
Mixed Grill, 274
Mocha Cake, Dark, 415
Monte Bianco, 112
Montezuma Pie, 216
Mornay Sauce, 424

INDEX

Moules à la Normande, 82
Mousse, Apricot, 306
Mousse, Instant Fruit, 429
Muffins, Blueberry, La Posada, 336
Muffins, Cornmeal, 285
MUSHROOM(S):
    with Braised Celery, Puree of, 278
    in Cream, 183
    Cream Sauce, 145
    Mary Victoria, Broiled, 406
    Pasticcio di Polenta, 110
    Puree of, 278
    Sauce, 95
    Soup with Parmesan Cheese, 110
    in Sour Cream, 248
    Truffle and Tongue Salad, 268
Mussels in Cream, 82
Mussels with Saffron, 163
Mustard Mayonnaise, 372
Mustard Sauce, 55, 146
Mutton and Cabbage, 142

N

Nantua Sauce, 57
Napkin Folding:
    Cactus, 418
    Fleur-de-Lis, 420
    Lily, 418
    Lotus, 417
    Mitre, 419
    Palm Leaf, 418
Nasi Goreng, 126
New England Boiled Dinner, 294
New England Clam Chowder, 296
Noisettes des Tournelles, 69
Noodle Casserole with Prosciutto, Green, 109
Noodles with Fish and Shrimp, 103
Noodles, How to Make, 106
Nusstorte, 246
Nut Bread, 437

O

Oatmeal Lace Cookies, 307
Omelet, Emperor's, 241
Omelet, Javanese, 126
Omelet, Lobster, 234
Omelette Norvégienne, 327
ONION(S):
    Sauce (Soubise), 69
    Soup, 46
    and Tripe, 159
Opakapaka, Baked, 358
ORANGE:
    Belle, 138
    Liqueur Cake, 61
    Pancakes, Harvey Girl Special
        Little Thin, 334
    Sauce, 306
    Zabaglione, 202
Osso Bucco alla Milanese, 102
OYSTER(S):
    à la Foch, 325
    à la Gino, 296
    Velouté, 327

P

Paella "Good Friend", 198
Paella à la Valenciana, 199
Panada, 217
PANCAKE(S): see also Crepes; Griddle
    Apple, 240
    Batter, 240
    Blintzes, 346
    Filled with Cheese, Little, 374
    Flambé Stonehenge, Banana, 286
    Flaming Soufflé, 45
    Kaiserschmarrn, 241
    Lüchow's German, 240
    Orange, Harvey Girl Special
        Little Thin, 334
Pannequets au Fromage d'Emmenthal, 374
Pannequets Soufflés Flambés, 45
Papaya, Candied, 363
Paprika Sauce, Hot, 201
Passion Fruit Chiffon Pies, 365
Pasticcio di Polenta, 110
Pasties, Cornish, 182
PASTRY, 46, 176
    Casseroles, 44
    Cream, Thick, 79
    Cream, Thin (Vanilla Custard), 212
    Danish, 147
    Rich, 438
Pasty, Currant, 175
Pâté de Brochet, 57
Pâté, Cold Pike, 57
Pavé au Chocolat, 430
PEA(S):
    with Artichoke Hearts, Ring Mold of, 305
    with Lettuce, Little, 82
    with Rice, Venetian, 105
    Soup, Famous Dutch Green, 120
Peperoni Don Salvatore, 392
Pepitas a la Curry, 204
Pepper Steak, 346
Pepper and Tomato Sauce, 335
Pesce Royal Danieli, Zuppa di, 104
Petite Marmite Henry IV, 343
Petits Pois à la Française, 82
Pheasant Sous Cloche, Breast of, 325
PIE:
    Apple, 438
    Blueberry, 438
    Cherry, 439
    Hunter's, 183
    Lemon Meringue, 439
    Melton Mowbray (Lancaster Pork), 176
    Montezuma, 216
    Passion Fruit Chiffon, 365
    Pineapple Meringue, 364
    Strawberry-Rhubarb, 439
    Two-Crust, One-Crust Shell, 438
Pig Roasted in Pit, 365
Pike Pâté, Cold, 57
Pike in Red Wine, 78
Pineapple Meringue Pie, 364
Pineapple Monte Carlo, 211
Pineapple Nut Bread, 364
Plaice La Belle Sole, Fillet of, 140
Planked Fish with Coconut Sauce, 358
Polenta, 110
Pollo alla Cacciatora, 105

INDEX

Pollo Disossato Valadier, 96
Polynesian Coconut Duckling, 361
Pomme de Terre Macaire, 268
PORK:
  Castilian Style, Roast, 195
  Chinese Roast, 233
  Cutlets Escorial, 198
  Forcemeat, 59
  Pie, Melton Mowbray, 176
  Skewered, 125
Pot de Crème Chocolat, 407
Pot Roast with Potato Dumplings, 242
Potage Tour d'Argent, 68
POTATO(ES):
  and Cheese Dumplings, 394
  Cottage Fried, 345
  in Cream au Gratin, 61
  Duchess, 316
  Dumplings, 242
  and Egg Salad Boulestin, 162
  Gratin Savoyard, Le, 61
  Hashed Browned, 276
  Sautéed Baked, 268
  Soup, Cold, 428
Potted Shrimp, 177
POULARDE:
  Dikker and Thijs, 124
  en Papillote, 70
  Pavillon, 267
Poulet en Civet au Vieux Bourgogne, Le, 54
Poulet Papa Bergerand, La Fondue de, 54
POULTRY DISHES:
  Boned Stuffed Duck, 59
  Breast of Capon au Whiskey, 395
  Breast of Chicken au Champagne, 344
  Breast of Pheasant Sous Cloche, 325
  Breasts of Chicken Tropical, 220
  Breasts of Guinea Hen Smitane, 385
  Caneton Tour d'Argent, 71
  Cannelloni au Gratin with Sardi Sauce, 257
  Cannelloni alla Passetto, 94
  Chicken Cannelloni with Cream Sauce, 94
  Chicken in Champagne Sauce, 267
  Chicken Chichén Itzá, 211
  Chicken Cooked in Leaves, 211
  Chicken Curry, 230
  Chicken with Curry Sauce, 54
  Chicken Fricassee, Spicy, 197
  Chicken Hunter's Style with Noodles, 105
  Chicken Livers en Brochette, 275
  Chicken Livers Sautéed with Apples and
    Onion Rings, 244
  Chicken and Long Rice, 362
  Chicken with Mushrooms and Lobster,
    Braised, 124
  Chicken Pepitoria, 197
  Chicken in Pineapple, 221
  Chicken Pyramide, 32
  Chicken in Red Wine, 122
  Chicken and Rice, 217
  Chicken and Rice with Almonds, Olives, and
    Mushrooms, 198
  Chicken and Spaghetti Casserole, 256
  Chicken and Steak in Red Wine, 142
  Chicken Sweet and Hot, 411
  Chicken Tetrazzini au Gratin, Émincé of, 256
  Chicken Valadier, Boned, 96
  Chicken and Virginia Ham Shortcake, 318

POULTRY DISHES: (continued)
  Chicken with White Wine Sauce in Paper,
    70
  Cocotte of Guinea Hen with Brandy Sauce,
    287
  Coq au Vin Rouge à l'Avergnate, 122
  Coquelet à la Moutarde, Le, 55
  Dodine de Canard, 59
  Fondue de Poulet Papa Bergerand, La, 54
  Frederic's Pressed Duck, 71
  Friday Chicken, 409
  Game Hens with Wild Rice and Orange
    Sauce, 306
  Garland of Chicken Breasts in Aspic, 53
  Grouse in Cream, 140
  Guirlande de Suprêmes en Gelée, 53
  Paella "Good Friend," 198
  Pollo alla Cacciatora, 105
  Pollo Disossato Valadier, 96
  Polynesian Coconut Duckling, 361
  Poularde Dikker and Thijs, 124
  Poularde en Papillote, 70
  Poularde Pavillon, 267
  Poussin en Surprise, Le, 36
  Pump Room Chicken Hash, 348
  Ragout of Chicken with Onions, Bacon and
    Mushrooms, 54
  Roast Chicken with Bread Sauce, 184
  Roast Game Hens with Mustard, 55
  Roast Turkey Wayside Inn, 284
  Rock Cornish Game Hens in Clay, 393
  Rock Cornish Game Hens with Grapes, 196
  Rock Cornish Game Hens with Sauce
    Diable, Boned Stuffed, 36
  Skewered Chicken in Sesame Soy Sauce, 359
  Spicy Chicken Fricassee, 197
Poussin en Surprise, Le, 36
Praline Powder, 430
Pressed Duck, Frederic's, 71
PUDDING(S):
  Apple, Steamed, 160
  Coconut Rice, 221
  Italian Tipsy, 107
  La Fonda, 338
  Molded Chocolate, 430
  Old-Fashioned Bread, 412
  Soufflé, Pierre, 231
  Yorkshire, 156
Pump Room Chicken Hash, 348
Pumpkin Seeds, Curried, 204
Punch, "Come Again!" Rum, 366

Q

Quenelles Ambassade, 47
Queso Relleno de Chiapas, 214
Queues d'Écrevisses, Gratin de, 56
Quiche Lorraine, 45

R

Rabbit, Welsh, 165
Raggedy Soup, 109
Ragout of Chicken with Onions, Bacon and
  Mushrooms, 54
Racquet Club Gazpacho, 373
Racquet Club Spiced Vinegar, 375

INDEX

RASPBERRY:
  Sauce, 37
  Soufflé, Fresh, 37
  Tart, 79
Ravigote Sauce, 425
RICE:
  Baked Saffron, 230
  Custard, 277
  Indonesian Fried, 126
  Meal Crullers, 219
  and Peas Venetian, 105
  Pudding, Coconut, 221
  with Saffron and Parmesan Cheese, 103
  and Seafood Casserole, 220
  Spanish, 220
  Stewed with Vegetables, 35
  Wild, 246, 306, 393
Rich Biscuits, 440
Rich Pastry, 438
Ris de Veau à la Crème, 350
Ris de Veau, La Terrine de, 59
Risi e Bisi alla Veneziana, 105
Risotto alla Milanese, 103
Riz Pilaf à la Valencienne, 35
Roast Beef, Bacon and Fried Onions Sandwich, 143
Rock Cornish Game Hens: see Game Hens
Rognons de Veau, 80
Rollmops, 162
Rolls, Dinner, 437
Rolls, Pan, 437
Roux, 435
Rum Punch, 366
Rye Molasses Bread, 437

S

Saboyan de Naranja, 202
Saffron Rice, Baked, 230
Salad Dressings: see Dressings
SALAD(s):
  Apple and Truffle, 53
  Asparagus Vinaigrette, 256
  Belgian Endive, 326
  Caesar, 185
  Charles Farrell, 375
  Chicken and Celery, 123
  Coleslaw, 376
  Cucumber, 139
  Curried Chicken, 373
  Egg and Potato Boulestin, 162
  Endive and Beet, 326
  Gauloise, 268
  Georgia, 276
  Herring, 144
  Jellied Madrilene with Egg Salad Dressing, 410
  Marinated Cucumber, 126
  Mixed Green, 304
  Mushroom, Truffle and Tongue, 268
  Peperoni Don Salvatore, 392
  Summer, 145
  Wilted Spinach, 402
Sally Lunn Bread, 440
SALMON:
  Butter and Asparagus Sandwich, 144
  Grilled Marinated, 146
  Kedgeree of, 158

SALMON: (continued)
  Levens Hall Poached, 174
  in Pastry, 167
  Smoked, and Scrambled Egg Sandwich, 144
SANDWICH(ES):
  Cheese, Shrimps, and Mayonnaise, 143
  Croque-Monsieur, 84
  Danish Open, 143
  Liver Paste and Ham, 144
  Roast Beef with Bacon and Crisp Fried Onions, 143
  Roast Veal and Cucumber, 144
  Salmon Butter and Asparagus, 144
  Scrambled Egg and Smoked Salmon, 144
  Sloppy Moe, 376
  Tartar Steak with Lumpfish, 144
  Tartar Steak with Small Shrimps, 144
  Toasted Cheese and Ham, 84
Sardines in Dill Sauce, 244
Sardi's Meat Sauce, 258
Sateh Babi, 125
SAUCE(s), SAVORY:
  Aïoli, 425
  Américaine, 47
  Aurorian, 426
  Béarnaise, 201, 351; blender, 426
  Béchamel, 424
  Bookbinder's Seafood Cocktail, 314
  Brandy, 287
  Bread, 184
  Brown, 425
  Butter, 78
  Cannelloni, 94, 257
  Cantonese, 317
  Caper, 160
  Cardinal, 70
  Caribbee, 351
  Champagne, 344
  Chicken, 33, 197, 211, 336
  Chicken Velouté, 424
  Cocktail, 200
  Cream, 80, 106; blender, 424
  Cumberland, 182
  Curry, 55
  Curry, Mild, 201
  Curry, Simple, 159
  Diable, 37
  Dill, 244
  for Fish, 56
  Fish Velouté, 424
  for Frankfurters, 400
  Garlic, 201
  for Ham, 58
  Herb, 167
  Hollandaise, 57, 383; blender, 426
  for Kidneys, 80
  for Lasagne, 106
  Livornese for Scampi, 392
  Madeira, 69, 325
  Madeira and Truffle, 47
  Mayonnaise, Blender, 424
  Mayonnaise, Green, 425
  Mayonnaise, Mustard, 372
  Meat, 92, 106
  Meat; Sardi's, 258
  Meunière, 295
  Mornay, 424
  Mushroom, 95

INDEX

SAUCE(S), SAVORY: (continued)
Mushroom Cream, 145
for Mussels, 163
Mustard, 55, 146
Nantua, 57
Onion (Soubise), 69
Orange for Game Hens, 306
Paprika, Hot, 201
Pepper and Tomato, 335
for Pork Cutlets, 198
Ravigote, 425
Sesame Soy, 359
Shashlik, Hot, 349
Soubise, 69
Soufflé, 68
Sour Cream, 385
Steak, 79
for Stuffed Cheese, 215
Supreme, 424
for Sweetbreads, 350
Tempura, 396
Tomato, 395; blender, 426
Velouté, Chicken, 424
Velouté, Fish, 424
Vermouth, 81
Vinaigrette, 256
Whiskey Cream, 395
SAUCE(S), SWEET:
Chocolate Rum, 349
Custard, 161
Egg and Wine, 347
Fruit, 385
Hard, 175
Liqueur for Crepes, 199
Raspberry, 37
Zabaglione, 347
Sauerbraten mit Kartoffel Klösse, Lüchow's, 242
Sauerbraten à la Mode in Aspic, Cold, 243
Saure Leber, 245
Sausage, Wayside Country, 284
Sauté de Scupions à la Niçoise, 36
Scallop Shells with Baby Lobster Tails, 383
SCALLOPS:
in Cream Sauce, 80
au Gratin, Veal, 94
Sauté Meunière, Cape Cod, 295
Scaloppine di Vitella alla Passetto, 94
Scampi Aurora, 108
Scampi Flamingo, 102
Scampi alla Livornese, 392
Scandinavian Fruit Soup, 148
Schlemmerschnitte, 245
Schnitzel à la Lüchow's, 241
Scones, Tea, 172
Scotch Shortbread, 177
Scrambled Egg and Smoked Salmon Sandwich, 144
Scupions à la Niçoise, Sauté de, 36
Sea Bass, Baked Whole, 316
Sea Bream Biscay Style, 194
SEAFOOD:
Assorted, on Skewers, 35
Cocktail, 211
Cocktail Sauce, Bookbinder's, 314
and Rice Casserole, 220
Senegalese, Quick, 428
Sesame Soy Sauce, 359

Shashlik, Flaming, 348
Shashlik Sauce, Hot, 349
Shell, One-Crust Pie, 438
Sherbet Castle, 415
Sherbet, Coffee, 203
Shortbread, Scotch, 177
Shortcake, Chicken and Virginia Ham, 318
SHRIMP:
with Hollandaise Sauce au Gratin, 108
du Jour, 315
and Mushrooms, Buttered Spaghetti with, 307
with Mustard Fruits, Crisped, 265
Noodles with Fish and, 103
Potted, 177
à la Sardi, Hot, 255
in Sherry Cream Sauce, 102
Sillsalad, 144
Skewered Chicken in Sesame Soy Sauce, 359
Skewered Pork, 125
Sloppy Moe Sandwich, 376
Snail Butter, 83
Snails, Burgundian, 83
Snapper Soup, Bookbinder's, 314
SOLE:
Cardinal, Filets de, 70
with Crayfish, Fillets of, 70
in Cream Aspic, Fillets of, 410
Fourrée au Fumet de Meursault, La, 56
Lasserre, Casserolettes de Filets de, 44
Little Pastry Casseroles of Fillet of, 44
Pierre Le Grand, Filets de, 121
Poached in Meursault, Stuffed, 56
Ritz, Cantábric, 196
à la Stephen, Fillet of, 143
au Vermouth, Filets de, 81
with Vermouth Sauce, Fillets of, 84
with Wine Sauce, Poached Fillets of, 121
Sopa de Ajo, 219
Sopa Poblano, 216
Sopaipillas, 337
Sorbete de Café, 203
Soubise Sauce, 69
SOUFFLÉ:
Custard with Honey, 203
aux Framboises, Le, 37
Fresh Raspberry, 37
au Grand Marnier, 72
Iced Lemon, 168
Pancakes, Flaming, 45
Pudding Pierre, 231
Rothschild (with Glacéed Fruit), 347
Sauce, 68
Topped Lobster, 218
Soup Anglaise, 212
Soupe à l'Oignon, 46
SOUP(S):
de Ajo, 219
Andalusian, Cold, 194
Bean, 68
Beef with Marrow, 247
Black Bean, 218
Bookbinder's Snapper, 314
Borscht, 428
Carrot Vichyssoise, 264
Chili Poblano, 216
Clear, with Meat and Vegetables, 343
Cold Beet, 428
Cold Cucumber, 382

INDEX

SOUP(S): (continued)
Cold Curried Chicken, 428
Cold Potato, 428
Consommé Farley, 200
Consommé Stracciatella, 109
Curried Lima Bean, 428
Famous Dutch Green Pea, 120
Fish, 104
Garlic, 219
Gazpacho Andaluz, 194
Gazpacho, Racquet Club, 373
Hare, 158
Lobster Bisque, 297
Lobster Bisque Dewey, 275
Mediterranean Fish, 195
Mushroom, with Parmesan Cheese, 110
New England Clam Chowder, 296
Onion, 46
Oyster, Cream of, 327
Oyster Velouté, 327
Petite Marmite Henry IV, 343
Potage Tour d'Argent, 68
Raggedy, 109
Scandinavian Fruit, 148
Senegalese, Quick, 428
Soupe à l'Oignon, 46
Vegetable Bouillon, 304
Vermont Cheese, 264
Vichyssoise, 428
Vichysoisse, Carrot, 264
Zuppa di Pesce Royal Danieli, 104
Sour Cream Dressing, 145
Soused Mackerel, 164
Soy Sauce, Sesame, 359
SPAGHETTI:
alla Bolognese, 92
with Meat Sauce, 92
with Shrimp and Mushrooms, Buttered, 307
Spanish Rice, 220
Spinach and Eggs Grisanti, 308
Spinach Salad, Wilted, 402
Spoon Bread with Virginia Ham, 305
Spumoni, 93
Squid with Tomato and Anchovies, 36
STEAK:
Chevillot, 79
Diane, 345
Flamed Mustard, 137
Hong Kong, Butterfly, 232
Moutarde Flambé, 137
au Poivre, 346
Sauce, 79
Skewers, Teriyaki, 358
Tartar, 245
Tartar with Lumpfish Sandwich, 144
Tartar with Small Shrimps Sandwich, 144
Stew, Javanese Beef, 128
STOCK:
Brown, 435
Chicken, 435
Fish, 57, 297, 436
Ham, 78
White, 435
Strawberries Puiwa, 232
Strawberry and Lemon Surprise, 186
Strawberry-Rhubarb Pie, 439
Streusel Bread, 439
String Beans Lyonnaise, 83

STUFFING:
for Duck, 60
for Eggplant, 328
for Fish, 32, 56, 197
for Ham, 411
for Veal, 412
Wayside Bread, 284
Wild Rice for Game Hens, 393
Summer Salad, 145
Sunshine Cake with Chocolate Almond Frosting, 414
Supreme Sauce, 424
Swedish Cream, 148
Swedish Tea Ring, 437
Sweet Dough, 437
Sweet Mouthful, 254
Sweetbreads in Cream, 350
Sweetbreads, Terrine of, 59

T

Tagliatelle Verdi Gratinate al Prosciutto, 109
Taheeni, 427
TART:
Apple, 111
Cheese and Bacon, 45
Raspberry, 79
Tarte aux Framboises, 79
TARTAR:
Steak, 245·
Steak with Lumpfish Sandwich, 144
Steak with Small Shrimps Sandwich, 144
TEA:
Hot or Iced, How to Make, 178
Iced, 413
Ring, Swedish, 437
Scones, 172
Tempura, 396
Teriyaki, Steak Skewers, 358
Terrine de Ris de Veau, La, 59
Terrine of Sweetbreads, 59
Tidbit, Grilled, 317
Tipsy Pudding, Italian, 107
Toad-in-the-Hole, 164
Toast Santa Fe, French, 334
TOMATO(ES):
Grilled, 276
and Pepper Sauce, 335
Sauce, 426
Sauce for Pasta, 395
Topping, Chocolate for Whitehall Roll, 343
Tortellini Palermitana, 395
Tournedos Masséna, 47
Trifle, 166
Tripe and Onions, 159
Trout with Cucumber Salad, Broiled, 139
Trout Fernand Point, Stuffed, 32
Truite Farcie Fernand Point, 32
Turkey Wayside Inn, Roast, 284

V

Vanilla Custard Cream, 212
VEAL:
Chops with Mushroom Sauce, 95
Cutlets Cordon Bleu, 386
Cutlets with Crab Legs, 384
Cutlets à la Lüchow, 241

INDEX

VEAL: (continued)
Kidneys, 80
with Mushrooms, Fillet of, 44
in Parmesan and Grated Lemon Zest,
   Medallions of Breaded, 265
Roast and Cucumber Sandwich, 144
Roast Stuffed Rib of, 120
Scallops with Crabmeat, 350
Scallops au Gratin, 94
Shinbones Braised with Vegetables, 102
Stuffed Crown Roast, 412

VEAU:
à la Duxelles, Carré de, 120
Marseillais, Escalope de, 350
Rognons de, 80
Vegetable Bouillon, 304

VEGETABLES:
Artichoke Hearts, Garnished, 95
Artichoke Hearts, Ring Mold of Peas with,
   305
Asparagus Dutch Style, 122
Asparagus Milanese, 257
Asparagus Vinaigrette, 256
Boston Baked Beans, 401
Broiled Mushrooms Mary Victoria, 406
Candied Papaya, 363
Carciofi Vignarola, 95
Celery, Braised, 278
Champignons Grillés Marie Victoire, 406
Colcannon, 184
Cornmeal with Mushrooms, 110
Cottage Fried Potatoes, 345
Duchess Potatoes, 316
Elote Con Crema a la Mexicana, 217
Fried Cucumbers, 130
Gratin Savoyard, Le, 61
Grilled Tomatoes, 276
Gnocchi, 394
Haricots Verts à la Lyonnaise, 83
Hashed Browned Potatoes, 276
Indonesian Fried Rice, 126
Kartoffel Klösse, 242
Mexican Creamed Corn, 217
Mushrooms in Cream, 183
Mushrooms in Sour Cream, 248
Nasi Goreng, 126
Pasticcio di Polenta, 110
Peas with Lettuce, Little, 82
Peperoni, Don Salvatore, 392
Petits Pois à la Française, 82
Pomme de Terre Macaire, 268
Potato Dumplings, 242
Potato and Cheese Dumplings, 394
Potatoes in Cream au Gratin, 61
Puree of Mushrooms with Braised Celery,
   278
Rice and Peas Venetian, 105

VEGETABLES: (continued)
Rice with Saffron and Parmesan Cheese, 103
Rice Stewed with Vegetables, 35
Rice, Wild, 246, 306, 393
Ring Mold of Peas with Artichoke Hearts,
   305
Risi e Bisi alla Veneziana, 105
Risotto alla Milanese, 103
Riz Pilaf à la Valencienne, 35
Saffron Rice, Baked, 230
Sautéed Baked Potato, 268
Spinach and Eggs Grisanti, 308
String Beans Lyonnaise, 83
Stuffed Eggplant (with Crabmeat), 328
Stuffed Green Peppers, 214
Stuffed Roast Breadfruit, 362
Zucchini Soufflé, 393
Velouté Sauce, Chicken, 424
Velouté Sauce, Fish, 424
Vermont Cheese Soup, 264
Vichyssoise, 428
Vichyssoise, Carrot, 264
Vignarola, Carciofi, 95
Vinaigrette Sauce, 256
Vinegar, Racquet Club Spiced, 375
Vitella, alla Passetto, Lombatina di, 95
Vitella, alla Passetto, Scaloppine di, 94
Volaille Pyramide, 32

W

Wafers, Chocolate, 34
Waffles, Buttermilk, 335
Walnut Cake with Marzipan, 141
Watercress Butter, 427
Welsh Rabbit, 165
Western Franks, 400
White Sauce, Basic Thick, 424
White Stock, 435
Whitehall Chocolate Roll, 343
Whole Wheat Bread, 286
Wild Duck Flambé Belle Terrasse, 137
Wild Rice, 246, 306, 393
Wild Rice Stuffing, 393
Wine, A Word About, 416

Y

Yeast Bread, 436
Yorkshire Pudding, 156

Z

Zabaglione, Orange, 202
Zabaglione Sauce, 347
Zucchini Soufflé, 393
Zuppa di Pesce Royal Danieli, 104

This book was set in Linotype Janson, a recutting of a charming old book face created by Anton Janson some time between 1660 and 1689.

Janson practiced typefounding in Leipzig, his types being shown for the first time in a specimen sheet issued there about 1675. There is some evidence that he was of Dutch ancestry. Most certainly the original matrices were purchased in Holland. For these reasons the face has often been regarded as a Dutch type.

The modern recutting used in this book retains the sharpness, sparkle and "beautiful clarity and comeliness" of the original drawing.

The bold-face characters are Caledonia, a modern American face created by the late W. A. Dwiggins, the man responsible for so much that is good in contemporary book design and typography.

The headings are Perpetua, another twentieth-century face, by the Englishman, Eric Gill, A. R. A.

This book was produced, printed and bound by National Publishing Company of Philadelphia from type composed by John C. Meyer & Son. The plates were made by Beck Offset Plate, Philadelphia, and Judd & Detweiler, Inc., Washington, D.C. Edward Stern & Company provided the color printing. Endpaper caligraphy by George Salter. The entire production was under the supervision of Curtis S. Ruddle.

Editorial concept originated and supervised by Bernard Geis.

Typography, design, art direction by Arthur Hawkins.

National seals courtesy of Petit Larousse.

A TREASURY of YOUR FAVORITE RECIPES

More than any other kind of book, a cook book is an act of collaboration between author and reader. And now, because we like this idea of personal collaboration with each of you, we carry it one step further by providing a baker's dozen of pages where *you* can write in your own favorite recipes. We hope that this will make our Treasury and yours a constant companion in the kitchen and the source of your most inspired entertaining.

RECIPE. . . . .

SERVES . . . . .

ingredients

. . . .

. . . .

. . . .

. . . .

. . . .

. . . .

. . . .

. . . .

. . . .

. . . .

RECIPE . . . .

SERVES . . . . .

ingredients

. . . .

. . . .

. . . .

. . . .

. . . .

. . . .

. . . .

. . . .

. . . .

. . . .

RECIPE . . . .

SERVES . . . . .

ingredients

. . . .

. . . .

. . . .

. . . .

. . . .

. . . .

. . . .

. . . .

. . . .

. . . .

RECIPE..

SERVES.....

ingredients

. . . .

. . . .

. . . .

. . . .

. . . .

. . . .

. . . .

. . . .

. . . .

. . . .

RECIPE...

SERVES.....

ingredients

. . . .

. . . .

. . . .

. . . .

. . . .

. . . .

. . . .

. . . .

. . . .

. . . .

RECIPE. . . . .

SERVES. . . . .

ingredients

. . . .

. . . .

. . . .

. . . .

. . . .

. . . .

. . . .

. . . .

. . . .

. . . .

RECIPE...

SERVES.....

ingredients

. . . .

. . . .

. . . .

. . . .

. . . .

. . . .

. . . .

. . . .

. . . .

. . . .

RECIPE..

SERVES.....

ingredients

....

....

....

....

....

....

....

....

....

....

RECIPE..

SERVES.....

ingredients

....

....

....

....

....

....

....

....

....

....

RECIPE..

SERVES.....

ingredients

....

....

....

....

....

....

....

....

....

....

RECIPE . . . .

SERVES . . . . .

ingredients

. . . .

. . . .

. . . .

. . . .

. . . .

. . . .

. . . .

. . . .

. . . .

. . . .

RECIPE..

SERVES.....

ingredients

. . . .

. . . .

. . . .

. . . .

. . . .

. . . .

. . . .

. . . .

. . . .

. . . .

RECIPE...

SERVES.....

ingredients

. . . .

. . . .

. . . .

. . . .

. . . .

. . . .

. . . .

. . . .

. . . .

. . . .

A TREASURY of YOUR FAVORITE WINES

The following pages have been designed for a convenient listing of wines that you have enjoyed. By recording the name of the wine, the vintner or bottler, the year—if it is a vintage wine—and any other necessary information, you will find it easy to order again a wine that pleased you and your friends. For more information about wines, see page 416.

RED WINES

WHITE WINES

_____

_____

_____

_____

_____

_____

_____

_____

_____

_____

_____

_____

_____

_____

_____

_____

_____

_____

_____

_____

ROSÉ WINES

SPARKLING WINES

MISCELLANEOUS WINES

YOUR FAVORITE GUESTS

So much of the pleasure of good dining depends upon the friends we break bread with that we felt this book would not be complete without some guest pages. When you have had guests to dinner, memorialize the event by asking each of them to write a line or so on the following pages. In years to come, these pages will be a treasured record of your hospitality and friendships.

DATE | **YOUR FAVORITE GUESTS**

YOUR FAVORITE GUESTS

YOUR FAVORITE GUESTS

DATE | **YOUR FAVORITE GUESTS**

YOUR FAVORITE GUESTS

DATE | **YOUR FAVORITE GUESTS**

YOUR FAVORITE GUESTS

YOUR FAVORITE GUESTS

DATE | **YOUR FAVORITE GUESTS**

DATE | **YOUR FAVORITE GUESTS**

YOUR FAVORITE GUESTS

TABLE OF EQUIVALENTS

Gertrude Stein's "Rose is a rose is a rose is a rose" does not apply to the measurement of foods. "Cup is a cup is a cup is a cup" is not necessarily so in the kitchen. Edibles that have been cooked, chopped, grated, or shelled become more in some cases, less in others. How many times have you wondered how much raw rice you'll need to make two cups of cooked rice? Or how much juice there is in one lemon or one orange? Or how many graham crackers to crumb for that cupful called for in your recipe? This handy table was designed to do away with much of the guesswork that arises from just such culinary puzzlements. Use it and cook with an unfurrowed brow.

	FOOD	AMOUNT	EQUIVALENT MEASURE
beverages	Coffee	1 pound—80 tablespoons	40 cups, brewed
	Coffee, instant	2-ounce jar	25 servings
	Tea	1 pound	125 cups, brewed
cereals	Cornmeal	1 cup	4 cups, cooked
	Flour	1 pound	4 cups, sifted
	Macaroni	1 pound—5 cups	12 cups, cooked
	Noodles	1 pound—5½ cups	10 cups, cooked
	Quick-cooking oats	1 pound—5 cups	10 cups, cooked
	Rice	1 pound—2½ cups	about 8 cups, cooked
crackers	Graham crackers	12 squares	1 cup fine crumbs
	Soda crackers	21 squares	1 cup fine crumbs
	Zwieback	9 pieces	1 cup fine crumbs
dairy products	Cheese, Cottage	½ pound	1 cup
	Cheese, grated	1 pound	4–5 cups
	Cream, heavy	1 cup	2 cups, whipped
	Eggs, whole	5–7	1 cup
	Eggs, raw, shelled	10 medium	1 pound
	Eggs, whites	8–12	1 cup
	Eggs, whites	1 egg white	1½ tablespoons
	Eggs, yolks	12–16	1 cup
	Eggs, yolks	1 egg yolk	1 tablespoon
	Milk, whole	1 quart	1 quart skim plus 3 tablespoons cream
	Milk, dry	3–4 tablespoons dry whole milk solids plus 1 cup water.	1 cup whole milk

	FOOD	AMOUNT	EQUIVALENT MEASURE
dried fruit	Apricots	1 pound—3 cups	4½ cups, cooked
	Dates	1 pound—2½ cups	1¾ cups, pitted
	Figs	1 pound—2¼ cups	4½ cups, cooked
	Pears	1 pound—2⅔ cups	5⅓ cups, cooked
	Prunes, pitted	1 pound—2½ cups	2 cups, cooked and drained
	Raisins, seedless	1 pound—2¾ cups	3¾ cups, cooked
dried vegetables	Beans, Kidney	1 pound—1½ cups	9 cups, cooked
	Beans, Lima	1 pound—2⅓ cups	6 cups, cooked
	Beans, Navy	1 pound—2⅛ cups	6 cups, cooked
	Split peas	1 pound—2 cups	5 cups, cooked
fresh fruit	Apples	1 pound—3 medium	3 cups, sliced
	Avocados	1 medium	2 cups, cubed
	Bananas	1 pound—3 or 4 medium	2 cups, mashed
	Berries	1 pint	2 cups
	Cherries, red	1 quart	2 cups, pitted
	Cranberries	1 pound	3–3½ cups sauce
	Grapefruit	1 medium	1⅓ cups pulp
	Lemon	1 medium	3 tablespoons juice, 2 teaspoons grated rind
	Orange	1 medium	6–8 tablespoons juice, 2–3 tablespoons grated rind
	Pineapple	1 medium	2½ cups, cubed
fresh vegetables	Beets	1 pound—4 medium	2 cups, diced and cooked
	Cabbage	1 pound	4 cups, shredded
	Carrots	1 pound—7 or 8 medium	4 cups, diced

	FOOD	AMOUNT	EQUIVALENT MEASURE
fresh vegetables	Corn	12 ears	3 cups, cut
	Mushrooms, fresh	1 pound—36 medium	5 cups, sliced, raw
	Mushrooms, dried	3 ounces	1 pound fresh
	Peas, in pod	1 pound	1 cup, shelled and cooked
	Potatoes, white	1 pound—4 medium	2½ cups, diced and cooked
	Spinach	1 pound	1½–2 cups, cooked
nuts	Almonds, whole	6 ounces	1 cup
	Almonds, ground	1 pound	2⅔ cups
	Almonds, slivered	1 pound	5⅔ cups
	Coconut	1 pound	5 cups, shredded
	Coconut, grated	3½ ounces	1 cup
	Coconut, dried	1 tablespoon, chopped	1½ tablespoons fresh
	Peanuts, shelled	1 pound	2¼ cups
	Pecans, shelled	1 pound	4 cups
	Walnuts in shell	1 pound	2½ cups, shelled
	Walnuts, chopped	¼ pound	1 cup
fats and oils	Bacon	1 pound, rendered	1–1½ cups fat
	Butter	1 stick	½ cup—8 tablespoons
	Fats, hydrogenated	7.3 ounces	8 ounces butter
	Oil	2 cups	1 pound fat
crumbs	Bread crumbs, dry	1 slice	⅓ cup
	Bread crumbs, soft	1 slice	¾ cup
	Cracker crumbs	¾ cup	1 cup bread crumbs

	FOOD	AMOUNT	EQUIVALENT MEASURE
sugar	Brown	1 pound	2¼ cups, packed
	Confectioners'	1 pound	3½ cups, packed
	Confectioners'	1¾ cups	1 cup granulated
	Granulated	1 pound	2 cups
	Maple	½ cup	1 cup maple syrup
	Noncaloric sweetener, liquid	⅛ teaspoon	1 teaspoon sugar
	Saccharin	¼ grain	1 teaspoon sugar
meat	Beef, cooked	1 pound	3 cups, minced
	Beef, raw	1 pound, ground	2 cups
	Chicken	3½ pounds, raw, drawn	2 cups, cooked, diced
miscellaneous	Baking powder	1 teaspoon	1 teaspoon baking soda plus ½ teaspoon cream of tartar
	Baking powder, double acting	1 teaspoon	1½ teaspoons phosphate or tartrate
	Chocolate	1 square—1 ounce	4 tablespoons, grated
	Chocolate	1 ounce plus 4 teaspoons sugar	1⅔ ounces semi-sweet chocolate
	Chocolate	1 ounce	3 tablespoons cocoa plus 1 tablespoon shortening
	Garlic powder	⅛ teaspoon powder	1 small clove
	Gelatin, powdered	¼-ounce envelope	1 tablespoon
	Gelatin, sheets	4 sheets—8 grams	1 envelope or 1 tablespoon powdered
	Ginger, powdered	⅛ teaspoon	1 tablespoon candied or raw
	Herbs, dried	⅓–½ teaspoon	1 tablespoon fresh

	FOOD	AMOUNT	EQUIVALENT MEASURE
	Horse-radish, fresh	1 tablespoon	2 tablespoons, bottled
	Thickening agents: Arrowroot	1 ½ teaspoons	1 tablespoon flour
	Cornstarch	1 ½ teaspoons	1 tablespoon flour
	Potato starch	1 ½ teaspoons	1 tablespoon flour
miscellaneous	Rice starch	1 ½ teaspoons	1 tablespoon flour
	Tapioca	2 teaspoons	1 tablespoon flour
	Yeast, fresh	1 package	2 tablespoons
	Yeast, dry	1 envelope	1 ¾ tablespoons to be reconstituted in 2 tablespoons water

CALORIE CHART

Calories are like the weather—everybody talks about them, but nobody does anything about it. Still it's helpful to know which foods have a high caloric value and which ones you can economize with to keep your daily count within bounds. The following chart is based upon information furnished by the U. S. Department of Agriculture. It is not meant to be a killjoy about the pleasures of the table. Simply use the calorie chart—along with your conscience—to be your guide.

	FOOD	AMOUNT	CALORIES
beverages	Beer	12 ounces	175
	Brandy, 90 proof	1 ounce	90
	Carbonated drinks, ginger ale	8 ounces	80
	Kola type	8 ounces	105
	Coffee, black	1 cup	0
	Tea, plain	1 cup	0
	Whiskey	1½ ounces	105-115
	Wine	1 wineglass	70-85
cereals and grain products	Biscuits, baking powder	1 biscuit	130
	Bread, Boston brown	1 slice	100
	Cracked wheat	1 slice	60
	Raisin	1 slice	60
	Rye	1 slice	55
	White	1 slice	60
	Cakes, Angel food	2-inch slice	110
	Chocolate fudge	2-inch slice	420
	Fruit	2-inch piece	105
	Cupcakes	1 cupcake	130
	Frosted	1 cupcake	160
	Cookies, plain	1 cookie	110
	Crackers, Graham	2 medium	55
	Saltines	2 2-inch squares	35
	Farina, cooked	1 cup	105

	FOOD	AMOUNT	CALORIES
cereals and grain products	Macaroni, cooked	1 cup	190
	With cheese	1 cup	475
	Noodles, cooked	1 cup	200
	Pancakes	1 4-inch cake	60
	Pies	a 4-inch sector	260-340
	Rice, cooked	1 cup	200
	Spaghetti with meat sauce	1 cup	285
dairy products	Butter	1 tablespoon	100
	Cheese, Cheddar	1 ounce	105
	Cottage	1 ounce	25-30
	Cream	1 ounce	105
	Swiss	1 ounce	105
	Cream, light	1 tablespoon	35
	Heavy	1 tablespoon	55
	Whipped	2 tablespoons	55
	Eggs, boiled	1 egg	75
	Scrambled	1 egg, milk, fat	110
	Egg white	1 white	15
	Egg yolk	1 yolk	60
	Ice cream	1 cup	295
	Milk, whole	1 cup	165
	Skim	1 cup	90
	Buttermilk	1 cup	90

	FOOD	AMOUNT	CALORIES
dairy products	Milk, evaporated	1 cup	345
	Condensed	1 cup	985
	Malted	1 cup	280
	Chocolate	1 cup	190
	Yogurt	1 cup	120
fruits	Apples, raw	1 medium	70
	Apple juice	1 cup	125
	Applesauce, sweetened	1 cup	185
	Unsweetened	1 cup	100
	Apricots, raw	3 apricots	55
	Dried	4 halves	40
	Avocados	½ avocado	185
	Bananas	1 banana	85
	Blueberries	1 cup	85
	Cantaloupes	½ melon	40
	Cherries, raw	1 cup	65
	Cranberry sauce	1 cup	550
	Dates	1 cup	505
	Figs, fresh	3 small	90
	Dried	1 large	60
	Grapefruit	½ medium	50
	Grapefruit juice	1 cup	100
	Grapes	1 cup	70-100

	FOOD	AMOUNT	CALORIES
fruits	Lemons	1 medium	20
	Oranges	1 medium	60
	Orange juice	1 cup	100–120
	Peaches, raw	1 medium	35
	Pears, raw	1 medium	100
	Pineapple, raw, diced	1 cup	75
	Prunes, cooked	1 cup	305
	Raisins, dried	1 cup	460
	Strawberries, raw	1 cup	55
	Watermelon	a 4-by 8-inch wedge	120
vegetables	Asparagus, cooked	1 cup	35
	Beans, baby lima, cooked	1 cup	150
	Green, cooked	1 cup	25
	Beets, cooked	1 cup	70
	Broccoli, cooked	1 cup	45
	Cabbage, raw, finely shredded	1 cup	25
	Carrots, raw	1 medium	20
	Celery, raw	1 stalk	5
	Corn, cooked	1 ear	65
	Cucumbers	1 medium	25
	Lettuce	2 large leaves	5
	Mushrooms, canned, with liquid	1 cup	30
	Parsley, chopped	1 tablespoon	1

	FOOD	AMOUNT	CALORIES
	Peas, cooked	1 cup	110
	Potatoes, baked	1 medium	90
	French fried	10 pieces	95
	Mashed with milk and butter	1 cup	230
	Radishes	4 small	10
	Sauerkraut, canned	1 cup, drained	30
vegetables	Spinach, cooked	1 cup	45
	Squash, Summer	1 cup, diced	35
	Winter	1 cup, mashed	95
	Sweet Potatoes, baked	1 medium	155
	Candied	1 medium	295
	Tomatoes, raw	1 medium	30
	Tomato juice, canned	1 cup	50
	Tomato catsup	1 tablespoon	15
	Fats, cooking, Lard	1 cup	1,985
	Vegetable	1 cup	1,770
	Margarine	1 cup	1,600
	Margarine	1 tablespoon	100
fats, oils	Oils, salad or cooking (Corn, Cottonseed, Olive, Soybean)	1 tablespoon	125
	Salad Dressings, Blue Cheese	1 tablespoon	90
	French	1 tablespoon	60
	Mayonnaise	1 tablespoon	110
	Thousand Island	1 tablespoon	75

FOOD	AMOUNT	CALORIES
Bacon, crisp	2 slices	95
Beef, lean and fat	3 ounces	245
Lean only	2.5 ounces	140
Hamburger, lean, broiled	3 ounces	185
Roast, lean	1.8 ounces	120
Steak, sirloin, broiled	3 ounces	330
Beef, dried or chipped	2 ounces	115
Chicken, broiled	3 ounces, boned	185
Fried, breast	2.8 ounces, boned	215
Fried, leg	3.1 ounces, boned	245
Chili con carne	1 cup	335
Lamb, chop, lean	2.6 ounces	140
Leg, roast, lean	2.5 ounces	130
Liver, beef, fried	2 ounces	120
Pork, cured, Ham	3 ounces	290
Luncheon meat	2 ounces	165
Pork, fresh, chop, lean	1.7 ounces	130
Roast, lean	2.4 ounces	175
Sausage, Bologna	4 slices	345
Frankfurter	1 frankfurter	155
Pork	4 ounces	340
Tongue, beef, simmered	3 ounces	205
Veal, cutlet	3 ounces, boned	185

meat,
poultry,
fish

	FOOD	AMOUNT	CALORIES
	Veal, roast	3 ounces	305
	Fish and Shellfish, Bluefish	3 ounces	135
	Clams, raw	3 ounces	70
	Crabmeat	3 ounces	90
	Lobster, boiled or canned	4 ounces	100
	Mackerel, broiled	3 ounces	200
meat, poultry, fish	Oysters, raw	1 cup	160
	Stew	1 cup	200
	Salmon, canned	3 ounces, drained	120
	Sardines, canned	3 ounces, drained	180
	Shrimp, canned	3 ounces	110
	Swordfish, broiled	3 ounces	150
	Tuna, canned	3 ounces, drained	170
	Almonds, shelled	1 cup	850
	Brazil nuts, pieces	1 cup	905
	Cashews, roasted	1 cup	770
	Coconut, fresh	1 cup	330
	Dried, sweetened	1 cup	345
nuts	Peanuts, roasted	1 cup, shelled	840
	Peanut butter	1 tablespoon	90
	Pecans, halves	1 cup	740
	Walnuts, Black	1 cup, shelled	790
	English	1 cup, shelled	650

FOOD	AMOUNT	CALORIES
sugars, sweets		
Candy, Caramels	1 ounce	120
Chocolate	1 ounce	145
Hard candy	1 ounce	110
Marshmallow	1 ounce	90
Honey	1 tablespoon	60
Jams, Preserves	1 tablespoon	55
Molasses	1 tablespoon	45-50
Sugar, granulated or brown	1 tablespoon	50
miscellaneous		
Bouillon cube	1 cube	2
Gelatin, plain	1 tablespoon	35
Dessert powder	½ cup	325
Ready-to-eat, plain	1 cup	155
Olives, Green	7 jumbo	65
Ripe	7 jumbo	85
Pickles, Dill	1 large	15
Sweet	1 small	20
Sherbet	1 cup	235
Vinegar	1 tablespoon	2
White sauce, medium	1 cup	430
Yeast, Compressed	1 ounce	25
Active dry	1 ounce	80
Brewer's	1 tablespoon	25